EDITED BY A. G. DICKENS

with texts by

A. G. DICKENS   SYDNEY ANGLO   C. A. J. ARMSTRONG

E. B. FRYDE   R. J. KNECHT   R. J. W. EVANS

NEVILLE WILLIAMS

JOHN H. ELLIOTT   PETER W. THOMAS   JUDITH A. HOOK

RAGNHILD HATTON   M. S. ANDERSON

E. WANGERMANN   J. H. SHENNAN

with 342 illustrations, 63 in colour

THE COURTS
OF EUROPE

POLITICS, PATRONAGE AND ROYALTY · 1400–1800

McGRAW-HILL BOOK COMPANY
New York   St. Louis   San Francisco

The picture on the half-title page is a relief showing the Emperor Maximilian I with a Counsellor and a Jester. It was made by Niklas Türing between 1497 and 1500 as part of the decoration of the Goldenen Dachl, Innsbruck. Now in the Tyroler Landesmuseum, Ferdinandeum, Innsbruck.

The drawing on the title page shows part of the balustrade of a staircase which once led to Louis XV's Cabinet des Médailles in the Palais Mazarin (now the Bibliothèque Nationale). It is of wrought iron and bronze, and incorporates Louis' emblem of interlaced Ls. The balustrade is now installed on the staircase of the Wallace Collection, London.

The crown at the head of the Introduction is the so-called St Henry's Crown (mentioned on p. 13), made about 1280 in France or south Germany and now in the Treasury of the Munich Residenz. That at the head of the Epilogue is the crown of Louis XV, now in the Louvre.

PICTURE RESEARCH: Georgina Bruckner MA

Library of Congress Cataloging in Publication Data
Main entry under title:

The Courts of Europe.

Bibliography: p.
Includes index.
1. Courts and Courtiers.   2. Europe—Kings and Rulers.   3. Europe—Politics and Government.

GT3510. C68   1977   940.2   76-55348
ISBN 0-07-016802-4

Published in the United States by McGraw-Hill Book Company, 1977.

Printed in Singapore by Times Printers

CONTENTS

Sources of illustrations and photographs

H.M. The Queen: 40, 141, 152, 158, 162, 163, 165, 202, 204, 207, 215, 216, 217, 218, 219, 220, 224, 225. Albertina, Vienna: 240. Archivo Historico Nacional, Madrid: 187. Bargello, Florence: 87. Biblioteca Medicea-Laurenziana, Florence: 85, 96. Bibliothèque de l'Arsenal, Paris: 56. Bibliothèque Nationale, Paris: 29, 102, 103, 104, 107, 118, 236, 250, 258, 262, 274, 275, 276, 277, 278, 280, 324, 336. Bibliothèque Royale de Belgique, Brussels: 49, 55, 65. Bodleian Library, Oxford: 30, 53, 57, 66, 67, 73. British Library, London: 26, 28, 30, 31, 37, 38, 43, 44, 45, 46, 79, 98, 139, 146, 147, 150, 156, 160, 161, 164, 170, 285. British Museum, London: 9, 10, 11, 12, 36, 108, 128, 134, 135, 136, 137, 155, 159, 167, 168, 205, 206, 209, 210, 226, 227, 230, 231, 232, 235, 272, 281, 282, 293, 296, 297, 298. Cambridge University Library: 239. Cronstedt Collection, Stockholm: 142. The Duke of Northumberland: 214. Escorial: 195, 196. Fitzwilliam Museum, Cambridge: 153. Galleria Borghese, Rome: 233, 238. Galleria Corsini, Florence: 234. Galleria Nazionale dell 'Umbria, Perugia: 41. Gemäldegalerie, Berlin-Dahlem: 51, 52, 54, 59. Germanisches Nationalmuseum, Nürnberg; 70. H.R.H. Prince Ernst of Hanover: 279. Herzog August Bibliothek, Wolfenbüttel: 105. Hermitage Museum, Leningrad: 283, 286, 294, 299. Historisches Museum, Bern: 60. Historisches Museum der Stadt Wien, Vienna: 318. Hungarian National Library, Budapest: 24. Hungarian National Museum, Budapest: 4. Jovellanos Collection, Gijon: 177. Kunsthistorisches Museum, Vienna: 68, 106, 121, 122, 125, 133, 138, 143, 145, 148, 190, 200, 309, 313, 316, 317. Lenin Library, Moscow: 284, 291. The Lord Sackville: 222. Louvre, Paris: 5, 47, 101, 115, 191, 223. Metropolitan Museum of Art, New York: Friedsam Collection: 71, 221. Musèe Condé, Chantilly: 104, 107. Musée de Carnavalet, Paris: 253, 320. Musée de Versailles: 208, 251, 252, 254, 255, 256, 257, 259, 263, 265, 266, 267, 270, 273, 326, 327, 328, 338. Musée des Augustins, Toulouse: 264. Musée Plantin-Moretus, Antwerp: 246. Musée royal des Beaux-Arts, Brussels: 72. Muse' d'Arte Antica, Castello Sforzesco, Milan: 78. Museo degli Argenti, Palazzo Pitti, Florence: 92. Museo di Palazzo Venezia, Rome: 229. Museo Mediceo, Palazzo Medici-Riccardi, Florence: 91. Museo-Monasterio de la Encarnación, Madrid: 199. Museo Municipal, Madrid: 178, 181, 193, 194. Museo Nazionale, Naples; 82. Museo Provinciale Campano, Capua: 15. Museo Topografico, Florence: 77, 84. Museum of Applied Arts, Prague: 124. Museum of Fine Arts, Budapest: 23, 25. Museum Meermanno-Westreenianum, 's-Gravenhage: 21. Nationalmuseet, Stockholm: 271. National Gallery, Prague: 22, 140. National Gallery of Art, Washington DC: 74, 333. National Museum, Prague: 131. National Portrait Gallery, London: 169, 171, 172. National History Museum, London: 144. Opera del Duomo, Florence: 87. Österreichische Nationalbibliothek, Vienna: 39, 69, 132, 182, 302, 303, 306, 314, 315. Palazzo Pitti, Florence: 247, 322. Prado, Madrid: 127, 175, 183, 184, 185, 186, 188, 191, 192, 198. Public Record Office, London: 99. J. D. Rockefeller jr. Collection, New York: 58. Regional Museum of History and Architecture, Novgorod: 300, Rijksmuseum, Amsterdam: 61, 288. Schatzkammr der Residenz, Munich: 2, 3, 123, 149, 248. Schloss Schönbrunn: 304, 305, 308, 311. Sotheby's, London: 126, Staatliche Künstsammlungen, Kassel: 173 Staatliche Museen, Berlin: 13. Trésor de la Cathédrale, Liège: 62. The Trustees of the Chatsworth Settlement: 211, 212, 213. Uffizi, Florence: 88, 89, 100. Vatican Library: 17, 18, 27, 179, 180, The Visitors of the Ashmolean Museum, Oxford: 117, 166. Victoria and Albert Museum, London: 48, 63, 76, 119, 151, 154, 174, 203, 249, 301, 323, 333, 334, 332, 340, 341. Wallace Collection, London: 268, 319, 321, 325, 331, 342. Weltliche Schatzkammer, Vienna: 130. Alinari/Mansell: 14, 16, 19, 20, 32, 75, 77, 79, 80, 86, 87, 88, 89, 90, 91, 94, 95, 97, 100, 228, 233, 234, 237, 238, 239, 241, 247, 322. Claude Arthaud/Studio Richard-Blin: 129. Arts of Mankind: 6, 7. Bildarchiv der Österreichische Nationalbibliothek, Vienna: 307, 312. Bulloz: 47, 253, 254, 266, 320. J. Allan Cash: 290. Foto Moderno, Urbino: 33, 34, 35, 42. French Government Tourist Office: 336. Giraudon: 107, 110, 112, 113, 116, 191, 197, 223, 251, 259, 261, 324. Hans Huber KG: 1. Institut royal du patrimoine artistique, Brussels: 50, 64. Victor Kennett: 287, 289, 292. A. F. Kersting: 50. Mas: 127, 175, 176, 177, 178, 181, 183, 184, 185, 186, 188, 192, 193, 194, 195, 196, 198, 199. Meyer KG, Vienna: 310. Reunion des musées nationaux, Paris: 5, 8, 101, 104, 109, 111, 114, 115, 117, 120, 208, 252, 255, 256, 265, 267, 269, 270, 273, 327, 329, 330, 338. Scala: 82, 83, 84, 243, 244, 245. Snark International: 263. Yan: 189, 264.

INTRODUCTION

THE ERA OF COURT LIFE most substantially covered by this book might be labelled 'Renaissance and Baroque': it ranges from Lorenzo de' Medici and the dukes of Burgundy down to the sunset of the *Ancien Régime* under Louis XV of France. Nevertheless the first chapter describes some medieval courts which clearly anticipated many characteristics of their Renaissance successors. The second essay, also of a broad general character, deals with the courtier in literature. Though it chiefly revolves around Castiglione and the writers influenced by his best-seller, it also looks back in its turn at medieval literature, which already in the twelfth century had made some sophisticated contributions to the theme.

Each of the remaining chapters surveys the context of a given ruler or dynasty, the choices being made not simply because these courts typified their periods, but also in order to display the rich contrast of styles which could mark near-contemporaries. For example, it will be seen that the ethos of Philip IV contrasted markedly with that of his son-in-law Louis XIV: the former stood reserved from the public eye, while the latter gave a continuous theatrical performance under the eyes of thousands. Again, what could differ more from the setting of Pope Urban VIII, the master of Bernini, than that of Peter the Great, in its harsh pragmatism almost deserving to be called a non-court?

That the courts of Europe exerted enormous historical influences cannot be denied, yet as institutional phenomena they present the historian with quite exceptional problems. Compared with parliaments, councils, law-courts, and other such bodies, they show ragged edges and shifting patterns. The greater ones pervaded their respective kingdoms and drew their fluctuating membership from diverse regions, political interests, and social groups. Again, their purposes were numerous and complicated. A court did not serve merely as the home and governmental headquarters of a ruler. It can also be observed as the nucleus of a ruling class, as a planned monumental environment, as a prime focus of culture. But its basic political function was to serve as a medium of propaganda suggesting power and stability. In an age when Church and State tended to be dominated by

physical symbols, a court naturally tried to become a permanent pageant: a concentration of grandiose buildings, art treasures, overdressed grandees so brilliant as to dazzle the beholder and to impress even the subjects and the foreign rivals who learned of it at second hand.

Throughout the present book my colleagues and I have been stimulated – indeed mentally taxed – by the sheer multiplicity of all these themes. We have sought to describe the ruler's dynastic background, his personal habits, his blend of tradition and innovation, his relations with the inner ring of nobles and ministers, his patronage of artists and intellectuals, his physical settings and architectural achievements. Again, we are often informative on such assorted topics as pageantry, religious observance, royal mistresses, and memoirists. Though we take more interest in serious themes than in court gossip for its own sake, we should have misrepresented our subject had we disregarded the personal quirks and intrigues, the anecdotes and the scandals. By the same token, the pictures seem to us no mere luxury but wholly essential to the subject. One would hardly publish a history of the theatre without illustrations! By its very nature and purpose, court life laid stress on the external rather than the internal life, and at this social level historians inherit a uniquely rich and informative array of visual evidence.

Such volumes as the present one demand prolonged collaboration not merely between the writers, but between these latter and the professional team appointed to the enterprise by the publisher. Such team-thinking, so expert, so varied, so indispensable, can attract little open prestige. But as general go-between, the present editor has been well placed to appreciate this contribution, and he duly records his gratitude. To thank the individuals best known to him would be most pleasurable, but also – in view of the complexity of modern publishing – not a little invidious.

Finally, I should draw special attention to a work which valuably supplements this present volume, yet which appeared just too late to be used. This is Hugh Trevor-Roper, *Princes and Artists: Patronage and Ideology at Four Habsburg Courts, 1517–1633* (London, 1976).   A.G.D

One

MONARCHY
AND CULTURAL REVIVAL
Courts in the Middle Ages

✳

A. G. DICKENS

T MUNICH THE HUGE RESIDENZ of the former kings of Bavaria has a treasure-chamber containing their unrivalled collection of crowns and other historic works in gold and pearls. Of its kind, this is the greatest show on earth. In the dimly-lit rooms the yellow metal smoulders under discreet spotlights: one begins to understand why misguided men have lost their souls for vastly less. Among these choice objects a special interest attaches to one officially entitled 'the Crown of an English Queen'. Admitting to a certain ulterior motive, I invite the reader to spend a few minutes studying its picture in detail, though the following description fails to cover the full complexities of this triumph of medieval design and craftsmanship.

The base of the crown consists of twelve major rosettes, each centred upon a near-hexagon consisting of six concave arches, the latter being alternated in red and blue enamels. From every hexagon, small golden three-tipped leaves grow outward, while within it an elaborate openwork design pushes forward a shallow funnel, from which, held by four claws, shines an uncut amethyst. Outside each hexagon further elaborate open patterns of gold support three rubies, which are counterbalanced by three groups of four pearls. The respective positions of the rubies and pearls alternate from one rosette to its neighbour so as to avoid monotonous repetition. Incidentally, each group of four pearls is arranged around a small diamond in a gold setting. So far I have described only the twelve rosettes, the main components of the ring which sat upon the Queen's head. But these rosettes are actually held together in a ring by as many links, consisting of oblong frames of gold, ending in a leaf above and another below. Each oblong frame encloses a blue enamel base, which in turn contains – here barely visible – a Gothic circular motif with a St Andrew's cross above and another below it.

From this frail but stable base there arises the intense but ordered efflorescence which is the glory of the design. Each of the twelve linked rosettes thrusts upward a golden stem culminating in a large lily. But a convincing crown – and also a sense of natural growth – arises from the fact that these upward-thrusting stems are alternately short and tall.

Sharply cut and with nicked edges, the stems shoot out side-leaves; but at the same time they push forward rubies and sapphires in clawed cups; or else pearls, some growing like fruit upon stalks, some (on the longer stems) in groups of four, each group with a small emerald at its centre. The strange harmony underlying this organic structure may somehow be enhanced by the play of numbers, though I cannot say whether any mystical significance was intended. From the threefold and fourfold patterns of the jewels arises the double-sixfold of the upward stems, culminating in the undulating twelvefold crown of lilies.

Like many notable works of art, this one combines harmony with some ambiguous, even comic, appeals to the imagination. Momentarily one may see it not as a bed of lilies but as a grove of prematurely fruitful saplings, or again as a ring of burning candles too grand for a wedding cake but too dangerous to adorn the head of a saint. More than other crowns, it is a fragile toy: it lacks a solid, strengthening circle, and seems intended to be worn by Titania at an elfin festival, rather than by a beautiful, uneasy head on some human state-occasion. One fact does not emerge from a mere photograph. Closer inspection reveals this to be a highly portable diadem, which in a few moments could be dismantled and locked away from the gross world of barons and burglars. In fact the upright stems detach from their bases and they are surreptitiously numbered I to XII, so that each may be slotted back into its rightful place.

The throne of Charlemagne *still stands in his royal chapel at Aachen, the plainness of its marble slabs contrasting with the richness of the surrounding decoration. Its position at gallery level is explained by the fact that the chapel was linked to the adjacent palace by an elevated passage, but this arrangement became the model for many subsequent Imperial chapels. (1)*

The imperial eagle *was a royal symbol inherited by the Middle Ages from the Roman Empire. This onyx cameo was made for the Hohenstaufen court in the thirteenth century. From here the image of the eagle was adopted by other dynasties – for instance the Habsburgs and the Romanovs – and survived into recent times. (2)*

When and where was this minor miracle created? To which English queen, if any, did it belong? Its first written record dates from 1399, when the new English monarch Henry IV listed the treasures of his royal predecessors. The stylistic evidence suggests that the crown had been made not very long before this time. This type of design also occurs in certain late-fourteenth-century depictions of holy maidens, while the cast and chiselled leaves point towards French or Burgundian goldsmiths of that same period. Clearly it was commissioned by a royal patron, and since the major rulers of that period often exchanged artists or summoned them from foreign countries, we cannot assume that the crown was made for the King of France or the Duke of Burgundy – or indeed that it must have been manufactured within these western lands. In old inventories it is called 'the Bohemian Crown', and this clue, together with its possession by Henry IV in 1399, comes near to proving that it had belonged to Anne of Bohemia, daughter of the late Emperor Charles IV (d. 1378) and sister of his successor Wenceslas. She probably brought it to England in or soon after 1382, when she arrived (carrying a Bible in Latin, Czech, and German) to marry Henry's young and hapless predecessor Richard II. But her crown seems the radiant symbol of a lost hope, for when she died in 1394 Richard was devastated. Deprived of her affection and merciful counsel, he stumbled thenceforth towards tyranny and disaster. There is no inherent improbability that Anne's brother – or deceased father – should have commissioned such a crown. The house of Luxembourg had the closest of ties with France. While her grandfather John had died fighting for France at Crécy, her father Charles had spent much of his early life in Paris, and in later years he attracted many French artists to his magnificent court. The crown is thus a sort of miniature parallel to the very French cathedral of St Vitus upon the Hradčany at Prague. As for Henry IV in England, he decided to utilize it again for another diplomatic marriage, since he sent it along with his daughter Blanche when she married Rupert of the Palatinate. Through this house it passed on to the Wittelsbachs of Bavaria: it recurs at Mannheim in an inventory of 1745 and has been at Munich since 1783.

My ulterior motive lies very close to the theme of this whole essay. It goes beyond the goldsmith's craft into more ethereal qualities expressed by this design: the growing sophistication, the secular spirituality, which marked medi-

The crown of an English queen, *now in the treasure-chamber of the Residenz, Munich, is one of the most splendid to have come down from the Middle Ages. It was probably made for Anne of Bohemia, wife of Richard II of England, towards the end of the fourteenth century. The crown is described in detail on p. 8. (3)*

For Matthias Corvinus, *King of Hungary from 1458 to 1490, Antonio Pollaiolo designed a fabric which was originally intended to form a set of throne hangings. Later it was made into a chasuble. Imperial symbols derived from ancient Rome included not only the eagles but also the oak wreath. (4)*

eval court life in Europe. We do not need to leave the Munich treasury to see the enormous advances made during the course of those centuries, advances which discredit that intentionally negative term 'medieval', coined by the humanists to cover this allegedly dark period between their noble selves and the ancient world. In fact the so-called Middle Ages do not correspond with any formula, religious or otherwise. Above all they were not culturally static, but moved along with increasing speed and force. Amongst the present neighbours of the Bohemian crown is that of the Empress Kunigunde (*c.* 1010–20), which shows only the 'natural' taste of a far less sophisticated age. Another neighbour is the so-called St Henry's crown, made in France or Germany around 1280. This piece, though far from technically naïve, lacks both unity and imagination, a flaw which relegates it to a different order of creation from the masterpiece made just a century later. And even as we pass along the room to the treasures of the Renaissance, the Bohemian crown still seems the fine flower of the collection. For example, nothing could be more dazzling than the St George and the Dragon of 1590, an ingenious confection of diamonds, rubies, and emeralds, yet like much else of its age a display of virtuosity masking a certain poorness of spirit.

Such comparisons illustrate my contention that this book should not be allowed to start suddenly around the year 1400; and moreover that the medieval courts must not be taken as humble stepping-stones to the glories of their Renaissance successors. I shall urge that several medieval courts and princes anticipated almost every aim and achievement of the later period with which the main body of this book is concerned.

The revival of Empire

An essay on the medieval courts of Europe has its obvious starting point with Charlemagne (r. 768–814) and his dynasty. For so early a period his court is well documented: it is also clearly identified with political and cultural aspirations destined to dominate the medieval centuries. While in Byzantium the surviving eastern portion of the Roman Empire prolonged yet subtly modified the legacy of Imperial Rome, the Frankish kings deliberately undertook to steer the barbarian peoples of western Europe back into the Roman tradition. They had not to rely upon imaginative genius alone. On their side stood papal Rome, northern Italy, and certain remoter areas which had preserved across the last three centuries more than a modicum of ancient classical learning. Again, much of western Europe was still studded with classical buildings and works of art bearing a readily available message. Extending their power into Italy, the Franks found there, it is true, a somewhat shaky bridge to the ancient world. As we may still witness at Ravenna, that bridge had hitherto been maintained by the outposts of Byzantium rather than by the rival enterprise of papal Rome. Nevertheless Byzantium lacked the power to return in force to the West; and when in 800 Pope Leo III unexpectedly crowned and anointed the King of the Franks as Emperor, he was acknowledging that the monarch already controlling western Europe should be entrusted with the protectorship of the Church and of Christian civilization. He had various good reasons to reject the continuing claims of Byzantium, at this time ruled by the evil Irene, who had blinded her own son to prevent his succession. Leo did not anticipate the enormous political pretensions to be made by his successors, let alone the resultant battles between Empire and Papacy. To modern observers both his own gesture and Charles's acceptance of the crown at his hands may well appear among history's more fantastic gambles; yet the episode remains intelligible, and for some time the alliance suited both sides. Thomas Hobbes saw the Papacy as the ghost of Roman Empire sitting crowned upon its grave. One must admit an element of truth in this brilliant simile; and in an age when Europe still seethed with barbarian movement, there were tasks which no mere ghost could undertake. Leo intended that Charlemagne should give the Papacy flesh and muscle, but in the event he gave it something more.

The coronation of the great Emperor came at the climax of a four centuries' process, whereby the various Frankish tribes did not merely coalesce but went on to generate a military force great enough to overpower their neighbours and to thrust back the new barbarian waves constantly pressing into Europe. The Frankish foot-soldier thus became the heir of the Roman legionary, while his compatriot on horseback became ancestor to the medieval knight. At first the Frankish expansion had ambivalent effects. On the one hand it had expunged the Latin language and the Christian religion from some areas of north-eastern Europe. On the other hand Romans and Franks had fought together against the Visigoths, the Saxons, and Attila's Huns. Ultimately in the twilight of Rome, King Clovis (d. 511) had become both a Roman consul and a Christian, while Pope Gregory the Great (d. 604) acknowledged the primacy of the Frankish kingdom. But for dynastic feuds and the promotion of the great magnates misleadingly called Mayors of the Palace, the successors of Clovis might have restored the western Empire a couple of centuries before Charlemagne's day. In addition the need for unity made little headway against the ingrained folly of Germanic family custom. Even Charlemagne's father, Pepin III (r. 751–68), divided the Frankish lands between his two sons. Hence only the fortunate death of Carloman allowed Charles to preserve the unity of a state which continued to depend upon the sword; upon ruthless campaigning against Lombards, Saxons, Czechs, Huns, Saracens; peoples in varying stages of cultural development and situated both within and beyond the frontiers of the new Empire. In the end that Empire stretched from the Atlantic to the middle Danube. It included all France except Brittany; and Germany so far as the Elbe, but with a precarious extension into Bohemia. Across the Alps it embraced northern and central Italy: it also thrust out a Spanish March across the Pyrenees so far as the Ebro. Yet the great majority of its subjects, though to some extent appreciating the benefits of peace, could not be expected to understand either the Roman ideal or its revitalizing under the ruler of the Franks. In his final years Charlemagne witnessed with grief the havoc made by the elusive and seemingly incorrigible Northmen; yet their descendants were to settle and become 'Normans', to display

a real genius for law and administration, finally to conquer the kingdoms of England and Sicily.

Within this huge and stormy landscape we observe not simply the gathering of scattered sub-Roman elements into a court, but a conscious and resolute attempt to diffuse those elements across a whole continent, a mighty effort to re-create the world of the first Christian Emperor, Constantine (r. 317–37). Beginning in the reign of Pepin III, this drive attained its greatest impetus under Charlemagne and his son Louis the Pious (r. 814–40). Thereafter the Empire was partitioned among the three sons of Louis, though the cultural movement had by now generated a certain momentum of its own. After 888, when the last Carolingian Emperor died, there followed a period of division and stagnation, while the frontiers suffered erosion under the assaults of Northmen, Magyars, and Muslims.

The unusual greatness of Charlemagne lay in his ability to think upon a European scale, overleaping tribal and national particularism. Even during the earlier decades of his reign, it became apparent that strength in arts and letters lay in centres well outside the fallow homelands of the Frankish nation. The scholars he called into that partial vacuum came from Byzantine-influenced Italy, from Visigothic Spain, from the British Isles, especially from Bede's Northumbria and from Ireland. Extending over three or four generations, these leaders and their pupils were imbued with the ideal they called *renovatio*: they had come to court holding in their hands the elements of a fragmented classical culture. Foremost in esteem and influence with the Emperor was Alcuin, who had begun his career as a pupil and then (766) as master of the school at York, a place where people somehow still wrote tolerable Latin poetry in classical metres. Charles met him at Parma in 781 and soon afterwards invited him to direct the library and palace school at Aachen. Abbot of Tours from 796, Alcuin created there a second major centre for the diffusion of classical studies. From Tours the young Rabanus Maurus (d. 856) went forth to found a third centre at Fulda, whence he became chief preceptor of all the German lands. In turn, two of Rabanus' students worthily maintained the tradition of Alcuin into an Indian summer at the court of Charles the Bald (r. 840–77). One was that monarch's tutor Walafrid Strabo; the other Lupus, Abbot of Ferrières (d. c. 862), who loved Cicero and collated classical manuscripts in a spirit not too remote from that of the Florentine and Roman humanists six centuries later. The group did in fact directly endow these remote successors with one useful tool, for it evolved the half-uncial script adopted by the Renaissance as authentically 'ancient'.

Though many Carolingian scholars were mainly concerned to produce what might be called high-school grammars and textbooks, the more advanced studies expanded during the ninth century. Between 848 and 858 the Irishman Sedulius Scotus wrote the best classical poetry of the age, while his countryman John Scotus Erigena (d. c. 877), the leading scholar at the court of Charles the Bald, led a revival of Neoplatonism and might be claimed as the first original philosopher of the Middle Ages. The Carolingian revival even produced a sympathetic and approachable heretic in Gottschalk of Orbais (d. c. 868), who strove without avail to withdraw from the monastic life at Fulda, and finally suffered life imprisonment on account of his unorthodox views concerning Predestination. Altogether the men of letters diversified their efforts in an impressive manner. And while many of them became heads of outlying monastic schools, there existed no division of purpose between these and the central establishment at Aachen. The great monasteries of that day were the very reverse of 'enclosed' houses, and some became nuclei of quasi-urban populations. Visited quite often by the Emperor and his magnates, they were in effect branch stores in the business of selling culture. The famous *Epistola de litteris colendis*, a circular mandate sent (*c.* 794–96) by Charlemagne to the Abbot of Fulda and others, instructs them to promote education throughout the surrounding areas.

This revival of letters directed from the court can hardly be dismissed as ephemeral. It persisted for more than a century, and though it slackened well before 900, the succeeding troubled period did not witness anything like a return to barbarism. Other criticisms of the Carolingian scholars deserve more attention. A rootless, Latinizing élite, they preached the divine origins of Imperial power, tending in some respects to divide court and government from the mass of subjects. A school of court theologians busily demonstrating the anti-Christian character of the Byzantine Empire had no direct relevance to the populace. Yet the clericalized official culture of the medieval centuries had come to birth, had already invaded the courts and civil services of the lay rulers. To display our socialist or rationalist nerve-endings when we witness this spectacle is at best an anachronism. And for that matter, what great cultural advance in history can reasonably be judged by popular diffusionist ideals which even our own elaborate educational media have so far failed to realize?

On the other hand, the Carolingian *renovatio* has sometimes been qualitatively overestimated, for it did not constitute a Renaissance in the same sense as did that giant expansion of the human mind initiated by Italian humanists in the fourteenth century and culminating in the age of Michelangelo, Shakespeare, and Galileo. In general it failed to appreciate ancient pagan culture as a world deserving of study in its own right, quite apart from its applicability to the practical tasks imposed by Church and Empire. Most of its enthusiasts were motivated by immediate aims: by a desire to standardize the Roman liturgy throughout Christendom, to instruct an ignorant secular clergy and discipline slack monks, to suppress heresy and recover the lessons of the Christian Fathers. Charlemagne deserved his canonization because he sought sincerely to regenerate the whole Frankish nation along the lines of Roman and patriotic dogma. But he blandly identified the sacral and the secular elements of the Latin *renovatio*. 'I wish,' he said to Alcuin, 'I had a dozen Jeromes and Augustines in my chancery.' Thus the disciplines of the Church became the legitimizing bases of rule and conquest, while *renovatio* seemed inseparable from the political duty imposed upon the Empire by God. On the other hand the Papacy now saw the western Emperors as agents for the promotion of a papal theocracy, which in course of time was to become more and more

King David *came to represent an ideal of kingship under the special protection of God. This ivory carving, showing David playing the harp, is part of the cover of the Dagulf Psalter and was carved by Charlemagne's court artists between 783 and 795. Few other Carolingian ivories can be so closely dated.* (5)

political, overthrowing that balance of powers achieved by Charlemagne. Wise after the event, we can see how this court culture became a theocratic rather than an Erastian weapon.

At the court of Charlemagne

Thanks largely to Einhard's biography of Charlemagne, modelled on the *Lives of the Emperors* by Suetonius, we have a relatively authentic picture of the Imperial court and of the remarkable man at its centre. In his physical life the Emperor took pains to keep fit on a moderate diet, as well as by swimming and hunting. He discouraged heavy drinking, but his clerical admirers did not rank chastity among his virtues. Of his five regular wives he repudiated two, while three died. In addition he had children by at least four ladies whom Einhard frankly calls concubines. While forbidding his daughters to marry, he turned a blind eye to their sexual irregularities, which became the subject of a commission under the Emperor Louis. One of them bore several children to Angilbert, learned administrator, literary intimate of the Emperor, and lay Abbot of St Riquier. Despite this atmosphere and despite the extreme devotion of Charles to his aged mother, the Carolingian women never attained an influence remotely comparable with that often prevalent at Byzantium. His third wife Fastrada is said by Einhard, perhaps unfairly, to have aroused much hatred and provoked two court conspiracies. But in general the role of the queens appears to have been limited to regulating etiquette and precedence, a sphere in which the Emperor allowed them influence. The court itself was headed by a group of great officers in close contact with Charles. The Arch Chaplain – in two cases an archbishop – was minister for ecclesiastical affairs, on which there came forth a great body of Imperial legislation. Alongside him a Chancellor and a Count Palatine supervised secular business, though the Emperor personally intervened to act both as appeal judge and as arbitrator on governmental problems. The Seneschal, the Constable, the Chief Butler, together with the Masters of the Horse and of the Wardrobe, served not merely as household officials but as general administrators. Below them, what amounted to a chancery provided a major connecting link between court and local officialdom; yet it seems to have been less formally organized than were the chanceries of later medieval times. To a surprising degree the innermost ring of the court consisted, not of military aristocrats, but of the Emperor's intellectual cronies: the greatest scholars of the day, whom he addressed by fanciful Christian names. Alcuin was 'Horace', Angilbert 'Homer', and Charles himself – with perhaps a richer suitability than he intended – 'David'. Certainly his mental curiosity went beyond its political uses. He transacted affairs of state in Latin and understood Greek. He attended lectures on grammar, took part in schemes to correct the Vulgate, was fascinated by Augustine's *City of God*, and maintained a passionate interest in theological issues. His learning remained oral: until his later years he did not seriously practise writing and even then made little progress. Educationally ahead of all save a few Frankish laymen, he never became a mere prisoner of the international Latin culture. He collected Germanic literature, began to compose a Frankish grammar, and refused to wear any save Frankish costume.

By the same token, Charlemagne knew that the centre of his power lay in north-west Europe, and he did not even bother to fit up a palace in Rome, much less transfer his capital thither. To reconstruct the various architectural settings of the Carolingian court is far from easy, since its secular buildings were nearly all destroyed or reconstructed well before the end of the Middle Ages. At the bottom end of the scale were a number of manor-houses, such as those in northern France described in the *Brevium Exempla* and in certain of the Capitularies. At these establishments, advanced horticulture, stock-raising, and clothmaking continued throughout the year. Despite the Emperor's mobility – which decreased in later years – they can have seen him infrequently if ever. In effect they formed part of the immense and highly productive royal estates which enabled Charlemagne to maintain a great following. More important, some larger residences were favoured by him at certain periods of the reign, for example, at Thionville on the Moselle and Herstal near Liège. Having mentioned his great palace-chapel at Aachen and his Rhine bridge at Mainz, Einhard remarks that 'he also began to build two magnificent palaces: one not far from the city of Mainz, near the township called Ingelheim; and the other at Nijmegen, on the River Waal'. Little remains from this period at Nijmegen,

but at Ingelheim the ground-plan (including a great hall) can be traced, and some fragments of the chapel have survived. Of course, at Aachen the magnificent polygonal chapel remains by far the most impressive memorial of the Carolingian age, but on its north side the area of the vanished palace has since the fourteenth century been occupied by the city Rathaus and other buildings. In his biography of Louis the Pious, the poet Ermoldus Nigellus enlarges chiefly upon the wall-paintings at Ingelheim, where frescoes in the Imperial hall depicted scenes of Frankish history from legendary times to the conquests of Charlemagne. Ermoldus also remarks that the nave of the palace chapel there was decorated on the one side with scenes from the Old Testament and on the other with Gospel pictures. Alcuin, Theodulf, and Florus of Lyons composed literary inscriptions for this scheme. Such reported splendours have been illustrated by modern discoveries of hitherto unknown wall-paintings of the period: for example, at Lorsch, St Germain of Auxerre, St Maximin at Trier, and S. Satiro at Milan. Perhaps the least spoiled domestic building is the gatehouse or guest-house at Lorsch, having on its upper floor a painted hall. This elegant building, designed outwardly along the lines of a Roman triumphal arch, was in all likelihood used by the Emperors when they exercised their privileges as founders and lodged at the abbey. The realistic paintings, uncovered early in the present century, do not fail to recapture the spirit of the age.

A design also suggesting Roman city gates occurs on the west front of the chapel at Aachen, the exterior of which is also enlivened by Corinthian pilasters. Inside, the splendid effect of the great octagon is not unduly marred by the modernity of the present mosaics, the seventeenth-century roof, the Gothic surrounding chapels, and choir. Some of the marble and granite columns, originally brought by Charlemagne's architects from older buildings in Rome and Ravenna, have been partially replaced and all their capitals restored. Even so, the whole building nobly illustrates the continuity of Empire, the more so because it forms an ingenious variation upon Justinian's great church of S. Vitale (526–47) at Ravenna. Amongst its more personal relics of Charlemagne it contains the marble throne used by him at divine service, and afterwards for the Imperial coronation at Aachen.

The vigour of the court-inspired revival is elsewhere attested by a host of churches, by very numerous surviving examples of metalwork and ivory-carving, above all by a great series of illuminated manuscripts running from the reign of Pepin to that of Charles the Bald. Deriving from both Anglo-Irish and Mediterranean sources, these illuminations have a warm and vital character, very different in spirit from Byzantine art and not very closely paralleled by the graphic work of any other period. The central patronage of the Emperors may have discouraged art and craftsmanship in the lesser monasteries, yet the rising volume of trade with the Islamic world and with Byzantium introduced unfamiliar forms of metalwork, glassware, and textiles which stimulated Western craftsmen. The remains of a foundry have been excavated near the palace at Aachen, and it is now believed that the fine bronze railings in the palace chapel, once thought to have been removed from Theodoric's mausoleum at Ravenna, were actually made here on the spot. As for the accomplished carvers of ivory reliefs, some were patronized by leading dignitaries like Alcuin and Einhard: they worked not only at Aachen but in some of the wealthy Imperial monasteries such as Lorsch and Trier. From other monastic workshops at Metz, Tours, Reims, Corbie, St Denis – and mainly under the fluctuating patronage of the later Carolingian rulers – came the magnificent ivory panels used as book-covers. Though the iconography of these reliefs is clearly based upon Roman Christian models, a new and subtle stylization becomes apparent, forming a landmark in the genesis of medieval art.

All in all, it remains hard to find anywhere else in history a comparable propagation of culture by any single court. Of course, the movement came too soon after the admired Constantinian age to achieve a vision of Graeco-Roman civilization as a whole. In particular, the winds which bore Greek science back into the West had not yet begun to blow. Furthermore a creative rebirth must involve reaction as well as conscientious imitation. Compared with Renaissance men, the Carolingians were unprovided with a genuine urban culture, worse-equipped intellectually to grasp the ancient heritage, less deeply stirred by the thrill of recovering it across a great gulf of time. Under these circumstances they could not conceivably have produced – on the rebound – a corpus of thought and art so original as that of Renaissance Italy. Yet within that urgent crisis of the eighth and ninth centuries, their achievement retains a unique significance in Western history, while even the rich legends soon to gather about the name of Charlemagne were the naïve tribute of generations which could not analyse cultural phenomena yet instinctively recognized greatness.

Henry versus Eleanor

Medieval rulers were saddle-kings with scores of residences; and despite an increasing investment in a few theatrical buildings, not many of their Renaissance successors became desk-kings like Philip II in his Escorial. On a number of grounds, mobile living was logical. The entourage could conveniently be shifted from one seat to another, and made to devour the stocks of food hoarded against their periodic arrivals. Besides, a state of warfare was no abnormality, and many rulers spent a fair proportion of their lives campaigning against foes and rebels. Alongside the rigours of war, the upper-class fanaticism of the chase took them abroad into distant forests, sometimes causing them to neglect their concurrent military objectives. At the same time travel taught a king his job, for he needed to study his territories, roads, rivers, and fortresses; above all to know the local officials and vassals upon whom his rule depended. Likewise he needed to show himself to his populace, to impose upon all a sense of his grandeur and ubiquity, his personal share in lawgiving, his gracious paternalism in peace, his power and wrath against dissidents and rivals.

The Anglo-Saxon Chronicle relates that when in England William the Conqueror wore his crown three times a year, spending Easter at Winchester, Whitsuntide at Westmin-

Architecture under Charlemagne *was consciously modelled on that of Rome. For the royal chapel at Aachen (top) columns were brought from Rome and Ravenna, though the dome they now support is a modern restoration. At Lorsch on the Rhine (bottom) only this gatehouse, including an upper hall, survives from an extensive monastery. (6,7)*

King Henry II of England *lies with his Queen, Eleanor of Aquitaine, in the royal abbey of Fontevrault – more peacefully than they lived together in life. Henry was not only a dynamic and colourful personality but a legal reformer and an organizer of genius, setting the pattern for English administration for generations to come. (8)*

ster, and Christmas at Gloucester. At each of these three places he had a great hall, suitable for entertaining in state his archbishops, bishops, abbots, earls, thanes, and knights. From time to time a ruler might stage some unique event. In 1184 for example, Frederick Barbarossa wanted to knight his sons Henry and Frederick, and to prepare for the former's succession as co-regent. So he built a festival town outside Mainz, complete with a temporary wooden palace, a church, guest-houses, and stores for provisions. By special messengers he summoned the spiritual and lay rulers from all over the Empire, even the civic leaders of the main Lombard cities. Splendidly dressed, they all attended performances by the leading poets, musicians, and entertainers. Barbarossa, his Empress, and his sons figured at a crown-wearing, followed by a banquet at which the great nobles acted as cup-bearers. The jousting and feasting would have continued for some weeks but for a freak storm which destroyed some of the buildings, killed many people, and induced the Emperor to curtail the festival.

Heir to the hard and practical Norman kings, the Angevin Henry II (r. 1154–89) scarcely needed to convince his subjects by such pageantry that he stood at the apex of English and Norman society. Unpompous and patient towards the humble, an intelligent reformer of government, he was nevertheless a victim of that restless *Daemon* which

seemed to possess all his family. Territorially regarded, Henry looked more like an emperor than a king. Before succeeding his uncle Stephen in England, he was already Duke of Normandy and Count of Anjou. But in addition he soon acquired about one third of France through his marriage with Eleanor, heiress of Aquitaine, following the annulment of her first marriage to Louis VII of France. Seeing him thus not merely as a Frenchman but as ruling more of France than Louis, we cannot without absurdity think of his French concerns as the 'foreign policy' of an English king. Nevertheless he inherited here a kingdom which his grandfather Henry I had made more absolute, more orderly, more productive of taxation than any other part of his dominions. Its administrative capital had already been located at Westminster, in effect an enclosed royal town west of London and still quite separate from that city. In his *Court Life under the Plantagenets* (1890) Hubert Hall describes a visit made in 1177 to the court at Westminster by the Hertfordshire gentleman Richard de Anesti, one of those many bound to follow the King in order to get justice in a private suit. With the aid of ingenious quotations, Hall makes Anesti meet with the leading literary lights of Henry's court: Walter Map, author of *De Nugis Curialium* (Courtiers' Trifles); the poets Wace, Jordan, and Benoît; the chroniclers Hoveden, Diceto, and Gervase of Canterbury; the philosopher and Bishop of Chartres, John of Salisbury; the treasurer Bishop Richard Fitznigel, compiler of the famous *Dialogue on the Exchequer*. Here we are introduced to an all-male cast of international repute and activities, a group which the visitor would have been lucky to find standing around in a conversation piece at Westminster. He would have been more fortunate still to find, as Anesti is made to do, the King himself transacting business in their midst, because among the peripatetic rulers of the day Henry was perhaps the most footloose of all. His courtier Peter of Blois remarks that if the King announced his intention to spend the whole day somewhere, one could be quite sure he would make off at the crack of dawn, upsetting everybody's calculations. Even people receiving urgent medical treatment had instantly to abandon it, risking their lives on the throw of a dice and preferring to lose their lives rather than the remote chance of securing some benefit.

You can see men running madly about, urging on the packhorses, hitching the teams to their waggons, everyone in total confusion: a perfect picture of hell. Yet if the King has proclaimed that he will set off early for a certain place, no doubt he will change his mind and sleep till noon. You will then see the packhorses waiting fully loaded, the waggons silent, the runners asleep, the court purveyors at loggerheads and everybody grumbling.

And when the court expected to spend the night in a place affording ample food and shelter, the King would again change his mind and press on to some other place where there was but a single house and no food for anyone but himself. He even seemed to enjoy creating havoc for others. Peter adds that the King's legs were constantly sore through being forever in the saddle, yet he never sat down even at Mass or in council. All this, remarks the sardonic observer, might be ascribed to his horror of growing fat; yet alongside his passion for hawks and hounds he filled his free time in reading or in discussion with his men of learning. Unlike the Norman kings, Henry had in fact enjoyed a sound literary education: as we shall see, he commissioned historical works and received the dedication of numerous treatises.

The notion that 'medieval men' thought and wrote within rigid theological frameworks would not survive a study of Henry's courtiers and officials. Even the conflict between Henry and Thomas Becket (d. 1170) involved far more than the legal problem concerning the trial and punishment of criminal clerics. Clashes of temperament and plain self-interest divided the factions, while many churchmen took the King's side against Becket and the Pope. Though a former monk and a convinced papalist, Gilbert Foliot, Bishop of London, backed Henry and fought Becket because he regarded the latter as spiritually inadequate to his office. Peter of Blois, Walter Map, and the informed chroniclers afford a strong impression of the cynicism and the competitive jealousies among Henry's *curiales*. Dr Lally has recently drawn attention to a network of court patronage having close similarities with its equivalent at any Renaissance court. Justiciars and bishops introduced lesser men to the King, who in due course might reward their service by offices, grants of land, or heiresses. At a time when landed estates provided by far the greatest source of wealth and power, marriages were business arrangements, and many were arranged at court. On the other hand, the loss of influence or royal favour could as rapidly lead to forfeitures and fines, in some cases so heavy as to necessitate loans from that eminent financier Aaron of Lincoln. Access to the King was largely controlled by a group of officials and courtiers close to his person, one of these being his physician and another Peter of Blois, who advised one petitioner 'not to approach the king to present your business, unless the ground is prepared either by myself or another who knows his ways'.

To learn more about the royal buildings and the physical setting of the Angevin court we can often collate archaeological investigation with the astonishingly detailed record of royal expenditure available in the Pipe Rolls of the Exchequer. At Westminster new residential and administrative buildings grew up around the hall left by William Rufus, still probably the largest in Europe. This hall, re-roofed by Richard II, has of course survived, but little else of the period can now be found in Westminster. Nearby a two-storeyed building overlooking the Thames housed the Exchequer, the complex procedures of which are so fully described by Fitznigel. But outside this rudimentary capital, many functions of central government continued to follow the person of the King. Already under the Angevins we can trace the early stages of the process whereby his Wardrobe and his Chamber both became mobile administrative departments, each with its staff of clerks handling part of the royal revenue and issuing commands under separate seals.

Westminster apart, the residences maintained by Henry II and by his sons Richard I and John might be divided into three types: castles, palaces, and manor-houses. They spent considerable sums on the living quarters within their castles, especially at Windsor, Winchester, and Notting-

ham, where in each case Henry erected a new hall. The Pipe Rolls show him spending sums large and small upon about ninety English castles, though much of this was straightforward military expenditure at strategic places like Dover and Orford, or along the Welsh Marches and the northern Borders. In the majority of such cases the Angevins were strengthening or making more habitable structures left them by their Norman predecessors. Under Richard I these activities slackened in England, since the King spent nearly all his reign abroad and was mainly interested in his monumental project at Château Gaillard. And then, after John lost Normandy in 1204 to the French crown, his building in England grew apace and clearly rivalled that of his father.

All the same, the Angevins did not need to spend their lives behind heavy defences, since they busily constructed and repaired numerous civilian residences, ranging from the palaces at Woodstock and at Clarendon near Salisbury down to timber hunting-lodges which could be erected in a few weeks for sums little in excess of a hundred pounds each. Except for a few convenient town-houses, at Bath, Guildford, Oxford, and Portsmouth, virtually all the rest stood within the royal forests, since the Angevins yielded to none in their passion for hunting. Of the little places, Kinver in Staffordshire happens to be recorded in especial detail, while the actual site of Writtle in Essex was excavated some twenty years ago. In addition to their royal chambers, these had smallish halls and kitchens incapable of accommodating any great entourage. A wooden palisade kept out the robbers of the forest. A *vivarium* supplied carp and bream for the meatless days prescribed by the Church, while the records show that the royal houses had their wine-cellars systematically replenished through the ports of London, Bristol, and Southampton. Amongst Henry's greater residences the plan of Woodstock may have been unique in northern Europe. Its site is near the great ornamental lake in the grounds of Blenheim Palace; but what remained of it by the eighteenth century is said to have been destroyed by Sarah, Duchess of Marlborough, when she heard that her architect Vanbrugh wanted it for his own quarters. By tradition Henry built it for his mistress Rosamund Clifford; but it was far from being (as one tradition relates) a secluded *nid d'amour* to guard her against Queen Eleanor's murderous designs. It centred upon a spring, from which water ran through a number of rectangular pools surrounded by cloistered courts. All this recalls the Saracen-style palaces of the Norman kings of Sicily, with whom Henry had numerous contacts.

Rather fragmentary information has survived concerning the domestic interiors of the royal castles and houses. Some stone-walled chambers were already being made warmer by panelling. Wall-paintings are occasionally mentioned, and Gerald of Wales in his work *On the Instruction of Princes* happens to have described a poignant decoration which Henry commissioned at Winchester. This painting depicted four young eagles preying upon their parent; and the sorely tried king explained that these represented his own rebellious sons. Pointing to an eaglet which awaited the moment to pick out its father's eyes, he added that this one symbolized his youngest son John, 'whom I embrace with so much affection', but who 'will sometime in the end insult me more grievously and more dangerously than any of the others'. Otherwise Henry's mental torments do not seem to have been softened by much physical comfort, light, warmth, and air. Though rich men were now beginning to glaze their domestic windows, frequent references were still made to 'linen cloth for windows'. We know too that the Barons of the Exchequer played their complicated games with the sheriffs in a room where the windows were covered with oiled cloth. More offensively, halls and chambers were still heated from central hearths, whence the smoke gradually found its way out through a louvre in the roof. The learned authors of *The King's Works* conclude that 'even the cosmopolitan and intellectually sophisticated court of Henry II was content with an architectural setting which, although superior to that of the previous age, was nevertheless to seem uncomfortably primitive to the more refined taste of the thirteenth century'. The considerable advances made in this later period we shall shortly observe on a visit to the Sicilian kingdom. Indeed, it seems hardly surprising that a good many Englishmen in both centuries emigrated to what Lord Norwich has called 'The Kingdom in the Sun'.

When Henry II had his eldest son crowned as joint king at Westminster Abbey in 1170 he had already become estranged from his wife Eleanor, who thenceforth devoted her energies to the task of separating the vain younger Henry and his brothers from their father. Supported by the rulers of France, Flanders, and Scotland, they raised in 1173–74 a massive feudal revolt on both sides of the Channel. Having won this struggle, the King behaved more like an educational psychologist than a lion of justice. Though he kept Eleanor under more or less dignified restraint, he tried to placate the three young miscreants by giving them greater responsibility. Nevertheless Henry and Geoffrey continued plotting until their early deaths (1183; 1186), and thereafter the unfortunate father's troubles merely continued, since Richard and John soon bade fair to dismember his dominions in that final rebellion which he did not survive. Eleanor then proceeded to fight and intrigue against the French crown in a praiseworthy effort to preserve the heritage for Richard and John. Active to the last, the dowager lived on well into her eighties and died in 1204. Apart from their exhausting clash of personalities she and Henry may well seem to stand for opposing outlooks upon society and culture. Essentially heirs of the Normans, Henry and his learned officialdom tended to identify court and law-court. They executed those great legal reforms which enabled the English monarch to reach a long arm down into society, brushing aside the feudal lord and touching the life of the meanest subject. By contrast Eleanor's court at Poitiers did not greatly concern itself with sober ideas of government. At all events we remember it only as fostering the development of courtly love, a code of ideals irresponsible, personal, and romantic, ostensibly opposed not only to ecclesiastical morals but to the world of state-builders and lawgivers.

While in some sense Westminster and Poitiers may thus appear opposite poles of twelfth-century Western society, a more minute inspection of the scattered and incomplete evidence suggests a contrast far less total. It is true that Henry worked and associated with the eminent jurists, philosophers, and historians we have listed. To him Adelard of Bath dedicated his work on the astrolabe, while Jordan of Fantosme presented to him the vernacular chronicle written in 1174–83. The King commissioned Lawrence, Abbot of Westminster, to write the biography of Edward the Confessor. Altogether, in the words of Peter of Blois, 'with the King of England there is school every day, constant conversation of the best scholars and discussion of problems'. Yet as Professor Elizabeth Salter has recently urged, Eleanor herself must be taken as more than a patroness of the troubadour lyric. She could read Latin and enjoyed intellectual relationships with learned men, especially with the more 'clerkly', moralistic poets of the day. Among these were the unknown author of the *Roman d'Eneas* (c. 1160); Benoît de Sainte Maure, who wrote the *Roman de Troie*; and the Norman clerk Wace, author of the *Roman de Brut* and the *Roman de Rou* (1160–74), respectively on British and Norman history. The otherwise unknown 'Thomas' probably wrote for her the Anglo-French *Tristan* (c. 1154–58), while about the same time Bernart de Ventadorn, a poet of lowly birth, was boldly comparing his separation from Eleanor with that of Tristan from Iseult! Having no real parallels in classical or barbarian history, romantic love had been largely invented by the southern troubadours, and its earliest known practitioner had been Eleanor's own grandfather, William IX of Aquitaine (1071–1127). All the same, many of those she patronized had moved on from this lyrical world and were possessed by a very different spirit.

The courts of love

Most clearly allied with Eleanor was Marie, her own daughter by Louis VII of France. This princess married Henry, Count of Champagne, a serious nobleman who possessed a good knowledge of Latin and corresponded on biblical scholarship with John of Salisbury and Herbert of Bosham. From about 1160 until Marie's death in 1198 this couple presided over a court which contained many scholars and theologians, and which has sometimes been wrongly dismissed, along with Eleanor's own household at Poitiers, as a mere purveyor of courtly love to northern France. It was, however, Marie of Champagne who allegedly presided at 'courts of love' when, during the years around 1170, Eleanor entertained at Poitiers a large group of her younger female relatives and friends. Besides Marie, these included three actual or prospective daughters-in-law. Margaret, the daughter of Louis VII by his second marriage, became the wife of the rebellious younger Henry, while her sister Alais was affianced to Richard, and Constance, Countess of Brittany, to Geoffrey. Eleanor's own daughters also joined the party: Eleanor, Queen of Castile, and Joanna, Queen of Sicily. So did her niece, Isabella, Countess of Flanders, together with the Countess of Narbonne and others of high rank, most of them below the age of thirty.

To learn what happened in these exclusive circles we are over-dependent upon a single treatise, the *De Arte Honeste Amandi*, written about 1190 by the royal chaplain Andreas

Courtly love *was always more a literary convention than a reflection of real life, but it did tend to exalt the status of women. Above: Tristan plays the harp to King Mark; a thirteenth-century tile from Chertsey Abbey. Right: a German ivory casket with another scene from the story of Tristan and Isolde, c. 1200. Below: the storming of the Castle of Love, from a slightly later French ivory casket. (9–11)*

Joanna, Countess of Narbonne, *was among those who attended Queen Eleanor's 'courts of love' at Poitiers around 1170. This is her silver seal. (12)*

Capellanus for the amusement of Marie de Champagne. It forms a code of sentiment and behaviour for courtly love, and derives not only from the troubadour poems but from the Arthurian legends and from Ovid's *Art of Love*, that light-hearted and cynical work which now seems so totally foreign to the solemn and delicate sentiments of these modish medieval aristocrats. Nevertheless the guide by Andreas enjoyed an intense and prolonged popularity. In view of its dubious moral implications it was fortunate to suffer no serious attack from the Church until a bishop of Paris suppressed it in 1277. Its themes harmonize well enough with those of the contemporary poets and are chiefly concerned to illustrate and idealize the humble devotion of the knight towards the married high-born lady, whom he could scarcely hope to possess. With feudal marriage a land-grasping or political transaction, this romantic passion tended inevitably to be adulterous, a feature which made the Arthurian story of Lancelot and Guinevere especially relevant. Chrétien's story *Erec et Enide* (later retold by Tennyson) remains exceptional in being a story of married lovers. Nevertheless the new devotion, though it might occasionally receive a carnal reward, remained cerebral rather than sensual, and its debt to Platonism requires further exploration. Though it exalted woman, its literature took a deeper interest in the tormented male: it cannot be dismissed as a mere feminist game of revenge. In terms of courtly and feudal society, the cult involved the emotional and spiritual re-education of a rude warrior-class by refined ladies. In France the actuality fitted the script, and more especially in the small provincial courts, where royal and aristocratic females found themselves confronted not merely by sordid husbands but by idle groups of noble

and knightly younger sons. Rather than suffering dysentery on crusade or repressing their sex in a monastery, these gallants preferred to hang around the fashionable courts. Here they could indulge a taste for impossible dreams and disputations about love, though doubtless some played a double game by keeping a shrewd eye open for a landed heiress, their one real hope of achieving worldly prosperity.

According to Andreas, problems concerning the behaviour of lovers became at Poitiers and elsewhere the subject of formal 'courts of love', at which the ladies occupied the platform as judges, while the men analysed cases and submitted pleas. This mockery of the law-courts of Church and State extended also to scholastic disputation, and provided for medieval minds a richly iconoclastic entertainment. More provocatively still, it was sometimes admitted that clerics themselves might become true lovers and (with suitable adjustments) enter the gallant world of the knight. Nevertheless, modern critics doubt whether any such 'courts of love' were actually held in the twelfth century: some treat the claim as a mere literary device of Andreas Capellanus. All the same, we cannot doubt the rising prevalence of a revolutionary cult with a subtle and ever-growing influence upon the mental relationships between men and women in the feudal and higher urban classes. For all its absurdities, it proved civilizing. Literature had invaded life, but then life fed back into literature a most powerful and permanent series of themes and attitudes. Ruined in southern France by the Albigensian Crusades, the world of the troubadours survived in their disciples, the northern French *trouvères* and the German *Minnesänger*. It likewise spread to the court of Sicily, and thence to Tuscany and the kindred worlds of Dante and Beatrice, Petrarch and Laura. Through such channels this twelfth-century convention became the inheritance of the Renaissance courtier, for even in Castiglione we cannot but recall the Duchess Elizabetta on her throne, the witty chairwoman Emilia Pia, and below them all the talkative males, whose actual lives fell so far below their platonizing poses. In still later times slightly updated forms of courtly love became one important ingredient in the romantic novel and the whole game of sentiment in bourgeois society.

The wonder of the world

Whoever seeks to delineate the 'advanced' elements in medieval court life is bound to linger upon the personality and the entourage of Emperor Frederick II (b. 1194; d. 1250). By any criteria except the moral sense he deserved the title accorded him by our own Matthew Paris: *stupor mundi*. His ancestry and early life form the perfect recipe for a man of complex motives and moods. Son of the astute Emperor Henry VI (r. 1190–97) and grandson of Barbarossa, he retained a deep reverence for the great office derived from his hero Charlemagne. His mother Constance, heiress of Roger II of Sicily, brought him an even more complex inheritance. The Norman kingdom of Sicily included not merely the island but also Naples and the southern third of the Italian peninsula. Even today this whole fascinating area bears heavy traces of its experience in the Middle Ages, when it remained an amalgam of Italian, Greek, Byzantine,

Arab, and Jewish groups and cultural traditions. Roger had been not merely a great Norman administrator and builder, but an outstanding patron of the arts and sciences. Through his court had come many of the Greek and Arabic scientific books which enlivened the West. Muslim scholars had worked under his patronage just as they continued to do under that of his grandson Frederick. Creating this marvellous monument of religious and racial tolerance, the Norman kings became deeply coloured by their southern environment at a time when the Papacy feared them and so did not shock Europe by exposing the Muslim life-style of these 'baptized Sultans'. Meantime they built the superb churches – predominantly Byzantine in style – which we can still see at Monreale, Palermo, and Cefalù.

Nominally King of Sicily since his childhood, Frederick grew up amid the medley of languages and ideas in Palermo. By 1198 the early deaths of both his parents left him a ward of the great Pope Innocent III. The latter tried to protect Frederick's Italian interests, but in Germany rival groups elected two Emperors, Philip of Swabia and Otto of Brunswick. As Frederick achieved a precocious maturity, he found his southern kingdom also under the backlash of anarchy; but in 1212, having cruelly repressed the incorrigible Sicilian nobles, he took the perilous road north to Germany, where the ecclesiastical princes secured his election to the Imperial crown. Otto had already overcome Philip, but in 1214 was himself crushed by the French at the Battle of Bouvines. He died four years later, and henceforth Frederick encountered no very formidable opposition north of the Alps; he could spend by far the greater part of his life contending for supremacy over Italy. Here, despite some fitful attempts to behave tactfully towards the successors of Innocent III, his luck at last deserted him and the latter half of his reign coincided with a ruthless phase of papal ambition. In Gregory IX (r. 1227–41) and Innocent IV (r. 1243–54) he encountered two popes so able, imperious, and unforgiving as to place even the saintly Louis IX of France on his side. Having impulsively promised to go on crusade, Frederick found himself with ample tasks at home and kept postponing the expedition. When in 1227 he at last sailed, pestilence genuinely forced him to put back for a time, but then Gregory excommunicated him without hesitation. Despite this serious handicap he went on to Jerusalem, and instead of wading in Saracen blood he negotiated every privilege needed to allow Christian pilgrims free access to the holy places. This unconventional victory availed him nothing with the pontiff, who now manipulated with great skill the old enemy of the Hohenstaufen: a numerous and powerfully defended group among the city-states of northern Italy. Frederick did not pursue any simple anti-municipal policy: like other major rulers of his day, he founded, chartered, and befriended a great many towns. Nevertheless he followed Barbarossa in seeking monarchical power over Lombardy. Amid desultory warfare punctuated by hollow reconciliation with the popes, he tended to lose military advantages through disastrous moments of over-confidence. His spectacular victory in the pitched Battle of Cortenuova (1237) was poorly followed up, while eleven years later, as he besieged Parma, the starving citizens burst

Frederick II, 'stupor mundi': *a marble head which has better claims than any other to be a portrait of the Emperor. (13)*

out while he was hawking and stormed his siege-base, the new city he confidently called Victoria. Here they captured even his regalia and his harem, slaying his faithful minister Thaddaeus of Suessa. Then in the following year the Bolognese took, and refused to ransom, his bastard son the poet Enzio, King of Sardinia, a great favourite since Frederick's legitimate heir Henry had raised a rebellion in Germany. Reduced to desperation by these disasters and facing plots against his life by some of his intimate associates, Frederick grimly struggled on; but in 1250 he died at Fiorentino, leaving Manfred, another estimable bastard, as regent of Sicily. Yet the dynasty now lay broken and his remaining legitimate descendants died before they could gain control of its former dominions. In 1266 the death of Manfred in battle against the papalist 'crusader' Charles of Anjou placed the Hohenstaufen cause beyond hope of revival. But in truth that cause never died in the hearts of many passionate admirers like Dante, who revered Frederick's achievements, sighed for Imperial rule in Italy and detested the political popes.

Compared with Frederick, no ruler in all European history had a keener intelligence or broader interests. He did not merely forestall his Renaissance successors in patronizing genius: he belonged in his own right to the select company of 'universal men'. Dante regarded him as the father of Italian poetry:

The illustrious heroes Frederick Caesar and his noble son Manfred followed after elegance and scorned what was mean; so that all the best compositions of the time came from their court. Thus, because their royal throne was in Sicily, all the poems of our predecessors in the vernacular tongue were called Sicilian.

23

East and West *met and mingled in the cosmopolitan atmosphere of Sicily. The royal throne at Monreale cathedral (left) has inlays of coloured marbles and mosaics in the Byzantine style, but with definite awareness of Islamic art, for instance in the frieze of key-hole pattern at the upper level. But Frederick's 'renovatio' entailed a deliberate revival of Roman motifs, as shown by the heads from his triumphal arch at Capua (top), and a female head in S. Pantaleone, Ravello. (14–16)*

Frederick helped to hand on the Provençal tradition of courtly love to the poets of Pisa, Arezzo, Siena, and Florence, all of which enjoyed close relations with his court. A little of his own poetry survives; but this pursuit formed a tiny part of his intellectual life, for he read widely in six languages and in all the contemporary fields of knowledge. Sending some translations of Aristotle to the University of Bologna, he wrote:

Since our youth, before we took up the responsibilities of government, we have sought always after learning and have breathed her balsamic perfumes. Now the cares of state demand most of our attention, yet the little time we have to spare . . . we spend in pleasurable reading, . . . meditating upon the manuscripts of all kinds which, classified in due order, adorn our cupboards.

In his constant travels he carried with him the bulky works of Aristotle and Avicenna on pack-mules; in the *débâcle* at Victoria, magnificently illustrated books bound in gold and silver were looted by the men of Parma. With the aid of learned Muslims and Jews, he developed a very fair acquaintance with the philosophical and scientific writings of both cultures. These he was able to review alongside a first-hand knowledge of Aristotle, whom he aspired to correct by independent researches. Frederick personally composed *De Arte Venandi cum Avibus (The Art of Hunting with Birds)*, no mere sportsman's handbook but also an original contribution to natural history based on his own minute and original observations. Such was its practical merit that it remained for centuries a standard treatise on falconry throughout Europe. His interest in animals induced him to collect and travel around with a menagerie: no doubt he also wanted to impress his subjects, and Germans were duly amazed to see his camels peacefully cropping their meadows. Expert in veterinary surgery and horse-breeding, he also studied and advocated the new agricultural methods of the Cistercians.

We have already seen that Charlemagne and Henry Plantagenet surprised contemporaries by their moderation in eating and drinking. Frederick went further: he was a valetudinarian who studied his diet and had a passion for hygiene. He offended devout Christians by bathing with such frequency – and worst of all, even on Sundays. Naturally enough, he patronized the writers of several medical treatises and made the famous school of Salerno the best in Europe, giving it control of the medical services throughout his kingdom. More important still, in 1224 he founded at Naples the earliest state university in Europe 'in order that those who have hunger for knowledge may find within the kingdom the food for which they are yearning, and may not be forced to go into exile and beg the bread of learning in strange lands'. He enabled it to compete financially for the best teachers, while also establishing cheap lodgings, food, and cash loans for poor scholars. That its outstanding faculty became that of Law should cause no surprise, since Frederick's court included a remarkable group of jurists, who enabled him to give his kingdom what one modern historian describes as 'the fullest and most adequate body of legislation promulgated by any ruler since Charlemagne'.

The art of falconry *was one of Frederick II's many attainments. His book on the subject became a standard work. These two miniatures from it represent Frederick and his natural son Manfred. (17,18)*

Frederick's 'renovatio'

While the Emperor shared the Carolingian passion for *renovatio*, his position, more distant in time from ancient Rome, enabled him to gain better perspectives, and so in some considerable measure to anticipate the historical and archaeological attitudes of fifteenth-century humanism. Excavating ancient buildings at Ravenna, he discovered classical statues and used them to decorate his castles. In his register for 1240 there is a letter from Foggia ordering ancient statuary to be taken from Naples to Lucera, where he had founded a new city based upon the crafts of some sixteen thousand Muslim subjects evacuated from Sicily. Though he inherited such magnificent Byzantine-Romanesque buildings from his Norman ancestors, he created a more closely neo-classical style amongst the architects and sculptors of his court. This he initiated with the Capuan Gate, which guarded the bridge over the Garigliano. Frederick is said by a reliable chronicler to have drawn the plan of this novel edifice with his own hand. Though the original suffered destruction in 1557, its design was preserved in the triumphal arch built by the Aragonese rulers at Naples, in some drawings at Vienna, and in some pieces of its actual sculpture. At Capua and elsewhere a flourishing school of sculptors produced works combining classical gravity with medieval liveliness. Most surviving examples are badly battered, yet in the cathedral of Ravello the superb head of a noble lady exemplifies the style at its best. The same school also produced semi-classical busts of Frederick, two of these having been recently discovered in Apulia.

While one cannot rely upon the shocking stories told by the papalist chroniclers, it remains evident that Frederick's involvement with Muslims, Jews, scientists, and dancing-girls played into the hands of his enemies. Too often did his talent for alarming the pious escape from those controls which more cautious and hypocritical rulers respected. The story that he dismissed Christ, Moses, and Muhammad as 'the three impostors', could be an unguarded epigram or even a scandal-monger's invention; yet numerous sources indicate that his theological speculations passed well beyond what the Church would tolerate, particularly from a layman. Gregory IX actually accused him of saying that he could only believe what was proved by the force of reason! It seems very possible that he disbelieved in the Virgin Birth and in the recently defined doctrine of Transubstantiation. Like many 'modern' men he probably fluctuated between religious doubts and pieties: by no means all his actions seem to spring from a single, consistent system of belief. Certainly he did not scruple to make bishops and German nobles sit down together with Muslim potentates, while his Saracen settlement at Lucera produced some excellent military detachments which fought reliably against the papalists. Such stories as the one which makes him dissect living criminals to study their digestive processes may well have been shrewdly concocted in accordance with his known scientific and medical interests. His occasional acts of ferocity against rebels or suspected traitors can have done little to darken his reputation among contemporaries, since devilish cruelties of all kinds were the small change of Italian politics in the thirteenth century.

So versatile and intellectual a ruler naturally collected an erudite and 'advanced' group of courtiers and protégés. Like Charlemagne, Frederick allowed his intimate friends to tease him at dinner-parties, and even pretended not to hear their more outrageous sallies. At the upper end of his court society stood the group of soldiers and administrators drawn from several countries; and for many years pre-eminent among them was Hermann von Salza, Grand Master of the Teutonic Knights and perhaps the greatest of all the heads of medieval military orders. One of the Emperor's 'good geniuses', Hermann strove all his life to preserve some semblance of cooperation between Empire and Papacy. On the other hand Frederick did not hesitate to promote *parvenu* advisers with outstanding ability. The prime example of a tragic careerist is Pietro della Vigna, by origin a jurist of Bologna and an exponent of the formal style of Latin prose called *ars dictandi*. This prototype of the lay civil servant seems to have contributed much to the clever anti-papal propaganda distributed throughout the contemporary courts of Europe. Why Pietro fell from power in 1248 has been much disputed. It happened at a time of nefarious plotting against the Emperor's life, and though it seems almost incredible that a minister so successful and honoured would have committed treason against his patron, it may well be that Frederick's suspicions were manipulated by the jealous group of German and Italian nobles then in the ascendant at court. Whatever the truth, the unfortunate ex-minister was condemned to be blinded – a favourite punishment of the period – and he subsequently committed suicide.

Despite occasional horrors and disasters, the court of the Sicilian kingdom was a school of manners which attracted

very numerous young nobles of Germany and Italy. But its most interesting element is the group of intellectuals close to the Emperor. Among them a leading part was played for many years by Michael Scott, astrologer, alchemist, and magician, whose demon horse, magic ship, and other alleged dealings with the occult provided material for many sensational passages ranging from Dante's *Inferno* to *The Lay of the Last Minstrel*. Frederick accepted astrological guidance throughout his career: he prompted Scott to write some of his works and even sent him on a tour of the universities of Europe to disseminate new versions of Aristotle. The Emperor's scientific interests were also stimulated by Elias of Cortona, the General of the Franciscans, who spent much time at the Sicilian court after his deposition by the Pope. Amongst the doctors, Master Theodore compiled Frederick's diet-sheets and wrote him a treatise on hygiene; another, Zaccaria, compiled from Greek sources a treatise on ophthalmology for his Imperial patron, who suffered from shortsightedness in his later days. Needless to add, Frederick also patronized Jewish physicians, held for centuries in high regard and employed by many distinguished Christians.

In one respect at least the Sicilian court of the thirteenth century differed from the High Renaissance courts: it gave no social or political scope to women. Frederick's three wives, Constance of Aragon, Yolande of Brienne, and Isabella, the handsome sister of Henry III of England, all lived in luxurious but almost Islamic seclusion. When Isabella's brother Richard of Cornwall visited her, he found her surrounded by new and hitherto unknown toys, games, and musical instruments ordered by her husband to keep her amused. It looks as if Frederick kept the refinements of courtly love to the literary compartment of his mind, though his canzone *Of his Lady in Bondage* – admirably translated by Rossetti – explores the mind of a captive and scornful woman with amazing sensitivity. But on this same occasion Richard of Cornwall himself was overwhelmed by kindnesses. Delighted by a court variety-show, he found especial pleasure in two lovely Saracen girls who danced upon rolling spheres to the accompaniment of castanets and tambourines. In one of his famous drawings Matthew Paris – who got such information directly from Richard – depicts these entertainers as most decorously clad, an impression which their employer Frederick attempted to implant upon the Pope and other suspicious critics. The mothers of his numerous illegitimate children are unrecorded, except for Bianca Lancia, the daughter of a Piedmontese nobleman and composer of Provençal poetry. She became the mother of Manfred and also of Frederick's daughter Constance, who eventually married the Emperor John Vatatzes, ruler of a part of the Byzantine Empire. It does indeed seem most probable that Frederick quietly married Bianca after the death in 1241 of his English wife: certainly he endowed her with large estates many years after the birth of her children. She must have occupied a unique place in his affections, and he likewise bestowed special pains upon the education of Manfred, who became his one important successor.

Though Frederick's court seldom stayed long in one place, it could in every province enjoy the amenities of several admirably appointed castles and villas. He referred to these as 'our places of solace'. Characteristically he added no important ecclesiastical buildings, though at Palermo he had the use of the exquisite Palatine Chapel built by his grandfather Roger. Several of his own residences were coast-defence castles, or, like Lagopesole, protected strategic routes. Others, such as the Maniace at Syracuse and the Ursino at Catania, also dominated cities. In the highlands of central Sicily, Enna was presumably a summer residence, while Gioia del Colle, one of his Apulian hunting-boxes, has even today an intimate modernity, with fireplaces like those of some Florentine palace in later days. Frederick personally designed the most striking of all: Castel del Monte, between the Murge hills and the coastal plain of Apulia. Standing on a conical hill, it forms a single octagon with eight projecting towers at its angles: within are sixteen state-rooms of moderate size but decorated by lavish stonework and sculpture. In many of these places the sanitation is strikingly modern and sometimes includes elaborate bathrooms. Frederick's court never lived amid that malodorous squalor which under Louis XIV enforced the annual closure of Versailles for elementary purification. Ample evidence attests the choice quality of his bronzes, marbles, furniture, and fabrics; or again, the delicacies both Italian and oriental which were served at his table. Nothing could have differed more from the film producer's image of medieval carousing against a background of crumbling stone walls. In addition, it should not be thought that – in Sicily at least – formal gardens date from the fifteenth century. At several of Frederick's residences, including those at Palermo, Cosenza, and Syracuse, he is known to have laid down gardens of great intricacy and elegance, and to have enjoyed a range of fruits, vegetables, and herbs unobtainable throughout most of Europe until much more recent times.

The central role of Frederick II in European history can scarcely be grasped by those who arrange that century around his kinsman St Thomas Aquinas, or around the Gothic North. The years of his political collapse and death did but mark the beginning of a deeper influence. Having inherited so much from King Roger II, Frederick bequeathed even more to the rulers of Renaissance Italy. Already in those years his sons and regional subordinates were establishing households full of poets, astrologers, and things of beauty. Around 1250 also there arose the first generation of the new *signori* who seized power in so many Italian cities, and who had learned from Frederick that the magnificence and wonder of a court could furnish a ruler with a political weapon of the first order. These autocrats were *epigoni*, not genuine originators; but ere long they joined the patrons of the rising new humanism. This latter preserved the old literary heritage – courtly love included, as with Petrarch – yet it also realized the further aspirations of Frederick and his circle by grasping ever more firmly, and then building upon, the achievements of the Ancient World. Meanwhile no medieval Emperor, Charlemagne apart, left livelier memories or more widespread anticipation of a Second Coming. In Frederick's case these were long to be accompanied by a passionate regret, when men reflected how nearly he had come to creating an all-Italian monarchy, the aspiration of

Frederick's life, *like that of most medieval kings, was spent travelling. Many of the castles which he erected are still to be seen throughout southern Italy and Sicily; but the most famous of them, Castel del Monte in Apulia (above), was built for pleasure rather than defence. He died in 1250, and is buried in a splendid porphyry tomb at Palermo (below). (19, 20)*

Dante, Petrarch, and Machiavelli alike. Even today one cannot easily forget him amid the castles of Apulia and Sicily; least of all in the streets of Palermo, where he wandered as a boy and began to assimilate the multiple cultures of the Norman kingdom. Fittingly enough, in Palermo cathedral a chapel off the nave holds his tomb, together with those of his parents, his Norman grandfather Roger, his first wife Constance of Aragon. All these massive structures of red porphry huddle together in the dim light, withdrawn from the rest of that ample but emasculated interior. And to this day one may seldom go there without finding a pathetic bunch of flowers on the step of the Imperial sepulchre.

The late medieval courts

The century which followed the death of Frederick II saw the extension into northern Europe of secularist and anti-clerical influences by no means dissimilar to those he had embraced. Philip IV of France (r. 1285–1314) burned the Grand Master of the Templars, bullied to death Pope Boniface VIII, and dragged the Papacy from Rome to Avignon, where it remained from 1305 to 1377. The main

Charles V of France *(r. 1364–80) epitomizes the monarch as social and cultural leader. In this miniature he is seen receiving an illuminated Bible from one of his courtiers, Jean de Vaudetar. (21)*

cultural interest attaching to this most uncourtly of rulers lies in the nationalist and Erastian campaign waged by his publicists. In 1306 the Dominican author John of Paris sought to restrict the powers of the Church to the spiritual field, while assigning to secular rulers a total control over the earthly lives of their subjects. More pointedly still, in his work *De Recuperatione Terrae Sanctae* (1307–8) Pierre Dubois aspired to the creation of a universal French Empire with its capital in the Holy Land and its king presiding over an international council of lesser Christian rulers. Needless to add, Dubois urged that the Papacy should remain at Avignon, governed by a French College of Cardinals. Meanwhile the clergy, no longer celibate, should become salaried officials supported by the former ecclesiastical properties, now fully nationalized. At least until the French Revolution, few anti-clerical writers went to greater extremes.

Such overwhelming ambitions and propaganda naturally constrained the enemies of France and of Avignon to adopt similar tactics. In the next generation the chief victim of the Avignonese Papacy was the Emperor Louis the Bavarian (r. 1314–47), who for twenty years retained in his court the two leading intellectuals of the century. Marsiglio of Padua (d. 1342) wrote the Erastian classic *Defensor Pacis* (1324), which in the event went on furnishing ammunition against Rome and was still useful to Protestant Reformers a couple of centuries later. The other celebrity at the court of Louis was William of Occam (d. *c.* 1349), who not only wrote anti-papal tracts but evolved a new philosophical system purporting to destroy the older models of scholasticism. He rejected the claim of Aquinas to reconcile reason with revelation, and placed Christian dogma solely upon the vulnerable basis of revelation. These court schools of propaganda, more sustained, more intellectual, more extreme than that of the Emperor Frederick, directly foreshadowed some aspects of the campaigns waged a couple of centuries later by Martin Luther and Thomas Cromwell, though with the important difference that these latter were to enjoy the resources of the printing press.

By contrast, several fourteenth-century rulers and their courts display the connoisseurship and the cool literary interests which we more readily associate with their humanist successors. The early Valois Kings of France Philip VI (r. 1328–50), John II (r. 1350–64), and Charles V (r. 1364–80) all became notable patrons of art and scholarship, while the brothers of Charles, the Dukes of Anjou, Berry and Burgundy, were also discriminating collectors. To grasp the courtliness of the period one cannot do better than study the *Très Riches Heures* of the Duc de Berry. Earlier still Popes John XXII (r. 1316–34) and Benedict XII (r. 1334–42) built up at Avignon a *curia* of several hundred officials and a renowned library of two thousand volumes. Hither they attracted a brilliant international society of scholars, artists, ambassadors, and visiting magnates. Already the Papacy was establishing that splendid yet worldly style which did so much to favour the humanist Renaissance and to provoke the Protestant Reformation. Among the secular courts of fourteenth-century Europe that of Charles V has an exceptional interest. He built himself apartments of unparalleled

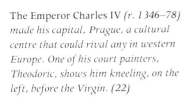

The Emperor Charles IV *(r. 1346–78) made his capital, Prague, a cultural centre that could rival any in western Europe. One of his court painters, Theodoric, shows him kneeling, on the left, before the Virgin. (22)*

magnificence in the Louvre, and at Beauté-sur-Marne and other palaces. He was the first French king to collect a great library, and towards the end of his life he owned some 1,200 manuscripts, many of them masterworks of the illuminator's art. It was he, not his Burgundian kinsmen, who first promoted the great tapestry workshops of Paris and Arras. The poetess Christine de Pisan describes a day in the life of Charles, whose public habits became as formalized as those of Louis XIV. His toilet finished, the King completed his early devotions by hearing a Mass set to music, after which he received petitioners or attended his Council. Taking his first meal at ten o'clock and being cheered by a little soft music, he entered his state-apartments for two hours of audiences with his magnates and visiting ambassadors. Having next rested for an hour, he inspected his jewels, manuscripts, and pictures, before attending vespers in the late afternoon. Then in summer he walked in his gardens, perhaps joined by the Queen and their children. In winter he read his books, took a very moderate supper with the nobles of his household, and so retired to bed. Occasionally he would relax his studious habits and provide a banquet with elaborately staged entertainments between the courses. And the advance of courtly ideals appears in the fact that this could now be regarded as an exemplary day for a good king.

Meanwhile in central Europe the outstanding type of a cultured, devout, and formalized court was afforded by the French-educated Emperor Charles IV (r. 1346–78), whose patronage we glimpsed at the outset of this essay. Though with his famous Golden Bull Charles did all he could to

regulate the constitution of the chaotic Holy Roman Empire, he is best remembered as a great ruler of his own kingdom of Bohemia. Though paying two brief visits to Rome, he avoided entanglement in the snares of Italian politics, and on this account incurred the wrath of Petrarch, upon whose shoulders the mantle of Dante had fallen. By judicious appointments to Bohemian court offices Charles gathered together at Prague the group of scholars responsible for polishing the official Latin usages and founding the *Kanzleisprache*, an improved High German which deeply affected the literary language of later days. One of the first acts of his reign was to establish (1348) the renowned Caroline University of Prague, the earliest to be founded east of the Rhine. Here he drew his ideas not only from the University of Paris, which he had known in his youth, but also from Bologna, which in 1372 provided the model for his Faculty of Law. As professors he admitted both Czechs and Germans, while students flocked in from all over the Empire, as well as from Poland and other Slavonic lands. Both scholarship and art remained close to the court of Charles IV. The first Chancellor of the Caroline University was Archbishop Ernest of Pardubic, the leading Bohemian classical scholar and a correspondent of Petrarch. He commissioned the famous Glatz Madonna for his own home town of Kladzko. Another patron at court was Bishop John of Středa, whose illustrated manuscripts are described by Michael Levey as 'in sheer artistic quality perhaps the finest of all work produced in the court circle'. The Emperor himself did not merely collect but also commissioned books: in particular he sought to create definitive histories of

The reign of Matthias Corvinus, *the humanist King of Hungary, joins two ages of Europe's history. To a court hitherto largely medieval in spirit he brought a Renaissance artist, Giancristoforo Romano, from Italy to make portrait reliefs of himself and his consort, Beatrice of Aragon. In the centre is an allegorical triumph from a manuscript of Philostratus' 'Heroica' made for him about 1480. (23–25)*

Bohemia, at first from the Florentine John of Marignola and then from a native, the Abbot Neplach, who compiled the *Summula chronice tam romane quam bohemice.*

Though Charles continued the building of the cathedral of St Vitus on the Hradčany and founded the 'New Town' of Prague, little remains of his secular buildings in either area, while even his great bridge across the Ultava has been transformed by Baroque statuary. To sense the atmosphere of his court, one should visit the superb castle of Karlštejn, some thirty kilometres to the south-west of Prague. Its evocative character depends upon the series of unspoiled and highly personal wall-paintings in the Emperor's state-apartments and chapels. Here one no longer sees the wily ruler with the low profile or the much-travelled patron of learning. Instead there emerges the religious visionary, the collector of holy relics – in crude terminology, the 'medieval' side of an almost 'modern' ruler. At court and elsewhere in Bohemia there had developed a strong native tradition of painting, though in some cases these artists had obviously seen the murals of Giotto at Padua and Assisi. In addition the Emperor sometimes bought pictures by Italians who probably never visited Bohemia, such as Tommaso da Modena, whose *Virgin and Child* can still be seen at Karlštejn. In this brilliant setting, one is tempted to think of Charles as a unique figure for his times in east-central Europe; but this conclusion would not be accurate, since his career forms part of a broader process: the penetration of advanced Western cultural motives not only into Bohemia but also into Poland and Hungary. The closest parallel to

Charles IV was his friend Casimir III of Poland (r. 1333–70), who also codified the laws, reformed the chancery, patronized the arts with intelligence, and saw university education as an urgent need for the erection of a strong Polish state. With this last ideal in mind – but also to stem the outflow of students to Prague – Casimir founded in 1364 the second great university in these eastern lands: that of Cracow. But these were not 'Renaissance courts' in the commonly accepted sense of that term. Contemporaries of Petrarch, such rulers and their men of learning came rather too early to partake of the new humanism, yet they did prepare the ground for its reception in the following century.

In Hungary the building of elaborate late Gothic residential palaces was succeeded after the middle of the fifteenth century by a rapid assimilation at court of Italian Renaissance art and architecture. Though in east-central Europe these developments were not limited to Hungary, they have recently acquired a special interest there, on account of dramatic rediscoveries by Hungarian archaeologists. After the catastrophic defeat and death of King Louis II at Mohács (1526), central Hungary underwent a century and a half of Turkish occupation; and though the conquerors built mosques and baths, they took little interest in the preservation of royal palaces in what had become a frontier province. Frontier warfare and natural decay thus conspired to ruin these buildings, while even after the Habsburg reconquest of the 1680s, archaeological reconstruction had still not become fashionable. Though interest revived during the nineteenth century, systematic excavation began less than fifty years ago: indeed, its chief results have emerged only since the Second World War. High above the Danube but directly beneath the vast modern palace of Buda, the exploration of its medieval predecessors has achieved remarkable success in the years following 1948. Here László Gerevich did not merely trace ground-plans but recovered major fragments of the late Gothic and Renaissance constructions, which went far to establish their elevations and architectural décor. The maladroit King Sigismund (r. 1387–1437; later also King of Bohemia and Emperor) created a splendid château, rivalling those of Paris, Avignon, and Prague. Then from about 1467, the great Matthias Corvinus (r. 1458–90) followed the ideas of his humanists – who knew Italy well – by a process of reconstruction in the Renaissance idiom. Today many features of both periods are exhibited with spectacular effect in the underground situations where they came to light. These discoveries harmonize admirably with the immense European fame of King Matthias as patron of scholars, and with his creation of the unique Corvina Library, a collection of some two thousand choice manuscripts. Of these about 180 survive in many libraries, forty being in Hungary itself, thanks to a beneficent restoration made in 1875 by the Sultan Abdul Hamid II.

Two parallel archaeological investigations have meanwhile progressed at Visegrád and at Esztergom, both some forty kilometres north of Budapest near the great southward bend of the Danube. At the former site about 1320 King Charles Robert began a large palace which his successors continued to develop until the time of Matthias Corvinus, who could simultaneously entertain there the suites of four visiting rulers. In 1536 Archbishop Nicolaus Oláh described in detail the courts, fountains, chapels, and three hundred rooms which he had seen at Visegrád in his youth. But by this date the place lay in the war zone between Christian and Turk, and the succeeding destruction became so complete that the prelate's description seemed a tall story – at all events until the excavations carried out from 1934 onwards proved him guiltless of exaggeration. At Esztergom, still the primatial see of Hungary, the medieval kings had long resided, yet on the removal of their capital to Buda, the palace there had been handed over to the archbishops. One of these, Vitéz János the humanist chancellor of Corvinus, reconstructed it about 1465–72 with the aid of Italian artists.

Here again excavation has extended the picture, while the beautiful Italianate burial chapel (1507) of another archbishop, Bakócz Tamás, has also been preserved within the present nineteenth-century basilica. I select for mention these Hungarian courts, partly because they remain unfamiliar in Western Europe and America, and partly since they illustrate the indivisibility of Western culture, which had expanded into the eastern borderlands with immense speed throughout the fifteenth century. Today the so-called Iron Curtain still looks a thin veil to the eyes of any historian.

Concerning the court of France under its curious fifteenth-century rulers, sound guidance is easily accessible both in French and English. The available literature on the English courts remains rather more patchy, though a few recent historians have done good service within certain areas of the late Middle Ages, notably on the households of Richard II and Edward IV. Throughout Europe as a whole the period remains one of great richness and variety: amid the stately ceremonial of the Teutonic Knights at Marienburg one may even observe a court without female influences. And as every visitor to the Doges' Palace would agree, Venice could boast one of the utmost magnificence, yet lacking both the advantages and the disadvantages of a genuine monarchy. Needless to add, a comparative study of fifteenth-century European courts would in itself form a fascinating and useful exercise. Here is a period when – especially though not exclusively in Italy – the close interdependence of municipal culture and princely patronage needs to be far better understood. Yet this preceding essay has not been concerned with the historical continuities: rather has it aimed to illustrate selectively the very solid and sophisticated foundations from which the life of the Renaissance courts arose. The rest of our book might otherwise fall badly out of focus without some recollection, however summary, of the great variety and opulence of all these medieval traditions.

The royal palace of Buda, *as it was about 1470: a woodcut from the Nuremberg Chronicle. Archaeological research is now recovering many details of the medieval building. (26)*

Two
THE COURTIER
The Renaissance and changing ideals

✦

SYDNEY ANGLO

HE REASON INDUCING ME to write of a courtier,' said Louis Guyon in 1604, 'is to take away a false persuasion, imprinted in common and popular judgment, in thinking that a courtier is none other than an affronter of merchants, a dissembler, a flatterer, incivil, a liar, a ruffian, a swaggerer, a troublesome fellow: in brief, a man made up of all vices.' To remedy this false opinion the author demonstrates 'what manner of man a courtier ought to be, and his ends'. For Guyon, a courtier should be noble by birth, good-looking, well-formed, and agile. He should be expert in arms and horsemanship; and just as he should be 'skilful in wrestling, leaping, dancing, playing on some or many instruments of music, so should he likewise readily sing any poet or historian'. He must be a linguist; a fluent conversationalist; witty but not offensive; and he must avoid 'bitter or unsavoury mocks', especially towards women who 'in regard to their imbecility, are to be respected'. His behaviour towards his prince must be attentive but not servile; he must wait for favours, not demand them; and he must never insinuate himself by 'serving in murderous or bawdy employments'. He should dress soberly; avoid gaming and drunkenness; and engage in amorous pursuits only with propriety and decorum. All these qualities are to be deployed to gain favour, so that the courtier may become a trusted adviser, able to express the truth without fear, and thus keep his prince on the path of virtue. A virtuous courtier makes a virtuous prince, whereas a vicious courtier makes his prince wicked and detestable: 'of this mind were all such as have meddled in writing of a courtier; and among others Balthazar the Castillannois'.

The ideal courtier was a concept that had been evolving all through the Middle Ages, but was given definitive form by Castiglione in 'Il Cortegiano' (1514). The book grew out of discussions held at the court of Urbino during the time of Duke Guidobaldo da Montefeltro. This frontispiece to a manuscript copy by Fra Simone Ferri da Urbino dates from a century after the book was written, but it is our only visual record of its setting. In the chair is the Duchess Elizabetta Gonzaga. To her left is probably one of the protagonists, the vivacious Emilia Pia. (27)

Guyon's essay has a twofold value as the starting point for this enquiry. First, it makes clear a tension in sixteenth-century attitudes towards court life: that is, between the extremes which saw courtiers as noble advisers, cultured, civilized, and civilizing; or which chastized them as

> Base sycophants, crumb-catching parasites,
> Obsequious slaves, which bend at every nod:
> Insatiate harpies, gormandizing kites,
> Epicures, atheists, which adore no God
> But your own bellies and your private gain,
> Got by your oily tongues bewitching train.

Secondly, Guyon's list of courtly virtues – despite his disingenuous closing remark – derives entirely from Castiglione; and, just as it is impossible to write of courts without writing of courtiers, so it is impossible to discuss the courtier without considering Baldassare Castiglione's *Il Cortegiano*. What then were the possible ways of regarding the lives and the purposes of courtiers? What traditions of courtly theory were available prior to the first publication of *Il Cortegiano* in 1528? To what extent did Castiglione utilize earlier traditions? How far did he transcend them? And, finally, what happened to the courtier after Castiglione?

'An evil life'

From remote antiquity it had been believed that the hierarchy of the heavens, with the sun surrounded by the planets and lesser stars, was represented on earth by the political hierarchy of the king surrounded by his magnates and servants working within the royal palace. Such a view was really concerned to magnify the position of the monarch; and the role assigned to those who served him was merely a corollary of the metaphor. When the focus wandered from the solar centre, the images of the court and its denizens became less flattering. Throughout the Middle Ages and the Renaissance, however much the sun imagery of kingship may have flourished, the court itself was deemed far more like Hell than like Heaven.

It was a place of danger, discomfort, and iniquity: a school for developing the worst features of human ambition. To Peter of Blois, in the twelfth century, the courtier seemed

The classical world *provided the Renaissance with a series of models which it interpreted in the light of its own conventions. In 1519 Francis I of France commissioned a manuscript of Albert Pigghe's 'Commentaries' on Caesar's 'Gallic Wars'. Caesar and his entourage are shown as a typical contemporary court, but Francis in his turn saw himself as another Caesar; on another page their two portraits appear side by side. (28)*

a martyr of the world, who, after many tribulations, enters at last into the Kingdom of Hell. For William of Malmesbury, the court was 'a death in life, a hell on earth'; and Walter Map based his *Courtiers' Trifles* (c. 1190) upon an analogy between the court and Hades where courtiers undergo perpetual and senseless torments. The theme continued without abatement in the fifteenth century: the humanist Aeneas Sylvius Piccolomini described court life as simply Hell; and early in the sixteenth century Jean Bouchet regarded it, if not as Hell itself, then certainly as an antechamber to that establishment.

If court were indeed a Hell on earth, then clearly little good could be expected of those who dwelt therein; and the terms in which court life and courtiers were attacked throughout the Middle Ages remained constant. William of Malmesbury's description (c. 1125) of William Rufus and his parasites might have provided a blueprint for those who discerned similar sins at the court of Henry III of France five hundred years later. William tells us that military discipline had been lost, so that the courtiers were free to plunder poor country folk. 'Then there was flowing hair,' he laments, 'and extravagant dress; and then was invented the fashion of shoes with curved points; then the model for young men was to rival women in delicacy of person, to mince their gait, to walk with loose gesture and half naked. Enervated and effeminate, they unwillingly remained what nature had made them; the assailers of others' chastity, prodigal of their own. Troops of pathics, and droves of harlots, followed the court.' John of Salisbury (c. 1115–80) was even more

colourful in his account of the courtier's unabashed sexuality. 'When the rich, lascivious wanton,' he writes, 'is preparing to satisfy his passion he has his hair elaborately frizzled and curled; he puts to shame a courtesan's make-up, an actor's costume, the dress of a noble, the jewels of a maiden, and even the triumphal robes of a prince.' And John continues with prurient relish to describe how the courtier, in plain view of others, caresses his paramour, with a hand that has been 'encased in glove to protect it from the sun and keep it soft for the voluptuary's purpose'. Even in a treatise on courtly love, Andreas Capellanus (fl. 1175–80) had been constrained to reprove men who adorned themselves like women; while, a hundred years later, within the context of a military ideal of knighthood, Ramon Lull had despised those who were proud of their physical beauty and who loved to 'hold the mirror in the hand'. The courtiers of fourteenth-century France were repeatedly pilloried by Eustache Deschamps for their exaggerated clothing, homosexuality, and fawning servility. In 1405, in a sermon preached before the Queen of France herself, Jacques le Grand denounced the debauchery and effeminacy of the court; and in 1442 Martin le Franc employed an assault on the latest fashion in men's breeches to introduce his diatribe against courtly lechery. Criticisms such as these abound; and they have sometimes been dismissed as literary commonplaces employed for moralistic effect. Such commonplaces may, however, represent permanent or recurrent truths. The flatterer – that 'cataract in the eye' of his victim – constantly attends upon those who have patronage to dispense, at any time and in any place. Similarly, exaggerated costume, effeminacy, and affectation seem recurrent features in human society wherever fashion becomes self-consciously effective. What would William of Malmesbury have made of

In the Faculty of Vice *the young courtier is instructed in swearing, slandering, drinking . . . an illustration from Pierre Michault's satire on court life, 'Doctrinal du temps present', Lyon, about 1484. (29)*

the permanent-waved, deodorized, reodorized, fashion-plate male of the late twentieth century, with his handbag, skin-tight trousers, and simulated orthopaedic boots?

The real point made by the medieval critic of courtiers is not merely that their life is degenerate, but that it is necessarily so. For a man to succeed at court, he must be corrupt. Pierre Michault reports a course of lectures given by professors of the Faculty of Vice, in which the aspiring courtier is instructed that, in order to become rich, he must lie, comply, swear, slander, and drink. This was the normal attitude towards court life, and we may take as typical the *Curial* of Alain Chartier, written early in the fifteenth century, and translated by Caxton in 1484. The author's brother desired a career at court; and Chartier tells him that he is better off in private life than in 'this servitude mortal'. The court is a place where deceivers, bullies, and flatterers abound; where virtue is mocked; and where success may only be achieved through corruption. Moreover, success itself brings fresh troubles: envy, hatred, and sudden ruin. The court forces a man to abandon his own manners and adopt those of others; good habits become bad; life degenerates into riot; and the courtier must forever be at somebody's beck and call. In marked contrast to all this are the pleasures and repose of private country life where one may enjoy good food, clean comfortable beds, and, above all, the independence and humanity lacking in the courts of princes. People often wonder at the courtier's rich robe; 'but they know not what labour nor by what difficulty he hath gotten it'; nor do they understand that, at court, a man does not rise by true merit. Court life is but a tissue of lamentable paradoxes: it is 'a poor richness; an abundance miserable; a highness that falleth; an estate not stable; a surety trembling; and an evil life'. Thus, for Chartier – as for all other anti-court writers – misery, hardship, envy, and ultimate failure were the courtier's rewards; while flattery, guile, falsehood, and corruption were the perverted prerequisites of even the most transient success.

Nevertheless, court life exerted an irresistible attraction for many ambitious young men throughout the later Middle Ages; and its rituals and forms became increasingly complex – especially under the dukes of Burgundy or the Italian princes. Court life grew intricate wherever lofty political pretensions were upheld by artistic and social buttresses; and it has sometimes been suggested that the disintegrating social strata of fifteenth-century Europe led to increasing formalization of court functions and public spectacle in an effort to maintain the old, or to legitimize new, hierarchies. One thing seems certain: that there arose a considerable and constantly growing literature devoted to the etiquette governing social intercourse. The range of this material is vast. Much of it is elementary in character and amounts to little more than basic instruction on how to behave at table, together with injunctions to comb the hair, wash the hands and ears, cut the fingernails, and refrain from picking the nose. On the other hand, specialized treatises prescribed the organization of state occasions, tournaments, festivals, and banquets; or were devoted to the meticulous daily administration of a mighty household, such as that of Charles the Bold, with its strict rules of conduct and inviolable orders of

A shower of gold *descends from the king and is eagerly gathered by courtiers and churchmen. This miniature from a 'Book of Hours' was made for Lord Hastings at Bruges about 1477. (30)*

precedence. Court life might be Hell on earth, and courtiers might be venal and vile. But everybody had his place; and he was expected to know it.

Only very occasionally was the courtier viewed more positively, not as a parasite but rather as a valued counsellor. Such a view is generally encountered in books, not about courtiers, but about kings and princes who, since they were apparently crawling with flatterers, had to be warned against them, and advised how to choose wise, reliable, and honest servants. One work, however, was devoted to the courtier himself in this capacity: Diomede Caraffa's *Dello optimo cortesano* (1479). Here the counsellor is given practical hints on how to judge the nature of his master, and how to choose the most propitious time and place to tender advice which might not always be popular. The manual is brief and offers no general prospect of the courtly profession. But it is worth noting, partly as representative of the minute fifteenth-century literature which did not despise

Ancient chivalry was the guide to modern courtly virtue. Raymond Lull's 'Order of Chivalry' describes in detail the qualities expected of a true knight. Nobility of birth was necessary, but so was physical and moral excellence. In this manuscript illustration the squire visits a holy man in his cell. (31)

courtiers; and partly because later courtly manuals were similarly to insist upon the importance of time, place, and person – though wholly for the adviser's own unworthy ends.

The apotheosis of amateurism

Castiglione's relationship with these antecedent traditions is curious. He condemns all the time-worn courtly vices: yet contrives to ignore the great mass of earlier anti-court writing. He is concerned with behaviour: but transcends the literature of etiquette. He believes that the courtier's principal mission is to serve his prince as an adviser: but devotes only a few passing remarks to this matter. The most significant feature of *Il Cortegiano* is that it creates a profession where, hitherto, none had existed. For his predecessors the courtier had been a mere aggregate of vices; or, rarely, he might appear as a sober adviser. After Castiglione, the ideal courtier is deemed vice-free and much more than an adviser. Castiglione achieved this transformation by a transcendent dilettantism exemplified by what he has to say concerning the 'principal and true profession' of his courtier: that he must be a warrior. 'The more excellent our courtier shall be in this art, the more shall he be worthy praise.' Yet this is immediately qualified: 'albeit I judge not necessary in him so perfect a knowledge of things and other qualities that is requisite in a captain'. This perfect courtier should be expert in this as in much else – but not too

expert. His knowledge is not to extend to that of the professional. And this amateurism is stressed throughout *Il Cortegiano* to such an extent that, in the end, it creates a profession of itself.

This new kind of courtier – a cultivated, full-time dilettante – was later satirized by Philibert de Vienne (1547), who wrote that it was 'singular good, to have some pretty sprinkled judgment in the commonplaces and practices of all the liberal sciences, chopped up in hotchpot together, out of the which we may still help ourselves in talk, with apt devices at essays, to have substance and matter to treat of and encounter with all manner of things, and no more'. Castiglione's *Cortegiano* is itself an exemplification of the very qualities it extols, and which Philibert attacks. Castiglione writes upon a great diversity of topics; and he writes superficially on all of them. He runs the gamut of courtly themes; and while these do not, for the most part, derive from antecedent courtier traditions, they frequently do derive from the literature of medieval chivalry, as is made clear by the hollow insistence that the perfect courtier must be a warrior.

The very form of Castiglione's work, though modelled on Cicero's *De Oratore*, is akin to the medieval *débat* based upon scholastic techniques of question and answer. *Il Cortegiano* reveals a double influence of chivalric literature on the one hand; and, on the other, of the feudal Italian courts, such as Urbino and Ferrara, where culture was dominated by women, and where, apart from war, there was little to do but practise refinement, politesse, and the art of elegant conversation. Castiglione skilfully reproduces not merely the rhythm of that conversation, but also its tangential quality. The debate, though waged by skilled practitioners, is deliberately discursive; and the author seeks to disarm criticism by adapting, from the *De Oratore*, the confession that he is recreating a series of conversations rather than writing a didactic treatise. Thus, through the accumulation of diverse arguments, stories, and exemplars, he is able to comprehend, within a discussion spread over four nights, what are in effect a whole series of brief, separate studies which otherwise might appear to have little in common. There is, for example, a long discussion of jokes, which arises from a consideration of the courtier's skill as a conversationalist: but it is really nothing more than a miniature joke-book deriving, by way of medieval *facetiae*, from the *De Oratore*. As an analysis of humour, its various manifestations, and its significance as a social virtue (which should be the principal point of this discussion), it compares unfavourably with the slightly earlier *De Sermone* of Pontano.

Even more revealing of Castiglione's eclecticism is his discussion of love and the role of women at court. Here we have a chivalric theme *par excellence*, although it was originally an Ovidian superimposition on the purely military qualities demanded of a knight. For example, in Lull's *Order of Chivalry*, written late in the thirteenth century, love plays no part in the system of knightly virtues; though it was already central in the romantic portrayal of the knight, and received poetic expression in the work of the troubadours, and a theoretical enunciation in the *Art of Courtly*

Love by Andreas Capellanus. Castiglione's treatment of the theme is highly unoriginal, and much of what he says may be found three centuries earlier, in Andreas. Both authors have a good deal to say about the wiles of lovers, and about the efficacy of speech, writing, and gesture. Both depict the sickly, love-lorn male and his complementary cruel, predatory female; while both, conversely, present arguments for the ennobling effects of love. Castiglione's debate, where women are alternately lauded and vilified, is within the tradition of Andreas's courts of love, his male-female dialogues, and especially his antithetical presentation of the joys of physical love followed by a bitterly misogynistic final book. Indeed, the parallel goes even further, for in both cases the necessary postulate for this antithesis is a free-thinking, open-speaking court dominated paradoxically by accomplished and witty women. There is less distance than might at first appear between the crisp exchanges of Gasparo Pallavicino and the ladies at Urbino, and the renunciation of love and womankind written by Andreas within the context of a Provençal civilization dominated by Marie de Troyes, who possibly even directed the composition of the work.

Much of Castiglione's discussion of women proceeds by the amassing of exemplars both noble and ignoble. However, when the theme is resumed towards the end of his work, the technique changes, and Castiglione covers his courtly love with a thin Neoplatonic veneer. The starting point for the final ascent, from the contemplation of physical beauty to a glimpse of the divine, is an argument concerning whether it is seemly for old men to indulge in physical love, together with a statement that passion is first stirred through the eye. Love, says Castiglione, is 'nothing else but a certain coveting to enjoy beauty' – a definition which, with the debate on aged lovers and the crucial significance of sight in exciting passion, is to be found in Andreas Capellanus. What is missing from the medieval treatise is the ascent from physical to divine love, and the ecstatic ultimate vision. For these Castiglione turned to the contemporary *Gli Asolani* by Pietro Bembo who – with a touch of verisimilitude – appears as the interlocutor for this section of the *Cortegiano*.

True nobility

However, though jests and love occupy a prominent part of Castiglione's work, they are not really the heart of a discussion primarily concerned to establish what sort of man the perfect courtier should be, and how he should develop his talents in order to enjoy a successful career in the service of his prince. More fundamental is the very first issue raised by Castiglione in the *Cortegiano*: should the courtier be of noble birth? The nature of rank and nobility had always posed problems to anybody who cared to think about them. If nobility were derived solely from birth, then what of those who, though noble and virtuous, were low-born? On the other hand, if the criterion were ability and worth, where did that leave many an ignorant and thuggish nobleman of long lineage? This topic, which had occupied the attention of several ancient philosophers, is sometimes discussed as though it only returned to men's consciousness in the late fourteenth century with the advent of civic

humanism in Italy: that is in a society – so the cliché runs – where traditional concepts of rank and worth were being challenged by 'new men' with new skills, and therefore with new values. But, of course, 'new men' (those rising to power and wealth outside the feudal system of military duty, allegiance, and land tenure) may be found at least from the eleventh century. Nor were medieval folk as obtuse as those who devote their lives to Renaissance studies often imply. Discrepancies between extrinsic rank and intrinsic worth must often have been evident. Certainly they were reflected upon. In the twelfth century Andreas Capellanus had suggested that it was excellence of character alone 'which blesses a man with true nobility', rather than beauty or high birth. All human beings, he points out, derive from the same stock so that, initially, rank must have been derived from worth; and just as there are many who trace their descent to the first nobles 'but have degenerated', so there are others of whom the converse is true. In contrast, Lull upholds lineage. Noblesse of courage, he agrees, must be sought not in words and appearances but in the exercise of virtue. Knights are not to be created simply from those who are good-looking and well-built. But here we have an explicit assumption that, however physically able they may be, the lower orders are incapable of virtue. Were physical attributes the only criterion for chivalry, says Lull, 'then should a squire be dubbed a knight of villeins; and of people of little lineage, low and vile, mayest thou make knights'. Thus, although a candidate for knighthood must be fit and strong – there is no place here for 'the lame, the over great or fat' – he must be

Mantua rivalled Urbino *in the brilliance of its court life. In Mantegna's famous fresco Ludovico Gonzaga turns to consult his secretary, Marsilio Andreasi; on the right is his wife, Barbara Hohenzollern. (32)*

rich enough to sustain the expense of rank lest he should be driven to crime by necessity. In the last resort, Lull was convinced that nobility was an inherited quality. 'Parage and chivalry,' he maintains, 'accorden together, for parage is nothing but honour anciently accustomed': a view which Aristotle may well have inspired.

The field of true nobility was tilled by Dante, and trudged into mud by a host of writers throughout the fourteenth and fifteenth centuries. There was little fresh to say in the sixteenth century; though, characteristically, this deterred no one. Nobility of birth is the first desideratum of Castiglione's perfect courtier – though neither the arguments in support of this view, nor those of its adversaries in the *Cortegiano*, take us more deeply into the problem than do the passing observations of Andreas and Lull. Indeed, one of the pleasures in Castiglione is derived from the sudden recognition of an old friend. Such, for instance, is the argument that a courtier of noble birth is encouraged to virtue for 'if he swerve from the step of his ancestors, he staineth the name of his family' – which had been the only virtue discerned by Boethius in inherited rank, a thousand years previously. Naturally, the topic was hotly debated wherever up-and-coming young men felt obliged to define rank. English writers of the early sixteenth century, such as Richard Moryson and Thomas Elyot, found themselves in the impossible position of trying to reconcile belief in the traditional social hierarchy and in the paramount need for order and degree, with that nobility of worth necessary to justify their own successful careers as non-noble 'new men'. The argument raged throughout the century, with an increasing emphasis on merit as against lineage; although even those who opposed nobility of birth tended to retain an element of ambiguity. This is well exemplified by the eclectic Pierre Charron (1601) who demanded: 'what good is it to a blind man, that his parents have been well sighted, or to him that stammereth, that his grandfather was eloquent?' Elsewhere, however, discussing the nature of valour, Charron reprimands those who, attributing it to subtlety and craft 'or to art and industry', profane it and 'make it play a base and abject part'. It is not fitting for a man of honour to 'try and adventure his valour in a thing wherein a base fellow instructed by rule may gain the prize'.

Only occasionally does one encounter an approach like that of Henry Cornelius Agrippa (1530), who could see nothing but vice both in the old nobility and in the new. The former, surrounded by a flock of parasites, waste their strength in whoring, and their wealth in riotous living. The base-born courtiers, on the other hand, are cringing sycophants: they flatter everyone; they worm secrets from their prey; they undertake jobs which the great men have abandoned through fear or indolence; and when 'conversant in treasons, deceits, sorrows, and labours' they have with 'painful and filthy practices gotten great riches, and aspired to high honours, then they set no difference between right and wrong, that their sons may be heirs, not so much of honour as of ravine and iniquity'. Finally, when the nobles have spent everything on 'queans, dice, hunting, jousting, feasting, pomp, apparel and pride', their possessions are bought up by the 'common or mean courtiers'

who usurp their position in society. Agrippa's observations ring truer than the traditional academic abstractions on this theme; and, though their effect is vitiated by being incorporated into a general attack on everything, they do come like a breath of fresh air into an ill-ventilated cellar.

Arms and letters

There are even fewer refreshing draughts in an adjacent, overstocked storehouse of platitudes, which demands our attention. The respective merits of arms and letters – of the soldier and the scholar – had been much debated in classical antiquity. For Cicero, *cedant arma togae*: a view which not unnaturally tended to be repeated by those who wore the toga, and did not bear arms. In the Middle Ages the hypothetical contraries were personified by the knight and the clerk; and, while it was normal to argue that both were necessary to society, it was difficult – in face of the lack of learning endemic in the warrior class – to postulate their perfect union. Lull's *Order of Chivalry* had, indeed, been undertaken partly in recognition of the need for chivalry to become a science. Lull wished to put the knight on an equal footing with the cleric. The latter's task was to teach and to demonstrate a life of goodness and devotion, to ordinary people. The knight was to maintain chivalry by 'noblesse and by force of arms', and to 'incline the small people by dread' to avoid wrong-doing. Lull desires a 'school of the order of knighthood', and recommends that the 'science were written in books, and that the art were showed and read in such manner as other sciences be read'. The *Order of Chivalry* was one of the most influential of all chivalric treatises: but the ideal warrior only slowly acquired learning; and, in the eyes of some at least, in so doing he lost his virility. Many knights remained armed but unlettered, and were frequently antagonistic to the values of the cultured.

Decadence, however, need not necessarily derive from culture. There were other contrasts which attracted critical attention. Already late in the thirteenth century, Lull had felt it necessary to counter a degeneracy which he perceived in contemporary chivalry. Two centuries later, Caxton concluded his translation of the *Order of Chivalry* with a passionate outburst against the knights of his own day, who had forgotten what chivalry was all about. 'O ye knights of England,' he cries, 'what do ye now but go to the bains and play at dice? Alas what do ye but sleep and take ease?' The contrast here is no longer between arms and letters, but between military vigour and self-indulgent flabbiness; and this, in turn, could easily shade off into another antithesis – the honest warrior and the slick official. Antagonism between the soldier and courtier was a prominent feature of the anti-court tradition, and in Jean de Bueil's *Le Jouvencel* we have a fifteenth-century illustration of this. The hero, in his youth, wishes to seek his fortune at court; but an old gentleman tells him that his only gain would be 'mockery, loss of time, and ill-spent effort'. A whole day would not suffice to describe the corruption and uncertainty of courts where princes' affections vary; where rivals seek to destroy you; and where the spirit is burdened by vice. In contrast to all this are the virtues, triumphs, loyalty, and courage of the

The prince between letters and arms: Federigo of Urbino's study is an epitome of his character. Lining the walls are cupboards in 'trompe l'oeil' marquetry apparently heaped with a profusion of objects. The Duke's library was among the most famous in Europe, while his prowess in arms made him one of the most sought-after condottieri. (33–35)

warrior – the foundation of all temporal power. Kings may always find new officials; it is not so easy to muster good fighters. War is more suitable for Le Jouvencel than to idle at court, noting who wears the best suit or the most fashionable hat. Besides, concludes the old man, nobody respects a courtier, whereas the good warrior is welcome wherever he goes.

This palpable untruth brings us back full circle to the nature of true nobility. De Bueil is not merely criticizing soft living; he is also defending the military ideals of the old *noblesse d'épée* against the encroachments of the *noblesse de robe*. He represents the antipathy of the warrior towards new men who gained position, prestige, and wealth by the exercise of unworthy qualities, such as brain power.

These problems are partially resolved by Castiglione, whose courtier is an idealization of the unity between arms and letters, of knight and clerk, of soldier and courtier: though his preliminary assumption of noble birth obviates protracted discussion of those whom Agrippa was to term 'common courtiers'. One is reminded of De Bueil when

Castiglione alludes to the fact that the French set store only in noblesse of arms, abhor letters, count all learned men 'very rascals', and think it 'great villainy when any one of them is called a clerk'. Nevertheless, Castiglione discerns some hope of improvement from the heir to the French throne – subsequently Francis I. There ensues a conventional summary of the arms and letters controversy: knowledge is proper to man; there are many examples of military leaders combining the 'ornament of letters with prowess of arms'; and, indeed, a soldier may find his greatest inspiration in the record of past deeds of greatness. There is just one counter-argument which Castiglione touches upon. 'The Italians,' he notes, 'with their knowledge of letters have shewed small prowess in arms for a certain time hitherto'; but he quickly passes over this depressing truth by laying the blame upon the 'offence of the few', before continuing with a succinct account of the type of reading indispensable to the soldier. Some discussion is devoted to whether arms are to be regarded only as an ornament to letters, since the body is inferior to the mind; but the matter is brought to a conclusion by a reminder that this 'disputation hath already been tossed a long time by most wise men'. The courtier must be primarily a warrior; but 'it is not so necessary for any man to be learned as it is for a man of war', and the ideal must combine 'these two points linked together'.

Castiglione's union of arms and letters is to be achieved by the combination of classical education and rigorous physical

Patronage of music was an essential function of the ideal king, as its practice was of the ideal courtier. The Emperor Maximilian I, who was careful that posterity should not remain unaware of any of his accomplishments, is here seen among his musicians in a woodcut by Hans Burgkmair. (36)

training recommended by many earlier authoritative Italian educationalists. Indeed, the system had become commonplace by the middle of the fifteenth century, and we may see it summarized by Aeneas Sylvius Piccolomini. 'Both mind and body,' he writes, 'the two elements of which we are constituted must be developed side by side.' And he gives rules on the discipline of the body; the need for 'every youth destined to an exalted position' to receive military training; the kind of reading best suited to their purposes; the teaching of eloquence both in speech and in writing; and the general value of the liberal arts. It is ironic that this same author – when Pope Pius II – felt obliged to write of Sigismondo Malatesta that (despite his great strength of mind and body, his eloquence and military ability, his knowledge of history and philosophy) 'the evil part of his character had the upper hand'. Sigismondo violated his daughters and his sons-in-law; he was an adulterer, a ravisher of nuns, and a pervert; he despised religion; he murdered his wives; he was a master of dissimulation; and he betrayed everyone who ever had dealings with him. He was, in short, the worst scoundrel who had ever lived, 'the disgrace of Italy and the infamy of our times'. So much for the universal man. A good education and a multiplicity of talents do not – despite the fond, eternal hopes of educationalists – inevitably result in moral excellence.

The ideal of the perfect all-rounder was not merely Italian. Nor was it solely humanistic. It may be found in northern Europe, and – despite Caxton's lament, and De Bueil's contempt – it was also chivalric. The skills and activities recommended by Castiglione, and enthusiastically adopted by his countless admirers – riding and hunting, tournaments and duels, dancing and festivities, and even the cultivation of eloquence, social ease, and artistic sensibility – were all part of the knightly tradition as it had evolved from its purely military origins. Castiglione writes of Urbino in the early sixteenth century; but there is little difference between the tone of court life as he describes it there, and what we may read of the hospitality accorded Don Pedro Niño by Renaud de Trie, Admiral of France. The Admiral had retired to Sérifontaine where his great household was organized by his accomplished wife. At a typical banquet, 'as long as the meal lasted, any man who, with due measure and respect of courtesy, could speak of arms and love, was sure of finding someone to whom to address himself'. During the meal there was instrumental music; and afterwards the minstrels played for dancing. Spices and wine followed, and then everybody took a siesta before going out for hunting and falconry. The afternoon's entertainment ended with a picnic, and then 'singing most delightful songs, they went back to the castle'. Supper was taken, and then guests could play bowls or dance until it was time for bed. This varied entertainment, which, we are assured, was normal procedure at Sérifontaine, antedates Castiglione's Urbino by a century, and itself represents a tradition of courtliness extending back at least to the thirteenth century.

Nor are we here dealing with uncultivated revelry. The association between knightly activities and artistic connoisseurship likewise has a long history which reached its apogee in the fifteenth century at the court of the dukes of Burgundy, and in the diverse interests of René d'Anjou, who combined the chivalric virtues and artistic prowess to a remarkable degree. An expert jouster himself, he was also the author of a treatise on tournament ceremonial; a connoisseur of painting, architecture, and the fine crafts, he was also a patron of these arts, and himself a painter, architect, and skilled miniaturist; an enthusiast for music, he himself composed and performed; a collector of manuscripts, he was also a patron of letters and a poet. This kind of accomplishment became the pattern for princes. Castiglione's contemporaries, James IV of Scotland, Francis I of France, and Henry VIII of England, all fancied themselves as warriors both on the battlefield and in the tilt yard. They all encouraged artists, craftsmen, and writers. They all danced, sang, and sometimes composed. And they all fancied themselves with the pen. Most striking of all was the Emperor Maximilian I, who took special pains to ensure that his manifold accomplishments, real or imaginary, should be passed on to posterity in their entirety. Under his personal supervision, a series of books was prepared illustrating his prowess as a military commander, scholar, author, jouster, hunter, fisherman, courtly lover, archer, swordsman, engineer, armourer, dancer, musician, and court reveller. There was, seemingly, nothing beyond the capacities of this emperor. And this idealized self-portrait is noteworthy because it comprises virtually all Castiglione's courtly prerequisites. In a very real sense, the dukes of Burgundy, René d'Anjou, James IV, Henry VIII, Francis I, and the Emperor Maximilian were the apotheosis of courtiership. Rulers such as these created the form of the perfect courtier who was really but an ape of his masters, not vice versa.

On the other hand, it would be misleading to underestimate the part played by Castiglione in systematizing these values and in transmitting them from princes to courtiers; or to overlook his part in the process whereby knights became metamorphosed into courtiers, and ultimately into gentlemen. This process was long and complex; but it may be vividly illustrated by comparing Lull's *Order of Chivalry* with a treatise such as Ansalone's *Il Cavaliere* of 1629. The subject remains ostensibly the skills and purposes of knighthood: but the purely military intention of the former, with its emphasis on the virtues necessary for leaders of men, has been supplanted by a strange creature who must ride, fence, dance, swim, hunt, and shoot; who must have knowledge of drawing, mathematics, letters, poetry, theatre, music, and history; who is given lessons in the joust, in running at the ring, and in every other equine exercise including horse ballet; and whose principal concerns appear to be excellence in participating in, and organizing, spectacles and masques.

Matter, manner, and appearances

Mention of this mutation from warrior to ceremonial puppet brings us to a fundamental and very original aspect of Castiglione's work. And this is the way in which he develops another debating topic which had been revived from antiquity: the antithesis between *Res* and *Literae* – content and literary form, philosophy and rhetoric, matter and manners. Cicero had expressed the problem succinctly in the *De Oratore*. He was, predictably, enthusiastic for polished style, but adds that 'this kind of diction, if there be not matter beneath it clear and intelligible to the speaker, must either amount to nothing, or be received with ridicule by all who hear it'. The most elegant words, devoid of sense and knowledge, are nothing but madness. Towards the end of the fifteenth century, the topic had been the subject of a famous controversy between Ermolao Barbaro, who had attacked the crude style of the scholastic philosophers, and Giovanni Pico della Mirandola, who had – somewhat paradoxically – defended their style for the sake of the truths concealed beneath it. Although, as in many Renaissance disputes, there was much empty posturing, the matter was of real importance when men were concerned to develop vernacular language as a precise, but pleasing, instrument for the expression of complex ideas. This was very much Castiglione's own concern, and he devotes a considerable part of his first book to a discussion of the nature of speech and literature which, as he puts it, is nothing else 'but a manner of speech that remaineth still after a man hath spoken'. In this section, as elsewhere, Castiglione is influenced by Cicero's *De Oratore*, maintaining that good style is absolutely dependent upon knowledge; and, although eloquence and elegance are challenged on the ground that they might obscure meaning, the classic and

sound response is that skill in language 'hindereth not the easiness of understanding'. Indeed, the converse is true.

An accusation commonly levelled against self-conscious oratory and literary style was that it was artificial and sought to influence the minds of an audience with carefully judged effects. Thus stylistic considerations could acquire moral overtones. Rhetoric was dishonest; it misrepresented the truth in order to persuade; it was a 'crafty and secret method'; and its procedures were 'deceits'. Castiglione analyses and defends stylistic devices, for he wishes his courtier to be furnished with eloquence. But he presses the argument much further than this. In fact, he so extends and elaborates the artifices of rhetoric that they embrace the very life of the courtier. The relationship between literary matter and manner becomes transfigured into the relationship between what a man really *is* and how he *seems*.

The stress placed upon appearances is the *Cortegiano*'s most striking feature. It first occurs during a discussion of self-praise which is held to be legitimate when discreet: 'speaking such things after a sort, that it may appear that they are not rehearsed to that end'. This artificial spontaneity is expressed by two principal qualities: *grazia*, or grace; and *sprezzatura*, or what we might term a studied nonchalance. These qualities are akin to the chivalric *franchise*, that is the naturalness and ease which could only characterize the well-bred. *Grazia* is employed so frequently to qualify the perfect courtier's actions that one of Castiglione's characters demands an explanation of the word which is 'put for a sauce to everything', together with

'Chascun tend à faulcer son visage' *wrote Guillaume de la Perrière in his 'Théâtre des Bons Engins', 1536. From the sixteenth century onwards the hypocrisy of courtly life provokes increasing comment, its virtues less. (37)*

instruction on how such a quality might be acquired. It seems that it can only be gained by close study with the acknowledged masters of each individual skill, for the courtier must steal his grace from those who apparently already possess it, 'even as the bee in green meadows fleeth always about the grass, choosing out flowers'. Difficult matters are to be accomplished with deceptive ease: 'that may be said to be a very art, that appeareth not to be art, neither ought a man to put more diligence in anything than in covering it: for in case it be open, it loseth credit clean and maketh a man little set by'. Nevertheless, nonchalance should never be so studied that it fails to conceal art. It is, for example, as bad to be slipshod and careless in dress as it is for the courtier to carry his head carefully, 'for fear of ruffling his hair, or to keep in the bottom of his cap a looking glass, and a comb in his sleeve, and have always at his heels up and down the streets a page with a sponge and brush'. Vice for Castiglione, as for Aristotle, is always rooted in extremes; and the purpose of nonchalance is to make everything appear natural. This is the fountain of all grace; and it affords another advantage since it makes even the slightest achievement seem better than it really is, 'because it imprinteth in the minds of the lookers on, an opinion that who so can so slightly do well hath a great deal more knowledge than in deed he hath'.

In war the courtier is to separate himself from the multitude so that he may perform brave deeds 'in the sight of noble men'. In the tilt yard he must ensure that he looks magnificent so that, like a magnet, he 'may draw unto him the eyes of the lookers on'. In athletic pursuits, or in skills such as music, the courtier must avoid all sign of effort; however expert he may be, he must convey the impression that he devotes little time to such matters. Reputation is of paramount importance and, when the courtier is required to venture where he is unknown, he must help himself with wit and art so that 'there goes first a good opinion of him before he comes in person'. Particularly valuable in impressing people is the art of conversation; and it is suggested that when the courtier is required to speak on some topic he should, whenever possible, prepare himself in advance while pretending 'the whole to be done extempore'. Similarly, when he must deal with matters where his knowledge is modest, he should touch upon them in such a way that his auditors may believe that he 'hath a great deal more cunning therein than he uttereth'. Only when entirely ignorant is the courtier to confess it – and then only because he might be caught out and lose reputation. The greatest effect of all is achieved by those who conceal their best ability by professing a lesser, and then, when opportunity presents itself, they surprise everybody. This particular ruse is challenged as deceit: and, although it is defended as 'rather an ornament', Castiglione stipulates that it should not pass 'bounds', and that the courtier should govern himself 'always with a certain honest mean'.

Castiglione's courtier is both artefact and autofact. He is fashioned by his author like some exquisite Frankenstein monster, pieced together from the choicest parts of divers chivalric and humanistic cadavers: but he is also constantly engaged in the act of self-creation. This courtier is always aware of an audience, admiring, criticizing, and judging him; and he is expected to fashion himself like a work of art. Just as skilled painters 'with a shadow make the lights of high places to appear, and with light make low the shadows of the plains' so the courtier must make a unity of all his good qualities, and arrange them to gain maximum effect. He must always weigh what he does or says, 'the place where it is done, in presence of whom, in what time, the cause why he doth it, his age, his profession, the end whereto it tendeth, and the means that may bring him to it'. He must, above all, be agreeable to 'great men, gentlemen, and the ladies'; 'pliable to be conversant with so many'; and, taking note of the differences between one man and another, 'every day alter fashion and manner according to the disposition of them he is conversant withal'.

The art of pleasing was not new. Etiquette books had been concerned largely with the manners necessary to smooth and facilitate courtly commerce. The venal purposes underlying attentive behaviour had been expressed with engaging ingenuousness in Caxton's *Book of Courtesy*, where a youth making his way in a noble household is advised:

> Await my child when ye stand at table
> Of master or sovereign whether it be,
> Apply you for to be serviceable
> That no default in you founden be.
> Look who doth best and him ensue ye,
> And in especial use ye attendance
> Wherein ye shall yourself best advance.

Castiglione is infinitely more sophisticated. But his courtier is concerned essentially with the same thing: to advance his career by ingratiating himself with authority.

This is not, of course, precisely how Castiglione expresses his courtier's purpose. As we have seen, the principal aim of the courtier, derived by Louis Guyon from Castiglione, is to give the prince sage counsel. However, Castiglione is less unambiguous, despite two separate attempts to define the relationship between courtier and ruler. In Book Two it is suggested that the ideal courtier must serve his prince with a devotion close to worship, and 'in his will, manners, and fashion be altogether pliable to please him'. One interlocutor exclaims that there are plenty such courtiers nowadays 'for (me think) in few words ye have painted us out a jolly flatterer'. This is staunchly denied: it is simply that 'to purchase favour at great men's hands, there is no better way than to deserve it'. The argument, however, runs into difficulties when confronted with the unworthy demands of a wicked ruler. Castiglione is evasive, and he attempts to justify obedience on the grounds that many things appear good which are, in truth, evil; while many seem evil but are, notwithstanding, good: 'therefore it is lawful for a man sometime in his lord's service, to kill not one man alone, but ten thousand, and to do many other things, which if a man weigh them not as he ought, will appear ill, and yet are not so in deed'. He adds that it is a dangerous matter for a courtier to swerve from the command of his superiors, 'trusting more in his own judgment than in theirs, whom of reason he ought to obey'. This savours of the sentiments of Placebo, in Chaucer's *Merchant's Tale*, who, though he had been a 'court-man' all his life, had never contradicted his lord.

> What he sayeth, I hold it firm and stable;
> I say the same, or else thing semblable,
> A full great fool is any counsellor,
> That serveth any lord of high honour,
> That dare presume, or else thinken it,
> That his counsel should pass his lord's wit.

Castiglione's slipperiness on this issue helps explain how it has been possible for a distinguished modern historian to mistake *Il Cortegiano* for *Il Principe* as the book allegedly offered by Thomas Cromwell to Reginald Pole, as an authoritative statement on the way in which a prince's advisers should behave. Pole had been horrified by Cromwell's pragmatism. 'If he had happened to live in the time of Nero who cherished the desire to murder his mother,' Pole exclaims, 'he would even have thought out some reason of piety for doing it!'

Castiglione does not go this far; and, when he returns to the problem at the beginning of his fourth book, he anticipates criticism of his courtier's accomplishments by accepting that these alone do not make for perfection. Were they an end in themselves they would not merit praise but discommendation, for they belong to the entertainment of women, and render men effeminate. We are here, momentarily, back in the mainstream of anti-courtier criticism; and Castiglione even anticipates a subsequent development when he maintains that such degeneracy has already brought the name of Italy into opprobrium. Nevertheless, when the courtly skills are directed towards a good end they are profitable and deserve 'infinite praise'. And what is this 'good end'? It is to gain the favour of the prince so that the courtier will be able to speak honestly to him and 'set him in the way of virtue'. Just as music, sports, pastimes, and all the rest, are the 'flowers of courtliness', so directing the prince towards goodness and away from evil is the 'fruit of it'. It was possibly with *Il Cortegiano* at his elbow that the cynical Francesco Guicciardini penned the following observation. 'When I was young I despised music, dancing, singing, and such frivolities. Also I despised fine writing, horsemanship, the art of dressing well, and all things which seem to be more ornamental than essential to man.' Later, however, adds Guicciardini, he came to regret this contempt, for his experience showed that the 'ability to do everything well adds dignity and reputation even to the best qualified'. In fact, the possession of such accomplishments 'opens the way to the favour of princes, and for those who abound in them it may be the beginning or cause of immense profit and promotion, since the world and its princes are not made as they should be, but as they are'. This sentiment is convincing in Guicciardini. In Castiglione it seems at least plausible, until we recall that in the third book of *Il Cortegiano* it has been argued that all comely exercises arise from a desire to please the ladies. Who learns to dance for any other reason? Who practises music or writes verse but for this purpose? 'Judge you how many most noble poems we had been without both in Greek and Latin had women been smally regarded of poets.' Noble birth; skill in arms,

'A Quip for an Upstart Courtier' *is the title of a pamphlet by Robert Greene, published in London in 1592. The honest sincerity of 'Cloth-breeches' is contrasted with the false vanity of 'Velvet-breeches'. (38)*

letters, and music; eloquence both in speech and behaviour – all constitute 'an instrument to obtain the good will of women'.

What then was the perfect courtier's real business: to ingratiate himself with his paramour in order to obtain her favours; or to ingratiate himself with his prince in order to influence him towards virtue? Admittedly, it might be deemed unfair to tax Castiglione too harshly with inconsistency. He himself stresses that he is merely reporting conversations. But this is a rhetorical technique of the kind he both advocates and employs elsewhere; and, although intention may be obscured by dialogue form, the author of a work must, ultimately, be accountable for the views he expresses therein. The general effect of *Il Cortegiano* is one of sparkling superficiality, and the serious intentions of its author are overladen with his own *grazia* and literary *sprezzatura*. Castiglione certainly sensed the danger himself and attempted to remedy offensive affectation by reiterated warnings against the vice latent in extremities, and by constant recommendations of the golden mean. He advocates pliancy and obedience towards the prince; but he cautions against flattery, and equivocates uncomfortably over whether or not the courtier should abandon a wicked ruler. He wishes his courtier to be noble by birth; but recognizes the solid claims of virtue to the title of true nobility. He stipulates that his courtier must be handsome, well-formed, and properly apparelled; but inveighs against effeminacy of dress, and narcissistic beauty-care. He will have his courtier eloquent; but he condemns affectation of speech. He will, above all, have his courtier constantly aware of his own effectiveness; yet he will not have him seem so. And, despite all Castiglione's caveats, the nonchalance relentlessly asserts itself as too premeditated. This perfect courtier simply tries too hard to appear not to be trying. One is reminded of early criticisms of Machiavelli's *Il Principe*: it is impossible, said his adversaries, for Machiavelli's prince to seem righteous while being wicked. Sooner or later the deception would be apparent, and, once revealed, he could never deceive anyone again. Similarly, once the courtier's *sprezzatura* is recognized as a device, how could it ever again convince? The parallel with Machiavelli goes further. *Il Principe* was either bitterly attacked because it recommended deceit as a conscious political programme; or defended on the grounds that it merely described how princes really do behave, and that it revealed their ruses. Castiglione's account of courtly accomplishments was open to similar interpretations: though, on the whole, few regarded it simply as an exposé of courtly wiles. Either it was accepted at face value as a desirable model of behaviour, or it was received with hostility. Its enemies were quick to seize upon the excessive concentration on manner, and to remark that this was achieved at the expense of matter – in terms of honesty, reliability, and loyalty. Nonetheless, like Machiavelli's prince, Castiglione's courtier aroused hostility by a paradox. He was immensely popular and influential. *Il Cortegiano* was without doubt the most significant book in the history of courtly literature.

Anti-courtiers and cynics

The crucial importance of *Il Cortegiano* has been questioned by recent scholarship, which has stressed not only the existence of a continuing anti-court literature fuelled by its ambiguous morality, but also the ways in which its ideals became outmoded in Italy by changing social situations. More especially emphasis has been laid upon a work such as Guazzo's *Civil Conversation*, which enjoyed a great vogue from the moment of its first publication in 1574, and which offers evidence both of hostility to Castiglione's dilettantism, and of a concern with practical social relationships rather than with elegant postures. This corrective is valuable: and exaggerated. Renaissance readers were just as capable as we are of reading more than one book, even at the same time. Keen students could read Castiglione as well as Guazzo; and they could combine this perfectly well with a strong admixture of Machiavelli. The fact remains that from the time of its first publication in 1528, there were few years, during the sixteenth century, which did not see an edition or translation of *Il Cortegiano*. Its popularity is strikingly attested by Roger Ascham, an inveterate hater of most things Italian, who himself wrote in his *Schoolmaster*, 'To laugh, to lie, to flatter, to face/Four ways in court to win men grace.' Yet he believed that the *Cortegiano* 'advisedly read and diligently followed but one year at home in England, would do a young gentleman more good iwis, than three year's travel abroad spent in Italy'. Certainly Castiglione's elegant and pleasing nobleman, with his martial skills, courtly graces, literary accomplishments, and – above all – his *sprezzatura*, became the pattern of the courtier and ultimately of the gentleman. Indeed, that pattern has only really been discarded within living memory, and not wholly with advantage.

While Castiglione's perfect courtier nonchalantly conquered fashionable society in Western Europe, older modes of thinking and writing about courtly behaviour showed themselves capable of endless repetition, or even some development. The etiquette book, for instance, received an extended expression when Giovanni della Casa's *Galateo* appeared in 1558. Here the aspiring gentleman is given an abundance of advice on the niceties of social behaviour, together with the not-niceties of unsocial behaviour: the necessary bodily functions and malfunctions; dressing and undressing; eating, drinking, and sleeping; speaking, jesting, and gesturing; tendering counsel, and knowing when to remain silent. The *Galateo* is lively, sensible, and well illustrated with citations from Dante and Boccaccio; but, that apart, it has little to say which might not be found in Caxton's *Book of Courtesy*, printed eighty years earlier. Traditional criticism of the courtier likewise continued unabated, receiving pithy pictorial and poetic expression in works which sought to summarize human experience in emblematic form. Guillaume de la Perrière (1536), especially, provides several views of court life – none of them happy. When the courtier is a simple and honest soul, he is shown as an ass ridden by monkeys. When, on the other hand, he is a skilled flatterer, he appears either as a birdcatcher trapping his prince with false sounds and rapid changes of countenance; or he is seen walking with his tongue held on a plate before him, and with his heart in his hand, behind his back. Even crows which feed on dead and decaying flesh are better than the courtly flatterer who devours his victims alive. If he seeks glory and reputation at court, then he is like a captive lion drawn on a lead; or like a swimmer struggling desperately to keep afloat while laden with a heavy pack. Other emblematists were equally sceptical. Courtiers might appear as mice gnawing a crown; they might be lost in a

---

The Emperor Maximilian goes fishing. *The court travelled in some luxury, and is here provided with a generous picnic on the banks of a lake. Miniature by Jörg Kölderer, 1504, from the so-called 'Tiroler Fischereibuch' compiled for Maximilian.* (39)

Humanism *grafted classical tastes upon the old chivalric values, a combination expressed most lastingly at the court of Urbino. Top left: a lecture by a humanist scholar, possibly Paul of Middelburg, to an audience which includes Federigo and his young son Guidobaldo. Below: part of a panel from the school of Perugino showing courtiers and an ecclesiastic in a setting strongly suggestive of Urbino architecture. The large photograph shows the courtyard of Urbino, built under Federigo's direction, one of the purest masterpieces of the Renaissance.* (40–42)

Courts in the north *shared many of the Italian ideals, but their imagery was their own. On a Flemish calendar page for February, painted by G. Hoornbuch in 1500, an unnamed nobleman presides over what must have been a typical evening's entertainment, with servants, guests, musicians, and a jester.* (43)

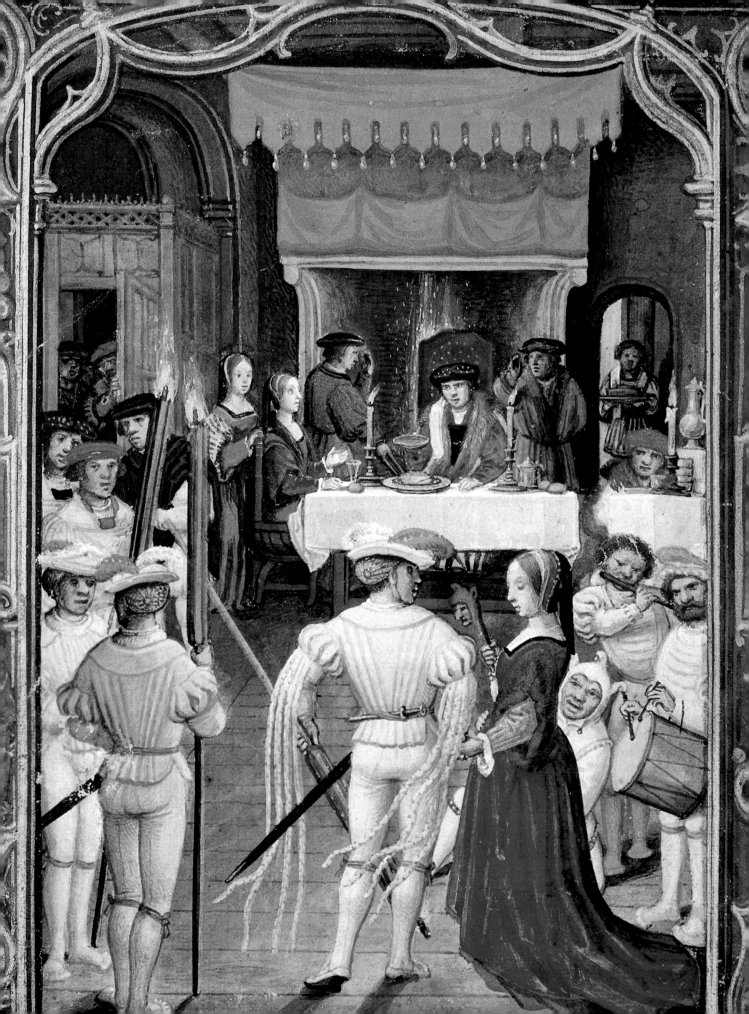

labyrinth; they might be in constant danger of being struck down by Jupiter's thunderbolts; they might be acceptable to princes, while still youthful, only to be cast out in old age; and their lives are of such misery that they might even be depicted as opening Pandora's box itself. Most common of all emblems was that included in every one of the numerous editions of Alciati (first edition 1531): the courtier sits with his feet trapped in a vice or within a pair of stocks. He has fine raiment; he eats well; he drinks plenty: but he is tied by a golden chain. This is the same thought as that voiced a hundred years earlier by Alain Chartier; and it was still being voiced more than a century later when an anonymous critic of the court of Charles II wrote that the greatness and magnificence of courtiers were 'only outsides, to amuse the ignorant; these stately escutcheons serve but to hide a dead corpse, and these excellent odours to perfume a sepulchre'.

The vices, discomforts, and dangers of court life, as contrasted with the pleasures of private retirement, were also constantly reiterated. They provide the theme of Antonio de Guevara's *Menosprecio de corte*, a work of elegant unoriginality, which enjoyed a remarkable popularity, especially in France, despite the availability of more interesting anti-court literature, and despite the fact that it was possible to breathe new life into the nearly defunct modes. New opportunities were offered by the increasing interest in Lucian's satirical dialogues, one of which, *The Parasite*, was particularly apposite for those wishing to attack traditional courtly vices and, at the same time, to mock at Castiglione's seeming idealization of those vices. For Lucian, sponging on the wealthy is an art superior to any other. The parasite does not pay to learn his skill, but is paid for it; the origins of his art are noble, for it is based upon friendship, that 'theme of the encomiast'; and it has been practised by distinguished men including Plato who came to Sicily for that very purpose. Nevertheless, the great philosopher only did a few days' sponging, for he 'found himself incompetent and had to leave'. Philosophers, in general, compare badly with spongers. In war, for instance, parasites are superior, for whereas philosophers are 'thin and white with underfeeding', the sponger is full-bodied and his 'flesh is a nice colour'. As his advocate points out: 'a noble pikeman that, and a noble corpse, for that matter'. When the well-nourished sponger falls none need feel ashamed 'of that great body, which now reclines as appropriate an ornament of the battlefield as it once was of the dining room'. By comparison, philosophers are withered squalid figures; these 'pallid hairy manikins scattered on the ground' reflect no credit on the city obliged to field them as troops. In peacetime, too, the parasite scores off the philosopher: 'who will contribute most to entertainment, he with his song and his joke, or a person who hasn't a laugh in him'. He is an ornament; and a rich man without his sponger is 'a mean, cheap spectacle'. The parasite sheds lustre upon his patron, never the patron upon the sponger.

The possibilities afforded by Lucianic satire to the anti-courtier were recognized, even before the publication of the *Cortegiano*, in Ulrich von Hutten's *Aula*: though, form apart, the work has little new to offer. Von Hutten's courtier is still ever the slave to others, a prisoner with a golden chain

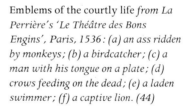

Emblems of the courtly life *from La Perrière's 'Le Théâtre des Bons Engins', Paris, 1536: (a) an ass ridden by monkeys; (b) a birdcatcher; (c) a man with his tongue on a plate; (d) crows feeding on the dead; (e) a laden swimmer; (f) a captive lion. (44)*

Right: a similar conceit from the French edition of Alciati's 'Emblemata', 1536: the courtier dressed in fine clothes, but helpless in the stocks. (45)

49

about his neck; and the court remains a sea of miseries where virtue is ineffectual, and where only vice can succeed. Courtiers have been corrupted by luxurious clothing and exotic foods; and the courtiers have, in turn, brought about the corruption of the German people. The *Aula* was popular; and there was even a plagiarism by Lodovico Domenichi, where it is the Italian people, not the German, who have been corrupted. However, the implications of Lucian's parasite were far better realized in a little book which did not, until recently, attract the attention it deserves: the *Philosopher of the Court* by Philibert de Vienne. Philibert's view of courtiers is, fundamentally, little different from that of other critics: but his intelligent reading of Lucian gives it a keener cutting edge.

Philibert writes for the instruction of the young who are of little use to the commonwealth 'till the scum and filth of youthful heat be boiled out of them'. Ancient philosophers encourage us to embrace virtue for its own sake, and to know ourselves. But court philosophy is very different: 'we ought to see and know the world'; and this requires some knowledge of all the arts, of music, dancing, and poetry, and indeed to have a smattering sufficient to maintain a mean between ignorance and seriousness. The drift of the satire is clear: Philibert is ridiculing Castiglione's golden mean while, seemingly, taking a similar stand against affectation. Thus Philibert despises the 'rude youths and minions of the court' who 'simper it in outward show, making pretty mouths, and marching with a stalking pace like cranes, spitting over their own shoulder, speaking lispingly, and answering singingly'. These creatures have curled hair, dress foppishly, and sprinkle their conversation with a few words of French, Italian, or Spanish. Yet they are but 'counterfeit courtiers', for their pretensions are too evident. Philibert moves on to deeper matters when he reveals that courtly justice is very different from either law or morality. At court we should not injure anyone 'if the injury be not covered, or held with some show or likelihood of reason'. Is not the man who fails to use a good opportunity to deceive a companion to be deemed an idiot? The courtly philosopher holds it 'tolerable to beguile, filch, and cog, and do the worst we can, so that neither law, judge, nor justice may touch or catch hold of us for it.' Nothing is of greater importance than 'reputation', though our word is only to be kept when it can be enforced by law: the 'promises of a gentleman', runs the proverb, 'are the holy water of the court'.

Humility, as extolled by the sages, is 'directly repugnant and contrary to our courtly virtue'; and the best way to achieve worldly honour is to be liberal, especially with other men's belongings. The only proviso is that all deeds should be done with a show of reason. Semblances and appearances are the 'principal supporters of our philosophy,' says Philibert, 'for such as we seem, such are we judged here'. Castiglione's art of pleasing is reduced to absurdity, as Philibert recommends the golden mean in bowing and scraping. This is the best route to advancement, but it must not be too little lest we be deemed arrogant; nor too much lest we incur the title of flatterers. With this caution in mind, the courtier must give advice according to the desires of his master – not according to the truth. Like Machiavelli in *Il*

Principe, Philibert recommends the path of conventional virtue when it is advantageous; but one must never hesitate to abandon 'such small trifling things' when they become a hindrance in our march towards riches.

Temperance is also given an individual definition by Philibert, who tells us that the temperate man is 'he that pleaseth every man, who taketh nothing in malice or displeasure, and frames quietness to all purposes'. Temperance produces 'good grace', and this, in turn, comprises the art of dissembling. Openness and simplicity are only suitable for 'beasts and idiots'. The Germans are thus esteemed, just as the French used to be before, 'God be thanked, they have prettily learned to live'. Deeds and gestures are but the external appearances of secret matters; therefore the 'gentleman courtier' must be pliant like wax, ready to receive any impression, 'for if it be needful to laugh, he rejoiceth: if to be sad, he loureth; if to be angry, he frowneth; if to feed, he eateth; if to fast, he pineth. And to conclude, he is ready to do whatsoever it be, according to the humours and complexions of his fellowship and courtly company, although his affections are clean contrary.' There is only one caution here. But it is crucial. All this dissimulation, all this pleasing, must be performed prudently. It must all seem natural. This is Castiglione's *grazia* and *sprezzatura* pressed to their logical conclusions; and Philibert goes on to underscore the anti-Italian purport of his work by describing the 'civility and courtesy' of the Italian, which are nothing other than the perfection of the art of dissimulation, and the scrupulous control or concealment of all ambition and emotions.

In France, Philibert's satire fell on ground already fertile and increasingly manured by Italophobia. Every aspect of court life, real and imaginary, was ridiculed and abused. Even the pronunciation of the courtiers was pilloried when Henri Estienne complained that certain sounds had been altered first by ladies who were afraid to open their mouths wide, and subsequently by the courtiers who affected the same trick. This accusation was repeated by Pasquier who believed that pampered courtiers were effeminating the French language; though it is strange to note that the altered pronunciation of words such as *roine* as *reine* were to become standard French. There were many observers for whom courtiers could do no right; and such opinion is exemplified by Maurice de la Porte (1571), who provides fifty-seven epithets for the word *courtisan*, all of them pejorative. The word, he affirms, derives honourably from *courtois*: but it has now become so infamous that 'to describe a man who is vicious to a superlative degree one calls him *courtier*'.

Moreover, Philibert's satirical philosophy of worldly success became readily identifiable with the topsy-turvy political morality advocated in Machiavelli's *Il Principe*; and increasingly ferocious attacks on the court became interwoven with hostility towards the Italian favourites of Catherine de Médicis. This process gained impetus after the Massacre of St Bartholomew's Eve; and from the welter of subsequent pamphlet literature there emerged the most ambitious of all sixteenth-century attacks on Machiavellism – Innocent Gentillet's *Contre-Machiavel*, where perverted Italian morality was held to have infected the noblemen of

France, and all but destroyed them. By this time Philibert's philosophy of court might have seemed more like a modest description than satire, especially if compared to the diatribes aimed at the Italianized court of Henry III. Courtiers were depicted not simply as rapacious, lying, and vicious, but as murderous perverts. The ladies of the court were execrated as harlots and whores who, clad in shameless apparel, displayed their quivering breasts in an attempt to stir the lust of those 'Heliogabalistes' still susceptible to heterosexual stimulus. And these latter were deemed few enough, since the King was an hermaphrodite smothered by a swarm of degenerates. This morass of vice seems a long way from the genial sophistication of Castiglione. Yet many commentators believed that they could recognize – in these mincing, posturing pathics – the debased progeny of *Il Cortegiano*.

'Degrees, dignity, power, wealth . . .'

A remarkable feature of the reception of Philibert's *Philosopher of the Court* is the way in which its patently satirical intention appears not to have been recognized in England – even by its skilful translator, George North. It was regarded simply as sensible advice on how to succeed within a competitive society. And the most bizarre development in the history of the idea of the courtier is the way in which such misunderstanding gave way, in its turn, not only to an acceptance of the topsy-turvy morality, but even to its systematization. There can be no more cynical work in courtly literature than Lorenzo Ducci's *Arte Aulica*, first published in 1601, and issued six years later in a chilling English translation by Edward Blount. Here Cornelius Tacitus is regarded as the 'excellent master of courtiers'; while Sejanus – with his energy, daring, cunning, dissimulation, and flattery – is the model of the courtier's art. The tone of the work is of such total cynicism that it might seem an echo of the most malicious passages in Philibert's satire were it not for the fact that there is no hint at any point that either Ducci or his English translator were not in earnest. If their purpose were satire, it is so covert as to remain impenetrable; and it seems more likely from Blount's dedication to the Herbert brothers that the book was considered relevant to any aspiring courtier. As Ducci writes in his prefatory letter, by the guiding star of methodical knowledge it is possible for a man to 'furrow the deepest seas of unknown discipline' and to arrive safely at the harbour of 'true and commendable doctrine'.

For Ducci, as for the emblematists, the courtier submits his neck voluntarily to the yoke of servitude. But his end is, blatantly, 'his own profit'; and all his service to a lord is only to achieve this. 'It appeareth then that the ends or scopes that the courtier hath are three, that is his *proper interest*, and this is that which chiefly he endeavoureth: next the *favour of the prince*, as the cause of the first end; and then, the *service of the prince*, as the efficient cause of that favour.' The courtier's proper interest is the good which 'can be obtained from a court', and is solely concerned with profit (riches and abundance of material possessions) and with honours which are 'degrees, dignity, power, wealth, and the reputation which spring from them'. Ducci ab-

The charge of effeminacy *was brought against the circle of Henry III of France, and continued to be a stock accusation against over-sophisticated courts. Above: from Thomas Artus' 'Les Hermaphrodites', published in Paris in 1605. (46)*

solutely excludes from his conception of honour the practice of traditional virtues for, as he remarks, these may be employed as well outside the court as within it and, therefore, have no specific relevance to the courtier. Like other men, the courtier knows no limit to his ambitions, and he must serve only those who have the power and will to help him, for princes vary in their generosity: though 'the illiberal, niggardly, and absolute not beneficial, are unworthy of life, since they live unprofitably in this human society'. Ducci advises his courtier to conceal personal ambition under the 'apparent desire of the prince's service', for this is the highway to remuneration. Beauty of body, learning, wealth, and nobility are only important to the extent to which they may be exercised in the prince's service. Nevertheless, service is not unlimited, and must not involve loss of life or possessions: for the courtier's own

*Henry III's court has an unmistakable air of decadence, even in
paintings not intended to be critical. Here the King sits under a
canopy on the left, at the wedding of one of his favourites, the Duc de
Joyeuse. (47)*

profit is his 'chiefest' end; the prince's interest is decidedly
the lesser.

Ducci's courtier is an unashamed climber insinuating
himself into the 'confines of other men's offices' so that, in
the end, he may aspire to control everything through his
own hirelings; for 'affairs are so little pleasing unto princes'
that they generally prefer to leave everything to some
employee. To achieve this position the courtier must master
not only his own job, but must strive in all things to please
his master. Again we see the logical conclusion of
Castiglione's art of seeming without being: many petty
services 'only accomplished with an effective shew, have
been the beginnings of rewards and incredible favours'.
Furthermore, while avoiding abject servility, the courtier
must be prepared to do difficult and unpleasant tasks which
are especially rewarding when undertaken *before* the prince
makes his intentions clear – the skilful courtier 'diving (as it
were) into his mind' and thus making 'an encounter with his
pleasure'. The courtier will constantly attend upon the

prince both to be seen and to observe the prince's nature.
Just as the tailor must know cloth, the smith iron, the mason
marble, and the physician the functioning of the human
body, so the courtier must have a perfect knowledge of his
master 'in order to induce and gently wrest into the prince's
mind a love and liking of him.'

Ducci, like Castiglione, has much to say about the art of
speaking well: but, again, it is as though we are seeing *Il
Cortegiano* through a distorting lens. Speech should fit the
humour of the prince, and should not, therefore, be too
clever where the ruler himself only cares for mediocrities.
One must distinguish between conference concerning affairs
of state, and speech for entertainment; and unlike those who
thought it possible to establish rules for jovial discourse,
Ducci considers that 'to be jovial and conceited is a gift from
nature which receiveth little help by art, howbeit many
have tried to give precepts of urbanity and merriment'. The
ability to speak eloquently is likewise brought 'from the
mother's womb', though, in this case, it may be improved by
study. Flattery, the constant target for moralists, is regarded
by Ducci as the best way to secure favour provided that it be
not too abject. Of course, praise is most effective when
legitimate; but where merit is deficient then the courtier
must have immediate recourse to flattery 'the which

52

consisteth in a little amplifying or enlarging, and to be not altogether disjoined from perfect commendations'. But, when there is no merit at all to work on, 'it is lawful to help yourself with that kind which makes an attribute of some good part where none are'.

Through skill in speech, Ducci's courtier may win his way into the prince's confidence and aspire to serve his master in 'excesses or extremes of some affection', such as ambition, covetousness, wrath, or the desire for revenge, and, above all, illicit love which can seldom be satisfied without some action 'disrobing the prince of decency and decorum'. Here the courtier must be at his most subtle, interpreting every hint from his master, while remaining heedful that the human mind is 'so full of lurking corners' that one can never be absolutely sure of another's innermost thoughts. One thing is certain: that the courtier will be required to play some evil part in the prince's designs; and Ducci reminds his pupils that, while virtue is all very well, service demands the execution of extraordinary things, and that no evil is so monstrous that it may not be 'washed away by the greatness of the benefits which by the prince's favour are many times obtained'.

There are yet other means for the courtier to ingratiate himself with the prince; and Ducci reviews the comparative merits of cultivating the prince's family, friends, and favoured servants. The last group are the most difficult to employ since they are themselves striving to hold their place and must, therefore, be given no cause to suspect that the newcomer regards them as a 'scaling ladder' to success. Ducci's aspirant must ensure that his progress is '*gnomon-shadow* like, invisible in his motion'; and, even when favour has been acquired, he must be vigilant in its retention, remembering that favours are not dues, and that they have been granted 'to the end that he *may* use them, not that he *should*'. Rivals must be bought off, or exploited by bribery. But where malignity is insurmountable then it is necessary for the courtier to 'extinguish or supplant his adversary' – simulate friendship, says Ducci, while plotting his downfall. Ducci shies away from the suggestion, which he himself raises, of encompassing a rival's death; and he refuses to discuss evil deeds since they are inhumane and, he adds thoughtfully, insecure. Nevertheless, where the rival is implacable, there is no remedy but to remove him from court, bearing in mind that 'howbeit the courtier be not by himself to perform any bad offices, he may pass them notwithstanding by means of his adherents'. Finally, Ducci reminds us that all his advice can only be termed a 'conjectural art'. It may fail absolutely; and, if it does, the courtier has no alternative but to leave his prince. This is a grievous step, but unavoidable if it becomes clear that the coveted ends cannot be achieved in that particular service.

If, ultimately, Ducci's purpose in writing must – like his courtly art – remain 'conjectural', there seems little reason to doubt the seriousness with which Blount undertook his translation of the latest Italian contribution to court literature. And the cynicism of the *Arte Aulica* seems to have been well in accord with the times if we may judge from secret jottings in the commonplace book of one early seventeenth-century aspirant to worldly honours. 'The merchants handle as sponges,' he jeered, 'when they are full wring them. Though you get nothing yet be still (if you can) in the prince's ear, it will be instead of a revenue unto you. If any man will have justice at your hands, let him buy it, serve not the commonwealth for nought. By no means take bribes yourself, let that be done by some trusty man. The offices of the crown, of the wars, of the law, and of the church, will bring in a reasonable harvest. Be not overfond of virtue, it hath hurt many of her doting lovers. Only carry an opinion of it. But above all things be not too religious. At that rock many have been made shipwreck.'

We began with Louis Guyon setting out to remedy, with his Castiglione-derivative, the current view that courtiers were full of vice. Yet, as Philibert's satire had demonstrated, Castiglione's courtly virtues were too prone to abuse; and, indeed, these very virtues could become the climbing-tools for cynical time-servers. And it is a sad fact that the systematic self-seeking, so coolly analysed by Ducci, remains too clearly recognizable as the sempiternal reality of what may crawl away when the stones of political life and polite society are unexpectedly stirred.

Perhaps the moralists were right. *Could a 'jeu d'esprit' like Palissey's sauce-boat in the shape of a lady taking a bath have found favour in any but a permissive society? (48)*

53

Three

THE GOLDEN AGE OF BURGUNDY
Dukes that outdid kings

❉

C. A. J. ARMSTRONG

HE BURGUNDIAN COURT of the fifteenth century was able to shine all the brighter because of the temporary eclipse of all its rivals outside Italy. The Imperial court at Prague is perhaps the most comparable case. During the fourteenth century that had been a cultural meeting-place where German and Italian influences could mingle; but it had been extinguished as a cosmopolitan centre by the Hussites before 1420. And from the artistic point of view Burgundy had a distinct advantage. Whereas the Imperial court could derive less than little from the native art of Bohemia, Burgundy could draw upon the virtually inexhaustible reserves of genius – musical, sculptural, pictorial – indigenous to the Low Countries. Nor did it merely assimilate. To its credit, Burgundy actively stimulated the arts of the lands which it dominated and exploited.

Of potential rivals, we may look briefly at two courts: those of the Valois and of the Lancastrians and Yorkists. The court of the Valois kings of France faded away as the monarchy sank into insignificance from 1413 onwards; and when Charles VI died (October 1422) there came the sad scene in which his court officers received a distribution of their late master's furs and silks. Although it retrieved great political importance when Charles VII became talked of as 'Le Victorieux' rather than, as formerly, 'Le roi de Bourges', the French court scarcely recovered its accepted status as a social centre. Certainly the Neapolitan exiles, busy inciting Charles VIII to invade Italy, enlivened the French court before 1492, and subsequently the ageing Louis XII preserved around himself some appearance of gaiety; but in practice splendour returned only with the accession in 1515 of Francis I, a fact which accounts for the reputation of this, in some respects, callow sovereign.

Philip the Good receives the 'Chroniques de Hainault' from the hands of Simon Nockart. Behind the Duke stands his Chancellor, Nicolas Rolin; in front of him his young son, the future Charles the Bold. This miniature epitomizes those qualities of the Burgundian court which made it in the mid fifteenth century the envy of most European kings. (49)

England: the Lancastrians and Yorkists

The court of England, from being phosphorescent under Richard II and sophisticated under Henry IV, was on its way to becoming paramount in northern Europe under Henry V. The King's early death at Vincennes (August 1422) ended the chances of England and France becoming united in a dual monarchy. But the late King's brother, John, Duke of Bedford, continued to administer English rule as Regent for his infant nephew, Henry VI. His wife was Anne of Burgundy, sister of Duke Philip the Good. Together they succeeded in maintaining Paris as a capital of arts and entertainments, re-animating a brilliant, if harsh, society. The remaining royal library of France, deriving from Charles V (d. 1380), was bought up by Bedford as a matter of connoisseurship. In the winter of 1423 (the winters of the 1420s were bitterly cold in Paris) the great lords of England, with their retinues, put on such a display of jewellery and furs that even the longest Parisian memory could recall nothing more splendid.

The marriage of John, Duke of Bedford, and Anne of Burgundy represented a vital political alliance. The Regent lived in the Hôtel Saint-Pol, the private residence of the kings of France. At the Hôtel d'Artois, his family's town house, lived Duke Philip of Burgundy. The two households kept up an incessant rivalry, vying with each other in the eloquence of their minstrels, the brilliance of their trumpeters and the agility of their tumblers. But it was English protocol which made the rules. In the streets the Regent and his wife took precedence everywhere, riding past ecclesiastical processions regardless of whether the clergy were splashed with mud. Even in Duke Philip's own house they presided over the parties where guests danced late into the night. On one of these occasions, a famous beauty and grand-daughter of the poet Chaucer, Alice, Lady Salisbury, narrowly escaped being abducted by her host, the Duke of Burgundy. Her husband Thomas Montague conceived such jealousy that Anglo-Burgundian relations were jeopardized. Unhappily, the Duchess of Bedford died in November 1431; and with her death, aristocratic gaiety in Paris ceased for many years. Parisians long remembered her kindness; she was said to take off her ball dress to hear Matins before dawn

The Gruuthuse Oratory *at Bruges provided Edward IV of England with the model for his royal pew at Windsor (right), evidence of the impression which Burgundy had made on him during his short exile in 1470–71.* (50)

and to hurry to minister to the sick at the Hôtel-Dieu, the major hospital of Paris, where, it was thought, she caught the fever that took her life.

But already England and Burgundy were moving apart. Valois prestige was reviving under Charles VII (crowned at Reims in 1429 with the help of Joan of Arc). In 1435 Bedford died, and in the same year the Duke of Burgundy changed sides. Burgundy wanted to be the arbiter of Europe, and this was as true culturally as politically. In England, the reign of Henry VI was a bleak period for courtly culture. The King grew up to become a saint – but not of that order of sanctity to which Louis IX of France had belonged. Louis was a *preudhomme*, possessing the ability to keep Heaven and Earth in touch, and therefore the power to hold a chivalrous society together. Henry had no such power, and culturally England soon became an extension of Burgundy.

During the long-drawn-out diplomatic wrangle between the two powers at least one Englishman, Edward Grymstone, seized the opportunity – either in 1446 or 1449 – while *en mission* in Burgundian territory, to have his portrait taken by Petrus Christus. Likewise Sir John Donne, based in Calais during the late 1470s, had Memling paint him an altarpiece in which he and his wife are included. In the brutal 1480s, well-born refugees from the despotism of Richard III or Henry VII continued the English patronage of Burgundian artists – for example Thomas Grey, Marquis of Dorset, a fugitive from Richard III, had what must have been an easel picture of himself made in Flanders between 1483 and 1485. The most extreme case of this cultural dependence are the panels containing portraits of James III of Scotland and his

sons, now in the National Gallery of Scotland. This is basically a magnificent work by Hugo van der Goes, with just the faces of the King and princes added later by a very much less gifted artist when the picture reached its destination.

In scholarship, however, particularly in classical or so-called humanistic studies, the honours lay with England. A cleric such as William Gray, Bishop of Ely, or a layman like John Tiptoft, Earl of Worcester, could not be matched for distinction by anyone, ecclesiastical or secular, at the Burgundian court. And Duke Philip, 'the Good', employed men of talent from wherever he could find them; from England he drew Somerset and Dunstable, two of his most notable court musicians.

Edward IV grew up without much courtly education, but in 1470–71 he and some of his personal friends, including William, Lord Hastings, spent six months as involuntary guests of Charles the Bold at Bruges. They returned home with a pronounced fondness for Burgundian culture. The two courts were in fact related through the marriage of Charles to Edward's sister Margaret. Edward made his brother-in-law a Knight of the Garter; Charles reciprocated by making Edward a Knight of the Golden Fleece. For over a decade after 1471 England saw a revival of court culture strongly influenced by Burgundy, detectable in numberless small details. In the Garter Chapel of St George at Windsor, for example, King Edward went out of his way to commission a royal pew, in the form of a raised oratory enclosed within the choir arcade. It is closely modelled upon an elevated oratory occupying both ground floor and gallery of the ambulatory arcades of the church of Notre Dame at Bruges, which was made to the orders of Louis de Gruuthuse, Knight of the Fleece, with whom King Edward had stayed throughout most of his six months' exile. Edward also founded a fraternity of minstrels, carefully associated in a royal corporation. This, too, was an English adaptation from the Burgundian court, where the ducal minstrels, from the time of Duke John in the early fifteenth century, had been banded together in a society ruled over by the king of the minstrels. Perhaps the most conclusive evidence for the dependence of the Yorkist monarchy on the Burgundian ducal establishment is furnished by the ordinance for the royal household of England, the outlines for which were obtained in the 1470s by Richard Whetehill, one of King Edward's men in Calais, from Olivier de la Marche, the chamberlain of Duke Charles.

Richard III was educated in the household of Warwick the Kingmaker, and may be thought therefore to have had some courtly advantage over his elder brother; but circumstances prevented him from showing it to much effect. With Henry VII, the first of the Tudors, Burgundian influence is once more apparent. Before ascending the throne in 1485 he had spent a protracted exile at the courts of Brittany and France; but from a cultural point of view there was little to be learnt at either. As king, Henry never set foot in Burgundian territory, but he became very susceptible to the chivalrous attraction of the court under Maximilian. Made a Knight of the Fleece in 1491, he was soon a more zealous enthusiast than most of his predecessors. He created more

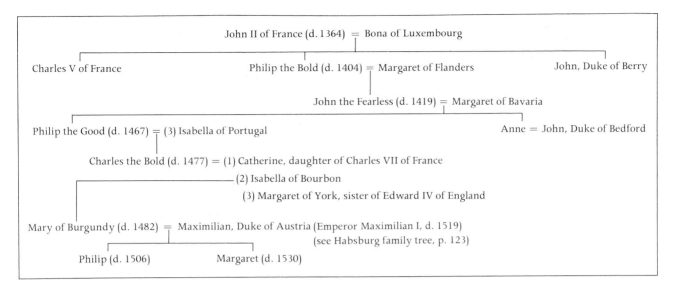

John II of France (d. 1364) = Bona of Luxembourg

Charles V of France   Philip the Bold (d. 1404) = Margaret of Flanders   John, Duke of Berry

John the Fearless (d. 1419) = Margaret of Bavaria

Philip the Good (d. 1467) = (3) Isabella of Portugal   Anne = John, Duke of Bedford

Charles the Bold (d. 1477) = (1) Catherine, daughter of Charles VII of France
(2) Isabella of Bourbon
(3) Margaret of York, sister of Edward IV of England

Mary of Burgundy (d. 1482) = Maximilian, Duke of Austria (Emperor Maximilian I, d. 1519)
(see Habsburg family tree, p. 123)

Philip (d. 1506)   Margaret (d. 1530)

Knights of the Garter than any English sovereign since the founder, Edward III; and he also had the knights wear the order as a chain around the neck – in imitation of the collar of the Fleece – instead of, as previously, displaying it as a true garter on the calf of the leg. Nevertheless, under this expatriate Welshman the pace of the English court was seldom more than pedestrian; and not until 1509, with the accession of Henry VIII, did a king of England surround himself with an ebullient social life.

Burgundy takes the lead

Well before the fifteenth century the royal Valois court of France had been surrounded by numerous feudal and appanagist sub-courts: Burgundy, Anjou, Berry, Bourbon, Brittany, Foix, and others. Normally these would regard the king's court as their model, but the sudden decline of that court as a result of civil war and the English invasion released them from royal control both politically and socially.

Burgundy was not alone in being ready to profit from this situation. The court of Foix was regarded by the cosmopolitan Froissart as the epitome of chivalrous life and imagination. That of Berry reached a peak of brilliance under Duke John (d. 1417), a civilized voluptuary, devoid of overriding ambition. Both Philip the Bold and John the Fearless recognized his pre-eminence in the arts – the first procured from him the designs of his *bergerie* (sculptured garden decoration showing flocks and shepherds) to reproduce in his own castle of Germolles; the second, less punctilious than his father, after besieging the Duke of Berry (his own uncle), forcibly removed his best choir-masters and boy singers to serve in the Burgundian chapel. Another appanagist court was Blois, where Charles of Orléans presided. Charles' father, Louis of Orléans, had been murdered on the orders of John the Fearless, Duke of Burgundy; John's son, Philip the Good, had in expiation ransomed Charles from captivity in England and given him his niece in marriage. Charles was an original poet, which none of the Burgundian dukes aspired to be, and directed a small court that

epitomized the Indian summer of French medieval literature. At Moulins another nephew of Philip the Good, John, Duke of Bourbon, kept what was by Burgundian standards a frugal court, but to his credit entertained the vagabond poet François Villon, the last medieval goliard and precursor of the French nineteenth-century romantics.

By the third decade of the fifteenth century, however, the court of Burgundy had surpassed not only these courts but also the royal courts of England and France, displaying a magnificence unseen in Europe since the fall of the Hohenstaufen Empire. Though a cadet branch of the Valois dynasty, it had virtually replaced the royal line. Nor was this entirely fortuitous. Since 1400 the dukes of Burgundy had done more than any other French princes to bring about the abasement of royal power. Now they presented their own court both as a centre of power politics and as a microcosm of chivalrous, gallant, and wealthy society.

Our picture of Burgundian court life has been deeply coloured by J. Huizinga's book *De Herfstij der Middeleeuwen* (published in 1919 and translated into English in 1924 under the wholly misleading title *The Waning of the Middle Ages*). Huizinga was one of the ablest and most fluent historians of this century, but the nostalgic charm with which he endowed his subject is the product of imagination, not scholarship. He saw the period as one of anxiety, of regret, of widespread misgivings about the state of society – as 'The Autumn of the Middle Ages'. His evidence should certainly be given its due weight. The qualities of romantic melancholy which he supposed to be universal north of the Alps were certainly present, as, for example, in the writings of René of Anjou ('dans la forêt de longue attente') and in the better-known poems of Charles, Duke of Orléans. Deception and disappointment were no doubt rife. There was plenty of anxiety in the courts, as in the Bourses of Europe at present. But the existence of the court and its survival were not called in question. About the Burgundian court in particular, there was little that could be called autumnal; on the contrary, it was enjoying a blazingly hot summer. It was opulent, ostentatious, self-confident. Indeed in 1477 after

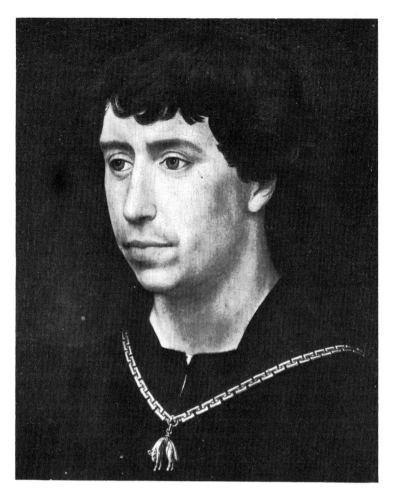

Charles the Bold *succeeded his father Philip in 1467. He reigned for under ten years before being killed at the Battle of Nancy. Roger van der Weyden's portrait suggests both his intellectual abilities and his instability.* (51)

their territory inherited an unbroken tradition associating a polite society with every form of artistic skill. The court, wherever it resided, was essentially a French court. However cosmopolitan in appearance, it retained this predominantly French character into the sixteenth century, when under the Emperor Charles V French was still the official accepted language for ordinances regulating behaviour and wages, and the current tongue of polite conversation and literature. The favourite parrot of the Emperor's aunt, Margaret of Austria, was respected under the gallant epithet 'l'amant en vert'.

Court and household

The backbone of the court was the ducal household, an administrative institution which imparted to it discipline and durability. Salaries were paid both to the highest dignitaries, the chamberlains, and to the 'valets', the humbler sort of attendants – 'yeomen of the body' as their equivalents were called in England – for their real or reputed household services. But court and household were by no means identical. Besides a number of hangers-on, who were frequently – three times in Charles the Bold's reign – ordered to depart, the court comprised numerous visitors: exiles like the Dauphin Louis or Edward IV, or travellers genuinely in transit, such as the Bohemian knight Leo of Rosmital. The household, on the other hand, constituted a body of picked ducal officers, councillors at the top and menials on the lowest rung of the ladder.

The household and its extension the court should be thought of as a compromise effected between the dukes, as sovereign princes, and the society in which they lived and which they desired to dominate. On the one hand the dukes as patrons or employers required a host of servants of all descriptions: aristocrats, councillors, soldiers, and diplomats to equal and excel those of kings; ecclesiastics to occupy territorial bishoprics and to represent Burgundian interests at the Roman Curia or at universal councils; clerks for their magnificent chapel; law and finance officers; physicians for themselves and their families; tutors for their children. These composed the élite at court and, consequently, the more regularly paid members of the household. Entertainers and craftsmen were also needed, the former ranging from theatrical producers to wrestlers and the latter from cobblers to cutlers.

From the other side of the counter, that of the employees, increasingly insistent pressure was exerted upon the dukes by claimants petitioning for ecclesiastical benefices, offices, pensions, food and wages. This insatiable demand for advancement was especially keen among the robust non-nobles of the duchy and county of Burgundy, who were running the Netherlands administration for the dukes' and their own advantage. Indeed, they forced their way into the court, but were a great deal less welcome there than the representatives of foreign banks, for example, Tomaso Portinari, the factor of the Medici at Bruges, who participated immediately in the anxieties of Duke Charles.

The insistence of the nobility on receiving entertainment and jobs at the dukes' expense was relentless and inevitable, and the dukes had to concede to it. Throughout their

the catastrophe of Duke Charles' death at the Battle of Nancy the Burgundian council, which had to act for his daughter Mary, seemed perfectly self-assured in negotiating with the Austrians for Mary's marriage and also with the more formidable King of France, Louis XI.

The vitality of the Burgundian court, exceptional as it was, can readily be accounted for by a few simple conditions. The dukes of Burgundy were not only determined from one generation to another to surround themselves with a vivid court life; they also controlled a skilfully organized system of highly trained servants directing inherited institutions. The resilience of these enabled them to survive such sudden crises as the murder of John the Fearless in 1419 and the death in battle of Charles the Bold outside Nancy in 1477; or such protracted strains as Philip the Good's period of governmental neglect from 1459 to 1465 and, more hazardous still, the blunderings of Maximilian, Duke of Austria, following the death of his wife Mary of Burgundy in 1482. In estimating other imponderable contributions to the brilliance and persistence of the Burgundian court, it should be remembered that, given the size of territory in relation to inhabitants, the dukes ruled the wealthiest lands in Europe outside Italy, and that

The pattern of life *at the Burgundian court is captured for us in a series of paintings and miniatures whose beguiling charm makes us forget its less attractive aspects. Right : Van Eyck's portrait of Baudoin de Lannoy, soldier, courtier, and ducal chamberlain, holding his staff of office. He and Van Eyck went to Portugal to negotiate Philip's marriage to Princess Isabella, and he was a founder-member of the Golden Fleece. Below : the birth of a prince. This miniature is unusual in showing the physician examining the mother. Below right : the choir singing Mass for the Duke who may be Philip the Good or Charles the Bold. Bottom : the jester, an essential part of the ducal household, with his horned cap and short jacket with bells. (52–55)*

In a formal garden *with neat brick walls, squares of grass and flowers, and a spacious summer-house, Duke Charles the Bold is presented with 'L'Instruction d'un jeune prince' by its author Guillebert de Lannoy. The man who wears his hat in the Duke's presence must be the chamberlain. (56)*

pearances of courtly life while performing military duties like professional soldiers.

No doubt the demands of Charles the Bold severely strained the loyalty of the court nobility, which goes far to explain the many defections, particularly under Maximilian's personal government from 1483 to 1492. During these years some of the leading figures of the court nobility – Jacques, Count of Romont and Philip of Ravenstein, to name only two – preferred an alliance with the urban patriciate of towns like Ghent and Brussels to service at court. This phenomenon serves to underline the fact that in the Low Countries there existed no real dividing line between court culture and that of the ruling class of the greater towns. It was not the well-to-do burghers but the dukes' highest civil servants, like the chancellor of Philip the Good, Nicolas Rolin, who were persecuted by the nobles, Thibaud de Neuchâtel savaging Rolin and Pierre Goux suffering attack by the local landlords around Châlon-sur-Saône. Nevertheless, although the in-fighting between nobles and the civil servants (*commis*) was more characteristic of the duchy and county of Burgundy than of the Low Countries, the tension between nobility and officialdom at court kept the nobles active, dutiful towards the prince, and intelligent. The official chronicler of Philip the Good and of Charles the Bold, Georges Chastellain, harps repeatedly on the hardships of the nobility; but though they had to work hard to please the dukes, as a class they suffered no serious crisis. Whereas their counterparts in Germany and to a lesser extent in England and France suffered the full effects of economic adversity, the Burgundian nobility was cushioned by remuneration for service at court.

Despite the strong-mindedness with which he ruled, even Charles the Bold in 1473 incurred a reprimand from his companion Knights of the Golden Fleece for recklessly granting away places at court. Charles disarmingly replied, however, that it was as much as he could do even to hear petitions from the endless stream of place-seekers; and it must be remembered that for every petitioner who succeeded in reaching the Duke probably a dozen had been weeded out by his ushers and chamberlains, a duty which Olivier de la Marche, himself a household officer, remembered as being especially incumbent on them. Ecclesiastics, particularly those with academic training, were among the most successful climbers at court. Two of the more conspicuous were tutors to the heirs-apparent of the dynasty: Antoine Haneron, brought from Louvain university in the 1440s to teach Philip the Good's legitimate and illegitimate offspring; and Frans van Busleyden, promoted – it would appear largely through the influence of Margaret of York – at some date before 1488 to be the tutor of Philip the Fair. One can see why Jean de Lannoy (1410–92), in many respects a model of paternal caution, warned his son not to let himself be exploited by ambitious courtiers, clerks, or laymen.

Above all the ducal court was the centre where all converged who sought to participate in the prosperity of the dynasty; and the Burgundian power, unlike the kingdoms of England or France, was something of a syndicate in which people took stakes so as to share in the fortunes of the house.

territories they were peculiarly harsh towards surviving feudal franchises, and the nobility of the Burgundian lands experienced all that the Tudor house held in store for their English counterpart. In throwing the court wide open for their employment and pleasure the dukes successfully seduced the majority of their noble subjects into becoming stout supporters of the dynasty. The history of the nobility in Western Europe is one of endless pursuit of magnificence and entertainment. Save for a few rugged characters, of whom the dukes had specimens among their subjects in Franche-Comté, the nobility was striving since at least the period of the Crusades to shed its rustic independence and transform itself into a pampered court élite. Indeed, it never had a finer opportunity than with the Valois dukes of Burgundy. 'Syche ger, gold, perle, stonys, they of the Dwkys coort neythyr gentylmen nor gentylwomen, they want non for . . . they have it by wyshys, by my trowthe I herd nevyr so gret plente as her is'; the quotation is taken from the admiring but envious John Paston. True, the noble courtiers of the dukes had to work increasingly hard for their princely masters as the military and diplomatic liabilities steadily increased. They reached an insufferable level under Charles the Bold, who, particularly at the siege of Neuss which lasted nearly a year (July 1474–June 1475), insisted that his nobles must maintain the outward ap-

One of the best reasons for coming to court was to make a useful marriage. If the dukes could not always find a lucrative office to give away, they were excellent match-makers. Among the highest nobility these marriages engin-eered at court were important in genetically blending the upper aristocracy of the various Burgundian-ruled ter-ritories of Germanic and Romance culture – as exemplified by the union of Reinoud II, lord of Brederode, and Yolande de Lalaing. The three first dukes were permanently con-cerned with the marriage of their courtiers, high and low, agreeing to bear the costs of the wedding festivities and to act as godfathers to the resulting offspring. Philip the Good may have overplayed his hand in this respect – for instance in his efforts to make a match between the family of Luxembourg, his most powerful vassals, and that of Cröy, of the lesser nobility of Picardy, but ducal favourites ever since one of their number, Agnes, had become a mistress of John the Fearless. On the other hand Charles the Bold, expecting everyone within his dominions to serve him for duty rather than reward, neglected the prince's role of managing the marriages of his entourage. Had the Duke provided Philip de Commynes with an opulent bride, he might never have defected; in the event less than six months after the arrival of Commynes at the French court Louis XI produced for him a splendid match with the heiress Hélène de Chambes.

Needless to say the court was larger than the ducal house-hold. Members of the household, whether the duke's chan-cellor or the duke's fool, were established; and they received 'livrée de bouche en cour' – something more than a subsistence allowance for persons of every quality. Ambassadors and knights-errant from abroad could move freely in and around. The Greeks had been conspicuous ever since the dynasty had committed itself to the rescue of Byzantium. In 1396 Philip the Bold had sent his son to deliver Constantinople from the Turks on a crusade which ended disastrously at Nicopolis. The majority of courtiers, however, were tepid in their support of the anti-Turk cru-sade, while the Greeks and their supporters constituted a divisive factor. For one reason or another the Wavrin family adopted Philip the Good's crusading or Levant policy; and one member of it, Waleran de Wavrin, enjoyed a spec-tacular cruise in 1444–45 along the Black Sea coasts, the Danube, and the shores of North Africa, anticipating the buc-caneering exploits of Sir Francis Drake around Spanish America. But despite this, and despite the anti-Muslim fervour of Jean Germain, Bishop of Châlon-sur-Saône, the court nobility was suspicious of crusading adventures, and like John, Duke of Cleves, preferred a pilgrimage to Jerusalem in the relative comfort of a Venetian galley.

The presence of foreign princes was a regular feature. Some of them were exiles, like the Dauphin of France in 1456 or Edward IV of England in 1470; one, a shoddy represen-tative of the Austrian house, Duke Sigismund, came to pawn his lands in 1469. But most were travellers of distinction – well-to-do Germans such as Eberhart the Younger of Württemberg or Ludwig, Pfalzgraf of Zwei-brücken, or Italians like Francesco d'Este and Rodolfo Gonzaga, who came to represent the interests of the despots of Ferrara and Mantua at this most active court north of

Court fashions *are represented with exactness in this Burgundian miniature of 1475–85. A sovereign, wearing the imperial crown, dictates to a secretary. The squire talking to the black page-boy wears a flat beret and close-laced shirt, a fashion imported from Spain which lasted little more than a decade. But the man in the foreground holding a staff is dressed in a costume that is wholly non-contemporary and intended to be antique. (57)*

the Alps. Foreigners, especially the frugal Italians, found living expensive at the ducal court, but many nevertheless remained for years. The presence of so many visitors from abroad does deserve special attention, particularly because in the fifteenth century they so rarely came to the court of England, or even to the court of France, if one excepts the Neapolitan exiles. Commynes, who had fled to the French court, remarked that in his day exiles from all over Europe had gathered at the court of Burgundy. This was indeed true, and not just because it was the best centre north of the Alps for receiving outside intelligences. The dukes distri-buted reasonably ample pensions to high-ranking refugees, though the dukes of Exeter and Somerset, the foremost Lancastrian exiles there in the 1460s, who had to quit when Margaret of York married Charles the Bold in 1468, do not seem to have received generous treatment.

One national group of exiles, the Portuguese, succeeded in establishing a veritable lobby at the Burgundian court. This was mainly due to the patronage of the Duchess Isabella of Portugal, third wife of Philip the Good. The connection with Portugal dated back to the time of John the Fearless; and well before the marriage of Isabella to Philip in 1430, her brother, Dom Pedro, as a knight-errant travelling across Europe, had been entertained in 1426 by the Duke in Flanders. When civil war broke out in Portugal and Dom Pedro perished at the Battle of Alfarrobeira (20 May 1449),

Isabella of Portugal, *Philip the Good's third wife, probably after Roger van der Weyden. She wears a brocade dress, a necklace of crystals and pearls, and one of the most extravagant coifs ever portrayed. It seems to be built over a framework of stiff cloth of gold, covered by diaphanous gauze. Front hair and eyebrows are plucked. (58)*

French crown – needless to say Charles VII as usual was far from the capital of France – viewed such gatherings as a return of Burgundian infiltration. Aliénor de Poitiers, daughter of the same Portuguese lady, preserved in precise literary form the niceties of protocol, as it was supposed to be observed in the Burgundian court.

Discipline, class and talent

The personality of each of the Burgundian princes was reflected in the type of court with which he surrounded himself. At that of Charles the Bold, courtiers had to attend in stiff para-military discipline, none daring to be absent, the Duke's pronouncements being like the formal promulgation of ordinances. The miniatures at the outset of these ordinances preserve a record of the rigidity of these occasions in which, despite the unwillingness of his servants, the Duke sought to sacralize the exercise of his authority. Everyone sensed the need to follow the Duke's lead, especially in matters of fashion. If in 1442 courtiers preferred to have their hair cropped close on the head, this was in deference to the Duke, who on medical advice had had his hair cut sharply back in imitation of the English and Italian fashion earlier in the century. Yet the Burgundian court was not in fact slavish in adulation of its ruler. There was no practice comparable to that of the English household under Richard II, who enjoyed sitting like a doll on his throne and expected any of his courtiers upon whom his gaze fell to genuflect.

The ducal chamberlains, who carried small sticks in token of authority delegated to them by the dukes, and the ushers, more formidably armed with metal maces, enforced upon the courtiers some standard of public behaviour. Conduct seems often to have verged on the rowdy. The gardeners in charge of the grounds at Germolles complained to Philip the Bold and John the Fearless of hedges broken down and flower-beds trampled; and judging by the repair accounts of Philip the Good's favourite pleasure residence at Hesdin, a good deal of hooliganism occurred in the castle and in the park when he and his courtiers were there. At the end of the fifteenth century a town like St Omer sought to restrict the number of princely entries per annum not only because of the cost of presents, mainly wine, to be offered to the Archduke Philip the Fair but also on account of the disorders occasioned by the court. The Burgundian courtiers were admittedly no more reckless than others: an envoy of the court of Brittany, who had come to negotiate a marriage between a sister of Philip the Good and the Count of Richemont, actually set fire to an inn at Dijon while celebrating the success of his mission.

Incidents involving honour and policy were treated much more seriously. When in 1407 Louis de Châlon Count of Tonnerre supposed that he could with impunity break into the Duchess's apartments and elope with one of her ladies – moreover a native of Aragon, which was friendly with Burgundy – he faced remorseless hatred from John the Fearless and confiscation of his lands. Both Philip the Good and his son Duke Charles were at pains to see that envoys of hostile princes were treated with something more than diplomatic correctness while at court or traversing Burgundian lands. The English herald and others crossing Brabant

two of his sons and a daughter later fled to Burgundy. One of the sons, Jaime, thanks to Burgundian support received in 1456 a cardinal's hat. The other João, Jean de Coimbre, became in the same year a Knight of the Fleece, while the daughter Beatrice married in 1453 Adolf of Ravenstein, nephew of Philip the Good.

Duchess Isabella and Dom Pedro were the children of John I of Portugal and his wife Philippa, daughter of John of Gaunt. Philippa had been a fanatic in support of chivalrous standards and courtly etiquette, and she successfully indoctrinated her children with the same values. Dom Pedro entertained the most extravagant notions about knight-hood, and Isabella found a spiritual home in the self-consciously chivalric court of Burgundy, bringing with her the idea of a literary cult with herself as patroness. One of her Portuguese ladies in waiting married John of Poitiers, lord of Arcy, and in 1456 had to accompany her husband to Paris on account of a lawsuit against him pending in the Parlement of Paris. The Portuguese Madame d'Arcy lost no time in setting up a salon in Paris to which she received the wives of influential officials. Her initiative was regarded with disfavour, since the stricter representatives of the in 1437 to reach the Rhineland were given special protection on the journey by the court chamberlains at Brussels and elsewhere; and when the herald of Lorraine defied Charles in the name of René II, the Duke of Burgundy offered the herald not only an escort but gold coin and a jacket of gold cloth. The duties which rested upon the ducal chamberlains in keeping order at court and escorting ambassadors and other visitors were not light; and while there were, at any given time, a number in attendance, the principal ones, *premiers chambellans*, such as Baudoin de Lannoy and Antoine de Cröy, who acted for Philip the Good, or Jean de Renty and Olivier de la Marche under Charles the Bold, were formidable men in their own right.

Members of the household, whatever their social origin, were equally servants of the prince. They were exempt from trial before any court other than the dukes' own commissioners (under the *committimus*, a privilege of French importation), but they were liable to be discharged any moment without notice – at the nod, as the saying went (*ad nutum principis*). Between the reign of John the Fearless and that of Philip the Fair at the end of the fifteenth century, there were at least six or seven occasions, excluding those

Adolf of Ravenstein *was a German satellite of the Burgundian dukes. Though himself a member of a ducal house, he wears lynx fur, not ermine, in deference to court etiquette.* (59)

brought about by disasters such as the murder of Duke John or the death in battle of Duke Charles, when the household and court were disbanded or at least so severely slimmed that only indispensable officers of the duke were retained. The reason was always the same: financial embarrassment. Only a few months after the superlative Feast of the Pheasant in February 1454, when it was said that the jewels worn by the Duke were worth 100,000 nobles, Philip the Good abruptly left for Germany to preside, as he hoped, over a conference at Regensburg for the launching of an anti-Turkish crusade. On the eve of his departure, which took place clandestinely, the Duke had ordered his chamberlains to disband the court. The sad occasion (for the courtiers) was celebrated by a farce showing a cold kitchen, put on by Michault Taillevent, the ducal entertainer.

Up to a point the relations between the duke and his personal circle of governing councillors on the one hand and the household court on the other may adequately be described as a bargain between mutually agreeable buyers and vendors. The court represented central government, a unifying factor binding together local society in the various territories of the Netherlands or the Burgundies, among whom no common bond existed. Relations between the court and this local society are reasonably well documented. Relatively obscure people wrote home to describe court festivities or their own situation, like the poor squire from the Franche-Comté who hastened to tell his family that he had been taken on to serve in the garrison of Dunkirk and hoped to make a good marriage.

The ducal policy aimed at distributing favours as widely as possible, while at the same time exercising parsimonious economy. For this reason members of the household, save those at the very top, served only half or a quarter of the year, sharing the honours with others who alternated with them. Early in the sixteenth century the Regent Margaret of Austria stated categorically that those who had done their annual stint at court were expected when they returned to their home in the provinces to defend and explain current government policy to their provincial neighbours. The Regent Margaret, whose statecraft was essentially Burgundian, undoubtedly inherited this formula from the Valois dukes, but they do not appear to have put it on record.

Household and court offered a unique opening for talent to display itself and afforded to artists and men of science an opportunity to show off their skill – an exercise which was normally difficult within a society criss-crossed by social barriers. The Burgundian court was more egalitarian in this respect than, say, the court of England, though this egalitarianism should not be exaggerated. The medallist, the musician, and the painter were all there essentially to minister to the taste of a ruling clique. Yet even on a cautious estimate it would be hard to deny that a fruitful cooperation between artist and patron did exist or to gainsay the success of artists in sharpening the taste of their employers, and in influencing through them a wider range of society.

Men of letters, being classified as 'clerks' (i.e. clergy), had enjoyed a privileged position in European courts for centuries; and it was therefore semi-traditional that an author in his own right and a publisher (in manuscript) of earlier literature, such as Jean Miélot, should receive a canonry, and that higher honours should reward the official historiographers Chastellain and Molinet. If poets had for long been viewed askance by ecclesiastical moralists, musicians, particularly minstrels, were doubly suspect. But in the long term, lavish patronage of devotional authors, coupled with extravagant expenditure on the choir of the ducal chapel, had the effect of raising the respectability and standing of writers, scribes, and musicians.

Both Burgundian court literature and music deliberately confused and intermingled the sacred and profane; while the Council of Basle was growling out old-fashioned sanctions against performers of music, Duke Philip was increasingly extending his protection to include musicians of all types. They composed and performed for banquets or for the chapel, where the setting of the Mass as often as not was taken from a secular tune familiar at court. Hainault, part of the Burgundian complex of territories, had been since the fourteenth century a conspicuous home of chivalrous society and music; in the Middle Ages the two usually coincided.

One of its main cultural and economic centres was Cambrai, and the cathedral of Cambrai functioned as a court 'conservatoire' where music was nurtured. From the late fourteenth to the early sixteenth century the bishop of Cambrai was invariably either a bastard or a councillor of the Burgundian prince, and ecclesiastical preferment was often a reward for musical achievement. The court musician Gilles de Binche (known as Binchois) was made a canon of Mons in Hainault, and Guillaume Dufay a canon of Cambrai. It is perhaps typical of the highly complex legal situation that Cambrai was strictly speaking not a Burgundian city at all but part of the Holy Roman Empire. In the same way, Tournai, where the finest tapestries of the Burgundian court were woven, belonged to the kingdom of France.

The dukes habitually went yet farther afield in search of talent. Music was international and cosmopolitan. Philip the Bold sent his wind players to be trained in Germany; but under his grandson Philip the Good, while trumpeters were still being imported from Germany, select virtuosi who had made names for themselves within the ducal household were already being taught to play wind instruments. The dukes' multi-national patronage of music extended to England where John Somerset left the chapel of Henry VI to serve Philip the Good. He was later followed by Dunstable and Roger Morton, who composed songs to be sung by Charles the Bold, whose voice, however, was said to be no more than indifferent.

Easy relationship between artists and their patrons provides one of the better criteria for an assessment of the maturity and informed taste of any society, past or present. Throughout antiquity and the Middle Ages a common religious aim, shared by patron and artist alike, had inspired both and mediated between their social disparity. At the court of Burgundy, as in contemporary Renaissance Italy, the ties linking patrons and their chosen artists are at once more personal and less idealized. In painting, a fashionable, though somewhat ingenuous, formula to represent the personal friendliness between patron and artist was the theme of the artist in his studio surprised by the visit of his patron. One miniature, or rather a book illustration – for Burgundian illumination is illustration rather than miniature – shows Charles the Bold concealing himself behind a column to catch the artist (either David Aubert or Loyset Liédet) unawares, but being detected by the artist's dog, a poodle or long-haired Pomeranian. Many miniatures depict artists at work with a dog at their feet, possibly a reminiscence of St Jerome's faithful lion, who guarded him while absorbed in study, but alternatively an up-to-date watchdog awaiting the patron's visit.

The best-known and best-documented instance of friendship between patron and artist is that which undoubtedly existed between the good Duke Philip and his *valet de chambre* Jan van Eyck. Van Eyck's household position, which implied the prince's confidence, earned for him the commission to make the future Duchess's portrait. This meant accompanying the ducal embassy (1429–30) to Portugal, where he was able to study from nature the exotic flora that he introduced into the panels reserved for the hermits and pilgrims in the Ghent altarpiece of the Adoration of the Lamb: two conifers – *Cupressus sempervirens var: pyramidalis* and *Pinus pinea* – the date-palm, the fig, and the pomegranate. Van Eyck's case was no isolated one, for Charles the Bold also had a favourite miniaturist, one Jean de Hennecart, who again acted as *valet de chambre*. It is possible to trace the stages by which the so-called 'Master of Mary of Burgundy' educated the taste of the Duchess Mary and that of her step-mother; but the 'Master' himself seems to have undergone a certain education through the extraordinary themes dictated to him for illumination by Adolf of Nassau, one of the Duchess's chamberlains.

The 'thousand flowers' tapestry *was made for Charles the Bold. In the centre are the ducal arms of Burgundy surrounded by the collar of the Golden Fleece. It was done by Jean de Haze in wool, silk, and gold and silver thread. (60)*

The Burgundian Golden Age *had already acquired a tinge of nostalgia when the duchy became united with vast territories in Spain. Philip the Fair, who is probably the duke featured in this Brussels tapestry, inherited Burgundy through his mother, Mary of Burgundy. His wife Joan (the Mad), who stands below him to the right, brought him Castile. (61)*

Charles the Bold *kneels holding a reliquary of St Lambert of Liège, probably made prior to the Duke's destruction of Liège in 1498. Behind him is St George, patron of chivalry, by whom the Duke was accustomed to swear – demonstrating his preference for England over France. (62)*

The world of the hunt *was a familiar part of Burgundian life. Many of the most splendid tapestries celebrate it. This one, made in the second quarter of the fifteenth century, is devoted to the art of falconry. (63)*

Men skilled in the arts were not drawn into the court circle by the dukes alone. The extreme case was the illustrator whom for want of a name we can but call the 'Wavrin Master'. He worked for Jean de Wavrin, lord of Forestel, who as a historian and author of the *Anciennes chroniques d'Angleterre* was more experimental than other patrons. He ordered manuscripts not on fine vellum but on paper, to be decorated with little pictures of an Impressionist type executed with pen and ink and touched in with watercolour, mainly sepia. The finest examples are at Brussels (MSS. 9631–9633) and at Ghent University (MS. 460). An authority so eminent as the late Comte Paul Durrieu considered the manuscripts cheap and the illustrations 'frequently childish'. But for all his fondness for rich material Duke Philip the Good recognized the originality of the 'Wavrin Master' and bought some of his work from the lord of Forestel.

Another ducal councillor, Louis de Chantmerle, from the Mâconnais, brought with him to court a trained scribe, who worked for him and accompanied him as the court moved about between Brussels and Arras in 1437 and 1438. He wrote what was the most legible script available at the time, indeed more easily read than that of the Italians. It was this script, adopted and standardized some fifteen years later by scribes working on texts for the ducal library, that produced the celebrated *lettres bâtardes* from which came the model for the type in which some of the earliest books in northwest Europe, for example those of Caxton, were printed.

The household constituted the backbone of the court and preserved the ceremonial cycle of its year. On May Day, for instance, Duke Philip the Good, who preferred black, either from affectation or out of mourning for his murdered father Duke John, clothed himself for the occasion in a green doublet: 'il te fauldra de vert vêtir c'est la livrée aux amoureux', as ran the old saying. And like a backbone, the household was made up of vertebrae, small groups forming compact societies of their own. The stable (*écurie*) had its little confraternity, whose patron was St Eligius, supposedly not a blacksmith but a goldsmith. His feast was punctiliously observed by the members of the stable – a preserve of the nobility – on 1 December, the day following that of St Andrew, patron of the Golden Fleece and reputedly the evangelist of the Burgundians.

The chivalric ideal

Neither the fact that numerous commoners were for their talent received at court, nor the grossly materialistic way in which both prince and courtiers pursued their pecuniary interests, in any way invalidate the essentially aristocratic and chivalrous nature of the Burgundian court. The ideal aimed at, first by the dukes and then whole-heartedly by the nobility, was to re-create an active chivalrous society along the lines of the literary romances of the twelfth and thirteenth centuries. This medieval renaissance of the fifteenth century probably did society less harm than the classical Renaissance; it was less aggressively exclusive and not at all anti-scientific.

Within limits, Burgundian court society did actually realize its ideal. The ambassadors of England, Hugh Mor-

The exotic trees *and fruits included by Van Eyck in the background of his Ghent altarpiece were sketched by him on his visit to Portugal in 1429. As Duke Philip's 'valet de chambre' he was included in the mission in order to paint the portrait of Isabella. (64)*

The anonymous artist *known as the 'Wavrin Master' was one of the original talents in the fifteenth century. His impressionistic caricatures of high society and his use of cheap materials, paper and watercolour, make him very unlike the other miniaturists patronized by courtiers. (65)*

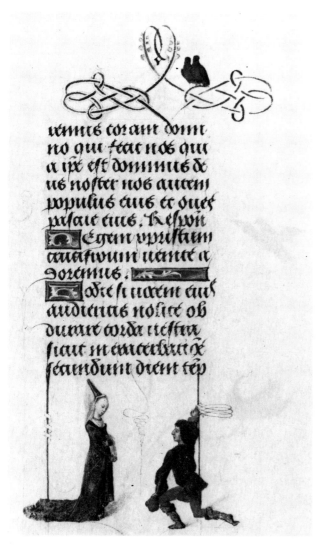

A falconer kneels *before a lady. The illustration is from a 'Book of Hours' of about 1485. The falconer becomes the lady's prey. (66)*

timer and John Catrick, returning from Paris in 1408, saluted Duke John and named him, apparently for the first time, John the Fearless. And after the jousts held in Bruges in 1468 to honour the wedding of Margaret of York and Charles the Bold, John Paston wrote to his mother: 'as for the Dwkys coort . . . I herd never of non lyek to it save King Artourys cort. By my trowthe I have no wyt nor re-membrans to wryte to yow halfe the worchep that is her.'

This admiration for chivalrous society was a re-assertion of the knight's value to society as a whole, then very much under fire from certain clerics who, in accordance with Marxist ideology, were the grave-diggers of their own culture. The Burgundian re-animation of chivalry was calculated to dispel the knight's own despair about himself. The dukes provided two antidotes: the elastic, embracive court and the rigid, select Order of the Golden Fleece. Politically speaking the statutes of the Fleece, founded in 1430 on the pretext of the wedding of Duke Philip to Isabella

of Portugal, were devised to retain the higher nobility for the Duke's camp and council, for war and advice; but the general intention was to revive what was wistfully believed to be the strict and pristine code of chivalry.

The knightly class, for long lampooned by burgesses and clerics, had come to imitate its critics by concentrating without any concealment upon monetary profits. Chivalry on the battlefield had become to an increasing degree a matter of seizing prisoners who had to buy themselves free, if they were not sold or exchanged for their ransoms, while the so-called law of arms lent a spurious legalism to such mercenary practices. The circumspect warrior quitted the stricken field, preferably with his prisoners, so soon as the ultimate outcome appeared to be in doubt. A notorious case was Sir John Fastolf, Knight of the Garter, who withdrew from the fight at Patay (1429) on perceiving, correctly, that there remained no hope of an English victory. Sir John's conduct was severely censured by the semi-official Burgundian chronicler Enguerrand de Monstrelet. When Duke Philip, who had refused the offer of the Garter, founded his own order in 1430, he set his sights higher. The statutes of the Fleece forbade a knight of the order to depart from any engagement with the enemy once banners had been displayed. The display of banners had been since the thirteenth century the sign of a fight to the death.

Ironically, in June 1430, six months after the foundation of the Fleece, Burgundian forces suffered a reverse at Anthon, where banners had indubitably been displayed. The battle was not excessively lethal, but it was a true battle on account of the show of banners, and ended by the flight of the two Burgundian commanders. Louis, Count of Chalon-Orange, owed his escape to his excellent mount, which swam him across the River Rhône; and Jean de Neufchâtel, lord of Montagu, retreated – in his own words – to prevent the enemy being enriched by his ransom. Both of them were designated members of the Duke's order, but neither was admitted to the first chapter of the Golden Fleece. Their exclusion was a serious decision both politically and socially. The Count of Orange, to whom the collar of the order was never sent, did not forgive the Duke of Burgundy, though his son, Louis de Châteauguyon, a Knight of the Fleece, fell at Grandson (1476) in an attempt to seize the banner of the Canton Uri. Jean de Neufchâtel, a chamberlain of both the dukes of Bedford and Burgundy, suffered the humiliation of having to return the collar to Duke Philip, as sovereign of the order. Pilgrimage was a juridical penalty for a crime, and knights who incurred dishonour undertook a distant pilgrimage for the same reason as their nineteenth-century successors retired to an obscure watering-place to atone for a scandal. Jean de Neufchâtel left at once on a pilgrimage to Jerusalem, where he died.

Under their statutes the knights were required always to wear the gold collar or at least the golden lamb on a velvet riband round the neck. In war the collar had to be worn and the sovereign was bound to replace those lost by enemy action. In 1478 at Guinegatte at least four knights lost their collars in hand-to-hand fighting, and Maximilian, Duke of Austria, sovereign of the order by right of his wife the Duchess Mary, had to replace them, however reluctantly.

All the while literary circles dependent on the court, particularly under the inspiration of the Duchess Isabella of Portugal during the 1440s and 1450s, were active in defining the theoretical qualities of chivalry. In doing so they produced an intriguing though over-voluminous literature in the vernacular; but in practice physical courage still remained the virtue most prized.

From the start the dukes had been book-collectors, a liberal prodigality inherited from the house of France. When they wished to give literary expression to their strife with Louis, Duke of Orléans, they favoured the archaizing verse form in *Le Geste des Ducs* and in *Le Pastoralet*, a pastoral romance with a vengeance. The elevation of chivalry was accompanied and fostered by the reintroduction (first in script, later in print) of medieval epics and romances in the *ancien français* of the older times, newly turned into prose versions in the currently understood *moyen français*.

It was a general passion of the time. John Talbot, Earl of Shrewsbury, who spent his life fighting for the Lancastrian cause in France, offered Margaret of Anjou (Queen of England, 1446) a superb manuscript, now in the British Library (Royal MS., 15 E.VI), containing stories of Guy of Warwick and the Four Sons of Aymon in French prose. Yet the Burgundian court stood out as the main centre from which emanated the impulses for the renewal of medieval mythology, though the classics were by no means neglected. Names like Lancelot, lifted out of the romances, were bestowed upon children of the nobility, while the exploits of the heroes of romances became the conversational small change of the day. When Philip the Good, beside himself with rage after an altercation with his son, rode off into the forest of Soigne and got lost, his chamberlain Philippe Pot, having at last caught up with him, addressed the Duke: 'Sire, are you now playing at Arthur or Lancelot or perhaps Tristan forever in the woods?'

The reinstatement of chivalry was clearly an ideal underlying the choice of publications, at all events up to 1483, made by William Caxton. He received 'a yearly fee' from the Duchess of Burgundy, Margaret of York, to whose household he was attached between 1471 and 1476. Until 1483 his collaborator in translating from the French works of chivalrous taste was Anthony Woodville, Earl Rivers. The jousts between this latter and Anthony of Burgundy staged in 1467 at Smithfield were among the most elaborate ever to occur in England and closely followed the model of contemporary Burgundian trials of strength.

Even men of much lesser means and rank than the dukes acquired some highly important manuscripts. Philippe de Loan, famous for his contribution to the *Cent nouvelles Nouvelles*, was Duke Philip's semi-permanent envoy in England during the first phase of the Wars of the Roses; yet he found time to buy a *Bible historiale* now in the Bibliothèque Nationale (MS. français 2) previously owned by Humphrey, Duke of Gloucester. According to his own note De Loan bought the volume on 15 November 1461 in London, being careful to add to the details of the purchase the fact that he was a squire of the stable, therefore a household officer of the Duke of Burgundy.

The revival of chivalry *constitutes a medieval Renaissance comparable to the classical Renaissance of Italy. One of the manifestations which Burgundy and Italy shared was jousting – practised with enthusiasm by the Burgundian court and its imitators. This miniature from a romance shows the fiercest form of joust, two knights armed with blunted lances and not separated by any barrier. (67)*

'The courtier' in northern Europe

Was there an ideal courtier of the Burgundian court comparable to *il cortegiano* of sixteenth-century Italy? One thing in common between the two societies was a respect for academic learning. From the 1440s onward an impressive number of the sons of the aristocracy in the Netherlands, who were regarded as eligible laymen to serve at court, in council, and in arms, were matriculated at the University of Louvain. Within a generation of its foundation Louvain was being attended by at least one son, not necessarily destined for an ecclesiastical career, from some of the noblest families: counting from north to south, Brederode, Borselen, Glymes, Lalaing, Lannoy, and Cröy. The 'Good Duke' had lent encouragement by sending there his eldest bastard, Corneille.

The sound education of the Burgundian ruling society in the Low Countries is clearly displayed in the person of Philippe de Commynes, a Fleming who wrote infinitely better French prose than any Frenchman of his day. No doubt it was his recollection of the well-tutored gentlemen in the Netherlands that led Commynes, as a 'transfuge' to the court of France, or a Marmaluke, as it was then politely termed, to take such pleasure in mocking the French nobility as a lot of blockheads. The court of France was evidently dull and unremunerative for a pleasure-seeker. Baudoin, one of the natural sons of Duke Philip, defected there from Charles the Bold, but soon crept back.

The inherited sports of the nobility were hawking and hunting, jousts and tournaments. The ducal hunting parties were highly organized, and each huntsman had his duties precisely defined. The duke's noble companions also had individual roles specifically assigned to them, so that a protocol almost as strict as that observed in the audience chamber was devised for hunting parties. The hunts were held in forests, above all the great forests of the duchy of Burgundy; but although some under Philip the Good lasted for several days around a particular residence, neither he nor any of his race were so addicted to the chase as some of the kings of France, notably Louis XI. The hunt seems to have been something of a pretext for outdoor festivities. Splendid open-air banquets attended by ladies – whether they hunted or not – occupied a great part of the day to the accompaniment of horns and trumpets. The practice was already growing up of hunting not across country but in an enclosed park, especially at Hesdin. Here in Artois an area of several square miles was enclosed and kept stocked with game of every sort from deer to partridges. Among the sportswomen of the court was the Duchess Margaret of York. Even after the death of her husband Charles in 1477, she kept a huntsman at Binche in Hainault, where she seems to have enjoyed the pleasures of the chase on a considerable scale, judging by the sums she paid her tenants whose property had suffered thereby.

Falconry and hawking was the peculiar sport of the court in the Low Countries. The moors of Brabant and Flanders provided a perfect setting for this sport, while Bruges was a principal market for the birds imported from the Baltic lands, for example Prussia. The Duchess Mary of Burgundy, the heiress of Charles the Bold, was so keen in tending her falcons that she had them brought into the bedroom within a few nights of her wedding to Maximilian Duke of Austria. The latter wrote to Otto von Prüschenk, who was of his own age and shared his interests, admiring his bride's sporting instincts but suggesting that they might be carried too far. Mary's death in the spring of 1482, which was such a personal tragedy for Maximilian and so great a calamity for the Low Countries, seems directly attributable to her passion for hawking.

Jousts and tournaments were the supreme spectacle at court, combining physical courage and skill with the utmost display of aristocratic pride in heraldry and ardent gallantry exhibited to the ladies among the spectators. The tilt yard was a test of nobility, so that German cities such as Nuremberg, wishing to prevent their patricians from aspiring to noble rank, prohibited them from participating in the sport. Onlookers crowded to see these combats for the sake of their own violence. Even townsmen turned out in numbers; although they preferred public executions or torturings to death, a highly developed taste among the artisans of the southern Low Countries.

The court's preoccupation with the revival of earlier chivalrous customs, comparable to the literary revival of the High Gothic romances, is evidenced by the reintroduction of the tournament. This was made to follow thirteenth-century practice, when one team fought another, as distinct from jousts, where one adversary tilted against an opponent, or combats in which single combatants fought each other with a variety of weapons. Such tournaments were sometimes fierce, and on the occasion of his marriage to Margaret of York in 1468 Duke Charles had to descend from his presidential chair into the arena to separate the combatants. Nevertheless they were also shows at which music expressly composed for the occasion by an artist such as Binchois or one of his pupils was performed, while horses and dromedaries were paraded and cheetahs on chains were displayed to the audience.

The champions of the joust were the heroes of the day, among whom none was more spectacular than Jacques de Lalaing, commemorated in a prose epic (a *biographie romancée* rather than a biographical study) probably written by Chastellain. Sprung from an ancient but not opulent family of Hainault, Jacques de Lalaing was spotted by the young Duke of Cleves, whose ambition was to be served by a squire possessing all the admired qualities. In company Jacques de Lalaing was remarked on for his gentleness, not to say docility, but also regarded as exceptional for the piety that sustained his devotion to the code of chivalry and the worship of ladies.

The *faits d'armes* also afforded a display of heraldry. Almost as severe as the blows struck in combat was the scrutiny which participants had to undergo before entering the lists. Shields, crested helmets, and pennons were submitted for examination by the president, either the duke himself or some other conspicuous champion, who, accompanied by heralds and ladies, inspected the armigerous title deeds of the contestants. Blasons if suspect were queried, and hammered when convicted. Duke Philip the Good, though not his son Charles, is represented in miniatures holding a hammer, the purpose of which was to knock out disqualified shields before the combats and to referee the contest once the fighting had begun. The hammer was a princely attribute; and this is why a princely visitor to the Burgundian court, Lionello d'Este, had Roger paint him with a toy hammer between the fingers of both hands. Another attribute of authority over the lists was the arrow, ranked only beneath the hammer as a symbol of power; and the Brussels picture of the *Man with the Arrow* – whoever he is, whether Burgundian or Portuguese – embodies the gravity and responsibility that Roger knew how to confer on his sitters.

Dionysius Cartusianus, a strict theologian admired and consulted both by Duke Philip and his son Charles the Bold, adhered to thirteenth-century tradition in condemning *hastiludia* on account of the spiritual risks of sudden unprepared death. He added that the lists encouraged the sin of pride, indeed the besetting sin of the Burgundian

Burgundy's wealth *made it a focus for the art of jewellery and precious metalwork. Above: an engagement present in the form of a brooch with the young couple in a garden surrounded by branches bearing pearls and precious stones. Below: detail from the Prayer book of Mary of Burgundy. Right: a clock owned by Philip the Good. The exquisite forms of Late Gothic architecture dominated almost every decorative art. (68–70)*

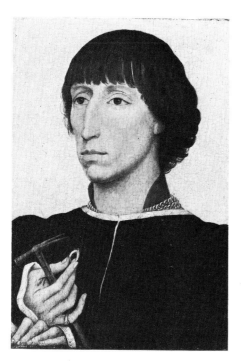

Two courtiers *portrayed by Roger van der Weyden. On the left, Francesco d'Este, who stayed at the Burgundian court from 1444 to 1475. On the right, probably Anthony, Bastard of Burgundy. Both men hold symbols of authority connected with the lists. The hammer was used to knock out disqualified shields before a tournament. The arrow was used to signify decisions by the referee. (71,72)*

court. Nevertheless, ecclesiastics certainly assisted at these dangerous sports; and Jacques de Lalaing was extremely well cared for by the clergy on the occasions when he challenged any knight to overthrow him. The eminent scholar and mitred Abbot of St Omer Guillaume Fillastre could attend jousts with a clear conscience, for he was chancellor of the Order of the Golden Fleece. Office-holding, like charity, covers a multitude of sins.

How was entry gained to this extravagant court? The German and Italian princelings infesting the ducal household arrived via diplomatic channels, furnished with credentials. The majority of the male arrivals from within seem to have been young. Jean de Margny, a scion of the rural nobility, just within Picardy but bordering Normandy, was presented in 1472 to Duke Charles by the Sire de Rambures, who held the finest castle in his own neighbourhood. His age would have been near to fourteen. At the same age Jacques de Lalaing was presented by the young Duke of Cleves, who as a trained courtier confronted the Duke as he emerged from Mass and briskly introduced his protégé. Philippe de Commynes was taken to court in 1464–65 at the equivalent age 'au saillir de mon enfance', but by whom we do not know. The memoirist of Burgundian etiquette Aliénor de Poitiers 'came to court', in her own words, at the age of seven; but in fact her Portuguese mother was in attendance on the Duchess Isabella. For others, entry to court might be less simple and more embarrassing, for Dukes Philip and Charles at times affected not to observe patrons seeking to introduce young men to them. The patron and his protégé might have to make as many as three running approaches to the Duke, and, much to the mirth of onlookers, fall on bended knee, before securing his benevolence. It may have been feared that without some chastening the young would carry all before them. This was certainly the view of Martin Le Franc, in his own

estimation philosopher to the court and indeed receiving quasi-official recognition as a moralist; and much the same opinions were expressed by Alain Chartier at the court of Charles VII of France. Duke Philip was probably something of a tease, for Jean de Lannoy warned his son that in order to put young men in their place the Duke had been known to ask the junior members of his council to speak before their senior colleagues.

The open air was the element proper to the court – not the tents or wooden huts used as shelter when the court was journeying between the Burgundies and the Low Countries – but the forests to hunt in and the moors to hawk over, above all the gardens around ducal residences, where rejoicings in varying degrees of frivolity and solemnity were conducted. The garden formed the symbol and reality of happiness. *Hortus inclusus* represented ultimate chastity, an attribute consecrated to Our Lady and borrowed by the Duchess Isabella for her device. The garden surrounded by hurdles presented also the ideal enclosure for amorous enjoyment: the *jardin d'amour* borrowed from the Germanic *Liebesgärtlein*. The Burgundian miniaturists saw the garden as a smart rectilinear shape, with pots of dianthus and topiary shrubs, opening out from an interior. Burgundian artists had abandoned, a trifle earlier than the Italians, the tradition received from the Byzantines of depicting an interior by showing it from outside, looking inwards. This exactly fitted the design of the gardens at Hesdin and Germolles, at both of which the residences opened outward as a planned extension of the castle; in Tuscany, likewise, high fashion was soon to relate the architectural planning of the house with the small garden.

The life of the court took place, in its most exquisite form, at night. The chroniclers (Chastellain and Monstrelet) reflect on the splendour of nocturnal entries into towns and, given the cost of illumination, any social event after dark was a conspicuous display of opulence. For the same reason the tapestry hangings were changed at least twice daily in the audience chambers to manifest the inexhaustible riches of the prince.

Courts cannot flourish without ladies. Abundant evidence shows that their presence was indispensable for the animation, etiquette, and politeness that distinguished Burgundian curial society. Some latter-day readers of the *Cent nouvelles Nouvelles* have conjectured that women were only wenches to courtiers; but these droll stories, whatever their literary merit, merely serve as a reminder that in a strictly disciplined society the coarser instinct for fun erupts in forms recognizable at the Burgundian court as in Edwardian smoking rooms.

Any assessment of courtly morality would be highly conjectural without medico-legal investigation into the behaviour of parallel social groups. The Abbé Jacques Toussaint has done something of the sort for the population of western Flanders; but a general investigation along such lines would be a formidable research operation. On the surface courtiers appear to have remained unperturbed by criticism. It was certainly the preachers who denounced them most warmly who attracted their attendance. A church interior with a fashionably dressed congregation gathered around the preacher was a subject often chosen for illustration, perhaps with veiled irony, by the illuminators of Burgundian manuscripts. Denunciation by one's fellow-courtiers was on the contrary much feared. Certain songs of Binchois reveal alternating fear and contempt towards his detractors: 'Mesdisans m'ont cuidie desfaire' followed by 'Qui veut mesdire, j'en fais la figue aux mesdisans'. The campaign of calumny that contributed to the removal from court of the ageing chancellor Rolin shows how damaging slander could be. Like other courts remembered by Aeneas Sylvius (Pius II), the court of Burgundy was not always a happy place.

The ducal court was not unsuccessful in solving the old problem of organizing around the prince's own person an artificial society whose members might enjoy a share in his wealth and magnificence as a reward for performing private services. Those services ranged from confidential to menial and from the aesthetic to the vulgar. The court produced its own style in many different fields. The severely individual portraits of Roger van der Weyden provide an example from the visual arts, the chapel choir and the composers in and around it from the musical. In historical literature the historiographers achieved their own concept of rhetoric. That the dukes and their courtiers were selfish and wasteful is all too obvious. Their more serious ideals were seldom realized: Constantinople remained unliberated. Yet they developed a culture which still exercises an attraction. It is doubtful, given the time and place, whether any alternative privileged society, for instance an urban confederation, would have shown greater enlightenment.

The late fifteenth-century garden *consisted of a series of small enclosed plots, carefully planned and planted, with many walls, fences, and hedges, rather like the rooms of a castle in the open air.*
(73)

Four

LORENZO DE' MEDICI
*High finance and the patronage of art
and learning*

❊

E. B. FRYDE

THE FIRST PERIOD of political ascendancy of the Medici over Florence lasted sixty years. They were not yet its lawful rulers, but merely private citizens of outstanding power and influence. It began with the return of Cosimo de' Medici from exile in October 1434 and ended in the precipitate flight from Florence of his great-grandson, Piero, on 9 November 1494. Throughout these sixty years the position of the Medici always depended on continuous cultivation of widespread support from other Florentines; on retention of old friends and securing of new ones. An exclusive Medici court, cut off from the outside world, would have been a formula for disaster. Piero's downfall was due in some measure to the fact that he was the first of his house to forget these realities.

The position of the fifteenth-century Medici as virtual rulers who yet had to behave as if they were private citizens affected their style of life and the pattern of their activities in all sorts of peculiar ways. Any attempt to reconstruct the authentic atmosphere of Lorenzo's preoccupations must start with a discussion of these special features of his position. It must partly be a study of how he adjusted to his inheritance.

Private fortune

Lorenzo's grandfather, Cosimo, had inherited from his father, Giovanni, who died in 1429, the richest and most influential bank in Florence. His entry into active politics was necessary in order to protect his business interests. In a city ruled by extremely competitive merchants a large business could only survive if it was not victimized by those in power, and the Medici bank could only continue to grow if the policies of Florence conformed to the interests of their firm. Cosimo's grandson Lorenzo expressed this lucidly in his intimate memoranda ('ricordi') by remarking that 'in

Lorenzo's was a court without a king. *The Medici had no constitutional position, and their power was derived wholly from a system of unofficial manipulation. In terms of real personal influence over the destiny of their state, however, they probably surpassed most contemporary monarchs. Bust of Lorenzo by Verrocchio. (74)*

Florence one can ill live in the possession of wealth without control of the government'. The first sixteen years of Cosimo's power over Florence were a time of impressive expansion of the bank's activities and profits. In his last years, however, Cosimo's grip was somewhat less sure and by the time of his death in 1464 the best days of the firm were over. His son Piero was much of the time an invalid and overmuch control was left to mediocre and quarrelsome business managers. When Piero died on 2 December 1469 he left to his two young sons, of whom the elder, Lorenzo, was not yet twenty-one, a bank which rested mainly on its past credit and its connection with the ruler of Florence and not on adequate capital assets. To survive as businessmen the Medici had to preserve their power in Florence. Lorenzo was probably quite sincere in the account of his motives in December 1469. He explains in his 'ricordi', written in 1472, that the second day after Piero's death he was asked 'to take upon myself the charge of the government of the city as my grandfather and father had already done. This proposal being contrary to the instincts of my age and entailing great labour and danger, I accepted against my will, and only for the sake of protecting my friends and our fortunes.' He then added the comment on political power, quoted above, about the impossibility of preserving in Florence one's wealth unless one holds political power.

Lorenzo estimated that his father left a fortune worth some 230,000 florins. This was considerably less than Cosimo's fortune at its peak and much of it was tied up in assets that could not be readily realized. Throughout his career Lorenzo was to suffer from a crisis of liquidity. His financial difficulties, which grew worse as time went on, imposed serious limitations on what he could attempt as a patron of artists and scholars.

Lorenzo had to pay out of his own pocket for many activities that formed part of his political position. He enjoyed, of course, important compensatory advantages, including even exemptions from taxation in moments of particular stress, as in 1481. But the state did not pay for much of the personnel that he had to employ. This was one of the reasons why Lorenzo had to do so many things by himself. While he soon learnt to discharge masterfully his heavy share of state affairs, he felt unable to spare much time for his bank. He had not been prepared for a business career and his tastes did not lie that way. In December 1469 Lorenzo knew very little about the Medici business and was not prepared to intervene in it. When shortly afterwards Angelo Tani, one of the most experienced retired Medici executives, appealed to him to deal with disputes at the bank's Bruges branch, Lorenzo replied that 'he did not understand such matters'. He had the ability to be an intelligent businessman, as he showed late in life when the disastrous decline of the bank forced him to revise somewhat his priorities, but this change came too late to effect any substantial improvement in his financial position.

Lorenzo could always find money for things which he regarded as essential, but one has the impression that he did many things only by choosing to forget for a while his real situation. He was never so desperate, however, that he could not indulge a particular fancy.

In 1469 the worst potential threat to the survival of the Medici bank lay in its over-involvement in papal finance; but Lorenzo had no inkling of this. The Medici enjoyed a monopoly of dealings in alum from the papal mines at Tolfa near Rome and their advances on the security of this mineral formed an important part of the papal budget. Lorenzo helped to finance the election of Pope Sixtus IV in August 1471; and his 'ricordi' (written in March 1472) mention his

The father and grandfather of Lorenzo *are represented in Benozzo Gozzoli's famous fresco of the 'Adoration of the Magi' in the Medici palace. Cosimo, 'Pater Patriae', is on the left; his son Piero rides in front of him wearing a brocade tunic and a turban. (75)*

visit to Rome to congratulate the new Pope. It is a very brief record dwelling chiefly upon Lorenzo's pleasure at acquiring on this occasion some antiques and a quantity of precious stones and cameos which had belonged to Pope Paul II, the immediate predecessor of Sixtus. Nothing delighted Lorenzo more than did such precious small objects, especially if they were of antique origin. He had probably seen Paul's collection on a previous visit to Rome in 1465. Sixtus made him a gift of two antique heads in marble. We know from other sources that Lorenzo advanced a loan of 35,000 ducats on the security of a selection of Paul's valuables. Among the things he carried off back to Florence was the splendid 'tazza Farnese', a beautiful engraved Hellenistic agate, probably of Egyptian origin. It is the most precious object in the inventory of the Medici treasures drawn up in 1492, where it is valued at ten thousand florins.

The friendship between Lorenzo and Sixtus IV soon turned to hatred. The feud was caused chiefly by political differences but the Pope was also bitterly disappointed by the failure of the Medici to market his alum profitably. By 1476 the alum monopoly had been transferred to the rival Florentine firm of the Pazzi. Probably with the Pope's knowledge the Pazzi plotted to murder Lorenzo and his younger brother, Giuliano. On 26 April 1478 the two Medici brothers were attacked at High Mass in Florence cathedral and only Lorenzo escaped alive.

This was the gravest crisis of Lorenzo's career. Sixtus declared war on the Medici. By the time it was over, in the early months of 1480, Lorenzo's position in Florence was indeed strengthened; but the Medici bank had suffered irreparable losses. In his tax return of 1481 Lorenzo had to make embarrassing admissions: 'In making out this report I shall not follow the same procedures as my father in 1469 because there is a great difference between that time and the present with the consequence that I have suffered many losses in several of my undertakings.' The Medici bank was only kept going because Lorenzo was able to use his position as the effective ruler of Florence to appropriate public and private funds which did not belong to him.

As soon as the nightmare of the 'Pazzi war' was over Lorenzo tried to resume his private pursuits. In July 1479 he had become the owner of a villa at Poggio a Caiano, some eleven kilometres north of Florence, which had previously belonged to Giovanni Rucellai whose son had married one of Lorenzo's sisters. It was reconstructed between 1480 and 1485 by Lorenzo's favourite architect, Giuliano da San Gallo. But there were also losses. When in 1485 Lorenzo's young cousins, the descendants of a brother of Cosimo, came of age they demanded the restitution of 53,643 florins which Lorenzo, their guardian, had appropriated to himself in the crisis of 1478. Lorenzo could not restore the cash and had to abandon to them instead the ancestral villa of Cafaggiolo, the oldest of the Medici country properties in the heart of the uplands of the Mugello from which the Medici had originally migrated to Florence. With Cafaggiolo had to be relinquished farms and other properties in the Mugello which had been carefully developed by his grandfather, Cosimo. Lorenzo loved this countryside, described it in several of his poems, and showed the mastery of its dialect in his youthful little novel of *Nencia da Barberino*. His cousins still regarded themselves as not fully compensated. They were henceforth enemies of Lorenzo.

The disaster of the 'Pazzi war' led to the liquidation of several Medici branches. The banks at Bruges, Avignon, Venice, and Milan had all disappeared by 1481. The Medici palace at Milan, which had housed the bank, was retained a little longer; but even this had to be sold by Lorenzo in 1486 for four thousand florins. Its elegantly sculpted doorway, executed for Cosimo by Michelozzo, can still be seen in the Sforza museum at Milan.

Lorenzo's favourite sculptor, Andrea Verrocchio, left Florence for Venice between 1483 and 1486. After the fall of the Medici regime in 1494 Andrea's brother, Tomaso, presented a detailed claim for the debts allegedly due from Lorenzo. It provides a very complete list of the works executed for the Medici by Andrea between *c.* 1466 and 1483. Tomaso may have been simply trying this on, but his claim must have had at least some plausibility. If he was telling the truth, Lorenzo had been chronically neglecting to pay his debts to one of the principal artists employed by him and had not even bothered to pay for the tombs of his grandfather Cosimo and his father Piero. Furthermore one of the works on Tomaso's list, the statue of David, had been promptly resold to the city of Florence for the considerable sum of 150 florins.

Historians are familiar with the statements of Francesco Guicciardini and other Florentine writers that Lorenzo had been misappropriating public funds. At least one archive document seems to corroborate this charge. In 1495 the

The family's roots *lay in the Tuscan countryside. It was from Cafaggiolo that they had originally migrated to Florence, but Lorenzo was forced to sell the ancestral estate in 1485 to pay compensation to his cousins. Painting by G. Utens, 1599. (77)*

government of Florence claimed from the administrators of the sequestrated Medici properties the large sum of 74,948 florins which, at various times, had been illegally paid to Lorenzo by the city steward in charge of the public debt fund.

Lorenzo's excessive neglect of his bank in his last years is vividly illustrated by an incident at the end of 1494. When Piero had to flee from Florence on 9 November of that year the only things that he could snatch away were some of the precious small objects from Lorenzo's collections, including a few which Lorenzo had brought from Rome in 1471. Piero counted on being able to receive help from such Medici agents as still existed in other parts of Italy. On his arrival at Venice he asked the local Medici factor to supply him and two companions with cloth worth a mere hundred ducats, but met with a refusal. This upset Piero terribly, as he confessed to the French ambassador, Philippe de Commynes. Obviously Lorenzo had failed to maintain loyal and dependable collaborators.

Manipulating the state

Throughout the fifteenth century the Florentine constitution could only work in practice if its normal regulations were continuously set aside or at least grossly distorted. The supreme government of the republic consisted of a committee of nine magistrates, known collectively as the Signoria. They were endowed with unlimited executive powers but held office only for two months. As soon as

The Pazzi plot *was a violent attempt (1478) to stop the Medici gaining supreme power. Lorenzo's brother Giuliano was killed, but Lorenzo escaped and was able to defeat his enemies. This medal was struck to commemorate the event. (76)*

Banking *was the foundation of the Medici's wealth and therefore of their political power. Top: the entrance doorway – all that survives – of the Medici bank in Milan, designed by Michelozzo. Below: a Florentine woodcut of a banking scene, 1490. (78,79)*

they left office they could be prosecuted and they usually dared not do anything controversial. Legislation needed the assent of a number of separate assemblies which were supposed to balance each other. The members of the Signoria and the majority of the other temporary office-holders were supposed to be selected by lot from among all the citizens eligible for these posts, that is from less than twenty per cent of the male population of Florence.

Continuity of policy was impossible under such a system unless it was somehow imposed from outside by an unofficial pressure-group. In the fifteenth century Florence was run in practice by groups of leading businessmen who manipulated the system to their advantage and were allowed to do so as long as they avoided major disasters. The main threat of instability came from factions within the ruling group. After one such crisis Cosimo emerged in 1434 as the man best fitted to assure a stable exploitation of the Florentine state by its oligarchy of richer citizens. Cosimo understood that the regime must try to assure at all times satisfactory food supplies at reasonable prices and that the principal Florentine industries must never be short of essential raw materials. Florentine businessmen, if they were friendly to the Medici, should be protected from bankruptcies and the Medici enterprise could operate as an unofficial 'central bank' of the Florentine business community.

Cosimo's never-ending task was to protect the regime from nasty surprises. The selection of office-holders by lot was suspended as often as possible and ingenious methods of great complexity had to be devised to ensure that only the supporters of the regime held key offices and that reliable majorities were maintained in the various legislative councils. It had all to be done under the guise of temporary measures that were not supposed to change permanently the normal constitution. But in practice the grip of the Medici oligarchy was tightening all the time and the intimidation of opponents by iniquitous tax assessments and all manner of other devious methods was being erected into a permanent system. Cosimo moved in a world of shifting expedients, of endless intrigues, of innumerable secret caucuses and of patient interviews with all who mattered politically. But he was a wise man who operated mostly under cover and the evil side of the regime was hidden by a façade of lavish ecclesiastical patronage, munificent charities, promotion of splendid buildings, and the high moral and intellectual tone of Cosimo's household. Lorenzo was able to record with approval that between 1434 and 1471 his family had spent 'an incredible sum' of 633,755 florins on 'buildings, charities and taxes'. In his opinion 'it gave great lustre to the state and this money seems to be well spent'.

Cosimo preserved to the end of his life a considerable measure of popularity among all classes of the Florentine population. This helped to save his son, Piero. In 1465–66 the regime nearly collapsed through a split within the ruling Medici faction. This crisis provided Lorenzo with his first close experience of the dangers surrounding his family; and, according to one story, his prompt action in sending a message about some suspicious happenings saved his father from actual assassination. It taught Lorenzo the danger of

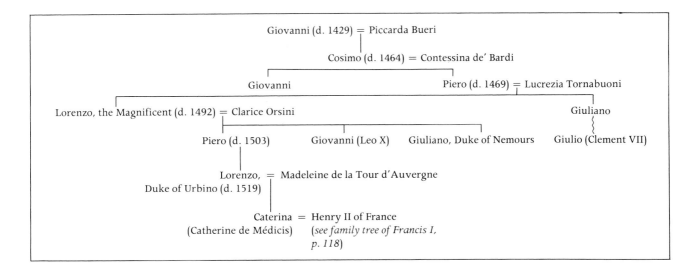

Giovanni (d. 1429) = Piccarda Bueri

Cosimo (d. 1464) = Contessina de' Bardi

Giovanni   Piero (d. 1469) = Lucrezia Tornabuoni

Lorenzo, the Magnificent (d. 1492) = Clarice Orsini   Giuliano

Piero (d. 1503)   Giovanni (Leo X)   Giuliano, Duke of Nemours   Giulio (Clement VII)

Lorenzo, = Madeleine de la Tour d'Auvergne
Duke of Urbino (d. 1519)

Caterina = Henry II of France
(Catherine de Médicis)   *(see family tree of Francis I,
p. 118)*

delegating too much political power to associates and may help to explain his obsessive personal attention to an immense range of political tasks.

In essentials Lorenzo still had to tackle the same job as had faced Cosimo, of synchronizing by mainly unofficial means the policies of Florence and of ensuring that his supporters never for a single moment lost control of all the key official posts and councils. Piero Guicciardini, the father of the historian Francesco, has left a fascinating account of the devious arrangements, in 1484, for the revision of the lists of citizens eligible for offices, the so-called 'Scrutiny'. Lorenzo stood at the centre of all the machinations. The thing that stands out is the ceaseless personal attention paid by him to minutest details, and the use of a mixture of official and private channels to assure that he got his way. He had to know well all the men who mattered in Florence and to form a personal judgment on what to expect from each. He was the head of a widely ramified mafia and could not be the aloof lord of a remote court.

Lorenzo's interventions in government, though ubiquitous, were mainly 'unofficial'. He held few specific public offices and there were frequent spells when he had virtually no official functions. Unlike his grandfather and father, he was never a member of a Signoria. Presumably he could never accept anything less than the chairmanship of that body; and the minimum legal age for that position was forty-five, while Lorenzo died at forty-three. But, especially after the failure of the Pazzi conspiracy, the grip of his supporters on power became quite unassailable, at least by any legal means. One of the most acute discussions of the regime is contained in the *Storie Fiorentine* of Francesco Guicciardini, begun in 1508. This has fewer illusions about the Medici rule than his subsequent writings, but tries to be fair and balanced. Guicciardini frankly recognizes that Florence had no liberty under Lorenzo, but adds that it would be impossible to find a better or more amiable tyrant.

Compared with Cosimo, or even Piero, Lorenzo was at a serious disadvantage because he lacked their ample supplies

of money and could not buy as much support as he would have liked out of his own resources. His supporters had to seek their main compensations out of state funds. Official corruption was a normal feature of fifteenth-century Florence. Machiavelli may have invented the speech in which Lorenzo's father allegedly castigates the oppressions and frauds of his former political associates; no contemporary Florentine, however, could have been surprised by the details of these denunciations. But the fiscal regime appears to have become extremely oppressive under Lorenzo. The wars and other ambitious enterprises were financed largely out of short-term loans advanced by some of his principal adherents at high rates of interest, while the rest of the population had consequently to bear higher taxes. According to Piero Parenti, who was not an opponent of the Medici, the news of Lorenzo's death was received in Florence with mixed feelings. The great mass of the people were relieved because they had been heavily taxed under Lorenzo. Memoranda submitted to Lorenzo show that he was aware of many abuses in the fiscal system. He was himself a member of two commissions that reviewed the administration of the public debt but made no radical improvements. He knew of the frauds perpetrated by the collectors of the indirect taxes. The whole regime rested on corrupt profiteering by the Mediceans and, as has been noted before, Lorenzo's own hands were apparently not clean.

The most serious contrast between Cosimo and Lorenzo lay in their different temperaments. Cosimo was content to live the part of a leading citizen. Lorenzo paid frequent lip-service to this ideal; but he was much more impatient of the restraints that this imposed upon him. Francesco Guicciardini thought that suspiciousness was Lorenzo's worst fault. As he acutely observes, this did not spring from Lorenzo's real nature but from the circumstances of his position: because he was well aware that he was controlling a city free by nature and where everything had to be done through the official organs and under semblance of continued liberty. This situation made Lorenzo obsessively secretive. He felt compelled to write in his own hand an appreciable part of his correspondence because, as he himself explains in one such missive in July 1478, 'I do not trust others.'

Lorenzo came to expect loyalty to himself rather than to the Florentine state; but he had no legal right to insist on this. Thence, as Guicciardini had correctly noted, sprang his constant suspiciousness about the attitude to him of all the major Florentine office-holders. He was extremely sensitive about being fully informed of all that happened, while fearing the communication to the official organs of the state of anything that he disliked. Some of the officials got the message quite quickly. As early as 1471 the captain of Volterra, a particularly sensitive spot at that date, enclosed the dispatches to the official Florentine authorities in private letters to Lorenzo, leaving it to the latter to forward them at his discretion. Gradually Lorenzo assured his control over the flow of information from the Florentine ambassadors abroad. In the last years of Lorenzo's life the extreme situation existed where certain ambassadors wrote, indeed, everything to Lorenzo, but were neglecting to inform the official Committee of the Eight at Florence ('Otto di Pratica'), who were supposed to be in charge of foreign affairs. On one occasion, Lorenzo's secretary, Piero da Bibbiena, had actually to warn Piero Alamanni, the official ambassador at Rome in 1491–92, that he must write more often and more

fully to the Eight, who 'had been heard to complain of the dryness of his dispatches', though 'of course he need not let them into affairs which should remain secret between him and Lorenzo'.

Woe betide an ambassador who forgot that certain things were fit only for Lorenzo's eyes. Failure to recognize this brought disaster upon Alamanno Rinuccini, one of the most distinguished Florentine humanist statesmen and a great admirer of Cosimo. He accepted an embassy to Rome in November 1475 at a time when relations between Sixtus IV and Lorenzo were already highly strained and he made the fatal error of reporting to the Florentine authorities, and not to Lorenzo personally, a violent denunciation of Lorenzo by the Pope. He was recalled from his mission and badly treated by Florentine authorities on Lorenzo's instructions. Rinuccini's feelings about Lorenzo found an outlet in his secret 'Dialogue on Liberty', written in 1479. The injustice of his treatment rankled deeply and he defends his conduct in corresponding primarily with his official superiors at Florence and not a mere private citizen like Lorenzo. Rinuccini expresses regret at the failure of the Pazzi to rid Florence of Lorenzo and piles up denunciations of the young Medici 'who exercises the tyranny which he inherited from his grandfather much more savagely and insolently than either his father or grandfather had done'. He survived to greet with delight the expulsion of Piero in November 1494 and to fill one of the key offices under the new regime.

Lorenzo could be very self-centred and impatient in handling his collaborators. The correspondence of his envoys amply confirms that he was a suspicious and fussy master. Inevitably the inexorable pressure of business affected him adversely. It sometimes left him exhausted. In a letter to Piero Alamanni he complains that he had been writing all day and was tired. Lorenzo's poems and letters show that he often hankered after a different way of life. He would have preferred to stay frequently away from Florence, dividing his time between his favourite outdoor pursuits of hawking and hunting and scholarly discussions with his learned friends or more relaxed literary and musical pastimes.

Guicciardini contrasts Lorenzo's conduct in important affairs, where he was reticent and ambiguous, with his ordinary amusing and pleasant conversation. This light-hearted side of Lorenzo endeared him to those in daily contact with him. On his progresses through the Florentine countryside his arrival was eagerly awaited by the small local communities. There is a delightful glimpse of one such occasion in May 1485. Matteo Franco, a household chaplain of Lorenzo, is describing to his colleague, Piero da Bibbiena, the return of Clarice, Lorenzo's wife, from the health resort at Morba. On the return journey to Florence she was passing through the picturesque little hill town of Colle di Val d'Elsa. The inhabitants had also expected Lorenzo, but he had already left by a different route for Pisa. A large group came to welcome Clarice and the notables introduced all their relatives. The Medici household was obviously completely approachable and its arrival was an occasion for joyful festivities.

In Florence *the family mansion had been designed by Michelozzo in 1444. Here Cosimo, Piero, and Lorenzo lived, here the bank's business was carried on and, behind the scenes of public life, the political decisions were made.* (80)

Lorenzo's artistic patronage: tradition and reality

General accounts of Florentine civilization in the age of Lorenzo usually ascribe to him an important share in most of the important artistic achievements of that period. This popular image greatly exaggerates the extent of his artistic patronage. As Professor Gombrich has pointed out, 'it comes as a shock of surprise to realize how few works of art are in existence which can be proved to have been commissioned by Lorenzo'. A reasonably precise and well-informed account of Florence's artistic treasures, written in 1510 by Francesco Albertini, manages to name Lorenzo only twice.

Specialized modern studies have reacted to the traditional vague generalizations about Lorenzo's role by sticking rigorously to the sources, especially the documentary ones. But this reaction can go too far. It is impossible to assent to Kenneth Clark's remark that Lorenzo 'although an enlightened patron of literature . . . took small interest in art'. Clark is nearer the truth when he observes that Lorenzo 'cannot be given credit for commissioning any of the great paintings of the day', though even this is not entirely true. Bad luck has played its part here. Some of the paintings that may have been executed for Lorenzo have been lost or at least cannot be securely identified. One particularly regrets the destruction of Lorenzo's villa at Spedaletto near Arezzo, where Botticelli, Domenico Ghirlandaio, and Filippino Lippi are known to have executed frescoes for him after 1482.

Two other important points must be borne in mind. Because Lorenzo was hampered by a shortage of funds, some of his patronage must be sought in works financed by the Florentine state. From 1479 to his death in 1492 he was permanently one of the officials in charge of the works at the Florentine municipal palace of the Signoria. In this capacity he was responsible for employing some major artists who are not known to have worked for him privately, like the brothers Benedetto and Giuliano da Maiano, sculptors and specialists in intarsia, who, after 1480, beautifully redecorated some of the chambers inside the Signoria. Lorenzo was also closely connected with projects carried out in Florence cathedral including, especially, the novel experiment of introducing mosaics into its decoration. Secondly Lorenzo's fastidious taste made him prefer unusual fields of artistic activity. His delight in classical antiques, in exquisitely carved precious stones, cameos and intaglios, ancient vases, mosaics, medals, and richly illuminated manuscripts was not a mere collector's mania. His choice of acquisitions was often highly selective and he commissioned admirable imitations of some of these antique objects.

At the root of some of the tenaciously surviving misconceptions and muddled generalizations about Lorenzo's real role lies the detailed *Lives of the Artists* by Giorgio Vasari, first published in 1550 and reissued in an amplified version in 1568. This contains a bewildering mixture of fact and myth. Vasari does provide a starting point for many suggestions that can be fruitfully explored from other evidence; but he could be shockingly careless and too often he imposed on his materials preconceived ideas. Most damaging of all was Vasari's illusion that he was near enough in time to Lorenzo's Florence to understand it correctly; while, in reality, he was viewing the past through

As a connoisseur *and a collector of precious antiques, Lorenzo stands high, though as a patron of contemporary artists he falls behind some other rich Florentines. One of the few whom he is definitely known to have employed continuously is Bertoldo, whose relief of a battle (above) is modelled on a Roman sarcophagus. (81)*

the veil of his mid-sixteenth-century prejudices. Vasari became the main artistic adviser to Duke Cosimo I of Tuscany and was entrusted with considerable authority over all the public buildings and principal churches of the Duke's dominions. His generation of ducal courtiers was probably genuinely unable to grasp that Lorenzo had no comparable authority. Duke Cosimo was surrounded by an increasingly exclusive and snobbish court where men of good birth had precedence over others and where sycophantic mediocrities were setting the tone. Vasari could not appreciate that no comparable official court existed around Lorenzo just as he could not recapture the real atmosphere of Lorenzo's household which, in comparison with Duke Cosimo's court, was much less socially exclusive and much more distinguished intellectually.

It was a part of the hierarchical outlook of Duke Cosimo that intellectual and artistic activities should be regimented through official academies. Vasari tried to justify his master's ideas by imagining that he had discovered precedents for them in Lorenzo's time. Hence the invention of a 'palace school' of artists allegedly organized by Lorenzo. The few crumbs of fact upon which Vasari reared his imaginative fantasy can soon be enumerated. Lorenzo did have valuable collections of works of art, including more classical antiques than anybody else in Florence. There is documentary evidence that he was in the habit of allowing the inspection of these treasures by people who seemed to merit such favour. Vasari knew that young Michelangelo first met Lorenzo on one such visit and this began Lorenzo's interest in this prodigiously gifted boy. All the rest was Vasari's invention. Judging by the inventories compiled after Lorenzo's death in 1492, most of the art treasures were concentrated in the old Medici palace in Via Larga (modern Via Cavour) built by Lorenzo's grandfather, Cosimo. Lorenzo's wife, Clarice, possessed a separate villa a few hundred yards farther to the north, opposite the church of San Marco. Vasari chose to place the 'palace school' in the garden adjoining this villa, which he imagined to be filled with Lorenzo's antique collection. The school was allegedly composed of promising artists of good birth like Michelangelo who were supposed to have studied and copied there the Medici collections under the supervision of Lorenzo's resident official artist.

The existence of such a personality was another figment of Vasari's imagination. The man cast for this role, the sculptor Bertoldo, was a skilled worker in bronze employed in the Medici household to repair antiques and other artistic objects. One of his bronzes, a statue of a centaur, is specifically mentioned in the Medici inventory of 1492, and two other works listed there can probably be identified with extant works ascribed to him. One of them is a skilfully contrived bronze relief of a classical battle. It was probably Bertoldo who in 1478 designed the medal commemorating the failure of the Pazzi conspiracy and another made for Lorenzo's ally, the Turkish sultan Muhammad II. He can hardly be regarded as an artist of the first rank and his status in Lorenzo's household seems to have been quite modest. He appears on a list of thirty-three attendants travelling in 1485 with Lorenzo to a health resort. He is mentioned in the tenth place between a performing musician and Lorenzo's barber.

Francesco Guicciardini remarked in his *Storie Fiorentine* that, compared with his grandfather Cosimo's numerous edifices, Lorenzo's building activities were nil. The only major ecclesiastical building which Lorenzo partly financed was the Florentine monastery of San Gallo. It was placed north of the city gate of that name and was destroyed during the siege by the Imperial army in 1530.

Lorenzo had inherited sufficient choice of residences in town and country. The palace in Via Larga sufficed for the main city residence. Careggi, in the hills north of Florence, lay near enough to the city to become the most convenient country house of the Medici. It was the scene of many of Lorenzo's convivial gatherings to read poetry or, more solemnly, to discuss Platonic philosophy, which some of Lorenzo's circle took very seriously. We know from Niccolo Valori, Lorenzo's friend and first biographer, that an incident on a journey from Careggi back to Florence inspired the 'Simposio', one of Lorenzo's most amusing poems. He narrates how he had encountered a party of drunken friends

hastening to yet another banquet and he uses the occasion to satirize pointedly this group of Florentine notables. Lorenzo apparently wrote or revised a good deal of his poetic writings at Careggi. Here the successive Medici retired in their last illnesses. Lorenzo's grandfather, Cosimo, died at Careggi, as did Lorenzo's father, Piero, and Lorenzo himself – all three killed by gout. There were also some lesser Medici houses on the southern slopes of nearby Fiesole, overhanging Florence. One of these was given by Cosimo to his protégé, the Platonist scholar Marsilio Ficino, who had played some part in Lorenzo's education. Farther north lay the excellent hunting country and ample hill pastures known as the Mugello. Mention has already been made of Lorenzo's loss of Cafaggiolo in the heart of the Mugello, alienated to satisfy the claims of his two cousins when they came of age in 1485. By that time Lorenzo had already acquired at Poggio a Caiano a suitable alternative residence on the edge of the Mugello. The older Medici villas with their towers and other warlike features all derived from medieval fortified houses; but Poggio was redesigned for Lorenzo by Giuliano da San Gallo as a purely civilian residence in the Renaissance style. One of the most striking features, dating apparently from Lorenzo's time, is the long frieze over the entrance in coloured glazed terracotta executed by the Della Robbia workshop. This is very different from most of their products and Professor Sanpaolesi has persuasively argued that it may have been designed by Giuliano da San Gallo himself. The frieze consists of a number of classical reliefs, the central scene being clearly copied from a Roman sarcophagus which today stands outside the Museo del Duomo at Florence.

The gem of Lorenzo's collection *was the 'Tazza Farnese', a Hellenistic agate, superbly carved on both sides. The story of its acquisition neatly illustrates Lorenzo's combination of aesthetics and finance. It was one of various precious objects from the papal collection given to him by Sixtus IV in return for a loan of 35,000 ducats. (82)*

An idealized Lorenzo *participates in Botticelli's 'Adoration of the Magi', a painting largely dedicated to Medici prestige, in which all the heads of the family, past and present, are portrayed. (83)*

The village of Poggio a Caiano *was -- alongside that of Careggi – the setting of Lorenzo's 'court'. Here he entertained his guests, wrote his poetry and relaxed. The house was designed by Giuliano da San Gallo. This view, another painting by Utens, shows it before the staircase was altered in the seventeenth century. (84)*

Scholarship owed more *than art to Lorenzo. Marsilio Ficino was only one of many humanists whom he encouraged and employed. The frontispiece to Ficino's 'Life and Works of Plotinus' records his dedication of the book to Lorenzo, who paid for its publication, and displays the Medici arms. (85)*

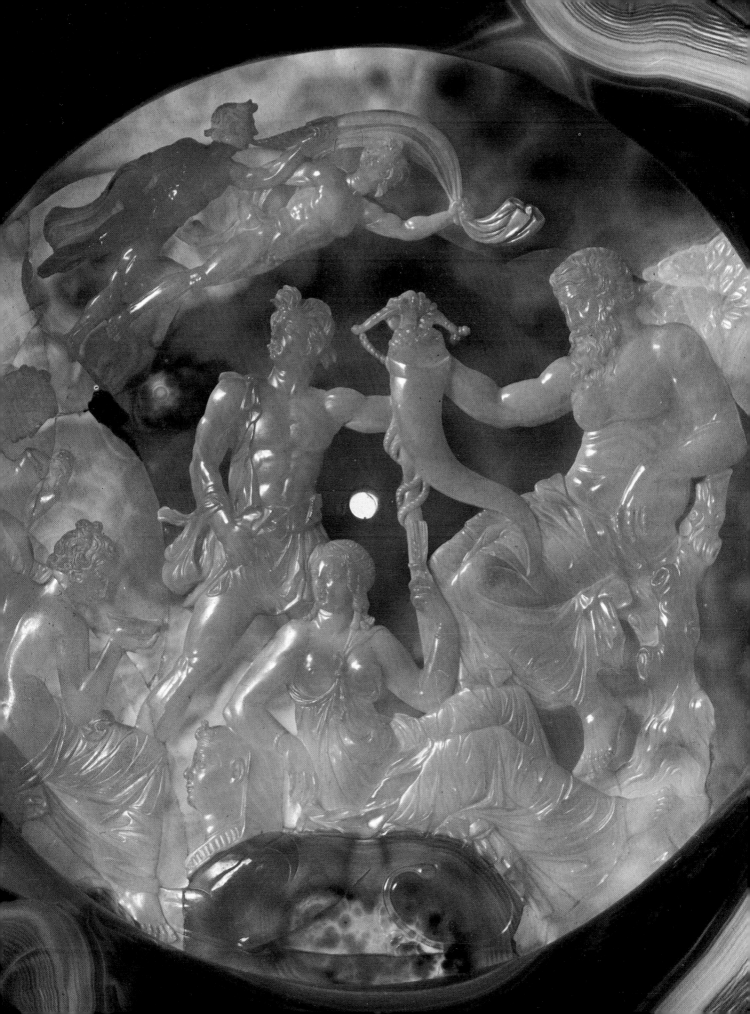

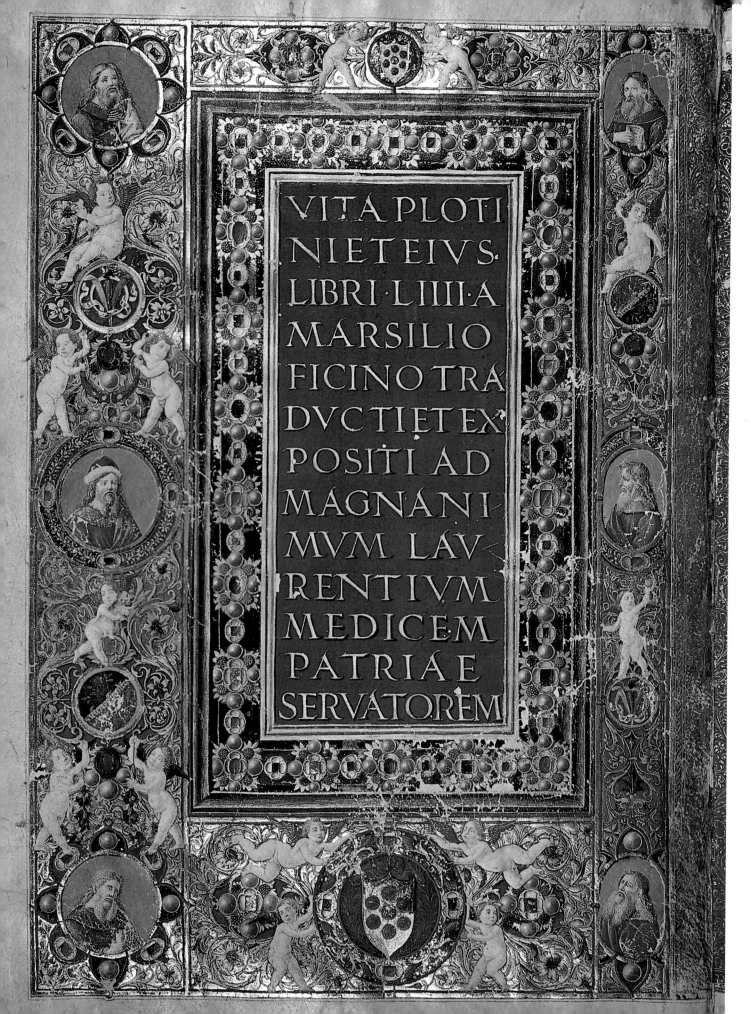

VITA PLOTI
NI ET EIVS·
LIBRI · LIIII·A
MARSILIO
FICINO TRA
DVCTI ET EX
POSITI AD
MAGNANI
MVM LAV
RENTIVM
MEDICEM
PATRIAE
SERVATOREM

Poggio was for Lorenzo not merely a hunting lodge and a favourite place of refuge but the centre of a highly profitable farm. Guicciardini notes that, in order to compensate for the decline of income from his bank, Lorenzo deliberately developed his country properties. This was much nearer to Lorenzo's real tastes and much more under his complete control. His poems reveal an acute observation of the countryside, and his descriptions of nature are among the most vivid and beautiful things in them.

The principal group of Lorenzo's estates lay nearer the sea in the territory of Pisa, where he possessed a summer palace at Agnano in the hills east of the city and properties in eleven other localities. This group of estates, which included extensive pastures, much arable land and a cheese factory at Vico Pisano, was valued in 1492 at some forty thousand florins. Here and at Poggio Lorenzo kept highly reputed herds of cattle, a specially fine breed of pigs imported from Calabria, and sheep with particularly long tails immortalized in one of Piero di Cosimo's pictures. Poggio boasted of its plantations of mulberry trees on which were reared large numbers of silkworms; and the place was over-run with golden pheasants specially imported from Sicily.

The principal inventory of the Medici art treasures, drawn up in 1492, lists only the contents of their main city palace in Via Larga. The majority of the paintings and sculptures represent the traditional Christian subjects. Most of these had been inherited by Lorenzo and included a particularly notable number of devotional paintings by Fra Angelico. But some of the religious works can probably be personally connected with Lorenzo. This is particularly the case with some portable mosaics. Seven of these are quite distinct from the Byzantine mosaics listed elsewhere and they were probably the work of the brothers Ghirlandaio, including a head of Christ and three heads of saints.

The inventory values most highly of all the antique carved precious stones, cameos, and intaglios and secondly the ornate vases in semi-precious materials. The foundations of this collection had been laid by Cosimo and Piero. Their delight in such antique carved jewels inspired the copying of designs from seven different cameos in the sculpted roundels decorating the first inner courtyard of the Medici palace. Lorenzo's acquisition of a part of the collections of Pope Paul II was followed, in 1483, by the purchase of at least 176 small precious objects that had previously belonged to the recently deceased Francesco Gonzaga, Cardinal of Mantua.

Lorenzo particularly liked cameos. His acquisitions from Pope Paul II's collections reveal a special preference for classical mythological subjects similar to the delightful myths which enliven his own poems. While portraits of emperors and emblems of state are prominently represented in Paul's inventories, Lorenzo was not interested in acquiring that part of the collection. Lorenzo was unique among the collectors of his day in inscribing with the letters LAU. R. MED his favourite carved jewels and precious vases. This has greatly facilitated the identification of his surviving treasures, but the choice of the objects that can thus be specially connected with him also brings out Lorenzo's unerringly good taste.

Across the portico *of Poggio a Caiano runs a terracotta frieze, probably designed by Giuliano da San Gallo. Its central scene is copied from a Roman sarcophagus.* (86)

The art of repairing antique engraved jewels and precious vases was deliberately fostered by Lorenzo. He appears to have been responsible for the remounting in silver of all the vases of the Medici collections, including the ones inherited from his father. Several of the silver mounts reveal the characteristic style of Giusto da Firenze, who was specially favoured by Lorenzo. One of his most distinguished younger protégés was Giovanni delle Corniuole who, in the generation after Lorenzo's time, became the most famous Florentine maker of cameos. Giovanni was probably responsible for a surviving cameo bearing Lorenzo's portrait. It is an idealized portrait and may have been carved after his death.

Lorenzo's passion for collecting ancient sculpture and pottery is exceptionally well documented. His agents in Rome busied themselves with securing recently excavated objects by methods that were sometimes most unscrupulous. Anyone who wanted to please Lorenzo knew that a gift of some classical object would be most welcome. In June 1491 Politian, the greatest classical scholar among Lorenzo's protégés, reported from Venice that Zaccaria Barbaro had offered 'a most beautiful, very ancient Greek earthenware vase', recently found in Greece, and two other 'little earthenware vases'. Politian was certainly a most competent judge of such things and Barbaro was grateful for Lorenzo's help in trying to secure the patriarchate of Aquileia for his son, Ermolao, an outstanding classical scholar. At the same time Barbaro had also tried to procure access for Politian to the collection of ancient Greek manuscripts controlled by the Venetian state. They had been given to Venice by Cardinal Bessarion, the most distinguished of the Byzantine refugees in Italy, and Politian wanted to copy them to fill the gaps in Lorenzo's library, but was seeking in vain as Lorenzo was out of favour with Venice.

Lorenzo was also interested in imitating some techniques of Byzantine art. The Medici inventory mentions at least nine portable Byzantine mosaics, two of which appear to have

89

been acquired since 1465. Vasari is particularly eloquent about Lorenzo's desire to revive this ancient Byzantine art. The necessary skills were not so completely forgotten in Florence as Vasari implied, but Lorenzo's fascination with this type of decoration can be independently documented. Mention has already been made of his possession of some modern works in mosaic, probably specially made for him by Domenico and Davide Ghirlandaio. The two brothers were certainly responsible for an *Annunciation* in mosaic over the northern Porta della Mandorla of Florence cathedral. In 1491 the two brothers were entrusted with the decoration in mosaic of one of the cathedral's principal chapels, dedicated to S. Zanobius. They were to collaborate with Botticelli and with the brothers Gherardo and Monte di Giovanni, two painters of some of Florence's most delightful miniatures. The surviving fragments of this work date, however, from 1504, twelve years after Lorenzo's death, and are the work of Monte di Giovanni.

The largest painting inherited by Lorenzo in the Medici palace was the fresco running along the walls of the private chapel, painted in 1459 by Benozzo Gozzoli. Under the guise

The art of mosaic *was one of Lorenzo's special interests. This panel survives from a scheme commissioned by him for a chapel dedicated to St Zenobius in Florence cathedral.* (87)

of the procession of the Three Kings journeying to Bethlehem it depicted the members of the Medici family and their followers against the background of the Florentine countryside in which can be discovered the principal Medici villas. The theme of the Adoration had a special significance for the Medici. They were the leading members of the influential Florentine religious confraternity of the Magi who, once a year, organized a great pageant in the streets of Florence. This secret association had its political uses for the Medici and it was abolished in the reaction against their rule in 1494.

Not surprisingly, at least five more representations of the same story existed in 1492 in the Medici palace, of which two were by Fra Angelico. Medici supporters repeatedly commissioned further *Adorations*. One of the earliest of Botticelli's five known treatments of that theme was commissioned in 1475 for an altar in S. Maria Novella by Gaspare del Lama; and, according to Vasari, it contains the portraits of Cosimo, his sons and grandsons. By 1477 there could be seen in S. Maria Nuova a very different kind of *Adoration*. It had been commissioned in the Netherlands from Hugo van der Goes by Tomaso Portinari, the head of the Medici branch at Bruges, and was subsequently brought by him to Florence. It is a much more devout picture. The more spiritual treatment of the shepherds and the more austere landscape profoundly impressed some Florentine artists. The earliest example of its influence is to be found in the *Adoration* commissioned by Francesco Sassetti, the general manager of the Medici bank, for his burial chapel in S. Trinita which was apparently completed in 1488. It is one of Domenico Ghirlandaio's greatest masterpieces and its shepherds are devout, humble peasants clearly reminiscent of the Portinari triptych.

To judge by the paintings hanging in Lorenzo's bedroom in the Medici palace and in the 'sala grande di Lorenzo', he liked works portraying movement, violence, and strength. In his bedchamber were the three panels of the Battle of S. Romano by Uccello, a battle between lions and dragons, apparently lost, by the same artist and a hunt by Francesco di Pesello, a popular painter of animal scenes. In the great chamber were to be found more lions by Pesello and four scenes of the labours of Hercules. These last were extremely violent indeed, to judge by copies preserved in the Uffizi, and were masterpieces of Antonio del Pollaiolo, the most expressive of the Florentine portrayers of violent action in painting and sculpture. In the garden of the Medici palace above a fountain stood Donatello's bronze Judith poised to kill Holofernes.

All these works, except perhaps for Pollaiolo's panels, had been inherited by Lorenzo, as was the case with almost all the other paintings and sculptures in the inventory of 1492. One of the few exceptions was the portrait of Lorenzo's ally, Duke Galeazzo of Milan, painted by Piero Pollaiolo, Antonio's brother, which decorated Lorenzo's bedroom. The portrait next to it of Duke Federigo of Urbino may also have been painted in Lorenzo's time. Only one picture by Botticelli is specifically mentioned in the inventory. None of Botticelli's most famous extant works can be connected with Lorenzo's patronage. The *Primavera* and

A streak of violence *seems to have been part of Lorenzo's taste. In his room in the Medici palace hung paintings of the labours of Hercules by Antonio del Pollaiolo (above, 'Killing the Hydra' and 'Suffocating Antaeus'), while in a garden stood Donatello's grim bronze of Judith decapitating Holofernes. (88–90)*

the *Birth of Venus* were most probably both painted for Lorenzo's cousin and future enemy, Lorenzo di Pierfrancesco. There may have been some closer contacts between Botticelli and Lorenzo's younger brother, Giuliano. For Giuliano's tournament of 1475, which inspired Politian's famous poem, Botticelli painted a standard with a figure of Pallas. This does not exist any more, but we have a portrait of Giuliano by Botticelli. It may have been painted posthumously in 1478 after Giuliano's assassination by the Pazzi. There was a tradition that Botticelli, as an official state commission, painted the effigies of the executed assassins for public display. Lastly there may be some connection between the Pallas on the jousting banner and the so-called *Minerva taming the Centaur*, one of Botticelli's most enigmatic pictures. This cannot any more be regarded as an allegory of Lorenzo's dangerous but ultimately successful mission to Naples in the winter of 1479–80.

From the back of the Medici palace can be seen the church of S. Lorenzo, rebuilt in the Renaissance style in the thirty years after 1420, largely at the expense of the Medici. In

return they were allowed to have a special funeral chapel; and here was buried Giovanni, Cosimo's father. Cosimo himself was buried, however, beneath the floor in the front of the high altar. He had prohibited all pomp and ceremony at his funeral and a tomb of great simplicity was made by Andrea Verrocchio. In 1467 Verrocchio also designed a marble roundel with the arms of the Medici which was placed on the floor of the church to mark the exact spot of Cosimo's burial. The simple inscription calls Cosimo 'pater patriae' (father of his country), as did the medals posthumously struck in his honour. In November 1495 the new government of Florence expressed its detestation of the fallen Medici by ordering the destruction of the inscription, as Cosimo 'did not deserve such a title but rather that of a tyrant'. It was, however, restored in the sixteenth century.

Verrocchio was also entrusted with the tomb of Lorenzo's father, Piero, and completed it in 1472. It is much simpler than the elaborate tombs of the Florentine chancellors constructed during the previous thirty years and it does not include any effigy of Piero or of his brother Giovanni, who

91

was also buried in it. But, compared with Cosimo's austere tomb, it is an elaborate and somewhat flamboyant sarcophagus in marble and bronze with a base in the shape of lions' feet out of which spring acanthus leaves.

Though Verrocchio's workshop was one of the most versatile artistic establishments of Florence, its master was primarily a worker in bronze. Two public commissions that may have been due to Medici suggestions bring this out. In 1468 he was asked to make the gilded bronze ball that was to crown the top of Florence cathedral. This was finally hoisted up in 1471. He also at least provided the bronze for the door of the sacristy on the left side of the cathedral choir. The sculptures on it were chiefly designed by Luca della Robbia, but it is possible that the actual casting of the door was also entrusted to Verrocchio's workshop. On 26 April 1478 that door saved Lorenzo's life. While his brother was being murdered inside the choir, Lorenzo, though wounded, was carried off to the sacristy by some of his friends including Politian. The door of the sacristy was slammed into the faces of the murderous pursuers and held firmly until help arrived from outside. There may exist yet another link between Verrocchio and the events of that terrible day. In the late nineteenth century a coloured terracotta of Christ's Resurrection was discovered at Careggi. It is clearly inspired by a terracotta relief on the same subject by Luca della Robbia that in 1478 already existed over the same providential door. It would have been natural for Lorenzo to commission the Careggi variant as a thanksgiving for his escape. Stylistically it might very well be Verrocchio's. Besides, the list of fifteen items executed by Verrocchio for the Medici, for which he was allegedly never paid, contains one undefined sculpture at Careggi that might correspond to this *Resurrection*.

Of these fifteen items only five can be securely identified with surviving works. Apart from the tombs, the two other identifiable sculptures are the bronze *David*, which Lorenzo resold already in 1476, and the bronze *Boy with the Dolphin*, which formed part of a larger group that once adorned a fountain at Careggi. All else must be surmise and some of the objects on the list do not seem to have survived. It shows that Verrocchio executed most varied commissions for Lorenzo. He had made various objects for Lorenzo's tournament of 1469 and Giuliano's similar enterprise in 1475. He had been responsible for some kind of portrait of Lucrezia Donati, once beloved of Lorenzo, and he had also restored an antique figure of Marsyas inherited by Lorenzo. On the other hand the list does not seem to include the two sculptured busts of Lorenzo and Giuliano. Lorenzo's portrait is only known from copies and cannot be dated. The terracotta bust of Giuliano, showing him as a young warrior wearing an antique breastplate, may have been an idealized portrait executed after his death.

Tributes to Lorenzo's good taste reached him from all sides, though one suspects that his political eminence accounts for much of the attention paid to his artistic judgments. Friendly rulers in Italy and beyond asked him to recommend artists or to transmit works of art; and Lorenzo gladly obliged. It was a part of his diplomacy, just as a giraffe that had come to him from the East in 1488 was to have been

sent on to the King of France – but unfortunately died at Florence early in the following year.

Lorenzo was deliberately responsible for the wide dispersal of Florentine artists and art treasures all over Italy and even farther afield to Portugal and Hungary. Florence lost for many years or even permanently some of its greatest painters and sculptors. In 1482 Leonardo da Vinci went, on his recommendation, to Duke Ludovico of Milan and stayed there for seventeen years. Lorenzo had the highest possible opinion of Antonio del Pollaiolo and described him in 1489 to the Florentine ambassador at Rome as 'the chief Master in this city and perhaps that has ever been'. Yet Lorenzo had no commissions for him and after 1483 Pollaiolo mostly worked at Rome on the tombs of two successive popes, Sixtus IV and Innocent VIII. Giuliano da Maiano was sent to the King of Naples to build palaces, and died there in 1490. Lorenzo's favourite architect, Giuliano da San Gallo, also travelled to Naples in 1488 on Lorenzo's orders. The palace that he designed for the future King Alfonso would have been the biggest that was ever built in fifteenth-century Italy, but the project was not carried out and Giuliano was preserved for Florence.

Nearer home, in the Florentine territory, every sort of artistic project was submitted to Lorenzo's scrutiny. He was most probably responsible for the building by Giuliano da San Gallo of one of the finest centrally planned Italian Renaissance churches, S. Maria delle Carceri at Prato. The head of the commission that entrusted the work to Giuliano in October 1485 was Carlo de' Medici, an illegitimate uncle of Lorenzo, who was provost of Prato. In 1478 the authorities of Pistoia cancelled a commission to Piero del Pollaiolo for a monument commemorating a deceased Pistoiese cardinal because Lorenzo had recommended the choice of Verrocchio. The men of Pistoia would have preferred the Pollaiolo design, partly because it was cheaper. Lorenzo's preference for Verrocchio outran their funds but his suggestion was law. When in 1483 the Florentine government assigned an altar to Ghirlandaio it was stipulated that it should be done 'according to the standards, manner and form as it will seem to and please . . . Lorenzo'. The most astonishing incident of all occurred in 1491. A competition was ordered for designing the façade of Florence cathedral. There were twenty-nine entries including projects from the greatest Italian artists: Ghirlandaio, Botticelli, Filippino Lippi, Perugino. There was also one from Lorenzo, who fancied himself as an architect. As the only possible solution the Florentine authorities requested Lorenzo to adjudicate. He had at least the good sense not to recommend his own project but to adjourn the decision. Florence had to wait for nearly another hundred years before its cathedral was given a façade.

Lorenzo the poet

If Lorenzo had been merely a private person, he would still have been appreciated today as one of the freshest and most original Italian poets of the fifteenth century. Students of Italian literature also assign to him an important part in the process that transformed the Tuscan dialect into the literary language of Italy, though here his own poetry was less

Medici art: *a medallion of Lorenzo in porphyry; an antique sardonyx cup, mounted and inscribed LAU. R. MED. by Lorenzo; a portrait of Giuliano by Botticelli. Below: part of Verrocchio's bronze sarcophagus for the brothers Giovanni and Piero de' Medici in the Old Sacristy of S. Lorenzo. (91–94)*

S. Maria delle Carceri *at Prato: a key work of Renaissance architecture by Giuliano da San Gallo, probably commissioned on Lorenzo's suggestion. (95)*

important than his patronage as a prince. Lorenzo's delight in poetry and in music brought into his circle some of his most gifted associates.

Lorenzo's mother Lucrezia herself wrote religious poetry. Lorenzo remained very close to her right until her death in 1482. She encouraged him to regard the writing of poetry as a natural activity of his moments of leisure. She also introduced to him two of his most original friends: the poet Luigi Pulci and the erudite scholar, who was also a considerable poet, Politian.

The chronology of Lorenzo's writings is never likely to be convincingly settled; but he certainly wrote some of his poems before his father's death in 1469 and he continued to turn to poetry at intervals throughout his busy years as the virtual ruler of Florence. The lively carnival songs were apparently written chiefly in his final years. To the last six years of his life belongs a sustained effort at revising much of his poetry and at perfecting his own commentary on some of it. This task of revision was far from completed at his death. Lorenzo clearly wanted to leave a lasting memorial to himself in his own poetry.

A great diversity of theme and mood runs through Lorenzo's writings. There are love sonnets chiefly from his earlier years and satirical novelettes delighting in the use of the juicy Tuscan popular dialect. There are also grave attempts at expounding in verse the Platonic doctrines of Lorenzo's former tutor Ficino. These do not display any philosophical originality; but Lorenzo had a clear grasp of problems discussed in the Ficino circle and a sound appreciation of methods of philosophical debate. We also have fresh and concrete descriptions of the Florentine countryside, and carnival songs at diverse levels of impropriety. At other times Lorenzo followed in his mother's footsteps by writing devotional hymns of praise, and, late in life, he produced his own religious drama which was publicly performed in February 1491. In this *Sacra Rappresentazione* Lorenzo used legends clustering round the memory of the Emperor Constantine and his descendants to utter, in passing, some sad reflections on the tribulations of power and the inexorable dangers surrounding a ruler. These precise references to the cares of a statesman are rare in Lorenzo's writings. Poetry was for him a refuge and a distraction, not a species of autobiography.

From his earliest childhood music was a natural part of Lorenzo's home background. His light poetry needed musical accompaniment, while Ficino's Platonic doctrines placed music at the centre of sublime activities. In Lorenzo's correspondence the lighter side appears more noticeably. As early as 1467 one of his love sonnets was being sent to a distinguished Flemish composer to be put to music. Lorenzo liked to accompany his poems on the viol; when he was away from Florence requests for despatch of this instrument recur in his letters. He also apparently played the lyre and the lute. We hear of repairs to his clavichord entrusted to no less a person than Antonio Squarcialupi, the famous organist of Florence cathedral from 1450 to his death in 1480. Lorenzo commemorated him by a portrait on the wall of the cathedral. It was sculpted in *c.* 1490 by one of Florence's most elegant sculptors, Benedetto Maiano, and Politian

Marsilio Ficino: *a portrait initial from his edition of Plotinus. At first a warm admirer of Ficino, Lorenzo seems to have become disenchanted with him and the relationship cooled.* (96)

composed an eulogistic epitaph. Antonio's son, Francesco, who succeeded his father as the cathedral organist, remained in close contact with Lorenzo. He was one of the thirty-three people who in 1485 accompanied their master to the medicinal waters at Morba. The cavalcade included also two singers and a player on the viol.

Lorenzo's educated contemporaries were very proud of the musical progress of their time. In 1477 a writer on the art of counterpoint could assert that no music more than forty years old was deemed worthy of performance. Distinguished composers and performers of the new polyphonic songs were eagerly recruited in Lorenzo's time into the service of the cathedral and of the Medici church of S. Lorenzo. Some were invited to come from the Netherlands, which was then the main home of this art. Heinrich Isaac was Lorenzo's favourite Flemish musician. By 1485 he had become one of the cathedral's singers. He put to music Lorenzo's carnival songs, and eminently singable they are. According to tradition he also composed the music for Lorenzo's *Sacra Rappresentazione* of 1491. His polyphonic songs are harmonious and dignified and yet very assured and fresh, like the best of Lorenzo's poetry. Politian asked Isaac to put to music his moving lament on Lorenzo's death.

Patronage of scholarship

The diversity of Lorenzo's literary interests is reflected in the wide variety of collaborators and intellectual associates gathered around him. They were not a harmonious group. There existed considerable differences of outlook among them, but the chief source of their quarrels seems to have been competition for Lorenzo's favour. There were intrigues and jealousies over appointments to offices and over preferments to Church benefices. Most of these men needed money and at times some of them, like Ficino, expected more from Lorenzo that he was willing or able to give. Lorenzo seems to have been a restless man whose affection for particular people was apt to cool off after a period, and this trait of character may have exacerbated the competition for his favour. But he also had the knack of keeping this quarrelsome group usefully in his service, in spite of their intrigues against each other.

Gentile Becchi, Lorenzo's principal tutor since 1454, remained his trusted adviser for the rest of Lorenzo's life. He was something of a poet and a very adroit orator. Lorenzo's principal secretaries were Piero da Bibienna and Niccolo Michelozzi. The latter was a son of Michelozzo, Cosimo's principal architect. Niccolo's brother, Bernardo, became a tutor of Lorenzo's second son, the future Pope Leo X. Bartolommeo Scala, as Chancellor of Florence throughout the period of Lorenzo's predominance, was one of the mainstays of the Medici regime. According to his detractor Politian, Scala's Latin dispatches were sometimes submitted by Lorenzo to Politian's expert scrutiny. Be this as it may, Scala was a man of great practical experience and massive good sense, while Lorenzo never cared to entrust any delicate or important mission to Politian. If the correspondence of these two men with each other is read dispassionately, Scala emerges as a more dignified and balanced man who respected Politian's superior learning and deplored his lapses from wisdom.

Apart from Politian himself, whom most people willingly recognized as the most accomplished scholar in Lorenzo's intimate circle, its two other major 'academics' were Ficino, one of Lorenzo's former tutors, and Cristoforo Landino, a Professor of Rhetoric at the University of Florence. Both these men were immensely industrious. Ficino's translations into Latin of the works of Plato stand out as one of the major intellectual contributions of Florence under Cosimo and Lorenzo. Landino seemed more distinguished to contemporaries than he now appears to modern scholars. Lorenzo seems to have noted at an early date the limitations of this unpractical and rhetorical scholar and he was not a member of Lorenzo's inner circle, though he had his uses. One of Landino's most famous works, published in 1481, was the commentary on Dante, written in Italian. It formed part of a cult of Dante, and of all Tuscan poetry, eagerly fostered by Lorenzo. The huge introduction is particularly superficial. Some sections of the commentary look very odd to a modern reader. Thus it contains an elaborate discussion of the site, form, and dimensions of Hell and of the size of the giants and Lucifer. Landino's professional colleague at the University of Florence, Politian, though he might indulge in some fanciful etymologies or philological hair-splitting, was by contrast a scientifically minded man who steered clear of any such unprofitable speculations, just as he was ironically distrustful of Ficino's Neoplatonist abstractions.

Frequent visitors to Lorenzo's household – rather than members – include the resourceful and original poet Luigi Pulci, and Giovanni Pico, member of a dynasty that ruled in Mirandola in Lombardy. Pico resided at Florence from 1484 to 1486 and again after 1488. A Neoplatonist disciple of Ficino, he wrote bizarre but impressively original works and certainly possessed mental powers of a high order. He was greatly beloved of Lorenzo, who specially summoned Pico to his deathbed, and is perhaps the most attractive member of the whole group. It is clear that Lorenzo surrounded himself with able people and could afford to do so because he was the intellectual equal or superior of almost all of them.

Lorenzo's initial experiments in the writing of poetry owed something to Luigi Pulci, though his exact share in Lorenzo's early poems still needs closer investigation. Pulci was sixteen years older than Lorenzo and was a friend of Lorenzo's mother. Witty, irreverent, full of verbal surprises and odd poetic devices, he outraged the more stolid defenders of traditional respectability. He compounded his crimes by denouncing Ficino's teachings as a fraudulent mixture of astrology and high-sounding but unscholarly nonsense. As Franco, Ficino's ally, bitterly complained in a letter to Lorenzo in January 1476, despite all Pulci's faults, he yet seemed indispensable to Lorenzo. Pulci's high spirits and riotous ways that masked a genuine vein of melancholy appealed to one side of Lorenzo's own character.

For more erudite literary studies Lorenzo found a scholarly assistant in Politian. He was four years younger than Lorenzo and became a member of the Medici household in 1473. One product of their collaboration is an anthology of Italian verse which Lorenzo sent in 1477 to his friend, Duke Federigo of Naples. It aimed at demonstrating the rich possibilities of the Tuscan language for expressing every kind of poetry. The anthology starts with thirteenth-century writers who had preceded Dante and ends with a selection of Lorenzo's own poems. The choice of the contents was probably due jointly to Politian and Lorenzo but the important preface was the work of Politian. It attempts a short but discriminating history of Italian poetry and recognizes the debt it owed to Latin poets. The same note is absent from Lorenzo's own writings. In his subsequent commentary on a selection of his poems he expresses a passionate preference for the vernacular as the language of poets.

Lorenzo's most serious poetry is dominated by the influence of Ficino. His *Altercazione*, which was probably written around 1474, reproduces the Ficinian arguments for the superiority of a contemplative life in the country to the distractions and miseries of an active existence in the city. In the commentary on his own writings, the most pompous and laboured thing that Lorenzo ever wrote, the scholastic distinctions learnt from Ficino have their full play, though they are refreshingly interspersed with more readable passages expressing in a concrete language Lorenzo's inmost thoughts.

Initially Lorenzo tried to look to Ficino for spiritual guidance. He accepts meekly Ficino's rebukes for forgetting the example of Cosimo and for wasting his time on frivolous activities. In a letter written in the autumn of 1474 Lorenzo disarmingly excuses himself. His foolish acts have not sprung from an evil nature but merely from a certain heedlessness and from bad habits. But Lorenzo gradually became disenchanted with Ficino. He resented Ficino's obsequiousness. In a letter written to Ficino before January 1474, he says that they ought to correspond as friends and equals, but Ficino was too insecure to follow this advice. Perhaps Lorenzo gradually glimpsed something of Ficino's basic unreliability as a man. Ficino became unduly

Politian *was a scholar more securely lodged in Lorenzo's favour.*
Besides being his librarian he was the tutor to his sons. In this detail
from a fresco by Ghirlandaio, he is with Giuliano, the future Duke of
Nemours. (97)

friendly with Lorenzo's cousins, who were no friends of
Lorenzo. At the intellectual level Lorenzo became sceptical
about some of Ficino's main tenets. Ficino tried to harmonize
the teachings of Aristotle and Plato. We know from an
exchange of letters between Pico and Politian that Lorenzo
did come to appreciate the considerable differences between
these two Greek philosophers. For whatever reason, Lorenzo
declined to finance the printing of Ficino's Latin translation
of all the works of Plato in spite of the fact that the principal
manuscript used by Ficino had been given to him by Cosimo.
The translation was published in the autumn of 1484 at the
expense of Filippo Valori. Lorenzo did, however, relent at
the end of his life and Ficino's translation of Plotinus
appeared at Lorenzo's expense in May 1492, a few weeks
after Lorenzo's death.

From 1475 onwards Politian acted as tutor to Lorenzo's
eldest son, Piero, who was thus entrusted to him when
barely three years of age. Politian's letters to Lorenzo about

the methods adopted by him in teaching Piero show how
misguided they both were in this matter. Piero was a
mediocre boy, mainly interested in outdoor sports, and to
entrust him to the foremost Hellenic scholar of Italy, who
had no special aptitude for dealing with little children, was a
forlorn enterprise. Lorenzo's wife, Clarice, certainly thought
so. She was an unintelligent woman and a strong antipathy
developed between her and Politian; but she was probably
right in regarding him as an unsuitable tutor for her
children. Before the full storm broke over Politian's head he
had already lost one of his main Medici protectors through
the assassination of Giuliano on 26 April 1478. Politian
seems to have been particularly attached to Giuliano. He
himself was nearly killed on that day. His earlier sense of
security had gone and his letters during the winter of
1478–79 reveal a tense, disappointed man. Clarice threw him
out of the household in Lorenzo's absence in May 1479.
Thereafter Lorenzo had no specific employment for him and
they drifted into a quarrel at the end of that year. Politian re-
entered Lorenzo's service in the summer of 1480, but he was
never again a permanent member of the Medici household.

Lorenzo was probably instrumental in procuring for
Politian a permanent professorship at the University of
Florence and he taught there from the autumn of 1480 to his
death fourteen years later. Contemporaries were particularly impressed by Politian's mastery of Greek. He was the
first Italian to be fully the equal of the best Byzantine
scholars. Today we are particularly impressed by features of
Politian's scholarship that anticipate modern methods to an
astonishing degree. He was apparently the first to grasp that
the reconstruction of a classical text cannot rest on inspired
guesswork but must depend on the recovery of the best
manuscripts, nearest to the original archetype. The way of
achieving this result lay in using as many manuscripts of the
text as possible, in carefully comparing them to establish
their possible interrelation, and in dating them approxi-
mately by handwriting and other means so that the correct
chronological sequence of manuscripts could be achieved.
Detailed and accurate description of manuscripts was
essential.

This type of work could only be pursued successfully by
a scholar who had access to plentiful collections of manuscripts. The Medici collections were the starting point for
Politian's researches. Lorenzo had inherited a considerable
library, partly consisting of beautifully illuminated manuscripts. Their production was a Florentine speciality and
Lorenzo employed the greatest miniaturists of Florence to
work for him. Authors in search of Medici patronage
presented splendidly illuminated copies of their works. But
printed books were not welcome. Like his contemporary,
Duke Federigo of Urbino, who did not possess a single
printed book in his library, Lorenzo had no use whatsoever
for this new technique. Printing was beginning to develop
in Florence in Lorenzo's time, but he was not at all interested
in its encouragement.

Ancient manuscripts were another matter. Lorenzo collected these as eagerly as he searched for all kinds of other
classical antiquities. He was glad to increase the stores at
Politian's disposal and financed his expeditions to other

parts of Italy in search of copies of rare works. In 1491–92 a learned Byzantine refugee, Janus Lascaris, was sent to Constantinople and the Greek islands in search of missing Greek works for Lorenzo's library, though his purchases only arrived after Lorenzo's death. By then the Medici collection comprised over a thousand manuscripts and covered almost the entire range of the then known Latin and Greek classical authors. It was one of the most astonishing libraries of Italy. Naturally enough Politian was in charge of it in Lorenzo's last years. All learned enquiries about its contents were passed on to Politian for answer.

Lorenzo encouraged Politian to demonstrate the quality of his perfected scholarly methods by publishing some of his discoveries. This is the origin of Politian's first *Miscellanea*, published in 1489. It consisted of a hundred articles, mostly quite short, clearing up some philological or historical problem connected with an ancient author. They read like contributions to a modern scholarly journal. Politian eagerly passed on to Lorenzo the many letters of congratulation that reached him from all parts of Italy. One dissenting note was struck at Florence by Bartolommeo Scala. He regretted that Politian was wasting his time on these trifles instead of demonstrating in a major work or in an edition of an important writer what could be achieved by such methods. In his replies to Scala Politian dealt with various minor points raised by the aged Florentine Chancellor but he never answered this basic charge of disappointing the expectations of humanist scholars. A few months later Politian was dead, cut off, apparently by a sudden illness, at the age of forty. He left behind fifty-nine partly completed articles for a second *Miscellanea*. They had been prepared after Lorenzo's death and it is sad to record that Lorenzo is hardly ever mentioned, and then only in passing, in contrast to the first collection of 1489, where fulsome praise of Lorenzo's generosity meets us in almost every article. By 1494 Politian was perhaps glad to forget what he had owed to Lorenzo.

Lorenzo the man

Lorenzo dressed soberly and lived frugally. Visitors from more splendid courts were astonished at the simple meals in the Medici household and at the absence of any strict etiquette. By contrast important guests were splendidly entertained and sumptuous banquets were given in their honour.

Nothing pleased Lorenzo more than a chance to be with his children. When away from them he was a fussy parent, worrying excessively about their health. His boisterous games with his children displeased Machiavelli, who could not understand how such a grave statesman could show such a lack of dignity in playing with his family. Guicciardini seems to have been less puzzled by Lorenzo's delight in the traditional festivities of his native city. He notes that in Lorenzo's time the people were kept content with numerous celebrations and festive pleasures. Every January Lorenzo threw himself with relish into the annual carnival. In his last years he always composed some new songs for these riotous occasions. Early in February 1492 one of his secretaries reported Lorenzo's sorrow at his inability to participate as fully as usual in that year's carnival because his gout had grown worse.

Within a few years Florence, rid of the Medici, was destined to experience under Savonarola's influence a dramatic reaction against such carefree festivities. Not for the first time in Florentine history a mood of fear swept through the city that God would punish His rebellious people for their backslidings. There is, however, little documentary warrant for interpreting these later events as evidence of latent conflict between Savonarola and the Medici in Lorenzo's lifetime. If we follow, as we should, Politian's account of Lorenzo's last hour we are told that Savonarola visited the dying man of his own accord. He tried to calm to the best of his power Lorenzo's anxieties and, when leaving the room, at Lorenzo's request gave him a final blessing.

Florence in 1500. *The Medici palace is near the centre, midway between the cathedral (with the dome) and S. Maria Novella (with the tall steeple). (98)*

The golden seal of Francis I *is attached to a treaty of amity drawn up in 1527 between England and France. Francis sits crowned and enthroned in a pavilion. Angels and cupids draw back the curtains. At his feet, lions. (99)*

Five

FRANCIS I

Prince and patron of the northern Renaissance

❊

R. J. KNECHT

N 24 APRIL 1547 Francis I appeared on a bed of state in the great hall of the palace of Saint-Cloud. He wore an ermine-trimmed mantle of purple sewn with fleur-de-lis, and on his head an imperial crown studded with jewels. Beside him on pillows lay the sceptre and hand of justice. Over the bed stretched a great tapestried canopy and, at its foot, two heralds-at-arms kept watch night and day. And, thus, the King remained motionless for eleven days. He had, in fact, been dead for more than three weeks and the figure on the bed of state was only an effigy. Francis' real body lay in a chamber next door. Yet, for eleven days his meals continued to be served as if he were still alive. The table was laid and the courses brought in and sampled by the King's servants in the accustomed manner. The napkin used to wipe his hands was, as usual, presented by the steward to the most eminent person present, and wine was served to the King twice in the course of each meal. At the end, grace was said by a cardinal with the addition of two Psalms appropriate to a funeral. On 21 May the King's body was taken to Paris for a funeral service at Notre Dame; then to the abbey of Saint-Denis. As it was lowered into the vault, all his stewards, save one, threw their wands of office into the grave. The one exception was the chief steward, who still had to officiate at the funeral supper. Only then did he snap his wand in half, after announcing the dissolution of the King's household. His gesture underlined the principal function of the court, which was to serve the King's person. In an age of personal monarchy the court was also the principal seat of government; it was there that the King conferred with his ministers and that policies were decided upon. In this essay, however, we shall be dealing with the court as an organization dedicated to serving the personal needs of the King rather than as one concerned with the administration of public affairs.

From the earliest times the kings of France had surrounded themselves with boon companions and servants; but it was only by degrees that their household became a well-regulated institution. Its development may be traced through a series of royal ordinances stretching back to the thirteenth century. In 1261 it was already divided into six departments, each with its personnel, and a distinction was drawn between services to the King's person (the *bouche*) and to his entourage (the *commun*). Household officials were paid in money, kind or both. Remuneration in kind included the right to eat at court and to receive allowances of fuel, candles, and fodder. Details of these allowances were carefully regulated by subsequent ordinances, usually with a view to eliminating abuses.

By the fifteenth century the court of France, though less magnificent than that of the dukes of Burgundy, had nevertheless become a vitally important political institution, providing the framework for a power complex of influence and favour. Whoever shared the King's ear shared to some extent in his power. Impoverished nobles went to court in the hope of obtaining offices, pensions, and other royal favours. This process received a boost in the early sixteenth century as inflation began to affect the value of the aristocracy's fixed landed revenues. The King, on his part, welcomed a trend which made the nobility more docile by increasing its dependence on his authority. Francis I's absolutism rested essentially on this arrangement.

By 1522 the King's household, which was the essential nucleus of the court, had doubled in size within half a century. It comprised 540 officials, more than twice the number inscribed on the payroll of Louis XI's household in 1480. The sixty categories of officials included confessors, almoners, doctors, surgeons, apothecaries, barbers, stewards, gentlemen of the chamber, valets, ushers, bread-carriers, cup-bearers, carvers, squires, grooms, pages, secretaries, a librarian, quartermasters, porters, musicians, sumpters, coopers, spit-turners, sauce-makers, pastrycooks, furriers, tapestry-makers, and laundresses. The court also included a substantial military establishment made up of independent units created in different reigns. Modelled on the King's household, though smaller in size, were those of the Queen, Queen Mother, and royal children. Finally, there were many hangers-on, including merchants and artisans, who were exempted from tolls and guild regulations in return for their promise to serve only the Crown.

Overall control of the King's household was vested in the Grand Maître, who was also an important minister of the Crown. Anne de Montmorency, who held the office after

By the 1540s *the King was no longer the handsome figure that he had been at the Field of Cloth of Gold and a serious illness in 1539 had aged him. But he still impressed visitors by his regal authority, reflected in the well-known equestrian drawing by François Clouet.* (100)

1526, was one of the richest men in the kingdom. He was also Constable of France and, between 1526 and 1536, virtually controlled royal policy. His household duties were necessarily performed by deputies, though he did introduce foreign ambassadors to the King's presence. Other senior court officials included the Grand Ecuyer (Master of the Horse), who controlled the King's stables and carried his sword on ceremonial occasions, the Grand Veneur and Grand Fauconnier, who organized the King's hunts, the Premier Médecin and Grand Aumônier, who looked after the King's bodily and spiritual needs respectively, and the Prévôt de l'hôtel, who maintained law and order at court.

An important structural innovation introduced by Francis I was the creation, early in his reign, of a new category of body servant, the *gentilshommes de la chambre*. These were invariably noblemen and were the King's constant companions. They had free access to his presence and followed him everywhere. Politically, too, they were important, for they were often employed as ambassadors. The *premier gentilhomme de la chambre* kept the King's privy purse, his wardrobe, and also the crown jewels.

An examination of the fragmentary household accounts for the reign of Francis I indicates a sharp increase in the size of its establishment and, correspondingly, of its expenditure. By 1535 the number of household officials had risen from 540 to 622 and the amount spent on wages had increased from 65,915 *livres* in 1517 to 214,918 *livres* in 1535. But the expansion of the household was not uniform. While some sections grew bigger, others were cut down in size and even dwindled to nothing. It seems that the court reached its maximum size about 1523 and that an effort was made to cut it down later in the reign, presumably for economy reasons.

The lure of Italy

The court of Francis I was not only larger than its predecessors; its manners were also more polished, at least on the surface, a change that can be directly related to the growth of Italian influence. When Francis came to the throne, in January 1515, France was already committed to a policy of armed intervention south of the Alps. The Italian Wars, which began in 1494, when Charles VIII conquered the kingdom of Naples, and lasted on and off until the peace of Cateau-Cambrésis, in 1559, were essentially dynastic. They were concerned with the affirmation of legal rights, some of them stretching back far into the Middle Ages, rather than the acquisition of natural frontiers or long-term economic advantages. Thus Francis could claim the duchy of Milan as the great-grandson of Valentina Visconti, daughter of the last duke of that name, and the kingdom of Naples as a descendant of the house of Anjou, which had ruled it in the thirteenth century. Both claims had already been advanced by Charles VIII and Louis XII to justify invasions of Italy. By 1515, however, the French had been expelled from the peninsula with the aid of the Swiss. A twofold responsibility thus weighed upon Francis at the start of his reign: he had not only to assert his rights, but also to avenge the humiliations recently suffered by French arms. Old commanders, whose pride had been dented, and young noblemen keen to prove their valour, looked to him for satisfaction. He did not disappoint them. Within a year of his accession he led an army across the Alps, crushed the reputedly invincible Swiss at Marignano, and restored French rule in Milan. But his spectacular triumph had a disastrous effect upon the rest of the reign. For when the French were again driven out of Italy, in 1522, Francis imagined that he only had to lead another invasion of the peninsula for his earlier triumph to be repeated. Instead, he was ignominiously defeated at Pavia in 1525, and taken to Spain as a prisoner. For more than a year France remained without her king. Even so, he never learnt his lesson, and Italy remained an obsession with him for the rest of his life.

A significant consequence of the Italian Wars was a change in the character of the French court. As the King of France became a key figure in the Italian political scene, Italians sought his aid or protection. A number of them attached themselves permanently to his entourage, notably Gian Giacopo Trivulzio, who became a marshal of France, and Galeazzo da San Severino, who served as Master of the Horse. Italians also visited the French court in consequence of the King's matrimonial diplomacy. In 1518, Lorenzo Piero de' Medici, nephew of Pope Leo X, came to Amboise to

The marriage of Francis' son, *Henry (later Henry II), to Catherine de Médicis strengthened the existing links between France and Italy. The wedding took place in 1533 at Marseille and was celebrated by jousts in the old chivalric manner. Drawing by Antoine Caron. (101)*

marry Madeleine de la Tour d'Auvergne. Ten years later, Francis' sister-in-law, Renée, married Ercole d'Este, son of the Duke of Ferrara. Last but not least, in October 1533, the King's eldest son, Henry, married Catherine de Médicis, niece of Pope Clement VII, at Marseille. This marriage, in particular, added substantially to the number of Italians settled at the French court. But the traffic between France and Italy was not one way only: the wars in the peninsula gave Frenchmen many opportunities, as soldiers, diplomats, or administrators, of observing Italian life and manners at close quarters. They found that women in Italy were considered an essential adornment of court society and that close attention was given to literature and the arts. As a result of the ideas which they brought back, the court of France became more refined.

Sophistication, however, entailed extravagance, especially with regard to buildings, clothes, food, and entertainment. Frenchmen tried to emulate Italians often at the risk of ruining themselves and many looked to the King's favour and munificence to rescue them from the consequences of their prodigality. This was grist to the mill of contemporary satire. Criticism of court life was, of course, not new. Its disadvantages as compared with life in the country were a common theme of French literature from the thirteenth century onwards. But in the sixteenth century criticism of the court and more especially of the professional courtier, whose extravagance and mannerisms marked him off from the rest of society, became wider in scope and also more barbed. Extravagance was criticized not simply as lack of thrift, but as a sign of physical and moral decay. There was also a strong reaction to the ideas contained in Castiglione's *Il Cortegiano*, a work that enjoyed a considerable success at the French court at this time. Castiglione's Neoplatonic idea of love came in for ridicule, as did his doctrine of social politeness.

The court on the move

In one important respect the French court in the early sixteenth century did not change: it continued to be peripatetic. A Venetian ambassador complained that it never remained in the same place for fifteen consecutive days during the whole of his embassy. But the impression conveyed by this report is not strictly correct; the King's movements, as one would expect, were seasonal. In the winter and early spring, when roads were little better than quagmires, he tended to stay put. In 1516, for example, he remained at Amboise (except for a brief stay at Blois) from 25 October until the middle of January. He then moved to Paris and remained there till 19 May, when he set off on a tour of Picardy. On 10 December he was back at Amboise, where he stayed till 2 June.

In the Middle Ages it had been customary for a king to be constantly on the move, feeding on the produce of his estates and dispensing justice to his vassals. But the peripatetic nature of Francis' court was not simply a mindless perpetuation of habits formed in a comparatively remote feudal past. There were compelling political and social reasons for its wanderlust. In an age of growing national unity and royal centralization it was vitally important for the King to know his kingdom at first hand and to establish personal contact with his subjects. Francis' wanderings were far from haphazard. At the start of his reign he systematically visited many French provinces: Provence in 1516, Picardy in 1517, Anjou and Brittany in 1518, Poitou and Angoumois in 1519, Picardy again in 1520, and Burgundy in 1521. He then became involved in a protracted war with the Emperor, so that his movements were henceforth largely determined by military exigencies. With the return of peace in 1526, however, he resumed his progresses. Even when his health seemed on the point of collapsing, he continued to roam about his kingdom at regular intervals. His movements, though often related to the political situation, were also inspired by more mundane considerations. Travel provided Francis with opportunities to indulge in his favourite sport of hunting. He was at his happiest, it seems, when he could shed cares of state and vanish into some deep forest, sometimes for days on end, with his hounds and a few trusted companions. Neither he nor his entourage enjoyed city life. By comparison with the cramped and unhealthy conditions of any major town in sixteenth-century France, the lure of the countryside and pure air of Touraine and the Île-de-France was irresistible.

In the course of his progresses Francis visited many churches and monasteries, inspected fortifications, castles, and harbour installations, and attended entertainments staged for his benefit. Whenever he visited an important town for the first time he was given an *entrée joyeuse*. This was a most effective form of royal propaganda. Neither royal proclamations nor official tracts could move the hearts of people as deeply as ceremonies in which the King appeared in person amidst a décor carefully designed to project his personality and the nature of his rule. A coronation or a royal funeral was impressive enough but it was seen only by a relatively small number of subjects. An entry had the advantage of being repeated several times within a reign and in a variety of places. Furthermore, it was organized by the townspeople themselves so that they were more closely identified with the mystery of kingship. Not all entries, however, were of equal importance; only the first in each town was solemn and costly.

From a comparatively simple affair in which victuals and sometimes fodder had been offered by the townspeople to the King, a royal entry had become, by the close of the Middle Ages, a magnificent spectacle with religious and political overtones. The King was met outside the town by the citizens, wearing colourful liveries, and escorted into it to the accompaniment of trumpeters and other musicians. The presentation of gifts, which might be money or some expensive *objet d'art*, was preceded by an exchange of oaths; the King promised to uphold the town's liberties, and the citizens to obey him. After receiving the town keys, the King rode through it in procession under a rich canopy or *dais*, along a route carefully prepared in advance. Its surface was usually covered with sand or rushes, and tapestries were hung over the façades of the houses. By the sixteenth century roadside theatricals had become the rule. The procession culminated in a thanksgiving service at the main church in the town, followed by a banquet and jollification that lasted well into the night.

One of the most spectacular royal entries of the reign of Francis I was held at Lyon, in July 1515, on the eve of his first invasion of Italy. As the King approached the city, he was greeted by a ship being towed across the Saône by a white stag. This was to remind him of the legend of Clovis, to whom a stag had indicated a ford by which he might pursue his enemies. The gateway of the city was decorated with a Tree of Jesse and the King's own emblem of a salamander flanked by figures representing Lyon and Loyalty. At intervals along the processional route, which had been decorated with the King's colours, young women stood on columns, each holding a letter of the King's name. Between them tableaux were performed by the city's leading families: one showed Francis defending Peace against the Duke of Milan and the Swiss bear; in another he appeared as Hercules gathering fruit in the Garden of the Hesperides. It was on this occasion, too, that a mechanical lion, made by Leonardo da Vinci originally for the city of Florence, performed for the King.

The canopy beneath which the King made his formal entry into a town was analogous to that carried over the Blessed Sacrament in processions on the feast of Corpus Christi. In fact, Frenchmen were never allowed to forget that their king was 'the Most Christian King'. The chrism with which he was anointed at his coronation conferred upon him an almost sacerdotal character. No French monarch ever claimed the right to celebrate Mass, but he took Communion in both kinds, a privilege enjoyed only by priests. He also had the miraculous power of healing. This originated in the early Middle Ages. The only other Christian monarch to claim this power was the King of England. In time it became restricted to curing scrofula, a disease more repulsive than dangerous and subject to periods of remission. The King touched the victim's tumours and sores with his bare hand, making the sign of the Cross over him and saying 'the King touches you and God cures you'. The victim was also given two small silver coins. This ceremony enjoyed a particular vogue during the Renaissance. People came from every corner of Europe to be touched by the King of France. Even when Francis was a prisoner in Spain, people sought his healing touch. He did not normally confine the ceremony to the four principal feast days of the religious calendar. On his progress through Champagne, in January 1530, he touched a few people at almost every overnight stop; he even touched a solitary man in the open countryside. The number of people touched by the King in the course of a year was considerable: in 1530, for example, it was at least 1,731.

Moving the court was like moving an army. According to Benvenuto Cellini, twelve thousand horses were used to transport it; and this was an unusually low figure. In peacetime, when the court was complete, eighteen thousand horses were normally used. Dr Taylor, the English ambassador, who witnessed the court's arrival at Bordeaux in 1526, noted stabling for 22,500 horses! The court's baggage train was, of course, enormous. It could include furniture, gold and silver plate, and tapestries. Only royal châteaux that were frequently visited by the court were kept furnished; the rest remained empty from one visit to the next. In 1533, when Francis met the Pope at Marseille, the sum of 4,623 *livres* was spent on moving the court's furniture, plate, and tapestries.

Finding accommodation for the court was always a serious problem. Wherever possible the King stayed in one of his own châteaux or accepted the hospitality of one of his courtiers. But sometimes there was no château available. He would then put up at an abbey or an inn and his followers would seek lodgings in the neighbourhood. This was often a mad scramble. In 1539 the Bishop of Saluzzo complained of the way in which an isolated house would be found for the King and the ladies, while the rest of the court were left to find shelter as much as three, four, or six miles away. Sometimes they were reduced to pitching tents.

The most famous occasion on which tents were used by the court was the Field of Cloth of Gold in June 1520. The small town of Ardres could not provide sufficient cover, having been seriously damaged in a recent war. It was, therefore, decided to pitch three or four hundred tents in a meadow outside the town. But these were no ordinary tents. Made specially for the occasion, they were covered with rich fabrics, emblazoned with the arms of their owners and surmounted by pennants and golden apples. An eye-witness described them as more magnificent than 'the miracles of the Egyptian pyramids and Roman amphitheatres'. In normal circumstances, however, less magnificent tents were used and, as Cellini discovered, the hardships imposed on the court's rank and file could be acute. 'Sometimes,' he writes, 'there were scarcely two houses to be found and then we set up canvas tents like gipsies and suffered at times very great discomfort.'

The court at Paris

If Francis I was a countryman at heart, he could not stay away from Paris altogether, for its political and economic importance was inescapable. The Parlement of Paris, one of the departments of state that had 'gone out of court' in the Middle Ages, was both prestigious and powerful. Though its primary purpose was judicial, it had important administrative and political functions. As an offshoot of the old *Curia Regis* it claimed the right to advise the monarch and to ratify his legislative acts. It could submit re-

Hunting was the King's passion, *as it was of almost all Renaissance monarchs. In this miniature of 1519, Francis rides through the woods of Fontainebleau with his huntsman Perot. (102)*

At Marignano, 1515, Francis beat the Swiss army defending Milan. Coming at the very beginning of his reign, it was a victory which made him the envy of other monarchs (particularly Henry VIII) but which only confirmed in his mind the disastrous policy of French intervention in Italy. (103)

Francis' courtiers were sketched in a series of vivid drawings by François Clouet. This one shows Galiot de Genouillac, appointed Master-General of Artillery in 1512. He was captured with the King at Pavia in 1525. (104)

monstrances which the King could refuse to implement, but in the last resort he could only override its opposition by coming to the Parlement and presiding at a ceremony, called a *lit-de-justice*. Thus, in order to carry through his more controversial policies, Francis was obliged from time to time to visit Paris. He also needed the financial support of its citizens. The time had long since passed when a King of France could hope to 'live of his own'. Neither the revenues from Francis' demesne nor the uncertain yield from taxation sufficed to cover his expenses, especially the rising cost of war. He, therefore, resorted to fiscal expedients including the sale of offices and titles of nobility, the alienation of Crown lands, and loans from foreign bankers and from his own subjects. His reign was one long exercise in fiscal ingenuity.

The picture that is so often presented of Francis living almost exclusively among the châteaux of the Loire or at Fontainebleau is not borne out by a close investigation of his itinerary. He visited Paris at least once in every year of his reign, except 1525–26 when he was a prisoner in Spain, 1541, and 1547. He spent more than a month there in each of seventeen years and less than ten days in four. Admittedly, he was not often there in the summer. In the course of his entire reign he spent a total of only thirty-one days in Paris during August. He stayed there usually in the winter or the spring.

Parisians probably viewed the occasional visits of the court with misgivings. An immature streak in Francis' character found an outlet, but only at the beginning of his reign, in senseless pranks at the expense of the good citizens of Paris. As Dauphin, he had been in the habit of putting on disguise with his friends and rampaging about the city at night. What is more surprising, is that Francis continued to behave in this way after his accession! In May 1517 he and his courtiers shocked the Parisians by riding through the streets at night, disguised and masked, and frequenting houses of ill-repute. Two years later some distinguished English visitors were invited to take part in the same kind of sport. They 'rode daily disguised through Paris throwing eggs, stones and other foolish trifles at the people which light demeanour of a king was much discommended and gested at'. Nothing could express more eloquently the contempt felt by courtiers for their social inferiors.

Royal disdain and extortion seriously undermined the King's popularity in Paris. The inhabitants also resented his absence in the autumn of 1523, when the English invaded northern France and almost reached the capital. The treason of the Duke of Bourbon enabled them to vent their feelings. Sympathy for the traitor was expressed in many popular songs, and the reprieve granted to Saint-Vallier, his principal accomplice, caused rejoicing in the capital. Parisians were not even moved, it seems, by the King's tragic defeat and capture in 1525. An unsuccessful attempt was made to unseat his mother as Regent, and the success of her foreign policy was imperilled by the capital's refusal to submit certain securities demanded by the English government in the peace treaty of August 1526. No wonder Francis kept away from Paris for more than a year after his return from Spain! When finally he did reappear, in April 1527, his mood was foreshadowed by the arrest of eight burgesses a few hours before his entry. But Francis was seldom vindictive. Recent events may even have opened his eyes to the growing political significance of the capital. For, in March 1528, he announced his intention to spend more time with and near his 'good people of Paris'. Though he continued to tour the kingdom as extensively as before, he shifted his main building activities from the Loire valley to the Paris region.

Francis' entry into Lyon in 1515 was the occasion for an elaborate allegorical pageant recorded for posterity in a series of miniatures. In this one Francis is represented as the flower of the royal line of France. Two angels hold an enormous crown above his head. Beneath him, on side branches, are 'Grâce de Dieu' and 'France'. The stem, guarded by Francis' emblem, the salamander, is flanked by 'Guide Loyal' and 'Léal Patron'. Beside them stand 'La Cité de Lyon' with a lock and 'Loyauté' with a key. At the bottom a cobbled road leads to 'Civitas Inviolata'. (105)

'The Unity of the State': one of the series of tapestries which repeat the designs originally carried out in fresco at Fontainebleau by Rosso. Francis is represented as a Roman emperor, holding in his right hand a pomegranate, symbol of unity and peace. (106)

To encourage learning was the duty of every Renaissance prince. Francis was generous in his patronage of scholarship, though his zeal needed occasional prompting. In this miniature of about 1530 he listens to Antoine Macault reading his translation of Diodorus Siculus. Next to him are his three sons. (107)

GRACE DE DIEV   FRANCE

FRANCOYS · I ·

LA CITE DE LYON   LOYAVTE

· CIVITAS · INVIOLATA ·

'Marvellously addicted to buildings'

Necessity as much as ostentation determined Francis' activities as a builder. The early sixteenth century was marked by a great outburst of architectural activity all over France motivated by functional and aesthetic considerations. With the return of peace after the Hundred Years' War the aristocracy began to build for comfort rather than defence. The old military features – angle towers, machicolations, *chemins-de-ronde*, water-filled moats and the like – were not discarded overnight, but were now treated rather as decorations and status symbols. At the same time, the Italian campaigns brought the French nobility into contact with classical architecture. Even if they did not immediately understand its language they responded favourably to its decoration. Classical motifs were imported into France and applied to buildings that remained structurally Gothic. Among pioneers of this trend was King Charles VIII who, on his return from Naples in 1495, set a team of Italians to work on his château of Amboise.

Under Francis I's patronage the classical influence ceased to be merely decorative and superficial; it began to determine the structure of buildings. Until 1528 his building activities were in the main confined to the Loire valley. At Blois, which belonged to his first wife, Claude de France, he enlarged one wing of the château, giving it loggias on one side and an exterior spiral staircase on the other. By taking Bramante's work at the Vatican as his model for the façade of the loggias, Francis showed his concern to keep abreast of Italian fashion. His most ambitious architectural undertaking, however, during the first decade of his reign was the château of Chambord, situated in a forest a few miles south of Blois. Though traditionally French in its overall plan, Chambord belongs to the Renaissance. The internal division of the keep into four blocks of *appartements*, each containing three rooms and a closet, is related to the plan of the villa at Poggio a Caiano built by Giuliano da Sangallo for Lorenzo de' Medici. The decoration of the roof at Chambord is also distinctly Italian: the chimney-stacks, dormer windows, and turrets are adorned with all kinds of classical motif, including panels of slate evidently intended to resemble polychrome marbles on Italian monuments.

Who was the architect of Chambord? Leonardo da Vinci's name has been suggested, but the evidence of his sketchbooks is scrappy. Furthermore, he died in 1519, before work on the château had seriously begun. A more likely candidate is Domenico da Cortona, a pupil of Giuliano da Sangallo, who, in 1531, was paid by Francis for wooden models of various buildings, including Chambord, made over a period of fifteen years. It was, of course, customary for an architect to submit a model of a projected building to his employer for comment and approval. Thus, it is likely that Francis had an important say in the final design for Chambord. His interest in architecture was more than superficial. He was, according to Androuet du Cerceau, the sixteenth-century architect, 'marvellously addicted to buildings'.

In 1528 Francis shifted the centre of his building activities from the Loire valley to Paris and its neighbourhood. He

Francis' buildings *mark a new era in French architecture. Italian Renaissance forms begin to influence the structure as well as the decoration, but the result is still unmistakably French. Above: the château of Madrid, just outside Paris. Below: the staircase which he added to the château of Blois. (108, 109)*

109

Chambord contains many Italianate elements in the decorative details of the skyline as well as its internal planning. It was begun in the first decade of Francis' reign, and may have been designed by Domenico da Cortona, a pupil of Giuliano da San Gallo. (110)

undertook work at the Louvre, in the Bois de Boulogne, at Saint-Germain-en-Laye, Villers-Cotterêts, Fontainebleau and elsewhere. The palace built in the Bois de Boulogne became popularly known as the château of Madrid for a reason that has never been satisfactorily explained. It certainly bore no resemblance to the Alcázar, in Madrid, where Francis had been imprisoned shortly before. Its high-pitched roof and spiral staircases were typically French, but it broke away from native tradition by having no central courtyard or water-filled moat. The plan again resembled that of Poggio a Caiano and the elevation, comprising two superimposed exterior galleries, also had distinctly Italian affinities. The most unusual feature, however, was the decoration, both interior and exterior, of brightly coloured terracotta. This was designed by Girolamo della Robbia, a member of the famous family of Florentine ceramists, who settled in France about 1527. It has been suggested that he was also responsible for the overall design of the château, but this has been disputed.

While Madrid was being built, Francis began to modernize the château of Fontainebleau, which his predecessors had frequently visited since the twelfth century. In April 1528 Gilles le Breton, a Parisian master mason, was commissioned to build a new entrance (the Porte Dorée), to add a long gallery to the rear of the keep, and to insert two blocks between the new entrance and the keep. It is possible that he was also responsible for the large courtyard (Cour du Cheval Blanc) that was added on the west side of the château. Le

Breton has sometimes been dismissed as a mere craftsman without originality. In fact, his additions to the oval courtyard of the old castle, notably a monumental staircase, show a more mature understanding of the classical style than French master masons had hitherto displayed. Another architect associated with Fontainebleau is Sebastiano Serlio, author of a famous treatise on architecture. No part of the château, however, can be attributed to him; it seems that he acted simply as an adviser, while continuing to write his treatise.

Work at Fontainebleau continued until the end of Francis' reign. By 1531, however, enough had been completed to allow the interior decorators to move in. They were led by two Italians, Giovanni Battista Rosso and Francesco Primaticcio. The former was a Florentine painter who had come under the influence of Michelangelo and Raphael whilst working in Rome. About 1529 he moved to Venice and did a drawing of *Mars and Venus* for Pietro Aretino. The drawing, an allegory on the peace of Cambrai, was presented to Francis and presumably paved the way for Rosso's invitation to France. He arrived there, in 1531, and, being not only a good painter but a cultivated man, immediately made a favourable impression on the King, who appointed him First Painter. Rosso's arrival was followed a year later by that of Primaticcio, who came recommended by the Duke of Mantua. A pupil of Giulio Romano, he was apparently particularly skilled in the art of stucco. Between them, Rosso and Primaticcio decorated many parts of Fontainebleau. Each had a large team of assistants; sometimes they collaborated, but more often they worked independently. Most of their work, alas, has been destroyed; it is known thanks to surviving preliminary sketches and to a large number of contemporary engravings copied from or inspired by their designs.

Fontainebleau *is Francis' most characteristic creation. Above right: the earliest part of the new work, the Porte Dorée (1528). Above: the Galerie François Ier, decorated, mainly by Rosso with (below and right) two details showing the combination of elongated stucco figures with paintings in panels. (111–14)*

All that remains of Rosso's work at Fontainebleau is contained in the Galerie François 1er. In spite of many alterations and excessive restoration over the centuries it remains impressive. The walls are divided into two roughly equal parts, the lower containing carved wood-panelling, and the upper, a combination of painting and stucco. Each space between the windows has a painted panel in the middle flanked by varied decorations in stucco. These include nudes, herms, *putti*, garlands of fruit, and also much 'strap-work'; that is to say, the stucco is made to look like rolls of leather cut into fantastic shapes. All this represents a rejection of High Renaissance classicism in favour of Mannerism. The meaning of the decoration in the Galerie François 1er has baffled generations of art historians. But, if the iconography is often difficult to interpret, its aim is evidently to glorify the King.

Francis' art collection *was one of the finest in Europe, and he managed to persuade several of the leading Italian artists to visit or settle in France. Among them was Andrea del Sarto, whose 'Charity' was painted for the King in 1518, and is still in the Louvre. (115)*

Part of a fireplace in the Chambre de la Reine is all that remains of work done at Fontainebleau by Primaticcio before 1540. But his drawings for the Chambre du Roi and other rooms are extant, and these show that he was at first strongly influenced by his master, Giulio Romano. In 1540, however, he was sent to Rome on an art-collecting mission for the King, and came into contact with ancient sculpture and the art of Parmigianino. On returning to Fontainebleau, he developed a style of figure-drawing exemplified by the caryatids in the Chambre de la Duchesse d'Etampes with their long, tapering limbs, thin necks, and small heads with excessively classical profiles. Primaticcio's main work after 1540 was done in the Salle de Bal and Galerie d'Ulysse, but most of it dates from after Francis' reign. He was, however, responsible for the mural decoration of the King's baths. These were situated under the Galerie François 1er and consisted of a bathroom proper and adjacent sweating-rooms. Sir John Wallop, who visited them in 1540, described the bath itself as 'like a pond railed about, and no more place therein, but for one person to go in front . . .'. The baths were filled with so much steam that the King had to guide the ambassador through them. Yet it was here, in the hot and humid atmosphere of the *appartement des bains* that Francis chose to display his collection of paintings! A cultivated Renaissance person, however, would have seen nothing incongruous in the dedication of a building simultaneously to the care of the body and the pleasures of the mind. But the baths evidently did not do the pictures much good. Some had been damaged beyond repair by the early seventeenth century, when Henry IV moved them to another part of the château, replacing them by copies. Eventually they formed the nucleus of the collection at the Louvre.

Painting and sculpture: Francis as patron

Francis I was not the first French monarch to collect pictures, but the royal collection was heterogeneous and of variable quality until he took it over. The art of painting in France was at a low ebb about 1500. The only two French artists of any significance were Jean Bourdichon, who illuminated Anne of Brittany's *Book of Hours*, and Jean Pérréal, a portrait painter, who also prepared pageants and designed works of sculpture and medals. Italian painters seldom troubled to visit France. In 1515, however, an important change came about as a result of Francis' conquest of Milan. He was able to see for himself some of the great masterpieces of the Italian Renaissance, amongst them Leonardo da Vinci's *Last Supper*, which apparently impressed him so much that he would have liked to take it home. This being impracticable, he did the next best thing: he invited the artist to settle in his kingdom.

Leonardo was sixty-five years old, in March 1516, when he accepted the King's invitation. He was given the manor of Cloux near Amboise and an annuity of five hundred *livres*. What the King expected in return is not known for certain. Leonardo's notes and sketches show that he was interested in canal-building, town-planning, and architecture and he may have been commissioned by the King to carry out some of his ideas at Romorantin, where the Queen Mother had a

Benvenuto Cellini made a number of outstanding works for Francis, including the famous salt-cellar now in Vienna and the hardly less famous 'Nymph' (above), intended for the Porte Dorée of Fontainebleau but eventually given to Diane de Poitiers for her château of Anet. (116)

palace; but nothing came of this. Nor is there evidence that he painted any pictures in France. By October 1517 his right hand had become paralysed so that he could not paint as well as before, though he could still draw and teach. Leonardo died at Cloux on 2 May 1519, but not in the arms of Francis I, as Vasari would have us believe. On the day in question, Francis was at Saint-Germain-en-Laye. The esteem in which he held Leonardo was nevertheless high. Twenty years later he described Leonardo to Cellini as 'a great philosopher'. No other man, he felt, had ever known as much about sculpture, painting, and architecture. By 1545 the royal collection at Fontainebleau included several important works by Leonardo.

Another Italian artist of major importance who visited France early in Francis' reign was Andrea del Sarto. He painted a portrait of the infant Dauphin for the King and also a *Charity*, now in the Louvre. But he soon returned to Florence, where allegedly he spent on himself a large sum of money which Francis had given him to purchase works of art on his behalf.

Francis' artistic interests were not exclusively Italian. For portraiture he turned mainly to Jean Clouet, an artist who hailed almost certainly from the Low Countries. Portraiture became very popular during the reign and many chalk drawings have survived of the King and of members of his family and entourage. Some are of high quality and are usually attributed to Clouet; others are contemporary copies of variable quality. These were put to different uses: they might be sent to friends and relatives of the sitter, as photographs are today, or be gathered into albums containing fifty to sixty drawings each. Although Clouet was almost certainly French-trained, his use of parallel diagonal hatching strokes to obtain a three-dimensional effect was of Italian origin. For this reason he has been described as 'one of the first artists in France to comprehend the principles of the Italian High Renaissance'. He died in 1540 and was succeeded as Painter to the King by his son, François, who continued the series of French court portraits.

By 1525 Francis' collection of works of art already comprised a significant number of paintings by Florentine and Roman artists of the High Renaissance. Thereafter its scope was enlarged. Agents were employed by the King to find him paintings, statues, books, and other rare and valuable items. Some were French diplomats like Guillaume du Bellay; others were Italians, like Battista della Palla and Pietro Aretino. According to Vasari, Della Palla ransacked Florence for the King of France, but the works which he is known to have sent him are few. His usefulness as an artistic agent ended in 1530 when he was imprisoned by the Medici. Even so, Francis continued to add Florentine works to his collection, including Michelangelo's *Leda and the Swan* and possibly Bronzino's *Allegory of Passion*. Though most of the artists represented in the Fontainebleau collection were Florentine, Venetians were not overlooked completely. In 1538 Aretino sent two pictures to Francis, 'one magnifying the honour of man, the other magnifying the glory of God'. The first was Titian's portrait of the King, now in the Louvre, which was painted from a medal, not from life; the other has not been identified but was obviously a religious work, possibly also by Titian. It was presumably on the evidence of these works that Titian was invited to France by the King, but the artist declined, allegedly because he 'never wanted to abandon Venice'.

Sculpture entered the royal collection later than painting. In 1520 it contained no statues, either ancient or modern. This prompted Cardinal Medici to order for the King a copy by Bandinelli of the recently discovered *Laocoön*. But it was never sent; perhaps because it was not thought good enough. Other ancient statues, so far unidentified, were sent to the King instead. His main supplier of statues in the 1520s was Della Palla; but the only one to survive is Tribolo's *Cibele*, which was given a place of honour at Fontainebleau. Michelangelo's *Hercules*, which Della Palla bought for the King in 1529, became part of a fountain. It was later removed to the Jardin de l'Etang and vanished, along with the garden, under Louis XIV. Francis twice invited Michelangelo to France, but the artist never made the journey. He promised, if he should live long enough, to execute for the King 'a work in marble, one in bronze, one in painting'. Ironically it was the King who died first.

Francis was also interested in ancient sculpture. In 1540 he sent Primaticcio to Rome to buy and copy antiquities. The artist returned with a number of plaster casts of ancient statues, mostly from the papal collection at the Belvedere. They included the *Ariadne*, *Laocoön*, *Apollo Belvedere*, *Cnidian Venus*, *Hercules Commodus*, two sphinxes, and two satyrs. These were turned into bronzes by Vignola, the future architect, who set up a foundry at Fontainebleau in 1541. They were displayed initially in the Galerie François 1er, and were much admired by the King and his entourage. The sight of Venus inspired Francis to flatter his mistress, the Duchess of Etampes; her body, he said, was no less perfect than that of the goddess. Not all Primaticcio's casts were turned into bronzes: Michelangelo's *Pietà*, reliefs from Trajan's Column, and a horse (possibly that of Marcus Aurelius on the Capitol) were reproduced in plaster only.

Francis' collection of works of art comprised many items other than paintings and statues. It included a perfume burner designed by Raphael, and a jewel casket with crystal panels showing scenes from the Life of Christ. The latter was made by Valerio Belli and given to the King by Pope Clement VII on the occasion of Catherine de Médicis' wedding in 1533. Some of the most valuable objects in Francis' collection were made by Benvenuto Cellini, the Florentine goldsmith and sculptor, who came to France twice, in 1537 and 1540. On the second occasion he was commissioned by the King to execute a life-size statue of Jupiter in silver and

given a workshop at the Petit Nesle, in Paris. Whilst the King took a close personal interest in Cellini's work, to the extent of visiting him in his studio, he delegated responsibility for the artist's welfare to subordinates, who were not always punctilious in discharging this duty. Yet Cellini's labours did not go unrewarded: in addition to cash payments, he received letters of naturalization free of charge, and possession of the Petit Nesle. But he created many enemies by his arrogance, bombast, and violent temper. Chief among them was the Duchesse d'Etampes, whom he offended by his tactlessness. She allegedly used all her influence to discredit him and even tried to sabotage the presentation of his *Jupiter*. He was ordered to bring it to the Galerie François 1er, where Primaticcio's bronzes had already been assembled. The Duchess hoped that their proximity would detract from Cellini's work. She also delayed the King's coming till nightfall so as to darken the gallery for the presentation. But Cellini's ingenuity outwitted her malice. He had mounted his statue on a movable wooden plinth, and inserted a wax torch among the flames of Jupiter's thunderbolt. As the King entered the gallery Cellini lit the torch and instructed his apprentice to push the statue forward. This made it seem alive and Primaticcio's bronzes were eclipsed. But the Duchess had not done yet. As the King praised the *Jupiter*, she replied that it would show to much less advantage by daylight and pointed to a veil concealing its faults. This threw Cellini into a rage. He pulled off the veil, which had been intended purely for modesty, and tore it to shreds. The Duchess, on her part, was outraged by his impertinence and only the King's timely intervention averted an ugly scene. Of the works for Francis actually completed by Cellini only two survive: a gold salt-cellar, now in Vienna, and a bronze relief of the *Nymph of Fontainebleau*, now at the Louvre.

The King and the scholars

What kind of a man was Francis I? The English chronicler, Edward Hall, who had no cause to flatter him, described him as 'a goodly Prince, stately of countenance, merry of cheer, brown coloured, great eyes, high nosed, big lipped, fair breasted and shoulders, small legs, and long feet'. Less terse but equally vivid is a description contained in a chronicle, written by Ellis Griffith, a Welshman in Henry VIII's service, who saw the King of France at the Field of Cloth of Gold in 1520. Francis, he states, was six feet tall. His head was rightly proportioned for his height, the nape of his neck unusually broad, his hair brown, smooth, and neatly combed, his beard of three months' growth darker in colour, his nose long, his eyes hazel and bloodshot, and his complexion the colour of watery milk. He had muscular buttocks and thighs, but his legs below the knees were thin and bandy, and his feet long, slender, and completely flat. He had an agreeable voice and an animated expression in conversation, marred only by the unfortunate habit of continually rolling his eyes upwards. Francis' eloquence and charm were frequently commented on by contemporaries. His affability delighted the Spaniards during his captivity. 'He bears his prison admirably,' wrote a Venetian, 'and in all places through which he passes is so well greeted by reason of the extreme affability and

The last portrait of the King is this drawing by François Clouet, which must have been made shortly before his death. Although only fifty-two, Francis already seems an old man (117)

courtesy evinced by him towards everybody, that he is well nigh adored in this country.' Yet Francis was apparently shy. 'If a man speak not to him first,' wrote Sir Thomas Cheyney, 'he will not likely begin to speak to him, but when he is once entered, he is as good a man to speak to as ever I saw.' Even at the end of his life, Francis still cut a fine figure. 'His appearance,' wrote Marino Cavalli in 1546, 'is entirely royal so that if one had never seen his face or his portrait, on first seeing him one would say at once: that is the king! His every movement is so noble and majestic that there is no prince like him.'

But Francis was not just a fine figure of a man; he also had a mind. Though not a classical scholar himself, he enjoyed the company of intelligent and well-educated men. Among the humanists in his entourage none was as distinguished as Guillaume Budé. Much as he disliked court life, where he had to endure the jibes of courtiers, he put up with it if only to foster the King's enthusiasm for scholarship, which was easily submerged by more urgent preoccupations. At the start of his reign the greatest need felt by French scholars was for a college devoted to the study of classical languages. Such colleges already existed outside France, at Louvain and in Rome. In February 1517 Francis announced his intention to found one and invited Erasmus of Rotterdam to take charge of it. The King's choice of a foreigner was understandable; only Erasmus had an international reputation commensurate with the prestige which the King hoped to

derive from his foundation. But the great Dutchman valued his freedom too much to tie himself to any master, however generous. He therefore declined the invitation, and Francis turned instead to Jan Lascaris, under whose aegis a college was set up in Milan, possibly as a first step towards the creation of a more ambitious one in France. It was soon starved of funds, however, and, in 1523, had to be dissolved.

Though genuine enough, Francis' interest in scholarship had to be continually kept alive by subtle promptings. 'I would not say,' wrote Budé in 1521, 'that his zeal is completely extinguished . . . but it is no longer alive. I do what I can to rekindle the fire which is only smoking at present, but I lack the ability to influence the courtiers who sometimes deride my plans and try unfairly to discredit me.' In the end, however, Budé's patience was rewarded. In March 1530 Francis created four royal professorships, the so-called *lecteurs royaux*, two for Greek and two for Hebrew. His action was widely acclaimed. 'It is a river that the king is going to let flow,' wrote a Flemish scholar, 'which will water many lands and make them fertile.' The establishment of the professorships, from which sprang later the Collège de France, was undoubtedly an important event in the history of French education. Additional *lecteurs* were soon appointed to teach mathematics, Latin, and Arabic. They included such famous names as Oronce Finé and Guillaume Postel. But the *lecteurs* were given no building of their own, and often had to teach in uncongenial surroundings. Moreover the salary each was supposed to receive from the Crown was seldom paid; and this detracted from their teaching, as they had to go to court to press their claims. Eventually, the King was persuaded to include them in the payroll of his household, but trouble over their remuneration continued till the end of the reign.

The creation of the royal professorships was only part of a programme that included the creation of a royal library and provision for the publication of its contents. In 1518, the royal library at Blois consisted mainly of medieval works. Of the 1,626 volumes only forty-one were in Greek, four in Hebrew, and two in Arabic. Under Francis many classical texts were added. The number of Greek manuscripts, in particular, increased to 560 by the end of the reign. These were in the main acquired by French diplomats in Italy and the Middle East, notably Guillaume Pellicier, French ambassador to Venice between 1539 and 1542. The library was further enlarged as a result of the ordinance of Montpellier (1537) which required printers and booksellers to deliver a copy of every new book to the librarian at Blois. Foreign books imported for sale were to be deposited for examination and purchased if found suitable. In 1544, when the library was moved from Blois to Fontainebleau, it comprised, in addition to a globe and a crocodile's head in a leather case, 1,894 volumes. Whether the King ever found time to dip into them is doubtful, but, in 1537, Pierre du Chastel was appointed Reader to the King with the task of reading aloud to him works on ancient history by Greek and Roman writers.

The appointment of Robert Estienne as royal printer first in Hebrew and Latin (1539), then in Greek (1542), helped to make the contents of the library at Fontainebleau more accessible to scholars. All his Greek texts, except one, were printed from manuscripts in the library. Francis himself is said to have chosen for publication the Roman history of Dionysius of Halicarnassus and to have suggested the small Greek type used for a pocket New Testament in 1546. Be this as it may, the King certainly paid for three special founts of Greek type – the so-called *Grecs du roi* – used by Estienne. These were cut by Claude Garamond and modelled on the calligraphy of Angelo Vergecio, a copyist and cataloguer on the staff of the royal library. Francis also initiated the rebinding of many of its books, an undertaking which culminated in the reign of Henry II in the production of some of the finest examples of the bookbinder's art.

Royal routine

Not enough is known about the day-to-day life of the French court in the early sixteenth century. It seems, however, that there was an established routine which was observed more or less strictly according to the temperament of each monarch. This, at least, is the impression conveyed by a famous letter written by Catherine de Médicis to her son Charles IX:

I would desire you, Monsieur my son, to fix the hour of your *lever* and to satisfy your nobles by following the example set by the king your father [Henry II]. When he took his shirt and his clothes were brought in, all the princes, lords, captains, knights of the order, gentlemen of the chamber, stewards and gentlemen-servants entered at the same moment, and he spoke to them and they saw him to their great satisfaction. That done, he attended to his affairs and they all withdrew except those directly concerned with those affairs and four secretaries. If you were to do likewise, it would please them greatly for it was a custom always observed by your father and grandfather [Francis I]; and afterwards you should devote an hour or two to dispatches and business which cannot be dealt with in your absence. Do not let ten o'clock pass without going to mass, as your royal father and grandfather were accustomed to do. Let all the princes and lords accompany you . . . and afterwards dine if it is late or take a stroll for your health, but do not dine later than eleven. After dinner, at least twice a week, give an audience, which is something infinitely satisfying to your subjects. . . . After remaining in public for half an hour or an hour, retire to your study or to your private apartments or wherever you wish. At three in the afternoon, go for a walk or a ride so as to show yourself and satisfy the nobility. Join the young people in some honest exercise at least two or three times a week, if not daily. This will please them greatly, since they got used to this under the king your father who loved them dearly. Then sup with your family and afterwards give a ball twice a week, for I have heard the king your grandfather say that two such days are necessary to live at peace with the French and that they like their king to keep them merry and engaged in some exercise.

Francis certainly gave his entourage plenty of exercise. No joyful event at his court was complete without tournaments and jousts. Mock battles reminiscent of those fought by him and his friends as children at Amboise continued to be a favourite pastime. A most elaborate one took place at Amboise, in April 1518, as part of the

celebrations for the Dauphin's baptism and the marriage of Lorenzo de' Medici and Madeleine de la Tour d'Auvergne. Six hundred men led by the King and the Duke of Alençon defended a model town in wood complete with a moat and a battery of guns against an equal number led by the Dukes of Bourbon and Vendôme. 'It was the finest mock battle that had ever been seen,' wrote Florange, 'and the nearest to real warfare, but it did not please everyone for some were killed and others terrified.' Another mock siege held at Romorantin as part of the Epiphany celebrations, in 1521, almost ended in disaster. A group of courtiers led by the King attacked a house occupied by the Count of Saint-Pol and his friends. As Francis tried to force open the door, one of the defenders dropped a burning log on his head. The King was knocked senseless and for several days his life was in danger; he refused, however, to punish the foolish courtier who had so nearly brought the reign to an untimely end. Francis' love of violent exercise made him particularly accident prone. He was nearly blinded, in September 1519, when he struck a branch while hunting in a forest; and, in February 1523, he suffered a dangerous fracture below the knee after being thrown by his horse.

Francis spent an inordinate amount of time hunting and was often criticized by foreign ambassadors for allowing it to interfere with his political obligations. 'This court,' wrote the Bishop of Saluzzo in 1539, 'is not like others. Here we are completely cut off from business, and should there be any, no hour, day or month is given to it for certain. One thinks only of hunting, ladies, banquets, [and] moving places . . .' Interesting glimpses of Francis' hunts are also contained in English diplomatic dispatches. In August 1527, Sir Anthony Browne sent the following account to his master, Henry VIII:

To advertise your Highness of such pastimes as the said French king useth, the most part thereof is in hunting, and that day that he hunteth, he is at dinner in some place in the forest by 8 o'clock in the morning to whom repair his veneers and hunts, bringing with them the scantling and fumishing of such deer as they have harboured, and the same lay on the table before him. Whereupon, aswell the gentlemen there present, as the said hunts, alledge many good reasons . . . to prove which should be the greatest deer, tracking the time at some seasons therein long; whom to hear, the king hath great pleasure. And after that he is resolved which deer he would hunt, he taketh his mule and rideth thither, and never faileth to kill his deer. . . . Furthermore the king's bed is always carried with him when he hunteth; and anon, after the deer is killed, he repaireth to some house near hand, where the same is set up, and there reposeth himself three or four hours, and against his return there is provided for him a supper by some noble man, as by Mons. de Vendôme, Mons. de Guise or other; whereunto a great number of ladies and gentlewomen, used to be in his company, be sent for, and there he passeth his time unto ten or eleven of the clock, amongst whom above, as the report is, he favoureth a maiden of Madame de Vendôme called Hely; whose beauty, after my mind, is not highly to be praised.

Women played an important part in Francis' life, though much that has been written on the subject is pure fiction. It has been alleged that he had a mistress at the age of ten and

Wife and mother: *Francis married Claude de France (left), daughter of Louis XII, in 1514. She died ten years later, aged only twenty-five. His mother (right) was Louise of Savoy, a strong personality who acted as Regent when Francis was on his Italian expedition. (118, 119)*

that his relationship with his sister, Marguerite, was incestuous. Neither story merits serious attention. Yet the King's private life was not irreproachable. He had the reputation of being dissolute, and the abcesses which began to plague him in the 1520s were probably syphilitic. Tavannes' comment on the King was that 'women rather than old age caused his death'. But the truth about his private life is elusive. Love poems and letters attributed to him and his first mistress, Madame de Chateaubriant, are uninformative and may not be genuine. The countess, in any case, was never allowed any political influence. On the other hand, her successor, Anne d'Heilly, Duchesse d'Etampes (the Hely mentioned in Sir Anthony Browne's letter), did acquire a great deal of political influence towards the end of the reign, perhaps as a direct result of the King's declining health. But, even if Francis' private life was not above criticism, he deserves credit for raising the status of women at his court. According to Brantôme, he insisted on their being shown respect and a courtier who disobeyed his ruling escaped severe punishment only by taking to his heels. The King's attitude may have represented a deliberate attempt to emulate Castiglione's ideal.

Apart from the Duchesse d'Etampes, three women were pre-eminent at the court of Francis I: his mother, Louise of Savoy; his sister, Marguerite d'Angoulême; and his first Queen, Claude de France. Louise had been trained in a hard school. She lost her mother at the age of seven, married when she was twelve, and was widowed at eighteen. Thereafter she devoted all her energies to bringing up her two children. She worked especially for the advancement of her son – her 'Caesar', as she called him. She was appointed Regent in 1515 and 1524, when Francis led his armies to Italy, and even in normal circumstances took an active part in government, especially foreign affairs. Wolsey called her 'the mother and nourisher of peace'. Her death, in 1531, removed a moderating influence at court and opened the way to faction. Francis' sister, Marguerite, is best known as the author of religious poems and of the *Heptaméron*, a collection of stories in the manner of Boccaccio. She came under the influence of Jacques Lefèvre d'Etaples, the great

French humanist and evangelical reformer, and was even suspected of Lutheranism. She certainly protected a number of scholars and preachers from persecution by the Sorbonne and Parlement of Paris, but was never a Lutheran. Her mystical faith was essentially her own; nor did she ever openly repudiate the authority of the Roman Church. Claude de France was renowned for her sweet, charitable, and pious nature. Even if her looks fell short of the King's ideal (she was described as 'strangely corpulent' and had a limp), she gave him no reason to complain on other grounds. Over a period of nine years she gave him seven children: three sons and four daughters. Of these, only two outlived their father: Henry, who succeeded him on the throne, and Marguerite, who became Duchess of Savoy. Eleonor of Portugal, Francis' second Queen, was the sister of his chief rival, the Emperor Charles V. She came to France, in July 1530, after the peace of Cambrai, and was given all honours due to her rank; but she never won a place in the King's heart. At her entry into Paris he stood at an open window with the Duchesse d'Etampes 'devising with her 2 long hours in the sight and face of all the people; which was not a little marvelled at of the beholders'. In 1533 the King's sister told the Duke of Norfolk that no man could be less satisfied with his wife than Francis. 'When he doth lie with her,' she said, 'he cannot sleep; and when he lieth from her, no man sleepeth better.'

The mortality with which the King's family was afflicted was not exceptional. Although the court could count on the best medical services available, it was frequently visited by sickness and death. An outbreak of plague at Blois, in October 1520, caused a near-panic. The King shut himself up in his room and refused to see anyone for fear of catching the disease. Normally, however, he was extraordinarily approachable. The preamble to a royal ordinance of 1523 boasted that 'a greater conglutination, bond and conjunction of true love, pure devotion, cordial harmony and intimate affection have always existed between the Kings of France and their subjects than in any other monarchy or Christian nation'. This may have been propaganda, but access to the court was remarkable free. Anyone who was decently dressed or could claim acquaintance with a

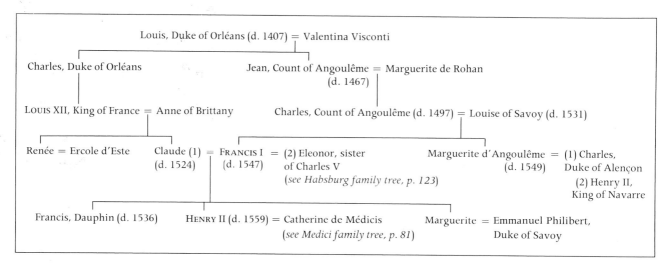

member of the royal entourage was admitted. In November 1530, Francis complained that such people had stolen ornaments from his chapel, silver plate and clothes belonging to himself and others. In future such thefts were to be punished by death regardless of the value of the objects stolen!

Reformers at court

Lutheranism was more successful in France than is commonly realized. It penetrated the kingdom as early as 1519 and despite the Sorbonne's official condemnation in April 1521 soon assumed the dimensions of an epidemic. The King was as much concerned about it as anyone else: he was bound by his coronation oath to defend the Catholic faith and repeatedly expressed his execration of heresy. But this was not always easily recognized in the early days of the French Reformation. As far as the Sorbonne was concerned any deviation from its own scholastic teaching was tantamount to heresy. Christian humanism, as exemplified by the writings of Erasmus or Lefèvre d'Etaples, was as dangerous, in its view, as Lutheranism. But the King was not prepared to endorse this opinion. There were Erasmians among the scholars and preachers of his court, and the Cercle de Meaux, a group of evangelical reformers including Lefèvre d'Etaples, had a powerful advocate at court in the person of the King's own sister, Marguerite.

There were consequently frequent collisions over religion between the King, on the one hand, and the Sorbonne and its ally the Parlement, on the other. In 1523 Francis obtained the release of Louis de Berquin, an aristocratic follower of both Erasmus and Luther, who had been charged with heresy. He also forbade the Parlement to ban Lefèvre's works. As his sister explained, he was determined to show that 'the truth of God is not heresy'. In 1525, however, his captivity enabled the Sorbonne and Parlement to gain the upper hand. A special tribunal was set up to deal with heresy, and censorship was taken further than ever before. The King was kept informed of the situation by Marguerite, who visited him in Spain; but an attempt on his part to protect the Cercle de Meaux was openly defied. Three of its members, Lefèvre, Roussel, and Caroli, fled into exile. In

January 1526, Berquin was again arrested, only to be released after the King's return home, in March. The Meaux exiles also reappeared in France: Lefèvre became royal librarian at Blois, Roussel joined Marguerite's household, and Caroli resumed preaching in Paris. Royal protection, however, was not foolproof. In April 1529, the ecclesiastical authorities took advantage of the King's absence from Paris to attack Berquin for the third time. He was found guilty, condemned to death, and burnt the same day. Despite this setback the King successfully resisted efforts by the Sorbonne and Parlement to determine the religion of his court. In 1530 he foiled an attempt to bring a heresy charge against Jean Du Bellay, Bishop of Bayonne, one of his most liberal councillors, and later successfully defended his own sister.

In Lent, while Francis was absent from Paris, Marguerite and her second husband, the King of Navarre, invited Roussel to preach at the Louvre. His sermons attracted large audiences and reduced the Sorbonniste, François Picart, to despair. 'It's all up with us,' he wrote, 'my chair is deserted. I am left with only a few old women. All the men go to the Louvre!' No record exists of what Roussel actually said in his sermons, but the Sorbonne accused him of preaching heresy and Marguerite and her husband of abetting it. Such impertinence caused Francis to intervene. While Roussel was committed to Marguerite's custody, his opponents were banished from the capital. But this did not end the dispute. In October students of the Collège de Navarre put on a satirical play in which Marguerite was shown receiving the Gospel at the hands of a fury called Mégère (a pun on Gérard Roussel's name), preaching heresy, and persecuting anyone who would not listen to her. The college was promptly searched by the Prévôt de Paris, but only some actors were arrested; the play's author was never found. Soon afterwards Marguerite again came under attack when her poem 'Le miroir de l'âme pécheresse' was included by the Sorbonne in a list of suspect works. Once again her brother intervened and the University had to beat a hasty retreat. It removed the 'Miroir' from the list of suspect works and sent an apology to the King.

The protection given by Francis to certain scholars and preachers is often misunderstood. It has been suggested that he began by tolerating Protestants and only turned against them after his sense of kingship had been offended by the Affair of the Placards of October 1534. This is incorrect. Whilst Francis protected evangelical reformers known to himself and the court, he never tolerated any form of dissent likely to disturb the peace. Thus, in 1527 he urged the Parlement to punish Jacques Pauvant, a young clerk of Meaux, who had insulted the Virgin, and, in June 1528, he reacted strongly to the mutilation of a statue of the Virgin and Child in Paris. He offered a large reward for information about the culprits, paid for a new silver statue, and led his courtiers in an expiatory procession to the scene of the sacrilege. Francis was hostile not only to iconoclasm, but also to sacramentarianism, the doctrine which treats the Eucharist not as a sacrifice but as a commemoration. If Protestantism in France began as a Lutheran movement, it soon turned to Zwingli rather than to Luther for inspiration, a shift of allegiance exemplified by the career of Guillaume Farel, Calvin's predecessor in Geneva. With this change-over to a more radical form of Protestantism, the borderline between orthodoxy and dissent became clearer and the King was better able to assert his orthodoxy unequivocally.

In 1534 the Reformation demonstrated its strength in France in a dramatic way. On 18 October Parisians found *placards* or broadsheets posted up in a number of public places. Written by Antoine Marcourt, a French Protestant exile, and printed at Neuchâtel in Switzerland, the *placards* were a violent denunciation of the doctrine of the Mass. Similar *placards* turned up at the same time in about five provincial towns and in the château of Amboise, where the King was residing at the time. One was allegedly found on the door of his bedchamber, and another in the pouch where he kept his handkerchiefs. Government reaction was swift and savage. Many suspects were rounded up and several executed. On 13 January 1535, however, copies of a heretical treatise on the Eucharist, probably also by Marcourt, were found scattered in the streets of Paris. This second act of defiance prompted the King to order a huge procession in Paris, on 21 January, partly as an expiation, partly as a demonstration of Catholic solidarity.

Contemporaries acclaimed the procession as the finest that had ever been seen in Paris. More relics were carried than ever before, including the Crown of Thorns which was normally kept in the Sainte Chapelle, and the court figured prominently among the participants. The King's three sons and the Duke of Vendôme carried the canopy over the Blessed Sacrament, and Francis walked behind it, bare-headed and holding a lighted torch. As he passed by, people in the crowd called out to him: 'Sire, do justice well!' to whom he replied with a gesture indicating that they could depend upon him. At Notre Dame he was joined for High Mass by the Queen and his daughters, who had watched the procession from a house opposite. Afterwards the royal family was entertained to a banquet at the episcopal palace and the King made a speech calling on everyone to denounce heretics, even if they happened to be friends or relatives. That same day six were burnt, but the King did not light the faggots, as was once supposed. This was followed by another wave of persecution that lasted till May. Among the martyrs was a chorister of the King's chapel who had allegedly put up the placards in the château of Amboise on the night of 17 October.

From 1534 onwards there was less friction between the King and the Sorbonne. But even after the King's death the Faculty's theologians were apt to take offence easily. On learning that Du Chastel had said in the King's funeral oration that his soul had gone straight to heaven, they promptly sent a deputation to the court to protest against this heresy. Anticipating their theological arguments, the late King's steward tried to reassure them with the following words: 'I can assure you of one thing, I who knew him [Francis] better than anyone: that is that he was not disposed to remain a long time in the same place, as agreeable as it might be. Thus, messieurs, if he went to purgatory, believe that he would scarcely have remained there, and that he would only have drunk a cup in passing.'

The heart of Francis I *was placed in a stone casket designed by
Pierre Bontemps, in the abbey of Saint-Denis. His body lies nearby in
a more splendid tomb by Philibert de l'Orme. (120)*

PIETAS

Six

THE AUSTRIAN HABSBURGS
The dynasty as a political institution

❋

R. J. W. EVANS

OURTS, IN THE POPULAR CONCEPTION, are usually associated with spectacle, pomp, exclusiveness, artistic effect. All these things belonged to their nature, but we need first to see the context which made possible, indeed demanded, the ostentation and aloofness. 'Court' in centuries past, like 'government' today, is not a precise word; it connotes two main ideas: the abstract totality of those serving a ruler, and the physical area occupied by the ruler. Neither element was fully stable: personalities could change, and so could locations. What held things together was ultimately the monarch alone, and thus – for any continuity to be given – the ruling dynasty. A court was a dynasty viewed as institution.

The Austrian court occupied a peculiar place during the sixteenth century. The Habsburgs were an international family with vast possessions in Europe and beyond. From the 1520s their realm became split between two brothers, Charles and Ferdinand: Charles ruled in Spain and all the Spanish dominions, and in Germany as Holy Roman Emperor; Ferdinand took over the old heartlands of the house (modern Austria) which were, nonetheless, formally part of the Empire, and, from 1526, Bohemia and Hungary, or as much of the latter as was free of the Turks and a local rival king. In 1558, with Ferdinand's succession as Emperor, his branch of the dynasty established itself in the central European territories. The Habsburg background was wholly cosmopolitan, and the dynasty itself, reigning locally as kings, dukes, margraves, or counts, formed the only permanent link between its various lands. Its court had the task not only of executing a sovereign will, but of binding together very disparate possessions.

The focal point of the Austrian duchies and, to some extent, of the neighbouring Alpine provinces, was Vienna

(though Graz, Innsbruck, even Linz were rivals); Prague, a greater city, was the unchallenged historic capital of Bohemia; Hungary, as a virtual rump, had no obvious centre, Pressburg (Pozsony, nowadays Bratislava), on the Danube below Vienna, serving as its metropolis. The German Reich was just as amorphous, its affairs being decided at several places, notably Frankfurt, Regensberg and Augsburg. The Habsburgs inherited, not one establishment, but a number of heterogeneous ones. In fact they brought little conscious pressure towards unity. After 1564 Ferdinand's three sons maintained separate courts with very extensive autonomy. Much the same happened with the offspring of Maximilian II, who married his cousin Maria, the daughter of Charles V, in 1548. They included the next two Emperors, Rudolf II and Matthias, although the principle of primogeniture gradually gained recognition. The Imperial crown fell next to Ferdinand II, from the Styrian line, a grandson of Ferdinand I, but Innsbruck continued in the hands of younger members of the family until 1665. Thus Habsburg rule only became concentrated during the long reign of Leopold I (1658–1705), and then only because of a progressive want of kinsmen, which was to lead by 1740 to the extinction of the house in male descent.

Leopold was also perhaps the first to make a definitive choice of Vienna as his residence. Ferdinand I and Maximilian II used it as the base for frequent travels. Rudolf II, most sedentary of monarchs, settled from 1583 in Prague: he chose a more vigorous city in a more prosperous region, and his immediate ancestors were buried under its cathedral. Ferdinand II had Styrian roots; brought up in Graz, he later built himself a mausoleum there. His son, Ferdinand III, was still too embroiled in the Empire and its wars to devote much attention to his Viennese surroundings. The ground, however, was well prepared. Vienna had been part of the Habsburg patrimony since 1282. Lying within the province of Lower Austria, it never enjoyed the same distinct identity as Prague or the German Imperial cities. Its senate and mayor were closely overseen by the local nobility and the Habsburgs' own representatives. It could easily accommodate itself to the dictates of an expanding court; indeed its livelihood depended on the monarch's presence.

The Holy Roman Emperor was formally elected by seven German princes, but by the middle of the sixteenth century the title had become virtually hereditary in the Habsburg family, who ruled the Empire in addition to their own considerable territories in central Europe. This miniature by Georg Hoefnagel shows Rudolf II, in 1599, surrounded by six of the electors. He himself, as King of Bohemia, was the seventh. (121)

Maximilian II *with his wife, the daughter of Charles V, and their three younger children. The artist was Arcimboldo, better known for his 'surrealist' paintings done for Maximilian's successor Rudolf.* (122)

The Imperial aura that grew up around Vienna owed as much to the weakness of the town's own traditions as it did to the exploits of the ruling house.

Hence we find a process of consolidation, accompanied by victories for Habsburg sovereignty over particular interests. In central Europe, as elsewhere, local organs of self-government were in decline. Although this was always a two-sided process – a change in the character and outlook of the noble estates rather than a direct assault on the regions – it went with the conception of Imperial power as absolute. The court was the notional centre of everything: of preferment in Church and society; of law and its implementation; of professions and guilds; of universities and publishing. However, while every subject owed his position in some way to the grace of the ruler, he nevertheless had his own rights as member of this or that corporate entity. The Habsburgs were always first movers and could intervene to grant privileges (even such things as university degrees), but only in terms of the whole organic system with its mutual safeguards and unwritten traditions.

At the same time the series of practical functions which the court embodied had not yet taken on a physical existence of its own. Administration and decision-making were still set within the Imperial purlieus: Vienna's Hofburg or Prague's Hradschin. Offices of state, 'ministries' which

outgrew the immediate embrace of the ruler and acquired bureaucratic values of their own, only developed in the eighteenth century. Thus the early modern Habsburg court, or rather fusion of courts, lay at the intersection of two evolutions: the rise of royal government at the expense of local powers and jurisdictions; and the decline of the royal household as source of this central authority in favour of modern institutions. Before the reign of Ferdinand I the task of monarchy was less complex; after Leopold I its implementation became less and less aulic in character. Add to this the union of diverse territories under one ruler, and it is clear how crucial was the role of the court in the polity of Austria.

The machinery of a multi-national court

The basic duties of the Imperial household were entrusted to four officers. Senior among them stood the High Steward (Obersthofmeister), charged with the general running of affairs, and having control not least over kitchen and cellar. The Marshal (Obersthofmarschall) exercised jurisdiction over courtiers, including foreign representatives, with the power to resolve disputes among them. He also arranged accommodation when the entourage travelled. The Chamberlain (Oberstkämmerer), with his symbolic key of office, ordered the affairs of the privy chamber, overseeing both the largely honorific retinue of Junkers attached to it and more active servants of the Imperial person, such as his jester. To him fell, naturally enough, the reception of envoys and the granting of audiences. Finally the Master of the Horse (Oberststallmeister) maintained, besides the stable, those who waited on the ruler's table. He was bound to attend his master on any journey, walking or riding alongside the carriage.

These dignitaries were evidently not adequate to wider administrative needs. Hence, from the early sixteenth century, separate court departments grew up under the Imperial aegis. At the highest level of decision-making stood the privy council, a body of close advisers to the sovereign, usually headed by the High Steward. In theory the privy council met daily to transact the immediate business of the Crown; in fact it soon grew too unwieldy for that purpose. The executive authority of the Empire was vested in a chancery, directed by a vice-chancellor (its nominal head was the Archbishop of Mainz). The Emperor's powers as fount of justice were interpreted by a group of aulic councillors (Reichshofrat). Financial affairs, above all the management of Crown estates and dues, fell to a treasury (Hofkammer). Organization of Imperial military forces passed to a war council (Hofkriegsrat) and a number of subsidiary bodies.

All these institutions were originally intended to serve the Holy Roman Empire. In some measure they continued to exercise a real function there; religious friction in Germany and the rise of autonomous territorial states did not eliminate Habsburg influence until much later. But the tension, implicit in their names, between Empire (Reich) and court (Hof) was genuine and growing. Some parts of the machinery, above all the treasury, came to have competence exclusively for the Habsburgs' own lands. Others were subdivided to take account of the realities of the·situation:

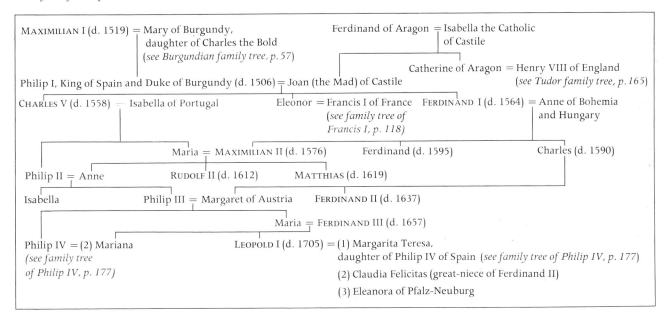

thus a separate Austrian chancery developed after 1620 which gradually assumed in addition the duties of supreme court. The war council and its subordinates tended, not surprisingly, to operate best where the Habsburg military presence was strongest, along the Ottoman front.

At the same time the bodies described so far had no authority *de jure* in Bohemia or Hungary. Bohemia belonged in some shadowy way to the Empire, but its internal affairs, like those of Hungary, were regulated by native servants of the Crown, as befitted two proud and ancient kingdoms. Of course the Habsburgs' powers as kings were very considerable from 1526 (Ferdinand I's accession) onwards, but the ruling structures of the lands of St Wenceslas and St Stephen still constituted a quite distinct establishment until the reforms of the eighteenth century. That proved true of Bohemia even after its abortive revolt in 1618–20: the Thirty Years' War and the collapse of Protestantism there brought radical changes which were hardly matched in government. But while the old estates survived, the High Burgrave of Prague, the chancellor, judges, councillors – all now became overtly royal nominees. The centre of gravity of political life shifted from Bohemia to Vienna, but its performers were still courtiers in the old mould. And the essence of the situation was still juxtaposition, not integration, whatever the dynasty might have wished. Members of the Bohemian chancery, for example, although they might live in Vienna (Fischer von Erlach built them a grandiose new palace at the beginning of the eighteenth century) asserted their continued independence of the Imperial Marshal in any matter of discipline. As for Hungary, its affairs remained turbulent, and even loyalists like the Esterházy or Pálffy families resisted the attempt to encroach on traditional forms of administration. In the seventeenth century, no less than in the nineteenth, we must remember that Hungarian politicians acknowledged a king as their ruler, never an Emperor.

The Habsburg court was then, first and foremost, a political centrepiece in the diverse realms of central Europe.

How many people did it employ? We can derive some idea from the lists of fixed personnel known as *Hofstaats*. In 1636 there were about six hundred attached to the various departments, ranging from councillors and chamberlains (about a hundred), through secretaries and clerks (about eighty), to scullions, messengers, and members of the palace guard. Beyond them came a larger floating population, unsalaried and probably uninvited: casual employees, factors and traders, informants and observers.

In fact the dividing-line between regular and irregular attendance could never be precise; therein lay much of the allure of the court. It presented an intriguing blend of the formal and informal, the aloof and the open-handed. The dynasty had notoriously acquired an austere code of manners from its Burgundian and Spanish ancestors, with niggling rules for preparing petitions and the rest. That went with a tendency to sobriety of dress and a certain unmistakable lack of humour; very few of the Habsburgs were ever unrestrainedly gay, at least in public, and there is little sign in their private dealings of spontaneous delight, though the correspondence of Leopold provides an exception. Yet their arrangements could be surprisingly flexible, and the domestic habits of most of them were frugal, even Spartan. No important Habsburg ever died of excess food or drink. Even the outsider might on occasion feel close to his sovereign. Rudolf in particular turned many conventions on their head. The system, however rooted in tradition, offered real opportunities to the ambitious.

The social character of the court

This 'system' is anyway not easy to define. Certainly no single group or ethos dominated the court. Of course the nobility enjoyed an entrenched position. Office-holding had long been balanced within the privileged orders of society: magnates assumed the greater dignities, being stewards or marshals, lieutenants in Bohemia or in the Austrian provinces; lesser nobles occupied as of right certain other political and legal positions. During the sixteenth and seventeenth centuries the aristocracy laid claim to more and more sinecure preferments at court, a miscellaneous aristocracy bound to the ruling house through grants of Imperial title. By the reign of Leopold the privy council had become almost a club for a few interrelated families, while the long list of honorary chamberlains embraced any count of the Holy Roman Empire who bothered to raise the money for his ceremonial golden key.

High nobility was undoubtedly secure at the top of the Baroque hierarchy of ranks. Yet it enjoyed no monopoly of influence. Careers were open to commoner talent throughout the period, especially in the earlier years. Maximilian II took many trusted servants from the middle, even the lower, classes: Zasius, Seld, Weber, Viehäuser. The obscure, but highly intelligent, petty noble Wolf Rumpf guided Rudolf's counsels for many years, and several low-born *arrivistes* – by no means so contemptible a crew as history, following contemporary hearsay, has readily assumed – found their way to the heart of that unorthodox Emperor. Throughout the seventeenth century all important heads of the Austrian chancery were commoners: Verda, Prickelmayr, Hocher, Strattmann. Lawyers, like priests, discovered channels of advancement in Vienna. Moreover control of finances never really fell into noble hands: members of the treasury were recruited from many sources; loans were provided by burghers like Lazarus Henckel, then increasingly by loyal Jews. The names of Meizl and Bassevi from the early part of the seventeenth century, Oppenheimer and Wertheimer from its end, point to the significance of these contacts. Indeed the dynasty showed personal regard for individual Jews, as it did for individual Protestants before 1620, though the logic of its evolution, as we shall see, was to turn the court into a bastion of Catholicism.

The Habsburg entourage, then, displayed elements of a bourgeois and commercial standard. It had not, however, reached the stage of true bureaucracy or proper economic management. Administration was still inefficient, its procedures ill-defined. Successful officials passed easily into the ranks of the upper nobility. During the seventeenth century it became difficult for intellectuals to meet the higher echelons of court on equal terms, still more so to realize any proposals, as the Cameralist writers Becher, Hörnigk, and Schröder found in the 1670s and 1680s, when they urged a reform programme on the dynasty.

Nor – to take a third set of values beside the noble and the bureaucratic – was the court in Vienna or Prague of markedly military persuasion. Evidently the power of the Habsburgs rested in part on control over an army. Their troops fought the Turks in Hungary again and again after 1526, while the seeds of a standing army and an international officer corps are to be found in the important but forgotten conflict around the year 1600, when Ottoman dominance was first shaken. A cosmopolitan band of generals – Piccolomini, Marradas, Leslie, Bucquoy, Butler, Aldringen, are names at random – served the Emperor with brutal skill during the Thirty Years' War, and their families received plentiful signs of the sovereign's favour. The war council represented a strong pressure-group, for all the devolution of functions to which its creaking apparatus

Thirteen Emperors *of the house of Habsburg figure on the bowl of a goblet made at Augsburg in 1645. At the top are Charles V and Ferdinand III. To the right there follow (not in chronological order) Ferdinand I, Rudolf II, Matthias, Ferdinand II, and Maximilian II. The portraits are in shell relief. In the centre: the four virtues, Piety, Fortitude, Liberality, and Temperance. (123)*

The city of Prague *including the Hradschin Castle: a mosaic picture in 'pietra dura' by the Italian artist Giovanni Castruccio, working at Rudolf's court about 1600. (124)*

Rudolf takes the waters *at a spa near Prague. The Emperor is in the centre, wearing red breeches. The painting, one of a series showing court amusements, is by Lucas van Valckenborch. (125)*

The great hall of the Hradschin Castle *of Prague was like an indoor market. Around its walls booksellers and printsellers had set up stalls. It comes as a surprise to realize how public most royal courts were, at least until the end of the eighteenth century. Painting by Aegidius Sadeler. (126)*

Jan Brueghel's allegory of the Sense of Sight *evokes the fantastic world of the Emperor Rudolf II, with its accumulation of jewellery, works of art, and instruments of science. The nymph leaning on a table is gazing at a picture of the 'Healing of the Blind Man', held up to her by a Cupid. The room is full of paintings and statues, both classical and modern, many by Rubens and his school – portraits of archdukes, Silenus, etc. On the tables and on the floor are strewn jewels, coins, and optical instruments. An ape wearing glasses examines a seascape. Through the door can be seen further vistas, with peacocks and buildings. This is one of a series representing the Five Senses which exists in many versions. (127)*

Clocks *were one of Rudolf's passions. None is more extraordinary than this one in the form of a ship, made in silver gilt at Augsburg, about 1580. Rudolf himself is represented standing in the stern, surrounded again by the six other German electors. (128)*

In a Tyrolean castle *overlooking Innsbruck the Archduke Ferdinand, brother of Maximilian II, brought together a bizarre collection of curios, works of art, scientific specimens, and freaks of nature. The castle is Schloss Ambras, and the collection is still intact, although at Ferdinand's death it was, characteristically, taken by Rudolf for himself. Shown here are Ferdinand's chess set, a 'trompe l'œil' painting of a medieval book, and two goblets, one made from a coconut shell. (129)*

Rudolf's crown *symbolized his triple royalty. He was Holy Roman Emperor, King of Hungary, and King of Bohemia. Three of the reliefs in the centre show the three coronations which consecrated him sovereign of these realms. Made in the Imperial workshops in Prague in 1602 and surmounted by a giant sapphire, the crown is among the masterpieces of the court goldsmiths, but it was in fact never used at a coronation. (130)*

succumbed (there was a separate command in Styria and local initiatives continually reasserted themselves on the Hungarian front). Yet no privileged caste of soldiers emerged. No Austrian Habsburg until the days of Joseph II (1780–90) really admired the military profession. Ferdinand II, however belligerent his convictions, left the fighting to lieutenants and to the confidently awaited intervention of heavenly powers. His son Ferdinand III, able enough on the field of Nördlingen in 1634, was too sophisticated to enjoy the life of camp and combat. Rudolf and Leopold felt a profound distaste for the actual business of war, the latter to the point of personal faintheartedness when the Turks besieged Vienna in 1683. Rudolfine Prague was unrewarding territory for ambitious generals; Hermann Rusworm, who alone gained the unreserved trust of the Emperor, found no clemency when sentenced to be executed for the murder of a fellow-officer in a brawl. The one Habsburg who made a career with the army, Ferdinand III's brother Leopold William, proved an unmitigated disaster.

The court regarded soldiering as an unpalatable necessity, and only welcomed its practitioners when they took on the more refined guise of landed proprietor or even intellectual. Many of the *condottieri* of the Thirty Years' War joined the Austro-Bohemian establishment on those terms. One reason for the mistrust was the Wallenstein affair of the 1630s. Albrecht Wallenstein, greatest and most self-willed of the war-lords, never really belonged among the intimates of the Emperor. He built up an essentially rival organization, with all the trimmings of an alternative court, centred in Bohemia. No pure outsider could have used his contacts and local expertise as did this member of the prominent Czech Waldstein family. His treachery and assassination left a lasting imprint on the character of the Habsburg court, as well as accentuating its estrangement from Prague, which had already begun. The two generals who later rose highest under the dynasty presented a far less martial face: Raimondo Montecuccoli (1609–80), long-time president of the war council, a subtle, well-mannered Italian, and the attractive Prince Eugene of Savoy, least pugnacious of men in his private life. They followed the model set by Maximilian's friend Lazarus Schwendi (1522–84), humanist commander and proponent of religious tolerance.

Thus no single class or set of standards dictated the atmosphere of the Austrian court. And what is true of social groupings holds also for individuals: no single person wielded the authority of the all-powerful favourite elsewhere. Central European history knows no Richelieu or Olivares, no Buckingham or Oxenstierna. One principal reason for this again lies in a general disposition of the dynasty. It was, by and large, remarkably hard-working and clung, however misguidedly, to a strict code of personal responsibility. Even Rudolf II, seeking prolonged solace in his laboratory or gallery, did not entirely neglect the affairs of state; rather his dilatoriness sprang from a dissatisfaction with the way those affairs were moving. His successors rarely took a day away from the minutiae of government. Nor were women crucial in the inner councils. The three Ferdinands and Leopold seem quite spotless in devotion to their undemanding consorts; Maximilian II and Matthias

Rudolf's army *swears fealty to him in 1611. The illustration is from Heinrich Hiesserle von Chodaw's 'Reiss-Buch'. (131)*

perhaps a little less so, but not markedly aberrant. Rudolf alone demonstrated open promiscuity; he at least had the excuse of bachelordom, and the women he gave himself to played no part either in politics or in society. More significant were one or two of the Empresses, especially the formidable Eleonora Gonzaga, dowager after the death of Ferdinand III, an Italian *grande dame* almost on the lines of the Médicis in Paris. Even she held no real power, though her own court enlivened the culture of Leopoldine Vienna.

The century between 1560 and 1660, however, that great age of the European *valido*, left its mark on the Habsburg household. It witnessed a string of major political figures, having the ear of the Emperor and aspiring to a plenitude of influence. First Rudolf, departing from the open counsel kept by his father and grandfather, leaned heavily on Rumpf and his court marshal Trautson, until he suddenly turned about and dismissed them both in 1600. Rumpf's hold had never been complete, though rumours were rife as to its nature, and Rudolf's moodiness meant that no one could be sure of his place. Matthias, by contrast, held firmly

133

The Emperor dines *in Prague with his leading courtiers. Rudolf is at the head of the table to the left. Next to him sits his uncle, the Archduke Ferdinand (the owner of Schloss Ambras). Food is served from a table on the right, while another table bears an elaborate display of plate, including a centrepiece in the shape of a ship. Note too the orchestra on the extreme right. (132)*

to one adviser, both before and after he took over government from his brother: Melchior Khlesl, bishop and cardinal, son of a Viennese tradesman, was the only Austrian cleric to play such a role. A shrewd and tenacious negotiator, he nevertheless exhausted himself in a remarkably successful campaign to revive the local Roman Catholic Church and scarcely saw beyond these horizons. Ferdinand II, a far more pious ruler than his ageing cousin, cast Khlesl aside in favour of a secular confidant, Hans Ulrich von Eggenberg (1568–1634), more a friend than a minister, upon whom the Emperor relied so much that he would pay daily visits to Eggenberg's lodgings when the latter fell sick. Others followed Eggenberg: Maximilian von Trautmannsdorf, Ferdinand III's plenipotentiary at the Peace of Westphalia; Johann Weikhard von Auersperg; Johann Ferdinand von Portia; Václav Eusebius Lobkovic – who each enjoyed a progressively shorter period of dominance. After the sudden disgrace of Lobkovic in 1674 no one person was to wield a like authority until the days of Wenzel Kaunitz.

Whereas no Emperor quite surrendered his freedom of political action, there were plenty of material rewards for the fortunate few. Payment to high officials was hardly regularized and could not cover the cost of semi-permanent residence at court. Instead they might receive *ad hominem* grants of land and money. Eggenberg affords a spectacular

example: a man of recent bourgeois extraction, he took over gigantic estates in the fertile south of Bohemia, together with a princely title. He was able to build a pompous Late Renaissance castle on the outskirts of Graz, as did Portia in his home province of Carinthia. Others compensated themselves in less approved ways. The levels of corruption acceptable to contemporary Europe were certainly exceeded at Rudolf's court, where large sums of money became necessary to secure audience, even at times from ambassadors and special envoys of foreign states. Later a vast fraud was discovered in the treasury, by which its president, Count Sinzendorf (d. 1680), had profited for years at the public expense.

With operators like Sinzendorf at work it is hardly surprising that the pay of lesser servants of the Crown often fell into arrears. Secretaries and heralds, artists and musicians might pass months or years without remuneration, surviving on the perquisites in kind which went with a fixed attachment to the court. When Rudolf sank into his last illness some of his instrumentalists were heard playing solemn melodies. Surely they should not anticipate the death of His Majesty? 'On the contrary,' retorted their leader, 'how can we be gay when we haven't been able to afford a square meal for months?' Their protest proved effective.

Overall, the most striking feature of this Habsburg court was its heterogeneity, the varied backgrounds and standpoints of its members. That in itself militated against lasting factions: rather we find a plethora of particular interests, spiced with temporary coalitions, like those which fought out the battle between Wallenstein and his critics. Only under Leopold were more consistent 'parties' formed, especially over the issue of the French alliance. Plurality of languages accompanied plurality of countries. The

134

By the time of Leopold I *the court had moved to Vienna and banquets were likely to be more lavish. Here the Emperor and Empress sit at the head of the left-hand section, and the scene is brightly lit by candles – on the table, round the walls, and on the chandelier. (133)*

sixteenth- and seventeenth-century Emperors showed considerable linguistic prowess; Maximilian II, for instance, learned good Czech and even some Hungarian. The main vehicles for court business were Latin and German, supplemented by Spanish and later, increasingly, Italian for refined intercourse. Rudolf conversed equally allusively in at least four tongues; Leopold wrote illegibly in three. Indeed, both ministers and scribes tended to acquire a macaronic vocabulary, mixing German constructions with Latin terminology, German circumlocution with Italian repartee. Meanwhile the official language of Bohemian departments was Czech until after 1620, and Magyar might be called for to expedite not only the business of Hungarian chancery and treasury, but also correspondence with the Turkish authorities at Buda.

The spiritual consolidation of an empire

The picture so far presented of an outward-looking court, open to many influences, must, however, be qualified. It holds true more for the sixteenth century than the seventeenth. Ferdinand I, Maximilian II, and – in his idiosyncratic way – Rudolf displayed a more genuinely cosmopolitan outlook than their successors. The change is reflected in the more settled Viennese life of the later rulers. The reigns of Ferdinand and Maximilian were spent in almost ceaseless travelling, with Vienna, so remote from Germany, so exposed to the Ottoman menace, merely a convenient resting-place. Rudolf flouted convention by going to dwell within the old stronghold of the Hussite heretics, choosing to recall the great epoch of Emperor Charles IV of Luxembourg. From the time of Ferdinand II court progresses, with their ever more elaborate protocol, grew less frequent: the Imperial coronation and an occasional diet in Germany; irregular visits to Bohemia, where the residence in Prague

was gradually abandoned; a little chivvying of the Hungarian estates at Pressburg, which, just forty miles down the river, was almost on home ground. Now the leisure resources of Lower Austria began to be exploited, a ring of gardens and *Lustschlösser* south and west of the capital: the Prater, with its woods and meadows; the elaborate Neugebäude, begun by Maximilian, destroyed by the Turks in 1683; Ebersdorf and Laxenburg; the Favorita palace of Empress Eleonora; the first diminutive Schönbrunn. Fewer Czechs and Hungarians were to be seen, either in them, or in the corridors of the Hofburg.

Along with this went the impact of the social evolution of the seventeenth century: the consolidation of a loyal, titled Imperial nobility at the expense of the other orders. Aristocratic families, local or foreign, which benefited from the Bohemian and German, then the Hungarian, wars gathered around the dynasty, lending it a more closed, exclusive character. The traditional privilege of being a courtier was that of enhanced legal status. Any accredited servant of the Crown carried about with him the right of exemption from arrest, from local taxes, and so forth; and this remained important – it was used by merchants and scholars as well as diplomats in the Habsburg retinue. But its basis was weakening, as new forces, including Roman law, worked to rationalize the judicial structure. By 1700 attachment to the court came to look much more like social

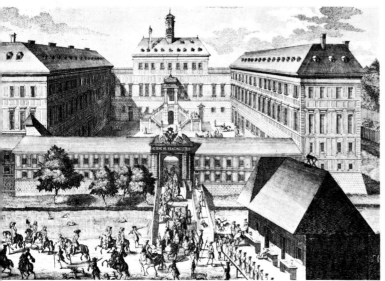

Two palaces *built by Leopold I in and near Vienna are typical of the contrast between the new capital and the old. The engravings are by S. Kleiner. Top: the Favorita, home of his third wife, Eleonora, on the outskirts of the city, and (below) Ebersdorf, a country palace just outside it.(134,135)*

prestige alone; and conversely the notion gained ground that only certain social groupings might enter the Imperial sanctum, seeds of the baneful *Hoffähigkeit* which so isolated Francis Joseph.

The change we are here seeking to apprehend amounts to the rise of an orthodoxy. It is part of the vital development whereby Protestantism was eliminated in central Europe and Counter-Reformation imposed. At the root of the process lies the religious affiliation of the Habsburg court, the dynasty's espousal of a failing Catholic cause. During the sixteenth century the Emperors were only lukewarm for Rome: Ferdinand I held firmly enough to its teachings, though he pressed the Pope for concessions over the lay

chalice and priestly marriage; Maximilian II did not openly dissent, but he kept his own conscience and persecuted no one; Rudolf combined moments of apparent spiritual wrath against the sectarians with wild invective directed at the Holy See and all its works. Many Protestants took office – often there was no substitute for them. Nevertheless all three rulers preserved a largely Catholic court. The old hierarchical Church, now suppliant, seemed a better option than variegated, intemperate Protestantism, with its tinge of Hussite fire and Calvinist dissent.

After 1600 a new generation came to power. It began with Matthias who, helped by Khlesl, had built up the nucleus of a Counter-Reformation court at Vienna while still merely Rudolf's representative there, before usurping the place of his brother in the rest of the Habsburg lands. But Matthias was a temporizer in whom ambition outweighed conviction; he owed his new position to the backing of Protestant estates, hence he could make no full identification of dynasty and Roman Church. He was outflanked by his cousins in Styria, who used the same tactics. The future Ferdinand II collected together his own fiercely Catholic court at Graz, to amalgamate it – when his time arrived – with the existing Imperial structure. The victory on the White Mountain over the Bohemian insurgents (1620) then confirmed him in his resolve and his slogan: heresy equals disloyalty. The Habsburg *imperium* must embody the principles of Catholicism: unity, hierarchy, piety, mystery. At its summit stands the orthodox court, the overseer of general purity. The significance of this ideal can hardly be exaggerated: it supplied the confidence to a wavering rule; in it is implicated, for better or worse, the Habsburg 'mission' for generations to follow.

The effects at court were immediate. Confessors and other Catholic advisers, especially Jesuits, multiplied. Under Ferdinand II two successive presidents of the treasury were abbots from local monasteries. Devotions proceeded twice daily in the court chapel, and the old offices and ceremonies revived all around the Imperial palace. Now the modern ecclesiastical topography of Vienna took shape: Augustinians and Capucins close by the royal precinct, together favoured as guardians of the earthly remains of all future Habsburgs; Jesuits on the square Am Hof, the original seat of Austria's dukes, and at the university across the city; St Stephen's cathedral raised for the first time to a position of real importance (its incumbent was made a Prince of the Holy Roman Empire in 1631); elsewhere regiments of monks and friars within and outside the walls, some very conspicuously placed, like the Camaldulensian hermits introduced by the Emperor atop the highest outlying summit of the Vienna Woods.

Most celebrated of the early Jesuit confidants at court was Guillaume Lamormaini. Lamormaini well illustrates the nature of this Catholic presence. He did not dominate the thinking of Ferdinand II: the actual influence of clerical politics has often been exaggerated; the Austrian Habsburgs never became puppets of Rome. Rather Rome and its lieutenants recognized their obligation, and ultimately their political subordination, to the Emperor. Lamormaini compiled a testimony, many times reprinted, to the virtues of his

Vienna took shape *in the later seventeenth century (top). The Hofburg, the Emperor's residence and the seat of government, is on the extreme right of the walled city (No. 28). The steeples of the Jesuit and Augustinian churches stand out next to it on the right (Nos. 30 and 31). (136)*

To celebrate the end of the plague, *the Viennese erected a symbolic column in thanksgiving to the Holy Trinity on the Graben in the centre of the old city. It was later replaced by the famous stone column by Peter Strudel, with a pedestal by Fischer von Erlach. (137)*

master, stressing the devoutly Christian government of Ferdinand. The close association of spiritual and material regimes, the *pietas Austriaca*, which definitely reduced the threat of corruption and excess in the aulic sphere, was further propagated by Ferdinand III, then by the Jesuit-educated Leopold. One of its motifs was the well-publicized meekness of the Imperial house, its gratitude for a bestowal of God's mercies. Ferdinand II expressed this in the pilgrimages he instituted to the Styrian votive church of Mariazell, the most solemn official journeys of the court. A later thanksgiving there by Leopold for victory over the Turks was celebrated in print by his librarian Lambeck. His offering after deliverance from the plague of 1679 was yet

grander: the magnificent symbolic column which still stands on the Graben in Vienna. Leopold also extended other public acts of Counter-Reformation piety: sitting at table with some local monks on feast days, and giving with great generosity to the indigent.

Such an atmosphere of open religiosity manifestly exerted great pressure on men to conform. By 1650 very few Protestants remained at court. Even those entitled to reside in Vienna, like the representatives of foreign powers – Holland, Sweden, some German Lutheran princes – found it difficult to arrange services. They tended to retreat to Hungarian territory at Sopron (Ödenburg) where their faith was still tolerated. Conversion became a necessary preliminary to acceptance; princes and scholars, artisans and secretaries showed themselves willing to take the step.

Religion thus complemented the Habsburg state in a peculiarly thorough way. Without the ruler's backing the Catholic cause in central Europe would have been hopeless; now Catholicism gave spiritual support to Imperial sovereignty. The Counter-Reformation introduced a new intellectual authority, but the cultural claims of the Baroque monarchy did not spring from nowhere: they gave a novel twist to a longer evolution. Religion is a bridge which leads us to consider the whole cultural predominance of the court, its growing power over artistic and spiritual life, towns and universities, even the manners of the noble in some distant château. To that context belong even the extraordinary manifestations under Rudolf II.

Though hesitant *at times in their religious loyalties, the Habsburgs never forsook the Roman Catholic Church. Ferdinand I is here shown listening to the papal nuncio in the Augustinerkirche, Vienna, in 1560. Courtiers, monks, and soldiers throng to hear a sermon which makes use of a particularly realistic figure of Christ Crucified. Painting by J. Seisenegger. (138)*

The role was much more than just pomp and circumstance; indeed the circumstances of the Habsburg court could appear distinctly meagre. Vienna before 1683 lacked any kind of finery in its Imperial buildings. The Hofburg, half-castle, half-palace, lay inconspicuously at the edge of the flat expanse of the fortified city, and travellers regularly comment on its modesty. Contemporary views of the town demonstrate well these limitations of site. An observer noted in 1636 that 'the Court of Caesar . . . hath no singular splendor or magnificens, and is somewhat straight for so great a Prince'. As late as 1705 a Frenchman reported: 'the Palace of the Emperor is a small thing, and the building which ought to be the richest of all corresponds in no way to the grandeur of the Master who inhabits it, and bears the title of first Prince of the world. The old courtyard is pitiful. Its walls are as thick as great ramparts, the stairs poor and without ornament, the apartments low and narrow, with ceilings of painted fabric, the floors made of fir-wood, as among the petty-bourgeois.'

Much of the area today consists of monumental eighteenth- and nineteenth-century architecture and only isolated elements preserve the earlier structure: parts of the late medieval chapel and inner courtyard (Schweizerhof), with its Renaissance gateway; the fine arcaded block built for Maximilian II, later turned into stables (Stallburg); the graceful Amalienhof designed for Rudolf II in his first days as Emperor; next to it the Leopold wing with a good façade of the 1670s. Three Gothic churches surround the Hofburg: one (St Michael's) served the courtiers; the others belonged to the Austin and Minorite friars. All are pleasing; nothing in them is showy, unless it be the exquisite vaulting of the Augustinerkirche. Appropriately enough it was the Augustinians who produced the most medieval of court chaplains in this period: the dynamic Abraham a Sancta Clara, who preached with crusading fervour against luxury and decadence within a stone's throw of the Imperial chambers.

Neither dynasty, nor Church, nor high nobility could expand in Vienna until the threat of Turkish occupation was finally banished. The leisure residences and monasteries outside the city remained equally restrained, even Leopold's favourite at Laxenburg, some ten miles to the south. But another reason exists for the paucity of good building earlier: the absence of most of the Imperial retinue in Bohemia during the peaceful and productive years of the late Renaissance. Prague's story was quite different. Here the Habsburgs inherited a grand citadel, the Hradschin (Czech: Hrad), which they beautified in the sixteenth century without changing its character of a massive royal stronghold. Ferdinand I raised an elegant Italian summer palace for his Queen on the far side of the steep castle moat, overlooking the city; his successors added tennis court and riding school, gardens and verandahs. Rudolf in particular, during thirty years of occupation, built the so-called Spanish wing and refurbished some of the interiors, but the rest remained haphazard: a mixture of chanceries, churches, and chambers, private lodgings and public concourses, which must have accommodated a large proportion of his court, even to the artisans housed in the tiny terrace – still intact – which legend has made the street of his alchemists.

After 1620 the rulers depart. Matthias' fine archway leading from the castle square (1615) proved to be an exit, not an entrance. Prague held memories too bitter for him or later Habsburgs to desire more than an occasional sojourn in the great courtyards of the Hradschin. They left the place to their stadholders, though the Bohemian capital was sustained another century or more in its accustomed grandeur by the prosperity of a loyal Church and aristocracy.

The cultural role

The physical conditions of the two main Habsburg centres bear witness to much insecurity and lack of money. Civilization, though, was always thought part of the representative functions of the Emperor. It had been given new stress at the beginning of the sixteenth century by Maximilian I, with his circle of humanists and artists, who tried – above all through Dürer – to reconcile the Italian and German roots of his claim to universal sovereignty. Maximilian's successors were well-educated, sometimes even erudite. Most indulged the traditional passions of ruling houses, particularly the hunt, for which the Vienna Woods offered peculiarly suitable terrain. At the same time they had plenty of opportunity for more elevating intercourse, and we have already noted the vein of solemnity in their character which prevented complete decline into the frivolous.

Certain positions at court were reserved to scholars. Historiographers appear as salaried employees in the *Hofstaats*, and some achieved respectable published work, albeit their chronicles were bound to favour dynastic views and could not probe very deep. A mathematician-cum-astronomer belonged among the regular servants of the Crown. When Tycho Brahe, the outstanding cosmographer of the later sixteenth century, found himself forced to leave Denmark, Rudolf received him in Prague with great warmth. Tycho was indeed supernumerary to the Emperor's establishment – hence the clashes between him and Raimarus Ursus, a mathematician of inferior talent already working at court. But Tycho's younger admirer Johannes Kepler, likewise brought to Prague by material necessity, succeeded Ursus and entered into a real partnership with the infinitely curious ruler from 1600 until 1612. It bore fruit in the *Rudolfine Tables* which, although only published much later, provided the basis for Kepler's discovery of his three laws of planetary motion.

An obvious centre of literary activity was the court library (Hofbibliothek), a celebrated collection which already had some – primitive – copyright arrangements for acquiring books. It attracted several learned curators, and while the Netherlanders Hugo Blotius (1534–1608) and Sebastian Tengnagel (1573–1636) never found close favour with Rudolf (the library remained in Vienna, whence the Emperor would order what he immediately required), Peter Lambeck (1628–79), an acknowledged scholar of north German birth, became the intimate associate of Leopold I. By 1700 the library, shortly to gain a splendid home in Fischer von Erlach's new extension to the Hofburg, had won a considerable erudite reputation, primarily for its manuscript riches.

The fruit *of Rudolf's interest in astronomy was the* Rudolfine Tables, *a record of thousands of systematic observations of planetary motions made by Tycho Brahe and published by Johannes Kepler, who used them to formulate his epoch-making laws, (Ulm, 1627). In this frontispiece the canopy is supported on posts (standing for astronomers), which grow progressively stronger from tree-trunks to classical columns (Copernicus and Tycho Brahe). (139)*

Other talented men might find a post which combined practical and intellectual opportunities. The botanist Carolus Clusius managed the Imperial gardens during the 1570s; the antiquarian Jacopo Strada supervised the Habsburg collections for many years, while profiting from Rudolf's proclivity for his pretty daughter Katherine. Medical training, combined with the right contacts, could bring employment as court physician (there were two categories: *Leibarzt* and *Hofarzt*, but no very obvious distinction). Many intellectuals of the period chose medicine as a career, while pursuing the study of natural philosophy and similarly speculative subjects. Doctors from all over Europe served the Habsburgs. For Rudolf alone the list would include Crato, Dodoens, Alexandrinus, Simon Simonius, three Guarinonis, two Rulands, Steeghius, Maier, Monau, Hájek, all of whom have left some record of scientific work.

Equally some persons of eminence in these spheres belonged to the main administrative and social echelons of the court. Ogier Ghislain de Busbecq, author of the *Turkish Letters*, acted as diplomat to three sixteenth-century Emperors. Two generations of aristocratic Khevenhüllers stood very near their monarchs: George represented Rudolf II in Spain for over thirty years (his fascinating correspondence has never been printed); his nephew, also an ambassador, compiled a gigantic history of Ferdinand II and his times, still our basic source for those momentous events. A number of interpreters and envoys to the Near East began Vienna's reputation in the field of oriental studies.

Certainly it was well for a scholar not to rely on the privy purse for his income – payments were notoriously irregular. He could perhaps combine attendance at court with teaching in the university, as did the prolific humanist Wolfgang Lazius (1514–65). A major part of his reward lay anyway in prestige. The poet hoped to see his eulogies bring him the title of *poeta laureatus*. Commoner intellectuals might achieve a grant of nobility, or even the higher dignity of count palatine which gave miscellaneous privileges like the power to legitimize bastards or award coats of arms to one's friends. Above all the Imperial aura itself offered a reflected glory; it could mean protection, even when no financial help was forthcoming and no contact made with the royal person.

Rudolf II *occupied the Imperial throne for thirty-six years. Adriaen de Vries presents him as a soldier and a leader; in fact he was an eccentric recluse, increasingly withdrawn into a world of ingenious craftsmanship, speculation, and magic.* (141)

Hence the widespread dedication to the Habsburgs of books, some published in Vienna and Prague, more at the leading centres of Germany and Italy. Much of course was merely hopeful flattery, buoyed up at best by the favour of a courtier. Yet the phenomenon is important: such dedications regularly enjoyed some kind of official approval, perhaps an Imperial privilege against plagiarism. They spread the wings of Habsburg patronage far beyond the immediate confines of the Austrian court.

Artists too found encouragement, though rarely great wealth. The portraitist was a standard ornament to any great household of the sixteenth century, and the features of Austrian archdukes were loyally reproduced by a number of pedestrian talents. Jakob Seisenegger now appears the most lively among them, but none stands comparison with the painters in the service of the Spanish branch of the family – Mor or Coello. Rudolf transformed this situation. Absorbed by the mysterious side of life, he sought out all the symbols and allusiveness in which contemporary Mannerism was so fecund. He did not succeed in attracting the most illustrious names; no Titian graced his chambers. But many artists of stature went to Prague: Bartholomaeus Spranger, most gifted of the conventional Mannerists; Hans von Aachen; Joseph Heintz; Giuseppe Arcimboldo; Rolant Savery; Jan Brueghel the Elder; the miniaturist Hoefnagel; the fine engraver Aegidius Sadeler; the sculptor Adriaen de Vries. A few, like Brueghel, did not stay long, but the majority, pampered by their ruler, took root. Arcimboldo enlivened

Artists in rock crystal, *the Miseroni family (above) enjoyed Habsburg patronage for many years, and acted as guardians for Rudolf's treasure.* (140)

Aspects of Rudolf. *Top: 'The Librarian' by Arcimboldo, one of several such fantasy portraits by this artist. Right: 'The Liberation of Hungary', a symbolic painting by Hans von Aachen; it celebrates the defeat of the Turks at Raab (Gyor) in 1598. Above: the Dodo, by Rolant Savery, one of Rudolf's natural history commissions. Below right: 'Rudolf II's Victory over the Turks', an allegory by Bartholomaeus Spranger with Rudolf in the role of Jupiter. (142–45)*

the earlier years of the reign with his famous surrealist portraits; Spranger married into a local burgher family and dominated the artists' guild in the city; we find Aachen, equally subtle as painter and as personality, in the toils of Imperial diplomacy.

In two further artistic fields Rudolfine Prague more than matched any rival European centre. The first was the production of applied art: works such as flagons, bowls, and dishes, salt-cellars and inlaid tables, clocks and mechanical toys, so characteristic of the late sixteenth century. These are objects of elaborate fantasy and great beauty. Their creators, mostly ordinary artisans, received much stimulus from the Emperor, who himself studied their techniques. The inventor of Bohemian cut-glass, for example, gained patents to promote his craft; the cleverest manipulators of rock crystal, an Italian family called Miseroni, became for several generations guardians of the treasures stored in the Hradschin.

They were thus custodians of another remarkable artistic achievement of Rudolf II: his collection. All the major artists of Renaissance and Mannerism appeared in it; no effort was spared to acquire their work. What a veritable distillation of European masterpieces adorned the walls of the Imperial palace! Yet how few outsiders could ever penetrate that fortress which surrounded the suspicious monarch. Dürer and Pieter Brueghel, Correggio and Tintoretto belonged among the Emperor's particular favourites. They hung in strange circumstances indeed, as modern taste would judge; for the Prague collection made no basic distinction between the wonders of art and those of nature. Curiosities of all kinds: exotica, stones, relics, antique sculptures, joined the canvases and automata, manuscripts and mosaics. *Multum in parvo*; the secret harmony of the universe: explanations of this mania for accumulated diversity do not belong to the present context. Suffice it to say that other courts of Europe indulged the same fascination for *Kunst- und Wunderkammern* on a lesser scale. Rudolf's own uncle Ferdinand assembled similar miscellaneous riches at his castle of Ambras in the Tyrol. When he died, a bitter family feud broke out about the ownership of certain items, notably an agate dish and the supposed horn of a unicorn which were prized possessions of the dynasty.

Patronage of the fine arts declined somewhat after the death of Rudolf. Wars militated against it. So did an inevitable reaction against the more eccentric fancies of the great Maecenas. Most of his artists melted away. His collections fell into neglect, along with the fine gardens and menagerie he had constructed in Prague. Part of his picture gallery was dispersed, or seized as plunder by the Swedes. But the trend was not decisive. Ferdinand II's son Leopold William amassed another impressive corpus of paintings and employed David Teniers as his personal artist. Ironically the best native talent emerged in the seventeenth century among the Czechs: the unjustly neglected school of Škréta and Brandl.

In other ways too the cultural sphere continued to develop, especially under the highly sensitive Leopold I. Now the visual arts played a supporting role as Emperors showed an increasing predilection for literature and music.

Both had a solid foundation from earlier reigns: Ferdinand I maintained the Spanish poet Cristóbal de Castillejo (d. 1550) as his secretary; the courts of Maximilian and Rudolf included composers whose reputation has become better established in recent years – Philippe de Monte, Hans Leo Hassler, Jacques Regnart, Jakob Handl (Gallus), Kryštof Harant of Polžice. Ferdinand II kept a staff of eighty musicians in 1636, despite the pressures of war. Leopold and his father Ferdinand III were active at versifying and composition; we have no reason to doubt the authenticity of works ascribed to them. Their protégés were brought mainly from Italy; the language and idiom of the Seicento – Roman and Venetian – determined the artistic atmosphere at court. Few of their names are remembered today, except for the organists Froberger, Pachelbel, and Kerll, though the stock of some others may yet rise again: the composer Johann Heinrich Schmelzer (d. 1680) for example, or the indefatigable Kapellmeister Antonio Draghi (d. 1700) who prepared more than two hundred large-scale pieces for Leopold. Each played his modest part in a larger enterprise: the seventeenth-century Baroque entertainment.

The most obvious constituent of these festivities was opera, brought to Vienna by pupils of Monteverdi, the works of Francesco Cavalli and Marc'Antonio Cesti becoming especially popular. But much else belonged: pageant, decoration, scenic invention, literary tribute, learned allusion, religious devotion. The whole public life of the dynasty – three different coronations (Imperial, Bohemian, Hungarian), homage, births, weddings, burials – was elaborated, presented as a gigantic fresco or apotheosis. Each carnival-time (*Fasching*) became a manifestation of worldly splendour, to be followed by the equally contrived abnegation of Lent. When Leopold married the Infanta Margarita Teresa in 1667 the court spent weeks in rejoicing, and the celebrations were crowned by two major dramatic events: an equestrian ballet in the middle of the Hofburg, and a theatrical performance entitled *Il Pomo d'Oro*. The former, announced as a '*Rossballett*', showed some of the Habsburg passion for horses and techniques of horsemanship which gradually came to be formalized in the so-called Spanish Riding School, with its associated Imperial stud at Lipica in Istria.

The *Golden Apple*, a highly complicated piece of jubilatory symbolism (it allegedly cost over 100,000 thalers to stage), had music by Cesti and a text by Francesco Sbarra which introduced not only political themes, but also a philosophical extravaganza based on the four Aristotelian elements. Its costumes and scenery owed their inspiration to a third Italian, Lodovico Burnacini (1636–1707), who built the earliest permanent theatre in Vienna beside the Hofburg (removed again during the siege of 1683). Burnacini, ennobled by the Emperor, typifies some of the main features of this Baroque: its inventiveness; its play of illusion and reality; its awareness, indeed exaggeration, of the spirit world; its strong sense of drama; its close identification with the role of the court. We are back with the outward show mentioned at the very beginning of this essay. Now, however, we can see something of its underpinning in the universal aspirations of the dynasty.

Court spectacle *grew more lavish as the seventeenth century progressed. These two entertainments were staged to mark the wedding of Leopold I and Margarita Teresa in 1667. Above: the 'Battle between Air and Water', an equestrian ballet in the Hofburg. Below: a scene from 'The Golden Apple'; Leopold is in the centre, flanked by personifications of his kingdoms and figures of former Emperors. (146,147)*

An astronomical clock, *made by Rudolf's court clockmaker, Jost Burgi. Its crystal case rests on an octagonal base with winged caryatids. Inside is an astronomical globe and dials telling the hour, the phases of the moon, and the movements of the stars. (148)*

The continuity of the aulic idea

The court Baroque, then, meant a blending of arts and learning, of visual, emotional, and intellectual effects. Much changed in the style of this official culture if we compare the years 1700 and 1600. Horizons narrowed – just as politics and society grew more restrictive. True humanism was replaced with much superficial allusiveness; conformity was enforced by a close censorship, particularly of thought and writing at the Jesuit-controlled universities. Whereas the climax of the earlier development was Rudolf's desperate search for harmony, Leopold's entourage proved more sophisticated in its manners, cruder in its intellectual content. While Rudolf strove ever more hopelessly to hold together traditional values, Leopold presided over a great forward leap and the exuberance of military success.

Yet there is demonstrably a continuity of evolution. Between 1500 and 1700 the Habsburgs became the arbiters of both taste and education in central Europe. The Renaissance tradition, which reached its climax under Charles V, was given a new dimension by Mannerist artists, then revitalized with the Counter-Reformation's dramatic flair. The realms of the dynasty were gradually transformed from fully-fledged, but peripheral, members of a Renaissance world into a conservative, but distinctive, Catholic civilization.

Perhaps we may say that this role of the court had two aspects: an outside and an inside; one for the people, and the other withdrawn, esoteric. The balance between them varied from reign to reign, but both were present in the sense of mystery which cloaked Habsburg sovereignty. The age of Leopold tended to lay stress on the expansive, popular functions. Rudolf's reign, on the other hand, represents the most extreme kind of inwardness. The Emperor notoriously patronized at Prague all kinds of purveyors of secret wisdom: natural magic, astrology, alchemy, emblems and hieroglyphics, Cabala and Hermetism. He came to live a largely private existence, shunning the commonplace human contact in favour of his collections, laboratories, and workshops in the recesses of the Hradschin.

Yet we should beware of accounting Rudolf's behaviour mere oddness, an abandonment of the dynastic idea; and that for two reasons. Firstly he himself by no means thought it an abandonment: to Rudolf the search for the philosopher's stone, the role of a King Solomon or Trismegistus formed rather an extension of the everyday political responsibilities embodied in the court. He did not anyway forgo the outward semblance of power, however incompetent the actions which allowed his ambitious brother to divest him of his crowns. Secondly other members of the family tended likewise to create an inner sanctum, a court within the court. Maximilian relaxed among his close humanist circle, where Lutherans were as welcome as Roman Catholics. Ferdinand II perhaps ascribed the same function to his religious coterie, his endless devotions in the company of theologians. Ferdinand III and his brother Leopold William return nearer to the mould of Rudolf: enthusiastic collectors and alchemists, men of some artistic and intellectual discrimination. Leopold too showed a penchant for alchemy and the mysteries of nature, beside his more conventional courtly pursuits. His adept Johann Wenzel Seiler, an unfrocked Augustinian from Brno in Moravia, conducted experiments with Imperial permission inside one of the old city gates of Vienna.

Persons who, like Seiler, gained the confidence of rulers – and not only the Habsburgs – as practitioners of the occult, are commonly dismissed as mere 'impostors' or 'adventurers'. That is too simple a view. Of course the court was an adventure, even for those of gentle birth. No one could be sure of the real esteem which compensated for irregular payment and often uncomfortable lodgings. Moreover the age had definitions of superstition utterly different from our own. Alchemy and astrology could appear perfectly legitimate when managed by the right hands. Many of the adepts who frequented Rudolf's court were fully convinced of their powers, however misguided the principles on which they operated. Almost all the occultists who penetrated the Habsburg entourage were genuine 'magicians'; that is to say, they possessed some trick or technique which other men did not possess and could not understand. Such abilities were not far removed from the wonders of art-creation or Baroque stage-management; their workings could come close to the miraculous element in life which the Counter-Reformation Church so emphasized. The inventor Cornelius Drebbel certainly had a remarkable grasp of mechanics, even if his claim to have discovered the *perpetuum mobile* can now be seen as a delusion. His colleague at Prague, Michael Maier, drew on surpassing imaginative gifts, even where his sense of the world's mysteries led him into errant paths of interpretation. Tycho Brahe was much given to prophecy. Kepler too, though his horoscopes do not, for the most part, belong to the Prague period, preserved a thoroughly mystical approach to the central problems of cosmology. Most famous of Rudolf's alchemical adepts for the English is Edward Kelley, who accompanied the celebrated Elizabethan mage John Dee to seek the favour of the Emperor. Dee's success proved short-lived, but Kelley prospered for years; to some extent a charlatan, yet one who probably believed in a good deal of what he purveyed. His impurities, like those of his gold, came to light at length, and he perished in a royal dungeon.

Patronage was necessarily an individual business: the whim of one sovereign could elevate an obscure figure, the accession of another might overthrow a whole establishment. But the *practice* of patronage was consistent. It belonged to the overall purpose of the court. Here too the court, however loose its structure or changeable its composition, appears as the only bond which preserved the fragile unity of the Habsburg monarchy in central Europe.

For what, after all, does 'Austria' signify during the period we have been examining? It means, to a contemporary, the 'house of Austria', in other words the dynasty; and the dynasty is equivalent to the court, considered in its enduring aspects. When the rule of the early modern Habsburgs is described as 'absolutism' – which frequently occurs – some words of qualification are needed. If anything exercised absolutism in seventeenth-century Austria, then the court did. The dynasty possessed no despotic powers, nor could it eliminate local bodies (above all estates), languages, or loyalties. But the court exerted an attraction on all levels of political society, so that estates, aristocracy, towns, Church, intellectuals in fact conformed. Its extended influence is the central feature in the evolution of the Habsburg lands, where consolidation brought a strengthening of traditional roles and ceremonies, of aulic values and competences. Austria may have had no Versailles, no Escorial. But equally it had no counterweight: no Paris, no parliament, no Puritan or commercial 'country'. Without the Habsburg court the Habsburg state would simply not have existed.

The double-headed eagle *crowned with the Imperial crown, surmounts a clock made in Augsburg in 1680. The town depicted on the globe may well be Vienna. (149)*

Seven

THE TUDORS

Three contrasts in personality

❋

NEVILLE WILLIAMS

N AN AGE OF PERSONAL MONARCHY the royal court of England was both the hub of the kingdom's affairs and the setting in which the sovereign lived out his public and private lives. Attendance at court became the social obligation of the nobility and the goal of lesser mortals, for this was the very fount of patronage. Essentially the court comprised the officers of the king's and the queen's separate households; yet ministers of state, peers of the realm, privy councillors, and senior government officials were also resident for much of the year, keeping terms, rather like the law courts and the universities. At the close of the Middle Ages the royal household was still of fundamental importance in the management of the kingdom as a whole and it was the normal source from which trained officials would be found for all kinds of administrative tasks; though the reforms of the 1530s were to bring considerable changes. It was still in the sixteenth century very much an itinerant court, as it had been from early medieval times, with sovereign and courtiers moving with the calendar from one royal residence to another, principally between Westminster, Greenwich, Richmond, Windsor and Eltham – though during the summer many of the great landowners would be free to return to their homes and the bishops to their dioceses, while the monarch made more distant progresses into the shires, partly to enjoy the hunting, partly to show himself to his people.

Within the king's household there was still a division of authority between the Lord Chamberlain and the Lord Steward, which had originated in early times and would

The Tudor dynasty *brought peace to England after the long internecine war between two branches of the Plantagenets. By marrying Elizabeth of York, Henry VII united the red and white roses (Lancastrians and Yorkists), and his son Henry VIII tied England dynastically to Europe by marrying Catherine of Aragon. In this frontispiece to a collection of motets in honour of Henry VIII, we see the crowned Tudor rose and emblems of England, Wales, and Spain. (150)*

long persist. Those who waited personally on His Majesty in his Privy Chamber and other private apartments 'above stairs' came under the direction of the Chamberlain; they included gentlemen of the Bedchamber and of the Privy Chamber, esquires of the body (who kept watch outside the bedchamber), cup-bearers and waiters at table, ushers, grooms, messengers and pages, physicians, barbers, and musicians. Such servants in regular contact with the king totalled about 170. Although the chaplains, gentlemen, and choristers of the Chapel Royal were immediately under the Dean of the Chapel, these forty-two men and boys fell within the Lord Chamberlain's jurisdiction.

The Lord Steward commanded the army of 'below stairs' staff who saw to the provision of the king's creature comforts and the needs of the inner man. With the help of his Treasurer, Vice-Treasurer, and Controller of the household, the Lord Steward directed the activities of twenty-five separate departments – pantry and bakehouse, acatary and poultry, cellar and buttery, saucery, spicery, wafery and confectionery, scullery, boiling-house, laundry, wood-yard, and the rest. Purveyors from each of the specialist victualling departments went to the markets in the city and country, and down to the docks, to supplement the supplies that came from the Crown estates. Under this system of purveyance the royal officers had the right to the pick of the market, naming the prices they would pay, and they could commandeer carts and horses to move provisions of all kinds. The Lord Steward had charge over a commissariat of some 220 men.

The Master of the Horse, the third great household officer, was served by a staff of sixty men who saw to the royal stables and the maintenance of carriages, while the Master of the Buckhounds, a man of much less weight, was responsible for the kennels.

A queen consort had her own staff of officials working in her separate apartments and here, too, there was a rigorous distinction between the men and women serving 'above stairs' and 'below'. From time to time there might be smaller additional establishments for one or other of the royal children.

Henry VII: economy versus ostentation

Much depended on the personality of the sovereign and his attitude towards display, no less than towards patronage. Henry Tudor, who continued to feel insecure on his throne, reckoned it was important to be seen wearing costly robes, to secure respect from his subjects and to impress ambassadors from foreign courts; whereas Louis XI of France had on principle gone about his realm wearing an old felt hat and shabby clothes. Though Henry VII acquired a reputation in his own day for miserliness, he spent considerable sums on buying cloth of gold and of silver, furs, fineries, and jewellery for himself, his consort, and his chief courtiers, for such were sound investments. He was expected to live in style and give the appearance of being sovereign of a powerful and wealthy kingdom. Perhaps, too, his long exile in the court of Brittany enabled him to see the importance of presenting the right image to men who thought him little more than a Welsh chieftain. In all this Queen Elizabeth of York played an outstanding part and when an ambassador once requested an audience with her at very short notice he found the Queen with thirty-two 'companions of angelical appearance, and all we saw there seemed very magnificent and in splendid style, as was suitable for the occasion'.

Pageantry was regarded as a very necessary prop to the throne and Henry continued the innovations in palace ceremonial which the Yorkist Edward IV had made 'after the manner of Burgundy'. Henry instituted a bodyguard, known as the Gentlemen Pensioners, modelled on the select *corps* maintained by the king of France, and devised for them a red livery with flattened black caps. Bearing their halberds they still enliven state occasions today. Nothing was skimped or makeshift about the splendour of the court of this King who patiently audited accounts himself; and it was the same with the food provided so liberally. 'Frugal to excess in his own person,' wrote one visitor, Henry 'does not change any of the ancient usages of England at his court, keeping a sumptuous table.' On red-letter days there might be sixty separate dishes served at a banquet; but on ordinary occasions, too, some seven hundred people fed at the King's expense in Westminster Palace. Dr Rodrigo de Puebla, Ferdinand of Aragon's agent, 'dined every day' at court out of choice, and a few years later John Skelton pointed to the blatant abuses of royal hospitality in his satire *Bouche of Court* – the term for the right to free meals at the palace which even servants of servants of royal servants reckoned they should enjoy unchallenged. This time-honoured system was to be completely overhauled, first by Cardinal Wolsey and then by Thomas Cromwell.

Henry's mother, the Lady Margaret, Countess of Richmond, had continued to patronize learning by supporting the scholarly editions which Caxton and his German assistant, Wynkyn de Worde, issued from their press in Westminster and by her great benefactions to the two universities. The King himself, though not a scholar, found places at court for learned men, poets, and musicians. Thomas Linacre, the humanist who had studied Greek at Florence before reading medicine at Padua, was appointed both the King's physician and Prince Arthur's tutor. John

Argentine, the Provost of King's College, Cambridge, served as physician to the royal princes, while the poet Skelton became tutor to Prince Henry and wrote for him *Speculum Principis*, a little manual on how royalty should behave. When Henry VII appointed Skelton his laureate he gave him a dress in the Tudor livery of white and green embroidered in gold thread with the name 'Calliope', the ancient muse of epic poetry.

Skelton was present at Eltham Palace in Kent in 1499 when Thomas More came with Lord Mountjoy to introduce Erasmus to the English court. Since the King was at Westminster and Prince Arthur was away at Ludlow Castle, it fell to the nine-year-old Henry, Duke of York, to receive the scholars. More knew he was expected to present an appropriate offering and had brought with him a well-turned Latin verse; but Erasmus had come empty-handed. The future Henry VIII, sensing his embarrassment, sent him a note during dinner inviting him to write something to commemorate his visit, and as soon as he had reached his lodgings Erasmus penned an ode praising Henry Tudor, his family, and his kingdom which was included in the first edition of his *Adages* that was issued the following year. On Henry VIII's accession Erasmus said he looked to him through his patronage of scholars to transform the court into a university.

Henry VII *possessed a shrewd economic judgment and a talent for administration, striking a balance between parsimony and ostentatious display. Torrigiano's terracotta bust was made posthumously, when he was working on the tomb effigy in Westminster Abbey.* (151)

Henry VIII *with his family: this schematic representation of the Tudor succession was painted after Henry's death and shows the King in the centre with his heir, Edward VI, and Edward's mother, Jane Seymour (who was also dead at this time). To left and right are the princesses Mary and Elizabeth.* (152)

The palace of Nonsuch *was Henry's answer to Francis I's splendid buildings. It was demolished in the seventeenth century, soon after this picture was painted, and only a few paintings of it are known. Although French and Italian artists were employed on its decoration, it was still basically medieval in structure and plan.* (153)

A writing desk *used by Henry VIII has come down to us. Made about 1525 of wood and gold-tooled leather, it includes the arms of Henry and Catherine of Aragon, as well as figures of Mars and Venus copied from a woodcut by Hans Burgkmair.* (154)

The young Elizabeth *meets a procession of members of the Order of the Garter. In front of her a nobleman carries the sword of state. In the background, Windsor Castle. Engraving after Marcus Gheeraerts, 1576.* (155)

De tresaulte trespuissante et tresexcel-
lente Princesse Elisabet, par la grace de
Dieu Royne d'Angleterre, France, et de
Irlande Souueraine de l'ordre de la
Jaretiere

Ceste place est tousiours supplice par vn
noble homme n'estant point de l'ordre de la
Jaretiere, lequel porte l'Espee.

Among the grooms of the King's Chamber was the poet Stephen Hawes whose allegorical verse romances on traditional themes enjoyed much popularity. In his *Pastime of Pleasure* Hawes presented a characteristic scene of a land of make-believe, peopled by lusty knights-at-arms, spotless damsels in need of protection from giants and foul fiends, and fantastic birds whose songs were rapturous; yet he wrote this as a 'book of moral virtue'. Its sub-title announces that the poem – it extends to 5,840 lines – contains 'the knowledge of the seven sciences and the measure of man's life' and Hawes endeavours to convince the reader that learning is an essential quality of a courtier. This was to be the theme that Baldassare Castiglione elaborated in his *Il Cortegiano*, which after its publication in 1528 was rapidly to become a manual of the courtier's behaviour throughout Western Europe. When Castiglione came to England in 1503 to stand proxy for his master, Duke Guidobaldo of Urbino, at his installation as a Knight of the Garter he may indeed have met Stephen Hawes at Windsor and discussed with him the ideals of Grand Amour, the hero of *Pastime of Pleasure*.

On special feasts during the first seventeen years of the reign there would be dramatic performances after dinner and for Twelfth Night in 1494 there was the novelty of masked dancing – 'a disguising' – which was introduced from Italy. Pageant plays on traditional themes were staged in the hall and women as well as boys took part in them. Nothing in the whole of Henry's reign surpassed the series of festivities that marked the wedding of Arthur, Prince of Wales, to Catherine of Aragon in November 1501. For the tournament in honour of the couple a 'Tree of Chivalry' was set up in front of Westminster Hall on which the challengers hung their shields and the procession of the Knights to the lists was devised with much ingenuity – some rode in pageant cars, others on floats decked out as ships, with cannons firing. In Westminster Palace after the banquets there were pageants, rich in allegory, interspersed with songs and dancing. Master William Cornish, a gentleman of the Chapel Royal, proved adept at designing ambitious stage sets to transform the hall into a fairytale palace. On one evening he had provided a tower that was pulled into the hall by 'sea horses', escorted by 'mermaids', and inside each of the 'mermaids' there was hidden a chorister 'singing right sweetly with great harmony'. The tower itself held bold knights on the lower storey and maidens on the upper, who surrendered to their entreaties to dance with them. William Cornish, the Chapel bass who wrote a number of songs at Henry's request, was in fact performing the duties of what would become the separate office of Master of the Revels, in charge of court entertainments, and while the court was still celebrating Arthur's marriage he staged around a pasteboard Castle of Love what was the very first masque in England – a form of production that combined singing, spoken dialogue, and dancing and was to develop in the next hundred years as a specifically English form of dramatic art.

As the founder of a dynasty Henry Tudor was anxious to leave permanent memorials behind him. The first was Richmond Palace in Surrey, near the River Thames, which

'Time' *from Stephen Hawes's 'Pastime of Pleasure', an allegorical treatise on 'the knowledge of the seven sciences and the measure of man's life'. Hawes's treatment of the courtier may possibly have influenced Castiglione. (156)*

he built in the grounds of Sheen Manor after its destruction by fire. This was a splendid residence in Gothic style, built round a paved courtyard, boasting a great many windows and turrets, and large enough to accommodate many courtiers. When it was ready for occupation at the end of 1500 Henry decreed that the new palace should be known as 'Richmond' to commemorate the title Earl of Richmond which he had held before his accession. Richmond was to prove a favourite residence for each of his grandchildren in turn. His secondary legacy was the chapel in Westminster Abbey which bears his name, though it was originally planned as a shrine for the murdered Lancastrian Henry VI. The foundation stone was laid in January 1503, but the building was not complete until sixteen years later and even then Torrigiano's elaborate work on the altar, and the tombs with their life-like effigies of Henry, his consort, and his mother, were unfinished.

The tragedy of Prince Arthur's death in 1502, followed within a year by the death of Elizabeth of York in childbed, took the merriment out of Henry's court. There was to be no occasion in the years which followed for Master Cornish to celebrate by producing spectacles and pageants; there were no more disguisings on Twelfth Night; and tournaments and banquets were rare. The court of those last six years of the reign had a sombre tone and lacked the presence of a woman to smooth manners and bring touches of gaiety. Despite efforts to find another wife Henry remained a widower; his elder daughter Margaret had left to marry James IV of

153

Richmond Palace *was built by Henry VII and named after the earldom he held before winning his throne. Like Nonsuch, it has mostly disappeared but a miniature of 1496 shows what was probably its covered walk. It may appear again in the background of an altarpiece (below) which once hung in the royal chapel there. In the foreground kneel Henry VII with his three sons (Arthur, Henry, and Edmund), and Queen Elizabeth with her daughters. (157,158)*

Scotland; his mother, the Countess of Richmond, again a widow, was rarely at court; and Catherine of Aragon was virtually exiled to Durham House while the vexed questions of her dowry and her future remained unsolved. The King became increasingly withdrawn and, past his prime, followed a staid routine. The tedium of the long winter evenings was relieved by gambling with the gentlemen of the Chamber and by watching the antics of a Flemish giantess or the fellow who ate coal. For his courtiers the month's stay at Windsor in 1506 of Philip the Fair of Castile and his Queen Joan, who had been wrecked on the Dorset coast, was an unexpected bonus, for there was again feasting on a scale that they had not seen since Arthur's marriage. Once Philip had left for Spain, the court returned to what many must have regarded as royal mourning. A tremendous change would come with the demise of the first Tudor monarch when Henry VIII, who had endured a confined and joyless childhood under his father's strict eye, threw off the traces.

Henry VIII: 'rich, ferocious and greedy for glory'

From the moment of his accession Henry VIII was determined to give his court a personal style that would make him the envy of Continental princes. With a full treasury, he could afford to be open-handed, and his coronation, with its accompanying festivities, set the tone of lavish pageantry that he loved. 'Our time is spent in continuous festivity,' wrote Catherine of Aragon to her father in those happy, honeymoon days when William Cornish was again busy devising entertainments. Yet although the King had a talent for enjoying himself in the company of others, whether it was in the tennis court or the tilt yard, the butts or the hunting field, the banqueting table or the hall cleared for dancing, and never hesitated about showing his concern if others did not seem to be enjoying themselves just as much as he, at heart Henry was still a serious-minded youth, interested in scholarship and the arts. He wanted to make his court the centre of cultural as well as of social life, largely for its own sake, but partly to show off and earn himself a reputation that would put his contemporary fellow-sovereigns in the shade.

Before Henry VIII had reigned for five weeks word reached Erasmus in Italy of Henry's promising intentions. His friend Lord Mountjoy told him that the new King of England 'does not set his heart on gold or jewels, but on virtue, glory and immortality. The other day he told me, "I wish I were more learned." "But learning is not what we expect of a King," I answered, "merely that he should encourage scholars." "Most certainly," he rejoined, "as without them we should scarcely live at all." Now what more splendid remark could a prince make?' After Erasmus had revisited England he wrote that since the King had gathered round him so many learned men for companions, 'it may seem not a court but a temple of the Muses', and the French diplomats, who were not renowned for paying compliments, noted the weight Henry attached to *les savants* and praised the elegance of the conversation at court. Now at last England seemed to be drawn into the mainstream of humanism.

In the arts there was less indigenous talent; so Henry set out to attract artists and sculptors from Italy, the Netherlands, and France to establish himself as a Renaissance prince. Some were dubious about the invitation and feared London was no place for an artist; Benvenuto Cellini, for instance, shuddered at the idea of spending a year's exile among 'such beasts as the English'. That phrase summed up the reputation for philistinism that the King was determined to bury, and he achieved considerable success in so doing. Torrigiano arrived in 1512 to work at Westminster Abbey; the Flemish glazier Galian Hone settled in 1517 to design much stained glass for the King; while artists such as Giovanni da Maiano came to his service after an apprenticeship ·with Cardinal Wolsey. Two years after Cellini's acid comment another Italian, Francisco Chieregato, the papal nuncio, found much to praise about the state of Henry's court, looking at much wider aspects of it than artistic patronage. 'The wealth and civilization of the world are here; and those who call the English barbarians appear to me to render themselves such. I here perceive very elegant manners, extreme decorum and great politeness; and amongst other things there is the invincible King, whose acquirements and qualities are so many and excellent, that I consider him to excel all who ever wore a crown.'

The King had a passionate interest in music of all kinds and where his father had been no more than a dilettante, Henry VIII was a skilled performer on as many as six instruments, boasted a good singing voice, and had some talent for composition. During his summer progress in 1510 he frequently played the recorder, flute, lute, and virginals, composed a number of songs, and 'did set two goodly masses, every of them 5 parts'. He was fascinated by the technical problems of making instruments and was something of an expert when it came to organ-building. Henry VII's twenty-five minstrels formed an *ad hoc* band for ceremonial occasions, but his son founded a regular group of instrumentalists and singers personally attendant on him, which he called The King's Musick. By the end of his reign these numbered sixty strong, quite apart from the gentlemen and children of the Chapel Royal. By providing generous stipends he could attract talented men from the Continent who found that in England musicians 'lived like gentlemen, not like servitors'. Friar Denis Memmo resigned his post of organist of St Mark's Cathedral, Venice, in 1516 to come to England, bringing with him 'an excellent instrument at great expense'. Henry was impressed by his virtuosity and would listen to him playing for hours at a time. From Italy, too, came the first members of the Bassano family, who were to dominate music-making at court down to the Civil War. Brass and woodwind players came from Milan, Cremona, the German states, and from Flanders, though most of the players for the lutes and viols and all but a few of the vocalists were English.

No English sovereign has spent more on music than King Henry, for he was bent on providing the finest opportunities for music-making. The King's Musick and the Chapel Royal combined to form what amounted to a great academy; in this stimulating atmosphere the court musicians led developments in instrumentation and composition and set standards

The King's Musick *was no empty phrase. Henry VIII was an accomplished performer and composer. This drawing of musicians at Whitehall is attributed to Holbein. (159)*

The rose set to music. *From the same manuscript book of motets and poems in honour of Henry VIII (1516) comes this witty and decorative pattern of music in a circle. (160)*

of performance for Europe as a whole. Visitors from abroad commented on the high place that music filled and the vital role of the King in every aspect of it. At the French court, by contrast, the choir failed to perform adequately because the conductor could not sight-read and was frequently drunk.

The choir of the Chapel Royal remained until 1533 an itinerant body, moving with the King from one residence to another. With the foundation of St James's Palace, however, the choir was at last settled. Its chief luminary in the first dozen years of the reign was Robert Fayrefax, who composed various motets and was the first English composer to write solos specifically for a counter-tenor. Towards the end of the reign Thomas Tallis, once organist at Waltham Abbey and then a lay clerk at Canterbury, joined the Chapel Royal at Henry's instigation. Now he had ample opportunity for composition, developing his skill as a master of counterpoint and in those years wrote his four-part Mass and the motet *Miserere Nostri*.

That shrewd commentator Machiavelli, who never met the King, reckoned he was 'rich, ferocious and greedy for glory'. Henry was certainly determined to outshine his rivals in every branch of endeavour – the rulers of France, Spain, and the Holy Roman Empire. In the early years of the reign the old guard was changing, for in 1515 the young Duke of Angoulême succeeded as Francis I of France and next year Charles of Ghent inherited the throne of a united Spain. As the senior in age and experience of ruling, Henry regarded himself as the natural leader of Europe as well as the embodiment of Renaissance chivalry, though this was to be so hotly disputed by the others that the rivalries between the three men were to dominate international affairs for thirty years. The elderly Emperor Maximilian I had inconsequentially talked about adopting Henry as a son and resigning the Holy Roman Empire to him, and this idea fed Henry's ambition – it would make his court truly imperial. Bishop Tunstall had warned him that if he accepted the Habsburg nomination imperialist lawyers could argue that the realm of England was henceforth subject to the Empire – a most unwelcome constitutional notion. 'The Crown of England' wrote Tunstall, in a pregnant phrase, 'is an empire in itself'; so further dignities were irrelevant. While the King accepted his argument he remained fascinated by the mystique of the Holy Roman Empire, which was, as he put it, 'the monarchy of Christendom' and apart from the Papacy the highest honour to which any man could aspire. With Maximilian's death, Henry was determined to stand as a candidate in the Imperial election against Charles and Francis, for he failed to grasp that no German elector wanted an outsider and the bribes his agent offered were derisory compared with the Habsburg and Valois offerings; Charles of Spain easily won the contest. In the same spirit Henry was twice to support Wolsey's candidature for the Papacy, convinced that a second English Pope was overdue, but here again he was thwarted and blamed his ill success on the machinations of Charles V and Francis I.

A summit meeting between the three sovereigns had been Wolsey's dearest wish, yet Habsburg–Valois rivalry in 1520 made it impossible for Charles V to be included in the Field of Cloth of Gold, which the Cardinal had arranged to be held in neutral ground in France between the English castle at Guisnes and the French fortress at Ardres. So rich were the costumes and pavilions of both courts that the name 'Field of Cloth of Gold' came as a natural description of the gathering, though the site of the first meeting between the kings had anciently been called the Golden Vale. Though the aim of the meeting was to foster 'eternal amity', the range of festivities afforded ample opportunities for displays of rivalry. The gathering had many facets: in part a political conference, the events of this month of mingling included athletics meetings, with jousts and wrestling, a festival of music and dance, and a series of state banquets. Richard Gibson, Master of Henry's pavilions, had erected a great field of tents to provide accommodation for courtiers and servants not sufficiently senior to be assigned lodgings in Guisnes Castle. Gibson's *tour de force* was a banqueting house, 'the most sumptuous ever', covered outside by cloth painted to resemble brickwork and decorated within with cloth of gold and of silver, interlaced with the Tudor colours of white and green. Leonardo could not have surpassed it, wrote one Italian, while another compared it with the palaces of Ariosto's *Orlando Furioso*. On this peaceful expedition to France Henry was accompanied by a retinue of 5,172 men and women.

Henry and Francis at last embraced in the Val d'Or on Corpus Christi Day, as trumpets sounded. Feats of arms in full pageantry followed. Those entering the lists had to present their shields at the 'Tree of Honour' and there was an awkward moment when the heralds could not agree on which branches the two kings should hang their own shields until Henry settled the matter by causing Francis' arms to be placed on the right and his own, equally high, on the left. It was so arranged that the two sovereigns would not be taking part in any joust against each other; but on the spur of the moment Henry asked Francis to wrestle with him and found his opponent a master of the art. On the first Saturday Wolsey celebrated High Mass in a temporary chapel built near the lists and he saw to it that the choirs of the two royal chapels sang alternately. Richard Pace preached on the theme of amity and afterwards the Cardinal laid the foundation stone for the Chapel of Our Lady of Friendship, that was to be jointly built and for ever maintained by the kings of the two countries. Alas, it was never erected and the treaties that were signed, for Princess Mary to marry the Dauphin, and for ending French intervention in Scottish affairs, remained a dead letter. Francis remained suspicious of Henry, largely because of his secret meetings with Charles V at Dover and Calais, just before and immediately after he came to Guisnes. As Erasmus had foretold, the great gathering altered nothing, and Bishop John Fisher lamented the fortunes the rival courts had wasted on their 'midsummer games', with the wind blowing dust in men's faces and shaking the 'strange houses build for pleasure'. The Field of Cloth of Gold was a glorious excuse for the two courts to show off; and the attempt at rekindling a departed chivalry was irrelevant to the problems of a nationalistic Europe.

We need not pursue the tangled skein of diplomacy which led to England's breach with Rome. The political origins of the English Reformation lay in Catherine of

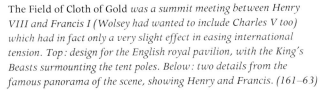

The Field of Cloth of Gold *was a summit meeting between Henry VIII and Francis I (Wolsey had wanted to include Charles V too) which had in fact only a very slight effect in easing international tension. Top: design for the English royal pavilion, with the King's Beasts surmounting the tent poles. Below: two details from the famous panorama of the scene, showing Henry and Francis. (161–63)*

Aragon's inability to give Henry the son for which he yearned; and their matrimonial dispute split the court. In the royal family itself Henry's sister Mary, the Dowager Queen of France, stood by Catherine while her husband Suffolk was one of Henry's chief supporters. Norfolk never ceased from furthering the claims of his neice Anne Boleyn, who had captivated the King, to wear a crown, yet his Duchess remained faithful to the Queen's cause. Once it was plain that the Pope would never allow Henry to divorce his wife and be free to marry Anne, it came hard for courtiers to resist the pressures which the King could exert. 'Leave of absence is never refused from court to those who take Catherine's part,' it was noted in 1531, and once she had been sent away to Ampthill he could make drastic reductions in her separate establishment. Too few stuck to their principles, such as Sir Henry Guildford, Controller of

the Royal Household, who had been warned by the Lady Anne that if he continued to oppose her she would have him dismissed when she became Queen; yet Guildford resigned his office forthwith and refused Henry's request to reconsider his decision. The chief penalty Henry paid for his affair with Anne was being cut off from his daughter Mary, and it was understandable that the rivalry between Catherine and Anne should be continued in the next generation by their respective daughters. Finding a solution to the 'King's great matter' involved first the fall of Wolsey and then the severance of England from Catholic Europe. After much shadow-boxing Henry looked to Thomas Cromwell to turn Parliament against the Papacy and to force the English clergy to accept the King's control of all legislation. Henry was to be supreme in his own domain and the preamble to the 1533 Act Restraining Appeals to Rome firmly denied the novelty of the new monarchy that Cromwell was creating:

This realm of England is an empire, and so hath been accepted in the world, governed by one supreme head and King, having the dignity and royal estate of the imperial crown of the same, unto whom a body politic, compact of all sorts and degrees of people divided in terms and by names of spirituality and temporality, be bounded and owe next to God a natural and humble obedience.

157

Henry as head of the Church *was an image that the King wished to imprint on the minds of his people. It is firmly expressed on the title page of Coverdale's Bible of 1535 where the King is shown handing down the book to his kneeling bishops. (164)*

If Wolsey, as Lord Chancellor and Cardinal legate, could engross into his own hands the effective temporal and spiritual power in England, then the sovereign he had served could himself exercise even greater authority. The 'imperial' theme of English monarchy was developed by such men as Polydore Vergil, Bishop Stephen Gardiner, and Lord Morley, the last of whom regarded Henry as 'the father of our country, one by whose virtue, learning and noble courage England is new born, newly brought from thraldom to freedom'. The image of the truly nationalist monarch had been created and the artists in Henry's service were able to sharpen the image. Nowhere was this more apparent than in the production of the English Bible. The title-page of Coverdale's Bible (1535) showed Henry in majesty, presenting the book to his bishops, a figure in the line of Old Testament prophets and New Testament apostles, while the title-page of Cranmer's Great Bible (1540) depicted him as the Supreme Head of the Church, ruling in the image of God. Though the Church of England in those early days lacked a specific doctrine, reformists took comfort first in the rapport between the Boleyn family and churchmen nurtured in Cambridge scholarship and then, after Anne's fall, applauded Jane Seymour's zeal for the Gospel.

Henry's matrimonial ventures continued to have a profound influence on the nature of his court. The cynic makes much of the fact that the traditional ground-plan of English palaces included a Queen's suite of rooms as well as a King's; duplicating the royal marriage-bed had increased the temptations for those with an inclination to unfaithfulness. Such an arrangement, hallowed by ancient usage, made it easy for Henry to take a mistress, such as Elizabeth Blount, and was to provide Catherine Howard with her death warrant. There remained, however, great continuity in

many of the personnel of the court, for instance Sir Edward Baynton served as Vice-Chamberlain of the household to each of Henry's six queens.

The reign was seminal in the reorganization of the royal household. By the Eltham Ordinances of January 1526 Wolsey promulgated long-anticipated reforms to rationalize the whole matter of service at court. He introduced notable economies and established a new principle of service; yet unfortunately his work was incomplete, for there was no guarantee that his reforms would be properly implemented, and the expectation that the chief officers – the Steward, Treasurer, and Controller – could solve every problem by meeting together but once a year shows a surprising lack of administrative grasp. Thirteen years later Thomas Cromwell carried forward what Wolsey had begun and on Christmas Eve 1539 the King gave his assent to a new series of ordinances which were destined to be in force with comparatively little change down to the days of the Prince Consort. Although Cromwell had to bow to Henry's demands for a sizable increase in the staff of the Privy Chamber, he succeeded in curbing the Chamber's expenditure by making it, and every other department of the household above and below stairs, subject to the Counting House or Board of Green Cloth, over which a new official, the Lord Great Master of the Household, was to preside. The duties of every official and the standards of performance required of them were set out in the Ordinances, often with a timetable, to ensure that tasks were no longer skimped or unnecessarily prolonged, and to provide the right degree of supervision. If Cromwell's Ordinances seem to underline discipline and fines, it is worth remembering how highly he valued professional service. He envisaged a ladder of promotion in every department and made it clear that no servant was to be engaged unless he seemed likely to qualify for promotion. This bureaucratic system swiftly took root and proved remarkably successful in securing honourable service at court and in eliminating waste.

The failure of the Pilgrimage of Grace to put back the clock in religion and politics and the isolation of England in a hostile Catholic Europe encouraged Cromwell to look to the German Protestant princes for a political alliance and a religious understanding. Hence the Cleves marriage in January 1540, which was expected to present Henry with a suitable bride and England with an ally. The failure of that marriage brought Cromwell's fall and after eight years of supreme power he was accused of being a 'sacramentary' in religion. Once his union with Anne of Cleves had been annulled, the King married the voluptuous Catherine Howard, niece of Cromwell's enemy Norfolk and the pride of Catholic orthodoxy, just as a few years back Anne Boleyn had been regarded as the handmaiden of Protestantism. It was not until Catherine's execution for adultery that Henry grasped the importance of keeping a *via media* between the Catholicism of Stephen Gardiner and the Reformist zeal of Archbishop Cranmer, and this was emphasized by his final marriage, to the devout blue-stocking, Catherine Parr.

The dissolution of the monasteries had brought into the King's hands property worth at least £100,000 a year; but by selling or leasing at realistic rentals many of these lands

Henry gained perhaps £1,500,000. Those who acquired spoils from the Crown became firmly committed to the Reformation settlement and the Tudor dynasty. Nearly all the larger grants went to men connected with the court: peers received 124 patents, other courtiers 183 grants, and royal officials 147. For instance, Sir Anthony Browne, Master of the Horse, was rewarded with vast acres in Surrey that had belonged to Chertsey Abbey; Sir Thomas Cheney, Treasurer of the Household, purchased the lands formerly of Faversham and Boxley Abbeys in Kent; while the Duke of Norfolk, Lord Treasurer, and his son Surrey secured valuable properties in the city of Norwich and estates in the eastern counties. All over the country the pattern was the same. The Cecils, Paulets, Russells, Wriothesleys, and other families paved their way to fame and political importance through their monastic lands and in every county there were men of middle rank who through their connexion with the royal court acquired a landed interest and by loyal service to the Tudors founded county families.

The new monarchy and its palaces

In April 1512 most of the residential quarters of the old Palace of Westminster, the King's principal London home, were destroyed by fire, and he remained desperately short of satisfactory accommodation in the capital. He made shift with the mansion of Baynards Castle in Thames Street, renovated by his father, and the White Tower of London, where his mother had died. Westminster Palace as such, the rambling home of medieval monarchy, was never to be rebuilt and in retrospect its destruction seems almost as

significant an event as the Reformation in dividing medieval from modern kingship. Few could have predicted in 1512 that Henry would double the number of royal residences in town and country, from eight to sixteen. His earliest building operations were at the Bridewell, by the Thames near Blackfriars; but before these had been completed he had begun the half-timbered King's House within the precincts of the Tower. Nowhere in London or Westminster, however, was large enough to house the entire court as had been the case with the ancient Palace of Westminster, and as a result Henry increasingly resided at Greenwich, where he had been born, or at Richmond. It was galling for him to inspect the magnificent home which Cardinal Wolsey had built at Hampton Court and even worse to see the splendid improvements the minister had made to York Palace, the traditional London home of archbishops of York, which was so centrally placed. When Wolsey feared he was losing Henry's confidence in 1525 he gave him Hampton Court; the King readily accepted this munificent gift, but would have preferred York Palace. The latter came into his grasp in 1529 on the Cardinal's fall and he at once began striking developments over a much enlarged site, transforming it into Whitehall Palace, which, by the time he had finished, covered twenty-three acres – twice the size of Pope Clement's Vatican and easily the largest palace in Christendom.

Whitehall was indelibly stamped with Henry's personality and it came to symbolize the new monarchy. This was the setting for a King who, having broken with Rome, was supreme in Church and State. Here Holbein decorated

Whitehall Palace *was largely Henry VIII's creation, though it remained a collection of parts rather than an architectural whole. The scene in pl. 152 is one of its galleries, and through a doorway (left) one catches a glimpse of the north side of Westminster Abbey and one pinnacle of Henry VIII's Tennis Court. This also appears (wrongly labelled 'Treasury') on the left of a sketch made in 1550 by Antony van der Wyngaerde. Next to it is the Holbein Gate and the octagonal Cockpit. (165,166)*

the Long Gallery, which served as the first art gallery in England, and a Privy Garden was laid out as one of the earliest known formal gardens. There was space here for tennis courts, the cockpit, and a tilt yard, and apartments were provided for a great many courtiers. Whitehall was essentially a waterside palace, close to London's principal thoroughfare, the Thames; and even Henry VIII felt he could not close 'Whitehall Stairs', from time out of mind a public landing-place; so there was to be access from the river through the palace grounds, along what had been the highway from Westminster to Charing Cross, and through the new gateway. The fact that ordinary folk could walk through the precincts gave Whitehall quite a different character from Greenwich or Richmond and helped to cement relations between king and subjects; there were always Londoners passing through the grounds eavesdropping on semi-private events and cheering at public occasions. In the summer of 1537, when Henry awaited the birth of his long-wished-for heir, he commissioned Hans Holbein to paint a fresco on the walls of the Privy Chamber, containing himself, Queen Jane Seymour, and his own parents of Lancaster and York. The figure of the King dominated this picture, which was Henry's earliest 'definitive portrait'.

To the west of Whitehall the King acquired the hospital of St James, a religious foundation which stood in open fields, and in 1533 began building a further palace round four courts, entered through a gateway beneath a clock tower that still stands. The octagonal turrets of this tower were decorated with the initials 'H' and 'A' for Henry and his second queen, Anne Boleyn, though Anne was to be more attracted to Whitehall during what remained of her life. As with Whitehall so at Hampton Court there were extensive changes once the palace had passed from Cardinal to King, for Henry constructed a new great hall, with its elaborately carved roof and musicians' gallery, and greatly enlarged the kitchens. He also acquired a number of manor-houses as retreats in safe country air from the smoke and infection of the capital; these also served as lodges from which he could hunt the royal deer and included Hunsdon and Hatfield in Hertfordshire and Oatlands, near Weybridge, in Surrey.

The most remarkable of all Henry's palaces was Nonsuch, a monument of royal ostentation on the most grandiose scale, which the wealth of the dissolved monasteries financed. Hitherto Henry's building operations had been limited to extending and embellishing existing residences in a piecemeal way, such as his alterations at Whitehall, where the sites had already been constructed, and he longed to design a palace from scratch, instead of having to build within the framework of an earlier architect's plans. Now at last he could afford to indulge his passion for building, and he selected the Surrey village of Cuddington, where the church, manor-house, and farmsteads were swept away to make room for this triumphant pleasure-dome amidst a spacious park:

> That which no equal has in art or fame
> Britons deservedly do Nonsuch name.

This was to be from its conception unique and incapable of imitation, though in fact Henry regarded it as an English answer to the château of Chambord, the great residence of Francis I – a challenge to the effect that the English King was capable of excelling his French rival in building as in everything else

Nonsuch was designed as a Gothic building profusely overlaid with classical decoration, and built round two courts. The inner court, containing the royal apartments, was entered through a gatehouse and up a flight of steps. A team of Continental craftsmen was assembled to garnish the half-timbered upper section of those lodgings with 'pictures and other antique forms of excellent art and workmanship', under the direction of Nicolas Bellin of Modena, who had worked at Fontainebleau. Bellin himself carved and gilded the slate panels that covered the timber frescoes, while William Cure from Amsterdam took charge of the intricate plaster-work, providing scenes from classical mythology. The gateway was decorated with statues of the most famous Roman emperors; yet these were dwarfed as the visitor penetrated the inner court and came across the massive figure of King Henry, seated on a throne, trampling underfoot a lion. Rarely can sculpture have been used so effectively for portraying monarchical power. 'Can harm befall the body politic,' asked one sightseer, amazed at the scene, 'when its most sagacious King, wielding the sceptre, is protected on the right by the arts and virtues and avenging goddesses, on the left by feats of Hercules and the tender care of the gods.' A foreigner noted 'one could imagine everything that architecture can perform to have been employed in this one work . . . that it may well claim and justify its name of Nonsuch'. The building was capped with sundry turrets and minarets. Its rooms contained unusual clocks, rich vases, and the costly bric-à-brac of majesty; while the two parks, running to 1,700 acres, were stocked with a thousand head of deer. Men soon referred to Nonsuch loyally as 'the very pearl of the realm', the finest jewel in Henry's crown. Yet the King was not to see it completed, but died while the outer courtyard was still under construction.

With Henry's passing, a court with a very different ethos came swiftly into being, dominated by Hertford as Lord Protector, who was advanced to the dukedom of Somerset in spite of all the provisions of Henry's will for entrusting the government of the realm during his son's minority to a well-balanced Council of State. The court of the boy King, who was separated from his two sisters, contrasted very markedly with what had gone before. His successor, after six and a half years, was Catherine of Aragon's daughter, determined to restore the old faith and the traditions at court which had been swept away under Edward VI. Her consort, Philip of Spain, chose to spend the minimum time in England, while her sister, Princess Elizabeth, as the focus of opposition to Mary, remained under suspicion and was never at the centre. Mary's was an attenuated court in consequence, indicating the disunity of England. Indeed, the two short reigns of Edward and Mary, from 1547 to 1558, formed an uncharacteristic interval in the development of the Tudor court, largely because of the fundamental religious issues.

Henry's was an extrovert court, *more deliberately organized for visual effect than either his father's or his daughter's. The genius of Hans Holbein the Younger was a necessary part of that effect. Above: 'Parnassus', a design for the celebrations of Henry's wedding to Anne Boleyn. Below: the King dining in the Privy Chamber of Whitehall, a pen and ink drawing by Holbein. (167,168)*

The definitive portrait *of Henry was Holbein's fresco on the wall of the Privy Chamber, showing him with his family. It was the original of innumerable copies and variant versions. Though the fresco is lost, Holbein's full-length cartoon survives. (169)*

'Fame' sounds the trumpet *for Elizabeth's triumphal car. So her subjects might have seen her on some triumphal progress. The drawing is from a book on calligraphy by William Teschel. (170)*

Elizabeth: 'the Sun Queen'

Queen Elizabeth I came to the throne on a wave of popularity no less remarkable that her father's; and she was determined to heal the rift which had divided court and subjects for the past eleven years. Everyone expected the Queen to marry and mother an heir as a matter of course, and no one would have foretold in 1558, and even much later, that she would remain a spinster. She regarded her court, as her father had done, as an extension of her personality, and though it was essentially a masculine society, she succeeded in dominating it and even persuaded not a few of the men around her that they must be a little in love with her. For much of her reign, indeed, she had not merely a single favourite, but three or four, and even in his prime the Earl of Leicester ranked no higher than *primus inter pares*. No sovereign has had quite so many endearing allegorical names applied to her, from 'Deborah' in the first weeks of the reign (when she was expected to side with the *revenants* from Zurich and Geneva in their demands to reform the Church radically) to 'Oriana' in her final decade, when at last she seemed to embody the novel idea of a Virgin Queen, whose only marriage was a symbolic union with all her subjects. To her courtiers, however, Elizabeth was the 'Sun Queen'. She shone, giving 'the common blessing' of light, and in consequence the warmth of her rays promoted a natural growth; she dazzled and at times burnt with a fiery intensity. 'Many make suit to have the twinkling of one beam of the splendiferous planet,' wrote one in Whitehall, knowing full well that those not in her presence lived as it were in a shadow. Sir Christopher Hatton, when absent from court, longed to see again 'the brightness of that sun that giveth light unto my sense and soul', and the Queen's favourite godson, Sir John Harington, used the self-same sun motif to portray Elizabeth's temperament: 'When she smiled, it was a pure sunshine that everyone did choose to bask in if they could,' yet he went on to point out that the

storm clouds could gather without warning, obscuring the sun, and then 'the thunder fell in wondrous manner on all alike.'

Of the Queen's favourites, Leicester remained in an exceptional position from the accession until his death shortly after the defeat of the Armada, and neither the suspicious death of Amy Robsart, nor his secret marriage to Lettice Knollys, put him out of royal favour for long. 'Sweet Robin' was the man to whom she remained attached, even though she never seriously contemplated marrying him. Raleigh, by contrast, lost all hope of preferment with his ill-advised marriage to Bess Throckmorton. Hatton was so sure he was in love with his sovereign that he never looked at another woman, consecrating a celibate life to the idyll of what might have been. Essex fascinated her when she was approaching sixty, and she struggled hard against overlooking the fatal weaknesses in his character. Others, too, were in high favour from time to time, such as William Pickering; Thomas Heneage, the seventeenth Earl of Oxford; and Charles Blount; and her relationships with each formed a regular succession of teasings, tiffs, and reconciliations. It is worth emphasizing that none of these achieved high office until he had proved himself to be absolutely worthy of it.

A female ruler who remained a spinster was a new experience for Englishmen. Her personal attendants numbered no more than eighteen – four gentlewomen of the Bedchamber, eight gentlewomen of the Privy Chamber, and six maids of honour. The first twelve were married ladies of high rank; but the maids of honour were young women whose ambitious parents considered they would vastly improve their chances in the marriage market through service at court – the finest of all finishing schools. The maids saw to her wardrobe, her toilette, and her creature comforts in the palace, and in their company she spent much of the day. With them she rarely discussed high politics but preferred to talk about religion and philosophy, would pull to pieces sermons preached before her, consider personalities of both sexes, and listen intently to court gossip. This was Elizabeth's family circle and she took an abiding especial interest in her young maids, teasing them cruelly about their love affairs. It would be wrong to portray the Queen as a sour old maid systematically putting obstacles in the way of the young who yearned to marry; yet she well knew that such matches broke up her own family circle. If all went happily and she approved of the suitor she would eventually become godmother to their offspring; but woe betide the courtier who took unwarrantable liberties with her maids of honour. In turn both Raleigh and Oxford went to the Tower for seduction, and quite late in the reign Leicester's son was banished from court for daring to kiss Mistress Cavendish. Elizabeth did often, according to Sir John Harington, 'ask the ladies around her Chamber if they loved to think of marriage. And the wise ones did conceal their liking thereto, as knowing the Queen's judgement.' Court, as the Queen intended it, was the place where subjects paid court to her, not the place where the young indulged in easy courtships. When Sir Henry Shirley secretly married Frances Vavasour, a lady in waiting, the Queen was furious and defended her fury, 'She hath always

Elizabeth's court *was less ostentatious than Henry's; she inherited her grandfather's instinct for economy, but she compensated for it by attracting an exceptionally brilliant entourage of courtiers. Right: the Earl of Essex, her last favourite, executed after a tragic and foolhardy rebellion, and Sir Christopher Hatton, Lord Chancellor. In a painting (below) by a visiting German of the reception of Dutch ambassadors, the Earl of Leicester is shown second from the left. (171–73)*

furthered any honest and honourable purpose of marriage or preferment to any of hers when, without scandal and infamy, they have been orderly broke to her.' The emphasis was on 'any of *hers*', and she would never relinquish her proprietary rights over these.

Her court resembled a large family, with its members closely knit by ties of kin and the obligations of allegiance. Foremost among her relations was Henry Carey, a Boleyn cousin, whom she created Baron Hunsdon, and his sister Catherine married Sir Francis Knollys. There was Sir Richard Sackville, whose mother was a sister of Sir Thomas Boleyn, the Queen's maternal grandfather, and whose son Thomas Sackville she made Lord Buckhurst. Then there were the Howard cousins of the Boleyns, who dominated the peerage in numbers, wealth, and honours. They were headed by Thomas, fourth Duke of Norfolk, until his execution for treason in 1572, and then by Charles, Lord Howard of Effingham, who married Hunsdon's daughter. The chief connexion stemming from Elizabeth's father's last marriage, with Catherine Parr, was the late Queen's brother, Thomas Parr, whom she created Marquis of Northampton. Finally, there were those with a measure of royal blood who were potential contenders to the succession: the Ladies Katherine and Mary Grey, grand-daughters of Henry VIII's sister Mary, and their cousin Margaret, Countess of Derby, who all caused the Queen much trouble, and Henry Hastings, Earl of Huntingdon, who caused none, despite his staunch Puritanism. Huntingdon was descended on his father's side from Edward III and on his mother's from George, Duke of Clarence; he married Leicester's sister, and when she came to court the Queen would 'give her a privy nip' about her husband's nearness to the throne.

As a family the court had its feuds where personalities clashed, its favourite sons, accorded nicknames, and its ill-favoured daughters. Round leading courtiers developed factions, the ancestor of political parties; but Elizabeth endeavoured to maintain a balance. The personnel of the court was far from being static, but was constantly replenished by fresh arrivals of men eager to seek their fortune through personal service. The luckiest newcomers had a father or an uncle to introduce them or a surname that carried weight; but others needed a patron for, as William Cecil put it, a man without a friend at court was like 'a hop without a pole'. To be noticed by his sovereign was very heaven. A young man with looks and wit as his sole assets could still make a favourable impression, as was the case of Charles Blount, to whom Elizabeth said at their first meeting 'Fail you not to come to court and I will bethink myself for to do you good.' The stakes were high, for the Queen was the outstanding source of patronage.

Preparation for court required more than an expensive wardrobe, for Elizabeth valued intelligence as no less important than courtly graces or skills in the tilt yard, and she expected a courtier to be a rounded Renaissance man. Sir Thomas Hoby's translation of Castiglione's *Il Cortegiano*, which appeared in 1561, was (as the title-page proclaimed) 'very necessary and profitable for young gentlemen and gentlewomen abiding in court, palace or place'. Castiglione's ideal courtier was expected to be a companion to his sovereign, not merely serving as a grave councillor or as a skilled soldier, but also showing himself to be a man of wit and fashion, able to discourse knowledgeably on a variety of topics, to play at least one instrument well, to sing a part in tune, to dance and to ride superbly, and to be always dressed for the occasion. Such all-round excellence was hard to achieve; but amongst Elizabeth's courtiers Leicester, Sidney, Hatton, Raleigh, and Essex would each have secured high marks in Castiglione's tests to become regarded as 'virtuosos of versatility'.

Progresses and prodigies

Much more than any previous sovereign, Elizabeth developed the summer progress, her annual holiday, as a piece of statecraft; for it enabled her to get to know much of her realm and also to show herself to her people. Whereas medieval monarchs had travelled simply to change residence and take advantage of provisions available in different parts of the royal estate, and while Henry VIII had escaped from the capital with a few chosen companions for a season's hunting, his younger daughter took the whole court on tour of the provinces. Nothing did so much to strengthen the average subject's bonds of affection to his sovereign as catching sight of her as she rode by with her train of followers, and Elizabeth's progresses became legendary.

In addition to staying at her own houses in the Home Counties, Elizabeth invited herself to her wealthier subjects much farther afield. Some courtiers made themselves bankrupt by building 'prodigy houses' large enough to accommodate great numbers of guests and, in many cases, following the ground-plan of a palace. Christopher Hatton dedicated Holdenby in Lincolnshire to the Queen as 'a shrine' for her to dwell in, and his invitations for her to visit him were frequent and pressing. William Cecil in 1564 began building Theobalds, near Enfield, in Middlesex, as a mansion suitable for entertaining Elizabeth; but he always shuddered at the costs of a royal visit. At Theobalds the dining-room would become her privy chamber, the Vine Chamber was transformed into her withdrawing room, the Tower Room served as the Lord Chamberlain's apartment, and so forth. The lesser fry had to make do with outhouses or tents at all but the largest mansions, and there was much bickering about rival claims to particular lodgings. Sir Henry Lee felt unable to rough it in a tent during the Hampshire progress in 1591: 'I am old and come now evil away with the miseries of progress,' he wrote. 'I followed Her Majesty until my man returned and told me he could get neither lodging for me nor room for my horse.' Elizabeth's favourites were extremely touchy about the quarters assigned to them. During the royal visit to Archbishop Whitgift's palace at Croydon, Lord Howard of Effingham, the Lord Chamberlain, was persuaded into allowing Raleigh to occupy the suite set aside for Hatton and there was a dreadful scene, with the Queen shouting at Howard.

The route to be taken was planned months in advance, yet the Queen kept changing her mind – 'every five hours', one official complained – and once she had set out would of a whim decide to alter course so she could pay a surprise visit to someone, and this last-minute change of plan would happily be called 'a by-progress', placing the unsuspecting host and the household officers in no little difficulty. But the general plan would have been carefully worked upon, with gentlemen ushers inspecting lodgings well ahead and mayors reporting on the prevalence of infection. While the itinerary was still indefinite, men in danger of having to play host to the court would make discreet enquiries of the Lord Chamberlain and offer excuses; few actually claimed that a royal visit would be financially awkward, such as the Marquis of Winchester – a Lord Treasurer's son – who wrote that the Queen's stay would make 'more charge than the constitution of Basing may well bear'. The Earl of Bedford pleaded with Burghley to ensure that 'Her Majesty's tarrying be not above two nights and a day' when she came to Woburn Abbey. So general was the wish to escape altogether from this honourable burden that few believed Lady Norris was in earnest about wanting the Queen to stay at Rycote. Once details were settled, supplies would be laid in at the prodigy houses, new ovens built, additional carpets, hangings, and plate borrowed, musicians and actors engaged, and everything 'made sweet against the Queen's coming'. Relations and neighbours were expected to cooperate with gifts of food and drink.

To send the court on tour was a formidable undertaking. Over two hundred carts formed an advance baggage-train on the lengthier progresses and heavy rains could necessarily upset the timetable. In 1574 when Elizabeth arrived safely at Bristol she publicly thanked the Almighty for 'preserving me in this long and dangerous journey'. If the weather were fine she would often ride side-saddle, otherwise she would travel in her coach; in front of her rode a noble bearing a sword and beside her were her bodyguard of henchmen. The entire train of officers of state, household officials, and servants rarely numbered less than five hundred individuals, forming a majestic procession that wended its way across the countryside at four miles per hour. Londoners understandably had the lion's share of the Queen, and country folk who came to gape and cheer as she went by knew they would be lucky if she passed their way again. It was a critical Spaniard, not a loyal subject, who dwelt on the popularity these personal appearances engendered:

She was received everywhere with great acclamations and signs of joy, as is customary in this country, whereat she was exceedingly pleased and told me so, giving me to understand how beloved she was by all her subjects and how highly she esteemed this. . . . She would order her carriage sometimes to be taken where the crowd seemed thickest, and stood up and thanked the people.

Another Spaniard in England shrewdly remarked 'in pompous ceremonies a secret of government doth much consist', but Elizabeth knew by instinct how to act the part of a crowned head in a way that would endear her to ordinary people. In Huntingdonshire Serjeant Bendloes said to her coachman, 'Stay thy cart, good fellow, stay thy cart that I may speak to the Queen', and though she laughed at the man's boldness she gave him her hand to kiss; at Warwick, when she realized how nervous the Recorder was about

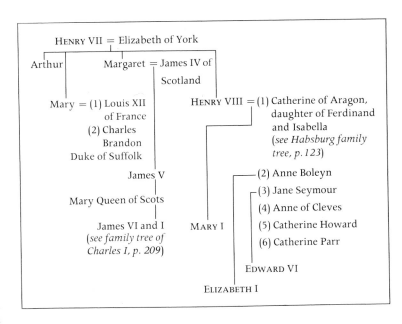

making his speech, she told him 'You were not so afraid of me as I was of you.'

In the first half of the reign a summer progress was the norm and was only cancelled in time of crisis – for instance, during the French War of 1562 – and when Mary Queen of Scots escaped to England in 1568, Elizabeth limited her travels to the Home Counties, 'as she is careful to keep near at hand when troubles and disturbances exist in adjacent countries'. She visited Southampton in 1560 and 1569, Cambridge in 1564, and Oxford in 1566. In 1572 she journeyed to the Midlands for the first time and, after spending the following summer quietly in Kent and Sussex, set out in 1574 for Bristol. Her longest progress was in 1575, when she stayed at the Earl of Leicester's Kenilworth for three weeks and then went on to Lady Essex's house at Chartley, north-east of Stafford. This was the most northerly part of her realm she ever visited; though she had hoped to extend her travels to Shrewsbury and Ludlow, this proved impracticable. Her last prolonged progress was to East Anglia in 1578, when she laid up in her head 'such goodwill as I shall never forget Norwich'. Other cities were anxious to receive her in subsequent years, including Salisbury, York, and Leicester, but they were disappointed. Even in her later years Elizabeth took to the roads, being fêted by the Earl of Hertford at Elvetham in 1591 and by the Sydneys at Penshurst in 1602. Her ministers, worrying about the Queen overtiring herself, tried to persuade her to stay put. Against all advice in 1600 she had gone to Nonsuch Palace and then on the spur of the moment had decided to go farther afield. 'The lords are very sorry for it, but Her Majesty bids the old stay behind and the young and able to go with her.' Like Alice's Red Queen she seemed restless, and right at the end of her long reign brought her court to stay with Lord Keeper Egerton at Harefield for a traditional round of feasts, allegorical plays, and other diversions. Henry VIII, by contrast, had undertaken progresses on this scale only once in his reign, when he visited York in 1541.

The Elizabethan Renaissance

Inheriting her father's interest in music, Elizabeth maintained a large musical establishment: apart from the choir of the Chapel Royal it comprised over sixty instrumentalists, including seventeen trumpeters, seven viol players, seven flautists and recorder players, two harpists, and three drummers. Musicians came in for a goodly share of royal patronage. Christopher Tye, who had taught the Queen the virginals, was appointed to the parish of Doddington, Cambridgeshire, which was the richest living in England; and his bishop was required to grant him almost permanent leave of absence so he could be at court. Those giants of composition, Thomas Tallis and William Byrd, were jointly granted the monopoly of publishing all vocal and instrumental music, including the ruled 'manuscript' paper. Byrd, at length organist of the Chapel Royal, was never in danger from his Catholic recusant tendencies. It is clear from Elizabeth's grants that besides performers and composers she attracted to court men skilled in making instruments, such as George Langdale, who perfected the sackbutt, and William Treasorer, the repairer of organs, who devised 'a rare musical instrument for our Chamber, such as we have not heard the like before'. Music in consequence played a key part in the everyday life of the court.

Poets were less fortunate. John Lyly won immediate success with *Euphues, or the Anatomy of Wit* (1579), which has some claim to be regarded as the earliest English novel; and he hoped for the post of Master of the Revels. To substantiate his claim he wrote a number of 'court comedies', such as *Woman in the Moone*, acted by the children of the Chapel Royal, and *Endymion*, a risqué drama dealing in a scarcely-veiled way with Leicester's passions. But rewards were so slow in coming to Lyly that he petitioned the Queen in 1590: 'After ten years' tempest, I must at the court suffer shipwreck of my times, my hopes and my wits.' Three years later he wrote in desperation and though he secured the reversion of the Mastership of the Revels, waiting for dead men's shoes was a painful business and the official in post outlived him. Edmund Spenser fared little better. He had hitched his waggon to Leicester's star, but his patron found him indiscreet and rewarded him with a junior post in Ireland, which seemed banishment from 'Cynthia's court'. In Ireland he wrote the earliest books of the *Faerie Queene*, which was dedicated to Elizabeth as a matter of course. The primary aim of this elaborate allegory (as he announced in his preface) was 'to fashion a gentleman or noble person in virtuous and gentle discipline', based on the twelve moral virtues of Aristotle. At one level, then, this was a 'Book of the Courtier', for instructing men in the ways of courtesy, though to avoid envy, instead of singling out a contemporary hero such as Philip Sidney, whom readers might take as a model knight, Spenser chose Arthur, the folk hero. A secondary aim was the glorification of his sovereign in her two personalities – as Queen and as 'a most virtuous and beautiful lady'. As a result fairyland became located in Elizabethan England and was peopled by characters that were readily identifiable; the Queen, indeed, appeared in the different guises of Belphoebe, the virgin huntress, of the chaste Britomart, and of Gloriana the Fairy Queen. Spenser

came over to present his first three books to her in person and she subsequently gave him an annuity of £50 a year, though there was to be no post at court for the laureate who had written the finest English poem since Chaucer. He made much of his miserable condition in his fable *Mother Hubberds Tale*:

> So pitiful a thing is Suitors state!
> Most miserable man, whom wicked fate
> Hath brought to Court, to sue for had ywist
> That few have found, and many one hath missed!

Spenser's friendship with Raleigh did him no good and he was thinking of Sir Walter's fall from grace rather than his own plight when he came to paint the court in sombre colours:

> And, sooth to say, it is no sort of life
> For shepherd fit to lead, in that same place,
> Where each one seeks with malice and with strife
> To thrust down other unto foul disgrace,
> Himself to raise . . . .

The Master of the Revels, the post Lyly had coveted, was much more concerned with masques than with drama proper during the first half of the reign, and what had under Henry VIII been 'masking after the manner of Italy' took firm roots, to develop under his daughter specifically English characteristics. There were set pieces, such as a fortress or a ship, chariots and triumphal cars, and elaborate costumes with dances interspersed with songs and spoken dialogue. Masques were invariably staged during the twelve days of Christmas, on Shrove Tuesday, and on Midsummer's Eve, and to stage such a production became the normal way of honouring an embassy or celebrating a courtier's wedding. These masques were rich in allegory, with characters representing 'Friendship', 'Peace', 'Purity', and 'Desire', and contained countless allusions to mythology, both classical and British. In the intervals of the masque the eight 'court interluders' played an *entr'acte*; but from about 1575 the boys from the Chapel Royal were much in demand for theatricals and became noted as much for their acting ability as for their singing. The popularity of the boy actors under their talented master, William Hunnis – distant successor to William Cornish – soon brought the future of English drama under attack from Puritans. As the subject-matter of drama broadened it was labelled 'mere bawdy fables', for the play was for Puritans a pagan thing, idolatrous, unseemly, and corrupting. The court plays were regarded as especially sinful since they began at the late hour of 10 p.m., were sometimes produced on the Lord's Day, and, worst of all, had boys playing female parts. One Puritan pamphleteer recognized the strength of his opponents: 'Plays will never be suppressed while Her Majesty's fledged minions flaunt it in silks and satins. They had as well been at their popish service in the devil's garb,' ruffed and surpliced in the Queen's chapel. At the same time the dramatic companies under the patronage of Leicester, Sussex, and others were under heavy fire. Had the Puritan city fathers had their way all the playhouses in London and the suburbs would have been closed – as they were to be closed in the Commonwealth – so no honest man would ever again have taken up 'the base trade of a mercenary interlude player'. The Queen's active support, political and financial, saved the drama from being sacrificed on the altar of Calvinistic principle and, indeed, nothing less than her own patronage could have sufficed to keep the drama alive against such unrelenting opposition.

In 1583 Elizabeth formed her own company, 'Queen Elizabeth's Men', by choosing a dozen of the best actors from the existing companies; and besides performing at court they went on tour. Even the City of London was forced to lease them a playhouse. Following her lead, Howard of Effingham formed the Lord Admiral's Company, led by Edward Alleyn and financed by Alleyn's stepfather, Philip Henslowe, who gave Christopher Marlowe his first chance. The 'Lord Chamberlain's Men' were also instituted in the same year, though it was not for another nine years, with Lord Hunsdon's reorganization of the company, that it became important and firmly associated with William Shakespeare. Elizabeth came with her favourite Essex to the first performance of *A Comedy of Errors* and a few months later was guest of honour at the earliest production of *A Midsummer Night's Dream*, performed for the wedding of the Earl of Derby and Lady Elizabeth Vere. No fewer than ten new plays were produced at court in the winter of 1601–2, and such is a remarkable testimony to the Queen's tremendous interest in the drama at the end of her life. By then Ben Jonson had established himself with *Cynthia's Revels*, which Elizabeth much enjoyed.

Until his fall from his horse in the Greenwich tilt yard in January 1536, Henry VIII had been a regular contender in the lists. His daughter appreciated the importance of favouring what was the only form of organized sport. She enlarged the tilt yard at Whitehall Palace in 1561 and on the west side built a high gallery for spectators. As the reign developed, the Accession Day tilt on 17 November became the principal contest of the year, held in an allegorical setting to honour the Queen, according to a scheme devised by Sir Henry Lee, who had invented for himself the office of Queen's Champion of the Tilt in 1580. There was great competition for seats in the covered stands, which cost 12d. each, and at Whitehall on that day 'not only very fine lords were seen, but also beautiful ladies, not only in the royal suite, but likewise in the company of the gentlemen of the nobility and the citizens'. Some days before, the seeded champions would have issued their challenges and on Accession Day they would process with their retainers in their distinctive colours into the tilt yard. A spokesman for each champion mounted the steps beneath the Queen's window to recite a well-turned speech and offer her an appropriate present; once this was accepted the contestant was permitted to take part. The victors received prizes from Elizabeth at the end of the day but were expected to present their shields for hanging in the Shield Gallery of the Palace, overlooking the River Thames. The prowess of knights at arms fighting for the love of a fair lady fitted in admirably with the concept that the poets had fostered of a Virgin Queen.

Where other queens had found their sex to be a matter of weakness, Elizabeth made it a source of peculiar strength and succeeded in evoking a remarkable emotional response from those around her, who felt bound to pay her a special kind of homage simply because she was a woman. This secular devotion owed most to the medieval idea of chivalry, which had kindled a deep respect for spotless maidenhood, and it was on quite a different plane from the religious homage paid to her as anointed Queen and as Supreme Governor of the Church. With the passing of the years this developed with her own encouragement into a strong personal cult of the Virgin Queen – a mystical romance lived out with her courtiers on a public stage, either in her palaces or on progress.

Three Tudors, *Henry VII, Henry VIII, and Elizabeth, in a slightly unusual situation – on the ivory handles of table-knives, made about 1607. (174)*

Eight
PHILIP IV OF SPAIN
Prisoner of ceremony

✳

JOHN H. ELLIOTT

HE COURT OF THE KING OF SPAIN cannot properly be called a court in comparison with those of France or England . . . or of many other lesser European princes. It is, rather, a private house with an enclosed style of life.' For a Frenchman like François Bertaut, on a mission to Madrid from the court of Louis XIV in 1659, the virtual invisibility of the King of Spain came as a surprise.

The king is seen only in private audiences which he gives on request, particularly one day a week, when he comes to a room specially designed for this purpose; or else when he attends the chapel or receives an ambassador. . . . The rest of the time he is shut up in his palace. The two cloistered courtyards of the palace are always thronged with people doing their shopping in the court-yard shops, or going to do business with the councils, which meet in the mornings in the ground floor rooms. This means that the palace square is always crowded with coaches. But one never sees anyone at the windows, or climbing the stairs, or coming and going – as if the king were not there at all.

By 1659 Philip IV was an ageing and melancholy monarch, living a more secluded life than in the early years of his reign, which in 1621 had begun so hopefully. But the relative seclusion of the King of Spain was no novelty; and the general pattern of Spanish court life, with its strange blend of magnificent but occasional public ceremony and its continuous but concealed domestic ritual, had developed long before Philip came to the throne.

Like other European courts, that of Habsburg Spain combined in rather haphazard fashion the functions of household and government. The government, in common with that of other sixteenth- and seventeenth-century states, was essentially that of the King. But the King of Spain was the greatest king in Christendom, and his dominions

spanned the globe. To administer this world-wide empire it had therefore been necessary to develop a massive bureaucracy, organized round a series of councils which sent up their recommendations to the King in the form of written *consultas*.

The councillors, the secretaries, and the proliferating hordes of officials, then, constituted an integral part of the court; and somehow they had to be housed and accommodated. But this had its difficulties. One of the peculiarities of the new Spain which emerged from the union of the crowns of Castile and Aragon in the late fifteenth century was that, for a long time, it lacked a capital. The court of Ferdinand and Isabella, although it settled down for periods in Toledo or Valladolid, remained peripatetic; and since the Emperor Charles V was even more of a traveller than his grandparents, and always had a number of important Spanish officials in his entourage as he moved around Europe, Spain had no fixed seat of government throughout the first half of the sixteenth century.

'Madrid alone is the court'

It was only with the return of the new King, Philip II, from Flanders to the Iberian peninsula in 1559 that the outlines of a definitive pattern began to appear. In 1563 that unconvivial royal bureaucrat set out to build himself an appropriately monastic residence, the Escorial, set in the foothills of the Guadarrama mountains. The Escorial was reasonably close to the still relatively insignificant town of Madrid, to which the court and the administration had moved from Toledo in 1561 – initially, perhaps, as no more than a temporary expedient. But Madrid's location at the very centre of the Iberian peninsula had obvious geographical advantages, and here the government settled down. On Philip's instructions the town's medieval castle, the Alcázar, was remodelled as a royal residence and as a home for the councils; and from this time onwards, except for a brief and abortive attempt in the reign of his son Philip III to remove the court to Valladolid, it could fairly be said that 'sólo Madrid es corte' – Madrid alone is the court.

Indeed, Madrid *was* the court in every sense of the phrase. In the 1530s it was little more than an overgrown

It was Philip's fate *to see Spain decline from the pinnacle of wealth and power which it had occupied during the reigns of his father and grandfather. The record both of that public decline and of his private disappointments is written in the series of portraits painted of him by Velázquez and his assistants. (175)*

village with fewer than five thousand inhabitants. A century later it had a population of well over 100,000 and had become a monstrous urban growth in the centre of Castile. Located on the banks of the undistinguished River Manzanares – scarcely more than a rivulet for much of the year – all its supplies had to be brought overland along the roads and mule tracks that criss-crossed the Castilian *meseta*. The price of foodstuffs was correspondingly high. Nothing, in fact, was cheap in Madrid. Housing was particularly expensive, and most of Madrid's houses were unimpressive constructions of brick and mud, for lime was scarce locally, and there were no stone quarries nearer than the Escorial.

In spite of the high cost of living and of building, Madrid expanded rapidly in the first two decades of the seventeenth century, especially after the definitive return of the court from Valladolid in 1606. It was in these years, during the reign of Philip III, that the town really acquired the character and the style of a capital city. The great landed nobles of Castile, who had been largely excluded from central government, played relatively little part in court life under Philip II, preferring a spacious existence on their own estates to the narrow and gloomy confines of the Escorial. But Philip III's court was both socially and financially far more attractive than that of his father, and grandees like the dukes of Infantado now hastened to build or acquire a residence in Madrid.

Armies of servants accompanied their masters to the capital, while the court itself proved an irresistible magnet to petitioners, place-hunters, and *pícaros* from all over

Spain. Consequently Madrid was soon hopelessly overcrowded and its crime rate soared. In a vain attempt to clear the capital of its hordes of idle and unemployed, the government in 1611 ordered the great nobles to return to their estates. The order was ignored. Instead, more and more of the flotsam and jetsam of a depressed and impoverished society flowed into the capital, where feverish building failed to keep pace with the demand for houses. There were already ten thousand private houses by 1623, according to a street census taken by royal officials. Not all these houses, however, were as private as their owners would have liked, for the King possessed the right to lodge foreign ambassadors, royal officials, and court servants in any Madrid houses which were more than one storey high – an imposition which naturally encouraged residents to keep their buildings low. With some 1,700 members of the royal households and nearly four hundred councillors and government officials to be accommodated, the requirements of the court therefore placed a heavy strain on Madrid's limited resources.

But the court, after all, had created Madrid; and the court acted, too, as the agency through which the wealth of Spain's dominions in Europe and the Indies was funnelled into the arid plateau of central Castile. This process was of less benefit to the Castilian economy than it might have been, since the highly privileged consumer society of Madrid looked to foreign imports to meet many of its luxury requirements – Flemish tapestries, Italian furnishings, glassware and silks, and high-quality northern cloths. Repeated

Madrid had become the capital of Spain during the reign of Philip II. It grew fast during that of Philip III. By the time of Philip IV it contained ten thousand houses and its streets were thronged with bulky coaches. But its royal palace continued to be the old and gloomy Alcázar (left, as it looked in the mid sixteenth century, drawn by Antony van der Wyngaerde). The centre of the city was occupied by the 'plaza mayor' (right), designed by Juan Gómez de Mora for Philip III, who is shown crossing it on horseback. (176–78)

attempts at sumptuary legislation, intended to check the alleged immorality of extravagant living and to curb the outflow of bullion, had little effect. But the demands of courtiers and of royal officials also helped to generate employment, both in domestic service and in the trades and professions. A horde of scribes and notaries recorded every contract of this intensely legalistic society; printers turned out a wide variety of books, tracts, and news-sheets for the entertainment and edification of a cultivated urban élite with time and money to spare; and masons and decorators, tailors, hat-makers, cobblers and furriers, confectioners and pastry-cooks busied themselves with the needs of a clientele which spent more than it had, and lived – as everyone from the King downwards lived – on credit and broken promises.

By the 1620s this urban élite had succeeded in turning an unpromising location – too hot in summer, too cold in winter – into a passable capital city. Foreign travellers, who were surprised by the absence of town walls, found distant views of Madrid impressive. Closer inspection, however, was less reassuring. The streets were wide, but, as an English visitor remarked, 'very foul and nasty'. Coaches bumped their way over hillocks of caked mud, and the stench of rubbish and excrement was so overpowering that it was necessary to resort to a liberal use of perfume. But the air of Madrid, like its water, was generally held to be good, and there were two fashionable public promenades where it could be savoured to advantage – along the banks of the Manzanares down by the palace, and on the eastern side of the town, in the Prado.

In the evenings the poplar-shaded avenues of the Prado would be thronged with the coaches of the ladies of the court – *maisons volantes*, as a French visitor described them, although with their mules, and their heavy Cordoban leather hangings, they were not exactly air-borne. Court gentlemen accompanied these coaches on horseback, and the Spanish court had an elaborate system, known as the *galanteo*, by which gentlemen, even if married, were permitted to pay public court to the ladies of the palace, waiting for them to appear at the palace windows, and following on foot beside their coaches when they took the evening air.

Coaches, of which there were nine hundred in Madrid in 1637, also cluttered the capital's principal thoroughfare, the *calle mayor*. This was the street where many of the nobles had taken up residence, and it also contained some of the more imposing of Madrid's numerous churches and convents. Nearby was the great *plaza mayor*, laid out in the last years of the reign of Philip III by the court architect, Juan Gómez de Mora. Symmetrically lined with uniform balconied houses built above arcades, the *plaza mayor* served not only as a market and a meeting-place, but also as superb forum for court, municipal, and religious activities. Close and constant involvement in urban life did something to save the Spanish court from the worst dangers of isolation, and fifty thousand people could be jammed into the *plaza* to watch spectacles that appealed equally to courtiers and people – bull-fights, javelin jousts (*juegos de cañas*), religious processions, and inquisitorial *autos-de-fé*.

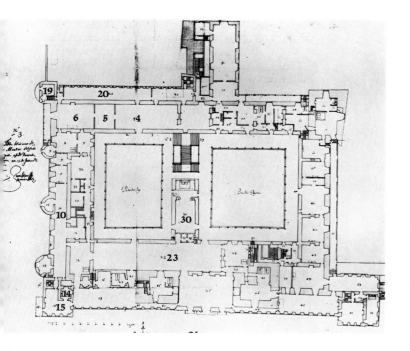

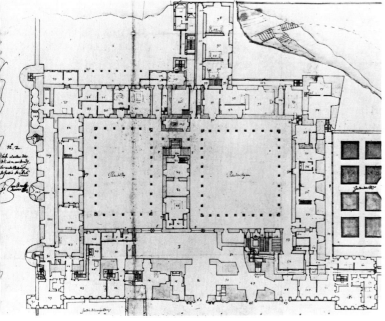

Philip's palace *of the Alcázar was destroyed by fire in the eighteenth century, but its plan is known from drawings made by Gómez de Mora when he refitted it in 1626. There are two courtyards, the King's on the left, the Queen's on the right. Their apartments were on the upper storey (top drawing), with the chapel (numbered 30) shared by both. Nos. 4, 5, and 6 are state-rooms; 10 the Gilded Gallery; 15 and 14 the King's study with its oratory. No. 23 is the 'salón de comedias', the principal hall, used for feasts and entertainments. On the northern side are the 'galería del cierzo' (20) and the Torre de Francia (19). The Count-Duke of Olivares had a suite in the northern wing, close to the royal apartments. The ground-floor rooms were occupied by the King's brother and sister and the leading officers of the court; those in the north wing were council rooms. (179,180)*

Life in the Alcázar

The *calle mayor* linked central Madrid to the royal palace, the Alcázar, which was built on a slight eminence on the western side of the city, looking out towards the Manzanares and the snow-capped Guadarramas. The palace was a gloomy and antiquated building, with small windows and ill-lit rooms. Basically it was a great rectangular fortress with an extended eastern annex which housed the kitchens, the bakery, and the so-called Treasury House, containing lodgings and studios for the court painters. Gómez de Mora gave the principal façade a face-lift around 1626, and he also made skilful use of the great vaulted spaces which ran beneath the Alcázar to carve out cool and pleasant summer quarters for the royal family. But the building as a whole remained obstinately intractable.

Much of the old Alcázar was destroyed by a great fire in 1734 and a new palace, the present Palacio de Oriente, rose on its site. But Gómez de Mora's ground-plans of the two principal floors give some idea of the appearance of the Alcázar in 1626, and of how space was distributed in a building which had to fulfil a dual function as a royal residence and as the centre of government. It was constructed around two large arcaded courtyards, those of the King and the Queen, in which, rather incongruously, shops were installed. Carriages, entering from the great *plaza* in front of the palace, drew up in a vaulted yard, where the occupants descended. From here they proceeded on foot to one or other of the *patios*. The King's courtyard was on the left; and in 1626 its ground-floor apartments were occupied by the King's young brother, the Cardinal-Infante Don Fernando, and by his sister, the Infanta María, who was courted in vain by the future Charles I of England in 1623, and was now known as the Queen of Hungary, following her betrothal to the son of the Emperor Ferdinand II. Other ground-floor rooms were allocated to the Countess of Lemos, as principal Lady of the Bedchamber to the Queen of Hungary, and to the Marquis of Heliche and his wife, who was the daughter and only child of the King's favourite and principal minister, the Count-Duke of Olivares. The rooms in the northern wing and along the northern range of the Queen's *patio* were reserved for the use of the various councils, and in the vaults beneath them there were further council rooms and secretarial offices. Only very rarely did the King attend a meeting of the Council of State, but in 1622 he had little windows let into the walls of the principal council chambers, so that he could listen in without being observed.

Between the two great courts was a monumental staircase, leading to the King's and Queen's apartments on the main floor. At the top of the staircase stood the royal chapel. Along the galleries and corridors of this floor were posted halbardiers of the royal guards – the guard of the archers and the Spanish and German guards – in their yellow- and red-striped uniforms. The King's apartments and those of his brother Don Carlos ran along the western and part of the southern sides, while the Queen's were to the south-east and the east. The Count-Duke of Olivares occupied a suite in the northern wing, with convenient access to the royal apartments.

A new façade was added to the palace by Gómez de Mora, giving it more light and a less military air. The earlier arrangement (seen in Wyngaerde's drawing) was left embedded in the new, as is evident from the lower plan opposite. (181)

When a foreign ambassador was summoned to an audience he would be conducted to the audience chamber through a succession of dark but handsomely furnished rooms, which were hung in the winter months with tapestries, and in the summer with pictures from the royal collections. As the door of the audience chamber was thrown open, the King would be revealed standing alone at a desk or table, and he would raise his hand to his hat as the ambassador made his entry. He remained standing, quite motionless, throughout the audience, which he would conclude with one or two impeccably courteous banalities, again touching his hat as the ambassador withdrew.

Further rooms, and a long 'Gilded Gallery' decorated with sixteenth-century frescoes, led to the Torre Dorada – the Gilded Tower – in the south-west corner. Here, with a private oratory adjoining, was the King's study, from the verandah of which he enjoyed splendid· views of the gardens, and, in the distance, of the royal summer-house, the Casa del Campo. Running off the Gilded Gallery were the two rooms in which he took lunch and dinner. The King, like the Queen, ate almost all his meals alone, which meant that no more than a small army of household gentlemen and servants was present to attend to his needs.

Sanitary arrangements are conspicuous from the ground-plan – as they may have been from the palace – by their absence, although there are one or two withdrawing rooms in the royal apartments which may have been used for this purpose. But other more informal arrangements were probably a commonplace. On one famous occasion Philip, not yet king, ordered the Count of Olivares, as a gentleman of his household, to fetch his chamber-pot. As he brought it the Prince turned to him and said: 'I am very tired of you, count,' at which Olivares, bowing deeply, kissed the exalted object and retired from the room.

The royal suite was separated from the King's bedroom by the great *salón de comedias*, splendidly decorated from the late 1630s with royal portraits of the kings of Castile and the magnificent tapestry series of Charles V's conquest of Tunis. The King and Queen ate in public in this hall on special occasions, like the marriage of a lady in waiting; but it was primarily used for the masques and plays which became a principal feature of court life under Philip IV. Between the *salón de comedias* and the main façade were further galleries and rooms, remodelled by Velázquez in the 1640s to make the famous hall of the mirrors and the octagon. These and the adjoining southern gallery contained some of the choicest pieces of the royal collections – Raphaels, Titians, Tintorettos, Veroneses; and Rubenses. Further pictures hung in the *galería del cierzo* along the northern façade, which also contained a studio where Velázquez worked until 1646 when he moved to a room made vacant by the death of Prince Baltasar Carlos. At the western end of this gallery stood the Torre de Francia, so called because Francis I had for a time been held here in captivity. This was now the royal library.

Above the royal apartments were two further floors. These housed the four hundred women of the Queen's household and that of the Queen of Hungary: – *dueñas* (all widows), ladies in waiting, maids of honour or *meninas* (so called because of their low-heeled shoes), and the innumerable female servants who worked in the palace. In theory the only married man to sleep in the palace was the King himself, but the ground-plan of 1626 shows that exceptions were made both for Olivares and his son-in-law Heliche.

Rank, ritual, and routine

The thousand or more servants of the King's and Queen's households constituted a well-disciplined army, precisely graded according to function and rank. This was an intensely hierarchical court, where each rank had its own finely marked distinctions. The grandees, for instance, of whom there were thirty-two at the beginning of the century

The theatre became a part of court life under Philip IV and he introduced many new refinements from Italy. This drawing is for 'Los Celos hacen estrellas' by Juan Vélez de Guevara. (182)

and almost a hundred by the end of the reign of Philip IV, were uniquely distinguished by their right to wear hats in the royal presence. But they themselves were differentiated into three distinct categories – those who could put on their hats before addressing the King; those who began speaking and then put on their hats; and those who remained bareheaded until they had finished speaking and had returned to their places. The remainder of the titled nobility (dukes, marquises and counts) were known as the *títulos*, and the status and precedence of each was a point of honour which led to endless quarrelling and required ministers to spend precious hours in attempts at arbitration.

In 1548 the Emperor Charles V had introduced Burgundian court ceremonial and organization into Spain, and although vestiges of the court structure of medieval Castile still survived, the court of the Spanish Habsburgs became essentially Burgundian in style, with all the formality which that implied. The King's and Queen's households had separate but parallel structures, each of them under the general management of a Lord High Steward, the *mayordomo mayor*. The King's *mayordomo mayor* (the Duke of Infantado in the early years of the reign) exercised an overall control over palace arrangements, and was also responsible for the massive operation needed to keep the court supplied with food. He was assisted by a number of *mayordomos* who were drawn from the ranks of the nobility and served on a weekly basis. Beneath him extended complex chains of command running from gentlemen of the household to the porters and from the chief cook to the scullery boys. They included, too,

the King's doctors, barbers, and surgeons; the army of officials with special responsibilities for the upkeep of the palace tapestries and clocks, the care of the jewels, and the supplying of candles; and the Grand Marshal or *aposentador mayor* of the palace. The *aposentador mayor* was in charge of the palace cleaning arrangements and the upkeep of the wooden furniture; and he also had the invidious task of allocating rooms and making the arrangements (including seating arrangements) for court ceremonies. It was to this office, which carried with it a key to every room in the palace, that the King appointed his painter, Diego Velázquez, in 1652, against the wishes of several of his councillors.

The other two principal household offices were traditionally those of Grand Chamberlain (*camarero mayor*) and of Master of the Horse (*caballerizo mayor*), although the first of these posts had remained unfilled for so long that it had come to be identified with another high household office, that of *sumiller de corps*. In the opening years of the reign the Count-Duke of Olivares acquired a uniquely privileged access to the royal person both inside and outside the palace by securing appointment both as *sumiller de corps* and *caballerizo mayor*. As Master of the Horse (and Olivares was an outstanding horseman, at least until he grew too fat) he accompanied the King when he went riding and hunting, took part with him in jousts and tourneys, and had the general management of the royal stables. As *sumiller de corps* (a post which he transferred to his son-in-law, the Marquis of Heliche, in 1626) he carried one of the coveted golden

Dwarfs *were for amusement, but Velázquez and other court painters painted them with a sense of dignity which reveals the sharp intelligence that could go with a deformed body. From left to right: 'El Primo' (Don Diego de Acedo, so called because the King called* him 'primo' – cousin); 'El Ingles' (possibly an Englishman, Nicholas Hodson, brought from Flanders in 1677); and 'El Niño de Vallecas' (Francisco Lezcano, seated under an overhanging rock and holding playing cards). (183–85)

keys which allowed him entry into the royal chamber at any time of the day. In 1636 he revived the office of Grand Chamberlain in his own person. The Grand Chamberlain, or, in his absence, the *sumiller de corps*, was expected to sleep in the King's bedroom. It was he who selected the King's clothes for the day, helped him to dress and undress, and – again in accordance with Burgundian usage – handed him his towel when he wanted to wash. He was assisted in the performance of these various intimate duties by the gentlemen of the Chamber, a select group of high-ranking nobles, who were also entitled to carry golden keys.

The King's spiritual requirements were as closely attended to as his physical needs. The royal confessor – for many years a Dominican, Fray Antonio de Sotomayor – naturally exercised great influence over a king with so tender a conscience as Philip IV. The principal chaplain (traditionally the Archbishop of Santiago) was nominally responsible for maintaining the standards of court religion and morals, and for the management of the royal chapel with its chaplains, organist, chapel-master, and choristers. The Grand Almoner distributed alms in accordance with the royal wishes, and dressed the poor whose feet the King ceremonially washed on Maundy Thursday. Specially nominated royal preachers – there were ten of them in 1623 – took turns to preach before the King and Queen in the palace chapel.

The elaborate ritual which accompanied every moment of the King's day – waking, dressing, eating, praying, receiving ambassadors, giving audiences, riding, hunting, attending public ceremonies – was all minutely regulated by written rules of etiquette, which stipulated the exact order of ceremony, the functions of every official, and the perquisites allowed him. The purpose of these rules was to protect and isolate the sacred person of the King; for kings were not as other mortals, and least of all the kings of Spain. Majesty was sacrosanct and must remain inviolate. This meant that for most of their lives the royal family were shielded from the public gaze, hidden away in the palace and surrounded always by the same few faces – those of the privileged group which had achieved the supreme object of all social aspiration, proximity to the King.

Court etiquette, while traditional, was not in theory unalterable; and Philip IV, who liked everything to be done with the maximum decorum, made certain modifications. But innovation inevitably threatened old-established privilege, and was fiercely resisted by functionaries who felt their precedence or perquisites endangered. Change was correspondingly rare, and the royal inhabitants lived out their lives within an iron cage of ceremonial. But there was relief, of a kind, in the antics and jests of court dwarfs and idiots, although even this could be taken too far, as Philip's young second wife, Mariana, discovered on arriving in Madrid from the Habsburg court of Vienna. When she burst into laughter at the antics of a dwarf, she was informed that laughter was unbecoming to a Queen of Spain. In that case, the Queen sensibly replied, they should remove the dwarf. But dwarfs and cretins, like everyone else, had their properly appointed place in the structure of court life. It was their duty to accompany and amuse the King, the Queen and the Infantes, and they lived with them in an easy familiarity

Sent as a present *by Philip's aunt, the Infanta Isabella, while Philip was still a prince, the dwarf Soplillo became one of the King's most trusted companions. The portrait is by Villandrando. (186)*

that bordered on the insolent. Villandrando's portrait of the young Philip IV while still a prince, shows him with his right hand resting on the head of his dwarf Soplillo, who had been sent to him from Flanders by his aunt, the Infanta Isabel, and became his intimate companion. There were others, too, who acquired fame or notoriety under such grandiloquent nicknames as Barbarroja, Calabazas, Pablillos de Valladolid, Don John of Austria. Licensed butts of ridicule, some of the court buffoons had wit enough to turn the tables on their mockers; and the stunted forms of the dwarfs occasionally hid an inner dignity which made the great men of the court look hollow and pretentious.

Even though the members of the house of Austria moved through the seventeenth century like marionettes amidst the interminable ceremonial of court and public occasions, the early years of Philip IV showed that the tastes and personality of a monarch – if he had any – could still find room for expression. The 1620s and 1630s were a period of sudden and unique brilliance, when for a moment the Spanish court became the focus of the country's social and cultural life before the storm-clouds gathered and Spanish power crumbled in the face of rebellion at home and of defeat abroad.

Spain's last Golden Age

This sudden brief blaze of splendour reflects a fortuitous conjunction of personalities and circumstance, unprecedented and unrepeatable. In the first place, the setting was unusually propitious. Exhausted by its long wars under Philip II, Spain had drifted into a period of precarious peace in the early seventeenth century. Although the Castilian economy was brittle, the ruling class was still sustained by the wealth of the Indies and of Spain's dominions in Italy. Psychologically, the return of peace, the replacement of the austere Philip II by Philip III and his young family, and the coming to power of the aristocracy under the weak and corrupt government of the Duke of Lerma, had all helped create a great sense of release and had inspired a wave of conspicuous consumption which carried everything before it. In the first two decades of the century the grandees and nobility, who had descended like birds of prey on the pickings of the court, vied with each other in the extravagance of their display and their lavish expenditure on clothes and jewelry. No career better exemplifies the heady excitement of these spectacular years than that of the Count of Villamediana, courtier, wit, and poet, who lived dangerously, spent recklessly, and died mysteriously at the hand of an assassin in 1622, hopelessly enmeshed in a web of homosexual intrigue.

Several of these nobles, whether in Madrid or in Spain's other cultural capital, Seville, were – like Villamediana – men of taste and learning. They regarded artistic and literary patronage as a function of their rank. Andalusian aristocrats like the Duke of Alcalá or the young Count of Olivares collected classical antiquities, built up great libraries and picture collections, and patronized artists and men of letters. The Duke of Sessa employed Lope de Vega as his secretary; the Duke of Osuna, Quevedo. But it was a happy chance that this great period of aristocratic patronage should have coincided with the appearance of a handful of poets, playwrights, and artists of genius – Cervantes, Lope de Vega, Góngora, Quevedo, Calderón, Tirso de Molina, and, in due course, Velázquez.

As long as Philip III was on the throne, this brilliant upsurge of creativity was only loosely connected with the court. Philip's personal interest in anything other than hunting tended to be minimal; and Madrid's vigorous cultural life owed its vitality to private patronage and to the existence of a literate and leisured class of citizens, courtiers, and government officials. But with the King's death at an unexpectedly early age in 1621, and the accession of his sixteen-year-old son as Philip IV, the climate was transformed. For the next two decades the court, with the new King at its apex, became the centre of Spain's cultural life as it had not been since the days of Ferdinand and Isabella.

If any single individual can be held responsible for the

The Count-Duke of Olivares *dominated the court for the first half of Philip's reign. A document dated 17 June 1629 shows him and the King working closely together. On the right-hand half of the page is a memorandum by Olivares on the international situation. On the left-hand side Philip replies in his own hand. Olivares' influence was not only political. It was he who encouraged Velázquez early in his career, and Velázquez' portrait of him (below) is one of his first masterpieces. (187,188)*

176

new directing role of the court in letters and the arts, it was the King's favourite and principal minister, the Count (later the Count-Duke) of Olivares. This Andalusian aristocrat, thirty-four years old at the time of the new King's accession, already enjoyed a reputation as a lavish patron of learning in his native Seville. On assuming power in Madrid in 1621 he brought with him not only the generous traditions of patronage of his native city, but also several of its more prominent cultural figures, like the poet Francisco de Rioja, who was both his librarian and his friend. As a result, the court of Philip IV in its early years produced a remarkable fusion of the talent of Madrid and Seville. This made it only natural that the young Diego Velázquez, like so many other ambitious Sevillans, should travel to Madrid in 1622 in search of fame and fortune. Although his first attempt proved unsuccessful, his compatriots in high places busied themselves on his behalf and in 1623 he returned with the active encouragement of Olivares, and with the commissions that were to launch him on his triumphant career as Painter to the King.

Olivares, however, did much more than simply bring together the two cultural worlds of Madrid and Andalusia. Imperious, assertive, restlessly energetic, and intensely ambitious both for himself and his royal master, he deliberately set out to create a king and a court worthy of the greatest monarchy the world had ever known. Himself a man of vast, if ill-assorted, erudition, his personal ties with many of the leading intellectual figures of his day were naturally close; but by bringing into the orbit of the court such luminaries as Lope de Vega, Quevedo, Antonio de Mendoza, and Calderón de la Barca, he was also consciously pursuing a skilful exercise in public relations for the benefit of the Crown. A 'palace academy' of Spain's most prominent men of letters would outshine the half-dozen or so private academies which flourished in Madrid, and would place at the Crown's disposal a formidable pool of literary talent which might otherwise be exploited by the enemies of the regime. Playwrights and poets would sing the praises of the

Four generations of Spanish kings lie below one another in the pantheon of the Escorial. Here, already, in the magnificent marble vault that he had himself commissioned, Philip had laid all his children except three. (189)

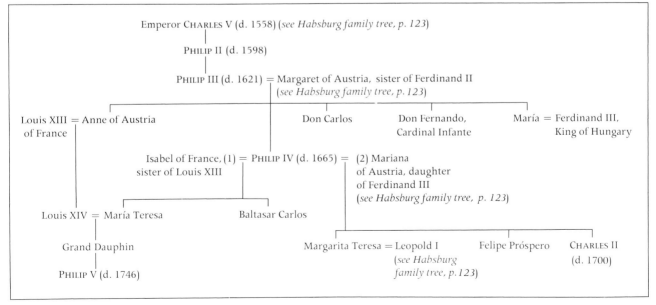

177

King and his ministers; historians like the Count of la Roca, or, in later years, the Italian Virgilio Malvezzi, would preserve the memory of their deeds for future ages. And all these luminaries would revolve around Olivares' supreme creation – the 'Planet King', 'Felipe el Grande', a monarch pre-eminent in the arts of peace as well as war.

The young King

The figure who was called upon to shoulder this heavy burden was not entirely unsuited to the part. With the fair hair, pallid complexion, and protuberant jaw of the Spanish Habsburgs there went a natural grace and a restrained dignity which impressed those who saw him on horseback or engaged in the performance of his ceremonial duties. Philip had been born in 1605, the eldest son and heir of a father who, apart from the accident of being King of Spain, was a nonentity, and of a mother, Margaret of Austria, who died when he was six. In 1612 he and his elder sister Anne were betrothed to the daughter and son respectively of the murdered Henry IV of France and the Queen Regent Marie de Médicis; and three years later, surrounded by glittering pageantry on the Franco-Spanish border, the two brides were formally exchanged across the River Bidasoa.

The future Queen Isabel of Bourbon, who was twelve years old at the time, was in due course to show the strength of character which her husband so conspicuously lacked. She brought with her to the Spanish court a taste for musical and theatrical entertainments, and a natural gaiety which would be sapped by the repeated unfaithfulness of her husband and by a long succession of miscarriages and the loss of children in early infancy. But she and the future Philip IV did not begin their married life together until 1620; and in the meantime she entered a royal family of children – Philip himself (who was ten at the time of his marriage); two brothers, Don Carlos and Don Fernando; and a younger sister, María. The survival beyond infancy of more than one male prince was a novelty in the Spanish ruling house, and in the 1620s the future employment of the two princes became a source of great preoccupation to Olivares. He feared, not without reason, that they would become the pawns of aristocratic ambition; but the royal brothers were, and remained, a closely united trio, which was only broken by the sudden death of Don Carlos, a weak and colourless figure, in 1632. The Infante Don Fernando, destined for an ecclesiastical career as Cardinal-Archbishop of Toledo, soon turned out to be hopelessly miscast. Lively, spirited, a great sportsman, and a patron of the arts, he at last succeeded in escaping from his constricting prison of Church and court to command the victorious Spanish army at Nördlingen in 1634 and to govern the Spanish Netherlands until his premature death in 1641.

Philip himself possessed the intelligence of the Cardinal-Infante, but not his dynamism. Outwardly at least he had all the virtues expected of a seventeenth-century prince. He was punctilious in his observance of the rites and ceremonies of the Church. An elegant horseman and a reckless hunter, he longed to take personal command of his armies, and envied his younger brother his military career. But he

also had a deep and lasting delight in literature and the arts. He surrounded himself with paintings, adding to, and appraising with a connoisseur's eye, the great royal collections which he had inherited; and he spent long hours in the company of artists – of Rubens, who visited Madrid on a diplomatic mission in 1628–29, and of the phlegmatic Diego Velázquez. He even indulged in a little painting himself, just as he also played musical instruments, wrote poems, and composed musical airs.

Above all he was fascinated by the theatre, and would slip incognito into one or other of Madrid's two playhouses to see the latest *comedia* (and the actresses). After he became King, plays and masques were regularly held in the palace. Some were amateur performances, staged in the royal apartments by courtiers and ladies in waiting, with the royal family sometimes taking part. Others were the work of professional troupes, summoned to appear before the King and Queen in the *salón de comedias*. Over the years these entertainments were mounted with increasingly elaborate scenery and mechanical stage effects devised by a Florentine designer and architect, Cosimo Lotti, who was brought from his native Italy to the Spanish court in 1626.

Philip's tastes were unfortunately not confined to Titian and the theatre. In 1621 the Archbishop of Granada rebuked Olivares for accompanying the King on nocturnal escapades through the streets of Madrid. If, as Olivares insisted, nothing improper occurred on these excursions, which were only intended to let the King see the world for himself, the fact remains that Philip's sexual urges were strong and uncontrolled. Most of the women with whom he had casual liaisons disappeared into the anonymity from which they had briefly emerged, but one, an actress known as La Calderona, secured a kind of immortality by giving birth in 1629 to a child who, as the second Don John of Austria (and a pallid replica of the first) would strut across the political stage in the reign of Charles II.

Philip incessantly reproached himself for his weakness, without however letting his self-accusation interfere with his pleasures. He was, he knew, setting a bad example to his subjects. 'For fornication and impurity they are the worst of all nations, at least in Europe,' wrote an English visitor in 1664, with no attempt to produce his evidence. If this had little to do with the King, the laxity of his court was startling, especially when taken in conjunction with its ostentatious piety. But there was another, and more serious, side to Philip's nature. The papal nuncio reported in 1633 that the King was trying to build up a personal library of French, Spanish, and Italian books on history, cosmography, military architecture, and poetry, and that every day after lunch he would retire for two hours of private reading. About this time, too, he set himself to translate Books Eight and Nine of Guicciardini's *History of Italy*, for reasons which he explained in an epilogue.

It might well seem strange, he wrote, that 'a king of Spain and of so many empires' should take time off to translate a history of Italy, but he had found this to be necessary in order to learn better his 'office of king'. Even kings had to acquire knowledge: 'and I do not presume to say that I know, but only that I am learning, stripping myself of my divinity in order to don more philosophy, moderation, righteousness and truth'. At least on paper this anthropomorphizing process appears impressive. Philip's reading programme consisted of the chronicles and histories of medieval Castile; the lives of Ferdinand and Isabella, and of Charles V; histories of the Indies and of the war in the Netherlands; the Roman historians – Livy, Sallust, Tacitus; and the history of France and the 'English schism'. He also read general books on geography and history (some of them for pleasure) and taught himself Catalan, Portuguese, French, and Italian. His own example would, he hoped, teach his descendants that the arts stood beside religion as a pillar of the state.

In many respects, therefore, Olivares had a promising pupil. Philip had plenty of native wit, and, within the limits of a rigorously conformist upbringing, a lively intellectual curiosity. In the early years of his reign he was lazy, and would spend six or eight hours a day out hunting, to the neglect of his royal duties. But rebukes by Olivares and a serious illness in 1627 combined to produce a change of heart. If he never became as conscientious a royal bureaucrat as his grandfather, Philip II, he seems to have spent many hours a day working on his state papers, many of which carry long marginal comments, often written in his own spidery hand. But he lacked the determination, and above all the self-confidence, to take personal charge of government. Although now and again he differed with the Count-Duke over questions of policy, the overwhelming force of Olivares' personality was too much for him. When Olivares eventually fell from power in 1643, Philip announced his intention to rule without a favourite; but the sheer complexity and weight of business, together with his own inner uncertainties, made this a forlorn undertaking. After a brief attempt at personal kingship he drifted into a dependence on the Count-Duke's nephew, Don Luis de Haro, which differed more in style than in substance from his dependence on the uncle.

This combination of a weak personality with strong cultural and aesthetic sensibilities made Philip IV an ideal subject for the kind of stage-management which Olivares had in mind. But the times were out of joint. Financial crisis, and war in central Europe and the Netherlands, prejudiced the chances of Olivares' programme almost from the outset of the reign.

Economy versus opulence

The slogan of the new regime of 1621 was *reformación*, which meant not only fiscal and economic reform, but also the reformation of manners and morals to prepare Castile spiritually for the difficult days ahead. But if austerity was to be the order of the day, it must clearly start at court. Consequently there existed an inherent contradiction between Olivares' schemes for the spectacular presentation of Felipe el Grande to the world, and his constant insistence on the need for economy and restraint. He would have liked, for instance, to revert to the old practice of an itinerant court, so that the various kingdoms of the Iberian peninsula could enjoy the royal presence by turns. But the sheer cost of getting the court on to the road made any such scheme

For Philip's brother, *the Infante Don Fernando, an ecclesiastical career was destined. He was made Cardinal-Archbishop of Toledo, but he was by temperament a soldier and a sportsman. Certainly, little spirituality can be read into Rubens' flamboyant portrait. (190)*

impracticable. A royal progress through Andalusia, which made heavy demands on the hospitality and purses of loyal vassals, was organized in 1624; and two years later Philip visited his territories of the crown of Aragon. But it proved difficult to scrape together sufficient money for the journey, and hereafter the King's travels beyond the immediate vicinity of Madrid were few and far between.

The nominal cost of the court – of the payment of the King's servants and the upkeep of the royal households – was around one million ducats a year, in a total annual budget of some ten million ducats. Military and naval expenditure therefore played a far greater part than court extravagance in Spain's financial troubles. But there were naturally many hidden costs in relation to the court which never found their way into the treasury balance-sheets, and Olivares made vigorous if sporadic efforts to prune their luxuriant growth. The King attempted several reforms of his household, and cut down sharply on pensions and financial grants. But the deserving still had to be rewarded – and what better way than to give them court offices, even if only on an honorific basis? So, paradoxically, 'reform' of the household went hand in hand with an increase in its size.

This kind of paradox constantly bedevilled the great reform programme of the early 1620s. In February 1623 the Crown promulgated with impressive fanfare its long-awaited reform decrees. These included drastic restrictions on the number of servants and the use of coaches; a ban on the import of foreign luxuries; strict regulations governing

179

Queen Mariana, *Philip's second wife, brought some light-heartedness back to his court in his later years. In Velázquez' portrait she is wearing the 'guardainfante', a vast skirt held on a frame of iron, osier, and whalebone. (191)*

the possession of silver plate, ornaments, and furniture; the closing of brothels, of which there were a large number in the alleys running out of the *calle mayor*; and sumptuary orders designed to curb the extravagance of men's and women's clothing. But one month later the Prince of Wales, to everyone's astonishment, appeared unannounced in Madrid to seek the hand of the Infanta María, and an order went out for the suspension of the sumptuary decrees for the duration of his visit. The expected austerity of a puritanical spring was therefore replaced by a round of expensive festivities in honour of the uninvited guest. For the best part of six months the Prince was royally entertained with bull-fights, tilting-matches, and tourneys in the *plaza mayor*, dances, masques, and comedies in the palace, and firework displays and torchlight cavalcades through the streets of Madrid.

The clothes worn and the gifts exchanged during the visit of the Prince of Wales and the Duke of Buckingham

effectively dissipated the puritanical atmosphere of reform which Olivares had been so anxious to introduce. But royal example, if not royal decree, did at least effect a striking change in fashion. The modish courtier of the last years of Philip III, distinguished by his curling locks and waxed moustaches, and colourfully dressed in close-fitting doublet with balloon sleeves, slashed breeches, padded stockings, and square-toed shoes, now gave way to a more austere and sombre figure. The King himself set a fashion for dressing in black. Capes became longer, the doublet shorter, and baggy breeches stretched to below the knees. Above all, the large and fragile blue ruffs of the age of Philip III were banished, to be replaced by that strange sartorial invention, the *golilla*, a stiff white cardboard collar which encircled the neck like a hollowed-out plate.

With feminine fashions, however, the new regime had less success. The *guardainfante* – that extraordinary descendant of the sixteenth-century farthingale, with its frame of iron, osier, and whalebone hoops – not only proved resistant to every attempt to legislate it out of existence, but grew wider and wider as the years went by. In 1637 it was already so wide that women could not get through the doors of churches, and in the second half of the reign the King's second wife, Mariana, adopted a still more voluminous version which made her look as if she was half enclosed in an enormous box.

The struggle between the urge for reform and the tradition of conspicuous consumption, between economy and opulence, therefore tended to be uneven. Occasional modest victories were no doubt won, as in 1630, when the court was reduced to a mere ten dishes for lunch and eight for dinner, with a maximum of four chickens, or fifteen eggs, to the plate. The most that can be said for Olivares' economy campaign is that it held court expenditure to its customary level at a time when he was attempting with some success to make the court the principal focus of Spain's literary and artistic life in a way unprecedented since the advent of the Habsburgs.

There was in any event a natural limit to the extent to which any court could be reformed without risking the loss of its essential purpose – the projection, both nationally and internationally, of the prestige and power of the prince. The Count-Duke was perfectly well aware of the propaganda value of impressive court festivities. In 1637, at a critical moment in the war with France, the most splendid *fiestas* in living memory were laid on in the court at an alleged cost of 300,000 ducats. Their purpose was said to be not only entertainment and recreation, but also ostentation, 'so that our friend cardinal Richelieu should know that there is still money both for spending, and for the chastising of his king'. But it was unfortunate that Olivares tended to be more preoccupied with trying to impress his neighbours than with gauging reactions at home. During the dark days of war Spanish public opinion turned sharply against ostentatious expenditure at court. In practice, many of the festivities were financed by private individuals like the Crown's Portuguese Jewish banker, Manuel Cortizos, rather than directly by the state, and represented a concealed form of taxation of the privileged and exempt. But the image of

The hunt *could be little more than a gory spectacle for the amusement of the court. Here the painter Mazo shows the Queen, Isabel, with her ladies at Aránjuez watching as deer and boars are driven down an enclosed track and slaughtered. In the foreground are Philip and Don Fernando, and on the right a black dwarf holding a dog which is surely the same one as in pl. 184. (192)*

court extravagance at a time of national penury provided Olivares' enemies with an easy weapon against him, and did much to destroy the credibility of his regime.

The King at home

Undeterred by the mutterings of discontented vassals, Olivares was determined that the King of Spain should live both in comfort and in style. Over the years, he and the King worked out a pattern of court life which was designed to strike a harmonious balance between the King's public functions and his private tastes. The Alcázar in Madrid remained the principal royal residence, and substantial sums were spent on improving and embellishing it. But it remained a forbidding building, and the King was delighted to escape whenever possible to other royal residences beyond the traditional confines of the court. Sometimes he would go to his grandfather's palace of the Escorial; but he

went primarily for the hunting, and he removed many of its art treasures to his other houses. The most attractive of these was at Aranjuez on the banks of the Tagus. With its enchanting gardens it was an ideal residence in the spring, and the royal family would settle here for a few weeks in April and May. These visits, like those to the other royal houses, became a fixed annual routine, although the actual length of the visits was not as rigidly determined by the calendar as foreigners believed.

Nearest to the Alcázar itself was the Casa del Campo, down by the River Manzanares. Philip preferred, however, to get rather farther away from Madrid, especially when the hunting season approached. Early in October there was splendid deer-hunting to be had in the rough wooded country around the royal house at Valsain. November and December were the months for hunting the wild boars, wolves, foxes, rabbits, and birds of prey which abounded in the hills and forests encircling the Casa Real del Pardo, some ten miles from Madrid.

It was in these forests that Philip built for himself in 1636 a small hunting-lodge, the Torre de la Parada, to which he became deeply attached. To decorate it, he commissioned 112 paintings from the studio of Rubens – a mythological cycle based on Ovid's *Metamorphoses,* together with wood-

181

land and hunting scenes and pictures of animals at play. These pictures, sent from Flanders by the Cardinal-Infante, reached Madrid in 1638. Although Rubens himself did the preparatory sketches for many of them, he left most of the work to his assistants – reasonably enough, in view of the remuneration he received. Much of the work was therefore of very indifferent quality, but in such an intimate setting the decorative impact must have been considerable. It was enhanced by ten paintings by Velázquez which also hung in the lodge. These included three royal portraits, in hunting dress, of the King, the Cardinal-Infante, and the King's young son, Baltasar Carlos; four paintings of court dwarfs; and, very probably, the *Tela Real* or *Boar Hunt*. This depicted one of the favourite rural pastimes of the court of Philip IV. The *tela* was a canvas wall surrounding a large enclosure. The boars caught in this enclosure would be driven into a smaller *contratela*, where the King and his gentlemen would repel their charges with blunt two-pronged forks. Once the boars had exhausted themselves, the huntsmen would dispatch them.

For all the number and variety of these royal houses and palaces, the King and the Count-Duke increasingly felt the lack of a residence in the capital itself, suitable for royal amusement and relaxation and for the entertainment of foreign dignitaries. The birth of an heir to the throne in 1629, Prince Baltasar Carlos – the first royal child with any apparent prospects of survival – may have given an impetus to the desire for a new palace located in a more salubrious quarter of Madrid, and set about with spacious parks and gardens. Early in the following year building began on what came to be known as the Palace of the Buen Retiro, on land adjoining the monastery of San Jerónimo, where the Countess of Olivares had kept an aviary: 'a thing of no great expense for such a king,' reported Arthur Hopton, the English resident at the Spanish court, 'yet murmured at by

the people, who will allow to their governors in time of misfortune nothing but care'.

By the autumn of 1633 a thousand men were working overtime to complete the palace by the end of the year, and it was duly inaugurated with splendid celebrations. The haste of construction showed in the building itself – a two-storied rectangular affair, with towers at the four corners, and a generally unimpressive façade. But inside it was sumptuously decorated and furnished with works of art brought from the other royal palaces and with priceless treasures sent from every part of Spain and Italy as 'gifts' to the King. In July 1634 Hopton reported that 'the whole court hath been at His Majesty's new house for a fortnight, which time hath been spent in all manner of entertainments, much to their king's contentment; wherein the Conde of Olivares took great pains, all things being ordered by himself, and so well as it savoured of his excellent judgment in all things, especially in the furniture of the house, which was such as it was not to be thought there had been so many curiosities in the whole kingdom'.

Olivares, as governor of the new palace, was clearly the principal driving force behind its construction and decoration. The master of the works was his favourite architect, Alonso Carbonel, while Velázquez was probably closely associated with the decorative design of the interior. During the 1630s the project continued to expand and develop, but the principal purpose of the Retiro was, and remained, recreational. This no doubt helps to explain the modesty of the façade, as it certainly explains the elaborate care taken over the layout and planting of the gardens. Essentially the Buen Retiro was a pleasure-pavilion set in an enormous park of formal flower-gardens, secluded groves, little pavilions and hermitages, and long avenues set about with statuary. Everywhere there was water, brought to the Retiro at great expense – fountains, terraced pools linked by canals, and a great lake, the *estanque*, used for water festivals. In the middle of the lake was a little island with a stage for theatrical productions. Here, as also in a new theatre, the Coliseo, opened in 1640 for the entertainment of a paying public as well as the court, the ingenious hand of Cosimo Lotti was much in evidence. Entranced audiences watched breathless as gods and goddesses descended from the clouds in triumphal chariots and Circe transformed Ulysses' followers into swine with a wave of her magic wand.

The Retiro was an ideal setting not only for the masques and pageants which played such a large part in the court life of the 1630s, but also for meetings of the King's 'palace academy'. Here, in the royal presence, Spain's leading poets and playwrights took part in literary and poetical contests, and exchanged the recondite epigrams that were expected of men of taste and letters. But if the Retiro was designed to allow the King to appear in his favourite role as patron of the arts, the more grandiose and martial aspects of kingship were not entirely overlooked.

The forecourt of the Retiro contained a superb equestrian statue of Philip by the Florentine sculptor Pietro Tacca; and one room in the palace was given over to the celebration of Spain's military and imperial tradition. This was the great

In the gardens outside Madrid *the court found a more congenial atmosphere than in the city itself. It was in the Prado de San Jerónimo (above), on land adjoining a monastery, that the King decided to build his palace of the Buen Retiro. (193)*

182

Three country retreats *near Madrid enabled Philip to enjoy the pleasures of hunting, masques, pageants, and poetry. Above left: the Torre de la Parada, a hunting lodge, decorated with paintings from Rubens' studio. Right: the Casa Real del Pardo, another centre during the hunting season. El Buen Retiro, the most elaborate of* Philip's palaces, set amid its gardens, groves, and fountains, was constructed in stages between 1629 and 1640. The panoramic view (below) shows it about 1636. Almost all the buildings were demolished in the nineteenth century, but the gardens have survived. (194–96)

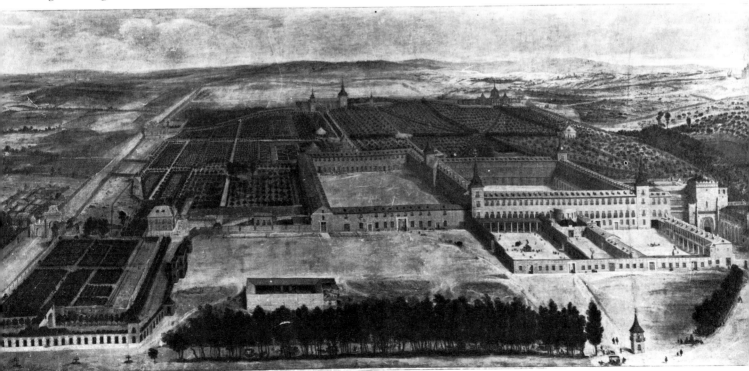

Philip's daughter, *the Infanta María Teresa, married Louis XIV of France, and in June 1659 a meeting between the two kings took place at the frontier. In this Gobelins tapestry of the scene Louis is on the left, with behind him Mazarin, Anne of Austria (his mother, and Philip's sister), and Monsieur (his brother). Behind Philip is the bride, María Teresa. (197)*

The end of greatness

It was one of the many ironies of a reign full of irony that the decoration of the Hall of the Realms was being completed at the very moment when Spain was entering on a devastating cycle of military defeats. France declared war on Spain in 1635; and after an initial run of victories the strain began to tell. As the government imposed still heavier taxes and resorted to more and more fiscal expedients to sustain Spain's colossal military effort, the general hatred of Olivares and his colleagues became almost palpable. Vicious lampoons were stuck up on the walls of the palace and passed from hand to hand, and the tone of court life – always obsessively preoccupied with petty quarrels over the most trivial points of precedence and etiquette – became increasingly acrid. Court correspondents, retailing the news of the capital to their country readers, filled their letters with stories of murders, attempted murders, and challenges to duels, as if, said one of them, 'the practice of duelling which has been banished from France had crossed into Spain'.

In his ruthless determination to prosecute the war to a successful conclusion, irrespective of the cost, Olivares succeeded in affronting the susceptibilities of one grandee after another. As more and more nobles fell out with the regime, the court was gradually abandoned by all but the Count-Duke's close friends and relatives, until the day came when the grandees' seats in the royal chapel were all but deserted, and scarcely any nobles remained to attend the King in his public functions or accompany him to the chase.

Shaken to its foundations by the revolts of Catalonia and Portugal in 1640 and by continuing reverses abroad, the days of the Olivares regime were clearly numbered. By early 1643, when the Count-Duke at last fell from power, the great age of the court of Philip IV was already at an end. Olivares, its directing spirit, had been overwhelmed in his last years in office by the disasters that were overtaking his country. The King in 1642 had left for the front in Aragon. The court festivities had ceased. Then, on top of national disaster,

Salón de Reinos – the Hall of the Realms – for which Velázquez designed a magnificent pictorial scheme. Many of the leading painters of the day were pressed into service for the occasion. Velázquez himself contributed five royal equestrian portraits – Philip III and IV and their queens, and Prince Baltasar Carlos, whose horse was given its strange barrel shape because of the placing of the picture, high up over the door. Zurbarán was called upon to paint what proved to be a curiously unsatisfactory series of the twelve labours of Hercules, although he executed only ten of them. The labours of Hercules were held to prefigure twelve great victories of the reign, the representations of which dominated the hall. Don Fernando Girón, as seen by Zurbarán, routed the English at Cadiz; Don Fadrique de Toledo, in a striking composition by Juan Bautista Maino, provided fresh laurels for the royal brow by reconquering Brazil from the Dutch; and Spinola's chivalry towards the defeated garrison of Breda was preserved for posterity by the genius of Velázquez.

Philip IV as conqueror. *On 1 May 1625 (St Philip's Day) Don Fadrique de Toledo recaptured Bahia, in Brazil, from the Dutch, and this curious painting by Fray Juan Bautista Maino was commissioned to celebrate the event. Don Fadrique exhibits a tapestry to the citizens of Bahia, in which Philip stands crowned by Victory and by Olivares and tramples on Heresy, Anger, and War. (198)*

The River Bidasoa *formed the boundary between France and Spain. Here in 1615, with immense pomp, two brides were exchanged to become queens. Brother and sister married sister and brother. Philip IV (aged ten) married Louis XIII's sister Isabel (aged thirteen). Louis (fourteen) married Philip's sister Anne (fourteen). (199)*

The Infanta Margarita, *born of Philip's second marriage, brought a touch of youth and gaiety to his later years. She was five years old when Velázquez painted this portrait. Ten years later she was to marry the Emperor Leopold I, and seven years after that to die. (200)*

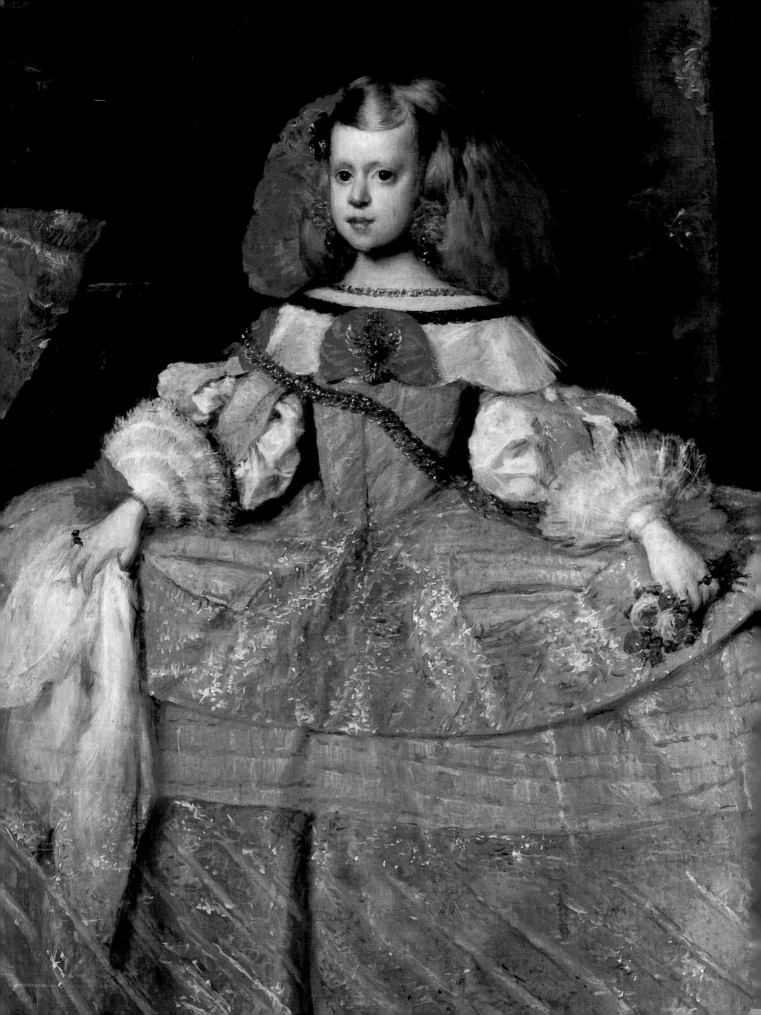

came personal disaster for the King: the death of the Queen in 1644, and, most devastating of all, the death of his only son and heir, Baltasar Carlos, in 1646 at the age of seventeen.

The King poured out his sorrow in agonized letters to a nun, Sister María of Agreda, who had become his confidante. A man whose extra-matrimonial affairs were notorious – he fathered at least eight bastards – he had always combined the weaknesses of the flesh with a high degree of religiosity. He was convinced that his own misfortunes and those of his country were the direct consequence of his sins, and fervently promised reformation while resigning himself as best he could to the blows rained upon him by a chastizing Providence. But contrition, for Philip, always came more easily than reform.

It was only with his marriage in 1649 to his niece Mariana of Austria – the bride originally destined for Baltasar Carlos – that court life began to recover something of its former splendour. The theatre of the Buen Retiro was refurbished after its long years of disuse; new masques and plays were mounted; and the birth of sickly children provided the occasion for spectacular festivities, which soon gave way to a fresh round of court mourning as they were laid to rest in the monumental building project of the second half of the reign – the marble, jasper, and porphyry pantheon of the kings, in the vaults of the Escorial.

But for a few years there was youth again in the palace – the Queen herself, the Infanta María Teresa (the only surviving child of the King's first marriage) and the new children, the Infanta Margarita (who later married the Emperor and died at the age of twenty-two), and the little prince Felipe Próspero, who lived to the age of four. This flickering return of life in the dimly lit rooms of the palace was caught by the brush of Velázquez, now the intimate of a King both ageing and disillusioned. When the French envoy asked the King's permission to present his condolences on the death of yet another Infante, Philip refused, saying that this was a child whom God had given and taken away again, and that he had lost so many that he was used to it.

The court ceremonial continued in all its frozen immobility; but at moments the royal table was reduced to fish or eggs by the refusal of merchants and shop-keepers to provide any more supplies on credit. The crippling burden of war had left both court and country hopelessly impoverished. In 1659, however, the terms of peace between France and Spain were at last agreed; and in April of the following year the King and court set out on a six-week journey to San Sebastián, where the Infanta María Teresa was to be married by proxy to the young Louis XIV of France. When the ceremony was over, the royal party moved on to the frontier fortress of Fuenterrabía, and embarked for the Isle of Pheasants on the River Bidasoa.

For months Velázquez had been busy with the ceremonial arrangements for the meeting of Philip IV and Louis XIV; but it was preceded by a more poignant meeting between Philip and his sister Anne of Austria, whom he had last seen forty-five years before as she was carried across this same river on the royal barge. Finally, on 7 June, in the island conference chamber hung with some of the best Flemish tapestries from the Alcázar in Madrid, Philip led his daughter to the line dividing the Spanish from the French side of the room, and formally handed her over to her new husband.

The marriage celebrations of June 1660 were to be the last court festivities arranged by Velázquez, who picked up a fever on his return to Madrid and died on 6 August. But there was to be one further round of festivities in what was now a dying reign – for the birth in November 1661 of a new heir to the throne, the future Carlos II. Four years later, on 17 September 1665, the King died in his summer apartments in the Alcázar. It came as no surprise to those who knew his court that a bitter dispute at once arose over questions of protocol in relation to the disposal of his body. But in due course everything was settled, and for two days, before being taken for burial in the pantheon of the Escorial, the dead King lay in state in the palace. The room chosen for the purpose was, appropriately enough, the *salón de comedias*.

Philip's signature: *'I the King'. (201)*

Nine

CHARLES I OF ENGLAND
The tragedy of absolutism

PETER W. THOMAS

O N A COLD JANUARY MORNING in 1649 Charles I set out across St James's Park towards his palace of Whitehall for the last time: on foot, under military escort, he urged the soldiers to step out, as was his wont, briskly. He knew to the last detail the part he had to play; and even an unnerving wait of some hours, in an ante-room, before the final act of his reign unfolded could not disturb his poise and self-possession. At last he passed through the great Palladian Banqueting House that some thirty years before had risen severe and stately above the rambling, rickety timber and brick of the old Tudor and Elizabethan buildings clutching at its skirts. Standing at the entrance to the royal palace, the building which Inigo Jones, the King's Surveyor, had conjured up to the astonishment, even to the alarm, of contemporaries had been from the first a kind of manifesto of the Stuart dynasty. Here, grimly, where many a royal audience and many a masque had been staged, the Army set the scene for the crisis of their dramatic *coup d'état*. The scaffold, draped in black and circled by armed troopers, stood in front of the hall; and to reach the window through which he must pass onto that stage, the King had to walk the length of the chamber beneath Rubens' magnificent painted ceiling. Securing this major achievement of the international Baroque style in 1635 had been among the most considerable (and costly) of the many artistic *coups* with which the royal aesthete had adorned his reign. As a work of art imaging in paint the ideas and aspirations so often rehearsed in royal masques, and as a tribute to his father's memory, it was dear to Charles's heart. Like the building it graced, it proclaimed – ironically now – the glory of monarchy by divine right. Rubens, as always, had risen heroically to his task: challenged to celebrate not military might or foreign conquest but the triumph of peace in the union of the three kingdoms, the painter crowned his

work, in the central oval, with the image of James I ascending, god-like, into the empyrean. Beneath this rich, recondite vision the son passed to his own very different apotheosis. With the steadfast, solitary man on the scaffold, encompassed by his enemies, we seem a far cry from the romantic prince who rode out in 1623 in search of his Spanish bride; a far cry, too, from the perfect gallant who two years later brought his teenage French wife home to share his kingdom. In the years between, a dream of Honour and Beauty, of admiring subjects united about a halcyon court, had dissolved into the air. Somehow, such a court (and such a King) as England had never before seen, flowered, flourished, and was cut down.

The making of a King

In 1625 Charles inherited a regime and policies already altered from the heyday of England's heroine Elizabeth. Among the nation at large her memory was stubbornly alive; her legend, a rallying point for resistance to Stuart polity, would be potent in the shape of things to come. At the centre matters were different. In the old Queen's time the maxims, occasionally even the practices, of pure monarchy were not unheard of: as long as government was useful and glorious the country accepted these pretensions; and at her court, for all the elaborate magnificence, a sense of social responsibility held. James I, by birth and habit attached to France, sought *his* allies and models in Europe, where England's rulers traditionally saw only enemies. He aspired to an absolutism none of the Tudors had practised. The Scottish King and his Danish wife presided over a far more exclusive circle of *arrivistes* and favourites (noble and otherwise), often nearly related to one another, and together bent on the pursuit of pleasure and self-interest. To them Gloriana's bellicosity, her pugnacious Protestant nation-alism, her accessibility, her parsimony, and the power of her Council were anathema. Determined to appear as the sole source of power and patronage, and confident they had come into a bottomless exchequer, James and Anne spent without stint.

Expensive wars were out of the question. In any case, like the sort of patriotic piracy Elizabeth encouraged, such

---

The image of kingship which Van Dyck created for Charles I owed as much to the artist's vision as to the King's sense of his own mission. In the great equestrian portrait of the King attended by his Master of the Horse, now in the Louvre, Charles rides through a triumphal arch like an English Caesar, proudly asserting his status as a monarch equal to any other in Europe. (202)

King James, Queen Anne, and 'Baby Charles': *this engraved silver plaque was probably made after 1612, when his brother Henry's death left Charles heir to the throne. (203)*

affairs were repugnant to the King's nature. They also impeded his dream of European reconciliation – so much so that he would not flinch from sacrificing Sir Walter Raleigh, greatest of Elizabethan courtiers, to the Spanish interest. On the day of Raleigh's execution the wily James mounted pageants in the streets to distract the disgruntled populace. He never lacked political cunning and recognized, however reluctantly, that even *his* policies sometimes called for a princely ruthlessness. Usually he preferred and practised a masterly prevarication: he knew how to flatter and be flattered; how to intimidate, charm, and bemuse; how to leave well alone; and, not least, how to buy off opposition. There was nothing aloof, sanctimonious, or priggish about the man. He displayed his anger, his robust, often blasphemous humour, and his deepest affections (to say nothing of his coarser instincts) quite openly.

His son was very different. He inherited some things in full measure, like the aversion of the people, and a passion for hunting and riding – two pleasures in which, as Frederick the Great remarked, the mind lies fallow. He also inherited his father's dependence on the feckless, glamorous Duke of Buckingham. The Duke excelled in swordsmanship, dancing, conversation, and love – in all of which the introspective Prince was deficient. He grew up, too, with natural disadvantages of speech and stature, in his brother's shadow. For Henry was (if we believe the propaganda) a paragon among princelings, and precociously skilled in all

the arts of peace and war. Charles's lifelong stammer tells something of what it cost him to survive such competition and to overcome ingrained inhibition. The stubborn determination and the temperate, chaste habits which enabled him to conquer his early physical weakness left him, moreover, intolerant of other men's frailties. His character showed that night at court in 1617 when James, who never shared Queen Anne's infatuation with masques, gave vent to his impatience. He was bored; and only a nimble courtier leaping forward to cut no fewer than thirty-four capers in rapid succession, followed by beloved Buckingham demonstrating his dazzling footwork, saved the day. Poor 'Baby Charles' could hardly compete with such agile gyrations: he took refuge in a series of impressively formal bows to his parents and to his partner. When his day came this grave young prince would set his own pace.

Little wonder the ageing King was somehow pleased when his son rode off with the irresistible Duke, to claim a wife. In his more lucid moments James was terrified to think where 'Steenie' and his headstrong heir would carry the kingdom. Against his better judgment he convinced himself that some good might come of their harebrained escapade. He set Inigo Jones to building a private chapel in St James's Palace for the Catholic bride-to-be. Meanwhile his 'sweet

When he was twenty-three *Charles went to Spain with the Duke of Buckingham to seek the hand of the Infanta. Reserved and unsure in his social relations (as this portrait by Mytens reveals more freely than Van Dyck would have done), he was impressed by the rigid formality of the Spanish court. (204)*

boys and dear venturous knights worthy to be put in a romance' descended on an unsuspecting Madrid. The Spanish court received its uninvited guests with a punctilious correctness and lavish gifts. In the streets enthusiastic crowds pressed round the Prince's coach, but 'took it ill he showed not himself to them in a more public manner'. He never learned winning ways or cared for popular applause. Kept at an equally proper distance from the Infanta (who was absorbed in her Lenten devotions), he watched her like a cat watching a mouse; he may even have used that perspective glass he took with him from England. His reckless attempt (more in Buckingham's line really) to woo her direct by clambering into her private garden when she was walking with her *duennas* completes the picture of a storybook silliness. Charles never outgrew the habit of sentimental gallantry. And though the vision of the Infanta rapidly faded and he shared a while in the spoilt favourite's childish pique against Spain, he never forgot the grandeur he had seen there. The memory shows in the punctilios of his behaviour and the austere stateliness of his deportment. Though Van Dyck imparted a Frenchified nonchalance to *Charles resting from the hunt* there was to the end something of the grandee about the straitlaced figure with the golden-headed cane.

Given the Spanish presence at the Jacobean court he hardly needed to visit the country to observe their haughty airs: besides, a touching dignity in the midst of debauchery came naturally to him. But he was impressed by the almost oriental formality of life in Madrid. Even at a play only the royal party sat in chairs: the court ladies reclined on turkey carpets, while the gentlemen stood at the rear of the room. He would have things somewhat this way too: ambassadors to Whitehall – and their wives – quickly learned that on formal occasions no woman, except the Queen, was permitted to sit in his presence. Not the King of Spain himself was waited on with such drill-like precision and subservience as England's monarch commanded. It is as though he had taken a leaf out of the Infanta's book: in 1623 giving audience to the Earl of Carlisle she sat aloft and unresponsive on her throne 'gloriously set forth . . . all the while as immoveable as the image of the Virgin Mary'. A main endeavour of Charles's reign would be to re-create in England the sort of hieratic *mise-en-scène* he found in Madrid.

Denied his bride, he brought back instead pictures and tapestry drawings, with a strong desire to compile a portraiture matching Velázquez, Titian, and Rubens' tributes to the Habsburg dynasty. His sympathies went deep: in the 1630s when Spain's overland access to the Netherlands was barred he opened a safe corridor through England for men and monies *en route* to stamp out Dutch Protestantism. The sight of Spanish troops marching from Plymouth to Dover was something most Englishmen could scarcely stomach. When the Spanish fleet, Tromp on its tail, hove to in English waters and English ships stood ignominiously by, succouring ancient foes instead of upholding maritime sovereignty and the Protestant cause, the country felt dishonoured. In the 1640s Charles hoped Spain would repay him by sending soldiers to his aid. Even

The Duke of Buckingham, *by contrast to Charles, could assume a variety of roles with the utmost ease. This engraving shows him at a military masquerade.* (205)

in captivity in 1647 he sat scrutinizing plans for a palace at Whitehall twice the size of the Escorial.

Meanwhile, of course, he had discovered France too, with its sophisticated style and the treasures of the Medici. From Europe, where the arts adorned and beautified the triumph of absolute monarchy over complacent (or subdued) peoples, the King took his model of splendour at court. For him the royalty of Madrid and Paris were the true type of the legitimate condition of a king. Had not his father told Parliament that England's sovereign 'must not be in a worse condition than his equals'? Charles would be as impervious to petition as the Habsburgs; as magnificent as the Medici; and every bit as fervent as his European counterparts to command a religious respect for his person, even if it meant extinguishing every untidy trace of Erasmianism. Given the actualities of the English situation – the power of the Commons, the vast wealth of London whose merchants and city potentates had ideas of their own, and the dominantly Calvinist temper of the Church – it was a formula for eventual calamity. The

The Queen's mother, *Marie de Médicis, visited the English court in 1638. She was received in the Presence Chamber of St James's, its walls hung with 'fleurs-de-lis' in her honour. Note that everyone except the three royal personages is obliged to remain standing. (206)*

Venetian ambassadors to Whitehall, who found much to admire in the cultivated, clean-living King, grasped that at the outset.

The court was certainly purged of riotous excess. The King and Queen dined in public as became great monarchs, and their tables were sumptuous. But Charles had a moderate appetite and a limited pocket; and general extravagance, drunkenness, and gluttony were curtailed. It was left to the Duke of Buckingham to stage the sort of prodigious blow-out that greeted the French ambassador Bassompierre at York House in 1626. He obviously meant, a contemporary remarked, 'to stop his mouth with a diet of meat': the 'excessive bravery on both sides' was a surfeit in itself. The cosmopolitan visitor was made of sterner stuff and survived Buckingham's bacchanal. At court he found, to his relief, magnificent company and 'order exquisite'.

All was not well with the marriage, however. At their first meeting Charles was all unspotted tenderness, Henrietta Maria the acme of modest affection. In true Petrarchan-Platonic fashion 'each others heart flew out at the windows of their eyes, and . . . lodged themselves in each others bosome'. The frisky young consort, alas, had none of the Infanta's self-control; and her entourage was noisy, wrangling, and frivolous. Her ladies, shockingly, were to be seen dancing in her presence while the King was being crowned. Repeatedly he rebuked her skittishness and their loudness; until in the end even his good manners were tried too far. Locking Henrietta Maria in her room where she proceeded, characteristically, to smash the windows with her fists, he sent her troublesome priests and attendants packing. It was not their ostentatious Catholicism he minded, so much as the unseemliness of the Queen's penances and the perpetual vulgar interference in his marriage.

Luckily for Henrietta Maria, her husband simply was not subject to amours; and even her hysterical tantrums could never dislodge his affection once fixed. She was never a great beauty and soon lost the bloom of youth, but her lustrous black eyes and her chic vivacity appealed from the first. Besides, he was determined to appear in the role of heroic lover. Buckingham's death in 1628 removed the one obstacle to a successful marriage. Their early contretemps past, Charles found in her the one intimate he needed. Rubens' fairytale *Landscape with St George and the Dragon* celebrates their idyll, while complimenting the King's addiction to the Order and religious ceremonies of the Garter. For the feudal knight-errant, a favourite persona, is a dashingly handsome Charles; the princess a plumped-up Henrietta Maria. In a scene from epic romance they stand at the calm centre of a dramatic vortex, heralding the dawn of Arcadian peace and plenty. Before the world's astonished gaze the daughter of the Medici and King James's son emerged as the archetypal couple of courtly love.

Even Daniel Mytens' altogether more documentary picture of the pair departing for the chase sees them off in a shower of roses, the flowers of Venus. Whatever lesser mortals might whisper of uxoriousness, courtiers steeped in the fashionable Platonics perceived in this match the mystical union of perfect beings. In the masque *Albion's Triumph* in 1632 the King appeared as Albanactus the Roman Emperor (another indispensable role) who is transformed by religious ceremonies into an ideal intellect, which then unites with the Queen, who is the idea of virtue. The 'Mary-Charles', the royal hermaphrodite, which emerges, reveals fundamental assumptions of personal rule: the country exists only as an object of sovereign affection; its sole choice is between passively worshipping from afar, or from nearer at hand. These masques and paintings were not for the common gaze, of course; their 'propaganda' was meant to define and sustain the identity of the initiated court.

No one would deny that the sexual coarseness of the Jacobean regime was a thing of the past. Charles showed an exceptional fastidiousness and privacy on his wedding night when he bolted his attendants out of his chambers with his own hand. Soon even those who could not abandon debaucheries 'retired into corners to practise them'. The

King was not amused when Old Parr, the oldest living Englishman, told him that the most remarkable achievement of his life was doing penance for a bastard when he was over a hundred. The ancient prodigy was silenced with a 'freezing reproof'. To friend and foe alike Charles was never spend-thrift with words – witness his enigmatic 'Remember' to Bishop Juxon as he handed him his Garter insignia on the scaffold; his brusque 'What care I for your debts?' to the Earl of Suffolk in 1633; or the exceptional note made by his Master of the Revels Sir Henry Herbert when once he was thanked for his pains more expansively than usual in a sentence of over a dozen words. Majesty need not talk, so much as simply be. Charles always accepted devotion as no more than his due, and as laconically as he did opposition. His was a feudal view of honour; and he scorned to threaten his inferiors. Conscious, in any case, of his stammer, his high falsetto, and his Scottish accent, he told Parliament at the outset that 'he loved not to hear himself speak'. He loved not hearing them speak either. His pedantic, intellectual father relished an argument: Charles disliked debate. He would engage in desultory theological talk or literary and artistic chatter; but he was baffled when political intricacies would not yield to his *idées fixes*. Over-sensitive therefore to dissent – for which he had an infallible memory – he always imagined that it must spring from personal hostility. He pursued his Parliamentary enemy, the fearsome mob-orator Sir John Eliot, petulantly at first, then with a cold ruthlessness, curtly refusing to permit the bereaved family to take his body home to Cornwall for burial. As Correr, the Venetian ambassador, observed in 1637, the King was 'extreme in nothing, except that he persists with his sentiments' and anyone he has once detested 'may be sure that he will never recover his favour'. Looking back in self-justification, Charles told his son that he had never sufficiently trusted his own judgment. In all essentials, whether touching daily deportment, plays, poems, paintings, or policy, the opposite was true. This 'truly royal spirit' who 'dares to the limit of daring', as Correr called him, 'changed the principles by which his predecessors reigned'.

Charles's Counter-Reformation

Charles I extended his 'revolution', as far as he could, over the whole range of life. The pattern of his programme for the arts, of his statecraft, his foreign and domestic policies, and of his religious aims is unmistakable and consistent. It was the objective of the personal rule he embarked upon in 1629, dispensing with troublesome parliaments, to knit all things inextricably about his divinely sanctioned monarchy. Religion inevitably became the top and bottom of the whole matter between King and Parliament, court and country. From his youth Charles was far stricter in his observances than his Calvinist father or the protean Elizabeth had been. Even the terrible news of Buckingham's death, reaching him at prayer, was not permitted to curtail his ceremonies. He watched his household like a hawk and backsliders were told to mend their ways or leave the court. In Laud he found a cleric after his own heart – 'as restless to establish his own innovations as to put down those of others'. He would insist on uniformity and decency of worship; on vestments, and

Mytens painted the King *without the Baroque bravura imparted to him by Van Dyck. This detail from 'The King departing for the Chase' with Henrietta Maria may be compared to Van Dyck's 'Charles resting from the Hunt' (see pl. 223). (207)*

candles, and the communion table altar-wise railed in at the east end; on the necessity of baptism; even on confession. These were the visible signs of a profound theological and political change. Together, Charles with his Archbishop and like-minded bishops set about shaping the English Counter-Reformation.

In the early seventeenth century most English clergy from Abbott of Canterbury down were Calvinists in doctrine; in the universities Predestinarian teaching prevailed; and everywhere preaching was regarded as the chief means of salvation. James, though reasons of state led him to attack extreme Puritanism, was in fact more sympathetic to Calvinism than Elizabeth had been; and though the Arminian Bishop Neile worked to wean him from that allegiance, he sustained the ameliorating bond that was the foundation of the English Protestant Church. Charles, who

Henrietta Maria *brought a touch of Parisian vivacity to the court of St James. In spite of difference of temperament, her marriage proved privately, if not politically, successful. The portrait is French. (208)*

in the Commons, rebuffed the Calvinists Bishop Morton, John Preston, Viscount Saye, and the Earl of Warwick. Despite them all he was foisted on Cambridge University as its Chancellor: Predestinarian teaching was forthwith forbidden. The King's bias was obvious: Laud's sermon at the opening of the 1626 Parliament attacked alleged Presbyterian conspiracy; a Royal Proclamation of the same year effectively outlawed Calvinism, for it taught the right of political resistance; Calvinist bishops were excluded from royal counsels; and the preface to the royal reissue of the Thirty-nine Articles expressly decreed that 'all further curious search' and theological debate were to be 'shut up'. The Cambridge and London presses swiftly succumbed. Oxford under the third Earl of Pembroke (most influential of the Calvinist Privy Counsellors, and a patriot suspicious of most things foreign) held out for two years. In 1628 it too yielded. The second session of Parliament, in that year, pointedly took up the issue of Arminianism. To orthodox loyalists like Pym, very much at the centre of the argument, to St John and the fourth Earl of Bedford, all of whom were anti-clerical Calvinists, the new Arminian autocracy was the path to Catholic absolutism. Charles might talk of maintaining 'the middle way between the pomp of superstitious tyrany and the meanness of fantastick anarchy'. These men did not believe him.

Significantly it was left to the Earl of Bedford to build the first Anglican church raised in London since the Reformation. At St Paul's, Covent Garden, Inigo Jones was inspired to his greatest achievement. If his lofty court designs are somewhat theoretical or stagey, this essentially works. The single rectangular room, with no screen dividing chancel from nave, was an auditorium for the pulpit – the sort of church, in fact, which Wren (himself a High Churchman) would build after the Restoration when the preaching function regained some of its lost ground. In 1633 this was an important departure from the medieval plan and

was never a Calvinist, soon showed his hand in the virtual transformation of the Garter sovereign's role. The Tudors had revived the Order to match the Burgundian Golden Fleece; and Elizabeth turned the St George's Day festivities into a great public spectacle at Whitehall. Averse to popular display, Charles removed the festival from London to the Chapel Royal at Windsor. He revamped the Garter badge, surrounding the Saint's red cross with a huge aureole of silver rays copied from the French Order of the Holy Spirit. Garter services became patterns of the new High Church liturgy, and its processions, which Van Dyck later sketched in oils for projected tapestries, were occasions of hierarchical splendour. In 1631 Peter Heylin, Laud's acolyte and a prelate of the Order, published his pietistic defence of the *Saint and Souldier of Christ Jesus; George of Cappadocia*: it cut little ice with Calvinist theologians. They would not have relished Rubens' canvas of 1629.

Buckingham's case is equally instructive. Until the early 1620s he cultivated close relationships with Parliament's so-called 'Puritan' leaders; but, ever the opportunist, he then began to entertain Laud's persuasions. On Charles's accession he soon discovered Arminian sympathies. His York House conference, which triggered proceedings against him

Charles's religious instinct *was towards a revival of High Church ritual, a liturgy that was virtually Catholicism without the pope. He saw himself as the champion of the Anglican Church, and after his death was widely regarded as its martyr. He is the only Anglican to have had churches dedicated to him. (209)*

The Queen's Catholicism *was openly practised, though confined to her own private chapel. In 1636 High Mass was celebrated in England for the first time in nearly eighty years, in a splendid setting devised by Inigo Jones. Something of its spirit is reflected in this French engraving by Abraham Bosse of Charles and Henrietta Maria offering their firstborn to the Virgin. (210)*

from Laudian priorities. The little hocus-pocus, intent on uniformity of worship, insisted that the altar be placed at the east end where the doorway should have opened onto the Piazza. The revision made nonsense of the architect's grand design; but Jones had given Bedford the plain and inexpensive church he wanted. Employing the primitive, natural Tuscan order he created a building with a solid, unaffected air: its restrained gravity caught something of the character of those pieties and disciplines so dear to the Earl and his clientele. This quite exceptional church reminds us, like Van Dyck's portraits of prominent 'Puritan' leaders, that even in the decade which ended in Civil War broad collaborations and accommodations were not impossible: but officious and narrowing insistences frustrated them.

The Queen's faith and taste, by contrast, were lavishly indulged at Somerset House. Her old confessors had been replaced by the more tactful, austere Capucins: the leader of their mission, Father Cyprian, believed their gravity and simple dress would 'disarm' Calvinist objections. There was nothing 'disarming' about the extremely sumptuous chapel Jones built for Henrietta Maria, nor about the astonishing inauguration of 10 December 1636. This, the first pontifical High Mass in England for nearly a century, drew tears of joy from the Queen; and little wonder, for Jones, alert to his patrons' predilections, had created a distinctly Frenchified setting. The French sculptor François Dieussant, hot from Rome, contributed 'a machine to exhibit the Holy Sacrament, and to give it a more majestic appearance'. This

amazing apparatus was a pure and stunning Baroque *tour de force*. Above and around the altar he erected an oval arch, some forty feet high, supported on pillars. At the centre of the arch was the Paraclete raised above seven banks of clouds; and all around, the host of archangels, angels, cherubim and seraphim, and other holy figures down to deacons – each order assigned to its distinct 'circle' or sphere within the design and each 'of a size proportional' to their capacities and duties – were ranged. These figures (some two hundred in all on the nine 'spheres') were 'painted and placed according to the rules of perspective', either adoring the Host or singing and playing musical instruments. Innumerable hidden lights, successively revealed, aided the illusion of depth and distance; while hidden musicians completed the deception of eye and ear. In front of the whole theatrical machine were two curtains, drawn dramatically back when the Queen entered the chapel. For three days the faithful (and others) flocked to see the spectacle: there were queues for confession and, according to the good father, abundant conversions. Unquestionably, as he claimed, his Capucins had 'insinuated themselves among those of the Court and palace, even to the King'. The following year Henrietta Maria's request for the readmission of a papal nuncio was granted; and she gave thanks with a High Mass to the Blessed Virgin. Charles did not concede this ground unwillingly: he may have denied Papal supremacy; he loathed the Jesuits' tolerance of regicide; but the faith's emphasis on uniformity, unity, and infallibility, its ordered hierarchy, its external splendour, its beautiful sacramental ceremonies were powerfully attractive.

His wife's cosmopolitan minority religion appealed too to the new cosmopolitan minority class they together cultivated. Charles encouraged Henrietta Maria's histrionic talent and interests, even on the Sabbath, though many (for Prynne was not alone) saw in this a terrible backsliding. By 1630 the King cared little any more to defer to the 1625

197

Court masques *flourished as never before or since in England. They were performed at all seasons, even on the Sabbath and during Lent, to the scandal of the Puritans. Above centre: Inigo Jones's set for 'Florimene', a pastoral romance acted by a French company in 1635. Left and right: the King and Queen in masque costumes by Jones, Charles as Albanactus in 'Albion's Triumph', Henrietta Maria as 'Divine Beauty' in 'Tempe Restored'. (211–13)*

statute against Sunday theatricals. Public regulations had never been strictly adhered to at court; and with its own remodelled Cockpit Theatre it systematically flouted them, adding insult to injury already inflicted by the Queen's 'daring' appearance in a play and by the first appearance ever of French actors in England in 1629. Their 'lascivious and unchaste comedye in the French tongue' had been 'hissed, hooted, and pippen-pelted from the stage'; but in 1635 Charles, undeterred, commanded another French company (equipped at the Queen's expense) to perform their pastoral romance *Florimène* on two sermon days during Lent. That, no previous monarch would have countenanced. At the same time censorship of the public theatre was severe: when Massinger in his *A New Way to Pay Old Debts* glanced at Ship Money, Charles magisterially excised the 'offensive' passage with his own hand. He prided himself on his critical acumen, and preferred the blander tone of university wits like Mayne and Cartwright. The reassuring empty bombast and display of court tragedy and pastoral appealed too. Royalty was well pleased with Sir John Suckling's *Aglaura*, with its magnificent scenes and high language, and 'clothes worth all the rest'. All this, as Thomas May the Parliamentary historian recalled in 1647, 'did not so much draw the Country to imitation, as reflect with disadvantage upon the Court it selfe'.

So did the company the King kept. He was too much at home with men like Sir Balthasar Gerbier, the mountebank painter-architect who moved easily through the world of European artist-diplomats and Papists; or like that other Buckingham protégé, the suave Endymion Porter, lesser hero of the Spanish adventure. With an eye for paintings and profitable projects – he had a hand in Star Chamber fines, in Petty Customs, in East India trade, fen drainages, and the hated soap monopoly – even in a grandiose scheme to build, in the Queen's name, a vast classical amphitheatre in London – Porter was well in the swim. His 'sweet temper' and 'brave style' were just what Charles loved in men about him. Endymion's sentimental sanctimoniousness (he hoped his infant son would prove a true 'Saint George'); his affected Platonic gallantry ('when my eyes by gazing after any other beauty, offend you, let them fall out'); his sycophantic disingenuousness (he claimed he was 'no politician') – these habits express the ambiance of the court. Waller might celebrate his Penshurst-like virtues as a landowner: at large he was the embodiment of the court's religion, its supine pacificism, its arbitrary and increasingly feudal fiscal policies, its commercial interference and irresponsibility, and its offensive administrative centralization. In short, he was a Jesuitical projector busy feathering his own nest. Such men and manners would appal Strafford when, like some furious Tamburlaine, that practical daemonic man returned from Ireland. Clarendon more coolly complained at the dearth of courtiers with 'larger hearts and more public spirits'. No wonder Sir Henry Wotton (old champion of the Venetian republic, a dedicated public servant and Calvinist, close ally of the great Erastian friar Paolo Sarpi) felt like an owl among the gay birds when he visited Whitehall in the 1630s. In a place where, as his secretary observed, 'idolatry is necessary', his witty outspokenness and crusading convictions were no longer welcome. Charles favoured people and practices that supported and mirrored his choice of non-intervention in Europe and absolute sovereignty at home.

In 1630 when the the old Earl of Pembroke died, Laud was duly installed as Oxford's Chancellor. He wasted no time in placing his *corps élite* of activists in positions of influence. Two years later Neile occupied York; and in 1634 Laud at last succeeded Abbott at Canterbury. An unprecedented onslaught on the lecturing movement followed: hot on the heels of the victimization of Bastwick, Burton, and Prynne came the closing of Chelsea College, a source of distasteful Calvinist propaganda. The country, as the zealous Nehemiah Wallington saw it, was in the grip of 'a mere usurpation'. Everything confirmed the Calvinist Episcopalian Francis Rous's definition of an Arminian as the 'spawn of a Papist'. He spoke for most Englishmen: in the 1630s even the popular stage largely abandoned its old habit of satirizing Puritans; and the Fortune Players mocked Laudian ceremonies to great applause. The authorities stopped the performance and confiscated the actors' 'properties'. By 1635, the year of *Florimène*, Bishop Goodman of Gloucester felt it safe to relinquish all pretence of being a Protestant. The King needed ritual; and through Laud he had, it seems, secured a Church which could comfortably coexist with Catholicism. He rejoiced that the triumphal arch of State had been closed, and went about his private business.

The royal image

The business of government, as such, was not quite to the King's taste. It always attracted him, Sir Philip Warwick claimed, much less than the Queen's person. With or without her, however, Charles would hardly have thrown himself into active administration. It was not exactly that he was lazy or negligent: he wished greatly to be admired by his fellow-sovereigns; and in his chosen sphere he was more than commonly energetic and tenacious. That was the sphere nearest to Heaven, where demi-gods disported or displayed themselves, like Apollo and Diana (the King and Queen) receiving the gift of the liberal arts from Mercury (Buckingham) in Honthorst's vast allegorical canvas. They might even condescend, as in masques, to move among mere mortals, not so much to exhort or extol (the sovereign need not speak) as to effect by their mere presence a magical transformation of the lower spheres of life. For Charles, patronage of the arts, and other princely sports, were not evasions of kingship but of its essence. It was a convenient theory for a man of his temperament. He obviously preferred the company of painters, designers, architects, musicians, collectors, and minor poets and playwrights – writers like Milton, Marvell, and the Metaphysicals, or Jonson were too serious and subtle for him – to politicians who petitioned and pleaded cases; or pressed arguments which, having long since made his mind up, he neither understood nor cared to hear; or pestered him for tactical decisions beneath his dignity. He remembered, moreover, what he thought he had seen in Spain and France.

We may feel that James, let alone Elizabeth, had a stronger sense of the realities of power; that Charles retreated into dilettantism, trying to live like a Belgian archduke or a duke of Florence. Yet he was shrewd enough to secure lieutenants far abler, steadier, and more energetic than his father's 'weathercock' favourite who governed,

Apollo and Diana – *Charles and Henrietta Maria – receive the seven Liberal Arts from Mercury – Buckingham. For Charles, patronage of the arts was the essence of kingship, and Honthorst's great allegorical painting is an evocation of the world in which he was most truly himself. (214)*

Charles's courtiers *formed a group of cultivated gentlemen with artistic tastes. Above: Sir Balthasar Gerbier, connoisseur, amateur painter and architect; Sir Charles Cotterell; and the painter, William Dobson. (215)*

199

Charles at home. *H. G. Pot's painting does nothing to disguise the King's small stature, and the symbols of peace and royalty do little to magnify his presence. Van Dyck's portraits, on the contrary, created an image of regal splendour which has outlived its model. (216)*

without political design, to gratify himself. After Buckingham's death and with Parliament finally prorogued, men like Wentworth, Noy, and Digges drifted back to Whitehall; and the execution of policy acquired a new skill and common sense. Charles had found his Richelieus. For he had studied the great French statesman closely, and believed that in Strafford and Laud (both of whom shared his admiration for the despotic Cardinal) he had established his government after that model. Certainly he would not, like the Tudors, turn a blind eye to irregularities: local government must be made to work as in theory it should. Justices of the Peace and Lords Lieutenant had other ideas: they regarded even 'progressive' measures like fen drainage and road improvements as encroachments. Their hostility and indifference to central government would eventually frustrate his plans. He set out, nonetheless, with high hopes that the policy of 'Thorough' would bring all things beneath his sway.

The King's ardent theoretic conceptions, that mythic view of himself which informed his every move, demanded that he delegate petty details and the execution of orders to his laborious, diligent ministers. Van Dyck's equestrian portrait expresses the whole matter: the dignified, sensitive warrior hero in shining armour, attended by his admiring Master of the Horse, the Frenchman De St Antoine, rides the great horse through a triumphal arch. The monarch's part is to be ceremonial, exemplary, and generally directive: it is the job of his Masters of the Horse and their grooms of the stable to keep the great Horse of State in fine fettle and

subject to discipline. This great symbol of sovereignty, steeped in recollections of Mantuan and Habsburg icons, was designed to hang on the end wall of St James's Gallery. There it created the illusion, startling in its lifelikeness, of England's Caesar riding into the company of those other emperors, ancient and modern, whose triumphal pictures by Titian and Guilio Romano hung along the walls on each side.

In 1633 Sir Henry Wotton's panegyric *Plausus et Vota* (translated into English in 1649) similarly hailed the King's 'joy in Chivalry and use of the great Horse' as symbolic of his skill in managing the tame and taming the furious. Life, alas, did not live up to these figures of speech: the Scottish 'progress' which Wotton celebrated had been no great success. Charles entered Edinburgh like a Roman emperor indeed, through a series of triumphal arches and saluted with a salvo of speeches, poems, pageants, and music. Even Bacon, who had little patience with most princely junketings, permitted these 'antique' ceremonies their place as a solid and instructive part of government; and they were an almost indispensable part of the apparatus of Renaissance kingship. Charles himself figured repeatedly in the required roles of classical hero and ancient (British) emperor in sculptures, paintings, and masques. Ironically and mistakenly, however, he avoided the common gaze if he could, repeatedly declining to gratify London's desire to acclaim him. In 1625 five triumphal arches erected at great expense were dismantled unused: they came down 'amid the murmurs of the people' and the disgust of those who had spent their money. Despite his readiness to let the Scots put their hands in their pockets in 1633, the pomp could not conceal uneasy mutterings. Charles's tampering with the Council of Scotland, his repeated changes of its personnel, pushing Englishmen into Scotsmen's places, was resented. He would have done better to keep out of Scotland and let sleeping dogs lie, as James did. Instead he insulted Calvinist leaders like the Earl of Rothes and persisted in imposing the Arminian sacraments and the Prayer Book in the teeth of opposition which eventually entrenched itself behind the Solemn League and Covenant. The King who rode into his northern territories as the incarnation of the state, God's anointed, the father of his people, heir of a great line, and, like the sun, the source of comfort and light could hardly leave the scene of his 'triumph' fast enough. He hastened home, avoiding London's greetings once again, to Greenwich and the consolations of the Queen's House.

Perhaps Wotton's panegyric was some consolation too; deliberately matching European praise of princes, it especially acclaimed Charles's artistic adornment of his palaces 'wherewith . . . Italy . . . may be seen by your magnificence to be translated into England'. Sir Henry, brilliant linguist and accomplished poet, among the first to recognize Milton's genius, was after twenty years in Italy one of the most genuine connoisseurs of his age. His was a profound and subtle insight into the naturalistic and perspective techniques of High Renaissance art, so unfamiliar to English eyes; and into the principles of Palladian architecture. No man was better equipped to appreciate the revolution in English painting, sculpture, and building which he so generously attributed to Charles's patronage. In fact the reorientation of courtly taste had begun before his reign, with James's interest in Rubens and Van Dyck, and his employment of Inigo Jones on major buildings in Whitehall, St James's, and Greenwich; with Prince Henry's gallery housing England's first systematic collection of classical antiquities and Renaissance pictures and bronzes; with the many activities of the insatiable Earl of Arundel, that absolute evangelist of the arts; and with Prince Charles's own acquisition of some of the greatest Renaissance masterpieces, among them Raphael's 'Cartoons', bought in 1623 for the Mortlake Tapestry Works, which he founded in 1619. Wotton's typically magnanimous praise was nonetheless just: for this King, the most enthusiastic 'amateur' of all the princes of Europe, as Rubens thought, had put the arts at the centre of his life. Sadly, Sir Henry found no answerable magnanimity at court: the offices of Church and State he sought after returning from his Venetian embassy were barred to him. Charles was determined to align high fashion with his unbending ideology, and behaved rather as though he had a monopoly of good taste. The story of his innovating patronage (its glamorous achievements and its curious blindnesses) is the same as the story of his politics.

All over Europe, as Professor Trevor-Roper has reminded us, this was an era of artistic acquisition and plunder: potentates vied to possess those antiquities and treasures which were 'part of the *mana*, the prestige of a particular system of government'. The *Kunstkabinett* itself was a form of propaganda; and artefacts and books, acquired by wealth, stealth, or better still, *force majeure*, were ferried about the Continent by cart and barge-load. In due course the kings of Europe, weeping crocodile tears over the sin of regicide, would swoop on Whitehall to get, in Clarendon's contemptuous phrase, 'shares in the spoils of a murdered monarch'. From all sides they dispatched their secret agents

Two of the King's Titians *hang in an alcove at the back of this scene — 'The Entombment' and 'The Supper at Emmaus'. The painting seems to be a sort of monument to the loyalty of the Earls of Pembroke and to the King's connoisseurship. Charles and his Queen enter accompanied by the fourth Earl, to be received by his predecessor, the third. (217)*

— as Charles himself had so often done — to outbid or undercut his rivals. When the dukes of Mantua fell on hard times and were forced to sell their paintings, the royal aesthete stepped in to buy the lot, with money voted for very different purposes. It was, a contemporary warned, dangerous to let him loose among your paintings if you had a canvas that might take his fancy. From the King's point of view, perhaps his greatest artistic *coup* – for it set the seal on his supremacy – was the acquisition of Van Dyck in 1632. Furnished with a knighthood, a studio at Blackfriars, and a royal patron who, unlike his father, was prepared to 'sit' for hours on end, the painter took up residence in London. There he performed a miraculous transformation.

The stiff little puppet of Robert Peake's old-fashioned painting, and the weak-kneed adenoidal youth of Mytens' portrait (done soon after the return from Madrid), emerged like a butterfly from a chrysalis. Beneath Van Dyck's immortalizing gaze he became a monarch elegantly at ease in his withdrawn grandeur. The same metamorphosis turned Robert Elstrack's engraved Jacobean doll on a horse, bedecked with sashes and ribbons, into a visionary *imperator*. Or we might compare Mytens' *King departing for the chase* with Van Dyck's *Charles resting from the hunt*. This rather dandified gentleman, elegantly but comfortably dressed, nonchalantly undisturbed by the horse and groom behind him, is the perfect *cortegiano*. The sword hints that he is expert in martial exercise but the bitted and bridled

Killigrew and Carew, *minor talents compared to Milton or Marvell, suited the King's taste for mannered sophistication and helped to create the genre known as 'Cavalier poetry'. (218)*

steed confirms his effortless self-control. Behind all this lies not only a change of fashion in costume and conduct, but also Van Dyck's easy mastery of symbol and allegory. We have only to compare Pot's canvas of the King *en famille* with any of Van Dyck's similar pieces to see how crucial the latter's technical skill was. Pot deploys the usual rich furnishings and symbolism of peace and war (in the olive and laurel sprigs), yet he hardly flatters his sitters' stature or looks. Even in Van Dyck's first picture for Charles, the 'great piece of our royal self, consort and children', things are stunningly different. Though the costumes are much the same, the texture and fall of materials, the scenery, the expressions and attitudes of the figures, their placing in relationship to each other and to the viewer's eye combine to create an illusion of beings at once lofty and supremely natural. Unlike Mytens and Van Somer before him, Van Dyck brought to the task a personal obsession with monarchy's mysterious authority, an infinitely refined aesthetic sense (looking away from Rubens towards Rococo), with a supremely seductive touch. He did for the Stuarts what he had already done in Brussels for Marie de Médicis' family. His cosmopolitan brilliance flattered the King's dream; and he changed the way a ruling caste saw itself and its leaders.

If Mytens' 1620 portrait of Martha Cranfield, Countess of Monmouth, was already something more than a lifeless

effigy, Van Dyck's picture of her in 1635, which understandably appealed to Gainsborough, belongs to another world. With its attractive accessories and delicate balance of movement, glance, and gesture, it answers exactly to Sir Balthasar Gerbier's view that painters must use perspective, setting, and shading to make figures real, but since 'all what is naturall is not always faire' must also remember to paint 'to please'. Even allowing for the passage of years the Countess emerged scarcely recognizable from Van Dyck's 'beauty shop'. This is the glittering silken image of womanhood proclaimed in the epicurean poetry of Herrick and Waller. The clothes and jewellery are naturally *à la mode*; but the face too is more refined and attenuated, almost simpering, with thinner lips and lighter eyebrows and no trace of the slightly bulbous nose. Its determination has been erased in favour of something more feminine, passive, and alluring: she is, in Waller's phrase, suffering herself to be admired. This 'actress' dressed for show is perilously close to a salon coquette – fit companion for a Richard Lovelace or for her cousin Sir John Suckling, or for Mytens' splendid befeathered Earl of Holland. No painter, however, was as adept as Van Dyck at flattering his sitter's sexuality: his Earl of Warwick has an air of glamorous virility quite undetected by Mytens, who was content with the shrewd, determined man he saw. Warwick, who stood with Parliament, reminds us that not all of Van Dyck's subjects were hypnotized by his vision of them. Nor did the practical Bedford, for all the magnificence of the portrait with his bookish headstrong brother George Digby, capitulate to the seduction. The painter brilliantly caught those two contrasting characters, as he did the fanatical fussiness of Laud and the suppressed violence of Strafford; but the withdrawn aloof air he casts over all his wealthy patrons was not wholly appropriate to the Calvinist businessman Earl.

On Henrietta Maria the marvellous illusionist lavished all his skill. Interestingly he ignores her energetic vivacity; and the small, thin, sallow woman who believed all girls lost their looks after eighteen becomes an enchanting radiant figure, the goddess of the Platonic love cult. Waller's poem 'To the Queen Occasioned Upon Sight of Her Majesty's Picture' obediently followed suit. His Queen is Venus, fairest of nymphs, the Hesperian dame to the King's Jove, Aeneas, and Phoebus: she would be, were she not a Queen and held in awe, the whole world's ideal mistress, in imagination at least. Waller, who knew how to flatter, stops just short of suggesting a super-courtesan. Sycophancy has, nevertheless, overcome the critical self-discipline of the older generation of courtier poets. We are a far cry from Wotton's lovely measured compliment ('You meaner beauties of the night') to Anne of Bohemia, James's daughter; and from Jonson's praise of Lucy, Countess of Bedford, who combined beauty and sweetness with a 'learned and a manly soul'. Donne's *Autumnal* to George Herbert's mother expresses the same regard for a womanliness where there is 'no voluptuousness, yet all delight'. Here 'Affection . . . takes reverence's name.' Cavalier poetry, much as it derives from Donne and Jonson, habitually attenuates their observation, diluting that serious intelligence which informs even their most sensuous verse. Suckling's knowingness and French

The genius of Van Dyck *has very largely conditioned the way in which we see the court of Charles I. Above: Henrietta Maria, probably less vivacious than in real life but a more hieratic queen. Above right: 'Cupid and Psyche', commissioned from Van Dyck to hang in the Queen's Cabinet at Greenwich. Right: Robert Rich, Earl of Warwick; the armour beside him alludes to his naval attack on the Spanish in 1627. Far right: Martha Cranfield, Countess of Monmouth. (219–22)*

libertin's airs are no substitute for that magnanimous self-knowledge. To the new men Jonson cared too much and let his learning show: Lovelace, the darling of the 'nymphs', was content to strike attractive poses and let sense take care of itself. Even Thomas Carew, most original and conscientious of court poets after Jonson's departure in 1631, contracted the self-absorption and hollowness. Van Dyck's picture of him with Killigrew catches the rather insipid mannered ease that passed for sophistication. His masque *Coelum Britannicum,* perfectly expressing the King's mind, flattered the court's sensuous pleasures, its self-conscious reformation of manners and its belief in its capacity to exorcise rebellion as by magic. Carew, past thirty, found that a simple hedonism had become the most painful of creeds. Failing to break free of Circean charms, he died wretchedly of syphilis in 1640. How easy it was for a man to lose his way at the court of love!

Looking at Van Dyck's luscious *Cupid and Psyche*, designed to hang in the Queen's Cabinet at Greenwich with a projected series on the legend by Jordaens and Rubens, we may understand how time-honoured reservations about pictures could grow from an ethical caution into political hostility. Jonson called painting 'the invention of heaven'; but precisely because it can 'penetrate the inmost affection' he urged artists to abstain 'from base pleasures, lest they should err from their end, and, while they seek to better men's minds, destroy their manners'. His earnest young 'disciple', Thomas Salusbury, was convinced that this had happened at court: gravely he denounced the 'varnisht Mistresses' and 'painted deities', along with the 'lewd adulterous fancyes' of the fashionable 'Follie in verse'. Such resistances were too easily degraded by fanatics to a philistine bigotry no better than the other extreme of self-indulgence. Men like the loyalist Salusbury were, however, anything but zealots; nor was their concern merely insular. They would have agreed with the Frenchman who in 1600 urged Henry IV to avoid the corrupt tastes of Francis I. His court at Fontainebleau had been adorned in a way that allegorically celebrated the divinity of princes and the happy proposition that refined eroticism (of a Neoplatonic cast) was the best reason for living. The English court never quite cultivated such overt sensuality; but onlookers would have agreed with the French 'Puritan' that 'it is a kind of pollution and sacrilege' to see in royal houses and palaces 'something . . . that is profane, vain, false, or immodest'. A conservative gentry largely concurred with the London Company of Painter-Stainers that modish 'foreigners', monopolizing metropolitan patronage, menaced the status quo. Stuart innovations once again went against the grain of native mores.

The court which had itself mythologized in oils regularly acted out the same apotheosis in the masque, where all the arts of architecture, design, sculpture, painting, poetry, and music met. In Inigo Jones it found a high priest who would elevate the old entertainment of masquing into a sacred rite. Believing passionately in the divine monarchy and his own role as the quasi-magical Vitruvian architect-engineer, Jones created an illusionary machine to transform his King and Queen into Platonic ideals. He reformed the English court theatre along French and Italian lines, introducing perspective and movable scenery, and an ingenious apparatus of wheels, lifts, and pulleys to achieve the desired effects. The action of the masque was firmly removed from the body of the court, placed at one end behind a curtain, and framed (a moving picture) in the proscenium arch. The power of single-point perspective (flattering to the King's stature) was used to focus all eyes on the sovereign as the mysterious transcendant source of love and wisdom, and keystone of the courtly hierarchy. Here most emphatically a fundamental revolution in the visual arts was aligned with an exclusive political philosophy. After two years of royal personal rule Jones finally dislodged the stubborn Jonson with his robust irreverent comedies, his habit of lecturing the court, and his claim that even in masques the expository text should have priority. He was replaced by tamer writers like Aurelian Townshend, Shirley, and Davenant. Turning his back on the world he had laboured massively to instruct, Jonson vehemently denounced the ascendant Jonesian masque as nothing but 'Painting and Carpentry', a 'body' without 'soul'. His Jones was guilty of 'Idolatry'. 'Politic eyes' might be flattered by the obscure symbols and stale court hieroglyphs; the old poet sees only that the once animating myths have shrunk to a mindless and pretentious hedonism. Platonic mysticism has turned to mumbo-jumbo; high-mindedness to self-importance; the celebration of an ideal to the flattery of the celebrants. Others (and in the 1640s they would have their way) noted that the plain, plump Hollanders eschewed these 'superstitious and heathenish gewgaws' altogether, preferring to grace the Sabbath with fast days and thanksgivings. As that suggests, masques were a sort of ritual bidding prayer – the High Mass of Neoplatonic monarchy performed by the whole clerisy of court.

The perfect courtier. *Van Dyck was able not only to express fully those qualities of intelligence, sensitivity, and dignity which Charles undoubtedly possessed, but also to endow him with an ease of manner and an air of commanding power which he probably did not. His long series of portraits build up an image of the King as a being apart from other men, a fitting memorial to one who died for the idea of divine right. 'Charles resting from the Hunt' is now in the Louvre. (223)*

Dining in public *was a usage which Charles probably copied from foreign courts. Here he sits with Henrietta Maria in a spacious room surrounded by courtiers and waited on by a small army of servants. The general atmosphere is authentic, but the setting is imaginary, based on Charles's ambitious plans for a great new palace of Whitehall. (224)*

Charles is St George *and Henrietta Maria the princess in this detail from a piece of romantic make-believe by Rubens. In the background is the Thames, likewise transformed into a river of Arcady, and on its banks a fairytale Lambeth Palace. (225)*

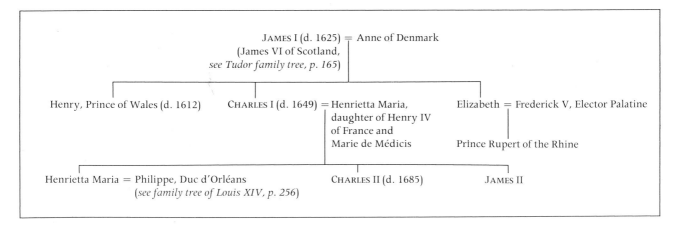

JAMES I (d. 1625) = Anne of Denmark
(James VI of Scotland,
see Tudor family tree, p. 165)

Henry, Prince of Wales (d. 1612) CHARLES I (d. 1649) = Henrietta Maria, Elizabeth = Frederick V, Elector Palatine
daughter of Henry IV
of France and
Marie de Médicis Prince Rupert of the Rhine

Henrietta Maria = Philippe, Duc d'Orléans CHARLES II (d. 1685) JAMES II
(*see family tree of Louis XIV, p. 256*)

The last masque of Charles's reign, *Salmacida Spolia*, performed on 21 January 1640, is revealing. It involved little speech and a lot of show, for this was Jones's most spectacular and mechanically ambitious work. England was no longer portrayed as the untroubled 'paradise of love' acclaimed in Shirley's *Triumph of Peace* in 1634. That masque, performed in Whitehall by the four Inns of Court at the King's command (he was in need of loyal reassurance after the attack on court theatricals in William Prynne's *Histriomastix*), was preceded by a magnificent evening procession, through the City, of the masquers in costume with elaborate chariots, horsemen, trumpeters, musicians, and attendants with flambeaux and torches to illuminate the way. Royalty was so pleased – Henrietta Maria took it as a particular compliment to herself – that a second performance had to be mounted in the City within the week. The citizens' bill, which came to some £20,000, was still unpaid eighteen months later. By 1640 even the masques no longer pretended all was perfect: kingly wisdom and queenly beauty still reign but are now portrayed as patient and suffering. Charles, as Philogenes, the merciful lover of his people, refuses to take up arms to tame their recalcitrance and ingratitude. The final transformation scene presented a prospect of the suburbs of a great city: it represented that translation to England of an ideal Roman civilization that was still the King's goal. Few now believed, however, that the 'savage' tribes of Britain would be pacified by these visions: three at least of the eight lords attending the King in the masque were vehemently opposed to his policies; and Charles had actually rehearsed his role in the intervals from Council meetings where he was drawing up very different plans to equip an army and bring his subjects to heel. Foreigners at court (like Marie de Médicis) were very impressed by the show: at least one practical Englishman, knowing the real dangers, was 'so wise as not to see it'.

Five years later, when events had confirmed men's worst fears, *A Deep Sigh Breathed Through the Lodgings At Whitehall* surveyed the desolation. This brilliant pamphlet reminds us how unpalatable to most contemporaries the splendour of court had become – and how fragile too. For the writer was no mere partisan, no upstart fanatic or obscure visionary: his was the authentic voice of an older anxiety and scruple that goes back through men like Wotton,

Sidney, and Spenser to the heart of Erasmian Christian humanism. Critical not out of envy but concern, it is altogether unembittered. Wittily ironic without railing, urbane but tough-minded, elegant but unaffected, it represents another sophistication, available (then as always) outside the princely regimen, but increasingly frustrated at the centre. The writer conducts us through the empty, echoing 'Pallace without a Presence', 'Court without a Court', which was all that remained. We see the very place where 'at a Play or Masque' amidst the lustre of torches and the sparkling of jewels which turned night into day the Sun King and his Queen sat enthroned in 'shining splendour'. Now we can go backstage unhindered, and 'view the Pullies, the Engines, conveyances or contrivances of each several Scaene. And not an Usher o' the Revels or Engineere to envy or finde fault with your discovery.' It was all, after all, only a grand illusion, a piece of theatre.

The final act

The King in due course would have need of Philogenes' example; meantime he had taken up another equally familiar role. In 1640, when no one else was preparing for war, he readied himself to play the *dux bellorum* of Van Dyck's great equestrian portraits: they had proclaimed symbolically his preference for peace and his complete willingness to fight if need be. It is easy to be misled by his non-intervention in Europe (that 'pernicious innovation', as the Venetian ambassador called it) into thinking that Charles was, like his father, unalterably pacific. Coexistence was certainly the whole aim of his foreign policy. Whatever he said or wrote of his desire to recover the Palatinate for his sister, his heart never wavered: especially after Buckingham's vainglorious failure at La Rochelle, he had no intention of recalling Parliament to vote supplies so that he could launch the country against his much admired Catholic fellow-princes. He was ready, however, to challenge his enemies nearer home, among the Calvinists of the north and in his own Parliament. His flamboyant Scottish crusades foundered on the popular reluctance to rally to his flag against the bastion of the Solemn League and Covenant. The attempt to master his enemies by a *coup d'état* in 1641 (conceived while Parliament pondered and negotiated; and urged on with typical Medicean energy by Henrietta Maria,

an EMBLEM of the ROYAL MARTYR KING CHARLES ʃ Jᵗ in his SUFFERINGS

'An emblem of the royal martyr, *King Charles I in his suffering.*' To the Royalists, Charles had laid down his earthly crown to wear a crown of thorns, but a heavenly crown awaits him. (226)

pamphleteers in 1642) may have hoped that to raise his banner with its motto 'Give Caesar his due' would be enough; and, indeed, a 'feudal' sense of loyalty brought many even of the reluctant to his side. He saw no reason to capitulate, and perhaps came closer to victory than, with the 'disadvantage' of hindsight, we commonly think. Yet in the event he found that even at home it was one thing to pose as *imperator*, another to drive the image home. For him it faded as the dream of Honour and Beauty had faded; until, as the Royalist John Cleveland lamented, only the House of Commons strode 'The stage in a triumphant sort'. But the drama was not yet done: in the wings stood Cromwell, the greatest Caesar of the age, who did not flinch from regicide.

And so, in January 1649, the 'royal actor', who so loved 'sad stories of the death of kings', was brought to the dénouement of his own tragedy. On the scaffold his aloof dignity, his fastidiousness, above all his habit of self-dramatization were entirely apt:

> *He* nothing common did or mean
> Upon that memorable scene.

His curtness, even his stammer, fell away. Yet in truth his last speech reveals all the old intransigence, the righteousness, and equivocation. Early in his reign he had announced that he would sooner see his kingdom in ruins than be subject to his own subjects: now, surveying the desolation, he denied encroaching on Parliament's privileges, reproached himself for Strafford's death and accused his enemies of starting hostilities. Reporters hung on his every word as, reaching through them to the subjects he had shunned, he engineered his own final transformation into a champion of patience and fortitude, a veritable Agonistes. Dying, as he had lived, ceremoniously, he proclaimed himself England's Counter-Reformation saint and 'Martyr of the people'. He was minutely prepared. At his last masque in 1640 Jones, who understood his mind, had adorned the proscenium with symbols of the suffering Christ's attributes; in 1642 Charles confirmed explicitly that he would rather 'wear a crown of thorns with my Saviour than . . . exchange that of gold which is due to me, for one of lead', and though in captivity he toyed with Scots, Army, and Parliament he never really intended compromise. In 1649 he completed the story of Philogenes.

Within the month *Eikon Basiliske*, the image of a suffering King at prayer, confirmed his canonization. In March, to complete the picture of his perfections, Henry Wotton's 1633 tribute appeared as *A Panegyrick of King Charles*. The legend was challenged by Milton who jeered at the stately King's 'ridiculous exit' as a piece of pure masquerade. In 1651 *The Non-Such Charles* recalled the 'millions of pounds' squandered on 'old rotten pictures, or broken nosed Marbles'. By then turncoat prosecutors were not hard to find: Charles's old agent Gerbier reformed with a vengeance, protesting an ancient hatred of Catholics, and that he had always said 'the English Court misrules would drive their affairs into confusion, and into an irreconsiliability'. Perhaps in the long run the King's death saved the monarchy and his son's future. Most assuredly he left behind a nation so divided against itself, so far gone in religious and

who threatened, not for the first time, to leave him if he delayed any longer) was thwarted by his wife's tongue: she crowed too soon, betraying the plot against the Five Members to Pym's friend the Countess of Carlisle. The execution of these and other such actions may have been inept and hesitant: Laud complained that Charles did not know how to be or to be made great. The iron Strafford (who once proposed – an unthinkable punishment for a gentleman – that John Hampden be whipped) told the King bluntly, 'Unless you hang up some of them you will do no good with them.' Ireland had taught *him* how to deal with troublemakers, and he proceeded to incarcerate members of Parliament and impose his vigilante justice on the City of London. He reassured the King, in the familiar language of imperial despotism, that he would get 'the wheel of your Majesty's triumph' rolling. Strafford reckoned without Pym and the power of the Commons; and Charles, his hand forced, sacrificed his ablest minister to the mob. But he had no objection in principle to playing Caesar in his own territories.

Perhaps intent on revenging the defeats of 1640 and 1641, he rode out in 1642 to plant his standard at Nottingham, like some feudal hero-king calling his robber barons' bluff. The resort to arms almost took Parliament by surprise; but it was not unprecedented and by no means out of character. Only 150 years before Edge Hill, rival armies had roamed the English countryside; and the Tudors certainly never imagined they had stilled internecine strife for ever. It was only later, when the need to close ranks against common enemies abroad became imperative, that civil war came to seem unthinkable. Charles I (who struggled far more vigorously to uphold his absolutist claims than did his predecessor Richard II, with whom he was pointedly compared by sectarian, even in aesthetic, antipathies that it could never be reunited under the precise dispensation he had died for. Ahead lay an era where the sort of limited monarchy Charles I disdained would restore at least the possibility of accommodation. It was, by comparison, a demythologized, even a disillusioned, world – one where his son, though feeling some twinges of the divinity of kings in his bones, would lead an astrologer, who proffered his services, down to Newmarket to spot winners. But there was something affirmative too, something more than cynicism, or a dyspeptic philistinism, in the growing conviction that other priorities, another sort of art, and a different view of human history must prevail. Marvell, whose remarkably even-handed poetry reveals so much of this crucial shift of sensibility, knew (as did Jonson before him and Pope in the next century) that the age of panegyric, the era of High Renaissance mystery and magnificence and of god-like princes, was over.

Cromwell, who gave the Calvinist Archbishop Ussher a state funeral, would retain the Raphael Cartoons and Mantegna's *Triumphs of Julius Caesar* for the service of the state: Puritan probity and imperial ambition were satisfied. Pictures like Honthorst's *Apollo and Diana* or Van Dyck's *Cupid and Psyche* were scarcely proper to keep. For the sort of Christian humanism that was (however haltingly) re-asserted at the centre resisted such blurring of identities. Milton attacked the King for still dwelling *in extremis* on Ariosto and Tasso, on French, even on Spenserian, romance. Following English antiquarians like Camden and Selden, who had discredited the absolutist legend of King Arthur, he abandoned his plans for a vast Arthurian poem. He proposed a more fundamental and explicit epic, a plainer, 'unromantic' heroism – something which he believed all Renaissance princes, from the first even to Cromwell

himself, had somehow missed. In *Paradise Lost* it is the Satanic false eloquence and overreaching imagination (preferring to reign in Hell than serve in Heaven) which seeks through self-absorbed role-playing to dominate and to distort man's authentic identity. The unimperious Christ of *Paradise Regained*, in order to find himself and take up his unequivocal and selfless mission, has to resist all that, even Athens and Rome, when Satan conjures up his dramatic visions: the transformation he must accomplish depends on his proclaiming, in a very different idiom, another order of knowledge, beauty, and fulfilment. Milton, the great classicist, is not dispensing with the past or rejecting the Renaissance, but assimilating all the history and art of man – pagan and post-pagan – into his radical, Christian experience. It was a poet standing outside all courts who achieved that fundamental reorientation of sensibility which even Spenser had stumbled at. Created on the verge of a world so altered, so increasingly fragmented that such comprehensiveness would scarcely be accessible to poetry, Miltonic epic, keeping the possibility of wholeness alive for succeeding generations, was an heroic achievement of the historical imagination fit to set beside Raphael's great masterpiece.

Like Shakespeare, Milton reminds us that essentially the concerns of history and literature are the same: we grow in their mutual strength; but when one weakens, the other fades and our identity is diminished. For the story of personal rule, with all its princely aspirations and achievements, its wasted opportunities, and its legacy of division and confusion, is in the end the story of a culture that (to borrow George Eliot's compassionate definition from *Middlemarch*), got its thoughts entangled in metaphors and acted fatally on the strength of them. The tragedy of the court of Charles I was rooted in a failure of moral imagination.

Charles died *on 30 January 1649, on a scaffold outside the Banqueting House, which had witnessed some of the most splendid events of his reign. (227)*

211

Ten

URBAN VIII
The paradox of a spiritual monarchy

❋

JUDITH A. HOOK

IN SUGGESTING IMAGES of splendour and magnificence, beauty and luxury, none of the courts of Europe can rival those of the great Renaissance popes. Nevertheless, combining enormous financial, economic, and political power with a unique spiritual authority, the papal court of the Renaissance inevitably embodied a glittering paradox. Aspiring, as it were, to make the flesh and the spirit gloriously one, such a court seems to symbolize those tensions which lie at the very centre of the Renaissance itself. In the seventeenth century, during the pontificate of Urban VIII, such tensions emerged with renewed intensity to create what was arguably the greatest and most spectacular Baroque court in Europe. Worldly pride and ambition, nepotism and financial extravagance, somehow combined with ideals of the highest aesthetic beauty and learning to produce a court which was itself a work of high dramatic art. In trying to understand and interpret that court, neither its worldliness nor its idealism may properly be neglected.

The origins of the papal court date back at least as far as the Carolingian era, but, as an institution, the court developed most rapidly during the period of the Avignon papacy (1306–74), and by the time of Urban VIII it had reached much the same form as it preserves today. Any comprehensive account of the papal court would have to include a description of the Curia, that vast complex of bureaux and committees through which the universal Church and the temporal estates of the Papacy were administered. But, although many members of the Curia were also members of the papal court, the papal court strictly defined comprised only members of the papal household (the Famiglia Pontificia) and the papal chapel (the Cappella Pontificia); that is, those ecclesiastics and laymen who had a recognized function by protocol in the papal residences, and those who had a right to participate in that category of liturgical acts traditionally and solemnly celebrated by the pope in person.

The court was always characterized by an elaborate protocol in terms of which the laws of precedence were strictly observed. First in importance and rank were the Palatine cardinals, those prelates who were assigned to the personal service of the pope within the apostolic palace. Second in rank were the members of the Noble Privy Antechamber: the Majordomo (known before 1626 as the *maestro di casa*), the Master of the Chamber, the Auditor of His Holiness, and the Master of the Sacred Palace, the pope's personal theologian who, by tradition, was always a Dominican. Then came the Participating Privy Chamberlains: the Privy Almoner, the Secretary of Letters to Princes, the Secretary of the Code, the Under-datary, the Secretary for Latin Letters, the Cupbearer, the Secretary of Embassies, the Keeper of the Wardrobe, the Sacristan, and the Master of the Sacred Hospice. In the seventeenth century only one of this group of offices – the last – was ever occupied by a layman. Laymen did, however, tend to be found at the papal court among the ranks of the Participating Privy Chamberlains of Sword and Cape, representatives of the old Roman baronial families who held a hereditary title to particular offices. These included the Quartermaster-General of the Sacred Palaces, the Master of the Horse, the Postmaster-General, the Bearer of the Golden Rose, the Colonel of the Swiss Guard, as well as the post of Captain-Commander, and the colonels and lieutenants of the papal noble guard. These then were the great offices of the papal court. A host of minor posts, the majority held by ecclesiastics, were also attached to the court, but what every office-holder shared, from the loftiest to the most lowly, was an ultimate dependence on the goodwill of that half-holy, half-imperial figure of the pope.

The Barberini family had been established in Florence since the fourteenth century and had acquired considerable wealth. Like every pope of the time, Urban used his position to benefit his family. The three bees of the Barberini arms, joined with the tiara and the keys of St Peter, proliferated all over Rome and the Papal States. This bronze relief comes from the base of Bernini's baldacchino (pl. 243). (228)

St Peter's in the 1640s *was structurally complete, but the interior still lacked some of its furnishings and the exterior the all-important piazza soon to be provided by Bernini. On the right is the Vatican palace and the clock tower of Paul V, later demolished.* (229)

Rome: the city and the Church

By its very nature the papal court was unique. Because of his office the pope was permanently surrounded by an aura of veneration accorded to no other monarch in Western Europe. This in itself would be sufficient to distinguish the papal court from all others. But there were other distinctive features; it was, for instance, the only court in Europe which was entirely male-dominated. Save in the most exceptional times, women played no part in the life of an institution whose dominant ethos involved devotion to the principle of celibacy. Unique too is the fact that the papal court was the centre of a vast variety of interests ranging from the universal and global to the most local and particular.

In the seventeenth century the papal court was the heart of a world-wide organization, one of whose major aims was to propagate a belief in a Papacy centred in Rome, and which constantly looked to that Papacy for direction in every area of its life. It was also the centre of a large territorial state, over which, as a Venetian had observed in 1595: 'The Pope rules . . . with complete authority and absolute power, for everything depends on his will.' Last of all, the court was the centre and source of all economic and political power in Rome itself, the Eternal City which was still widely regarded in Western Europe as 'the common country of all men' and as 'the mother of us all'.

Retaining none of her former secular greatness, seventeenth-century Rome was completely controlled by the pope. The old Roman commune, already dying by the early sixteenth century, had lost all independence of action by the beginning of the seventeenth. Chronically impoverished, it only continued to exist because the popes willed that it should do so and were prepared to make substantial contributions to the finances of the communal government. Typically, during the pontificate of Urban VIII, the Roman

Senate, heir to all the glories of Republican and Imperial Rome, passed its time in doing little more than voting the erection of various monuments dedicated to perpetuating the glories of the Barberini family; indeed the ultimate subordination of the commune to papal ambitions was symbolized in 1635 by the Senate's revocation of a decree of 1590 forbidding the erection of statues of popes on the Capitol during their lifetime, and its commissioning of a marble statue of Urban VIII from Bernini.

Yet, although Rome was subject to the popes, it did not, as a city, suffer from that mastery. The text of the resolution by which the city agreed in 1641 to vote a subsidy of fifty thousand *scudi* for the papal war coffers began: 'The glory of this Eternal City and the magnificence of this illustrious people rests entirely in the governance of this best of princes . . .' It was clearly recognized, in other words, that it was the presence of the Papacy in Rome that made it the wealthiest city of Italy, an international centre and great metropolis, attracting visitors and permanent residents from all over Europe.

Rome was still the most important diplomatic centre in the Christian world, for the popes had to be informed regularly and reliably about world affairs, and Catholic princes still liked to maintain a direct link not only with the pope but also with many of the cardinals. Contemporaries were also aware that Rome attracted a constant stream of talent because, 'No place is more adapted to making one's fortune', and, 'everyone can hope to reach a high position'. Certainly, there were a multitude of career opportunities associated with the papal court, where any man of ability and learning might well aspire to make his name.

Moreover, Rome was still the greatest artistic centre in Europe, and no pope could afford to ignore the fact that a large part of the impact that Rome made on foreign visitors was the result of the grandeur and magnificence of the city. The splendours of Rome resulted from the deliberate encouragement of the arts and the financing of great architectural projects, of which the most important and the most spectacular had been the rebuilding of St Peter's, which, after more than a century, was still incomplete. The popes were well aware that in financing such projects they not only enhanced the reputation of Rome as a great international centre but also contributed to the stability of the society over which they ruled. They knew that, directly or indirectly, the vast bulk of the population of Rome were dependent on them and on the papal court for employment. Unlike most Italian towns, Rome had never been an industrial city; it lived off pilgrims, tourists, artists, and theologians, and the nearest thing to an industry it could lay claim to was the building trade. The furtherance of artistic projects might therefore be both a measure of social control – preventing unemployment and consequent social unrest – and an act of Christian charity. Had not Gregory XIII remarked that it was public charity to build and that all princes should do so because it brought assistance to the citizens and people?

Many princes, both temporal and spiritual, seem to have shared Pope Gregory's views on the advantages of building. Whether in doing so public charity was what they had most

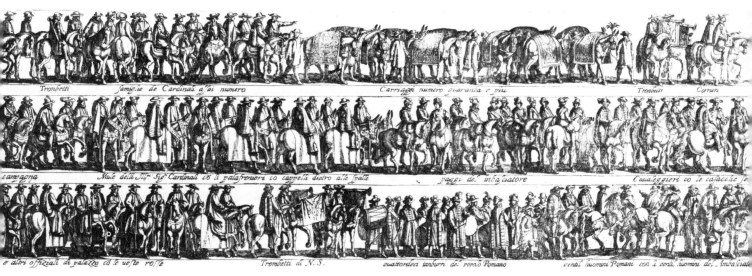

Tronbetti   famiglie de Cardinali assai numero   Carriaggi numero quaranta e piu   Tronbetti   Cornet

cavagona   Mule delli Ill.mi Sig.ri Cardinali co li palafrenieri co cappelli dietro alle spalle   paggi del imbasciatore   Cavalleggieri co le casacche jo

e altri offiziali di palazzo cō le veste rosse   Trombetti di N.S.   quattordeci tanburri del popolo Romano   venti huomini Pomani con i venti huomini del Imbasciata

Competitive display *played as large a part in Rome as in other European capitals. Cardinals, heads of houses, and visiting diplomatic missions vied with each other in expensive pomp. In February 1632 an embassy from Spain under the ambassador Cardinal Borgia arrived to conduct some hard bargaining with the Pope over Philip IV's rights to tax the Spanish clergy. This engraving, dedicated to Urban's nephew Taddeo, Prefect of Rome, shows part of the train of dignitaries, officials, servants, and military escorts which could be seen progressing through the streets of Rome.* (230)

in mind, is more open to question. In fact the popes, like contemporary secular rulers, seem to have believed that the expenditure of money for prestige purposes was a necessary aspect of the art of government. Remarking that 'Poor princes, and above all, poor popes, come to be despised even by children, particularly in this age when one can do anything with money', Sixtus V was stating no more than a simple truth. As far as the upper classes were concerned, the last decades of the sixteenth and the first half of the seventeenth centuries in Rome were an age in which luxury was deliberately cultivated. It was expected of an aristocrat, whether secular or ecclesiastical, that he should live with great pomp and splendour, and one aspect of this luxurious living was a desire on the part of the wealthy to display their riches in conspicuous expenditure. Their aim was to build themselves sumptuous homes and to decorate them magnificently; to purchase rare and expensive jewels, not for purposes of investment, but to wear on festive occasions; to purchase carriages of more and more fantastic designs, made out of more and more improbable materials; to give their daughters and nieces in marriage with princely dowries and, since the Counter-Reformation had made charity fashionable, to outdo each other in ostentatious gifts to confraternities and other religious foundations, in building churches, restoring convents, and paying for sumptuous memorial chapels. This language of luxury was well understood by contemporaries; magnificence in expenditure was

equated with greatness. So, in 1625, the returning Venetian embassy from Urban's court had to assure its Senate that they had in no way demeaned the Republic: 'The saving of money played no part in our calculations, and, in the name of the Serenissima we displayed great pomp, on our tables, on our decorations, with quantity and profusion in all things, merely in order to preserve the name of Great to the Republic.' Though a world in which expenditure on such a scale was the norm might in the end impoverish the Roman aristocracy, and eventually even the Papacy, and though its maintenance did lead to the exploitation and punitive taxation of the Church State, in the short term it did appear to benefit the Roman populace by the provision of manifold opportunities for employment and profit.

Courts of the cardinals

Papal cultivation of the doctrine of magnificence can therefore be said to have done much to embellish and enrich Rome. The city's prestige and status were further enhanced by the development of papal power and authority in another area. During the early seventeenth century Rome became not just the theoretical capital of Christendom but, as has been said, the actual and effective capital of the Church State. Largely because the papal court was resident there, Rome became the dominant political and cultural centre within the area, to which all cities which had once challenged its supremacy – Perugia, Bologna, and Ancona in particular – were subordinated.

This evolution of Rome into a capital city had an important impact on the nature of the papal court, for it meant that Rome now exercised a magnetic attraction, not only for all power-seekers in the Church, but also for the traditionally turbulent feudal nobility of the Church State, who for centuries had posed a challenge to the Papacy's territorial control of the area. But, as Rome became more and more important as a social, administrative, financial, and economic centre of the Church State, the papal court came to play a role similar to that of Versailles in the history of the development of the French monarchy. For prestige reasons

215

Coaches gather *for a 'medieval joust' organized in February 1634 by Urban's nephew, Antonio Barberini. Antonio, made a cardinal at the age of twenty, shared his uncle's enthusiasm for the arts. The setting for the joust was designed by Andrea Sacchi, who subsequently drew this illustration of it. (231)*

Three great-nephews, *children of Taddeo Barberini, present Urban with a book bearing his emblem the sun on the binding. The eldest, Carlo, was made a cardinal in 1653; Maffeo inherited the family estates; Niccolo became a Carmelite friar. (232)*

the old feudal nobility came to live in Rome and to compete in the contemporary display of luxury. Essentially *rentiers* and living off fixed incomes in an age of rising prices, they inevitably fell into debt, and from these debts only the Papacy could rescue them, with favours, loans, gifts, and sinecures.

Because of the peculiar structure of administration in the Church State the Roman aristocracy could not look to the fruits of office to finance their increasingly expensive tastes. The administration of the Church State was, in fact, unique in that it was reserved for the clergy. The function of the feudal aristocracy in the state and at the papal court was purely a decorative one, for of the major state offices only the Postmaster-Generalship was, by some bizarre tradition, reserved for a secular aristocrat, and the only other positions the aristocracy could hope to fill were as guards or chamberlains in the papal household. The profits of office were, therefore, denied to the Roman barons and aristocrats; but by constant attendance at court they could bring pressure to bear to have members of their families elevated to the Sacred College, and thus hope to recoup some of their lost fortunes. Nor were these hopes always disappointed. In the seventeenth century there did tend to be an increasing representation of these old families among the higher clergy and particularly among the cardinals.

In previous centuries the Sacred College had acted as an effective limitation on the absolute power of the Papacy, but, by the time of the pontificate of Urban VIII, the political power of the cardinals had collapsed. Consistory, which had formerly acted as the main administrative body in the Church, had steadily declined in the course of the sixteenth century, until it could be described in 1598 as serving only, 'to publicize decisions already arrived at by the pope'. There were a number of reasons for this decline. The first was deliberate policy on the part of successive popes who had always resented the control which the cardinals endeavoured to exercise over them. The second was Consistory's increased size which made it too unwieldy a body for concerted political action; and the third was the bypassing of its functions by the use of the Congregations, first introduced in the mid sixteenth century and later systematized by Sixtus V. By the end of the century the cardinals had become little more than decorative court aristocrats exercising no real power over the destiny of the Church except in the exceptional circumstances of a conclave.

Yet, as court aristocrats and as leaders of society, the cardinals continued to be very important in the life of Rome. The same aura of reverence which surrounded the pope also surrounded the cardinals, each of whom had the chance of one day becoming pope himself. As the pope was always accompanied by pomp and magnificence so were the cardinals. None took a step outside his palace without being followed by a magnificent cortège, and throughout the streets of the city a cardinal's carriage was given absolute precedence, the papal guards presenting arms as it passed. Each of the cardinal-palaces sheltered within its walls what was, in fact, a little 'court' of clients, servants, pages, gentlemen, chamberlains, chaplains, and masters of ceremony. The size and quality of this court would depend on the individual cardinal, but from the beginning of the seventeenth century it had been accepted that a household of twenty was the absolute minimum for a cardinal, and it was common to find households of two or three hundred persons. Like the papal court itself, these households maintained artists, musicians, scholars, and writers, reflecting the interests of the presiding cardinal-prince, for Maffeo Barberini was not the only cardinal to be practised in the arts. The Roman Cardinal Gaetano, for instance, was a distinguished writer, well known for his satirical poems.

Within their own households, the cardinals might be the centre around which all things revolved; but they, in turn, were the glittering, but essentially subordinate, ornaments of the papal court, 'a proud crown for the person of the pope'. It is true that the cardinals normally filled all the most important executive and administrative posts in the Church and in the Church State and that they presided over the governing Congregations. The right to rule, both in Church and State, was reserved to them, but that right they exercised only during papal pleasure and in the name of the pope, in whose hands all power was in fact concentrated. Increasingly, the sole source of both wealth and power at Rome was the person of the pope, and everything depended upon his will. Examples may readily be seen in the pontificate of Urban VIII. Throughout his reign, for instance, the decoration of St Peter's was nominally under the control of a permanent committee – by this time known as the Congregazione della Fabrica – just as the whole rebuilding project had been since the days of Julius II. But no one, for one moment, would consider that it was this committee which was the inspiration, or even the directing intelligence, behind the works done in St Peter's in Urban's reign. From the beginning the records of the Congregation make it clear that it was the Pope who controlled the whole project.

Another example of the all-importance of the papal will is the prominence of Bernini as the leading Roman architect in Urban's reign. Urban's protection and patronage of the young Bernini, his determination to discover in him another Michelangelo, were certainly significant since the interest of the sculptor was directed by the Pope to architecture and painting, with positive and beneficial results. But Urban's attitude also led to the subordination of all other artistic talent in Rome, as Bernini was elevated as an overriding genius. Those who might have challenged his artistic supremacy were not allowed to, for the cardinals and the aristocracy followed the Pope's lead; thus, despite his manifest genius, Borromini was simply unable to emerge as an independent architect until after the death of Urban.

With only one particular group of people did all popes share both their wealth and their political power. This group was composed of their friends, clients, and, above all, their relatives. The history of the Papacy at this time was dominated by a series of power revolutions, for, as each new pope was elected, his friends and relatives converged on Rome from all over Italy to seize what could be got out of the Papacy in the shortest time possible. For as long as a pope ruled, the opportunities for his family to make money were virtually unlimited; although Gregory XIV ruled for only a

'It is a piece of good luck *for you, Cavaliere,' said Urban to Gianlorenzo Bernini (above), 'to see Cardinal Maffeo Barberini pope, but far greater is our good fortune that the lifetime of Cavaliere Bernini should fall into our pontificate.' (233)*

year, his family, the Sfrondati, managed to make 210,000 *scudi* out of the Church during the period. Once a pope died these opportunities came to an abrupt end, and the relatives of the deceased pope would overnight be reduced to positions of political impotence, if not positive disgrace.

Since pontificates tended to be short, for popes were usually already old when they were elected, it was essential for papal dependents to grab as much as possible while time allowed. This is why the Barberini seem so spectacular in the gains they made from nepotism; not because they were any worse than their predecessors, but because the length of time for which Urban VIII ruled (1623–44) gave them unparalleled opportunities for profit.

The fortunes to be made by papal dependents were one of the great avenues of social mobility in the seventeenth century. Inevitably, therefore, a pope like Urban VIII who lived, as it were, too long, was bound to court unpopularity and even danger. On at least one occasion Urban's life was theoretically threatened by the ambitions of a relative of a *papabile* cardinal. This was Giacinto Centini, a youthful nephew of Felice Centini, the learned and pious Cardinal Ascoli. Giacinto provides an excellent example of the pressures placed on the relatives of cardinals by a society constantly prepared to gamble on the outcome of a future papal election. Despite his humble birth, Centini was able to find a bride among the Malaspina, once his uncle was

The young Maffeo Barberini *first rose to prominence as an astute lawyer and administrator with a keen interest in poetry and the arts. In 1595 he commissioned his portrait from Caravaggio, then barely known. (234)*

elevated to the purple, and gradually became surrounded, according to Urban's biographer, Nicoletti, with a crowd of flatterers and hangers-on who encouraged him to believe that in the next conclave his uncle would be sure to be elected, and that their fortunes would be assured. But Felice Centini was already over sixty and Urban VIII seemed as well and healthy as on the day of his election; so Giacinto became convinced that there was no time to lose. With two friars, a Sicilian hermit, and some other conspirators, he plotted to get rid of Urban by means of sorcery and astrology. Over a period of two years between 1633 and 1635 the conspiracy developed until one of the friars panicked and revealed the story to the Inquisition in exchange for a promise of his life.

Perhaps the real significance of this sad little story is that it partially explains the practice of nepotism. For, within the circle of the papal court, whom could any pope trust save his own relatives? It had become common practice for many of the cardinals to accept pensions from foreign monarchs and to act as their political agents in Rome. Such connections inevitably rendered their advice suspect. Then again, the traditional power-structure of the Church's governmental machinery had to be bypassed, the cardinal-nephew had to become the repository of the pope's secret confidences simply because the holders of the great offices of the Church were, too often, automatic enemies of the pope. The practice of the sale of offices, which impoverished or greedy popes had resorted to, had tended to alienate whole areas of the

traditional bureaucracy from effective papal control, and only too often the most important office-holders would be relatives of an earlier pope. Thus Urban inherited as head of the Penitentiary, Cardinal Borghese, the nephew of Paul V, and as Vice-Chancellor, Cardinal Ludovisi, the nephew of Gregory XV.

Urban and the arts

Much of what has so far been said would be generally true of any papal court in the seventeenth century. What distinguishes that of Urban VIII is the magnificent patronage of the arts which is associated with it and which was at least one cause of the flourishing Baroque culture of seventeenth-century Rome. Even without the active interest of the Pope, it is probable that the pontificate of Urban VIII would have marked a high tide in the development of the arts of Rome. It was largely fortuitous that elaborate structures of patronage which had been developed for more than a century reached their apogee during this pontificate and that Roman art should have reached its cultural culmination at about the same time. Several of Urban's predecessors had already shown a marked interest in urbanization programmes and the arts, most notably Sixtus V and Paul V. By the beginning of the seventeenth century, the high social status of the artist at Rome was generally accepted, and an increasing number of men of noble birth, like Gian Battista Crescenzi and Paolo Giordano Orsini, the Duke of Bracciano, were taking up painting professionally. Even the young Cardinal Antonio Barberini and his brother Taddeo did not disdain taking lessons from practising artists. All things, therefore, were working together to favour the arts in Rome and for more than a generation distinguished artists had been attracted there, not only from other parts of Italy, but from all over Europe. Rome, at this time, was full of flourishing little communities of foreign artists.

Yet the election of Urban VIII was not without importance for the history of artistic developments in Rome at this time. In the previous century, cynical observers had not been slow to notice a sudden conversion to sanctity and piety among the cardinals of Pius IV and Pius V, once it became recognized that these qualities were the ones most admired by those particular popes. A switch to an interest in arts and letters on the part of the members of the Sacred College was no more difficult and often a great deal more congenial than the ostentatious practice of sainthood, and was equally certain to find favour with Urban VIII. Did not a contemporary proverb advise that: 'he who is no good at double-dealing will get nowhere in Rome'?

And it was clear from the beginning that the keynote of the Barberini pontificate would be the encouragement of scholarship and the arts. It is probable that no more civilized or sophisticated a man than Maffeo Barberini ever ascended the papal throne. He had been born in Florence in 1568 into a wealthy merchant family, and, after an early and very successful training in the law, he entered the priesthood. Once in the Church, where his career was fostered by a careful uncle, his rise was swift; at twenty-four he was governor of Fano, at thirty-five an archbishop, at thirty-six apostolic nuncio to France, and, at thirty-seven, a cardinal.

At fifty-five, he was still a relatively young man when he became pope.

Throughout his career, Urban had nourished an interest in the arts. He was famed as a more than competent poet, who wrote in Italian, Latin, and Greek, as a friend of scholars and scientists, and as a passionate lover of antiquity. In all these areas he was an established patron long before he became pope. The house on the Via de' Giubbonari which he inherited from his uncle became a kind of academy for all the most learned persons of Rome and his courtiers and clients included some of the most cultured men in the city. While he was still a cardinal, Maffeo Barberini possessed an art collection which included sculptures by Bernini, paintings by several great Renaissance artists, including Raphael and Correggio, and recent works commissioned from Guido Reni and Caravaggio.

As pope, there was a dual aspect to Urban's court life. He was both ascetic and self-indulgent. The asceticism revealed itself in the ordering of his daily life, which, as far as lay in his power, he kept simple and businesslike. He operated, of course, within an already existing framework in that the papal court, as the centre of papal government, was an established institution with an independent life of its own. It was a vast rambling organization which represented one of the major perennial drains on papal expenditure. Something like 100,000 *scudi* a year had to be spent merely on running the Vatican palace and the papal chapel and in paying the Vatican officials. And the Vatican was only one of the palaces whose upkeep was a papal responsibility. The Lateran and the Quirinal also employed vast populations of bureaucrats and servants of their own.

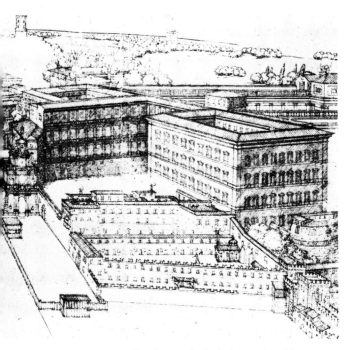

The Vatican *was a confused network of administrative offices, galleries for the popes' works of art, and apartments for the armies of officials. But in its midst Urban was able to lead a personal life of comparative simplicity. (235)*

These palaces were never homes in any real sense of the word. The Vatican was really a great network of art collections, galleries, chapels, and administrative offices, linked together by dark corridors, tiny tunnels, and more than two hundred staircases. It was a backdrop for the magnificence which was built into the papal system of government. It was a central feature of papal government that the Holy Father was constantly on display, and that this display should impress by its splendour. Every major festival in the Church's year had its own established forms for the pope to observe; on Christmas Eve, for instance, he said Mass in his private chapel, and then gave Communion to all members of the court, before proceeding with a full papal retinue to St Peter's for vespers. On Christmas Day, accompanied by all the cardinals, and his entire court, he sang Mass at the High Altar of St Peter's and then passed out to the Loggia to give the annual blessing, 'To the city and the world'. On New Year's Eve, the pope said vespers and then, by tradition, the new officials of the city of Rome came to swear fealty to him. Similar obligatory festivals and customary observances throughout the Christian year, culminating in all the pageantry of Holy Week, together with extraordinary ceremonies like the official consecration of St Peter's in 1626, the ceremonies connected with the Jubilee of 1625, or the celebrations on the integration of Urbino into the Church State in 1634, meant that there were regular occasions on which the pope and all his court were on show, and when all those present in Rome could become temporary participants in papal magnificence.

Yet behind all the outward display which was clearly inherent in the papal office, Urban VIII lived with relative simplicity. He invariably rose early and often before dawn. He began his day by reading his breviary, and then heard or said Mass. The rest of the morning was devoted to business of Church or State, which he always conducted with the greatest application and diligence.

Only on Mondays did this pattern vary; every Monday morning the Pope held a public audience. In Urban's pontificate admission to an audience, whether public or private, was given relatively freely, for if there was one thing above all else the Pope delighted in it was talking. Even ambassadors often found it difficult to get a word into the conversation or to stem the flow of the Pope's instructive discourse, and one cardinal was driven to complain that he went to the Vatican, 'not to receive an audience but to give one since his Holiness would rather discourse than listen to any one'.

After his midday meal, the Pope either retired to rest, passed time with his family or close friends, or listened to performances of his own Latin poems, set to music. Urban always tried to devote a portion of each day to writing new poetry, but the evening was reserved for exercise. The Pope prided himself on being an excellent horseman and greatly enjoyed riding in the extensive grounds of the Vatican palace, or through Rome to inspect some new architectural project.

Further opportunities for relaxation, in a more congenial atmosphere, were opened up when, in 1626, the Pope purchased the villa of Castel Gandolfo in the Alban hills and

Cardinal Francesco Barberini, *the Pope's eldest nephew, was also a lavish and discriminating patron and a scholar with wide humanist and antiquarian interests. The French artists Vouet and Valentin owed much to him. This 'apotheosis' of the Cardinal – notable for containing no Christian allusions whatever – is the work of Vouet. (236)*

addition to his already princely salary as architect of St Peter's. Impressively eclectic in his tastes, Urban VIII provided opportunities not only for Bernini, but also for the more strikingly original Borromini, in architecture, while as far as painting was concerned, he was a simultaneous patron both of the emerging Baroque painters – Giovanni Lanfranco, Pietro da Cortona, and Domenichino, as well as the more classically inclined Guido Reni, Poussin, and Vouet.

These men the Pope insisted on treating as his friends, for he had an almost over-exaggerated respect for genius and prided himself on his ability to mix with artists as an equal. Both as a cardinal and as a pope he delighted in making surprise visits to Bernini's studio, where he is reputed to have enjoyed such menial tasks as holding the mirror while the sculptor worked on his self-portrait for the famous *David* statue. The story of the relationship between Urban and Bernini is one of the most remarkable in the whole history of patrons and artists. For Bernini all the elaboration of court protocol was laid aside; the artist was allowed free access to the Pope's private apartments, and 'During the dinner hour the Pope used to have pleasant conversation with him until it was time to retire. When sleep brought an end to discussion, it was Bernini's task to pull the blinds, close the windows, and take his leave.'

The relationship between Urban and Bernini was exceptional in its intimacy, but not markedly different in type from the relationship which the Pope enjoyed with his other court artists. Scholars and men of letters were equally honoured and were frequently entertained in the garden of the Belvedere, at the Villa Borghese, or at Castel Gandolfo. Here, they came in contact with painters, sculptors, and architects in a very free atmosphere and something very like the ambience of the High Renaissance courts of Julius II and Leo X was re-created with beneficial results for the arts. Paintings acquired a new strength and intellectual rigour; there was a return to elaborate visual allegory with recondite allusions and hidden meanings. It was in this kind of atmosphere that Urban's close friend, the epic poet Francesco Bracciolini, could be charged with providing the poetic themes and the programme for the famous decorations of the ceiling in the great hall of the Barberini Palace painted by Pietro Cortona.

The ability to write poetry was clearly one avenue to favour at Urban's court. The Florentine poet, Giovanni Ciampoli, who shared the Pope's views on the necessity for Christian, rather than pagan, themes in poetry, was appointed a papal secretary, and, although he fell from favour in 1632 because of his close association with Galileo, he was at first so intimate with Urban that even the cardinal-nephews were said to be jealous of his influence. Two other poets distinguished for their erudition, Antonio Quarenghi of Padua and Giambattista Doni of Florence, were named as secretaries of the Sacred College; Virginio Cesarini was appointed *maestro di camera* in the first year of Urban's pontificate; the oriental scholar Pietro della Valle was made papal chamberlain, while Agostino Mascardi, author of the *Arte istorica* (Rome, 1636), became private chamberlain to the Pope with an annual salary of five hundred *scudi* a year.

had it extensively altered and modernized. Twice a year, for two weeks in May and in October, he would retire there for a holiday. It was at Castel Gandolfo that he felt most relaxed, and there, in a more informal atmosphere, that he delighted in the poets and artists who were to make his pontificate famous.

Artists and poets and art-lovers always formed a part of Urban's entourage and his court. There was, in fact, little that was exceptional about this, for Roman society was permeated throughout by *virtuosi*, men who lived by their skill, wits, and talents and as hangers-on at the courts of the great cardinals or the Roman barons, often working as secretaries or librarians in one of the great palaces of Rome, and making a profession of their erudite antiquarian knowledge. They, like Rome's countless artists, expected to be supported by patrons of one kind or another and they were rarely disappointed.

Urban was merely the greatest patron of them all, revealing in the company of these *virtuosi* and artists the self-indulgent aspect of his nature. Immune to influence in matters concerning the Church or the State, he was always susceptible to sycophancy and flattery in questions relating to the arts, and, in particular, to praise of his own poems. Sparing of himself as far as physical needs or pleasures were concerned, he was prepared to spend unstintingly on the arts and on scholarship. For the baldacchino alone, for instance, Bernini was rewarded with ten thousand ducats and a number of life-pensions for himself and his family, in

Given these conspicuous success stories and the known delight of the Pope in antiquities, poetry, and the visual arts, it was likely that those who sought advancement or political influence would follow his lead as an art patron. The Spanish ambassador wisely cultivated the entire Barberini family by putting on spectacular dramatic performances at his palace at Trinità dei Monti, and ambitious cardinals imitated him. Flattery and sycophancy came to play a large part in the life not only of the court but of the whole of Rome. It is difficult to believe that the Roman reading public needed all those editions of Urban's poems which poured from the press during his pontificate, even though they culminated in the great Jesuit edition of 1631 with its illustrations by Bernini, or that anything save desperation should have driven Odoardo Farnese to write odes in the Pope's honour.

Barberini fortunes

The anxiety of Urban's courtiers to be seen to share his interests and attitudes expresses in exaggerated form the general truth that the quality of life at the papal court was very much dependent on the personal qualities of the pope at its head. But in Urban's case there is a danger of distortion here. If flattery and sycophancy had been the only motives at work then the intellectual and aesthetic tone of Urban's court would ultimately have been superficial and fraudulent. In fact the most important men at the papal court do genuinely seem to have shared Urban's interests. Most prominent in court life were the Pope's own family, who, from the beginning of his pontificate, served as a hedge about his person. Even by contemporary standards, the rise of the Barberini family to power, fame, and fortune was meteoric. Urban was elected on 6 August 1623. In October

When Bernini *was carving 'David',
according to tradition, Maffeo Barberini
held the mirror so that he could use his
own face as a model. (237)*

The Barberini Chapel *in S. Andrea
della Valle, commissioned by Urban in
1600 as a memorial to his uncle, was in
the forefront of a new fashion for rich
marbles and striking polychromy. (238)*

221

'*Aedes Barberinae*' *is a large illustrated volume by Girolamo Teti describing, room by room, the Barberini Palace and its treasures.* (239)

he created his nephew, Francesco, who was only twenty-six years old, a cardinal. Since Francesco was still so young the Pope gave him a personal adviser. This was Urban's brother-in-law, his closest intimate and most important political adviser, Lorenzo Malagotti, who was made Secretary of the Letters to Princes – the equivalent of a secretary of state. In 1624 Malagotti became a cardinal. In the same year the Pope's saintly brother, Antonio, was also raised to the purple. These elevations were followed in 1627 by that of another nephew, also called Antonio, to the intense and openly expressed annoyance of the Sacred College, and in violation of a series of former papal bulls which had forbidden the elevation of more than one papal nephew at any time. Antonio's brother, Taddeo, the weakest of all the family, was set up as the founder of the Barberini dynasty. He was showered with prestigious political offices; in 1630 he was made General of the Church, in succession to his uncle Carlo, governor of the Borgo, and governor of Castel Sant'Angelo, and a year later he became Prefect of Rome. Wealth flowed as freely upon him as did honours. By 1631 he was already said to have an income of 143,384 *scudi* a

year, and certainly by the end of Urban's pontificate he was one of the richest men in Italy. In 1627 he was found a bride from the Colonna family and in 1629 purchased the status of Prince of Palestrina.

Meanwhile, very considerable sums of money from the papal treasury had gone to endow every other member of the Barberini family which, before Urban came to the papal throne, had already enjoyed an annual income of twenty thousand *scudi* a year. Since at this time no distinction was made between the papal treasury and the pope's private income, the opportunities for papal nephews to acquire a fortune at the expense of the Holy See were known to be unlimited; but contemporaries held that the Barberini, while they exceeded no legal limits, had certainly exceeded those of reason. By 1627 Cardinal Francesco Barberini alone was reputed to have an annual income of 100,000 *scudi*, and while this suggested figure must be seen as an exaggeration, there can be little doubt, judging by his annual expenditure, that his income was very substantial indeed.

Yet contemporaries fully understood the motives of the Barberini. While recognizing that Urban's brother, Carlo, was largely interested in the Pope's position as a means of enabling him to make money, the Venetians commented: 'He knows well that the possession of money enhances one's reputation, and raises a man above the common herd, and he thinks that it is neither becoming nor reasonable that a kinsman of the pope should find himself in straitened circumstances after the pontiff's death'. Money, that is, could be used to establish the permanent status of the Barberini family. This was done in two ways. The first was to replace the old feudal aristocracy, by buying them out of such fiefs as they had managed to retain. In 1624 the Orsini sold their estates at Monte Rotondo to Carlo Barberini; in 1625 it was the turn of the Colonna, who sold him their castle of Roviano; in 1634 that of the Sforza, who sold Valmontone to Taddeo Barberini. The most important purchase, however, came in 1629 when, for 575,000 *scudi* Taddeo Barberini, as we have noted, bought the principality of Palestrina from the hopelessly indebted Francesco Colonna and so established himself in a pre-eminent position among the Roman aristocracy.

The second means by which the Barberini established themselves in Rome was through their patronage of the arts. Ever since the time of the first Cosimo de' Medici in Florence, the Italians had recognized that the surest way of insuring the immortality of a family name was to pay artists to commemorate it. Thus, long before the Barberini, all papal nephews had been conspicuous builders of great palaces, and highly competitive art patrons. Now, under Urban VIII, all the arts in Rome were to be engaged in celebrating the Barberini family. In this, as in everything, the Pope himself was the moving spirit; what other aim, after all, could so successfully have united the two most powerful emotions of his heart: love of the arts and family pride? While he was still a cardinal he had begun the process of glorifying the Barberini family by decorating the Annunciation Chapel in Sant'Andrea della Valle as a memorial to his uncle. For all the Barberini were to be included in this general apotheosis, both the living and the dead. Urban commissioned Bernini

In the Barberini Palace *lived the two cardinal nephews, Francesco and Antonio. As well as being a cultural and intellectual centre for the whole of Roman society (it included a theatre capable of holding three thousand people), it also inaugurated a new phase in the story of secular architecture. Maderno, Borromini, and Bernini all worked on it. Right: the street front in 1665; the fountain is by Bernini. In the garden front (above) the window on the extreme left with double pediment containing a shell is characteristic of Borromini. (240,241)*

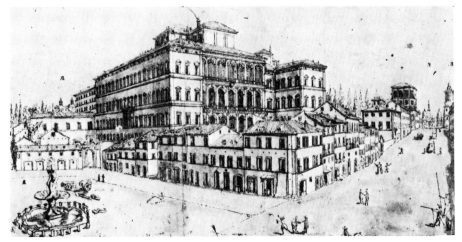

to carve commemorative busts of his deceased mother, father, and uncle, to be placed in the Annunciation Chapel, and, when his brother Carlo died in 1630, commissioned a memorial plaque for him also. As for himself – at the very beginning of his pontificate Venetian observers had noted in him a 'hunger for glory'; and in his determination to follow any course, 'which could raise his name in public opinion and make it famous in the future', the Pope left nothing to chance, history, or family piety – within three years of his accession he had commissioned his own tomb from Bernini, now one of the most striking monuments in St Peter's.

In other acts of artistic patronage, however generous, the desire to perpetuate the Barberini name was never entirely absent. Even Bernini's great baldacchino in St Peter's, one of the most famous and influential pieces of Christian art in the world, is also a memorial to the Pope's family: bees, the well-known Barberini emblem, crawl up the twisted columns and decorate the bronze leaves on the cornice, while the leaves on the column are not the traditional vine but the Barberini laurel, and a sun, another Barberini emblem, blazes from the capitals.

The baldacchino is no isolated example. All the works of art paid for by this family were expected to glorify and immortalize their name. That art of this nature should also have been great was not merely fortuitous; the Barberini were discriminating as well as generous patrons. The charming and courteous Carlo Barberini, the Pope's brother and the business genius of the family, was a student of all the arts and particularly well read in history. Cardinal Francesco Barberini was a man of even greater intellectual achievement. He continued to retain his uncle's confidence and in 1632 became papal Vice-Chancellor, thus holding the most lucrative office in the Curia and a post which, in terms of precedence and tradition, made him the second most important person in the Church's hierarchy. His income was vast, but much of his wealth was spent magnificently, for Francesco Barberini, who was described by contemporaries as having, 'nothing so dear to his heart as the greatness and good government of Rome', was always a most generous friend and patron and a munificent alms-giver. To his generosity would certainly have testified the clergy of his own titular church of San Lorenzo in Damaso, on which he lavished splendid artistic gifts as a setting for spectacular religious services which were the talk of all Europe. And Francesco was not merely a generous but also a sensitive patron. Deeply read in theology, history, and botany, he had translated the works of Marcus Aurelius, and was a collector of antiques and rare objects, of ancient inscriptions and coins. His court was remarkable for its erudition; among his closest friends he counted the famous antiquarians Luke Holstein and his secretary, Cassiano del Pozzo, himself a distinguished patron of the most cultivated artists working in Rome, including Cortona, Pietro Testa, and Poussin. It was in Cassiano's own private museum of antiquity that Poussin first studied when he came to Rome and through Cassiano that the painter Vouet first met the poet Marino, another of Cassiano's protégés. The distinguished intellectual circle which gathered round Cassiano and his patron Francesco Barberini, and thus ultimately formed part

of the papal court, included Francesco's Secretary for Latin Letters, Jean-Jacques Bouchard, one of the leading mathematicians of his day; and his librarian, the historian Gabriel Naudé, who was later to enter the service of both Richelieu and Mazarin. It also included distinguished disciples of Galileo, among them Benedetto Castelli and Gian Battista Doni. All these men doubtless helped Francesco Barberini to gather together the collection of books and manuscripts which formed the core of the Barberini Library, second only in importance to that of the Vatican and distinguished by the number of foreign – particularly French – works that it contained. This library was opened to the general public.

Francesco Barberini was equally generous in his patronage of the visual arts and, like his uncle, remarkably catholic in his taste, as his simultaneous patronage of Vouet, Le Valentin, Poussin, Cortona, and Bernini reveals. In 1627 he set up the Barberini tapestry works in the family palace and, three years later, commissioned Cortona to design cartoons for it. The most important of these designs was the *Life of Constantine* series. It was Francesco, also, who was the moving spirit behind the building of the spectacular new Barberini Palace at the Quattro Fontane, the first of the great Baroque palaces of Rome, where, in 1633, he and his brother, Antonio, established their courts. The Barberini

---

The immense baldacchino *designed by Bernini as a canopy for the high altar of St Peter's, itself built over the Apostle's tomb, is a glorification of the Barberini family as much as of St Peter. The coats of arms at the base have already been illustrated (pl. 228); bees also climb up the twisted columns and settle in threes on the fringe at the top. The sun and the laurel, other Barberini emblems, are also prominent. (242)*

Urban's own tomb *was commissioned from Bernini only three years after he became pope. At the top Urban (in bronze) raises his right hand in blessing. Below, two allegorical virtues, Charity and Justice (in stone), flank a sarcophagus from which Death emerges bearing a scroll which reads URBANUS VIII BARBERINUS PONTIFEX MAXIMUS. (243)*

The centenary of the Jesuit Order *fell in 1639 and large-scale celebrations were organized at the expense of Cardinal Antonio Barberini. Andrea Sacchi decorated the great Jesuit church in Rome, the Gesù, and afterwards commemorated the occasion in this painting. Pope Urban VIII himself attended, and is shown in the centre. (244)*

Glorification of the Barberini family *reached its climax in the great Baroque ceiling by Pietro da Cortona in the Gran Salone of the Barberini Palace. Its complex allegorical programme was the work of a minor poet, Francesco Bracciolini. The figure in the centre is Divine Providence, mistress of Time and Fate, who crouch in the two lower corners. She looks upward towards the Barberini emblems, the three bees within a wreath of laurel, which is being borne aloft by Faith, Hope, and Charity, and commands Immortality (left centre) to crown them with a halo of stars. At the very top are the Church (holding two massive keys) and Rome (holding the papal tiara). (245)*

Palace, which had been designed by Maderno, Borromini, and Bernini, and was decorated by Lanfranco and Cortona, thereafter became one of the great show-pieces of Rome as well as a meeting-place for scholars from all over Europe, whatever their nationality or creed; even the young and censorious John Milton was a welcome guest in 1638.

Francesco's brother, Cardinal Antonio Barberini, shared the family enthusiasm for the arts almost to the point of excess. His exaggerated respect for genius led him to shelter in his court a number of disreputable artists whose open defiance of the law led to scandal on more than one occasion. As a prolific writer of vacuous Latin poetry himself, Antonio naturally favoured poets and numbered among his clients the famous poet and antiquarian, Delio Guidiccioni. Of the visual arts Antonio was an even more munificent patron. His clients included the Viterban painter Gian Francesco Romanelli, to whom he gave a house on his country estate; Claude; Poussin; Bernini; and Andrea Sacchi, whom he maintained for at least twenty years. For Antonio, Sacchi decorated the interior of the new villa the Cardinal acquired at Bagnaia in 1632, painted his *Giostra di Piazza Navona*, which was subsequently presented to the Roman people; and, at Antonio's expense, in the Gesù the *Celebrazione del Centenario della Compagnia di Gesù*. To the Jesuits, in fact, Antonio was always generous. It was he who paid for the centenary celebrations of the order and who paid more than five thousand *scudi* for the new altarpiece to decorate the Gesù, as well as for many other embellishments to the church. It was Antonio Barberini, also, as the family's most enthusiastic patron of the theatre, who was the moving spirit behind the creation of the first modern theatre in Rome, added to the Barberini Palace in 1632. It opened with a melodrama, *Sant'Alessio*, written by another of the papal literary courtiers, the young Giulio Rospigliosi, later to become Pope Clement XI. The performance was an immediate success and Rospigliosi was to write many more operas for the theatre, with music by such varied composers as Marazzoli, Cornachioli, Michelangelo Rossi, and the Mazzocchi. Bernini too would be encouraged by Cardinal Antonio to use this theatre in order to embark on yet another successful career, as the composer, creator, and producer of plays, and it was to be Barberini money which would underwrite Bernini's spectacular, famous, but very expensive stage effects.

Even Taddeo Barberini, the least able and the least interested in the arts of all his family, managed to behave as a great patron as a result of the influence of his friend, Cardinal Guido Bentivoglio, patron of the poet Marino, whose taste was impeccable, and whose interest in the arts was long-established. Only Urban's brother, Antonio, the sternly ascetic Capuchin, Cardinal of San Onofrio, held aloof from the artistic concerns and magnificent living of the rest of his family. Although Urban insisted on Antonio's presence at court, apart from a period between 1627 and 1629 when he was absent in his diocese of Senigallia, the Cardinal continued to live the austere life demanded by the rules of his order. *His* income was devoted to charity – including the building of the Capuchin church and convent of Santa Maria della Concezione, and the church of the

'Out of the strong *cometh forth sweetness.' Rubens' design for the frontispiece of Urban's 'Poems', published in Antwerp in 1634, uses the image of Samson finding a bees' nest in the throat of a dead lion – an allusion both to the Barberini arms and to the sweetness of the poetry. The title was to go in the grotto at the bottom. (246)*

Propaganda Fide – to which he left a legacy of 25,000 *scudi* – and the only memorial he willed for himself was the epitaph on his tomb: 'Here rest dust, ashes and nothing.'

Former friends of Maffeo Barberini, who were admitted to the inner circle of power in the papal court, also tended to share the Pope's artistic interests. Most prominent among these were the two Sachetti brothers, Marcello and Giulio, the sons of a prominent Florentine businessman, who were the leaders of the Tuscan community in Rome. Urban VIII never forgot his Tuscan background, and Florentine interests tended to play a prominent part in court life, since, all other things being equal, a Florentine would naturally patronize another Florentine. Giulio Sachetti was made a cardinal in 1626, while Marcello became papal treasurer and was given the coveted monopoly of the papal alum mines at Tolfa. The prominence given to these men only strengthened the existing bias of the papal court, for the Sachetti had long been known as patrons of the arts, scholarship, and poetry, and Marcello had been responsible for introducing Cortona, whom he virtually discovered, to Urban VIII.

Although as a corporate body the cardinals were ruthlessly excluded from power, there were, of course, prominent individuals with whom Urban regularly chose to consult. These included Cardinal Mellino, the Papal Vicar, an extremely able man as well as a generous patron of the arts; the Florentine, Cardinal Bandino, a *papabile* cardinal, with a wide range of political experience, and a distinguished career already behind him; and the Venetian subject,

229

Cardinal Guido Bentivoglio *possessed a degree of scholarship and an aesthetic taste that made the Borghese Palace, where he lived, a rival to the Barberini. This portrait was painted by Van Dyck in 1623, when the artist was in Rome before beginning his career in England.* (247)

Scaglia. The interests of all these men were essentially centred on a successful court career. Apart from these political advisers, Urban also numbered among the cardinals some of his own most intimate friends. The most important of these was Pietro Aldobrandini, the Cardinal Camerlengo, one of the most important officials of the Church, since during a vacancy many of the most important papal powers would devolve upon him. Very fat and often ill, Aldobrandini was, nevertheless, a person to be reckoned with at the papal court; by virtue of his office; by virtue of his friendship with the Barberini – based upon a common love of poetry; and by virtue of his great wealth. Another close friend of Urban VIII was Cardinal Borromeo, the strict, austere, and pious nephew of St Charles, but he played little part in the life of the court as he was normally resident in his diocese of Milan. Cardinal Montalto, one of the most famous patrons in Rome, was also considered to be a close friend of the Pope, as was Cardinal Ginetti, an old legal colleague who was made Majordomo of the papal court in 1627, and, subsequently, on the death of Cardinal Mellino, Vicar of Rome. On this occasion Urban made his famous statement: 'We have made Ginetti Vicar, and we could really do no less, for in the twenty years which he has served us, he has always expressed the same opinions that we have held, and has never contradicted us on any occasion', a remark which forced people to conclude, reasonably enough, that the certain road to success at the papal court was to support all of the Pope's ideas and to flatter him without ceasing.

Mellino's office of Majordomo was one of a number of household offices at the papal court whose holders were

inevitably brought into close daily contact with the Pope; the papal cupbearer, the papal steward, the captain of the papal guard, were others. With all these men the Pope had close, often intimate relationships; but in no case did any of them wield any political power simply by virtue of holding office. Their function was largely decorative. Like the entire papal court they served as a magnificent backdrop to the person of Pope Urban VIII Barberini.

Behind the façade

Life at Urban's court seems to have flourished in something of a hot-house atmosphere, which, while it might, as we have seen, produce great art, also bred pettiness, faction, intrigue, and strife. It was universally recognized that what was essential for success was to be constantly under the eye of the Pope, and yet always to give pleasure, never offence. It was a world in which social pre-eminence became all-important, a pre-eminence which was largely measured in terms of external display, by the number of one's carriages, the size of one's palace, and by the number of one's clients and hangers-on. These hangers-on might include, as in many cases they did, *virtuosi*, singers, musicians, artists, and writers; but they could also include less attractive figures. The nobility, the ambassadors, and even some of the cardinals, like the younger Antonio Barberini and Carlo de' Medici, attempted to enhance their prestige by surrounding themselves with armed men and ex-bandits, who were constantly getting embroiled in street fights. These usually centred on questions of precedence and involved constant squabbles between ambassadors, between old and new noble families, and between different office-holders in the Curia. In September 1634 a dispute over precedence – whose carriage should pass first in the street – led to a duel between Carlo Colonna and Gregorio Caetani, in which Caetani lost his life. Far more serious were the squabbles sparked off by the appointment of Taddeo Barberini as Prefect of Rome, and his insistence that the position gave him precedence over all the Roman nobility and all foreign ambassadors, a claim which few were prepared to accept.

Among those who refused to tender to Taddeo Barberini the respect which he believed was owed to his sinecure, just as he had always refused to treat Cardinal Francesco Barberini with the respect that strict court etiquette required, was Odoardo Farnese, the Duke of Parma. Urban's indignation against Farnese for the slights offered to his close relatives certainly played a precipitating part in the war which took place between the Pope and Farnese over the district of Castro between 1640 and 1644.

That war revealed the slender basis on which the edifice of papal magnificence was built. The intervention of foreign powers meant that Urban was forced to accept a compromise peace; but the cost of the war led to the virtual collapse of papal finances at the end of his pontificate. The Venetians described Rome as a city where gold passed rapidly from hand to hand; but it was a city whose credit was overdrawn. Urban had spent with great generosity – on the arts, on the defences of Rome and the Church State, on bread subsidies, and on war both local and international. But, in doing so, he overreached the resources of the papal treasury, just as surely as his policies of encouraging luxury and magnificent expenditure tended to encourage his courtiers to overspend. The papal see was heavily indebted when Urban became pope. His pontificate aggravated the situation to the point of crisis. In 1623 the funded debt of the Papacy was already between fifteen and sixteen million *scudi* and the interest payment on this debt accounted for two thirds of the annual papal income. In the next four years Urban spent 300,000 *scudi* on military preparations alone; the papal debt was increased by some eighty thousand *scudi*, and the Pope was described as being in 'great need of money.' The new interest rates could only be met by raising the tax on salt throughout the Church State. By 1629 the debt had risen to something in the region of twenty million *scudi* and Urban had been forced to increase taxation on meat and salt, on wine and on incomes by a further 380,000 *scudi*. Even this proved to be insufficient; in January 1630 the Pope set up a congregation of cardinals, 'to consult about ways of raising money for present needs', but they seem to have been unable to make any positive suggestions for alleviating the situation, and Urban, on his death, left an accumulated debt of thirty million *scudi* .

Although only a portion of this increased debt was a result of the Pope's nepotism and patronage of the arts, the bulk of the money raised being used for war, it was inevitable that within Rome what should come under attack should be his most obvious forms of expenditure – the endowment of his own family and his expensive artistic projects. Throughout Urban's pontificate a flood of pasquinades attacked these areas of papal policy with relentless bitterness. As early as 1625 Pasquino proclaimed:

> *Urbano ottavo della barba bella*
> *finito il giubileo, impone la gabella.*

> (Urban VIII of the handsome beard,
> As soon as the Jubilee was over, put on a tax.)

The Barberini bees became a favourite theme:

> *Queste d'Urban si scriva al monumento*
> *ingrasso l'api e scortico l'armento.*

> (Write this of Urban on the monument
> That he fattens his bees and starves his flock.)

And the expenditure on the Trevi fountain provoked:

> *Urban, piochè de tasse aggravò il vino*
> *ricrea coll'acqua il popolo di Quirino.*

> (Urban, since burdening wine with taxes
> Entertains the Roman people with water.)

Finally, on Urban's death, the Roman mob, as was its wont, vented its hatred on the Barberini family and showed its relief at being freed from the onerous taxation burden associated with Urban's pontificate.

Much of modern Rome is the creation of Urban VIII. At the very least, his lavish patronage of the arts established and glorified the Eternal City and helped to make it one of the great urban centres of the world: a fitting and permanent monument to the splendours of his court. In economic terms the cost was high – no doubt too high. But can we honestly regret today that Urban chose to incur it?

Golden roses *were special tokens of papal favour. This one was given by Urban VIII in 1635 to Maria Anna, bride of Maximilian called 'the Great', Elector and Duke of Bavaria. (248)*

Eleven

LOUIS XIV
At the court of the Sun King

❋

RAGNHILD HATTON

THOUGH THE COURT OF LOUIS XIV stands forever identified with Versailles, it is worth noting that the Sun King, born in 1638, was in early middle age when, by stages between 1678 and 1682, he moved his household, his court, and his government officials to Versailles. Until then the Palais Royal, the Louvre, and the Tuileries had housed him in Paris, with Saint-Germain as a favoured country residence and occasional visits to Fontainebleau in the summer and to Vincennes and Chambord in the hunting season. Even after 1682 the chief courtiers and ministers moved with the King when he visited other châteaux in the perambulatory older tradition. Saint-Germain, however, no longer figured on the list of available palaces, Louis having lent it as a residence for his exiled Stuart relatives from 1688 onwards.

There were several reasons for Louis XIV's change of his main residence from Paris to Versailles. One was the fire of 1671 in the Louvre which made it uninhabitable for some time and necessitated the court's transfer to the Tuileries. Another was the rapid growth of the population of Paris which made for overcrowding, pollution of the River Seine, and for difficulties of communications: ministers found it increasingly hard to make their way to the Louvre or the Tuileries on time, given the frequent pile-up of carriages in the narrow streets. Private properties, which their owners refused to sell, made it impossible to widen the palace precincts or to effect the desired junction with the Tuileries (an event not achieved till the reign of Napoleon III). Finally, Louis' personal delight in fresh air and exercise, as well as the challenge to build a new royal palace – the first of the Bourbon dynasty – exerted a powerful pull. Here was a field of endeavour, a chance to give architectural expression to the concept of harmony and order which Louis shared with, and encouraged in, the artists and designers of his time; an

opportunity through conscious symbolism to glorify and strengthen the monarchical idea against anarchy, a way to indulge personal taste whether it was for a profusion of children in the park statuary ('toujours les enfants', ran the royal order) or for the placing of a sculptural masterpiece – like Puget's *Milo of Crotona* (1683) and his *Perseus and Andromeda* (1685) – not acceptable to the majority of the King's artistic advisers. It was not only in minor matters that Louis defended his own view concerning Versailles. As a ruler, continuity was important for him. Just as he, in his so-called *Mémoires*, which were in reality 'Instructions for the Dauphin' begun shortly after the birth of his eldest son in 1661, wished to prepare the boy for his future task, so he valued his own father's hunting lodge at Versailles and insisted that it should be incorporated into the plans for the new palace. It was in this older part, kept as the very centrepiece of the façade towards the growing village, that he chose to have his own set of rooms. He refused throughout the blandishments of his architects, who wanted to destroy the brick structure of Louis XIII in favour of an imposing stucco façade in symmetry with the garden front of the palace. Changes were made in the reign of his great-grandson Louis XV (his direct successor) in the internal arrangement of rooms; in part because Louis XV's taste was not that of Louis XIV but also because Louis XV had a large brood of legitimate children who needed appropriate private apartments as they grew older. Louis XV's abandonment of his great-grandfather's set of rooms had also necessitated reconstruction. The famous King's Staircase was lost, though luckily the shape and decorations of Louis XIV's apartments were largely kept. The pillaging of Versailles which took place during the French Revolution has robbed posterity of the furnishings of Louis XIV's time, though individual pieces of furniture and hangings, as well as designs and sketches, enable us to visualize much of what has been lost.

The young Louis

Until Louis XIV was declared of age (as soon as he had entered upon his fourteenth year) he was in effect a member of the court of his mother the Queen Regent, though he had

The image of the sun dominates the iconography of Louis XIV. In an ivory plaque by Mollart of 1683 he wears a helmet crowned by a figure of Apollo. Underneath are medallions of Henry IV and Louis XIII, his grandfather and father. The cloak is covered with fleurs-de-lis, while on his shoulder are allegories of Industry and Justice. (249)

Louis was crowned *and anointed in Reims cathedral on 7 June 1654. In this contemporary engraving we are looking west. Two ceremonial stairs have been constructed and extra seating placed above the stalls. Louis' throne is on the choir-screen itself. (250)*

the dance training which Louis XIV received is sometimes overlooked by present-day historians who tend to emphasize only the symbolic significance of the young Louis costumed as the Sun in the ballet of 1653; but from a purely practical point of view this training was invaluable for one whose *métier* included making an entrance, assuming a mask for his public persona, and controlling demeanour at all times when he was on public view. The King, who by his very office would have to hold court, had inculcated in him in these early years the prerequisites both of court life and of statecraft. He was a willing and apt pupil, though somewhat shy and lacking in self-confidence as an adolescent, particularly in his relationship to Mazarin and to his mother.

Growing freedom came with the royal progresses to the centre and south of France in 1658 and 1660. Both were connected with the search for a suitable bride, but more importantly part and parcel of the tradition whereby a new king showed himself to his subjects and learned by personal experience to differentiate between regions, their problems as well as their potential value for the kingdom as a whole. Happy in his romantic love for Marie Mancini, collecting round him a group of young friends who frequently managed to travel ahead of the Queen Mother's party, Louis grew in stature: he was treated as the king on all occasions, fêted even where royal power was feared. There is a historically important painting of the royal coach halted outside Toulon, while the *échevins* of that city kneel in homage beside it. Queen Anne and Louis' brother Philippe are sitting inside as modest spectators; the young King, clearly the central figure, is by the open window, extending his hand. He had indeed beautifully shaped hands, which nearly astonish in the perfection of their rendering in this painting which, though endearing, is somewhat primitively realistic. It is one of the few portraits which, perhaps because it is so much less studied than most, give an impression of the charm that was Louis' as a young man. It corresponds closely as far as shape of features are concerned to a medal engraved at the time; but is given life by the colour of the hair and the stance of the half-figure. The painting is interesting also in two other contexts. The town dignitaries all kneel before the King, a customary obeisance which Louis, more of a reformer than often realized, dropped from court etiquette: we meet it in his personal reign only for the solemn entry, with its religious overtones, of new knights into the orders of chivalry and at the submission of conquered towns when officials hand over the keys of the gates to Louis in person. Conversely, in the painter's minutely correct portraiture of the *échevins*, each with his coat of arms and his full titles flowing as streamers beyond his glorious red mantle, we see exemplified that concern for rank and privilege which was deeply embedded in French social consciousness and which persisted throughout Louis XIV's reign – even though the King brought writers, artists, and men concerned with commerce into the charmed circle of nobility, thus shocking the more conservative members of his court.

Louis himself was conservative enough not to tamper too much with rank and privilege. He felt bound by his coronation oath to uphold the privileges of individuals,

his own household from the age of seven. After his coronation at Reims, which by its religious ceremonial bound him to defend the Catholic religion and keep the fundamental laws of France while bestowing on him the powers to heal by his touch sufferers from scrofula, he became in theory more independent. But his mother and his godfather Mazarin, the first minister, continued to make decisions at court and to teach him in their various ways the craft of kingship. The Queen stressed the observance of etiquette and ceremony, particularly religious ritual; Mazarin introduced him to matters to be discussed in council meetings and made sure that he had plenty of time for the physical exercises, especially riding and dancing, which would give him command of his body. The importance of corporations, and cities. He took care, for instance, to consult the Law Faculty of the Sorbonne whether he had the right – in wartime – to tax those members of French society who were traditionally exempt. He was meticulous when bestowing the coveted title of *duc et pair* of France in observing that the promotion should be justified on grounds of old nobility as well as deserved politically: it has been shown that promotions which fell below the customary number of noble quarterings during his reign were all made before 1661 or rested on firm promises made before that date by Mazarin and the Queen Regent.

Marriage, children, and mistresses

With his marriage to the Spanish Infanta María Teresa in 1660 and the birth of the Dauphin in 1661, Louis XIV achieved a considerable measure of independence in his court life. The Queen Mother, who got on very well with her Spanish niece and daughter-in-law, could no longer reckon with a monopoly position; she had her own court, but so did Queen Marie-Thérèse (to use the French form of her name) and Louis – while keeping on good terms with both – found freedom to go his own way. He had been quite favourably impressed by the physical appearance of the bride chosen for him. She had the much admired luxuriant blonde hair of the Austrian branch of the house of Habsburg; she was petite and cried out for protection; she doted on him from their wedding-night onwards. Her education had not been neglected and she was not as stupid as often suggested; but she did not hold his attention for long. For this there were several reasons. She did not share his delight in open-air exercise and her imperfect command of French grated on Louis, whose love and concern for his native language and its literary expression in prose and verse was deep and enduring. A measure of cynicism had become part of Louis' character after his platonic and nerve-racking affair with Marie Mancini; if he for reasons of state were not free to marry her – and of this he had been convinced by his mother and by Mazarin – then he felt free, after marriage, to seek consolation outside the union blessed by State and Church. His marriage never broke down, but it became incidental to his sensual life. The need to perpetuate the dynasty was a bond between Marie-Thérèse and himself. Five children were born to them after the Dauphin, two boys and three girls. They both grieved at losing all of them, most acutely at the death of Prince Philippe in 1671, at the age of nearly four, and Princess Marie-Thérèse in 1672, when five years old; but whereas the Queen sought comfort in good works and religious devotion, Louis found diversion and joy in the children born to him outside marriage; first those of Louise de la Vallière and then those of Françoise, Madame de Montespan, usually known as Athénais because of her intellectual bent. Of the two surviving children from his love affair with Louise, both legitimized, Louis, Comte de Vermandois (who died at the age of sixteen), proved something of a disappointment; but the girl, Marie-Anne, the first Mademoiselle de Blois, became a person of some importance at court; as did the four children of Louis by Madame de Montespan who reached adulthood. Louis had great difficulty in having these legitimized since Athénais,

Louis' Queen *was María Teresa – or Marie-Thérèse – daughter of Philip IV of Spain. The wedding, depicted here on a Gobelins tapestry now at Versailles, took place at St Jean-de-Luz. (251)*

Queen Mother and Queen *were also aunt and niece. In this painting by Simon de St André, the Queen Mother wears symbolic armour, expressing the fact that she had acted as Regent during Louis XIV's minority, while her daughter-in-law carries the olive-branch and the fruits of the peace of 1659 between Spain and France. (252)*

1679 to Marie-Anne-Christine-Victoire of Bavaria had produced Louis' first legitimate grandchild, Louis, Duc de Bourgogne), and his household of three sons, and, in time, their respective wives; though the Dauphin had his own palace at Meudon.

Any description of the court must take into account Louis' legitimized children, the joy they afforded him in their childhood, unmarred by the responsibility attached to his bringing up the heir to the throne and the tension which the quarrels attendant upon their rank brought to the King's later years. The marriages of the children of the Grand Dauphin were more straightforward; the Duc de Bourgogne married [Marie-] Adélaïde of Savoy in 1697; the Duc d'Anjou (when already King Philip V of Spain, so that he and his wife formed no part of Louis' court) her sister Marie-Louise; and the Duc de Berry, Marie-Louise-Elisabeth, daughter of Philippe II d'Orléans, in 1710. The great-grandchildren of Louis by the eldest and youngest of the three legitimate grandsons were on the fringes of the King's life as an old man, though the deaths in quick succession, first of the Duc de Bourgogne (Dauphin since the death of his father in 1711), then of his eldest son, then in 1714 of the Duc de Berry, left the succession hanging on a slender thread: the life of the remaining great-grandchild, Louis, born in 1710. Louis XIV therefore became directly responsible for the upbringing of the third Dauphin of his reign. One of the most touching paintings in the Musée Carnavalet is by an anonymous artist: it shows Louis supervising the lessons of the five-year-old boy who within months was to become Louis XV. The precarious character of the succession explains the step which Louis XIV in July 1714 took to safeguard it by his decree, generally regarded as unconstitutional, which rendered the Duc de Maine and the Comte de Toulouse and their heirs capable of succession if the legitimate collateral branches of the houses of Orléans, Condé, and Conti should die out. Philippe, the son of Louis' brother (who had died in 1701) and Louis' son-in-law by his marriage to Françoise-Marie, had but one son, while the other princes (four in all) were either children or unmarried. So quite apart from Louis' fondness for the Duc de Maine and the Comte de Toulouse there were sound political reasons for making provision for the succession; though, to the *ducs et pairs* of France who already bitterly resented Louis XIV's decision that the legitimized princes should take rank immediately below the princes of the blood and before the *ducs et pairs*, it seemed the last straw. Louis XIV's will, whereby he seemed to have weighted the honours and the powers in favour of the Duc de Maine, already head of the household and thus in charge of the royal guards regiments, by giving him charge of Louis XV's education, was upset by the Parlement of Paris in cooperation with the Duc d'Orléans, Regent by Louis XIV's will for Louis XV. The regency council, on which the legitimized princes had places beside experienced ministers and marshals, was suppressed; the right of the Duc de Maine and the Comte de Toulouse to succession was declared null and void along with their precedence above all *ducs et pairs*, while they now took their rank according to date of creation of their respective titles. Before long the Duc de Maine, more

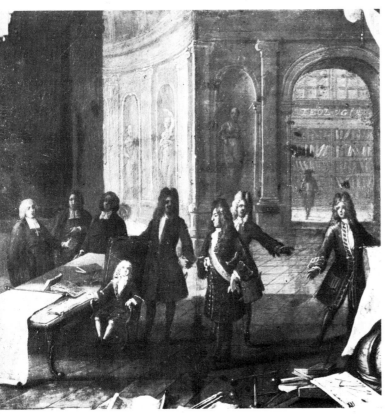

The Dauphin, *Louis' great-grandson, born in 1710, became an object of intense concern to the old King after 1712, when his son, grandson and elder great-grandson had died. Here he attends one of the boy's lessons; on the floor lie scientific instruments, and through the arch one glimpses a vast library. (253)*

unlike Louise, was a married woman. Adultery in a king could be condoned, if with some heart-searching on the part of the theologians and lawyers; double adultery was a different matter. Moreover, the Marquis de Montespan was not at all anxious to divorce his wife; but after considerable pressure the Paris Parlement in 1673 agreed to a legal separation of Athénaïs and her husband, and the legitimization followed of Louis-Auguste Bourbon (b. 1670, created Duc de Maine), Louis-César (b. 1672, created Comte de Vexin), Louise-Françoise, Mademoiselle de Nantes (b. 1673), Louise-Marie, Mademoiselle de Tours (b. 1676), Françoise-Marie, the second Mademoiselle de Blois (b. 1677), and Louis-Alexandre (b. 1678, created Comte de Toulouse). Louis' legitimized children married well: in 1680 Marie-Anne, the first Mademoiselle de Blois, to the Prince de Conti, nephew of the Grand Condé; in 1685 Louise-Françoise, Mademoiselle de Nantes, to Louis III, Duc de Bourbon; the second Mademoiselle de Blois to Philippe II, Duc d'Orléans; the Duc de Maine to Louise-Bénédicte, grand-daughter of the Grand Condé; the Comte de Toulouse (but post-1715) to Marie Victoire Sophie de Noailles. All these children, and their spouses once they had married, formed part of the court. So did the only legitimate surviving son, the Dauphin Louis (known as the Grand Dauphin once his marriage in

On the heights of Olympus: *Louis
and his family depicted as Greek gods
and goddesses in a painting by Nocret,
c. 1669. The King is enthroned as
Apollo. Behind him is his cousin,
Mademoiselle, and in front of him his
wife Marie-Thérèse and their children.
The Queen Mother is in the centre. The
group on the left consists of his brother,
Philippe d'Orléans, with his wife and
mother-in-law. The two children in the
framed painting in the front had died in
infancy. Right: two of the royal
mistresses, Louise de la Vallière (by
Werner) and Madame de Montespan
with her children (by Mignard).*
(254–56)

Witty, intelligent, and pious, *Françoise, Madame de Maintenon,*
became Louis XIV's morganatic wife some time in the 1680s and the
valued companion of his middle years and old age. This portrait by
Mignard shows her in about 1694. Note the devotional book and the
hourglass. Louis teasingly called her 'La Sainte Françoise'. (257)

ambitious than his younger brother, forfeited all his offices.

Such contentious issues lay in the future, however, at the
time when Louis fell in love with Louise de la Vallière. She,
an officer's daughter, was an exceptionally skilful rider and
a fine musician who sang with a sweet voice. Her successor
as *maîtresse en titre*, Madame de Montespan, a more sultry
beauty, was if anything of even better stock, being a
Rochechouart-Mortemart. She proved more responsive to
the King's political plans and was forever investing in his
ventures, fitting out naval ships for example, and giving him
moral courage and support. Neither influenced political
decisions or important appointments, but they set the tone
of the court. The *grandes fêtes*, apart from the famous
carousel in Paris in 1662 which celebrated the birth of the
Dauphin, were – as all the court knew – in their honour,
though the Queen presided at the King's side over the
festivities. Louis' mistresses appreciated more than his wife
the allegorical and symbolic content of the *fêtes* and of the
decorations and statuary of Versailles. The lady who in
Louis' middle age became his closest woman friend and,
after the Queen's death in 1683, his morganatic wife, was
less concerned with frivolities and tried with some success
to make Louis a 'moral being', concerned with his eternal
fate. The year of Louis' marriage to Françoise Scarron (born
d'Aubigné and created by him Marquise de Maintenon) is
not known, some scholars thinking 1689 as likely as the

more usually accepted 1683 or 1684; but her private
standing in the royal family was demonstrated by her being
seated, even in the presence of princes of the blood, and at
court by the deference paid to her and her relatives. She
came of an old family, her grandfather having been the
Huguenot friend and adviser of Henri IV. Widowed, she was
given charge by Athénais of the two eldest of her children
by Louis, and her strong attachment to the Duc de Maine
(handicapped in childhood by a weak leg caused by
poliomyelitis) formed a bond between herself and Louis.
The King, whose attachment to Louise de la Vallière had
lasted from 1661 to 1667 and whose love affair with Madame
de Montespan endured with some fluctuations from 1668 till
1679, was ready to move into calmer waters by 1680.
Madame de Maintenon persuaded him to take no more
maîtresses en titre and to make a show of fidelity to the
Queen; and though Louis had at least one intense love affair
– with Mademoiselle de Fontanges – after his conversion to
morality as defined by Madame de Maintenon, it is
significant that no children apart from those with Louise and
Athénais were legitimized or even recognized. From his long
union with Madame de Maintenon there was no issue (she was
already near the menopause when their sexual relationship
began); but they both treated the young Duchesse de
Bourgogne, only twelve when she arrived at court, as their
own child. She lived with them until her marriage was
consummated some two years later, and after that their
concern for the younger generation was channelled into
their joint efforts on behalf of the school for young
gentlewomen at Saint-Cyr founded by Madame de Maintenon in 1686.

Louis regarded it as axiomatic that a ruling monarch (as
opposed to a *fainéant*) should not be guided by either male or
female favourites. In his instructions to the Dauphin he
claimed that he would never let his mistresses – though he
found them a needful relief from the burden of kingship –
influence his policy decisions. In practice he seems to have
been able largely to follow theory: Louise and Athénais
helped some applicants to positions of honour and even
minor office; and Françoise' apartments became in Louis'
old age a refuge where he could go through papers and
discuss affairs of state with one or two ministers in peace.
But though at least two of the three women desired power,
none wielded influence over Louis' policies.

Louis' government

Louis XIV's political independence was achieved after his
marriage and before the birth of the heir to the throne. The
timing was accidental, fixed by the death of Mazarin on 9
March 1661; but the aim had been preconceived and
encouraged by Mazarin himself. On 11 March Louis announced that he would govern without a first minister. He
held council meetings where ministers informed and advised him; but the final decision was reserved for him alone
and no one minister had the right to regard himself as more
privileged than others in the weight which attached to his
advice. The most important council already in existence was
the *conseil d'en-haut* or *conseil d'état secret*, in everyday
parlance called the *conseil du roi* or the *conseil du ministère* or

even simply *le conseil*. No adviser, not even a secretary of state, had the right to be called to this council; every member became a minister of state by virtue of being called to the council by the King, and relinquished office if the King's invitations to attend ceased. Louis liked to keep this council small. In 1661 there were only three ministers, and though the number increased to four and then to five, and usually included the more important secretaries of state and the Chancellor, the highest-ranking officer of the Crown, it is worth noting that during the long reign there were only seventeen ministers in all and that the King reverted to three councillors towards the end of his reign. No man of the Church was ever a member; and the only three members of the nobility of the sword – the *noblesse d'épée* – were, significantly enough, those who had been charged with the education first of Louis himself and then of the 'sons of France', that is, the direct descendants of Louis with right to inherit the crown: the Ducs de Villeroi, father and son, and the Duc de Beauvilliers. The nearest heir to the crown was admitted to the council to learn his *métier* as soon as he was of age. This small council met on Sundays, Mondays, and Wednesdays in the early afternoon at least every other week, though it could be called also on other days and at other times if the King thought it necessary. Louis himself was in the chair and discussions were generally initiated by questions posed by him. Foreign matters requiring secrecy were debated and the great decisions of the reign taken. Dispatches or reports from diplomats, commanders, and other military experts were read in extracts or summaries, and draft answers or orders outlined. More important in domestic affairs, the *conseil des dépêches* (created in 1630) met on Tuesdays, but later also, or alternatively, on Saturdays. Here again, the King presided, but the Chancellor, the ministers, and the secretaries of state attended by virtue of their offices. The secretaries were four in number: one for foreign affairs, one for the army, one for the navy including the merchant-marine, and a fourth for the Maison du Roi, the household, including the court, the palaces, the royal guard and even – if religious affairs had to be discussed at the *conseil* – for the Church. Here were read reports from provincial governors and intendants. Draft orders and decrees for the internal administration were planned, though, as for the high council, drafts were often amended and finalized by the King in consultation with individual ministers or secretaries. For both councils the King sought, if he so wished, the advice of men who were not members. In the early years of the personal reign, Turenne was often approached; in the later years Vauban, and the Marquis de Dangeau, colonel of the *régiment du roi* from 1665, a member of the Académie Française since 1668, and grand master of the orders of chivalry after 1693.

Beside the two councils that ranged over the whole spectrum of foreign and domestic affairs there was a more technical *conseil des finances* instituted by Louis XIV in 1661 to bring order into the finances and prepare the state budget. He himself used to attend its Tuesday and Saturday meetings regularly, but he did not take the chair; and later on in the reign he left its work in the hands of the Chancellor, the Controller of Finances, and other experts,

finding it difficult to spare the time for such specialized work. Louis also instituted a *conseil de commerce* in 1664 to discuss ways and means of increasing manufactures and trade. On it, apart from certain royal officials, twelve deputies from the more important towns had seats. This *conseil* has frequently been underestimated, as it wilted away after a few years; but it was reconstituted in 1700 and played an increasingly important role during the last decade and a half of Louis' reign. The *conseil privé* (also called the *conseil des parties*) was in 1673 reorganized as a supreme legal and administrative authority. It was a huge council, consisting of some thirty councillors of state and some eighty masters of requests, and its business was large enough to need seven *bureaux* to prepare its work. There was yet another council, the *conseil de conscience*, which advised the King on religious matters. Though its formal meetings were rare – the most important one of the whole reign being that which in October 1685 preceded the revocation of the Edict of Nantes – it became a convention that Louis, every Friday, would see at least the Archbishop of Paris and his own confessor to settle vacancies and generally discuss affairs of the Church.

With this organization of the King's own working day and the more or less systematic handling of official business, it is not strange that the nineteenth-century historian Lavisse should have labelled Louis XIV 'le roi bureaucrat', although truly bureaucratic forms inside the various departments of the administration were slow to emerge. The officials were, in form, on the staff of the individual secretary of state and paid by him; but there was a well-recognized ladder of promotion whereby young men, who generally received their first chance through private patronage, were brought to the King's notice when they did well and thus earned the chance of royal promotion in careers and marriage alliances. There was a lively interchange between home and foreign service. Men from the office of the secretary of state for foreign affairs were sent abroad as diplomats, but so were military men and those experienced in commerce; and every expert was looked upon as available in times of need whether for advice on missions-to-be, for propaganda activities, or for military, trade, and financial ventures.

The need to train the younger generations of officials by systematic studies focused on their special fields of work as well as by practice helps to explain the revived *conseil du commerce* in 1700, and also the foundation of the Académie Politique in 1712. Like most of the other academies this was housed in the Louvre. Its establishment coincided with the decision to move the archives (except those for the last ten years) of the foreign secretariat from Versailles to Paris: with the private collections which the Crown had assiduously been buying up, these papers would provide the academy's students and teachers with material to work on. All Louis' academies were given a practical slant. The royal academy of science had, as a kind of sub-title, the Académie des Arts et Métiers. The task of the Petite Académie – originally comprising only four members of the Académie Française – was soon defined by an official title, the Académie Royale des Inscriptions et Médailles. The teaching duties of the

The Académie Française, *founded in 1635, was taken under Louis' special protection. Sessions were made public in 1671 and women were admitted in 1702. Its monumental dictionary of the French language appeared in 1694. (258)*

Académie Royale de Peinture et de Sculpture and the Académie Royale de Musique (at first more restricted as Académie d'Opéra) are clearly enough identified by their titles, though they have perhaps been overshadowed by the fame of the Académie Française de Rome, where young French painters, sculptors, and architects were taught. The Jardin des Plantes was in effect an academy for the research and teaching of botany. It should not be overlooked that some of the sessions of the Académie Française were made public in 1671 and that women were admitted to meetings in 1702. Towards the end of Louis' reign he conceived a plan for rehousing the academies and the royal library in a magnificent square of specially designed mansions. The present Place Vendôme, then Place Louis le Grand, was laid out, and nearly all its buildings were completed before 1715; though after the King's death they were put to other uses.

This undertaking alone gives the lie to the stereotype of a Louis XIV who deserted Paris and starved it of development because he had conceived a dislike for the city during the civil wars of the Fronde and wished to punish it. Paris was, and remained, the capital. Important ministers maintained *hôtels* there, the secretary for foreign affairs received diplomats on given days to gather news at first hand and to guide them in their negotiations at Versailles. While the city authorities and private individuals helped to beautify the capital (the Place des Victoires, for instance, was laid out by the Marquis de Feuillade to honour Louis XIV), Louis himself did a great deal. Work on the Louvre improvements continued; the Hôtel des Invalides was completed; the old city walls were torn down to permit growth; broad

boulevards, magnificent in conception, were laid out (the Champs-Elysées among them); and splendid *portes* defined the city boundaries, glorifying by their decorations the achievements of the Crown in the post-Fronde period. Nor was Paris neglected in matters of hygiene and safety. Louis donated fountains to give the citizens unpolluted water to drink, street-lighting and pavements were provided, and the newly instituted office of intendant of police with far-reaching powers to initiate improvements of all kinds gave the capital 'a minister for Paris'. The intellectual and artistic life of the city was rich. Theatre, opera, and ballet benefited from royal patronage, though Louis rarely journeyed to the capital in person, giving the task of representing him to younger members of the family who were less busy than himself after 1672. He came on solemn occasions or when he wished to give emphasis to a project, visiting the Académie Royale des Sciences in 1681 to support it against the jealousy of the Académie Française; attending a banquet at the Hôtel de Ville given in his honour by the city authorities; and taking part in religious services.

The court at Versailles

That these and other visits after the King's move to Versailles were brief and well spaced can be explained by the fact that the court of Louis XIV was a place of work for the monarch and it was not easy for him to get away. The 'Dutch War' of 1672–78 found Louis in the field during the campaigning season for the major part of the war, and with an increased desk-burden as soon as he returned. That war had escalated in a way which neither he nor his generals had expected: instead of a speedy victory over the Dutch Republic Louis found that the state he had attacked received ever more allies, and that the competition to be first in the field for the next campaign grew ever more fierce. And when peace had been concluded, the move of the court and the administration to Versailles chained the *roi bureaucrat* to his new palace. That he was a willing slave is clear. The restarted building programme and the extensive embellishment of the gardens fascinated him. Here was everything that enabled him to enjoy his spare time. He hunted with his sister-in-law Liselotte of the Palatinate, his most intrepid companion while they were still fit enough for the chase. Both had stamina for a great number of years, whether the sport was for stag or wolf. It was only with the beginning of old age, when plagued by gout, that Louis followed the hunt from his wagonette. He was also an exceptionally good shot and felt a strong need for outdoor exercise: a walk round the gardens he loved so much that he wrote in his own hand a guide to its treasures of vistas and statues; and a visit to the kennels or the falconry, or to discuss pruning and pollination of fruit-trees with the expert La Quintinière. *Le roi propriétaire*, the King as a country gentleman, is another of the labels bestowed on Louis XIV which fits. The flowers he ordered to be planted convey something of this to us; thousands of tulips were bought from the Dutch Republic even in wartime; the heliotrope, which by its colour symbolized royalty – and not, as is sometimes assumed, the sunflower – was ubiquitous, its scent (since it had been so plentiful at Fontainebleau) possibly reminding him of his

The court moved to Versailles *by stages between 1678 and 1682, and building operations were virtually continuous throughout Louis' reign. In a large painting by J.-B. Martin (above) Louis is shown inspecting plans for a reservoir about 1689. In the far background is the new palace of Versailles and on the right the old village with its parish church. The palace chapel was not finished until 1709; it is seen on the far right of the smaller engraving. The buildings flanking the forecourt are the stables. (259,260)*

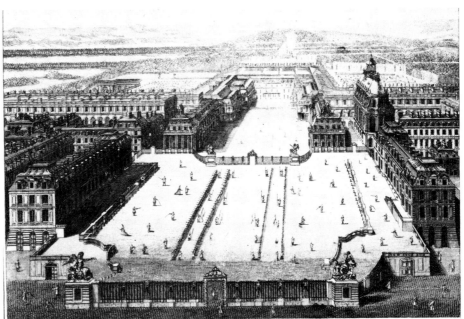

summer courtship in 1661 of Louise de la Vallière. Orange blossom was another of his favourite flower scents. Nor, as a good *propriétaire*, did he ignore the fruit and vegetables. The herb garden provided the tisane he drank at breakfast-time, globe artichokes and asparagus were prized delicacies, and when the tiny sweet peas – a recent import from Italy – ripened in May and June, the whole of the court (according to Liselotte, whose own taste was rather coarser) 'went mad'. The apples and pears which were developed with Louis' encouragement became famous strains, some of which have survived to the present day. Stays at other palaces were something of a necessity from the point of view of hygiene and the maintenance of Versailles. Apart from brief visits to nearby homes – to advise Madame de Montespan at Clagny or to admire the works he had set in progress for the Dauphin at Meudon – longer visits to Fontainebleau and to Chambord gave the Versailles domestic staff a chance to clean the vast palace, already becoming overcrowded outside the royal apartments because of the multitude of those who claimed the right, or were by their office or position forced, to have lodgings there. While the King, his ministers, and most important court officials and their respective staffs and servants were away, Versailles could be aired: that the smell of urine in some of the staircases in the wings was abominable is mentioned by more than one commentator. Building work continued whether the King was there or not. There was hardly a year – except during the worst financial periods of war – when the noise and muddy lanes connected with construction were absent from Versailles, though the last building, the chapel, was finished by 1709. The painting of Louis inspecting Versailles being built is typical of his reign. The dampness of the region, the very refashioning of the landscape

The statuary *of the Versailles gardens combines classicism and sensuousness. This nymph in the fountain of Diana is by Le Hongre.* (261)

itself, claimed victims among workmen and soldiers from various agues and swamp fevers. This, as the continued presence of beggars in Paris, was kept from the King as much as possible.

Embodying the new style of monarchy, built on old traditions, Versailles by 1682 was almost complete. The state apartments of the King and Queen, in use from 1674 onwards, celebrated the arts of war and peace. The formal staircases impressed by their finely wrought iron balustrades, their marble and bronze decorations, and their *trompe l'oeil* paintings which told of far-off lands explored by French mariners and cartographers. The widespread use of Apollo, the sun god, to symbolize the French monarchy seems to have been promoted by the preoccupation with classical statuary following the discovery in 1651 of an antique *Venus* in Arles; and it received positive encouragement from the members of the Petite Académie. The emblem of the sun was an old one, appropriated in medals and devices by rulers of all ages, most recently by Philip II of Spain. Now it was more systematically applied, and the Apollo-legend was, at least within France, reserved in poetry and in statuary for Louis XIV. In the early Versailles period it was signified by the Grotto of Thetis, finished in 1668, which displayed Apollo and the muses. The building of the chapel necessitated the destruction of this feature in 1694, and it is now known to us only through paintings and engravings. The allusion was not lost on contemporaries. Louis had set it as one of his aims to reward arts and learning throughout Europe. As soon as he began his personal reign his diplomats were asked to suggest men worthy of support. Those who did not wish to travel to France were as welcome to gratuities (such as the Florentine scholar who used part of his pension to build a house which in an anagrammatic inscription thanked Louis) as those, like the Italian astronomer Cassini and the Dutch physicist Huygens, who accepted invitations to pursue their research in Louis' academies. For the English reader it is of some interest that Louis tried to find out whether Milton, 'the greatest English living poet', would accept a token of his regard in the form of a bill of exchange, though nothing came of the gesture since Milton died before an answer could be sent back to France. Voltaire regarded it as Louis' most potent claim to *la gloire* that he gave financial support to some sixty foreign scholars, quite apart from the great number of French artists and *savants* whom he rewarded with money, titles, and preferential treatment at court so as to raise their reputation and enforce respect for them, at least outwardly, by his noble-born courtiers.

Three groups of statuary from the 1660s embodying the Apollo-legend have survived to our own day. Most direct in impact is the sun god in his chariot, perfectly placed and reflected in a wide sheet of water. From the terrace of the garden front Apollo, the horses, the dolphins, and the tritons are low enough not to obstruct the view; seen at close range Tuby's creation is equally imposing, the horses as realistically modelled as the muscles of the tritons blowing their seashells. Two fountain groups convey the legend more subtly, though the political messages are more potent. That Python in his fountain is slain by the arrow of Apollo might not be immediately grasped by those unfamiliar with Greek myths, since only the piercing arrow shot by Apollo is shown, not Apollo himself. But the fact that children are swimming happily and safely in the basin of the dragon fountain could not be lost even on the less educated. The Latona fountain celebrates the Crown's victory in the civil wars of the Fronde. Latona, the mother of Apollo and Diana, successfully protects her children against those who have attempted to harm them: her enemies, as in Ovid's *Metamorphoses*, are in the process of being turned into frogs. Political messages could also be read into many other works of sculpture at Versailles. The personification of the rivers of France – the Saône and the Rhône, the Seine and the Marne, the Garonne and the Dordogne – as male and female water gods is accompanied by the symbols of plenty: ears of corn, every species of fruit and flowers, and the most adorable *putti* and children. The many nymphs are tributes to female beauty, though the realism of the sculptors, Le Hongre and Coysevox in particular, should not be missed; one of the nymphs of the former in the fountain of Diana has the ugliest of thumbs and Coysevox's celebrated *Vénus accroupie* has flaccid abdominal muscles as well as deformed toes. Yet both are utterly beguiling and convey the sensuousness which reigned at Louis XIV's court in his youth and early manhood.

This sensuousness was equally evident in the *fêtes* for which Versailles first became famous; in the poetry and music of the tragicomedies enacted, in the splendid fireworks which ravished the night sky, in the carousels which perpetuated the ceremonial of chivalry. Yet from the first, at Louis' insistence, realism and satire also had their place at these spectacles. Molière was encouraged to ridicule the pompous, the bullies, and the would-be know-alls in all walks of life: the medical man, the priest, the hypocondriac, the scolding wife, or those ladies who aped the *précieuses* without their application to the task of learning and the improvement of manners. Concern for quality was a prerequisite at court, the search for perfection unending. Louis himself had been brought up on Corneille's tragedies and had an abiding love for and interest in the beauty and clarity of the French language. He related the struggle between duty and inclination, one of the main themes of these plays, to his own position; and their demand that the ruler should set an example as an *honnête homme* was one that he tried to meet both in his own conduct and in the upbringing of his sons and grandsons. He found for them teachers of moral fibre; and it is sometimes forgotten that his critic Fénélon was chosen by him to supervise the Duc de Bourgogne's education. Louis tried personally to teach his heirs the principles he held to be important in the exercise of the *métier* of a king. He did this by practical example and also by written instructions and letters. The heir to the throne attended council meetings and could observe that the King had picked men of intelligence, energy, and probity. The Dauphin and his sons, as well as Louis' legitimized sons, took part in the big manoeuvres at Compiègne in 1698; and, as his sons after him, became the recipient of frequent letters from Louis XIV once they joined the French armies in wartime. The guidelines Louis laid down for his grandson

Louis in the costume of a Roman emperor, *as he appeared at a tournament in 1662 to celebrate the birth of his first son, the Dauphin. The King's whole public life was in a sense a theatrical performance, and his training in ballet, which may seem odd to modern eyes, was a useful professional technique. (262)*

Philip V after he had become King of Spain are as illuminating for Louis' concept of kingship, matured by greater experience, as his instructions to the Dauphin of the 1660s and 70s. Since after 1700 Louis had to guide Philip V by correspondence, the 503 letters sent to him form the longest sequence that we possess of this particular educational type; and they still repay investigation.

Louis' taste for reform extended to the court itself. He rationalized the functions of his courtiers and created new offices where these were needed, as for instance the *grand maître de garderobe*, a mark of the importance of royal robes in the early and more sumptuous years of the King's reign. Court dress, as defined by Louis, became fixed for as long as the *Ancien Régime* lasted; the red-heeled shoes, the ladies' dresses in rich material, the men with embroidered waistcoats and a coat of military cut, favoured courtiers wearing the blue coat which proclaimed them as the King's chosen companions. There were minor changes from time to time, in the fashion in ladies' hair-styles and in the cravats of the gentlemen; but when one changed, all changed. Louis also brought a greater variety of court officials into closer contact with himself, the most obvious examples being those who catered for his musical and theatrical entertainments and the historiographers-royal with whom he collaborated because of his interest in French prose and his concern that the historical record of the reign should enhance his *gloire*, or at least explain the motives behind his actions. He did not choose subservient men. Boileau, much disliked by members of the Académie, was made a historiographer just because of his strong streak of independence.

In outer forms little was changed. The French court had long been built round the daily routine of a royal *lever* during which the king said his prayers in public, was dressed in public, walked to Mass attended by courtiers, dined in public (even though Louis ate at a small separate table and not at any of the larger tables he kept for courtiers, ministers, and guests), admitted certain courtiers – usually by virtue of their court office – to his leisure relaxations whether at the hunt or when visiting stables or kennels or gardens, welcomed the whole court for more formal evening entertainments, ending the day with a royal *coucher* in the same public manner. In Louis' case this routine had little to do with his work as a ruler, in which courtiers as such had no share: the councils and the discussions with individual ministers and secretaries of state which took up so much of his time were outside the time-honoured court sequence.

Yet the court of the courtiers remained of the greatest importance, for historical as well as practical reasons. It retained traditional ceremonial and formed an ordered frame round the work of the ruler and his ministers. Of the great officers of the Crown the Chancellor straddled the line between court and councils; while the Grand Maître de France, the Grand Chambellan, and the Grand Ecuyer tended to merge with the great officers of the king's household: the Grand Maître de la Garderobe, the Grand Maître des Cérémonies, the Grand Aumônier, the Grand Veneur and the Grand Maréchal des Logis. Each was supported by the various departments (twenty-two in all) which had been organized by Louis XIV; each had jurisdiction and control over and responsibility for a given number of these departments; each was distinguished by emblems of office, whether these were ivory-tipped batons covered in different coloured velvet or ceremonial keys; each had his given place and duties at coronations and other state occasions. But some special aura still clung to those who were technically officers of the Crown. The Chancellor represented the continuity of the Crown. He could not lose his post even if he were exiled from court. He alone did not wear mourning on the demise of the sovereign. The Grand Master of France was responsible for the many departments (seven, grouped together under the title *bouche du roi*) that guarded the physical well-being of the king. He administered the oath of loyalty to most other great officers and it was he who, at the funeral of the king, broke his baton and declared to all the king's servants present, 'Messieurs, le roi est mort, vous n'avez plus de charges.' The Grand Chamberlain controlled the routine of the king's daily life and regulated access to the state bedroom and the outer and inner cabinet, differentiating between the six forms of *entrées* granted by Louis XIV. The royal banner was in his keeping and he had the privilege of riding at the king's right hand in ceremonial processions, taking care that the head of his horse stayed level with the royal leg. The Grand Master of the Horse carried the lance royal when the king went to war; and had responsibility for the stables in general. The royal heralds worked under his direction. In regard to the great officers of the civilian part of the Maison du Roi, we have already touched upon the duties of the Grand Master of the Wardrobe. The Grand Master of Ceremonies supervised all functions in which the king took part, from royal baptisms and marriages and Te Deums to *fêtes* and receptions for foreign ambassadors. The Grand Almoner organized the

religious life at court, though not the music at services. He also had some control over the king's alms and scholarships; and what we might term welfare, for example hospitals. The Grand Master of the Royal Hunt was responsible for the king's safety when out hunting, as well as for the supervision of the various departments connected with hunting in all its forms. The Grand Marshal of Lodgings allocated rooms wherever the king took his court, or part of it, whether on travels or on campaigns. It was his chalk which put the coveted *pour* on the door of princes of the blood and foreign princes.

All the great officers, and their immediate deputies and subordinates, helped set the tone at court and thus contributed to the training of the next generation of courtiers. The custom, general at most European courts, for pages and *gentilhommes* to serve at court by rotation (for a period of

---

The living likeness *of Louis XIV in old age is caught in Antoine Benoist's life-size wax medallion portrait, made in about 1706. To add to its slightly bizarre realism, the figure wears Louis' actual wig (faded from its original black), lace collar, and red velvet coat. Benoist was famous for his waxworks, and exhibited a cabinet in which one could see the ladies in waiting of Marie-Thérèse. (263)*

Outside the gates of Toulon, *the young King receives the homage of the 'échevins' of the city. He stands at the window of his coach, and lays his hand on a book, swearing to maintain the ancient privileges of Toulon. Behind him are his mother and brother. The 'échevins' are identified by their coats of arms and full titles. (264)*

The Grotto of Thetis *was part of the Versailles gardens, finished in 1668 but destroyed in 1694 to make way for the chapel. It was decorated with symbols of the sun. In this painting Louis (on horseback, centre) is about to set out with a party of courtiers. (265)*

Versailles grew *from a small hunting-lodge to the largest palace in Europe. This panorama (left) shows the arrival of the King. The château has reached the stage at which Le Vau's work is complete but Mansart's not yet begun. (266)*

On a marble table-top *are depicted all the provinces of France as they were in 1684, the moment when French territorial expansion reached its peak. The veneered oak cabinet (below), probably an early work by H. C. Boulle himself, was made for the French crown. It has ebony and tortoiseshell inlay and a gold medallion in the centre containing a portrait of Louis XIV. (267,268)*

The Queen's staircase *is among the grandest of the surviving parts of Louis XIV's Versailles, with its coloured marbles, gilded reliefs, and 'trompe l'oeil' painting, which leads the eye into further magnificent vistas. (269)*

The Bassin d'Apollon *formed the climax of Le Nôtre's immense garden, with the sun god in the centre driving his chariot amid jets of water. In the foreground of this painting by J.-B. Martin, the aged Sun King, a sad contrast to his youthful image, is being propelled in a wheelchair. (270)*

NOBLE IEAN
DALBO
BOVRGEOIS.

MOB CARTHEL
CHARLARE
TEVRGEOIS.

NOBLE IEAN SOI
IVIARRIC
POVRGEOIS.

ANNE PERE
ERES AVOCAT
S DE BAR
TRES

months or for a year) was much used at Louis' court. This accounts, in part anyhow, for the great number of well-born persons who lived at court – most of them with titles of comte, vicomte, marquis, chevalier – and came within its codes of etiquette and service.

The spatial relationship between ruler and court found in England, where the monarch was approached through a series of apartments increasingly restricted of access, was not significant in France, where access to the king's person at given times of the day indicated the standing of particular members of the court.

Courtiers and administrators

The move to Versailles increased the size of the court, because all those who served in rotation moved with the King, not wanting to be left behind since this proximity had real advantages, even outside one's period in waiting. Those 'known at court', both men and women, had the privilege of presenting petitions to the King, and most of them increased their income by acting as commission agents and marriage-brokers, taking a given percentage for their services. For this, as well as for introducing someone to the King or to an influential minister, a fee was charged. Courtiers also found it necessary to stay at Versailles whenever Louis was there, lest opportunities be lost to further the prosperity of their own relatives and protégés: an office here, a marriage alliance there, might be missed even during a brief absence, since competition was fierce. Louis himself is reported as saying, 'Every time I fill a post, I make ninety-nine enemies', adding with the light cynicism of his later years, 'and the successful candidate invariably turns out ungrateful.'

It is usually assumed that Louis chained his courtiers to Versailles in order to prevent a repetition of the Fronde: if he kept an eye on them and kept them busy they could not plot against him. This is somewhat crude, but contains a grain of truth in that Louis taught his courtiers, and even those who served him in the administration of government, to regard banishment from court as the ultimate disgrace. There were plenty of French nobles who lived on their estates and only occasionally visited Versailles; but those who aspired to be courtiers did not like to leave for any length of time; they visited their estates in the provinces, preferably if they could combine this with the King's service, yet they did not stay long lest they might be thought to have fallen out of favour. Those who needed money or were just plain greedy did not wish to forego opportunities to exercise what social and economic power they possessed at court; for who knew when the chance would come to urge a certain measure, to present a given petition, to recommend a promising young man, to earn a reward by reporting to the King some malfunction in the financial administration? There was also the attraction of being in the know, so essential to the well-being of the courtier; but to ferret out the latest news, to pick up and pass on the latest *bon mot*, even to enjoy the gossip of the moment, one had to be present. The evening entertainments, the so-called apartments, were also an important consideration. These took place several times a week, with music, dancing, card-playing, and splendid buffets, quite apart from the occasional lotteries, *fêtes*, and

receptions, particularly when a foreign embassy was received. Above all, there was the privilege, deeply felt by most, if not all the courtiers, of serving the King and thus France. To be part of the daily routine of the King's *lever* and *coucher*, to wait on him at table, to play billiards with him, to accompany him at the hunt or during his walks in the grounds or – as Louis got older and plagued by gout – to walk alongside his wheeled chair, was a signal honour highly prized. This royal routine was so meticulously timed that courtiers boasted they could say where the King was and what he was doing every minute of the day, from the moment of his waking to his ceremonial return to his bed. They made it their business to know when the councils broke up, what the King's plans were for his outdoor activities, where and what he was hunting, what palace or estate he was visiting to note improvements or discuss plans for embellishments, whether he was to review his guards or to be present at the pruning of the Versailles fruit-trees. The King's hours, usually in the later afternoon, *entre les draps* with his mistress of the moment, were noted as part of the routine.

The nearest Louis came to having a private life was in late middle age with Madame de Maintenon when he, as far as the responsibility of government was concerned, was busier than in the days when Colbert and Louvois had eased his burden. He called ministers to her apartments for discussions and drafting of dispatches while she read or did her needlework, and but for her letters to her confessor we should not know that Louis even in old age frequently demanded two *bonnes bouches* (Madame de Maintenon's euphemism for sexual intercourse) before leaving for his formal *coucher*.

When the King was on campaign or on his travels, court ceremonial was usually simplified. In Franche-Comté in 1677 for instance, though Louis had a magnificent tent for an audience chamber, he did not dine alone but with his aides-de-camp and principal military officers. When, however, the occasion demanded splendour, this was laid on, most strikingly in 1670 when Louis, his Queen, Madame de Montespan, and a large entourage accompanied Monsieur's wife Henrietta (the first Madame, known as Henriette d'Angleterre) as far as Dunkirk on her journey – a secret diplomatic mission to her brother Charles II. Comfortably sprung coaches with large glass windows moved in procession. Louis, who rode horseback on his campaigns, at times used one or other carriage as a compliment to its occupant. Throngs of officials and servants rode ahead of the royal party to prepare for the evening's food and entertainment, while a mobile theatre for plays, operas, and ballet, as well as musicians, actors, and dancers, formed part of the large retinue. The court had in any case become larger when in 1668 it was decided that the Queen, no longer a young woman, should have married ladies (*dames de la reine*) for her entourage rather than the *filles d'honneur* who had hitherto been in attendance upon her. The *filles* had not been able to claim membership of the court for relatives, but the *dames* received the right to introduce their husbands, children, and even other relatives to the court, thus making them 'known' persons to the King, and in effect courtiers.

253

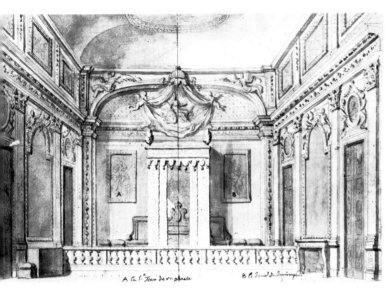

Inside Versailles: *Louis' bedchamber is known today through the drawing made of it in 1701 by the Swedish artist Tessin. Below: the Grande Galerie (Galerie des Glaces), with its famous silver furniture, melted down later in the reign; similar pieces, however, have survived in Germany (see pl. 279). (271,272)*

It has been estimated that those who lived at Versailles, in the palace and outside, with employment or residence at court, numbered some 25,000. A great many of these were servants, gardeners, stable- or kennel-boys, and specialized craftsmen of various kinds who saw to the daily upkeep of the palace and its grounds. They made the Versailles routine possible by their physical labour, so that the falconry and the menagerie, the ships and gondolas on the canal should be ready for inspection at a moment's notice, that meals and receptions should be properly prepared and that theatricals could be mounted with little advance warning, whether in the open air or in the Grand Ecurie. This last, as at other European courts, fulfilled the double function of a *manège* for equestrian display and a space which could be transformed into a theatre. Others, some eight thousand in all, were soldiers in the picked regiments which made up the Maison du Roi as reconstituted by Louis XIV: the Swiss bodyguard (*les cent-suisses*), the French guards regiments of foot and horse where each private was a *gentilhomme*, young and of good bearing if not of good looks, as well as companies of halberdiers, musketeers, and light horse. In their resplendent uniforms they kept guard outside the King's tent when he was on campaign, displayed their expertise at drill before him at Versailles, formed the nursery of an officer-corps for the rest of the army, and were called upon as élite troops to defend French military *gloire* in battle. These men, and especially the French royal bodyguards and life-guardsmen, stood socially far above the servant and craftsman groups; but they did not by virtue of their service rank as courtiers, though their officers usually were courtiers as well as military men.

Those who composed the narrower court of some ten thousand persons included men who were not thought of as courtiers. The ministers, the secretaries of state, the councillors and *maîtres des requêtes* employed by the King, formed part of his court, yet their positions were functional in that they served the King as political or legal advisers, their standing being related to their office. Equal in status with the ministers were the high military and naval officers, the marshals and admirals of France and the officers of the Maison du Roi from whom Louis usually picked his aides-de-camp when he went on campaign. The courtiers proper were those who held either traditional court offices or the offices created (or given added significance) by Louis XIV in his reorganization of the court. The Grand Master of the King's Household, the Grand Almoner, the Master of the Hunt, the Master of the Wolf-hunt, the Grand Falconer are examples of the former; while the Master of the King's Robes, the Grand Master of the orders of chivalry, and the *surintendant des bâtiments* represent the latter. The innovation of Louis XIV's reign lay in the fact that while these titles were usually bestowed on men of high nobility, the offices were robbed of political importance; such men were not advisers of the King as ruler. Yet the court offices remained of the greatest social significance and gave men of the high nobility the opportunity to serve the Crown without interfering with the developing professionalism of the ministers and the administrators, and without the attendant danger of political intrigues against the policies which the King wished to pursue at home or abroad. That they also provided a worthwhile career for men of high nobility in peacetime is clear from the hard work accomplished by his last *surintendant des bâtiments*, Louis Antoine, Marquis d'Antin (son of Madame de Montespan by her husband), work which was deeply appreciated by the King. Louis did not scruple, if he so wished, to put a minister into a court office: the great Colbert had been superintendent of buildings between 1664 and his death in 1683. But generally speaking, Louis wanted the *gentilhommes* of old nobility, the nobility of the sword, to be the holders of the great court offices and their sons to form the officer-corps of the French armies. In the wars of the reign (1666–67, 1672–78, 1688–97, 1702–13), the court emptied of young men and of older courtiers too: they went to their regiments, or accompanied the King, who did not give up campaigning till 1693. Louvois' death more than Madame de Maintenon's entreaties that the King should spare himself the effort of campaigning, was responsible for this change: with his experienced and immensely hardworking war minister gone, Louis increasingly had to perform that office himself. Marshals and admirals, and lower-ranking officers as occasion demanded, reported to the King at court; and in the brief interval between campaigning seasons in the Nine Years' War and the War of the Spanish Succession the court was replenished by officers on leave from their regiments.

Louis remained personal commander *of his armies until 1693. In this engraving he presides over the siege of Namur in 1692, surrounded by his officers and with a comfortable armchair to sit in. (274)*

Strasbourg was 'the key *to the door of the French house'. Louis occupied it in 1681 to prevent its being useful to Leopold I. Here the magistrates kneel in submission and offer him the town keys – a ceremonial which Louis had discontinued except for occasions such as this. (273)*

That Louis still regarded himself as commander-in-chief is shown by his words to Villars when Marlborough in 1711 had succeeded in breaching the defensive lines of the *barrière de fer* of the northern frontier of France: he would not take the advice of those who suggested that, if the enemy came closer, King and court should move to Orléans, but would rally and lead the *noblesse d'épée* in defence of the capital. His consciousness of the need to train the prospective future rulers, the Dauphin as well as the Dauphin's sons, had also its military aspects. At the 1698 Compiègne manoeuvres – a vast exercise camp in which mock battles were staged – ten thousand troops took part; a number indicative of the armed strength which France could muster in wartime: 220,000 in the Nine Years' War, 350,000 in the War of the Spanish Succession. Within the army, Louis worked to make men of humbler origin obeyed by those of high birth and rank. This is especially striking in the case of Vauban, the great specialist in fortification, equally important when places had to be captured and when the defensive ring of fortresses, the so-called *barrière* or *frontière de fer*, in the north, the east, and the south was forged by stages, but never fully completed. If the King, his son, or one of his grandsons were in nominal command, Vauban could be given his head even when officers superior to him disagreed with his decisions. Another example of Louis' concern to reward military merit irrespective of birth is his institution of the Order of Saint Louis in 1678. This order of chivalry took its place beside that of the Saint-Esprit where noble rank, whether old or new, was a prerequisite.

The hierarchy of privilege

The ranks of the nobility were widened in Louis XIV's reign. His ministers came generally from the *noblesse de robe*, but tried hard with the help of genealogists to trace their pedigrees far back in order to find an ancestor of old nobility, whether French or foreign. They were rewarded with titles of marquis and comte, and were given equality of treatment in etiquette, by virtue of their office, with *ducs et pairs*; but none of them were created dukes. Their daughters frequently married into the high nobility, helped by rich dowries in part paid by Louis himself; but their sons found it more difficult to obtain the hands of daughters of *les grands* in marriage. The elevation of able ministers into the nobility was a common enough occurrence at all European courts. Where Louis differed from his fellow-monarchs was in admitting writers and artists to the rank of chevalier, baron, and vicomte (and even to that of marquis or comte),

much to the chagrin of members of the high nobility who regarded them as *viles personnes* (low-born persons) disfiguring the face of the noble estate. They did not resent Louis rewarding such persons with pensions and other gifts; but they felt humiliated when he accorded them favours to which high-born courtiers often aspired in vain. The King stood godfather to a son of Molière, the actor and playwright; and Racine, one of the historiographers-royal, was regularly invited to Marly, that much sought-after place where, from 1680 onwards, the King increasingly sought relaxation from the tyranny of court etiquette. Marly, the successor to the porcelain Trianon (so-called because of its tiles) of Madame de Montespan's time and to the marble Grand Trianon, displayed in its layout a new variation on the sun-king theme: the guest pavilions which flanked the central royal palace symbolized satellites circling the sun. When he visited Marly Louis invited only those with whom he felt at ease and whose conversation he found stimulating.

Etiquette and ceremonial at the palace of Versailles were of necessity strict, the court being hierarchically arranged. On top of the pyramid was Louis, as king symbol of the state of France. By virtue of their personal relationship to the King, the Queen and the immediate heir to the Crown, the Dauphin at any given time, had a special position. After 1688, when Louis supported the Stuart court in exile and housed it at

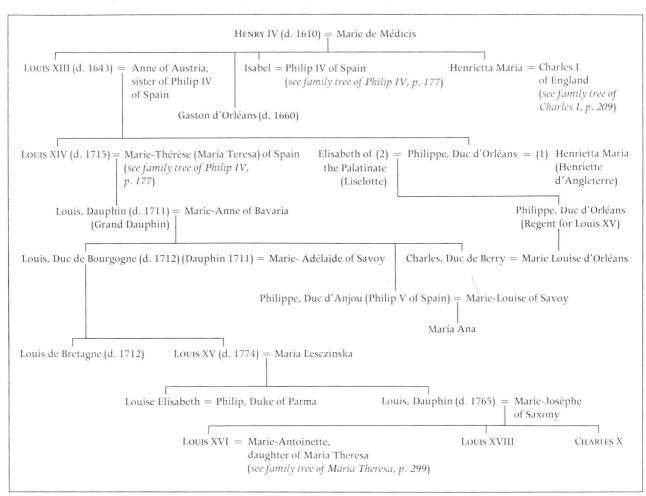

The family gathers *for the wedding of Louis' grandson, the Duc de Bourgogne, to Marie-Adélaïde of Savoy. The young couple hold hands in the centre. To the left stand Louis and the Grand Dauphin, both of them noticeably gaining in embonpoint. To the right, in the black wig, stands Monsieur, the King's brother, with his second wife Elisabeth of the Palatinate (Liselotte). (275)*

Saint-Germain, James II and his Queen were treated with royal honours when visiting Versailles. Next came *les enfants de France*, the sons and daughters of France: that is, the legitimate descendants of the present or former kings of France in the male line. In Louis' case this was his brother Philippe, with his children. His wife, in court parlance Madame (to match his Monsieur), partook of this rank by marriage; first Henriette d'Angleterre, who died in 1670; and then his second wife (from 1671), Elisabeth Charlotte of the Palatinate, who retained the court title even after her husband's death in 1701. Louis' first cousin, Anne-Marie-Louise d'Orléans, Mademoiselle de Montpensier (who died in 1693), was a daughter of France in her own right, her father having been Louis XIII's brother, and so were her three half-sisters, the issue of Gaston's second marriage. After the children of France followed the princes of the royal blood, comprising all those who reckoned their descent in the male lines to kings of France as far back as the Capetian house. In Louis' reign these were the princes of Condé, the head of the house at any given time having the court title of Monsieur le Prince and his heir that of Monsieur le Duc; and the princes of Conti. In 1711 Louis' legitimized sons were permitted to represent, with the princes of the blood, the body of *ducs et pairs* at certain ceremonies; and in 1714 they were declared to be 'true princes of the blood royal'. Cardinals and holders of some specific bishoprics were at court given rank with the princes of the blood, though it should be noted that papal nuncios who happened to be cardinals were not treated as cardinals, but as foreign diplomats at court: they, as other nuncios of lesser Church rank, had to lay aside their ecclesiastical robes when coming to Versailles, court dress being demanded of them as of all other visiting European representatives.

Below the princes of the blood but with privileges above the main body of *ducs et pairs* came the so-called foreign princes, whose substantive title was that of *ducs et pairs étrangers*, the descendants of foreign houses, or former foreign houses which had served France well and which were deemed to owe a special loyalty to France: those of Bouillon, Rohan (Brittany), Lorraine, Soissons (Savoy), Gonzaga-Nevers (Mantua), Grimaldi (Monaco), and La Trémouille (Neuchâtel). Their position often led to awkward situations. Louis' proposal, embodied in the Treaty of Montmartre of 1664, that Duke Charles IV of Lorraine should will his duchy to be incorporated with France in return for his promotion into the group 'princes of the blood', met with implacable opposition not only from Duke Charles' nephew – who stood to lose Lorraine – but from all the French princes of the

The will of Charles II *of Spain made Louis' second grandson, the* Duc d'Anjou, *King of Spain. Louis sits on the left; next to him is the* Dauphin, *with his two other sons, the* Duc de Bourgogne *and the* Duc de Berri. *The* Duc d'Anjou *and the Spanish ambassador stand on the right.* (276)

blood. This treaty was not ratified. And when Louis chose the Prince of Monaco to represent him at the Vatican in 1698, that prince – contrary to instructions that he should act as a French *duc et pair* on a diplomatic mission – chose to behave as a sovereign ruler: an already difficult situation was reduced to hopeless immobility.

At court the 'foreign princes' took precedence over all other *ducs et pairs*. These, the descendants of families which from the very dawn of the French monarchy had held hereditary fiefs, with a few *comte-pairs* of illustrious families, were ranked according to the seniority of the creation of their titles and took their seats at coronations and in the Paris Parlement according to the dates when the Parlement registered their peerages. Below the *ducs et pairs* came the *ducs à brevet*, dukes whose titles had not been registered in the Paris Parlement; and after these followed the so-called *simples ducs*, 'ordinary dukes', whose titles were reckoned social rather than legal.

Distinctions at court between these various groups were jealously guarded both by the titleholders and by the King, who, like his ancestors, had a vested interest in such gradations as outward marks of rank achieved by exceptional service to the Crown. *Ducs et pairs* had permission to enter the forecourt of royal palaces either on horseback or in their carriages. They walked immediately behind the princes of the blood and the 'foreign princes' in all processions such as Te Deums, royal marriages, baptisms, and funerals. They wore their ducal coronets and ducal

mantles on ceremonial occasions and carried their swords when attending the Paris Parlement. They had the right to address the king as 'my cousin', and their wives had the privilege of being seated on *tabourets* in the presence of the queen. The children of France and the princes of the blood, all of whom were *ducs et pairs* by birth, had extra privileges which were augmented in Louis' reign. They had long been permitted to cross the parquet flooring of the Paris Parlement to reach their seats, and the first president of that assembly uncovered his head when inviting them to speak. Their wives also had the privilege of bringing two carriages into the royal courtyards, one for themselves, another for their entourage. From 1688 males of this group received preferential treatment at the ceremony of the Order of the Saint-Esprit, and from 1711 their wives could have their parasols carried by an attendant in certain religious processions, while wives of *ducs et pairs* had to hold their own sunshades aloft.

But quite apart from the privileges attaching to their rank courtiers valued their proximity to the king. To the greater *lever* and the greater *coucher* only certain members of the royal family and the princes of the blood were admitted; to the lesser version of both ceremonies courtiers attended according to their office in the rotation described above: it was minutely laid down who should present the king's shirt at his *lever*, who should hold the candlestick at his *coucher*, and similar services of a formal nature. Many of the new court offices created by Louis XIV did not bring such proximity, though they brought the Crown income (such titles as Guardian of the Royal Carp and Chief Goblet-holder to the Queen were sold) and a measure of loyalty and commitment.

Offices of a more personal nature than the purely ceremonial ones did in any case rank higher in close attendance on the King. Louis' various physicians, for instance (whose importance for the medical historian is great since a running journal was kept of the King's health), attended both *levers* and *couchers* and were given a considerable freedom of advice. His first *valet de chambre* (virtually a hereditary office in the Bontemps family) and his personal secretary (particularly Rose Toussaint, who died in 1701), served on a different level from the grander courtiers who shared, so to speak, only one compartment of the King's activities and interests. The servants at a humbler level sometimes saw the King close at hand without the official mask. The courtiers at large saw him with the mask of royalty, though those to whom he felt personally close (as the Marquis de Dangeau, who had started off as his aide-de-camp in 1672 and who from 1684 kept a journal of the King's activities) noted that the mask dropped when a particular ceremony or interview was over. In either case Louis' studied concept of kingship was noticeable. Even when relaxed he would not permit himself to speak ill of anyone, and his reported outbursts of anger or loss of control are extremely rare at a court which was avidly alert for any lapse.

For the general subject the King was in practice not easy of access. He was always surrounded by those 'known at court', and though the grounds of Versailles were open to

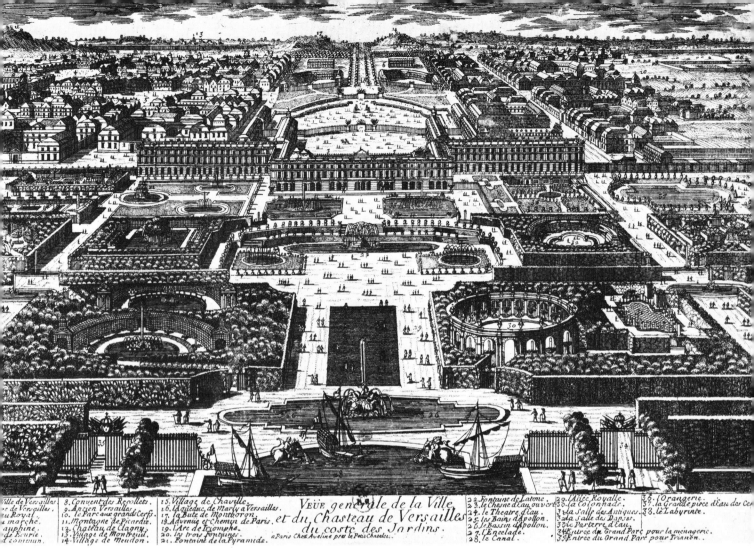

VEÜE generale de la Ville et du Chasteau de Versailles du coste des Jardins.
à Paris Chez Aveline pres le Petit Chastelet.

Ville de Versailles.	8. Convent des Recollets.	15. Village de Chaville.	22. Fontaine de Latone.	29. l'Allée Royalle.	36. l'Orangerie.
de Versailles.	9. Ancien Versailles.	16. l'Aqueduc de Marly à Versailles.	23. le Chesne d'eau ouvert.	30. la Colonnade.	37. la Grande piece d'eau des Ce...
u Royal.	10. le Parc aux grands Cerfs.	17. la Bute de Montboron.	24. le Theatre d'eau.	31. la Salle des Antiques.	38. le Labyrinte.
marché.	11. Montagne de Picardie.	18. Advenue et chemin de Paris.	25. les Bains d'Apollon.	32. la Salle du Dancer.	
auphine.	12. Chateau de Clagny.	19. l'Arc de Triomphe.	26. le Bassin d'Apollon.	33. le Parterre d'eau.	
Ecurie.	13. Village de Montreuil.	20. les trois fontaines.	27. l'Encelade.	34. Entrée du Grand Parc pour la menagerie.	
commun.	14. Village de Meudon.	21. Fontaine de la Pyramide.	28. le Canal.	35. Entrée du Grand Parc pour Trianon.	

'The perfect setting *for an open-air concert' said the Duc de St Simon of the colonnade at Versailles (No. 30, near centre, right). Together with many original features of the garden, it has now been swept away. (277)*

Like planets round the sun *guest pavilions surround the château of Marly. Begun in 1679, it was an escape from the grandeur and formality of Versailles. (278)*

A silver table *now at Schloss Marienburg, modelled by Augsburg silversmiths for the ducal house of Brunswick-Wolfenbüttel on those made for Louis XIV, gives some impression of the original splendour of Versailles. (279)*

any visitor dressed as a gentleman – and the sword, the then outward mark of a gentleman, could be discreetly hired at the entrance to the palace – influence and patronage were necessary to be presented to the King inside the royal apartments. Once outside, Louis was, in the words of a foreign observer, surrounded by as tight and buzzing a swarm as any queen-bee. There was a security element in this at least outside the palace. Researches into the papers of the Master of the Hunt have shown how stringent were the precautions taken during Louis XIV's hunting expeditions: roads were so constructed, guards so posted, rules for shooting so defined that no would-be-assassin might be given a chance to endanger the life of the King. Louis was also in some measure guarded against the reality of the situation outside Versailles. Whenever he went to Paris, some twenty-four visits in all between 1670 and 1715, care was taken that beggars and vagabonds should be prevented from lining his route of approach. Naturally, as he got older, and as those on whom he had relied in youth and middle age died, he became more dependent on the developing bureaucracies of his secretaries of state. It is symptomatic that in his later years the *conseil d'en haut* – increased from three to five in the middle years of the reign – again decreased to three. Yet the material which has survived,

including the journal of Torcy, Louis' last minister for foreign affairs, gives ample evidence of the King's conclusive influence in decision-making until his last illness of the summer of 1715. Then France – and Europe – held its breath. The British ambassador, true to the gambling mania across the Channel, was reported to have laid a heavy bet that the French King would not survive the month of September. He died on the first of that month.

Louis was known to have made a will and to have stipulated a regency council for the minority of the future Louis XV which would keep a necessary balance between his nephew, the Duc d'Orléans, and his legitimized sons, in particular the Duc de Maine, whom he had made head of the Maison du Roi and governor of the future King. But who could guarantee that the will would be obeyed? The will of Louis XIII, instituting a regency council at the side of the Queen Mother during Louis XIV's own minority, had been flouted. And what would happen to Versailles? Custom decreed that the new king should leave the palace as soon as possible after the old king had expired. The younger generation at court had found Versailles boring during the last years of Louis XIV's reign: would Versailles, the perfection of the court of the *Ancien Régime*, be deserted?

Versailles as model

In the event, Louis XV was moved to Vincennes immediately upon Louis XIV's death. The Parlement, spurred on by the high nobility who believed with some justification that the Duc d'Orléans – if given untrammelled powers as a regent – would uphold ancient privileges against Louis XIV's innovations, upset the late King's testament and rob the Duc de Maine of the role which his father had allocated him. The court moved to Paris and did not return till Louis XV was nearing the age when he would be declared to have entered his majority.

Versailles easily surmounted this neglect of some seven years. Already in Louis XIV's lifetime it had become an example to be imitated by the courts of Europe. These courts did not abandon the arrangement of their palaces fashioned more on the ancient Burgundian spatial relationship than on the 'timing' schedule of Louis XIV's court; but in externals, as in the atmosphere of their courts, the majority modelled themselves on what they had heard of Versailles. Their gardens were laid out anew, the fountains (and the mining engineers necessary to produce the desired volume of water for the fountain displays) became the objects of vivid concern; drawings of the uniforms of Louis' Maison du Roi and of the Sun King's throne and embellishments at court were eagerly sought via diplomatic channels. Indeed, our knowledge of some of the arrangements at Versailles (as for example the King's bedchamber) depends upon sketches taken for the Swedish court and still surviving in the archives of Stockholm. Louis' love of theatre, of music, and of opera stirred minor courts to emulate him, and major courts, where such entertainments were already the rule, strove to follow Louis' example in the founding of academies and in the preferential treatment of, and care for, the native language. French which had become accepted as a universal language in diplomacy alongside Latin and which all over

Europe remained the language of polite society, was 'demoted' for prestige reasons by monarchs in their official capacities as rulers; however well they understood or spoke French, they would use their native tongue (or Latin) in discoursing with French diplomats lest contempt of the native language and official subservience to France should be inferred. Simultaneously and consequentially, concern for the vernacular, for its purification from foreign loan-words, for its elegance and expressiveness, was consciously sought. The manners of the French court and the entertainments of Versailles were also eagerly studied. French actors were invited to all courts. Louis' taste in furniture and *objets d'art* was transmitted by French Huguenot refugees in Protestant countries as well as throughout Catholic Europe by general osmosis. While Louis XIV melted down his silver art treasures in the Nine Years' War and the War of the Spanish Succession, other courts kept theirs. The silver furniture of the Wolfenbüttel house of Brunswick, now magnificently displayed in the grand hall of the Marienburg castle of the Prince of Hanover, is a living example of the splendour and grace of this type of console tables and mirror frames, as are the imitation silver tables which George I as King of England had fashioned for Hampton Court, and the silver furniture, transmuted to

The court bids farewell to Louis. At the head of the funeral procession from Versailles to Saint-Denis come the coaches of Louis' legitimized sons, the Duc du Maine and the Comte de Toulouse; then that of the Duc d'Orléans (Regent for Louis XV), followed by the coffin and the royal household. The new King was never present at the funeral of the old. (280)

some extent by Rococo influence, which Frederick II of Prussia had made for his palace at Potsdam.

The long personal reign of Louis XIV largely explains the impact which Versailles made on other European courts. The Sun King's separation of the courtier side of the palace from the departments which served the King's *métier* as a ruler ensured that Versailles became a progressive institution and example, assisting at the birth of the professional bureaucracy based on promotion or merit.

In a wider perspective the very power and resources of France in Louis' reign, compared with those at the disposal of other dynasties, exerted an enormous influence. Twenty million Frenchmen constituted a formidable reservoir of manpower, together with the geographical extent of the country and its general fertility despite the static state of its agriculture. Enemies might well fear France as an exorbitant power dangerous to the balance of Europe, and diplomats inimical towards Louis might rail at the French King as this new comet – an allusion to Halley's comet of 1682 – lately risen, which 'expects not only to be gazed at but to be adored'.

Yet the court of Versailles had impressed itself, once and for all, as the very model of European courts during the early Enlightenment: forward-looking in its support of commerce and social mobility, in practical measures such as the building of the canal connecting the Atlantic with the Mediterranean, in the codification of the laws, in its encouragement of the arts and sciences. Those reluctant to give Louis XIV his due for these advances might do well to remember Voltaire's words: 'Not only were great things done in his reign, but they were done by him.'

The Tsar as military leader *was an image of himself that Peter the Great sought to propagate both in Russia and abroad. His apotheosis is represented in this engraving together with his victories (the steps), the fortresses he established (the garland behind him), and Russia's previous tsars. (281)*

Twelve

PETER THE GREAT
Imperial revolutionary?

✻

M. S. ANDERSON

FOR A GENERATION, from the middle 1690s to his death in 1725, the court and much of the central government of Russia were largely reflections of Peter's own personality. Over them he exerted a direct personal dominance unmatched by any of his contemporaries on the great thrones of Europe and perhaps unequalled in the entire modern history of the continent. By his later years he seemed, to many of his own countrymen and nearly all foreign observers, to have raised Russia single-handed from the position of a backward, obscurantist, semi-Asiatic country on the fringes of Europe to that of a new great European power with almost unlimited potentialities. It is impossible to understand the country's history during his reign, and in particular the life of the court and the incessant changes in the central government in this period, without some understanding of Peter the man.

'That was a tsar, what a tsar!'

No facet of his personality impressed contemporaries more than his tireless energy and his indifference to the elaborate network of custom and tradition within which his predecessors on the Russian throne had been in general content to live. One aspect of this energy and unconventionality was his incessant travelling – endless movement within Russia, long visits to Poland and Germany during the Great Northern War, journeys to western Europe in 1696–97 and 1717. 'He has I believe,' wrote in 1716 an Englishman with much experience of Russia, 'for the Proportion of Time I was in the Country, travell'd twenty Times more than ever any Prince in the World did before him.' The same energy showed itself in the daily routine of government. 'His Majesty might truly be called a man of business,' reminisced a Scottish doctor who had observed him in his later years, 'for he could dispatch more affairs in a morning than an houseful of senators could do in a month. He rose almost every morning in the winter-time, before four o'clock, was often in his cabinet by three o'clock, where two private secretaries, and certain clerks, paid constant attendance. He often went so early to the senate, as to occasion the senators being raised out of their beds to attend him there.' There is no doubt that this praise was justified. In the preparation of the *Morskoi Ustav (Naval Regulation)* of 1720, for example, Peter is known to have worked for four months, four days a week, from 5 a.m. to midday and from 4 to 11 p.m. The decree of 1722 which established the duties of the new office of procurator-general, one of the most important of those created by the Tsar, was copied out by secretaries four times, Peter making many corrections and alterations to each draft in his own hand. This restless itch for action, this passion for doing, for physical activity, meant that he could never be a tsar in the traditional mould – remote, hieratic, at one remove from the real world. His intense interest in technical achievement, in learning skilled trades of many kinds, was a highly unorthodox characteristic which again caught the eye of contemporaries and often astonished them. When his second marriage was publicly solemnized in 1712 (a private ceremony had taken place five years earlier) one of the decorations was 'a sconce with six branches of ivory and ebon-wood, which he had turned himself'; this had taken him about a fortnight's labour to produce. Such tastes were highly unaristocratic: from his early adolescence one of the Tsar's most striking and unconventional characteristics was his liking for the society of foreigners and men of low birth and the direct personal response which his energy and unconventionality were sometimes able to arouse in them. In March 1690, already conditioned by years of contact with foreign officers and technicians in the German Suburb of Moscow, he took the unprecedented step of dining in the house of a foreigner, General Gordon. A few years later, at a New Year banquet, a foreign observer was astonished to see 'several common sailors, with whom the Czar repeatedly mixed, divided apples, and even honoured one of them by calling him brother'. 'That was a tsar, what a tsar!' exclaimed after Peter's death an unknown peasant of Olonets. 'He did not eat his bread for nothing, but worked like a peasant.' This may not be the highest form of praise for a monarch; but it is one which again sets Peter apart from his fellow-rulers.

His energy and ceaseless activity sprang in part from a deep sense of his responsibilities. His unconventionality went hand-in-hand with a high view of the importance of his position and a determination to tolerate no infringement

Impulsive violence was part of Peter's aggressive personal energy. Despite his attempt to civilize the usages of the imperial household, his own reputation as a brawler endured, as demonstrated in this posthumous depiction by Chodowiecki of him at a German court. (282)

of it or belittling of Russia's prestige. It is significant that his decrees, unlike those of his predecessors, usually begin with an introduction stressing, in terms of the 'general good', the necessity of the measure or instructions which they embody. He felt deeply that he and his subordinates had a duty and right to watch over all aspects of communal and individual life. 'You must love all that contributes to the welfare and honour of the fatherland,' he wrote to his deeply unsatisfactory son Alexis in 1704, on the capture of the fortress-city of Narva from the Swedes, 'and spare no labour for the general well-being; and if my advice is lost on the winds – I do not recognize you as my son.'

However this drive towards action and achievement had other and less desirable results. It made him throughout his reign a deeply impatient man, one who believed that very far-reaching social and intellectual changes could be achieved quickly by more or less mechanical methods, by legislation backed by coercion. Of society in Russia, or for that matter anywhere else, as an organism, and of the difficulties inherent in this fact, he never had an adequate

grasp. Impatience helped to make him severe, indeed brutal, in his treatment of opposition. Coupled with other factors, notably his very limited formal education, it may help to explain the deep and undeniable vein of coarseness (though it was coarseness rather than the more serious flaw of vulgarity) which is visible in him. Peter was not naturally a cruel man. Where political offences were concerned he seems to have preferred the beating and exile of the culprits to the infliction of the death penalty. But he believed unquestioningly in the rightness of his own absolute rule and in the sacred obligation laid by God upon the subject to obey the monarch. 'His Majesty is an autocratic ruler,' said the *Voinskii Ustav (Military Regulation)* of 1716, in one of the best statements of the ideology of absolutism produced in Russia during his reign, 'whom no one in the world ought to criticize regarding his affairs, for he has the power and authority to rule his empire and lands as a Christian ruler according to his own will and good pleasure.' Conspiracy and revolt were therefore repressed ruthlessly. It is significant that one of the most stable and long-lived of Peter's new organs of administration was the Preobrazhenskii Prikaz, which early in 1697 was given jurisdiction over political crimes and retained this function (in spite of the creation of the College of Justice in 1719) until the end of the reign. In particular the savagery with which the revolt in the summer of 1698 of the *streltsy*, a privileged and highly conservative military force, was punished after the Tsar's return in September of that year from his journey to western Europe startled contemporaries and has passed into legend. For months the corpses of some of the 799 men put to death dangled from the walls of the Kremlin, while others lay in pools of frozen blood in the Red Square: seven years later 320 other would-be rebels were executed after an unsuccessful rising in Astrakhan.

Even with his closest associates Peter was capable of sudden and unpredictable outbursts of violence, especially at moments of severe strain. Thus at dinner at the house of his best-loved friend, the Swiss Franz Lefort, in September 1698 when the punishment of the *streltsy* was beginning, he suddenly became furious with General Shein, one of his most important military subordinates, over his alleged selling of army promotions. When other guests tried to defend Shein Peter 'grew so hot that he startled all the guests by striking right and left, he knew not where, with his drawn sword'. At least three of the guests were wounded; and Lefort, by catching the Tsar in his arms, barely prevented his striking a very serious blow at Shein. 'But the Czar, taking it ill that any person should dare to hinder him from sating his most just wrath, wheeled round upon the spot, and struck his unwelcome impeder a hard blow upon the back.' Almost at once, however, 'merriment followed this dire tempest; the Czar, with a face full of smiles, was present at the dancing'. No incident better illustrates the remark of a great Russian historian that Peter's associates were like travellers walking on Mount Vesuvius and from moment to moment waiting for the eruption of the uncontrollable forces under their feet.

His liking for the crudest sort of practical jokes, and the grossness of many aspects of life at the Russian court, were certainly not without parallels elsewhere in Europe. Nevertheless they were carried to lengths which foreign observers witnessed with a mixture of horror, amusement, and astonishment. One of them noted in October 1698 that at another banquet 'Boyar Golowin (Golovin) has, from his cradle, a natural horror of salad and vinegar; so the Czar directing Colonel Chambers to hold him tight, forced salad and vinegar into his mouth and nostrils, until the blood flowing from his nose succeeded his violent coughing.' The Hanoverian envoy has given an account of the entertainment offered by Peter nearly two decades later at his new Peterhof palace which illustrates vividly the rigours of imperial hospitality. Each guest, already hardly able to stand after a long drinking-bout, was forced to empty a bowl containing a full pint of wine, 'whereupon we quite lost our Senses, and were in that pickle carried off to sleep, some in the Garden, others in the Wood, and the rest here and there on the Ground'. They were then awakened and forced to follow the Tsar in cutting down trees to make a new walk to the seashore. At supper they drank 'such another Dose of Liquour, as sent us senseless to Bed'; but an hour and a half later they were roused to visit the Prince of Circassia (himself in bed with his wife), 'where we were again by their Bedside pestered with Wine and Brandy till four in the Morning, that next day none of us remembered how he got home'. At eight o'clock they were invited to breakfast, but given brandy instead of tea or coffee. This was followed by a fourth drinking-bout at dinner, after the guests had been forced to ride very poor horses, without saddles or stirrups, for the amusement of the Tsar and Tsarina. When the party sailed back to the island of Cronslot (part of St Petersburg) Peter showed great skill and courage in face of a dangerous storm; but when they had landed his guests could find neither dry clothes nor beds and had to make a fire, strip naked, and wrap themselves in sled-covers while their wet clothes dried. We are here not merely geographically distant from Paris or Vienna but in what was still, in many essentials, a different world.

The wedding of two court dwarfs in 1711, *celebrated at the new Menshikov Palace in St Petersburg, was an occasion for the display of Western European fashions, still relatively unfamiliar in Russia. Bride and groom sit in separate groups, numbered 6 and 5. (283)*

A folk artist's view of the new military of the eighteenth century registers many small if not entirely correct details of their Westernized appearance. Persistent in his efforts to enlarge and modernize his army, the Tsar aimed to enhance Russia's status by foreign conquest. (284)

Royalty without ceremony

Some of the strength and strangeness of Peter's personality can almost certainly be attributed to the pressures to which he was subjected in childhood. The palace revolution of 1682, in which the Moscow *streltsy* hacked to pieces a number of his mother's relations in the courtyards of the Kremlin and placed the ten-year-old Peter in fear for his life, made a deep impression on him. Many years later he still shuddered when he thought of these events and admitted that 'I cannot bury the memory of these days.' The fact that throughout his adolescence he lived not in the Kremlin (which he always disliked) but in villages belonging to the imperial family in the neighbourhood of Moscow, meant that he did not receive the education now beginning to be considered appropriate to an Orthodox man of high social rank. Unlike his brothers and sister he did not study Latin, rhetoric, and theology with Semyon Polotskii, probably the greatest Russian scholar of the period. Though he learned to read Russian fluently and to do simple arithmetic his writing and grammar remained bad throughout his life. Instead he interested himself in technology, in fortification, boatbuilding, military affairs. He thus received, or rather gave himself, an education relatively free from traditional influences. In this sense as in others he was a new phenomenon on the Russian throne.

Any court life which revolved around a man of this stamp, so furiously active, so wilful, so contemptuous of traditional restraints, was certain to be very different from the glittering show of Versailles or the elaborate etiquette of Vienna and Madrid. Indeed in the sense in which the term was used in western or even central European capitals Russia under Peter had little court life at all. The fact that the Tsar travelled so incessantly meant that the real capital of the empire, the centre of decision at the highest level, was also in constant motion. Under these circumstances it was hardly possible to maintain an elaborate apparatus of court officials, ceremonies, and etiquette. Peter had little wish to do such a thing. Nor was he ever able to provide the money which such a structure would have required. He was unquestionably anxious to raise his own prestige and that of Russia, particularly in the eyes of foreigners. He therefore did his best to disseminate news of his victories and achievements – through the work of agents in Europe; through the foundation, in 1703, of what is usually regarded as the first Russian newspaper, the *Vedomosti*; and through such means as the publication of engravings showing his battles and the public ceremonies which celebrated his victories. (A collection of these appeared in the *Marsovaya Kniga (Book of Mars)*, the first Russian book to be printed in St Petersburg, in 1713.) He also dreamed of erecting a great memorial to himself, a perpetuation of his fame to posterity as the monarch of a great state, though these plans were never realized during his lifetime. (A bronze statue of him, designed for this purpose, was not cast until after his death and was not mounted on its pedestal until 1800. A great triumphal pillar surmounted by his statue and covered with bas-reliefs representing the main events of his reign (he may have been inspired in planning this by descriptions he had read of Trajan's column in Rome) was finally raised only in 1938.) But expenditure on advertising the glory of the empire and on his posthumous reputation was one thing; money squandered on the day-to-day costs of an elaborate court was quite another.

On ships, artillery, fortifications, harbour-works, arsenals, canals, Peter was willing to spend to the limits of his ability. It has been calculated that in the years 1705–9, the most critical ones of the great war with Sweden, over nine tenths of the revenue of the Russian state went to meet military and naval costs; and though this proportion fell somewhat after these years, it remained very high. To waste scarce and painfully acquired money on clothes, jewellery, elaborate meals, many servants, in a word on a court in the normal sense of the term, was quite foreign to the Tsar's nature. Like virtually all monarchs of the period he greatly admired Louis XIV, whom he regarded as in many ways a paragon of kingship. But he never contemplated creating a Versailles of his own. His tastes ran, in the words once more of the Hanoverian envoy, Weber, to 'a plain Dress and a small Retinue'. He never appeared, noted another foreign observer with admiration, 'in a dress-suit of cloaths' except on important festivals and holidays: and 'when he was dressed, he wore the order of St Andrew; at other times, he had no badge, or mark, of any order, on his person'. When he was in St Petersburg he used no more showy vehicle than an open two-wheeled chaise and was attended normally only by two soldiers or grooms, and by a page who often sat in the chaise with him and drove it. In winter he used a sledge drawn by a single horse, with the same unostentatious number of attendants. It seems well established that when his second wife and successor, Catherine, made him a new coat of blue *gros-de-tours* decorated with silver braid he thought the braid too extravagant and wore the coat only once, at Catherine's coronation in May 1724. As a final demonstration of the almost unkingly plainness of his tastes, he presented to the admiring gaze of Europe the unaccustomed spectacle of a great ruler who neither hunted nor gambled.

The Tsar's family

There was yet another way in which Peter differed from virtually all his fellow-monarchs, another factor which made it difficult for him to maintain, even had he wished to, a court of the normal European type. This was the small part played in his life by family relationships and his lack of any strong family feeling. His half-brother, Ivan V, ruled with Peter as co-tsar, at least in theory, from their joint accession to the throne in 1682 until his death in 1696. But he was mentally subnormal, almost blind, and afflicted with a speech defect. He could never play any role in government and with him Peter had never any personal relations of significance. Peter's half-sister Sophia, who was the effective ruler of Russia from the revolution of 1682 until her overthrow in 1689, was always his enemy. It was probably her unwillingness to educate a potential rival which led to his being left so much to his own devices in the 1680s, while it was her fall in 1689 which opened the way to his achievement of real personal rule in 1695–96. The *streltsy* revolt of 1698 was intended to restore her to power; and until her death in 1704 she remained a prisoner in a nunnery. Another half-sister, Maria, was later also despatched to a nunnery in 1718, accused of having fomented opposition to the Tsar. Peter's first wife, the conventional and not very attractive Evdokia Lopukhina, was never able to arouse any sympathy in her husband. The marriage, in 1689 when Peter was only seventeen, was arranged by his mother. Nine years later the unfortunate bride was forced to take the veil; and though she outlived her husband she never counted for anything in politics or public life. In 1707, with the disregard for tradition which was so important a part of his makeup, Peter took as his second wife a foreigner, and one of low birth at that, the Livonian servant-girl taken prisoner at the capture of Marienburg who became after his death the Empress Catherine I. Peter had her crowned in 1724, a year before his death; and there is no doubt that he found in her real help and support. But she was hardly the woman to preside successfully over a glittering and elaborate court, even had she been allowed to make the attempt. Above all, Peter's relations with his only son, Alexis, born in 1690, were always strained. Their mutual incomprehension and dislike were to culminate in the most spectacular tragedy of the reign.

The Tsar was determined from the start that his son should continue his own work of strengthening and

The infant Peter *here accompanies his half-brothers Feodor III and Ivan V, the Patriarch, and the Metropolitan of Moscow, in a religious ceremony. Peter's loyalty to the Orthodox Church was constant if equivocal. (285)*

The servant-girl *who became Empress Catherine I of Russia gave Peter valued personal support as his second wife. In this contemporary engraving of the marriage's public celebration, in 1712, Peter is shown upper centre, opposite Catherine, who turns to face us. (286)*

267

modernizing Russia, of rejecting the aspects of the Muscovite past, and above all the clerical influences, which stood in the way of these things. It seems clear that as early as the winter of 1698–99 he had decided to send Alexis abroad, to Germany, to be educated (a breach with the past, had the decision been carried out, even more complete than Peter's own journey to the Netherlands, England, and Austria in 1697–98). For reasons which are still unclear, the idea was abandoned. The Tsarevich was educated in Russia; and though he received an ambitious and wide-ranging intellectual training he never shared his father's outlook and aspirations. In 1710 he married a princess of the house of Brunswick-Wolfenbüttel, since Peter was determined that he should take a foreign bride. He was given a number of official tasks and positions; the last of these was to superintend the building of ships on Lake Ladoga in 1713. But after that year Alexis lived quite privately, with no official position, in St Petersburg. It was now clear that he was totally out of sympathy with the father who was to him a remote and terrifying figure whom he had never really known. Deeply attached to Orthodox tradition, he had no interest in making Russia a European power and deeply disliked the efforts of his father at internal reform. Moreover in spite of his weakness and mediocrity he could not but be a figure of political importance. He was the obvious rallying-point for the forces of resistance to the Tsar and his policies. The fact that Peter was by no means in good health increased the danger which Alexis represented to the future of his father's reforming efforts and to the position of those in Russia, such as Prince A. D. Menshikov, Peter's most important and active subordinate, who had supported and applied them. It seems clear that by 1715–16 the Tsarevich had come to believe, and probably to hope, that his father could not live for longer than another two years.

At the end of 1715 the situation began to come to a head. The Tsar increasingly pressed that his son either change his attitude radically or become a monk; to allow him to remain in his present position was too dangerous, even though he offered to renounce his right of succession to the throne. In August 1716 a letter from Copenhagen, where Peter had been taken by the needs of the war with Sweden, demanded an immediate decision. The result was the flight of Alexis, first of all to a castle in the Tyrol and then, after Peter had put pressure on the Habsburg government to surrender him, to Naples. Events now moved swiftly to a conclusion. The Austrian ministers, who seem genuinely to have feared a Russian invasion of Silesia and Bohemia, agreed to allow Count P. A. Tolstoy, one of the most subtle of all Peter's agents, to interview Alexis; and in October 1717 the Tsarevich agreed to return to Russia. He was won over by a promise that he would be allowed to live on his estates and that he would not be separated from his mistress, a Finnish peasant-girl who was pregnant and to whom he was genuinely attached. These promises were not kept. Though Alexis solemnly renounced, in a ceremony in Moscow, all claims to the throne, Peter was deeply disturbed by his flight; and with reason, for the Imperial, Prussian, and Hanoverian representatives in Russia all felt in the summer of 1718 that there was a real possibility of serious unrest.

The Tsarevich had never planned or conspired for the overthrow of his father. He was too weak, too afraid of Peter, and perhaps too unintelligent to aspire to such a role. But it was now difficult to leave him alive. So long as he lived he would remain, whatever formal renunciations he might make, the symbol of the very widespread and pervasive forces – pious traditional Orthodoxy; noble families disgusted by the Tsar's promotion of foreigners and commoners; landowners suffering under the increasing burden of compulsory state service – which loathed Peter's policies. The alleged conspiracy of which Alexis had been the centre was broken up; nine of its members were publicly put to death, many others punished less severely. As for the wretched Tsarevich, he was declared guilty of plotting against his father and of attempting to procure, by his flight, foreign help in Peter's overthrow. A special assembly of high officials, ministers, and military men, called together in the offices of the senate in St Petersburg to consider his fate, unanimously recommended his execution. Early in July he died in the Peter-Paul fortress. The exact circumstances of his death will never be known; but there is no doubt that he had been tortured twice in the preceding week and most contemporaries believed that he had been killed on the orders of his father.

The little, domestic Summer Palace *in St Petersburg, built by Peter very much for living in, contains a quantity of its original furnishings. They include the boat-shaped cradle, patterned with inlay and lined with padded leather, that was used for his short-lived son Pyotr Petrovich. (287)*

The Russian embassy of 1697–98, *seeking to obtain Western help against the Turks and to recruit technicians and specialists for service in Russia, took Peter, as an incognito 'volunteer' accompanying it, to England, Austria, and the Netherlands. There his private studies included gunnery and ship-building. While Peter was in Amsterdam Aert de Gelder executed this portrait of him, now in the city's Rijksmuseum. (288)*

The Dutch style *so favoured by Peter was in the case of the Summer Palace in fact the work of an Italian, Domenico Trezzini. Catherine's apartments were on the first floor; the ground floor comprised the reception rooms and Peter's living quarters and workshop. (289)*

Peterhof palace, *thirteen miles outside St Petersburg, is the climax of a park established in a wilderness. The fountains, completed in 1721, were fashioned after those of Versailles. A spring several miles distant supplies them; and a short canal joins them with the sea. (290)*

Sartorial changes *legally enforced reveal Peter's limited understanding of the origins of real social change. In this woodcut a folk artist shows a barber cutting off the beard of an Old Believer, an adherent of the most conservative wing of Orthodoxy in Russia which was strongly opposed to the Tsar's policies. (291)*

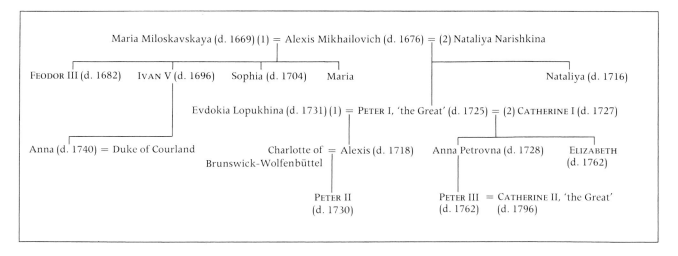

Inevitably this spectacular and scandalous story produced comment and speculation in Europe. This Peter, now increasingly secure in the prestige of victory over Sweden and at the height of his effectiveness as an administrative reformer, could afford to disregard. But nothing illustrates better than the fate of Alexis the psychological gulf which separated the Tsar, with his towering energies and impulsive ferocity which no minister or institution could control, from the rulers of Western Europe. Four years later, in 1722, he asserted in the most striking possible form his unlimited autocratic power. A law of succession promulgated in that year empowered him to name his own successor; and though in fact he never exercised this power such a formal declaration of it contrasts starkly with the reverence for inalienable hereditary right which was the cornerstone of Western European legitimism.

Routine, religion and reform

Peter's reign thus does not present us with the picture normal in Western Europe, that of a ruler limited by law or tradition and performing largely ceremonial functions against the background of an elaborate court. It shows us rather a dynamic and impetuous individual working in a highly informal environment provided in the main by a small number of close associates. His first collaborators in the middle and later 1690s – Prince B. A. Golitsyn, L. K. Naryshkin, T. N. Streshnev – were merely typical representatives of the upper bureaucracy of the day; and the difficulty of finding competent and trustworthy subordinates was one which he never solved. Rapid change, the development of new policies and new institutions, meant that high positions, particularly in the earlier part of the reign, had often to be given to men with little relevant training or experience. Thus B. P. Sheremetev became a field-marshal in 1701 and A. D. Menshikov achieved the same rank some years later without either having much knowledge of military affairs. In the same way F. M. Apraksin became in 1706 an admiral without any knowledge of the sea. Such men were chosen largely for their energy and loyalty to Peter and were often supported by foreign experts who did much of the real work – Field-

Marshal Ogilvy in the army, Vice-Admiral Cruys in the navy, the Polish Jew P. P. Shafirov and later the German H. J. F. Ostermann in foreign affairs. However the importance of such foreigners declined after the first decade of the eighteenth century; and perhaps there was an improvement in the quality of Peter's main subordinates in the later years of his reign, with the rise to prominence of such men as P. P. Yaguzhinskii, who became in 1722 the first occupant of the great new office of procurator-general, and as such the supervisor of the workings of the central government in general. Nevertheless among the Tsar's associates there remained to the end a marked element of the adventurer and the *parvenu*. Menshikov, the most successful of them all, almost certainly did not begin life, as his enemies claimed, by selling pies in the streets of Moscow; but his origins were humble enough to draw upon him, as he accumulated wealth and honours, the resentment and envy of many of the old noble families. Yaguzhinskii, his greatest rival, was also of modest birth and of Lithuanian extraction; while A. M. Devier, who became Generalpolizeimeister of the new capital of St Petersburg, was born in Amsterdam, the son of a converted Portuguese Jew (he was one of the three foreign members of the assembly of notables which recommended the death of Alexis in July 1718). Shafirov's Jewish origins were never forgotten by his enemies, while A. A. Kurbatov, who became vice-governor of Archangel, was born a serf.

From men of this kind Peter received in general loyalty so long as he lived, though a good many of them had little belief in reform for its own sake and were willing to serve later rulers who abandoned many of the great Tsar's policies. Honesty was another matter. Bribery in particular was so deeply engrained in Russian administration that it could not be rooted out even by the most severe punishments. Many of Peter's subordinates suffered, some of them on the scaffold, for accepting bribes. Prince M. P. Gagarin, governor of Siberia, and even Alexis Nesterov, who as Oberfiskal was the official chiefly responsible for stamping out corruption, paid with their lives. Shafirov was disgraced for the same reason; and even Menshikov, after being forced in 1715 to disgorge some of his ill-gotten gains, appeared with Apraksin before a court-martial three years later. They

273

object of veneration in Russia, was to him at best an unsocial being, at worst the inspirer of active opposition to his aims and policies. The extent to which his attitude to religion differed not merely from that of the ordinary Russian but also from that of his fellow-rulers elsewhere in Europe is illustrated most clearly by the creation at least as early as 1692 of the 'Most Drunken Council', which continued to flourish through his reign. This was a group of his friends and associates which performed, to the accompaniment of heavy drinking, gross parodies of religious rites in which some of the participants assumed mock ecclesiastical titles and wore costumes which imitated Church vestments. The purpose of this notorious institution remains one of the enigmas of Peter's reign; but it is best regarded as a reflection of the grossness of the Tsar's taste in amusements and of his desire to mock and weaken religious tradition. It was certainly not merely the product of youthful high spirits, or a simple reaction of disappointment to his failure in 1690 to have his own candidate made Patriarch and head of the Church in Russia. Nor is it likely that it was underlain by any far-sighted scheme for Church reform. Such a reform was indeed carried out by the *Dukhovnyi Reglament (Spiritual Regulation)* of 1721, which made the administration of the Church in effect part of a single great centralized bureaucracy centring on the monarch; but this came a generation after the setting up of the 'Most Drunken Council', whose antics continued to the last days of Peter's life. In religion, as in everything he touched, his politics cannot be separated from his personality.

It is true that even Peter could not disregard totally the power of traditional religious feeling in Russia. His new capital of St Petersburg accordingly had, as a matter of policy, to be linked, as Moscow and Kiev had been for centuries, with a great monastery. Thus the Alexander Nevskii monastery was founded there in 1710, and five years later made the centre for the training of the higher clergy in Russia. But it is notable that the saint to whom it was dedicated had been in life a warrior-prince, and that Peter specifically decreed that he be depicted as a warrior, not a monk. Moreover such a foundation was very much the exception rather than the rule where the Tsar was concerned. For Peter's desire to divert Church lands and money to state use (an objective which he went far towards realizing) there were plenty of parallels elsewhere in Europe. For his open contempt for many of the religious beliefs of his subjects there were none. Every other great European monarch of the period paid at least outward respect, and often much more than that, to the traditional religious decencies. Peter alone took pleasure in deriding them. 'Now, who would believe that the sign of the cross – that most precious pledge of our redemption – was held up to mockery?,' wrote a scandalized Austrian envoy in 1699, after seeing one of the Tsar's cronies, masquerading as a bishop, parody religious rites with two pipes placed at right angles to simulate a cross. No other monarch of the age would have wished or perhaps dared to expose an important foreign diplomat to such an exhibition.

His personal tastes; the overwhelming strain placed for many years upon his limited resources by the demands of the great war with Sweden; his constant travelling; the

With his own hand, *Peter made a variety of ornaments and pieces of furniture, including this mirror-stand in the ballroom of the Summer Palace. Carved in walnut, it shows devices and animals of the chase. (292)*

were sentenced to dismissal and loss of all honours, but were so indispensable that they were soon restored to their former positions. Peter was justified though unoriginal in his conclusion that 'there is little honesty among men and much deceit'.

There was yet one more way in which the Tsar differed from other rulers of the period. This was in his ostentatiously ambivalent attitude to religion. Peter was not an unbeliever. His letters are full of biblical allusions; and he retained throughout his life a simple, soldierly, and untheological faith in the importance of religion as a social cement and a prop of government. Nevertheless he had no feeling whatever for traditional Orthodox piety, a fact which raised a high psychological barrier between him and almost all his subjects. To him monasticism meant merely the diversion to unconstructive purposes of resources and energies which should be devoted to the strengthening, development, and enrichment of Russia. The hermit or holy man of irreproachably pious and ascetic life, a traditional unimportance to him of family ties; his dislike of elaborate religious ritual: all combined to make Peter prefer an unpretentious physical environment. He created no Versailles, no Nymphenburg, no Schönbrunn. He was certainly not altogether indifferent to outward appearances and to certain types of ceremony. This can be seen in his liking for firework displays and for complex ornamental waterworks (tastes he shared with many other rulers of the age) and in the elaborate triumphal processions (based on classical models) which celebrated his most important victories. Moreover a taste for Western European luxury, for larger palaces with bigger rooms, for more ornate decorations and more elaborate furniture, had been seeping into the Russian ruling classes long before Peter was born. In the 1660s the Tsar Alexis Mikhailovich had listed the luxuries which he would like to import from abroad; 'lace like that worn by the Spanish king, and the French one and the Emperor', skilled musicians who 'can play the trumpet as the birds sing in the trees', and experts capable of organizing a theatre. In 1666–68 he had built at Kolomenskoe, outside Moscow, a new palace with many distinctively Western characteristics. Later, in the 1680s, Prince V. V. Golitsyn, the favourite and chief minister of Sophia during her tenure of power, had lived very much in the Western European style. In his great house in Moscow could be found Western furniture, mirrors, lifelike portraits both of Russians and foreigners (a highly significant innovation which was rapidly gaining ground in Russia), many clocks and thermometers, a large library, and on the ceilings paintings representing the planetary system. When he fell from power in 1689 the list of its contents filled an entire book. In the same way the palace built for Lefort in the German Suburb in the last years of the seventeenth century foreshadows in its size and rich furnishings, its gilt leather, silks, damasks, and Chinese rarities, the ostentatious luxury of the reigns of Elizabeth or Catherine II in the middle and later eighteenth century.

Peter, however, had for most of his reign little liking for this sort of thing. In April 1694, when he accompanied his half-brother Ivan in the Easter procession, he took part for the last time in a traditional court ceremony in the Kremlin; henceforth he made virtually no use of the palaces there (several of which had been redecorated, with the use of such Western innovations as gilt leather, in the 1680s and 1690s). Though handsome, the palace which he built at Peterhof, near the new capital of St Petersburg, was by the standards of Western Europe relatively small and unpretentious. Moreover it was begun only in 1718 and was not quite complete at his death: another at Strelna, also near St Petersburg, had then scarcely been commenced. The Winter Palace in the city itself, which was begun in 1711, was a small two-story wooden building which bore no relationship to the magnificent present-day edifice of that name. Even the 'second' Winter Palace, which replaced it in 1716, though modestly attractive to judge by the plans (it was pulled down in 1726) was far from imposing by Western European standards. The house which Prince Menshikov built at Oranienbaum, near St Petersburg, was far more of a true palace than anything in which the Tsar indulged.

Russian access to the sea *had preoccupied more than one of Peter's predecessors. This, and the desire for a port and metropolis facing on to Europe, induced Peter in 1703 to found St Petersburg, a vast undertaking celebrated in this miniature of twenty years later. (293)*

The beginnings of St Petersburg

But if the Tsar did not build a great palace he associated his name, as no ruler since Alexander the Great had done, with a new city. St Petersburg, proclaimed in 1712 as the capital of Russia, was the most unmistakable physical manifestation of Peter's demonic urge towards creation and novelty and of the complete ruthlessness with which he gave expression to it. The most truly symbolic event of his entire career was his burial, not with his predecessors in Moscow, but in the new cathedral of SS. Peter and Paul in the city which owed its existence to him. The building of the new capital shows the impulsiveness with which, at least until the later years of his reign, he embarked upon new enterprises without adequate study of the problems and costs involved. The site of the city was chosen by him after only two short visits to the estuary of the Neva and without any grasp of the enormous difficulties which flooding was to cause to the inhabitants of the new capital. Yet the building of the city, once decided, was pushed on with unsparing energy and total indifference to the human costs involved; for years, indeed for decades, on end, thousands of conscripted workers living in appalling conditions in huts and dug-outs (*zemlyanki*), or in the open air, laboured on its construction. There were incessant difficulties in raising men on the scale required. In 1710, for example, the Moscow province sent for work on the new capital only a quarter of the number Peter had demanded, and in 1714–15 the proportion sent by other provinces was only about a third of what the Tsar thought necessary. In 1714 he tried with only partial success to meet this situation by 'ascribing' to the admiralty in St Petersburg, which was now by far the largest single productive enterprise in Russia, 24,000 peasant households in the St Petersburg and Archangel provinces. Even more brutal coercion was used to populate the new city. From the summer of 1705 onwards the forcible settlement there for life of skilled workers (above all carpenters and smiths) with their wives and children became a settled official policy embodied in a long series of decrees. In August 1710, for example, the sending

The Winter Palace *took very different various forms before the surviving, sixth version was erected. The first palace (above), begun in 1711, was found too small for its official functions, much less, had there been one, for an extensive court; and in 1716 it was replaced. (294)*

to the new capital of almost five thousand such workers was ordered. Later yet another form of coercion came into play. In 1719 all landowners who possessed more than forty serf households were ordered to build a house on Vassilievskii island, which Peter now wished to make the centre of the city, and to live there themselves. These measures inevitably encountered resistance, above all in the form of flight by those marked down as forced settlers. Of a thousand carpenters brought to the new capital in accordance with a decree of 1713, over half had run away within a year: of a group of just over 2,200 workers received in 1710–12 at least 365 fled. To this sort of passive resistance the government had no answer except the issue of new decrees calling for even more forced settlement and the use of more overt and brutal coercion. Thus conscripted settlers were often brought to St Petersburg in chains and under military guard, while those engaged on shipbuilding and other admiralty projects were branded on the left hand in

order to make escape more difficult. Only in the last years of Peter's reign was the situation somewhat eased when a new source of conscript labour became available in the form of army recruits no longer needed for the war against Sweden.

Even the economic life of St Petersburg was to be provided by compulsion from above; from 1713 onwards there were sustained though not completely successful efforts to develop it as a trading centre by ordering that many Russian products – tar, potash, caviar, certain types of leather – should be exported only through it. From 1720 onwards it was systematically favoured as against its main rival, Archangel, by differential customs duties. But though the cost in human suffering was appalling the result was achieved. In spite of the death of thousands of wretched conscripted peasants, in spite of the dislike of the whole enterprise felt by most of the noble and landowning families, who found the city remote, expensive, and un-Russian, St Petersburg was built. At Peter's death it was still, in the main, a city of wooden houses. Already, however, it was the object of increasing admiration. 'At present,' wrote a foreign diplomat in the early 1720s, 'Petersbourg may with Reason be looked upon as a Wonder of the World, considering its magnificent Palaces, sixty odd thousand houses [the real number was much less than this], and the short time that was employed in the building of it.'

Peter, then, is a personality of abiding interest to the historian. But personal peculiarities alone, however striking, would not have won him the historical stature which he was seen to possess in his own day and which he has enjoyed ever since. For this, lasting achievement was essential; though only the barest sketch of his policies, and of their successes and failures, is possible here.

Russia's first public museum, *the Cabinet of Curios, or Kunst-Kamera, was established in St Petersburg in 1714. It at first contained the Tsar's different collections, including such exhibits as the stuffed animals shown below. Subsequently it was incorporated in the Imperial Academy of Sciences. (295)*

St Petersburg *was a fortress city as well as a mercantile port. In this engraving, forges, arsenal, and shipyards are all depicted, consequences of the Tsar's preoccupation with his largely superfluous new navy.* (296)

An intellectual revolution

No aspect of his reforming activities in Russia has been more written about than his efforts to develop and strengthen the country's intellectual life. Certainly these efforts were numerous and persistent: they continued throughout his life and became, like many other aspects of his work, more systematic and considered in his later years. Some of them had an importance which was in part symbolic, as rejections of tradition and the past. Such were the adoption of the Julian calendar and the abandonment of the traditional method of dating events from the alleged creation of the world in 5508 BC. Such again were the adoption of a reformed and partly new alphabet, so that from 1710 onwards the Old Slavonic one was used only for the printing of liturgical works; or perhaps the establishment in St Petersburg in 1714 of the Kunst-Kamera, the first public museum in Russia. Others were more directly utilitarian in their inspiration. Such was the creation in the first years of the eighteenth century of a wide range of specialized schools intended to produce technicians and experts for the armed forces and the development of economic life – an important school of mathematics and navigation, the artillery school founded in 1701, the school of medicine set up in 1707, the

engineering school created in 1712, the naval academy established in 1715. These institutions were of widely varying importance and effectiveness; but taken together they undoubtedly injected into Russian intellectual life an element of science and rationality larger than had been known before. Even elementary education was not totally neglected. An effective system on this level was quite beyond the reach of Peter or any of his successors; but the garrison schools for the teaching of the sons of soldiers and the 'ciphering schools' which attempted to give the sons of provincial landowners and officials the ability to read and write and a smattering of mathematics were an effort, though a very limited and ineffective one, in this direction. It was under Peter that there appeared the first arithmetic textbook in Russian (at Amsterdam in 1699), the first important Russian primer for the teaching of reading (in 1701), and the first Russian work on dynamics (in 1722). Most impressive of all in purely intellectual terms was the foundation in the new capital in 1725, after several years of enquiries and planning, of the Imperial Academy of Sciences, which was later to become one of the great intellectual institutions of eighteenth-century Europe.

Of the Tsar's own involvement in every aspect of this process of intellectual development there is no doubt whatever. He was personally interested in the exploration and mapping of his vast and still largely uncharted dominions, above all in Siberia; and in this respect as in many others his interests became wider and less narrowly utilitarian in his last years. From 1719 onwards, for example, he inspired a series of efforts (urged on by the earlier proposals of the great German scholar and philosopher Leibniz) to discover whether or not eastern Siberia was joined to North America. He was personally interested in the translation of books from foreign languages into Russian, an activity which grew greatly in scope during his reign; and though a high proportion of these translations were of technical and semi-technical works on such subjects as engineering and fortification they were none the less one of the most important means by which a new outlook and new ideas filtered into Russia. He was personally interested in the recruitment of foreign technicians and experts of all kinds for work on his projects. A whole network of agents abroad, very often merchants – Henry and Thomas Stiles in England, Thesing, Ermen, and Kintsius in the Netherlands, Lefort (nephew of Peter's close friend of the 1690s) in Paris, Caretta in Venice – recruited people of this kind for him,

Educational reform *was given imperial encouragement; over seven hundred books were published and a newspaper founded. The letter 'psi' of the Russian alphabet is here illustrated from an early eighteenth-century primer, with an assortment of objects beginning with it. (297)*

especially in the early years of the eighteenth century; and though the inspiration of the entire enterprise was utilitarian it had intellectual and cultural overtones. He was personally interested in the writing of Russian history, and more especially in that of his own reign. There was undoubtedly a large element of self-glorification in this. But it none the less produced results of some intellectual value. It inspired in particular the writing of the most important historical work in Russian produced during the first half of the eighteenth century, the *Yadro Rossiiskoi istorii (Essentials of Russian History)* by A. I. Mankiev, and of a detailed official history of the Great Northern War of which the part dealing with events down to 1715 was revised by Peter, though neither of these was published until long after the Tsar's death.

Yet the real importance of all this can be exaggerated. These efforts at intellectual development were sincere, sustained, and up to a point impressive. They caught the eye and aroused the admiration of contemporaries; they have drawn the attention of historians ever since. But it is important to remember how small a proportion of the population of Russia was affected by them, even indirectly, how traditional and resistant to change this huge, land-locked, isolated society still remained. Peter was, in this field, as the great Marxist theorist Plekhanov remarked two centuries later, 'attaching European extremities to a body which nevertheless remained still Asiatic'. This limitation also applied, at least so far as his own lifetime was concerned, to the most striking of all his cultural innovations, if the term is used in a wide sense; his efforts to improve the status of women, at least in the higher ranks of Russian society. At the 'assemblies' in St Petersburg established by decree in 1718 the attendance of women was compulsory (it is supremely typical of Peter that such a change should have been attempted in such a way). The amusements provided there – dancing, chess, draughts – together with the presence of women, would, it was hoped, generate in the new capital a polite society of a new, Western European type. Efforts to bring women out of the seclusion of the *terem*, in which hitherto they had been isolated in almost Asiatic style, went back to the early days of the reign. Some had appeared at a dinner given by the Tsar, and taken part in dancing afterwards, at least as early as March 1699. By 1714 it was already possible for one acute foreign observer to feel that so far as appearances went high society in St Petersburg was little different from that of London or Paris (though he was struck by the fact that women's teeth were still stained the traditional black). The decree of 1718 was therefore merely the culmination of a long rejection of tradition so far as the position of women was concerned. But it is necessary to stress once more how superficial and limited much of this was. The same observer pointed out that even in the early 1720s Peter's efforts in this respect had had no effect outside a limited circle in St Petersburg. He also made the telling point that it was one thing to dress a woman in Western European style and quite another to give her the self-confidence and social sense appropriate to her new clothes. Though the ladies of the court were 'perfectly well dressed after the foreign fashion'

The Great Northern War of 1700–21
ranged Poland, Denmark, and Russia
against the recently aggrandized power
of Sweden. Russia's military success,
celebrated in this contemporary
engraving of Peter, won all Sweden's
territories east of the Baltic, and made
Russian power a potential threat to
Germany. (298)

ПЕТРЪ ВЕЛИКІЙ
ОТЕЦЪ ОТЕЧЕСТВА ІМПЕРАТОРЪ ВСЕРОСІЙСКІЙ

he found that 'in Conversation with Strangers they cannot yet conquer their in-born Bashfulness and Awkwardness'.

Russia and Europe

The real importance of the reign transcended such St Petersburg novelties. The Tsar's work was a response to the needs of Russia, or what he saw as such; and these were inherent in the country's history and geographical position and owed nothing to Western ideas or inspiration. Better outlets to the sea were needed, as had been seen by several of his predecessors since at least the second half of the sixteenth century. To achieve these and overthrow the Swedish power which stood in Russia's path a much more powerful army was essential. Such a force, organized on Western European lines and using foreign officers, had begun to emerge during the seventeenth century; and from 1699 onwards Peter continued and greatly accelerated this development. To satisfy the voracious appetite of this great army for men, money, and equipment a system of conscription which bore very heavily on the peasantry had to be built up, many new taxes had to be raised, efforts to develop new industries had to be made. To enforce these unprecedented and bitterly unpopular demands Russia had to be equipped with a system of administration more effectively centralized, more complex, and more military in spirit than any previously known. The senate, established in 1711 as a general supervisory and regulating body; the nine administrative colleges set up in 1718–19, each to direct an important aspect of government activity; the Synod, established in 1721 to subject the Church finally to the State; important though short-lived efforts at reform of provincial administration in 1708 and 1719: these were merely the most significant aspects of incessant institutional change. The years 1718–22 in particular saw a sustained effort, after years of chaotic experiment, to systematize the administration. To run this great bureaucratic machine and to provide officers for the armed forces the landowning class was turned, to its own great dismay and with real suffering to many of its members, into a caste of hereditary state servants, a group which maintained its status and possessions only at the price of life-long liability to service in the armed forces or the administration. By the operation of the system of army levies, and above all of the new poll-tax introduced from 1718 onwards, the complex distinctions which had hitherto existed between different groups of peasants were more and more obliterated and a vast class of unfree 'bonded people' (*krepostnie lyudi*) created. In this way Peter created, almost unwittingly, a new monarchy, more bureaucratic and more military than anything previously known in Russia, and a new society, more simple, more tragically and completely divided, than any the country had seen before. Yet these developments were, it may be argued, in some sense forced on the Tsar if Russia were to develop as a great state or even to safeguard herself against foreign attack or interference; and for most of them there were important seventeenth-century, or even earlier, precedents. Serfdom had been developing for generations and had been systematized by the law-code (*ulozhenie*) of 1649. The need for greater military strength had been recognized and responded to generations before Peter was born. Of all his innovations only two, the subjection of the Church and the creation of the new and largely useless navy

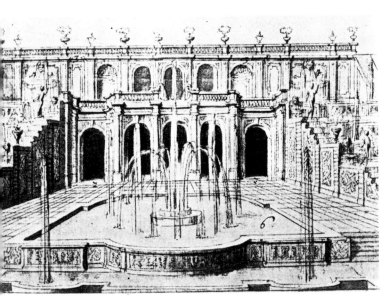

Peter's architectural designs, *recorded in his own hand, combine natural ability with an awareness of contemporary developments. His drawing of the projected Peterhof palace, already shown centred on a cascade, is recognizably similar to the finished building (pl. 290). (299)*

of large sailing-ships which was always in essence largely the Tsar's personal toy, were genuinely unprecedented. Peter carried out no revolution in Russia. What he did was rather to accelerate, brutally and often unthinkingly, developments which were already well under way.

Though court life of the Western European kind was not in general attractive to him nevertheless the foreign influences which he encouraged, the building of St Petersburg, even his 'assemblies', were in one way at least highly significant. They, and the veneer of Western culture which they represented, symbolized the new Russia in the eyes of the outside world. This had important practical results. Peter was able, in particular, to alter drastically the relationship of the Romanov dynasty to the other ruling houses of Europe, and also to bring about a great improvement in Russia's international standing and raise his personal prestige to unprecedented heights. The first of these developments is seen most clearly in the growing willingness of the greatest European dynasties to contemplate intermarriage with the Romanovs. During the seventeenth century no member of the Russian ruling family had married a foreigner. Yet the Habsburg Emperor Leopold I seems to have thought as early as 1701 of a marriage of one of his sons to a Russian princess; and for this purpose efforts were made in Vienna to procure portraits of Peter's sister Nataliya and of one of his nieces. Nothing came of the idea; and neither the marriage of Alexis in 1710 to a member of a minor German house nor that of Peter's niece Anna in the same year to the Duke of Courland could be said to reflect fully Russia's developing status as a great European power. The last years of the reign, however, saw a striking change in the position. In 1722 Philip V of Spain thought seriously of

marrying one of his sons to a Russian princess; while Peter in his later years had real hopes of a marriage of his daughter Elizabeth to the young Louis XV of France. Already in 1716 the French *Almanach royal*, one of the standard reference books of the age, had begun to list the Russian ruling house with those of the states of Europe: no longer did it occupy in works of this kind the ambiguous and peripheral position to which it had usually been relegated in the past. The Romanovs could now be seen, and could see themselves, as in some sense the equals of the Bourbons or Habsburgs among the European dynasties, a development symbolized by Peter's assumption of the title of Emperor (*Imperator*) in 1721.

For Russia's standing in Europe, and for the personal prestige of her ruler, the turning point was the decisive victory over the Swedes won at Poltava in July 1709. This transformed the country's international position with startling suddenness. The threat of Swedish invasion and a possible collapse of Peter's power (Charles XII of Sweden had been urged by some of his advisers to proclaim Sophia as ruler of Russia) was now at an end. The Swedish Baltic possessions, already partly in Russian hands, could now be conquered at leisure. Poland, more than ever divided by factional rivalries and weakened by war and disease, was now largely at Russia's mercy. From a powerful but semi-barbaric and largely unknown despot on the fringes of Europe Peter changed into a great European ruler whose alliance was valuable and whose enmity was to be feared.

The transformation was immediate and unmistakable. Foreign states were compelled to accept and adjust to it. In 1707, when a marriage between the Tsarevich Alexis and Princess Charlotte of Brunswick-Wolfenbüttel was first mooted, the father of the prospective bride had been warned by one of his officials against such a scheme on the grounds that the Tsar as a European ruler was of virtually no significance. After Poltava the negotiations, which had hung fire for some time, were rapidly brought to a successful conclusion. Almost on the morrow of the Russian victory, in another illustration of the changed position, Frederick of Prussia suggested an agreement to partition Poland and thus advance Russia's frontier into Europe farther than ever before. Most striking of all, within a few months of the battle Louis XIV himself was openly hoping for Russian mediation between France and her enemies in the War of the Spanish Succession; a French minister was sent to St Petersburg in 1710 with this as his main objective. The tide of military success did not flow uninterruptedly in favour of Peter. In particular a rash invasion of the Danubian principalities in the summer of 1711 ended in a potentially disastrous defeat by the Turks and the acceptance of some very irksome peace terms – the loss of his southern naval base at Azov and of the fleet painfully accumulated there; an undertaking not to intervene further in Poland. But this setback made little difference to his position and prestige in Europe. In 1697–98, when with a large retinue Peter had travelled through Germany on his 'Great Embassy' to the Netherlands and England, the curiosity he aroused had been obviously mixed with patronage and even amusement. When he visited Paris two decades later, in 1716, he came as the greatest European monarch, though he failed to obtain the French alliance which he sought. The fact that both he and his country were still largely unknown quantities in France added, if anything, to the impression which he made. Even the enmities which Russia now aroused were a tribute to his achievement; she might be feared and even hated but could hardly be ignored as in the past. The fears aroused in London during the last years of Peter's reign by possible Russian dominance of the Baltic and hence of the supply of naval stores on which Britain depended so heavily, or by the threat of Russian influence in north Germany, or even by the possibility of Russian aid to the Jacobites, would have been almost incomprehensible a few years earlier. In the same way the acute uneasiness aroused in Vienna by the spectacular growth of Russian power was an involuntary tribute to the Tsar and his achievements.

The last years of his life saw Peter's international stature, consecrated by political and military success, grow steadily. A child on the French throne, a melancholic on that of Spain, a mediocrity enthroned in Vienna, an uninspiring German prince established in England, could not compete effectively with him for the position of greatest ruler in Europe. By the end of his reign some of the praise lavished on him had become positively fulsome. An English newspaper in 1724, the year before his death, described him as 'the greatest Monarch of our Age . . . whose Actions will draw after him a Blaze of Glory, and Astonishment, through the latest Depth of Time! and warm the Heart of Posterity with the same generous Reverence for the Name of this immortal Emperor, which we now feel at Mention of Alexander the Great: or the first, and noblest, of the Caesars'. This tone was as yet hardly typical; but such works as Fontenelle's famous *éloge* of the Emperor, delivered to the Académie Française after his death, and later still more Voltaire's *Histoire de l'Empire de Russie sous Pierre le Grand* (1759–63), were to implant in the mind of Europe an uncritically favourable view of Peter which was not to be seriously modified for over a century. He had created no great court. His efforts at the intellectual development of his country had often merely skimmed the surface of Russian life. Many of his domestic policies had been appallingly costly in terms of human suffering and had left his country a heritage of problems greater in many ways than those he had tried to solve. But his place in history was now secure beyond serious challenge.

Peter's achievement *is naively expressed in this wood relief of the sculptor A. Kreptikov at work on a statue of him. Over his head, a sunburst. Around him, images of his role as architect and naval leader. (300)*

Thirteen

MARIA THERESA
A reforming monarchy

❋

E. WANGERMANN

'NO ONE WILL, I THINK, DISAGREE that it would not be easy to find in history an example of a crowned head acceding to the government in more un-favourable circumstances than I did myself.' In these words Maria Theresa referred in retrospect to her accession. With respect to dynastic law and diplomatic arrangements, her father, Charles VI, had done all that could be done to ensure his daughter's peaceful succession to the entire Habsburg inheritance. But the policies he pursued from about 1733 had resulted in wars against France and Turkey, in which the decline of Habsburg military power since the great victories of Prince Eugene had been clearly revealed. Therefore his sudden and unexpected death at the height of his misfortunes in October 1740 presented an irresistible temptation to the competing powers to go back on their solemn commitments, and to advance claims to substantial parts of the Habsburg inheritance. So numerous were Maria Theresa's enemies, so weak and demoralized her own forces, that few contemporaries would have been surprised, if her accession were to have marked the disintegration of the Habsburg monarchy and the end of the court at Vienna as one of the great centres of political power.

In this perilous situation, most of the aged ministers inherited by Maria Theresa from her father favoured compromise with the invaders of Habsburg territory rather than resistance to them. The survival of the monarchy and the continuance of Vienna as the capital of a 'great power' came therefore to depend on the young Queen Maria Theresa herself. This was a formidable challenge for a new sovereign who was only twenty-three years old, and had not been given any kind of political training or experience. Maria Theresa ascribed this astonishing omission in her

education to her own respect for her father which, she felt, precluded her from showing any interest in matters of government during his lifetime.

In confronting the invaders and mobilizing the latent resources of her territories, Maria Theresa revealed great strength of character and political acumen, as well as a certain 'genius of femininity' reminiscent of Elizabeth I of England. She imparted some of her own courage and determination to her ministers. She discovered how to win the confidence and arouse the enthusiasm of the Hungarians, whom her ministers tended to distrust more than they did the Prussians or the Bavarians. She was quick to realize that the province of Silesia, conquered from her by Frederick II in 1740–41, would not be regained without recourse to new policies at home and abroad, and she picked out the men who had the will and the ability to carry out new policies. Her closest advisers during these crucial early years of her reign were her husband Francis Stephen of Lorraine, her cabinet secretary Ignaz Koch, and the state secretary and *de facto* foreign minister Johann Christoph Bartenstein. The sources unfortunately do not enable us to assess precisely the respective contribution of these three men to the young queen's achievement.

In order to mobilize the latent resources of her territories to sustain greater military power, Maria Theresa had to effect a revolution in government. Under the existing system, as she discovered to her profound indignation, the central government's objective could be frustrated by the provincial Estates, who controlled direct taxation, recruitment, and army supplies, and generally used this control to serve the interests of province and nobility. Individual ministers sought prestige and popularity by advancing the interests of the province in which their own estates lay, treating other provinces as though they were foreign lands. Habsburg government during the wars of the 1740s was little more than a competitive struggle of province against province to minimize the burdens and inconveniences of sheltering, supplying, and moving armies. 'This was the sole reason,' Maria Theresa wrote, 'why I quickly realized what was going on, and why, step by step, I took my measures to carry out a complete change in the form of government.'

The young woman of twenty-three who unexpectedly inherited the Habsburg domains in 1740 faced a situation that would have daunted more experienced monarchs. Yet by 1745, when this porcelain plaque was made, Maria Theresa had begun to reorganize the state and to initiate a foreign policy that gave it new prospects of survival. (301)

Francis of Lorraine and her cabinet secretary Koch drew her attention to the man to whom she was later to refer as having been sent to her by Providence to enable her to 'break through' and to achieve the necessary revolution in government. It was Friedrich Wilhelm, Count Haugwitz, formerly a government official in Silesia, and described by the court diarist Khevenhüller as a man who 'was in harmony with her humour', 'loved all innovations', was industrious and energetic, and 'overcame seemingly insuperable obstacles'. He established a royal 'Representation and Chamber' in every province except Hungary to take over the bulk of the functions which the Estates had been carrying out so unsatisfactorily. These were made responsible to a single central government department, the Directorium, under Haugwitz' own presidency, which replaced the Bohemian and Austrian chanceries as well as the treasury, and which was to submit weekly protocols for Maria Theresa's resolution. Maria Theresa sustained Haugwitz against the determined and almost unanimous opposition of the Estates and her ministers. Thus the work was completed by May 1749. Henceforth the court became the administrative nerve-centre of the monarchy to an unprecedented degree. For the new authorities in the provinces not only took over functions previously carried out by the Estates, but gradually extended the scope of governmental authority into areas not previously subject to it, such as public health, schools, and many others. This tight central control over provincial affairs was not affected by the frequent subsequent changes in the allocation of functions between the central departments. When the Council of State

(Staatsrat) was set up in 1761 as a result of the second great crisis of the reign, and began to control and coordinate the work of all the internal departments, this was intended to provide Maria Theresa with an overall view of the monarchy's government. In fact it tended to become merely a further channel through which the swelling torrent of administrative detail passed on its way to Maria Theresa's desk.

Maria Theresa's revolution in government was accompanied by the adoption of a new 'system' in Habsburg foreign policy. This, too, originated in the sovereign's personal initiative. As soon as Maria Theresa had reluctantly signed the Treaty of Dresden in 1745, ceding Silesia to Prussia, the recovery of the lost province became the principal long-term objective of her policy. For the sake of this objective, she decided to 'change the system of this House', i.e. to abandon the traditional European role of the house of Habsburg of maintaining the balance of power against France. Habsburg territories in Italy and the Netherlands, the possession of which inevitably entailed the burdensome obligation of countering the expansion of Bourbon power, were now to be regarded as of secondary importance in the development of Habsburg foreign policy. Hence Maria Theresa was prepared to accept the terms agreed by Britain and France at Aix-la-Chappelle in 1748, despite the loss of some of her Italian territories which this entailed.

As a result of this fundamental reappraisal of the objectives of Habsburg foreign policy, the maintenance of the traditional alliance with the Maritime Powers, Britain and the United Provinces, became increasingly problematic. But neither the members of the Conference nor Francis of Lorraine (who had been crowned German Emperor in 1745) would seriously consider a system of foreign policy jeopardizing the traditional alliance which had proved itself in practice, as long as there was no guarantee that an

Prague had been occupied *by the forces of Charles Albert of Bavaria, a rival claimant to the succession. He was not ousted until 1743. On 29 April, Maria Theresa entered the city in triumph (below), to receive the crown of Bohemia a few days later. (302)*

alternative alliance could be forged to take its place. If acquiescence in the Prussian possession of Silesia, which Britain had guaranteed at Aix-la-Chappelle, was a condition for maintaining the traditional alliance, they would accept even that.

Once again, therefore, Maria Theresa had to look beyond the circle of her ministers to find a man who, like Haugwitz, was 'in harmony with her humour', 'loved all innovations', and was able to 'overcome seemingly insuperable obstacles'. Only this time he had to be a diplomat rather than an administrator. She found such a man among her ambassadors. He was Wenzel Anton, Count Kaunitz. Acting as her plenipotentiary at the Congress of Aix-la-Chappelle, he demonstrated his willingness and his ability to negotiate in the spirit of the new system of foreign policy. Immediately after the conclusion of these negotiations, in January 1749, Maria Theresa appointed Kaunitz to the Conference. He was the youngest member of this supreme advisory council. When Maria Theresa asked the Conference to consider the policy to be adopted after the conclusion of peace, Kaunitz approached the problem from the angle of the new system. He demonstrated the inadequacy of the traditional alliance with the Maritime Powers, and tried to show how it might be replaced by an alliance with the Bourbon dynasty on the basis of making the dismemberment of Prussia an objective of Bourbon foreign policy. Soon after Kaunitz had demonstrated on paper how the new system might be brought into effect, Maria Theresa appointed him ambassador to France and subsequently head of foreign affairs under the distinguished title of Chancellor of State (1753) so that he could turn his ideas into reality. Though the French response to his advances was by no means encouraging, Kaunitz and Maria Theresa deliberately allowed the alliance with the Maritime Powers to lapse, presumably in the hope that this would improve the chances of a positive French response to Austrian advances. When clashes between British and French colonists made war seem imminent again in 1755, Kaunitz told the French ambassador that the Habsburg monarchy would remain neutral in the coming Anglo-French conflict, even if the French were to occupy the Netherlands. Immediately afterwards he launched the plan which was designed to win the French King's support for the Habsburg objective of Prussia's dismemberment – the offer of at least a part of the Austrian Netherlands as an appanage for the King's son-in-law Don Philip.

Kaunitz' patient and daring diplomacy now quickly produced the long-awaited results. Britain, obliged to fill the breach in the defences of her Continental interests caused by Maria Theresa's defection, concluded an alliance with Frederick II, who was willing to perform this task in order to escape from his threatened isolation. Louis XV and his advisers reacted to the defection of their ally to France's arch-enemy by responding positively to Kaunitz' alliance proposals. The recovery of Silesia now seemed assured.

On the strength of this achievement, Kaunitz became Maria Theresa's most influential adviser on all aspects of policy. His position was not even undermined when after the costly sacrifices of the Seven Years' War the recovery of Silesia seemed as far removed from realization as ever. In the

Wenzel Anton, Count Kaunitz, *became the most powerful of all the Queen's advisers. His first major post was that of plenipotentiary at Aix-la-Chapelle in 1748 (he was thirty-eight). Soon afterwards, in 1753, he was appointed Chancellor of State. (303)*

reorganization of the central government departments made necessary by the monarchy's crisis of exhaustion, it was not the architect of the diplomatic revolution, but that of the earlier revolution in government, Haugwitz, who was demoted. Kaunitz, indeed, attained a virtually prime-ministerial position.

After the conclusion of the Seven Years' War, Maria Theresa abandoned the objective of recovering Silesia, and adopted a peaceful foreign policy not geared to territorial ambitions. But as the war effort had grossly over-strained the available resources of her monarchy with near-disastrous results, there was no question but that the revolution in government would be extended. Even more of the monarchy's latent resources would have to be mobilized to increase further the regular revenues of the state.

The ultimate objective of reform therefore remained the same. Yet Maria Theresa's government now evinced a more comprehensive conception of the task in hand. This may be seen from the General Instruction for the reorganized court chancery, which established the principle that 'the increase of the Monarch's power and revenues cannot be sought except in the furtherance of the common welfare and prosperity'.

Maria Theresa and some of her ministers came to realize how much was involved in a serious effort to further the common welfare and prosperity. They realized that it could

The Queen's home *life was relaxed, informal, and bourgeois. These two groups were both painted by her daughter Maria Christina in 1762. The first shows Maria Theresa with her husband and three youngest children, Ferdinand, Marie-Antoinette, and Maximilian. The second (below) celebrates the next generation: Joseph (later Joseph II), wearing a dressing gown, sits with his young wife Isabella of Parma soon after the birth of their daughter Theresa. (304, 305)*

not be done without drawing extensively on the ideas and the men of the Enlightenment, and that it could not be done without raising the cultural and educational standards of all the people. Much would have to be sacrificed in the service of such a comprehensive educational effort. All this doubtless helped to strengthen the Habsburg monarchy as a power. But the unintended results were probably more significant in the long run.

The situation facing Maria Theresa at her accession drastically affected the life of the Habsburg court. The economies required to sustain the defence of her threatened inheritance were facilitated by the fact that, for the time being, the court had ceased to be the residence of the Holy Roman Emperor. Charles VI's Spanish followers were now dismissed from the court, as were most of the fine musicians who had contributed so much to the magnificence with which Habsburg power was represented at the court of Vienna.

When the immediate threat to Vienna had passed, and Maria Theresa's armies had won their first victories, some splendour returned to the court. In the carnival season a mood of gaiety erupted which was unknown under Charles VI, but which was natural at a court presided over by a sociable young couple with a capacity for enjoying themselves. Maria Theresa indulged a veritable passion for dancing, and permitted the organization of masked balls which had been prohibited under her father.

There was no return to the old solemn magnificence, not even after Francis of Lorraine had been invested with the Imperial dignity in 1745. Indeed, it soon became apparent that the simplification of court ceremonial and conventions suited the taste of the new ruling couple, whose personal and family style of life had in some ways developed along lines corresponding to contemporary bourgeois ideals rather than aristocratic traditions. The Prussian ambassador referred to Maria Theresa's 'bourgeois marriage', which in the context of the time was an apt description of the couple's shared bedchamber as well as of the generous amount of time they gave to their children. The delightful scene described by the Dutch ambassador Bentinck in 1750, when Maria Theresa yielded to Francis' insistence and sang a few songs accompanied by Wagenseil on the piano, singing each song better than the last as her embarrassment subsided – this scene has no precedent at the court, but anticipates the amateur music-making in the Viennese salons which was to become an important feature of bourgeois social life later in the century.

Maria Theresa would not tolerate aristocratic levity and debauchery at her court, whatever might be the practice at other courts. Ready to compromise in most other matters, Maria Theresa became a fanatic in this. Her concern for moral standards quickly developed into an inquisitive censoriousness in respect of the matrimonial practices and religious observances of all persons admitted to the court. For a number of years, a special department, the notorious 'chastity commission', operated the moral inquisitions, causing much suffering, provoking much ridicule, and compelling even independent-minded men like Kaunitz to adopt an attitude of obsequious pretence.

The Queen's passion for dancing *brought new gaiety to the Hofburg in Vienna. Sumptuous masked balls were held in the Redoutensaal, the former Hofoperntheater, adapted as a ballroom in 1745. (306)*

The architectural achievement

The development of court architecture during Maria Theresa's reign reflected the transition from solemnity and the symbolization of power to a simpler informality and the growing emphasis on moral responsibility. It has frequently been noted that the style in which Maria Theresa's palaces were rebuilt or restored marked a change from grandeur to a serene and joyous gracefulness. The architect chiefly associated with the 'Theresian' style is Nikolaus Pacassi, who was put in charge of the rebuilding of Schönbrunn palace, just outside Vienna, in the 1740s. After the completion of this work, Schönbrunn became the regular summer residence of Maria Theresa, her court and staff. The palace in Innsbruck was rebuilt in the 1750s and 1760s in a strikingly similar style. It is therefore assumed that the architect in charge of this work, the army officer Constantin Johann Walter, was acting under Pacassi's general direction. If in these two palaces there is little evidence of a striving for simplicity, the decorative detail expressed the splendour rather than the power of the court.

The completion of the décor inside and around the rebuilt palaces was the work of many years. The later stages of this work reflect a continuing process of transition. And during the last decade of Maria Theresa's reign, we can detect, as in foreign and domestic policies, the increasingly pervasive influence of Kaunitz.

The main ceiling frescoes in Schönbrunn and Innsbruck are characteristic products of the process of transition, in that the 'programmes' to which the artists had to keep somewhat incongruously attempted a synthesis of the traditional and the new values. Both Gregorio Guglielmi in Schönbrunn and Franz Anton Maulbertsch in Innsbruck had to devise an allegory in the traditional manner on the military prowess of the house of Habsburg-Lorraine. In each case, however, these allegories, placed in the central areas of their respective ceilings, were flanked by a number of natural terrestrial scenes representing the material resources of the Habsburg lands and the human skills by which they were exploited. The style in which these terrestrial scenes were painted clearly reflects the insistent demand of Enlightened publicists and Neo-classical art critics for plain truth and likeness to nature.

The programme to which Maulbertsch worked in the Innsbruck palace has survived. It was written by Joseph Freiherr von Spergs, the Tyrolean geographer who was one of Kaunitz' principal assistants in the state chancery. Enumerating the agricultural and industrial products of the Tyrol, it expresses that intense delight in nature's bounties and man's productive energy which is so characteristic of the Enlightenment, and which was to find expression again in a different form in Gottfried van Swieten's adaptation of 'The Seasons' which was set to music by Haydn:

The Tyrol's natural wealth *and the military prowess of the Habsburgs are the themes of a series of allegories devised by Joseph von Spergs and executed by Franz Anton Maulbertsch in the Riesensaal of the palace at Innsbruck. Here Ceres and Pomona benignly watch the activities of the industrious Tyrolean people.* (307)

In the first oval sit Ceres and Pomona who look smilingly at the industrious country people . . . From the mines the coined gold and silver, metals from the forges . . . From the fertile Alps cattle, milk and cheese, the most select fruits of trees and earth, the precious wine, and also manufactured silk. In the second oval . . . Mercury, the inspirer of commerce appears, the merchandise of the traders, manufacture of wool, the hunt of chamoix and wildfowl, the felling of timber and its transport along the rivers, spinning, fishing, the lemons and other fruit of the Italian Tyrol, and lastly the transport of goods by packhorse.

The uneasy juxtaposition of Baroque and Neo-classical elements in the interior decoration of Maria Theresa's palaces seems to symbolize the contradictory character of a reign in which radically new policies were adopted, and radical new theories encouraged in justification of these policies – all in the service of highly traditional objectives.

The complete triumph of the neo-classical style in the last decade of Maria Theresa's reign may, similarly, be seen as symbolizing the changing conception of the ultimate objectives after 1763, in which, as C. A. Macartney has suggested, the purely dynastic element receded, and the sovereign attempted a real identification of herself with her subjects. It also reflected the over-riding influence achieved by Kaunitz, who seems to have had a philosophically coherent view at least of internal policy, and who had developed strongly neo-classical tastes. But Maria Theresa would not accept advice which contradicted her own strong feelings even from Kaunitz, and we may safely assume that her own taste

was moving with the times in the direction of Neo-classical simplicity. Her instructions concerning the triumphal arch which was to be erected in Innsbruck on the occasion of the court's visit in 1765 indicate this clearly enough. It was to be like one she had seen and liked in Waitzen (Vác), 'very simple and wholly in the Roman taste', as she herself put it in a letter. And so it was designed by Constantin Walter. It still stands today, in marked contrast to the cheap ostentation of the new buildings which surround and overshadow it.

The scene was set for the triumph of neo-classicism, when Maria Theresa agreed to go ahead with the 'beautification' of the park of Schönbrunn palace. This work took place in the years from 1772 to 1778, and at Maria Theresa's request Kaunitz took on the overall direction of it. We may assume that the choice of the artists to be engaged for it was his. The architect who created the basic plan and design was Ferdinand Hetzendorf von Hohenberg. In his work in Schönbrunn, he gave full reign to that 'nostalgia for classical antiquity' which had come to express at its emotionally most potent level the Enlightenment's challenge to the traditional values of feudal society. He rebuilt Pacassi's Rococo stairway on the park side of the palace on classical lines. Opposite, at the foot of the slope, he placed a monumental Neptune fountain. From the fountain two serpentine paths were taken up the sides of the hill, which was crowned by the Gloriette, a magnificent symposium of antique themes. As nostalgia arouses an insatiable appetite, Hohenberg erected a Roman ruin and an obelisk in other parts of the park.

Joseph (later Joseph II) married Isabella of Parma *in 1760 and after a proxy wedding in Italy the bride was welcomed to Vienna with a dazzling series of feasts and entertainments. Here, in the Redoutensaal, a theatrical performance is being given of Hasse's 'Alcide in Bivio' and Gluck's 'Tetide'. The painting is by Meytens.* (308)

Rococo taste *reached an extreme of elaboration and artifice in the Vienna of Maria Theresa, though by the end of her reign it had yielded to the austerity of Neo-classicism. The bouquet made of silver, rock crystal, and precious stones was fashioned in 1736 by the court jeweller Grosser as an engagement present from Maria Theresa to her future husband Francis of Lorraine.* (309)

The Chinese Cabinet *in Schönbrunn palace: the walls are panelled with black and gold lacquer in gilt frames; above ornaments in Chinese porcelain, the wall brackets bear flowers of enamel. The Rococo style of decoration merged with fashionable chinoiserie to the advantage of both.* (310)

The old chapel of the Hofburg *witnessed the wedding ceremony of Joseph with Isabella of Parma on 6 October 1760. Maria Theresa and her husband stand on the left. Painting by Meytens.* (311)

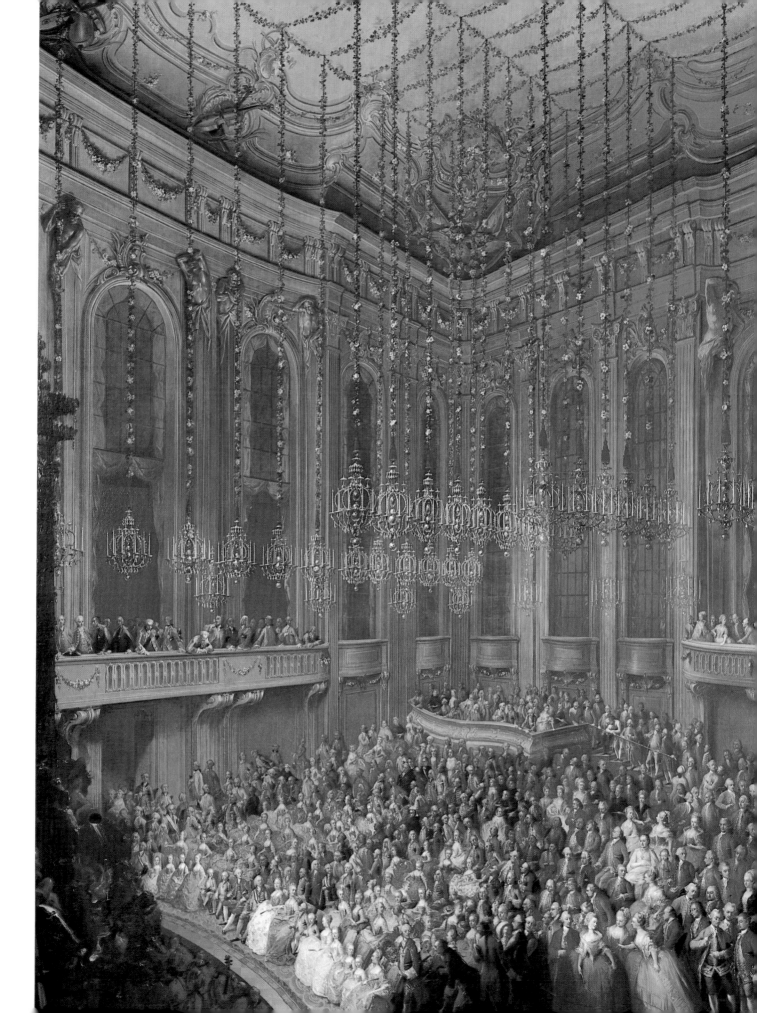

The commission to provide the statuary both for the Neptune fountain and to line the sides of the avenue leading to it from the palace, was given to Johann Wilhelm Beyer who had established his reputation as a Neo-classical artist by his designs for the Ludwigsburg porcelain factory. No less than thirty statues were required to realize Kaunitz' programmatic concepts. Beyer had to engage a number of Austrian collaborators to complete this gigantic task.

If Hohenberg's structures had catered for the insatiable appetite for antique forms, the statues of Beyer and his collaborators evoked the qualities and ideals of which the men of ancient Greece and Republican Rome were believed to have been the most inspiring example. And this makes the statuary of Schönbrunn park unique. In the parks of Versailles, Trianon, and Marly, as Joseph Dernjač has pointed out, there are statues recalling the great figures of Roman Imperial history, such as Augustus, Titus, and Commodus; but one would look in vain there for the heroes of the Republican age. The avenue of Schönbrunn is lined by the heroes of Republican Rome, including assassins of tyrants and generals of peasant origin. Taken from the pages of Plutarch, they represented the qualities of character which were thought to have made ancient Rome great. A few years later, J. L. David would paint the Horatii and Brutus in a similar spirit. Neo-classicism thus brings us close to the ideas of the French Revolution even at the residence of the Habsburg dynasty.

Court theatre and the development of opera

The development which we have traced in the architecture and styles favoured at Maria Theresa's court – from Baroque grandeur and display to stylish and elegant entertainment, and from there to a new emphasis on moral responsibility to which entertainment is subordinated – this same development can, I believe, be seen in the changes affecting the court theatre. Among the economies which had to be effected because of the crisis facing Maria Theresa after her accession, was the discontinuance of the lavish and costly productions of Italian *opera seria*. The last court production of this kind, Metastasio's *Ipermestra*, set to music by Johann Adolf Hasse and with sets by Galli Bibiena, took place on the occasion of Maria Theresa's sister's wedding to Charles of Lorraine in January 1744. Not long after this production, the opera festival hall in the palace, where all the famous productions of this kind had taken place, was rebuilt to serve as the main court ballroom (Grosser Redoutensaal).

As Maria Theresa was no longer able or willing to maintain a court theatre directly, she leased an unused house next to the palace to an impresario, Joseph von Selliers, for dramatic productions to which the public were admitted for payment, while the better boxes were reserved for members of the court, who also had their own entrance accessible directly from the palace. On court occasions, such as birthdays or saints' days of members of the royal family, Von Selliers had to make the Theatre Next to the Palace, as it was now to be called, available for the traditional court entertainment at an agreed fee. At the same time Von Selliers took over the lease of Vienna's public theatre, the Kärntnertortheater (on the site of the present State Opera),

the home of Vienna's still flourishing popular comedy with its traditional knockabout farce and improvisations. The main significance of this development was that it established regular contact between the cultural life of the court and that of the ordinary theatre-going public, a contact that was to become ever closer in the course of Maria Theresa's reign. Henceforth, members of the court and the general public would meet regularly in both theatres, and many new Kärntnertor productions were given a first performance at the Theatre Next to the Palace.

The new 'regular' German drama, as reformed by Johann Christoph Gottsched, was first introduced to the Viennese public in the time of Von Selliers' lease of the Vienna theatres. Among a number of translations from the great French dramatists, Mylius' *Schäferinsel* and Gottsched's own *Cato* were produced. It is a measure of Gottsched's growing influence in Vienna that the first performance of *Cato* in February 1748 was honoured by Maria Theresa's presence. There is little evidence as to the reception of these German productions. On the other hand, the improvised

The gardens of Schönbrunn *reflect that 'nostalgia for classical antiquity' which succeeded Rococo. Following a programme drawn up by Kaunitz, Johann Wilhelm Beyer produced thirty life-size statues for the Neptune fountain and the avenue leading to it, representing figures from Greek legend and Republican Rome. (312)*

293

Maria Theresa's Versailles – *Schönbrunn* – owed its original form to
the great Baroque architect Fischer von Erlach. But the Queen's
retinue was larger than her uncle's and her architect, Nikolaus
Pacassi, was obliged to sacrifice grandeur to convenience. Rooms
were reduced in size, and the central pediment was replaced by an
attic half-storey. The painting by Bellotto shows the palace in 1759.
At the summit of the garden Hohenberg built the 'Gloriette' (far right),
a composition of columns and arches entirely in the Neo-classical style.
(313,314)

German comedies were as popular with the great nobility at
the court theatre as with its home audience at the Kärntnertor.

Despite these new developments, traditional Italian
opera, both *seria* and *buffa*, and Italian comedy, sung and
performed by Italians, continued to provide the staple
repertoire of the court theatre. Pietro Metastasio, the most
renowned Italian poet of his time, provided the majority of
libretti in his capacity as resident court poet. But the music
for many of the Italian operas was composed by Germans
who, like Hasse, had attained a fluent mastery of the musical
conventions of this genre. In 1748, the brothers Lo Presti,
Sicilian adventurers who had made their fortune by gambling, took over Von Selliers' lease and considerably
enlarged the Theatre Next to the Palace. The opening of the
new building coincided with Maria Theresa's birthday and
was celebrated with Metastasio's *La Semiramide Ricono-
sciuta*. This work was selected because it could be produced
particularly lavishly. The music for this august occasion was
composed by Christoph Willibald Gluck. It was his first
major commission for Maria Theresa's court. 'Never,'
comments his biographer Einstein, 'was Gluck more baroque than in this opera.' His attitude to Metastasio's
'monstrous comedy of intrigue and disguise' was 'ingenuous
and uncritical'. Gluck had recently (1745) had the opportunity to study the taste of English audiences, and, as he
later told Dr Burney, had found that 'plainness and
simplicity had the greatest effect upon them'. Setting this
artificial libretto to music may, therefore, have been a
frustrating experience for him. After all, the *Impresa* of the
court theatre was keeping alive an art form, which, in the
changing context of these years, must have seemed to many
increasingly anachronistic.

The overdue change was not delayed much longer.
Festive Italian opera as the staple repertoire of a theatre was
no longer financially viable on any basis. The brothers Lo
Presti went bankrupt in 1752, and we may safely assume
that it would have been difficult to find anyone to take their
place. There was no choice for the court but to resume direct
control and financial responsibility. However, in conformity with changing tastes as well as with changes aspired to
in foreign policy, French drama was to replace Italian drama
on the court stage. The Genoese Count Giacomo Durazzo was
appointed dramatic director of what was now to be called
the Théâtre français près de la Cour. A company of French
actors led by Hébert arrived from The Hague and became
the resident company of the court theatre. French designers
were recruited from Paris. To make sure of a steady supply
of the best French plays, Durazzo carried on a *correspondance
littéraire* with the French playwright Charles Simon Favart,
who became his faithful agent in Paris. Plays by Molière,

Marivaux, Le Sage, Destouches, and others now made up the regular repertoire of the court theatre.

The main problems of the new French theatre arose from the increasingly puritanical attitudes of Maria Theresa. On fifty days in the year there were to be no performances for religious reasons. The French actresses were the object of anxious supervision, because Maria Theresa suspected them collectively of immorality. Above all, most of the plays selected by Durazzo had to be adapted so as not to offend her moral susceptibilities. Durazzo had to explain the position to Favart:

The changes which have to be made if a play is to be transferred from Paris to Vienna, consist of cuts rather than additions. Every double meaning . . . spoils morals or assumes them to be spoilt. Every satire against the clergy can harm religion. Every epigram on the subject of financiers is lost on audiences outside France. Every description of that commerce of gallantry which supplements marriage, and which is generally referred to as 'doubles ménages', would be a scandal in Vienna.

Despite these arbitrary proceedings, the French theatre at Maria Theresa's court provided a stimulating cultural experience for those who saw its productions. The standard of acting was high, even if the excessively declamatory style was slightly dated. The wide range of subject-matter and the high level of dramatic composition expanded the cultural horizons of the Viennese audience. Most important of all, the French comedies, which were really comic operas, as they included light-hearted musical numbers (*vaudeville*), were performed with new musical scores composed by Gluck.

Gluck was engaged by Durazzo in 1754 as court conductor at a salary of two thousand florins. From 1758 onwards, when *L'Isle de Merlin* was produced, this composer, from whom so far nothing but conventional Italian opera had been commissioned, turned to the completely different task of composing 'airs nouveaux' for the French comedies. This meant turning from heroes and heroines involved in complicated plots to a great variety of humbler types in more natural situations. In the light of Gluck's comment on the English audiences' response to 'plainness and simplicity', we may assume that the new task was more in line with his artistic inclinations. According to his biographer Einstein, he achieved it with complete success:

The composer of Italian *opera seria* . . . is to be recognized only in the ease with which he acquitted himself of his musical task. He is here concerned with stupid, mean, or grumbling old men, shy pairs of lovers, roguish girls, merry lads, beatific drunkards – all of whom are characterized in a masterly way by delicate strokes, and from among many conventionalities emerge little melodic blossoms, tiny melodic piquancies of the utmost charm. The spirit which Rousseau called 'the return to nature' is to be perceived everywhere; in the orchestra nature's ways are painted by means of figuration and tone colour.

Gluck's style developed rapidly. In *La Rencontre Imprévue*, Dancourt's adaptation of *Les Pèlerins de la Mecque*, which was first performed in 1764, he created a new type of comic opera. He adorned a French *opéra comique* plot with a musical score of the richness and amplitude derived from the Italian tradition, and thus combined comic action with nobility of characterization and feeling. The work was widely performed in a German version in the 1770s, and inspired Mozart to attempt the same combination in *Die Entführung aus dem Serail*.

The success of the French comic opera stimulated the demand for a reform of *opera seria*. The critics of *opera seria* believed that in its original seventeenth-century form it partook of those qualities of naturalness and simplicity it so conspicuously lacked in their own time. In 1761, the Livornese author Raniero Calzabigi arrived in Vienna. He had published a critical commentary on the dramatic poetry of Metastasio. Calzabigi argued that the only music suitable for dramatic poetry was music which came as close as possible to natural declamation. Natural declamation he saw as itself a kind of music which, because incomplete, required musical supplementation. Therefore, he argued, the simpler, the more passionate and moving the poetry, the more the music, written to give added expression to it, would approach perfection. In other words, Calzabigi was applying to music drama the criteria and values of the Enlightenment, with their emphasis on naturalness and genuine feeling, which helped to stimulate the changing tastes in architecture, painting, and sculpture referred to earlier in this chapter.

Durazzo, who was probably acquainted with Calzabigi, wanted to produce an *opera seria* based on these 'reformed' aesthetic principles in the court theatre. Convinced that Gluck was the appropriate composer for this project, he introduced him to the recently arrived author. According to his own later account, Calzabigi did indeed discover that Gluck's artistic aspirations corresponded closely to the aesthetic theories he was trying to propagate.

'Gluck thought little of Metastasio's meticulous dramas,' he later recalled.

> He was of opinion that this high-flown poetry and these neatly manufactured characters had nothing that was great and elevated to offer to music . . . Gluck hated those meek political, philosophical and moral views of Metastasio's, his metaphors, his garrulous little passions, his geometrically devised word-plays. Gluck liked emotions captured from simple nature, mighty passions at boiling-point . . .

The result of the two men's exchange of views was that Calzabigi offered Gluck his libretto *Orfeo ed Euridice*. Here the story is presented in its simplest outlines and with a minimum of dialogue. A sequence of simple scenes or 'pictures' provides the framework for the expression of the deepest human emotions, from which nothing is allowed to distract the audience. Librettist and composer collaborated in unprecedented closeness in the creation of the work in pursuit of the over-riding objective of truth to nature.

'I read him my Orpheus,' Calzabigi recalled, 'and declaimed several pieces to him repeatedly, drawing his attention to the inflections I put into my delivery, the suspensions, the slowness, the speed, the tone of voice, now full, now restrained and slurred over, which I wanted him to take account of in his composition. At the same time I begged him to banish *i passaggi*, *le cadenze*, *i ritornelli*, and all the gothic, barbaric and extravagant accretions from our music. M. Gluck accepted my views.'

Gluck drew on the forms he had developed in his compositions for the French comedies to achieve the desired effects in *Orfeo*. In the simple melodic line he found the most authentic expression of deep emotion. Thus, as Patricia Howard has put it, he 'exalted an originally plebeian language to serious opera'.

In the rehearsals Calzabigi directed the acting of the singers to ensure that their style was not at variance with the desired emotional effect. Poet and composer acknowledged themselves fortunate that in Guadagni, who created the role of Orpheus, they had a singer of sufficient sensibility and understanding to enter into the spirit of the work, renouncing all virtuoso effects. The dancers, directed by Angiolini, likewise confined themselves to pantomime, grace, and expression of feeling, eschewing technical feats not in keeping with dramatic truth.

Orfeo, the first great neo-classical *opera seria*, had its opening performance in the court theatre in October 1762. Five years later, Calzabigi and Gluck cooperated in the creation of *Alceste*, which was based on the same principles, now fully spelt out in a preface. The audience reaction to the new art form was divided. Those who wrote in the periodical press, both reflecting and helping to shape an increasingly influential 'public opinion', understood the intentions of poet and composer, and found themselves deeply moved. 'The characters and the passions are expressed clearly and effectively,' wrote the anonymous reviewer of the *Wiener Zeitung* after the first performance of *Orfeo*. Sonnenfels, Vienna's most renowned literary critic, wrote after the first performance of *Alceste* that Gluck had discovered 'the accents of the soul'. Another article in the *Wiener Zeitung* referred to Gluck as 'the leader of our hearts' who can take them where he will.

The reaction of the court audience was by comparison reserved in the extreme. Maria Theresa, it was reported, disliked *Orfeo* at the first hearing, but took to it after hearing it a second time. Count Zinzendorf complained in his diary of its rapid changes of passion. The court diarist Khevenhüller, whose diary for 1762 is unfortunately missing, thought *Alceste* 'excessively pathetic and lugubrious'. Clearly, the courtiers missed the ostentatious sparkle of conventional *opera seria*. The Neo-classical conception of the theatre as a mirror of nature and a school of the emotions seemed to them, as Sonnenfels scornfully noted, merely a formula for mournful and depressing productions. The fact that Maria Theresa's court theatre had launched 'reform opera', which actually silenced Metastasio as a dramatic poet, demonstrates to what extent it had become something more than a court theatre long before the change in its official title acknowledged the fact.

The triumph of German drama

By the time Gluck and Calzabigi were introducing neo-classical opera in Vienna, the future of the Théâtre français près de la Cour was already in serious doubt. The expenses incurred as a result of the Seven Years' War (1756–63) overstrained the resources of Maria Theresa's territories, and brought the monarchy to a state of near-bankruptcy.

Already in 1759 Maria Theresa was compelled to reduce her expenditure on the theatre. But as there had to be a theatre, she reluctantly agreed to the establishment of a gambling saloon in the Theatre Next to the Palace, to which only the higher nobility were admitted, and the profits of which were used to cover the theatre deficit. By this device, the French theatre, which was far more expensive than the German theatre at the Kärntnertor, was given a short reprieve.

After the unexpected death of her husband in August 1765, Maria Theresa ordered that both Viennese theatres be closed indefinitely. The German actors were paid a modest retaining fee, and the French company was dismissed. After a period of eight months, the German theatre was allowed to reopen at the Kärntnertor, but found itself once again on lease to an impresario. The Theatre Next to the Palace reopened after a closure of more than two years under the same lease. The German actors, under the dramatic direction of Heufeld, took advantage of their presumably temporary monopoly of the Viennese stage to concentrate on the regular German drama, favoured by the spokesmen of bourgeois opinion, at the expense of the improvised farces. Among their rapidly growing repertoire, they presented Lessing's early plays, though not without some arbitrary cuts and adaptations. Nevertheless, the nobility clamoured for the return of a French company. For, in truth, the only German drama the nobility appreciated was the improvised farce, now loudly condemned by the spokesmen of bourgeois opinion as unworthy of a self-respecting nation. Giuseppe d'Afflisio, the impresario who had the lease of the two theatres, responded to the insistent clamour, and engaged a French company in 1768. During this second reprieve, the French drama in Vienna enjoyed an 'Indian summer'. The standard of acting was higher than before, and the repertoire impressively wide. But the expenses involved in maintaining a French company quickly exhausted d'Afflisio's resources, and he surrendered his lease to the young aristocratic theatre enthusiast Count Kohary. By early 1772, Kohary found himself in exactly the same position. As no one else was now willing to take on a lease which spelt speedy financial disaster, Kohary staved off bankruptcy by dismissing the French company. Thus the French theatre staged its 'definitely last' performance in Vienna in February 1772 with Goldoni's *Bourru Bienfaisant,* the play he had written for Marie-Antoinette's wedding.

The field was at last clear for the German bourgeois drama. But if the nobility had been unable to finance *their* theatre without court subvention, how much less were the modestly circumstanced Viennese bourgeois in a position to finance theirs! The only German theatre which could cover its expenses from receipts was the traditional popular comedy with its mass plebeian audience. This was now hamstrung by increasingly strict government prohibition of improvisation. Kohary, threatened with bankruptcy, repeatedly pleaded with the government for a relaxation of the prohibition. In this situation, so full of both promise and peril for his aspirations, Sonnenfels addressed himself directly to the government to submit on behalf of the middle class the case for state support for their theatre:

Music *underwent the same revolution as art, based on the search for simplicity and truth to nature. The new movement found a leader of genius in Christoph Willibald Gluck, who was appointed court composer in Vienna in 1754. (315)*

Is the high nobility the only object of public concern? Is it fair that the needs of the citizen [*Bürger*] who contributes no less to the general welfare, should be totally ignored? The middle classes have a far stronger claim that the state should provide them with decent entertainment than the nobles whose large fortunes enable them to provide for their own. The limited means of the middle classes confine them to the theatre as their main entertainment. If they are deprived of that, they will turn to other forms of entertainment harmful to morality.

The phrasing suggests that the appeal was addressed to Joseph II. The theatre was the one sphere of public affairs which Maria Theresa, lacking a strong personal interest, was prepared to leave to the Co-Regent's exclusive control during the last decade of her reign. Joseph was adamant in his refusal to relax the prohibition on improvisation. But that was tantamount to condemning Kohary to imminent bankruptcy. He no longer had the resources to cover the deficit incurred by productions of regular German drama. Only four years after the dismissal of the French company, Kohary declared total bankruptcy. As in 1752, the court was compelled to resume direct control and financial responsibility. In deciding what kind of drama to sponsor, Joseph characteristically considered the needs of 'national education' rather than of court entertainment. In other words, he was going to give the middle classes, as Sonnenfels had pleaded, *their* entertainment, for they, in contrast to the nobility, conceived of it as a kind of education. He gave the German actors a permanent home in the Theatre Next to the Palace, which was renamed Hof-und Nationaltheater. The Italian actors and singers were dismissed. The Kärntnertor-theater was put at the disposal of travelling companies performing in any language.

This was a development of momentous importance for the history of German drama. It was the first example of a major theatre being exclusively dedicated to German drama since Lessing's failure to establish a German national theatre in Hamburg. Nothing could have added more to the prestige of German drama than the theatre of the Imperial court becoming a Nationaltheater. It was clearly Joseph's example which was being followed when the Elector Palatine established a Nationaltheater in Mannheim less than a year later.

However, the example would have been of little significance in the long run, if Joseph II had not made a success of the reorganized theatre. Regular German drama in Vienna had been gaining in prestige during the last ten years or so of its coexistence with more favoured forms of dramatic art. The German actors had developed a sense of professional dignity which had made them increasingly reluctant to participate in the crude antics which were all that remained of the popular comedy after the censorship had suppressed the ambiguous allusions and the witty dialogue. The standard of acting improved markedly when J. H. F. Müller, Joseph Lange, and the Jacquets joined the German company of actors in the 1760s. At the same time, the supply of plays of reasonable dramatic quality and based on themes of general interest also increased. There is no mistaking the profound impression made on middle-class audiences by such plays as Lillo's *London Merchant*, Lessing's *Miss Sarah Sampson* and *Minna von Barnhelm*, and the latter's translation of Diderot's *Père de Famille*.

However, any real flourishing of German drama was precluded until the foundation of the Nationaltheater in 1776 by the feud between the rival dramatic genres and the uncertainties and frequent changes in management and dramatic direction to which this gave rise. Joseph II made such a flourishing possible by offering the German actors financial security, official recognition, and consistent dramatic direction.

This brings us to one of the most remarkable aspects of Joseph II's reorganization of the court theatre. The general manager and to some extent the dramatic director of the Hof-und Nationaltheater was none other than Joseph himself. He looked out for competent actors and singers to be engaged. He laid down the long-term policy in relation to repertoire. In particular, it was his decision that regular German drama or good translations should continue to provide the bulk of the programme, despite the small audience for this type of entertainment at the start. His own regular visits to the theatre and the rising standard of acting due to his insistence on adequate rehearsals, was quickly rewarded by larger audiences, though the mass of the population patronized the new suburban theatres founded in the 1780s, where a remarkable revival of the popular comedy took place. In

1778 music drama was restored to the repertoire to attract a bigger audience, but in the form of German opera (*deutsches Singspiel*), which had never before been heard in Vienna. The standard of musical performance seems to have been very high. Mozart's *Entführung* was commissioned for the German opera at the Nationaltheater. In the field of music, however, the nobility's strong preference for Italian fare could not be ignored indefinitely, even by Joseph II, and in 1783 Italian *opera buffa* replaced the German *Singspiel*.

Despite this setback in the field of music drama, the Vienna theatre under Joseph II's direction became one of the great centres for the cultivation of the German spoken drama. Many of the great German plays written in this period were introduced to the Viennese public in good productions – Lessing's *Emilia Galotti* and Goethe's *Clavigo* to name but two. Soon, the first of the new Shakespeare translations were produced. Many of the plays written for the Nationaltheater, which have not stood the test of time, were successful, because their authors raised topical issues and wrote in accordance with the prevailing aesthetic norms. That the German theatre before long won the support of Kaunitz, hitherto the staunchest protagonist of the French theatre, is the most eloquent testimony to its success.

A stain on Joseph II's record as a reformer of the theatre was his censorship policy. Hardly any play brought in from outside escaped arbitrary cuts and adaptations to make it conform to the numerous, often pedantic and absurd censorship regulations. The actual wording of the regulations was that of the theatre censor Karl Hägelin, appointed in 1774. But in the mixture of moral prudery and concern for the prestige of traditional authority underlying them, it is possible to discern the influence of Maria Theresa, from which Joseph II, contrary to common belief, never completely emancipated himself. Under these regulations, Lessing's last and greatest play, *Nathan der Weise*, with its assertion of the ethical equivalence of all religions, and Schiller's early revolutionary plays could not be performed.

Literature: 'a useful influence in matters of state'

With the establishment of the *Nationaltheater*, the court at Vienna had, in the end, fulfilled the high hopes expressed by the German writers of the time. The hopes that the court at Vienna would similarly sponsor other forms of cultural endeavour, however frequently kindled in the course of Maria Theresa's reign, were always in the end disappointed.

It is difficult to avoid the impression that Maria Theresa's interest in the theatre reflected a sense of its importance as part of the 'representation' of a great court, rather than a deep personal appreciation of this particular art form. This impression is reinforced by the fact that, apart from maintaining, directly or indirectly, a court theatre, she gave little encouragement to men of letters and learning. In this respect, too, Joseph II followed in her footsteps.

There was a widespread and frequently expressed feeling among the German writers of this time that Vienna, as the closest approximation to a capital that divided Germany had, should become the cultural centre to which German arts and sciences could look for patronage and encourage-

There were sixteen children. *Four died in infancy. This family group by Martin van Meytens shows eleven of them. Marianne, the eldest, stands next to her father; Joseph, the heir, the future Joseph II, is in the centre near his mother. Note, by Francis' elbow, the Imperial crown and orb, and next to the Queen the two crowns of Hungary and Bohemia. (316)*

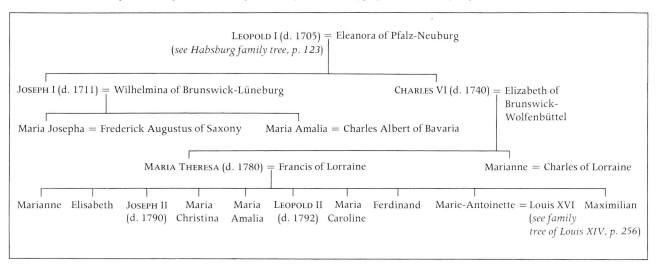

299

ment. The tendency to look to Vienna was, of course, reinforced by Frederick II's openly advertised contempt for German culture. The wish tended to become father of the thought, and it is astonishing how easily some writers' hopes were kindled that a plan for the advancement of German culture was being seriously considered at the court in Vienna. Sometimes such hopes were unduly encouraged by sincere admirers and well-wishers of these writers in Vienna.

The first of the hopefuls was Johann Christoph Gottsched, the Protestant Leipzig professor, who almost single-handedly laid the cultural foundation for the revival of German self-confidence and German literature. During the 1740s, he came into contact with some of his followers in the Habsburg territories, who sent him all the evidence they could find of his growing influence, including the news that Maria Theresa had attended the first performance of his *Cato* in 1748.

Encouraged by these reports, Gottsched urged one of his Viennese correspondents, the poet Franz Christoph Scheyb, to establish a German Society in Vienna in order to make the Habsburg monarchy more fertile ground for German cultural endeavours. Scheyb's reply, with its lively description of the methods employed by the Jesuits to nip such developments in the bud, may have suggested to Gottsched the idea of coming to Vienna in person. Together with his famous wife, he arrived in Vienna in September 1749. Through the efforts of their supporters at court, the couple were granted an audience of three quarters of an hour with Maria Theresa and Francis. They were treated with all due respect; Maria Theresa agreed to accept the dedication of Louise Gottsched's history of the Paris Académie des Inscriptions et des Belles Lettres; and after their return they received the customary gifts. This added greatly to Gottsched's prestige and literary authority throughout Germany; but his project for a learned society or academy on the Parisian model was nevertheless rejected. The ministers consulted by Maria Theresa on this question expressed doubts as to the availability of a sufficient number of learned men of the Catholic religion, and they pleaded lack of funds.

Hopes of an academy and similar institutions were rekindled when Joseph became Emperor in 1765. The young Emperor's entourage contained men whose attachment to German culture was well known. The Austrian ambassador to Copenhagen was in touch with these men, and had established a close friendship with Friedrich Gottlieb Klopstock, the famous author of the epic *Messias,* who was stirring the German literary world with his bardic poetry. In 1768, Klopstock transmitted a project for the advancement of German culture to the Emperor. This differed considerably from the usual concept of an academy. It included the idea of an officially sponsored monumental history of Germany, a system of national prizes for great achievements in the arts and sciences, and a national theatre. There was an unspoken implication of an appointment for Klopstock to supervise it all.

Klopstock embarked on negotiations concerning his project with the rather original idea of exchanging a

dedication to Joseph II of his intensely patriotic bardic drama *Herrmanns-Schlacht,* which he had just completed, for a firm commitment to carry out the project. The dedication was so worded as to make an acceptance of it tantamount to entering upon such a commitment:

When a historian speaks, it is not he who praises, but the deed. And I may call deed that which has been decided and will happen soon. The Emperor loves his country and he wishes to demonstrate this, not least by giving his support to the sciences . . . I know of no stronger expression of the admiration in which I approach Your Imperial Majesty with the presentation of this poem than to wish my fatherland and Your Majesty success for all that you want to do for the sciences. Never have I been more proud of my fatherland than now as I think of this prospect.

Joseph, it seems examined the draft dedication from an exclusively diplomatic point of view, in the light of which he considered a sharply critical reference to Frederick II's contempt for German culture undesirable. Kaunitz, submitting his opinion on the matter, agreed on the necessity of striking out the reference to Frederick, and did not attempt to conceal his contempt for most of Klopstock's project. Nevertheless, he strongly advised Joseph not to decline the dedication on the following grounds:

In my humble opinion it would be unwise to give Klopstock a negative reply, because this man has gained a particular respect throughout Germany, and the words of such a poet usually determine the attitude of the public and arouse its enthusiasm. To win this enthusiasm is not to be regarded only as vainglory, but as a useful influence in matters of state. Therefore a golden chain or medal might also be appropriate for the said Klopstock.

The condition implied by Klopstock in the wording of the dedication evidently escaped both Kaunitz and Joseph.

Klopstock was naturally overjoyed when he heard of the acceptance of his dedication. He arranged for the printing of the *Herrmanns-Schlacht,* convinced that its publication would be the signal for the official announcement of his project, and for an invitation to himself to come to Vienna. Not until the middle of 1770 did he begin to realize that Joseph had either misunderstood the dedication or broken his promise. In order to justify his conduct and to explain the dedication which must have been puzzling to most readers, Klopstock published extracts from the project and from the correspondence to which it had given rise, as a kind of appendix to his next major publication, the *Gelehrtenrepublik.*

After these disappointed hopes, it need not surprise that Lessing was deeply sceptical about the chances of an appointment in Vienna. As he fiercely resented his treatment at the hands of his employer, the hereditary Prince of Brunswick, and as he was getting into debt, and could not endure the isolation of his existence in Wolfenbüttel, he certainly would have welcomed an offer from Vienna. There he would at least enjoy human companionship again; and, as it happened, an appointment in Vienna would have made possible a speedy marriage to his betrothed Eva König, who had moved to Vienna after inheriting two factories there. But Lessing, like Klopstock, never received a firm offer.

Science was well served both by Maria Theresa and her husband. Here Francis sits among his natural history collection, with four of the men whom the court employed and encouraged: Gerard van Swieten, the Queen's doctor, and reformer of the University; Jean de Baillou (from whom Francis acquired the nucleus of his collection); Valentin Duval, the director of Francis' coin collection; and Jean François Marci, mathematician and numismatist, who taught mathematics to some of Maria Theresa's children. (317)

Efforts, probably originating with Kaunitz, were made in 1771–72, to revive the project of an Academy of Sciences, and Austrian ambassadors sounded out possible candidates. Gottfried van Swieten, ambassador in Berlin, established indirect contact with Lessing, held out glowing prospects, but lacked the authority to make a concrete offer. Lessing subsequently lost interest, as Eva König made it clear that she would prefer to live with him in quiet Wolfenbüttel rather than in Vienna, and took steps to sell her factories. Thereupon, as a study of Lessing's letters makes clear, he

was interested in offers of appointments, whether in Vienna or elsewhere, only as a means of improving his bargaining position in securing a rise in his salary from the 'frugal' Prince of Brunswick. The trip on which he embarked early in 1775, which took him to Vienna in April of that year, must be seen in that light. As Franz Mehring has said, Vienna and Maria Theresa demonstrated that they at least knew how one received and treated a man of Lessing's stature. His plays were performed at the court theatre in his honour (and performed rather better than he expected); he was given ovations when he appeared at the theatre; and Maria Theresa received him in audience, just as she had received Gottsched a quarter of a century before. But as she had just declared her unwillingness to provide any funds for the endowment of an academy, the question of an appointment for Lessing was not raised. Lessing, in his turn, deliberately avoided a meeting with Kaunitz, who was almost certainly the moving spirit behind the efforts to win him for Vienna. After his return to Wolfenbüttel, Lessing did secure his rise in salary.

301

Its relationship with the men of letters, then, is not a very creditable aspect of the history of Maria Theresa's court. If men of science fared rather better, this was due to a large extent to Maria Theresa's good sense in matters of health. She was able to recognize and bring to her court two of the greatest medical practitioners of the time. The Dutchman Gerard van Swieten, Boerhaave's greatest disciple, combined the task of caring for the health of Maria Theresa and her family with that of reforming the universities of the Habsburg monarchy, where he introduced not only up-to-date medical science, but Wolffian philosophy, chemistry, botany, and history. After the terrible smallpox epidemic of 1767, which wrought such havoc among Maria Theresa's family and of which she was herself a victim, she asked George III to recommend to her a successful practitioner of inoculation. As a result of this request, the great Ingen-Housz came to Vienna. He successfully inoculated Maria Theresa's surviving children, and organized an inoculation campaign in the Habsburg provinces. Maria Theresa was so profoundly grateful to him that she granted him a large pension for life. This afforded him the leisure he had long desired to carry out scientific experiments in the course of which he made the momentous discovery of photosynthesis, i.e. the fact that green plants absorb carbon dioxide from the air in daylight, but not in the dark. Later he developed the science of plant nutrition.

Science at the court of Vienna also profited from the scientific interests and hobbies of Francis of Lorraine. He observed the electrical experiments of the Jesuit physicist Joseph Franz, and established a chemical laboratory in his private residence in Vienna. Above all, he was a passionate collector. He bought and expanded the celebrated natural history collection of Jean de Baillou, and employed the Dutch naturalists Adrian van Steckhoven and Van der Schot to establish in the grounds of Schönbrunn a botanical garden which contained one of Europe's richest collections of tropical plants. It was here that Nikolaus Joseph Jacquin, whom Van Swieten had invited to Vienna, gained his basic botanical knowledge. The Emperor commissioned Jacquin to publish a descriptive flora of the Schönbrunn garden. In doing this, he became the first botanist to apply Linnaeus' method of classification. In 1755, Jacquin and Van der Schot left on an expedition to the West Indies and South America, on which Francis spent thirty thousand florins. They returned in 1759 with many species of live plants and animals rarely, if ever, seen before in Europe. As a result of this success, it became possible to get a comprehensive idea of West Indian flora. The 'Dutch botanical garden' at Schönbrunn became famous throughout Europe, the palm house being a particular attraction. Half a century later, Alexander von Humboldt was to make a point of visiting it before setting out on his South American expedition.

Art and academies

The greatest beneficiaries of patronage at the court of Maria Theresa were the practitioners of the fine arts, the painters, sculptors, and engravers. In the fine arts, Maria Theresa's own inclinations harmonized with Kaunitz' ideas. Thus, while thwarted in most of his efforts on behalf of literature

and science, the Minister was able to translate all his ideas on the fine arts into practice.

An Academy of Fine Art had existed in Vienna since the late seventeenth century, but in the reign of Joseph I the court assumed control and financial responsibility. Like so many other cultural institutions, the Academy fell victim to the crisis which followed Maria Theresa's accession, and formal teaching was discontinued. After the conclusion of the War of the Austrian Succession, teaching was resumed. The directorship rotated among the more prominent painters for a time. But in 1759 Martin van Meytens, Maria Theresa's chief court painter, obtained the directorship and then retained it until his death in 1770.

After the conclusion of the Seven Years' War, the government embarked on a comprehensive policy of raising the level of economic activity. In the context of the prevailing mercantilist ideas, artistic production was regarded as a 'native industry' which should be encouraged and protected against foreign competition. From this point of view, the graphic arts, for which there was then a rapidly growing market, seemed the most important of the fine arts. As the existing Academy did not cater for them, Maria Theresa provided the money to send the two leading Austrian engravers Jakob Schmutzer and Johann Gottfried Haid to Paris to perfect their art. When they returned, Schmutzer was appointed to head a newly established Academy of Engraving. Imports of etchings from the traditional suppliers in Augsburg and Nuremberg were now actively discouraged.

The number of students increased so rapidly that there were soon problems of accommodation, and an unhealthy rivalry between the two academies developed. The time was ripe for reorganization, and Maria Theresa transmitted a proposal for the unification of all the art academies to Kaunitz for his opinion. In justifying his approval of the proposal, Kaunitz fully developed his ideas on the political importance of the fine arts and their contribution to industrial development:

Good taste . . . has an effect on manufacture and trades. It can bring into existence new sections of the economy. It stimulates industry. A lot of money . . . which previously . . . flowed out of the country, remains inside it, and more and more money flows in from outside. France provides a convincing example of this. For Louis XIV greatly enlarged the French kingdom through his military campaigns and conquests, and thus established his glory. But his memory would be . . . abominated by the nation today, because his victories exhausted its treasure, its men and its resources to such a degree that the after-effects are still felt, if he had not at the same time . . . encouraged . . . the arts, and with them the manufactures of his kingdom, and raised them to such a high level of excellence. The Academy in Paris and Rome which he founded and richly endowed, were the first of their kind and laid the foundation for the prosperity which . . . has put France ahead of all other countries. It is certain that the great masters Poussin, Le Brun, Girardin, Mansard and many others have contributed more to the welfare of the nation through improving taste in manufactured products and training good students, than Condé, Turenne, Luxembourg, Vauban, Villars and other generals. The latter would have impoverished and ruined France . . . despite her territorial expansion, if the former had not raised her up again by their very different activity. The genius of innovation is awakened by the arts and taste is refined, so that France has now attained a dominant position in . . . the whole field of luxury goods.

If good artists could thus revolutionize a country's economic position, the sovereign could make no better investment than to endow the school in which they were going to be trained. Maria Theresa sanctioned the proposal, and a single Academy of Fine Arts with sections for painting, sculpture, architecture, and engraving was established in November 1772. Kaunitz became its president, Sonnenfels its secretary.

Detailed proposals on methods of teaching were made by Anton Maron, an Austrian neo-classical painter residing in Rome. He persuaded Maria Theresa that copying from the ancients and from the great masters of Italian painting was an essential part of the training for a good artist. In accordance with this advice, Maria Theresa endowed a number of Rome scholarships of six hundred florins each, to be held by students recommended by the Academy. As the Habsburg collection, since the acquisitions of Archduke Leopold William, was particularly rich in the great Italian masters, it was now taken out of the inaccessible Stallburg, rearranged, and hung in the Belvedere, where not only the students of the Academy but also the general public were admitted free of charge – if their shoes were clean. The enormous task of rearrangement was carried out by the gallery director, Joseph Rosa, with the help of the Basle engraver Christian von Mechel. The aim was to use the rooms in the Belvedere in such a way that the gallery became 'a visible history of art', providing lasting instruction rather than ephemeral pleasure. This was a very neo-classical objective, and it corresponds exactly to what Joseph II was trying to achieve in his reform of the theatre. The new gallery, exhibiting more than a thousand works, was opened shortly after Maria Theresa's death, and was visited by large numbers of the general public.

In the course of Maria Theresa's long reign, her court underwent a far-reaching transformation. Having been a means for the display of Baroque grandeur and the representation of dynastic power, it eventually became a centre for the promotion of instruction and moral improvement in the spirit of neo-classicism. Though Maria Theresa's own understanding and feeling for the arts was limited, she always allowed men whose understanding was larger and whose feelings were more deeply committed than hers, to manage the cultural side of court life, and she gave these men just sufficient latitude to make success possible. As a result, the court of Maria Theresa was throughout her reign one of those great centres of European culture, which helped to stimulate the period's most important and lasting cultural achievements.

THERESIENS LEZTER TAG.

Maria Theresa's last day: *a charming vignette, with figures in silhouette, showing Maria Theresa, mortally ill, in a chair with her family around her. (318)*

Fourteen

LOUIS XV
Public and private worlds

✴

J. H. SHENNAN

OUIS XV was King of France for fifty-nine years, only thirteen fewer than the epic span of his great-grandfather; and the two reigns have more than longevity in common. In particular each has come to be so dominated by the personality of the ruler that merely to recite the King's name suffices to invoke an image – however inaccurate or distorted – of his age. At first glance it may seem surprising that Louis XV, who was irresolute, withdrawn, and easily bored, should make as indelible an impression as his strong-minded and extrovert predecessor, whose highly regulated routine left no time for boredom. The fact is that in this matter Louis XV owed a great deal to Louis XIV. The latter had worked particularly hard not at making the Crown the social and political cornerstone of the state – it had been that for a long time – but at publicizing and ritualizing the fact. Although in 1715 the young Louis inherited a bankrupt and hard-pressed kingdom, he also succeeded to the greatest leading role available in Europe, and it would have taken a far poorer actor than he to muff his lines. For some time to come the audience remained captive, dazzled by the *coup de théâtre* provided at Versailles; becoming aware nevertheless, slowly and hesitatingly, that that particular entertainment no longer had any meaning for them. Thus Louis XV's court basked in the time bought for it by his great-grandfather. Though it operated according to the rigid rules of the previous reign it focused a new spirit, sensuous and inventive and burgeoning, which, unbridled, offered mere wanton extravagance, a Roman feast; but at its best an elegance and refinement to catch the breath and elevate the name of Louis Quinze even above that of his illustrious predecessor.

The Regency

The first eight years of the reign were spent under the regency of the late King's nephew, Philippe of Orléans, for Louis was only five years old at the time of his great-

grandfather's death in 1715. Until his majority therefore, the royal court was effectively the Regent's. This period marked an incipient break in Bourbon government in a variety of ways: Philippe was among the most original and gifted members of the family and in other circumstances his short rule might have produced a radical realignment of French policy. That it did not do so may be attributed in part to flaws in his own character, though they were no more to blame than the intellectual and personal preferences of the new King. Aside from the might-have-beens of Orléans' regime one tradition was indubitably broken, albeit temporarily: even before the old King's body had been laid to rest at St Denis the new sovereign had left Versailles on 9 September 1715 for the palace of Vincennes and later the Tuileries. He was followed at once by the court and the great palace was left empty for almost seven years, a symbol, or so it seemed, of an outmoded regime. The Palais Royal became the new hub of the social and political world, libertarian, epicurean, licentious. It was no place for the *dévots* of the last reign: Madame de Maintenon withdrew to the tranquil environs of Saint-Cyr.

Orléans' lifetime reputation has pursued him through the generations following his death and, unjustly treated by historians, he remains the 'fanfaron de crimes' of Louis XIV's striking phrase, a sinister influence on the young King. He certainly inherited the Bourbons' sexual appetites; though it was less the number of his conquests, impressive as that figure was, than the publicity with which he conducted his *affaires* and the unimpressive lineage of his paramours which caused offence. The ladies of the court did not appeal to Orléans: he much preferred *chanteuses* and actresses from the Opéra and the Comédie Française. Similarly his infamous 'suppers' at the Palais Royal offended polite society as much by their notoriety and their guest lists as by their undoubted lubricity. Yet, like Louis XIV before him, Orléans strictly separated business from pleasure, and though he became intoxicated after very little wine he could never be induced to discuss matters of state during his frequent bouts of junketing.

There were other aspects of the Regent's reputation which rendered him suspect as the custodian of the kingdom during Louis XV's minority. He was a sceptic and a deist

A profile medallion of Louis XV *surmounted by the French royal crown forms the back of a turquoise Sèvres clock of about 1770. The porcelain factory at Sèvres was established there in 1756 under the patronage of Madame de Pompadour. (319)*

who allegedly read Rabelais in church; and, worse even than that, indulged in chemical experiments which, according to malicious gossip, had turned him into a poisoner intent on eliminating his rivals for the throne: hence the sudden deaths of the Dauphin in 1711 and of the Dauphin's son and grandson in 1712. The grosser charges levelled against Orléans, including the accusation of incest with his daughter, the Duchesse de Berry, were groundless. He was a freethinker, however, whose intellectual inclinations leant towards the Enlightenment and away from the divine right orthodoxies inherited from the former regime. Yet those orthodoxies, which were to become less meaningful as the century progressed and *le roi très chrétien* gradually lost his awesome hold over his subjects' minds, remained at the heart of French government in 1715. Orléans was determined that his charge should inherit the kingdom with authority undiminished, and so began to appear the dangerous gulf between absolute power and its outmoded justification. Orléans proved to be an efficient administrator of the kingdom and a conscientious guardian of the young Louis, but he was too honest and intelligent to seek to portray himself as a latter-day Bossuet.

The contradictions in the Regent's character make him a fascinating though difficult subject for the biographer. In giving due weight to the coarseness and vulgarity of Philippe's behaviour with his *roués*, for example, it is tempting to play down the refinement of taste and delicacy of feeling which he also displayed, and which was reflected in the changing fashions of the Regency. He had a special affection for the fine arts, and painting in particular; his collection of some five hundred canvases, ranging from the

The Regent Philippe d'Orléans, *contrary to the will of the late King Louis XIV, gave France absolute, albeit competent, government during Louis XV's minority. His gesture indicates the young King, who is accompanied by his tutor. (320)*

306

Italian Renaissance masters to the contemporary Watteau, was of major artistic significance. A considerable part of it may be found today in the National Galleries of London and Scotland. It was while this complex personality presided over the French state that *rocaille* became the definitive decorative style of the age – though it had struggled to assert itself in the last years of Louis XIV's reign. Later given the derisory name of Rococo, the art of Louis XV's reign was at first restrained and delicate, free from the eccentricities which ultimately threatened to turn the style into self-caricature. It is impossible to find a precise definition for it: most suggestive perhaps is the analogy with the crest of a wave frozen at the instant of its unfurling. Characterized by a sense of elegant disorder, its curved lines embody subjects largely abstracted from nature, a cascading profusion of shells and vines and foliage. It was to be found in the decoration of aristocratic salons, in painting, embroidery, and furniture. If it reflected something of the Regency's lack of restraint, of its exuberance and sensuality, it still maintained a sense of order and discipline which would only diminish as its aristocratic patrons lost their own sense of purpose. Under Orléans the new style made a particularly noteworthy contribution to the rich bronze decoration of the commode, a piece of furniture characteristic of the eighteenth century which made its first appearance as the commode *à la Régence*.

In the shadow of the exciting, febrile, and contradictory world of the Palais Royal with its mixture of elegance and vulgarity, taste and tastelessness, Louis XV grew up. His governor was the elderly Marshal de Villeroy who, having been born only six years after Louis XIV, sought to make his new master a replica of the old. Despite being an orphan from the age of two Louis did not become deeply attached to Villeroy, who was a conventional, inflexible old man of limited intellect and a most undistinguished military record. The King was fonder of Madame de Ventadour, his governess, to whom he believed he owed his life. In 1712 with his elder brother, the Dauphin, he contracted what was thought to be smallpox, and with great resolution she had refused to allow the doctors access to him. His brother died after treatment and he survived without it. There was a tearful scene when, at the age of seven, the time came for Louis to leave his governess's care. The third of the triumvirate with particular responsibility for watching over the King in his formative years, and the most influential by far, was the future Cardinal Fleury who in 1715 as Bishop of Fréjus was appointed the royal tutor. He was a conscientious teacher and a good many of his pupil's exercises, duly corrected, have survived. His influence over the King was assured when, in 1722, Villeroy was exiled from the court. Orléans himself also played a part in instructing Louis, especially towards the end of the Regency when he inaugurated a series of daily sessions at which to inform the King about the state of the realm which he was shortly to inherit. He was a kind man and Louis, who was genuinely fond of him, wept at the news of his death.

Louis XV was an attractive child with a broad forehead, symmetrical features, and wide, brown eyes, strikingly like his great-uncle, the Duc du Maine, an illegitimate son of

The royal succession: *in the famous painting by Nicolas de Largillière, the aged Louis XIV sits with predecessors and his heirs. Behind him is his symbol, Apollo. On the left and right are busts of Henry IV and Louis XIII. Standing are the Grand Dauphin; the King's grandson Louis, Duc de Bourgogne (far right); and Madame de Ventadour, governess to both princes. The child is Louis de Bretagne, Louis XIV's eldest great-grandson. In 1711 and 1712 all three princes died, leaving the second son of the Duc de Bourgogne as the heir, the future Louis XV. (321)*

Louis XIV and Madame de Montespan whose hopes of controlling the young King's education himself had been thwarted by the Regent. He was a clever youth who grew into an intelligent man. A popular child with his subjects, he did not relish the public nature of his office, remaining shy and secretive throughout his life. In the ceremonial-ridden atmosphere of Versailles he would introduce changes to take some account of his distaste for exposure.

In fact, with the approach of the King's majority Orléans decided that the royal court should return to its most spectacular setting; and in June 1722, Louis came back to Versailles. The palace had an affectionate place in the King's memory as a result of his early years spent there in his great-grandfather's time and he re-entered his new home with enthusiasm, even to the extent of lying prone in the Galerie des Glaces the better to admire Le Brun's magnificent ceiling. However, the first momentous event to occur there was an unhappy one for Louis. On 2 December 1723, his first minister and former Regent, Philippe of Orléans, collapsed and died from a heart attack while awaiting a routine audience with the King on matters of state. He died in the arms of his latest mistress, the Duchesse de Falari, a symbolically apt demise which provided what seemed to many a literally heaven-sent opportunity for homilies of divine retribution. On a more mundane level Orléans' death left the unattractive and talentless Duc de Bourbon as the King's first minister. His 'reign' lasted for three years and added only one piece to the mosaic of Louis' personal life, though that was an important one: he arranged the King's marriage.

The young king

Louis was not an unusual male adolescent in that he combined precocious physical maturity with acute diffidence and shyness in his relations with women. It had been decided in 1721 that in order to strengthen the link with the Spanish Bourbons the King should be affianced to the

religion or their mental stability debarred them (the latter a predictable result of generations of royal inbreeding). Finally, Louis had to make do with Maria Lesczinska, daughter of Stanislas, the dethroned King of Poland, who was living in exile with her father in Alsace. The match transformed the fortunes of the Lesczinski family. Stanislas was to become Duc de Lorraine and in return would bequeath to France one of the most superb monuments to the Rococo, the elegant town centre of Nancy. For the Bourbons it was a far from brilliant alliance. Yet Maria was a strong young woman, a devout Catholic, and though no beauty, pleasant to look at; and at twenty-two, seven years older than the King, she was ready to produce a much-needed heir.

Louis fell in love with his Queen at once and a Dauphin was born in 1729. Indeed, between 1727 and 1737 Maria gave birth to eight daughters and two sons, of whom one son and six daughters survived the rigours of an eighteenth-century childhood. At the same time Louis' old tutor, Fleury, became the undisputed chief minister, retaining affairs of state in his own capable though increasingly fragile hands (he had been born in 1653) until the eve of his death in 1743. Inadvertently he owed his success to the new Queen for she, an innocent in political affairs, had allowed herself to be used by Bourbon and his ambitious mistress, Madame du Prie, in their efforts to rid themselves of their only serious rival. The scheme miscarried and in June 1726 the Duc de Bourbon was dismissed.

For the next decade life at court followed a tranquil and predictable pattern. Each day was divided, as it had been under Louis XIV, into a variety of ceremonial occasions framed by the royal *lever* and *coucher*. At the former the King greeted a succession of visitors beginning with the Queen, the royal children, and the princes of the blood (whom he received while still in bed), followed by his personal

The need for an heir *prompted marriage negotiations for Louis at an early age. However, his first intended bride, the three-year-old Infanta María Ana, was too much his junior, and the alliance was cancelled. Trappings of state, in the children's portrait, fail to conceal the artificiality of their affianced pose. (322)*

Spanish Infanta, María Ana, daughter of Louis' uncle, King Philip V. Since the bride-to-be was only three at the time of the betrothal the marriage was deferred for ten years, although the Infanta arrived at the French court in the following year. The miscalculation of this proposed union became increasingly apparent, for Louis had inherited his family's robust appetites and seemed unlikely to wait ten years without seeking interim solace elsewhere. In addition France needed an heir and Louis' health was causing many anxious moments. Eventually, after the King had suffered a bout of fever in 1725, the Duc de Bourbon decided to risk Spanish wrath by sending the Infanta home and the search for a more suitable replacement began. The European courts turned out to be surprisingly lacking in eligible young ladies worthy to grace the title of Queen of France: either their

Brilliance of colour, *delicacy of composition, and charm of subject characterize the essentially aristocratic art of Rococo as patronized by the court. The royal factory at Sèvres produced porcelain that was copied all over Europe. In this finely observed enamelled Sèvres plaque of 1764, painted by Dodin, a child feeds sweets to a parrot. (323)*

The 'Bal des Ifs', *given to celebrate the marriage of the Dauphin to María Teresa of Spain, marked the beginning of the King's long liaison with Madame d'Etioles, later the Marquise de Pompadour. The name of the ball alludes to the yew-tree costumes worn by Louis and seven of his courtiers. Other guests wear enormous heads with turbans. (324)*

The pleasures of ordinary life *had a particular attraction for Louis. In hunting he was able to escape from some of the oppressive formality of his official role. This sketch is for 'The Hunt Breakfast', executed for the King in 1737 by Jean-François de Troy, and was designed as decoration for the dining-room of the 'petits appartements' at Fontainebleau. (325)*

officers, the gentlemen of the Bedchamber and the masters of the Wardrobe, and then more utilitarian figures including the royal barbers, apothecaries, and dressers. Other privileged officers arrived for the *premières entrées* and eventually the royal suite was crowded as almost every inhabitant of the palace claimed his or her rightful part in the elaborate procedure. During this time the King was washed, shaved, and dressed, prayed, and had his breakfast in accordance with an unvarying ritual which succeeded in protecting both the sensibilities of the court and the modesty of the sovereign. In the evening at the *grand coucher* the performance was repeated in reverse. Immediately after the *lever* the King attended Mass in the chapel. The rest of the morning was given over to state business in the royal study, the *cabinet du roi*, where the King met official deputations, discussed political affairs with his ministers, and received distinguished visitors. At the end of the morning it was customary for him to eat alone. Louis inherited his great-grandfather's prodigious appetite, and his Queen too was a formidable *gourmande*. The *grands couverts* at which the royal family regularly partook of their evening meal in the presence of the court were little more than public exhibitions of gluttony. In the afternoons the King took exercise, usually in the hunting field, and in the evenings after dinner he would play cards or chat with his friends. Even the devout Maria gambled at the card-table, though not being a very competent player she wisely preferred *cavagnole*, a game played for low stakes, to the more fashionable *comète* and *piquet*.

There was little privacy at Versailles. Even while the King slept a valet attended him in the bedchamber, a bell-pull attached to his wrist and to the King's bed. Nor was it only the high points of the day which were conducted according to an inflexible ceremonial; life itself was at every level a public performance. Matters of precedent were a daily obsession: the King and Queen and all their attendants from the highest to the lowest still danced to steps devised for them by the old puppet-master, Louis XIV.

Louis XV did not enjoy this regime, though he acknowledged his obligation as King to put up with it. His innate shyness disqualified him from an imitation of the *bravura* performance of his great-grandfather. He disliked so many strange faces, so much display, so little intimacy. The cold draughty corridors responded to the mood of a bygone age: they were too severe and sombre for the light and delicate *ambience* of the new century. Besides, the King was bored. Like his kinsman, the Regent, he became bored very easily, a fact which could be interpreted to suggest that he was empty-headed and fickle or equally (bearing in mind the overwhelming monotony of his role) that he was a man of intelligence and sensitivity. The latter was in fact the case; but Louis had the increasingly thankless task of trying to act out another man's part. Whereas Louis XIV worked hard at the substance of politics his successor was left with little more than the trappings. That was not simply because Louis XV was lazy but because in changing times the Crown had not yet realized that its overwhelming significance at the centre of French life and government which in the seventeenth century was assured, was now no longer so.

Marriage with Maria Lesczinska *brought no political advantage to Louis. She was the daughter of the exiled Polish King Stanislas I. But Louis was in love with her, and remained faithful to her for at least eight years. Even after the reign of his successive 'maîtresses en titre' began, she was treated with loyal respect. (326)*

The King's boredom increased as his ardour for Maria Lesczinska turned to disenchantment. The rift was neither altogether Louis' fault nor his Queen's. Having produced ten children in twelve years Maria was showing understandable signs of diminishing interest in sexual relations, a state of affairs unimaginable and intolerable to the King. He was excluded from her bed whenever a sufficiently important feast day came along and the number of significant saints in the Church's calendar tended to increase year by year. Her inclination towards religiosity also grew. She encouraged the fashion of acquiring a death's head to assist the contemplation of man's inevitable destiny. Louis himself was inclined to melancholia, though he was quick to seek distractions to dissipate his morbid fancies. He may have felt that, unlike Louis XIV, he had met his Madame de Maintenon at the wrong end of his life. For at least eight years he remained faithful to Maria, finding his pleasures in eating and hunting and in frequently moving about from one royal residence to the next, to Rambouillet, Marly, Fontainebleau, Compiègne, and especially Choisy after its purchase in 1739. Yet in the end Louis' sensuality overcame his feelings of loyalty to the Queen, his well-known dislike of new faces, and his awkwardness with women. The reigns of the royal mistresses began.

313

Louis depended on women *for private reassurance, and to a lesser extent for political guidance. Some of his mistresses remained in the background of state affairs; others almost assumed the role of unofficial ministers. Left: Louis, by Van Loo, in his martial character as leader of the nation's army. Centre: the Comtesse de Mailly, by Nattier. She amused the King but made the mistake of introducing him to her two sisters, who then took her place. Right: the younger sister, Marie-Anne, Duchesse de Châteauroux, also by Nattier. Louis repudiated her in a fit of piety when he thought he was dying.* (327–29)

The royal mistresses

The first serious contender for this title was the Comtesse de Mailly, the eldest daughter of the Marquis de Nesle and a member of Maria's household. She was the first of an unique family trinity, for two of her younger sisters followed her in the King's favour. Thus it is possible to treat as a whole the period of the Nesle ascendancy at court. It coincided with changes in the interior construction and decoration of Versailles reflecting Louis' desire for greater privacy and marking the first hesitant and informal break with Louis XIV's palace regime. The crucial change was of the King's bedchamber, the focal point of the ceremonial at Versailles. Upon his return to the palace in 1722 Louis had inherited his great-grandfather's bedroom which symbolically occupied the very centre of the original building, its windows looking out over the Cour de Marbre and away towards the Avenue de Paris and the modern town. It was too cold and monumental for its new occupant's taste, especially when his liaison with Madame de Mailly whetted his appetite for a more intimate retreat. So began the construction of the King's new apartments in 1735 for which the architect,

Jacques-Ange Gabriel, supplied the drawings and the wood-carvers, Verbeckt and Rousseau, the superb embellishment. A small group of rooms formed the kernel of the King's private world within the palace. His new bedroom, the Petite Chambre, was so constructed that it could be reached from his former one, the Grande Chambre du Roi, by way of the council chamber. From this new room he entered the magnificent salon adorned with the *boiseries* of Verbeckt which from the mid-century was known as the Cabinet de la Pendule from the clock presented to the King by the Académie des Sciences. From there he reached his study, set in the angle between the Cour de Marbre and the Cour Royal, from which a balcony offered a view of the road to Paris. One of the clearest images of Louis XV to have come down to us concerns that balcony and that view. In effect this suite constituted part of the first floor of the northern wing of Louis XIII's old hunting lodge; in shifting the balance of the château from the town to the garden side Mansart's grand design had nevertheless incorporated the earlier residence. The new apartments were hardly less grand than Louis XIV's salons and their air of intimacy and informality was of course strictly relative: in fact they represent an outstanding example of the decorative art of the Rococo. Above the first-floor suite were some fifty more rooms, the veritable *petits appartements,* which offered even more privacy, and gradually a series of ever smaller *cabinets* proliferated under the eaves of the north wing of the château, 'rats' nests' as they were called by the son of Louis XIV's architect, Robert de Cotte, whose classical upbringing no doubt blinded him to their exquisite decoration.

Louis moved into his new suite in 1738 while still involved in his liaison with Madame de Mailly. His mistress was no beauty but she was amusing and undemanding and she suited the King well enough after the somewhat lugubrious company of Maria Lesczinska. He himself had matured into a most handsome man, as his portraits reveal, with a fine open countenance and the sensuous lips of the Bourbons. Not surprisingly, he was the cynosure of a good many female eyes, including those of two of Mailly's sisters. He met one of them, the Duchesse de Vintimille, in 1739 and she quickly ousted her sister from the King's affections. She died in 1741 after giving birth to Louis' son. For a while the Duchesse de Mailly regained her former place, but the foolish woman repeated her earlier mistake by introducing a second sister to the King. This one, Marie-Anne, was a far more formidable character than either of her sisters. Ambitious and beautiful, as we may judge from her portrait by Jean-Marc Nattier, she had no difficulty in having her unfortunate but imperceptive sister relegated once more.

Marie-Anne, who was already at twenty-four a widow of the Marquis de Tournelle, was not herself destined for a long life. However, she lived long enough to infatuate the King and to dominate him. Her strength of mind revealed the essential weakness of Louis' character, masked as it was by his stubbornness and the authoritarian setting in which he moved. Marie-Anne persuaded the King to give her a title, Duchesse de Châteauroux, and to admit her formally to the court. Thus she became his first *maîtresse en titre*. She was not a woman to wear her triumphs modestly, and the humiliated Queen loathed her abrasive and arrogant rival. Her rise to power coincided with the decline of Cardinal Fleury's hold on affairs. Thus her position was one of potential political significance and indeed she encouraged the King to take political matters firmly under his own control. Louis had never been unwilling to play his part, though his preference was to work in the privacy of his own apartments, where he applied himself with diligence and a fair intelligence to affairs of state. Accusations of laziness levelled against the King around this time are not borne out by contemporary observers close to the throne. The acid-penned Marquis d'Argenson noted in the spring of 1738 that the King seemed willing to work of his own accord and not because he had to, and by the summer of that year the same diarist was remarking on Louis' personal filing system which the King had organized in his study. Some five years later the Duc de Cröy observed that the King worked on his own 'assez despotiquement'. In addition he worked each day with his ministers and met his councils faithfully at the appointed times. Yet he lacked self-confidence in his public role and was inclined to allow his professional advisers to have the last word. With Fleury's disappearance rival cliques were bound to develop around the King, each seeking to become the dominant political influence at court. The new favourite, Châteauroux, held the King in thrall and thus promised a rosy future for her chief backer, the Duc de Richelieu, engagingly described by the late Dr Gooch as 'the champion rake of eighteenth-century France'. Their chief antagonist among the King's ministers was the Comte de Maurepas, an urbane and witty figure whose hold on power was facilitated by Louis' fondness for him.

War provided the opportunity for Châteauroux to demonstrate the extent of her influence. She persuaded the King to seek martial glory, if not actually at the head of his troops then at least in their vicinity. In 1744 he set out for the Austrian Netherlands, soon to be joined by his mistress at Lille; together they went on to Metz. And there, in a most unlikely setting far from the gossip and intrigue of Versailles, the Duchesse de Châteauroux suddenly, and, as it turned out, irrevocably lost her authority with the King. The cause was a sudden illness which seemed to threaten Louis' life. In this parlous situation, as his Most Christian Majesty faced the next world, there was no room for a royal mistress. Louis judged matters to a nicety, and having decided that he was indeed about to die, with that mixture of honesty and hypocrisy which he would reveal on more than one occasion in the years ahead, he dismissed the Duchesse and received the last sacraments. In fact he recovered quickly and returned to Versailles ready to resume his interrupted liaison. To his chagrin Maurepas was forced to deliver in person the royal summons back to favour. However, before Châteauroux could make the short triumphant journey from Paris she too was forced to take to her bed. She died after a short illness, probably from peritonitis, at the age of twenty-seven.

Madame de Pompadour and the rule of taste

Louis was upset and the court was agog with expectation. Sooner or later he would have to replace the Duchesse, since he could not live a celibate life for very long and his wife showed no desire to take his mistress's place. That position was all the more attractive with the King currently enjoying

A private world for the King within the immense palace of Versailles became desirable when he began his liaison with Madame de Mailly. The so-called 'petits appartements' consisted in fact of some fifty rooms, luxuriously decorated but comparatively intimate in scale. (330)

Madame de Pompadour was the King's mistress for seven years and the dominant personality at his court for nearly twenty. In the field of the arts her most famous protégé was François Boucher, from whose portraits we can divine something of her magnetic charm. (331)

flee the country. Fortunately for Jeanne her mother established a new relationship with a rather more successful financier, Le Normant de Tournehem, who supervised her education and enabled her to acquire all the social arts and graces as she grew up. She learnt to play the clavichord, to sing and act, to paint, to dance, and to ride. No expense was spared in providing expert tuition: the dramatist Crébillon was her elocution teacher. Soon to be an actress of outstanding talent, she was in fact being groomed for a role to which members of her class had no business to aspire: her pet name within the family was 'Reinette'. In 1741, at the age of twenty, she married Le Normant's nephew and thus became Madame d'Etioles. By this time she was a woman of outstanding elegance and allure. President Hénault, a close friend of the Queen, saw her for the first time in 1742 and remarked of her: 'I met one of the prettiest women I ever saw. She sings with gaiety and perfect taste, knows a hundred songs, and acts in comedy at Etioles in a theatre up to the standard of the Opera. She has a lovely complexion, chestnut hair, wonderful eyes and teeth, a fascinating smile, dimples, animation and a perfect figure.' Perhaps had he known this paragon's future his loyalty to Maria Lesczinska would have made him tone down his enthusiasm. As it is, the description conveys no more than the lawyer's honest recollection of what was clearly for him a spectacular encounter.

This young lady possessed intelligence as well as beauty and taste and in the capital she attracted the attentions of Fontenelle, Montesquieu, and Voltaire himself. By the end of 1744 Madame d'Etioles had begun to make a name for herself in Parisian society. Her marriage provided her with a château close to Louis' favourite hunting lodge at Choisy from which she calculatingly drove out on occasions when

great popularity following his recovery from illness at Metz. In return for this signal service his subjects bestowed upon him the title of 'Bien-Aimé'. Besides, the political vacuum brought about by Cardinal Fleury's death remained to be filled, and Châteauroux had demonstrated the potential power awaiting the successful candidate. Through the early part of 1745 – the year of Fontenoy – speculation continued to grow. At the time it appeared simply that Louis was about to choose mistress number four to replace mistress number three, but hindsight offers a different perspective: the most deeply felt and permanent relationship which Louis was ever to experience began in that year with the captivating Madame d'Etioles.

This formidable young woman, born Jeanne-Antoinette Poisson, a surname which Parisian doggerel-mongers were to recall unsubtly and *ad nauseam*, was the daughter of a notorious beauty and a middle-class financier who ran into economic difficulties after the Regency and was forced to

A sofa of c. 1750, bearing the arms of the Marquise de Pompadour at the top, is typical of the Rococo's fluent, arabesque lines. The shell, or rocaille, motif, which gives the style its name, appears on the lower edge. (332)

The 'Louis Quinze style' *was very largely the creation of Madame de Pompadour's taste. Above left: a Boucher study for decoration to the château of Crécy. Left: one of a pair of Sèvres pot-pourri covered vases. Above: Pompadour as 'Venus of the Doves' by Etienne-Maurice Falconnet. Below: the marquise in Lully's 'Acis and Galatea' at Versailles. (333–36).*

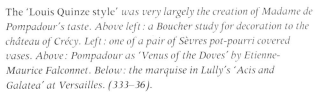

the King was in the vicinity. There can be no doubt that he knew something of her by the beginning of 1745. The date on which it is generally considered that the famous liaison was established is 25 February 1745 when a grand ball was held at Versailles in honour of the Dauphin's marriage to the Spanish Infanta, María Teresa. This was a spectacular ball even by Versailles' standards; the engraving of the scene by Cochin gives some impression of the fancy-dress splendour of the evening. As befitted the occasion, Madame d'Etioles was dressed as Diana the Huntress (a metamorphosis also favoured by her late rival, the Duchesse de Châteauroux), while Louis and his friends appeared in the bizarre uniform of clipped yew trees, inspired by the décor of the palace gardens, after which the ball has been named. Several days later the two met again at a ball in Paris given by the municipality, and thereafter Madame d'Etioles appeared regularly at Versailles. She was installed in the suite once occupied by Madame de Mailly which communicated directly with the King's rooms by a private staircase. Her first public appearance at court was on 3 April when she attended a performance by the Italian Comedy. Then in the early summer Louis departed for the campaign leading to the Battle of Fontenoy which would mark the high point of his popularity with his subjects. Madame d'Etioles withdrew to the château near Choisy and during her stay there this talented and ambitious *bourgeoise* heard that the King had revived for her an extinct title: that she was to become the Marquise de Pompadour.

Madame de Pompadour dominated Louis XV's court from 1745 until her death in 1764. She provided the King with emotional support long after their physical relationship had ceased, offered him diversions to counter his frequent bouts of boredom, influenced his political judgments, and stamped her taste indelibly upon the Louis Quinze style. In fact Pompadour found only limited pleasure in physical love-making and – like a latter-day Madame de Maintenon – would have preferred to exercise her influence over the King's mind. However, despite his attacks of melancholia the thought *timor mortis conturbat me* had not yet taken hold of the still youthful sovereign, and for fear of losing his affections the marquise resolutely accepted his advances until 1752 when their intimacy – though not her influence – came to an end. It was of course her ability to dominate the scene when she was no longer *maîtresse en titre* which indicates the formidable nature of her personality. For almost two decades she shrugged off the opposition of ministers and would-be favourites as she herself became increasingly involved in politics and especially in foreign affairs. Yet her supreme attribute was taste: the Pompadour style would prove to be her most lasting though insubstantial memorial.

She brought her love of the theatre to Versailles and in 1746 Louis had built for her the Théâtre des Petits Cabinets which opened in January 1747 with a performance of *Tartuffe*. There was only room for some fourteen people in the audience and the competition for places was predictably fierce. Among the distinguished names failing to gain admission for the first night were the Comte de Noailles and the Prince de Conti. Subsequently the marquise drew up her own set of rules for the company and for five seasons plays were performed to the highest professional standards of the time with Pompadour herself excelling in a series of leading roles. In the summer of 1748 a second, larger theatre was built at Versailles to accommodate the successful troupe and a rather bigger audience. However, escalating costs at last brought the venture to an end in 1750, although by that time Pompadour herself may well have been ready to retire in any case.

One of the ingredients contributing to the success of the Théâtre des Petits Cabinets was the cooperation of the artist François Boucher, who decorated the theatre and designed some of the costumes. Boucher had been a royal painter since 1742 and his career was to be closely linked with that of the marquise. His next important collaboration with the favourite was in 1750 when he helped Van Loo, the official court painter, to decorate the new château of Bellevue, built on the Seine between Sèvres and Meudon and destroyed during the French Revolution. Its destruction was a great loss, for as well as the work of these two artists it contained Verbeckt's panelling and sculptures by Pigalle and Falconnet. With the splendid grounds complete with china flowers smelling like real ones, it represented in its totality the elegant though extravagant taste which Pompadour imposed upon the environs of Louis XV's court. There can be no doubt about her extravagance, the chief source of her unpopularity in Paris, where she gradually came to symbolize the feckless irrelevance of an outmoded society. She collected houses as the poor garnered their loaves: the Hôtel d'Evreux, now the Elysée Palace; the Duc de la Vallière's château at Champs; St Ouen; Crécy; and the château of Ménars on the Loire, the old home of the distinguished *robe* family of Charron. In addition she approved the plans for Gabriel's Petit Trianon, though she did not live to see it completed, and built the elegant retreat of Brimborion in the grounds of Bellevue and the hermitages at Versailles, Compiègne, and Fontainebleau. Everywhere she indulged in expensive rebuilding and luxurious interior decoration. To condemn her extravagance is to make a judgment *sub specie aeternitatis* which does less than justice to her actual situation. Pompadour was the arch-parasite in a parasitic milieu where considerations of social and economic justice had little relevance. Certainly, the King was expected in his actions to reflect and respect a kind of Christian equity, but increasingly he seemed too puny a figure to play that giant role. Meanwhile his mistress added what she could to the glories of his court, and relieved him of boredom.

Boucher figures again in the history of Sèvres. Through Pompadour's intervention the soft-porcelain factory at Vincennes was transferred to Sèvres in 1756 and thereafter Boucher and Falconnet were both involved in the production of porcelain which rivalled the great factory at Meissen. The famous Sèvres colours of royal blue and Pompadour rose still remind us of the patronage of Louis and the marquise. Louis himself was not indifferent to the arts and Pompadour's flair provided the stimulus he needed to exercise a generous patronage. Her brother, created Marquis de Marigny in 1754, exercised the office of Director of the King's Buildings. The English abbreviation of his title conceals the scope of his office for he was in fact the Directeur et Ordonnateur Général des Bâtiments, Maisons, Châteaux, Parcs, Jardins, Arts et Manufactures du Roi. After Pompadour's death the King wisely refused to accept the resignation of this modest and cultured man, who continued in his undemonstrative way to support and nurture the artistic life of his age. Not the least of Pompadour's achievements was to provide an *entrée* for her brother into public service.

The marquise interested herself increasingly in public affairs, especially after 1752 when her hold over Louis was no longer based on physical attraction. She was closely concerned, for example, with the commissioning of plans to be drawn up by Gabriel for the building of a school in Paris for future army officers, the Ecole Militaire, which is now linked to the Right Bank of the capital by the Pont d'Iéna, a name permanently inscribed in French history by the school's most celebrated pupil, Napoleon Bonaparte, who was admitted in 1784. But her public interests extended far beyond such isolated though enlightened gestures: she also immersed herself in affairs of state. For some time the King had been conducting his own secret foreign policy parallel with his government's official diplomacy. He instituted this practice shortly before Cardinal Fleury's death in 1743; indeed, it was a reflection of Louis' new-found sense of independence. It was also in keeping with the King's own character that he should prefer to work with a few intimates behind the scenes. Chief of these intimates was Madame de Pompadour herself, who began to exercise political influence in the nomination of ministers and diplomats. She played a major part in the appointment and dismissal of Machault d'Arnouville as secretary of state for the marine; she rid herself of one of her fiercest and ablest critics, Maurepas, also a navy minister; and through her influence the Duc de Choiseul was sent as ambassador to Rome and the Abbé de Bernis to Venice. In particular she concerned herself with the policy of effecting a *rapprochement* between the old enemies, Bourbon and Habsburg. In 1755 she was approached as an intermediary by Count Kaunitz, the Austrian chancellor and chief architect of the so-called diplomatic revolution, to convey a note from the Empress, Maria Theresa, to the King. Subsequently Pompadour was present at a meeting in Brimborion, her retreat in the grounds of Bellevue, between Bernis and the Austrian envoy, Count Stahremberg, which was to lead eventually to the signing of the Treaty of Versailles between France and Austria. Three years later Maria Theresa signified her gratitude by presenting to the marquise a writing desk inlaid with the Empress's portrait in precious stones. Even King Frederick of Prussia thought it worth offering her a bribe in 1757, nothing less than the principality of Neuchâtel. However, the Peace of Paris which concluded the Seven Years' War brought her efforts at diplomacy to an inglorious end. She died in the following year, aged forty-two.

Her twenty years of power at the court of Louis XV encapsulated all that was worth preserving and all that was hollow and counterfeit about that era; in fact the two aspects cannot be viewed apart: each belongs with the other

The Petit Trianon *by Jacques-Ange Gabriel in the grounds of Versailles, marks a change in taste from Rococo to Neo-classicism. Its plan was approved by Madame de Pompadour, though she did not live to see it completed in 1766. (337)*

like the vibrant colours in a stormy sky. A splendid patron of the arts and sciences, she left a superb library, a beautiful collection of engravings in precious stone, and a wealth of furniture and crystal. Her patronage inspired great works of beauty in Gobelins tapestry and Sèvres porcelain. She employed the greatest decorative artist of the age as her personal painter, and the Ecole Militaire and the Petit Trianon remain her monuments, though she did not live to see either completed. All this represented that frothy crest of the Rococo wave which showed itself to the best effect in the moment before plunging into the void. At court she came to be accepted even by the Queen, whom she was always careful to treat with consideration and respect, a trait which Maria Lesczinska appreciated the more because of the cavalier treatment she had undergone at the hands of the Duchesse de Châteauroux. In 1756 Maria accepted the marquise as a lady in waiting – not with enthusiasm, certainly, but with a degree of tolerance and resignation. Yet, as Pompadour edged the Queen towards a policy of peaceful coexistence, made easier by the latter's increasing preoccupation with the next world, nobody could doubt that the favourite's relationship with the King remained the crucial factor at court. She fashioned a private world for Louis, this insecure and diffident sensualist, into which he fitted more comfortably than ever he did into the great public shell of Versailles. Yet Pompadour's world of intimate suppers in the *petits cabinets*, of a galaxy of private pleasures and entertainments designed to offset the tedium of being King of France, offers a clue to the approaching tragedy.

With the passage of time Louis XV's reign had become a sham, a facade, an illusion purporting to represent a kind of

Jeanne, Comtesse du Barry, *became Louis' 'maîtresse en titre' during his last years. Without Pompadour's intellect or resources of character she nonetheless found herself in a position of political power. (338)*

his successor preferred to act in secret and often in opposition to his professional advisers at a time when the mounting complexity of affairs of state had greatly reduced the scope for amateurs – even royal ones – in the King's government. Even in religious matters there was a degree of dissimulation: the King sent away one favourite, Châteauroux, in 1742 when he believed that his death was imminent and the need to make his peace with God imperative; and in 1764 he similarly bade farewell to another, Pompadour, when he saw how near she was to dying. Not that Louis should be judged too harshly on this score, for there were precedents enough among his Bourbon forefathers for conduct finely balanced between the urge to religious devotion and illicit sexual satisfaction. But the overall impression inescapably conveyed by the long reign is one of creeping disillusionment and unconscious deceit held at arm's length by a dazzling display of Rococo elegance, which enriched the next generation even if it did not deceive it. Although Madame la marquise, as she came universally to be known, provided Louis with the environment in which he could live as a more private man than his great-grandfather, she could not offer him an alternative public role. Thus she helped inadvertently to compromise the concept of kingship in France. Louis would not himself suffer for that and we cannot know to what extent her death represented in his eyes the end of an epoch. He may have had some such sense as from the balcony outside his study he watched her cortège move away towards Paris: but his tears then, as for the Regent some forty years earlier, were for a trusted friend lost.

Madame du Barry and the decline of authority

In the last decade of Louis XV's reign the King's reputation continued to decline. He had long since lost the 'Bien-Aimé' image of the 1740s and the barrister Barbier records in his *Journal* the increasingly unenthusiastic response of the public to Louis' personal appearances in the capital. By 1764 the spendthrift reputation of his court at a time of severe financial hardship for the unprivileged had lost him the sympathy of most of his subjects. Nor did his personal conduct do anything to restore their faith. Now in his mid-fifties, Louis' desire for sexual gratification remained as compulsive as ever and led him into the last celebrated liaison of his life, with Madame du Barry. It is something of an injustice to Pompadour that posterity should link her name with that of her successor as the two great courtesans of eighteenth-century France. For in almost every way Du Barry was a pale reflection of her famous predecessor, a far less important and impressive personality. Her origins were humbler even than those of the marquise, since she had been born Jeanne Bécu in 1743, an illegitimate daughter of an unknown father and an impoverished mother. Like Pompadour she grew into a striking beauty, yet she possessed few intellectual or aesthetic gifts to back up her physical allure. She worked as a prostitute in Paris, eventually becoming the mistress of a dissolute nobleman, the Comte du Barry, who introduced her to a succession of aristocratic lovers until the interest of the King himself was aroused in 1768. However, according to the increasingly

authority and a way of exercising it which properly belonged to the previous century. There is no better symbolic example of the illusion than the ceremonial *grand coucher* and *grand lever* as practised by Louis after 1738 when he vacated his original suite for the new private apartments. It was still considered necessary for the King to retire publicly in Louis XIV's bedroom, the Chambre de Parade, which his great-grandson found so austere and grand. So the nightly performance went on with the King finally getting into bed and the courtiers withdrawing. No sooner had they gone however than the King got up again and made his way to the bedroom in his private suite or to the marquise's room or even left the palace altogether in search of entertainment. After a while he omitted to take off his clothes during the *grand coucher* in order to make a speedy exit when the moment came. Similarly with the *grand lever* the King would arrive in the official bedroom from his own room simply to get out of bed again, on the second occasion under the ceremonial eye of the court. It was a ridiculous performance which reduced the King and his court to the level of players acting out an old and meaningless ritual: Louis XV playing at being Louis XIV.

A similar deception attended his political role. Whereas the old King had worked with and dominated his ministers, discredited and hypocritical-seeming protocol of Versailles the office of *maîtresse en titre* could only go to a nobleman's wife. Hence Jeanne was married to Du Barry's obliging brother and thus became eligible to succeed Pompadour at court. One contemporary pleasantry relates an apocryphal conversation between Louis and a courtier: 'They say that I am succeeding Sainte-Foix in Du Barry's affections.' 'Yes Sire,' came the response, 'as Your Majesty succeeds Pharamond!' (Pharamond was the legendary founder of the French monarchy.)

The new favourite's interest in, and understanding of, affairs of state was limited but inevitably her position made her an important counter in political intrigue at court. She threw in her support with the enemies of Choiseul, who had once enjoyed the patronage of Pompadour, and he was dismissed in 1770 despite his long and successful career in diplomacy and at the ministries of the marine and war. However, it would be misleading to suggest that Choiseul's fall should be laid at the door of the favourite alone. She spoke for others, notably for the Duc d'Aiguillon, who was to be foreign minister for the last three years of the reign. Significantly D'Aiguillon was a well-known enemy of the magistrates, having been involved in a long and bitter feud with the Parlement of Brittany, and one of the chief reasons for Choiseul's fall was his unwillingness to stand firm against *parlementaire* pretensions, which had been steadily mounting during the course of the reign. In particular the magistrates began to invoke the theory of *robe* solidarity whereby all the Parlements in the kingdom claimed to be part of a single body, a kind of national Parlement which by implication possessed rather more political significance than a royal court. The King was affronted by such a claim, and indeed he had a positive attitude to the Parlement of Paris, the chief of these courts, which was not apparent in his handling of other aspects of government. In 1756 he remarked to the Dauphin in words reminiscent of his great-grandfather's quest for *la gloire*: 'My authority is given to me only for the duration of my life; I must preserve it in its entirety for you, my son: I am obliged so to do.' To prevent the magistrates from challenging that authority in 1753 he had four members of the Parlement of Paris arrested and imprisoned and the rest of the company exiled in towns at a distance from the capital; and in 1757 sixteen councillors of the same court were deprived of their offices. The most famous of the King's confrontations with the great Parisian court was that of March 1766, the *séance de la flagellation*, at which he formally rejected the Parlement's constitutional claims, reminding the magistrates that sovereign power belonged to the king alone, 'sans dépendence et sans partage'. In Louis' eyes the magistrates compounded their offence by their Jansenist sympathies and he was determined to move against them. Choiseul, whose inclination was for rather than against them, was not the man to carry out the assault.

In addition, the King was still pursuing his own secret diplomacy; and in this area too he crossed swords with Choiseul. During the final ten years of the reign Louis was obstinately convinced of the need to remain at peace. His minister's support for Spain against England towards the end of 1770, with the consequent risk of involving France in war, was another factor of some importance in Choiseul's dismissal.

Du Barry's part then in the eclipse of one of the reign's chief ministers should not be given undue weight. Of more significance was the fact that by 1770 Choiseul apparently stood athwart the two paths along which the King was keen to exercise his authority untrammelled. In one of these directions he made spectacular headway. In 1768 Louis appointed as chancellor René-Nicolas de Maupeou, who was to be his instrument in bringing the Parlement of Paris, of which Maupeou had been the first president, finally to heel. In January 1771 the magistrates' offices were confiscated and they themselves were sent into exile. For the remaining years of the reign new courts staffed by royal nominees proved to be far more amenable. Yet this *coup de force* only highlighted the King's essential dilemma: could he at one and the same time cut through the outmoded legalism which hedged him about and yet continue to claim authority according to the ancient rights of his dynasty? Not for the first time in the reign was the growing uncertainty about the nature of royal authority demonstrated. The same point can be made about the King's other main political pre-occupation, foreign affairs. For all the time and energy employed in the *secret du roi* only twice could the royal conduct of affairs be said to have produced significant results: in 1768 when Turkey declared war on Russia and in 1772 in support of the *coup d'état* by Gustavus III in Sweden.

Louise O'Murphy represents a yet more 'private world' – Louis' need to escape even from his mistresses. The girls of the Parc-aux-Cerfs had no social position and are mostly quite unknown. Miss O'Murphy owes her fame to Boucher's delicately erotic portrait. (339)

Marie-Antoinette *(portrait by Drouais), the daughter of Empress Maria Theresa, married Louis' grandson, the Dauphin, in 1770. The Bourbon–Habsburg rapprochement which this represented almost came to grief through the young bride's insulting hostility to Madame du Barry. In the end it was Marie-Antoinette who gave way. (340)*

How far removed was that record from the conduct of foreign affairs in the previous reign when Louis XIV had scrutinized, regulated, and controlled every aspect of policy however important or trivial, and taken all the decisions. Once more the credibility gap – to borrow a useful though anachronistic phrase – between the theory and practice of government under Louis XV was exposed, and as it widened so did the King's isolation increase. Kingship was in danger of becoming irrelevant.

By this time death, which had always exercised an obsessive fascination over him, had begun to harvest his own generation. The King himself had survived an attempted assassination by Damiens in 1757 which left its psychological scar. The faithful Maria Lesczinska died in 1768, her last years warmed by a closer and more tender relationship with the King, following Pompadour's death. In 1765 his only son, the Dauphin, died and two years later his daughter-in-law, Marie-Josèphe. Yet in the absence of a Madame de Maintenon to concentrate the King's attention on eternity he continued to seek diversions from his own fears by indulging his passions for food, hunting, and women. Where the last were concerned he shared with his former mentor, Philippe of Orléans, a liking for those of low birth; indeed he had access to what was virtually a private brothel at the Parc-aux-Cerfs. This notorious residence in

the village of Versailles was acquired by Louis in 1755 and he continued to visit it until 1771 when at Madame du Barry's request he agreed to sell it. The girls who lived there in those sixteen years are for the most part unknown, though one of them, the delectable Louise O'Murphy, 'la belle Morphise', for a brief moment seemed poised to move from the Parc to the palace. It was not to be, though her son became a general and she herself achieved immortality in the canvases of Boucher.

In the last four years of the reign, as the state of the royal treasury became more parlous and the King's prestige diminished further, Louis seemed determined to assert his family's public authority more extravagantly than ever. In May 1770 his grandson, now the Dauphin, was married to Marie-Antoinette, the fifteen-year-old daughter of the Empress Maria Theresa, and the occasion was marked by spectacular and expensive celebrations including a supper in Gabriel's new opera-house at Versailles, a performance of Lully's *Persée*, a great ball, a public festival in the park, and a giant display of fireworks: all at a cost of some five million *livres*. Hardly less spectacular were the festivities accompanying the marriages of his other two grandsons, the future kings Louis XVIII and Charles X. In June 1773 the new Dauphine made her official entrance into the capital; in April 1774 she led the court to the Paris Opéra to attend the first performance of *Iphigénie* by her countryman Christoph Gluck. All these grand occasions would serve in retrospect to feed the terrible anger of the Revolution and so would the heady, gem-laden opulence displayed by Madame du Barry during her years as *maîtresse en titre*. Of the Controller-General's desperate efforts to stop the financial rot at this time the Duc de Cröy wrote ironically, half-perceiving the dangers in the situation, 'as if one went in for retrenchment at Versailles!'

It was fitting that to the end Louis XV's court should be dominated by women, and in particular by the rivalry of two of them, the King's mistress and the prospective Queen of France, Marie-Antoinette. On her arrival at Versailles the Austrian princess was still an adolescent, in part a proud and mettlesome young woman, in part a tomboy fretting under the stern gaze of her lady-in-waiting, Madame de Noailles, whom she christened Madame Etiquette, and the malign influence of the three spinster daughters of the King, Mesdames Adélaïde, Victoire, and Sophie, a petty and lugubrious trinity. Though their influence on the Dauphine was fleeting it did encourage her to embrace a cause to which her own sentiments inclined her: that of total opposition to Du Barry. She resented the dominating position of this woman at the King's court, where she was entitled to be the first lady, and no doubt she felt too that the presence of the royal mistress emphasized her own humiliatingly un-

The Rococo theatre was in a sense only an extension of the great theatre that was the court. Actors and audience both had their roles to play, each came to be seen as much as to see – a function reflected in the form of the auditorium. This engraving shows a performance in the theatre built in the Versailles riding school for the wedding of the Dauphin Louis to the Infanta María Teresa of Spain in 1745. (341)

satisfactory – and all too well publicized – relationship with the Dauphin. At all events the rivalry between the two women became the consuming topic of conversation at court. It revealed itself, predictably at Versailles, in a matter of court etiquette. The young princess simply refused to speak to the favourite and therefore to recognize her existence, much less her privileged status. The quarrel was brought to the ears of the King, who let his displeasure reach the Austrian ambassador. It even seemed a possibility that the Bourbon-Habsburg alliance would not survive the insult. That fear stimulated the wayward Dauphine's mother, the Empress Maria Theresa, to write to her daughter requiring that she accept Du Barry as a lady admitted to the court by the King and therefore worthy of respect. Grudgingly Marie-Antoinette gave way, and on 1 January 1772 she addressed to Madame du Barry the unremarkable though avidly recorded phrase, 'there are a lot of people at Versailles today'. The mistress thus achieved her revenge for past slights, though it was a pyrrhic victory, since from that day to 1793, when both perished in the Place de la Révolution, Marie-Antoinette did not speak to her rival again.

The age of Louis XV drew to its close in an atmosphere of political, financial, and moral crisis. Even in aesthetic terms the exuberance of the Rococo style faltered before the stern neo-classical reaction: David renounced the patronage of Boucher. French kingship faced an insupportable burden, for it was Louis' misfortune and his grandson's tragedy to be called to rule over subjects increasingly sceptical of values long held as absolute. Virtues and vices were as mixed in Louis as in most men and if in the end his vices outweighed his virtues that was because however hard he worked at being king he could not restore to his role the meaning which had gone out of it. Besides, he was something of an introvert, who found communication difficult. He was tempted therefore to settle self-indulgently for pleasures readily available to kings, and he succumbed. The Duc de Cröy, commenting on Louis' boredom during the 'reign' of Madame du Barry, truly observed that 'the king who is bored and to whom one speaks only of the misery in work, who is captivated by a pretty woman, who has eyes only for her and for her advantage is doubtless to be pitied and having lost his grip he will find great difficulty in regaining it. To whom can he appeal when he distrusts everybody except the one he loves? He is a being isolated in the midst of a crowd, and for him the crowd is nobody.'

In April 1774 the King was taken ill with smallpox, from which at his age there was scant likelihood of recovery. He lingered in great pain for a fortnight and died at half-past three in the afternoon of 10 May, aged sixty-four. Two days earlier Madame du Barry had left the château so that the King could make his peace with God; to the end he retained his fine appreciation of the respective lures of this world and the next. Most of his contemporaries cheated the Revolution. That old rake, the Duc de Richelieu, judged the moment of his exit to perfection, choosing to depart this life at the age of ninety-two on the very day that Louis XVI summoned the fateful meeting of the States-General. The guillotine did claim the wretched Jeanne du Barry, a surrogate victim for Philippe of Orléans and Maria Lesczinska, for the Duchesse de Châteauroux and her sisters, for Boucher and 'la belle Morphise', for Madame la marquise, and all the others who had graced or demeaned the court of the once-loved King.

The arabesque line *of Rococo: brass detail from a chest of drawers made for the bedroom of Louis XV. (342)*

EPILOGUE

THIS SHORT EPILOGUE is not intended to systematize the findings of my colleagues, much less to evolve some comforting synthesis, which might, for example, divide courts into types, relate them to their causal factors, and analyse their impacts upon national and international life. Doubtless one might make the attempt, beginning with dynastic traditions, the personalities of rulers and their intimates, the recruitment of talent, the backgrounds provided by regional cultures and legal systems, urban growth and sophistication, aristocratic codes and life-styles, political exigencies and fiscal resources. Yet I doubt whether such an analysis would produce more than a few trite and predictable observations, while even these would need to be based upon a much larger corpus of information. Of course, without passing outside early modern Europe, or entering the more esoteric corners of its history, one could produce at least four or five further collections of the present size. Moreover, Europe never constituted a closed system. We cannot think of Spain without the Moors, or south-eastern Europe without the Ottoman Turks. Just as this book was being finished, I happened to be in Sarajevo, with its sixty mosques, where thousands of Muslim Slavs still worship alongside other Slavs of the Orthodox and Catholic faiths. I could not help reflecting what a different shape this book would have taken if some of its contributors had been Bosnians, and how very different again had we been Croats or Serbs, living a few hours' drive along the winding valleys to the north or the east. Again, any typological survey of European courts would become much more meaningful if it could be laid alongside a similar survey of extra-European courts, especially those of the more sophisticated Asian states and cultures. What do they know of Europe who only Europe know?

Even, however, when a vast body of data and comparisons has been collected, it may still remain unfruitful to attempt systematization. We began by observing the problem of human boundaries. Monarchy was a stone dropped in the pond of a society: the rings filled the pond, even if the outer ones were barely observable. So exactly what people, institutions, and settings should be regarded as belonging to a given court? Equally daunting in some cases are the changes occurring throughout a long reign: not only ministers and favourites but habits of consultation and household structures can change markedly over the years, as they did even under the conservative Philip II of Spain. To compare the parliamentary institutions of one country with those of another presents formidable tasks, yet to compare monarchical courts is to compare phenomena worse recorded, more protean, less easy to define. In the period we have discussed, a royal or princely autocracy – often somewhat modified by Estates and other corporations which rulers created for their own purposes – had become the most common and successful instrument of government in Europe. Nevertheless in practice policy emanated not from a single person but from a complex group not necessarily coinciding with the official councillors. Doubtless the study of political history and its social concomitants should more often begin with this large group, 'the court', rather than with the formalized structure of councils recognized by 'constitutional history'. Many circles, unsteady and evanescent as they were, have not reached the textbooks; yet they have their places in the history of a state, and our essays suggest that they deserve closer inspection from the political standpoint alone.

Yet whatever the claims of the political historian, many readers will have found more attractive those passages wherein we have tried to describe the varied cultural influences exerted by the rulers and courtiers of Europe. That European art, architecture, music, literature, and 'philosophy' owe much to court patronage cannot be gainsaid. How did this happen within a group ostensibly dominated by spoiled princes and mutton-headed military aristocrats? Should we not regard it as a delightful miracle of history that courts became places where birth paid an ever-increasing homage to brains? And must this not count among the greatest of our debts to the Italians, firstborn of the children of Greek intelligence and Roman oratory? Of course, many writers have asked how much princely patronage was worth, and have pointed to the spectacle of Leonardo devising elaborate pageant-machinery for the court of Milan. Others have exalted the sterling qualities of republican Florence, forgetting a little too readily that the 'freedom' of Florence involved centuries of squalid political intrigue, not to mention the long exiles of Dante and many others of her great sons. Certain American historians in particular would have done well to remain on guard against their own subconscious republican affinities. After all, a good many of the monarchs, including some with little political achievement to their credit, possessed not merely money but grand ideas: they had vicarious intellectual ambitions, or at least saw works of genius as the best magnification of their fame and authority. Without the popes, Michelangelo's, Raphael's, Bernini's masterpieces would have been immeasurably diminished: Leonardo died (more or less) in the arms of Francis I, while the world-monarch Charles V stooped to retrieve the fallen brush of Titian. We may fairly claim that the plastic arts and the pride of the eyes were better served at court than letters, imagination, scholarship. Nevertheless, later in the story, one recalls that Louis XIV personally interceded with Madame de Sévigné, teaching her to love the newcomer Racine as she already loved the established Corneille. And speaking of our less brilliant British monarchs, we should recall, not that George III twitted Gibbon with writing yet another 'thick square book', but rather than George's library still forms a major glory of the British Library. Among the patrons, the political failures had at least an even chance of becoming the cultural successes. In the essay by Peter Thomas we may read how Charles I created what might have been the nucleus of our National Gallery, had not his enlightened republican enemies sold it abroad. By the same token the plutocrats of Amsterdam turned away from the sublimity of the ageing Rembrandt, while his contemporary Velázquez painted superb masterpieces under the patronage of that pathetic 'failure' Philip IV. All in all, history affords no guarantee that 'liberal', 'republican', or 'constitutional' groups will compete successfully with court patronage. And so far, democratization, socialism, protest – in whatever senses we employ these abused words – have since Goya achieved relatively little in the cultural field. In fact, one's disillusion with the post-monarchical governments of our own century arises not merely from their all-too-widespread inhumanity but from their lamentable failures of patronage. Altogether, there seems to exist no simple, moralistic zone where society interlocks with inspiration.

When, however, we have given such examples and dozens more, it would seem we have not yet attacked the subtler sociological problems of early modern patronage. One of these, for example, concerns the relationship of court life with city life. After all, during the later Middle Ages the major cities of Europe developed a new sophistication and to all appearances took a unique part in changing the whole tenor of European culture. They had a secular spirit and were governed by laymen who had expelled their bishops, were controlling their own city clergy, and in several cases had successfully defied kings and great feudal lords. In addition many also harboured universities and supported scholars, artists, and heretics. Their revolutionary test-cases came in the form of the Hussite, Lutheran, and Zwinglian Reformations, which movements arose, despite some de-

ceptive appearances to the contrary, from urban society at least as much as from monarchs, nobles, and ministers. Again, according to the extensive statistics lately compiled by Peter Burke, the majority of leading artists and scholars in Renaissance Italy – whatever types of patronage they may have needed and received in later life – came from the big cities, some of which were at least nominally republican, others ruled by princes. Such claims could certainly be supported elsewhere by reference to capitals like Paris, London, and Prague, the last-named forming in its heyday a first-rate example of interaction between municipal and courtly influences. Hence, whatever praise may be awarded to princely patronage, it cannot be regarded as an isolated or self-supporting phenomenon: it demands to be related to its urban sources of talent; indeed also to the growth of essentially urban cultural forms.

A further general topic must already have occurred to many readers, and it perhaps demands my final paragraphs. Why should this book virtually come to an end with the courts of Maria Theresa and Louis XV? Initially, it must be admitted, we did consider closing it with a chapter which should somehow 'cover' the nineteenth-century sequel, and receive some apologetic title like 'The Twilight of the Courts'. In the end it was decided not to attempt this feat, not merely because it might disturb the unity of the book, but because its implicit claims would seem rather fraudulent. To achieve any genuine coverage, several new chapters would have been required and would have added fifty per cent to the length of the volume. Far more significantly, they would have been concerned with a 'different' subject, since the French Revolution and its sequels so radically changed not only the courts but the whole surrounding world. After the ephemeral pantomime of the First Empire, it is true, the restored monarchies purported to exercise functions and powers similar to those of their predecessors. Splendid ceremonial continued or revived, intimate memoirs proliferated, court intrigues flourished, quasi-absolutist monarchs dismissed ministers, while even in a constitutional state like Great Britain, the prejudices and intellectual limitations of a widowed Queen had their effects upon public life. Nevertheless monarchies of all types were steadily becoming institutionalized in the face of ever more complex societies and problems. And when we turn to the cultural aspects of monarchy, do we not find a still stronger case for treating the nineteenth century as a story separate from that of the *Ancien Régime*?

The loss of cultural influence by the post-Napoleonic courts did not result from conscious abnegation, though it did so happen that only a very few of their sovereigns could be described as educated and sensitive men with a strong sense of their debt to civilization. Most were not gilded figureheads but plain wooden figureheads. Civilization pushed them aside, and its important movements did not even apply for support to monarchs and courtiers. With a few exceptions and nostalgic survivals such as Goethe at the miniature court of Weimar, the great rationalist and Romantic men of letters wanted to be Byronic individualists or else members of independent cliques. Some were notably anti-royalist and desired to continue in one sphere or another the

326

thrust of revolution. From this point the leap-frogging *avant-gardes* began their often tiresome yet often creative rhythms. With an increasing rapidity, progressive art and literature tended to detach themselves not merely from the courts but also from most of those assorted groups and layers we call the middle classes for these latter had developed their own types of conservatism, or even through the revival of Christianity had become less receptive of 'advanced' thinking than the old aristocracies. Théophile Gautier coined the popular slogan *épatez le bourgeois*, and within a few decades some creative characters went further still by seeking to cut themselves loose from the whole Western tradition. The bourgeoisie remained unimpressed, the working classes uninvolved. Skilled mediocrities like Winterhalter painted the courts of Napoleon III and Victoria. Yet Manet's *Olympia* scandalized both the academicians and the respectable humbugs. Cézanne and Van Gogh did not even attract notoriety, while with a harsh logic Gauguin departed for Tahiti. Faced by this chaos, middle-class taste settled for a spirited and often delightful trivialization. Great music was still written; yet all too adequately, Offenbach represented the spirit of Paris and Johann Strauss that of Vienna. Courtiers and noblemen did not, however, leave their traditional spheres of patronage in order to embrace science and technology. Though here Victorian Britain claimed to lead the world, after the most lamentable death of the Prince Consort science received little encouragement either from Windsor or from the Dukeries.

Even had the individual rulers of the last century attained great intellectual stature, their capitals had become too big and too complicated to admit of an effective central patronage. But on this plane it is fair to add that there remained a few tolerably useful monarchs. Though the ballet has a long history, the Imperial Ballet at St Petersburg occupied a most crucial phase of its modern development. Even the stodgy Habsburgs founded a great public art museum with their family treasures, while more impressively still, the kings of Bavaria built theatres, opera houses, and galleries. Following upon these triumphs of an informed but largely antiquarian enthusiasm, the medieval fantasies of the Wagnerian Ludwig II may well seem as remote as those of the *avant-garde* artists. But I must confess that his grandfather Ludwig I (r. 1825–48) would have been one of my heroes, had I been compelled to write that chapter on the courts of the nineteenth century: this not because he abdicated rather than discard Lola Montez, but because, in the teeth of a mean-spirited parliamentary opposition, he made Munich one of the finest cities of Europe; and above all because he founded that peerless collection, the Alte Pinakothek. On acquiring the famous Boisserée collection of Netherlandish and German pictures, the young Ludwig exclaimed in private to his brother:

What a collection I have now! Just wait until it is all set out together! My only wish is that there should be no mention of this in the newspapers, and especially that no one should get to know the price I paid for it. People nod their heads approvingly when you lose your money gambling, or spend it on horses, but if you use it to acquire works of art they start talking of extravagance.

And on a more public occasion he added, 'Long after the works of statesmen have passed away, the works of artists will continue to gladden the hearts of men.' Is it not this happy combination of flair, money, and achievement for future generations which has done most to palliate the sins of the old monarchies? And today, has not the work of preserving this achievement become one of the strongest ties between Eastern and Western Europe? Since 1945 astronomic sums and fantastic skills have been expended in the Soviet Union on the restoration of Tsarist palaces and treasures. If one demands the reason, one's Soviet friends reply that these, after all, were the handiwork of the Russian people. I suspect that this important half-truth forms by no means the whole justification they feel; yet the shining deed is the essence of the matter, whatever democratic emotion or strict logic may suggest. And whoever receives the lion's share of the credit, one prophecy cannot fail: nothing resembling our marvellous legacy from the courts of Europe will ever come this way again!

BIBLIOGRAPHY

One **Monarchy and cultural revival**

On the crowns at Munich, see Herbert Brunner, *Kronen und Herrschaftszeichen in der Schatzkammer der Residenz München*, Munich, 1971, in the series *Aus Bayerischen Schlössern*. The literature on the Carolingian *renovatio* is extensive, as will be observed e.g. in E. Panofsky, *Renaissance and Renascences in Western Art*, Paladin edn., London, 1970, especially pp. 43–54. On its art and architecture, see R. Hinks, *Carolingian Art*, London, 1935, and the superbly illustrated J. Hubert, J. Porcher, and W. F. Volbach, *Carolingian Art*, London, 1970. On scholarship and letters, several older works are still useful; e.g. M. L. W. Laistner, *Thought and Letters in Western Europe, A.D. 500–900*, London, 1931, and F. J. E. Raby, *A History of Secular Latin Poetry in the Middle Ages*, vol. I, Oxford, 1934. Recent works of importance in English are D. A. Bullough, *The Age of Charlemagne*, London, 1965; W. Ullmann, *The Carolingian Renaissance and the Idea of Kingship*, London, 1969; J. M. Wallace-Hadrill, *Early Germanic Kingship in England and on the Continent*, Oxford, 1971. A translated selection from the sources will be found in H. R. Loyn and J. Percival, *The Reign of Charlemagne: Documents on Carolingian Government and Administration*, London, 1975. The biographies by Einhard and Notker are well translated and edited by L. Thorpe in *Two Lives of Charlemagne* in the Penguin Classics series, Harmondsworth, Middlesex, 1969.

W. L. Warren, *Henry II*, London, 1973, provides the best general account and includes a generous bibliography. Angevin buildings are fully described in H. M. Colvin, R. A. Brown, and A. J. Taylor, *The History of the King's Works*, 2 vols., London, 1963. On the cultural side, see C. H. Haskins, 'Henry II as a Patron of Learning' in *Essays in Medieval History presented to T. F. Tout*, ed. A. G. Little and F. M. Powicke, Manchester, 1925. Walter Map's *De Nugis Curialium* has been translated into English by M. R. James, Oxford, 1914, and by F. Tupper and M. B. Ogle, London, 1924. H. Hall, *Court Life under the Plantagenets*, London, 1890, is a clever and unconventional attempt at reconstruction, still worth reading. On courtly love there is a very extensive literature. Perhaps the best short account in English is Elizabeth Salter's 'Courts and Courtly Love' in *The Medieval World*, ed. D. Daiches and A. Thorlby, London, 1973: it contains fresh insights upon the cultural positions of both Henry and Eleanor. R. Barber, *The Knight and Chivalry*, London, 1970, Cardinal edn., 1974, has useful bibliographies and is more realistic than the very speculative and literary classic by C. S. Lewis, *The Allegory of Love: A Study in Medieval Tradition*, London, 1936; Oxford paperback, 1958, 1973. Andreas Capellanus, *The Art of Courtly Love*, is a translation by J. J. Parry, New York, 1941. Concerning Eleanor and her associates, see also Amy Kelly, *Eleanor of Aquitaine and the Four Kings*, London, 1952, and the same author's article 'Eleanor of Aquitaine and her Courts of Love' in *Speculum*, xii, 1937. The following are also relevant: F. M. Chambers, 'Some Legends concerning Eleanor of Aquitaine' in *Speculum*, xvi, 1941; J. F. Benton, 'The Court of Champagne as a Literary Center' in *Speculum*, xxxvi, 1961; A. J. Denomy, 'Courtly Love and Courtliness' in *Speculum*, xxviii, 1953.

Probably the most helpful introduction to Frederick II and his background is the readable and well-informed biography by Georgina Masson, *Frederick II of Hohenstaufen*, London, 1957. It owes not a little to the scholarly but over-dramatized work by E. Kantorowicz, *Frederick the Second 1194–1250*, trans. E. O. Lorimer, London, 1931, 1957; only the German edition, Berlin, 1927, has a proper account of the source materials. For specialists, T. C. van Cleve, *The Emperor Frederick II of Hohenstaufen*, Oxford, 1972, now outstrips both, taking full account of recent researches; it includes most concise bibliographies. On Frederick's essential foundations in Norman Sicily, see the two volumes by J. J. Norwich, *The Normans in the South: 1016–1130*, London, 1967, and *The Kingdom in the Sun: 1130–1194*, London, 1970. For Frederick's *De Arte Venandi cum Avibus* see A. Wood and F. M. Fyfe, *The Art of Falconry*, London, 1943. An important survey of life and literature at court is A. de Stefano, *La Cultura a la Corte di Federico II Imperatore*, Palermo, 1938. A stimulating but sometimes incautious treatment of medieval ideas will be found in F. Heer, *The Intellectual History of Europe*, trans. J. Steinberg, London, 1966, chs. VI–VIII.

For Burgundy and Florence see the essays and bibliographies by C. A. J. Armstrong and E. B. Fryde below. S. Harrison Thomson, *Europe in Renaissance and Reformation*, New York, 1963, ch. III, provides initial guidance on the Papacy at Avignon. On Charles IV and Karlštejn see M. Levey, *Painting at Court*, London, 1971, ch. 1. Note also the brief but useful G. G. Walsh, *The Emperor Charles IV*, Oxford, 1924; B. Jarrett, *The Emperor Charles IV*, London, 1935, and S. Harrison Thomson, 'Learning at the Court of Charles IV' in *Speculum*, xxv, 1950. An introduction to the French and English courts in the later Middle Ages, together with remarkable illustrations, will be found in K. A. Fowler, *The Age of Plantagenet and Valois*, London, 1967. The court and background of Charles V are fully treated in R. Delachenal, *Histoire de Charles V*, 5 vols., Paris, 1909–31. On the semi-independent principalities, see J. H. Le Patourel, 'The King and the Princes in fourteenth-century France' in *Europe in the Late Middle Ages*, ed. J. R. Hale, J. R. L. Highfield, and B. Smalley, London, 1965. P. S. Lewis, *Later Medieval France*, London, 1968, and M. G. A. Vale, *Charles VII*, London, 1974, have valuable material on later French courts. On England see e.g. G. Mathew, *The Court of Richard II*, London, 1968; C. Ross, *Edward IV*, London, 1974; and A. R. Myers, *The Household of Edward IV*, Manchester, 1959. On the excavations in Hungary, see L. Gerevich, *The Art of Buda and Pest in the Middle Ages*, Budapest, 1971; Rózsa Feuer-Toth, *Château royal du moyen âge à Bude*, Budapest, n.d., recent; Miklós Héjj, *The Royal Palace of Visegrád*, Budapest, 1970. On the Hungarian Renaissance see especially Csaba Csapodi and Klára Csapodi-Gárdonyi, *Bibliotheca Corviniana. The Library of King Matthias Corvinus*, Shannon, Ireland, 1969.

Two **The courtier**

The most valuable and richly documented general study of courtly literature, despite the apparent limitations of its title, is Claus Uhlig, *Hofkritik im England des Mittelalters und der Renaissance*, Berlin, 1973. Pauline Smith, *The Anti-Courtier Trend in Sixteenth Century French Literature*, Geneva, 1966, is a useful if limited survey of its subject; and Ruth Kelso, *The Doctrine of the English Gentleman in the Sixteenth Century*, Urbana, Ill., 1929, offers a good bibliography of primary sources: though one should beware of the still popular, but misleading, term 'courtesy books'.

Representative examples of medieval criticism of court life are Walter Map, *De Nugis Curialium*, trans. as *Courtiers' Trifles* by F. Tupper and M. B. Ogle, London, 1924; John of Salisbury, *Frivolities of Courtiers and Footprints of Philosophers*, trans. J. B. Pike, Minneapolis and London, 1938; Alain Chartier, *The Curial*, trans. William Caxton, ed. P. Meyer and F. J. Furnivall, London, 1888; Aeneas Sylvius Piccolomini, *Miseriae Curialium*, trans. Alexander Barclay, as the first three of his *The Eclogues*, ed. B. White, London, 1928; and Jean de Bueil, *Le Jouvencel*, ed. L. Lecestre, Paris, 1887–89. The more positive view of Diomede Caraffa may be read in his *Dello optimo cortesano*, ed. G. Paparelli, Salerno, 1971. Etiquette books are legion: but elementary examples may be seen in Caxton's *Book of Curtesye*, London, 1868; and in *Early English Meals and Manners*, London, 1868; and *Queene Elizabeth's Achademy*, London, 1869 – all edited by F. J. Furnivall for the Early English Text Society. These should be compared with the popular sixteenth-century essay in this genre, G. della Casa's *Galateo*, 1558, trans. R. S. Pine-Coffin, Harmondsworth, Middlesex, 1958. For the ritualistic organization of a great fifteenth-century household, see 'L'Estat de la maison du duc Charles de Bourgogne dit le Hardy' in Olivier de la Marche, *Mémoires*, IV, ed. H. Beaune and J. d'Arbaumont, Paris, 1883–88.

Basic texts on the military and courtly-love aspects of chivalry are, respectively, Ramon Lull, *Book of the Ordre of Chyvalry*, trans. Caxton, ed. A. T. P. Byles, London, 1926; and Andreas Capellanus, *The Art of Courtly Love*, trans. J. J. Parry, New York, 1941. The chivalric background to our problem may be studied in R. Barber, *The Knight and Chivalry*, London, 1970, a good general survey of a difficult field; S. Painter, *French Chivalry*, Baltimore, 1940, a remarkable feat of compression; and in a wide-ranging collection of essays edited by E. Prestage, *Chivalry. A Series of Studies to Illustrate its Historical Significance and Civilizing Influence*, London, 1928. Two essays by Gervase Mathew are helpful to the reader seeking out the chivalric resonances in Castiglione: 'Ideals of Knighthood in late fourteenth century England' in *Studies in Medieval History presented to F. M. Powicke*, Oxford, 1948; and 'Ideals of Friendship' in *Patterns of Love and Courtesy. Essays in Memory of C. S. Lewis*, London, 1966. The medieval background to the arms and letters controversy is the subject of C. Oulmont, *Les débats du clerc et du chevalier dans la littérature poétique du moyen âge*, Paris, 1911; and fifteenth-century views on education may be studied in W. H. Woodward, *Vittorino da Feltre and Other Humanist Educators*, revised edn. by E. F. Rice, New York, 1963. The courtly-love traditions are elegantly elucidated by C. S. Lewis, *The Allegory of Love*, Oxford, 1936; and G. Luck, '*Vir facetus*: a Renaissance Ideal' in *Studies in Philology*, lv, 1958 offers an unusual insight into joke literature, and especially on Pontano's contribution to the analysis of humour.

The decline of the knight, or his metamorphosis into a courtier or gentleman, is studied by R. L. Kilgour, *The Decline of Chivalry as shown in the French Literature of the Late Middle Ages*, Cambridge, Mass., and London, 1937; and by A. B. Ferguson, *The Indian Summer of English Chivalry: Studies in the Decline and Transformation of Chivalric Idealism*, Durham, N. C., 1960. The extent to which this transformation took place may be illustrated by reference to Antonio Ansalone, *Il cavaliere descritto in tre libri*, Messina, 1629, where all the courtly arts are attributed to the knight. O. Cartellieri, *The Court of Burgundy*, London, 1929, remains a helpful survey of a topic crucial in the evolution of the courtier; while, as an illustration of the range of chivalric activity, it is worth reading Gutierre Diaz de Gamez, *The Unconquered Knight. A Chronicle of the Deeds of Don Pero Niño*, trans. Joan Evans, London, 1928. For the prince as the archetypal courtier, see S. Anglo, *The Great Tournament Roll of Westminster*, Oxford, 1968. More specifically on the Emperor Maximilian, see L. Baldass, *Der Künstlerkreis Kaiser Maximilians*, Vienna, 1923; and G. E. Waas, *The Legendary Character of Kaiser Maximilian*, New York, 1941. On René d'Anjou, see R. A. Lecoy de la Marche, *Le Roi René: sa vie, son administration, ses travaux artistiques et littéraires*, Paris, 1875.

Baldassare Castiglione's *Il libro del Cortegiano* may be studied in the oft-reprinted text by V. Cian, 4th edn. 1947; or the more recent versions edited by Bruno Maier, *Il Cortegiano con una scelta delle Opere minori*, Turin, 1955; or S. Del Missier, *Il Cortegiano*, Novara, 1968. The most accurate English translation is by L. E. Opdycke, London, 1901; though Sir Thomas Hoby's translation, which first appeared in 1561, is more colourful if less exact. The standard critical study is E. Loos, *Baldassare Castigliones 'Libro del Cortegiano': Studien zur Tugendauffassung des Cinquecento*, Frankfurt a. M., 1955. For biographical details, see V. Cian, *Un illustre nunzio pontificio del Rinascimento. Baldassare Castiglione*, Vatican City, 1951. Julia Cartwright, *The Perfect Courtier*, London, 1908, retains value as a picture of Castiglione's life and times. Louis Guyon's distillation of Castiglione, referred to at the beginning of my essay, is to be found in his *Les diverses leçons*, Paris, 1604, trans. Thomas Milles, *The Treasurie of Auncient and Moderne Times*, London, 1613–19.

Examples of continuing traditions in anti-courtier literature may be seen in Ulrich von Hutten, *Aula. Dialogus*, Augsburg, 1518; and in Antonio de Guevara, *Menosprecio de corte y alabanza de aldea*, ed. M. de Burgos, Madrid, 1915, trans. Sir Francis Bryan, *A Dispraise of the Life of a Courtier and a Commendacion of the Life of a Labouryng Man*, London, 1548. The changing direction of courtly interests and their social context may be studied in Stefano Guazzo, *La civil conversatione*, Brescia, 1574, trans. G. Pettie and B. Young, London, 1581, 1586, ed. Sir E. Sullivan, London, 1925. On Guazzo, see J. L. Lievsay, *Stefano Guazzo and the English Renaissance 1575–1675*, Chapel Hill, N.C., 1961. This is an important study, but its overstatements should be modified in the light of D. Javitch, 'Rival Arts of Conduct in Elizabethan England: Guazzo's *Civile Conversation* and Castiglione's *Courtier*' in *Yearbook of Italian Studies*, i, 1971.

Lucian's influential *The Parasite* may be read in *The Works of Lucian of Samosata*, trans. H. H. and F. G. Fowler, Oxford, 1905, III, pp. 167–90; and an outstanding example of Lucianic anti-court satire is Philibert de Vienne, *Le Philosophe de Court*, Lyon, 1547, trans. George North, *The Philosopher of the Court*, London, 1575. Philibert's significance was first pointed out by C. A. Mayer, 'L'Honnête Homme, Molière and

Philibert de Vienne's *Philosophe de Court*' in *Modern Language Review*, XLVI, 1951. D. Javitch, '*The Philosopher of the Court*: a French Satire Misunderstood' in *Comparative Literature*, XXIII, 1971, is an illuminating examination of the text. The most striking instance of a purely cynical approach to court life is Lorenzo Ducci, *Arte Aulica*, Ferrara, 1601, trans. Edward Blount, *Ars Aulica or the Courtiers Arte*, London, 1607. Finally, the later history of our subject receives detailed treatment in M. Magendie, *La Politesse mondaine et les théories de l'honnêteté en France au XVIIe siècle de 1600–1660*, Paris, 1925.

Three The golden age of Burgundy

There exists a superabundant documentation of narrative and record material about Valois-Burgundy, though rather less after 1483. For a brief survey, see R. Vaughan, *The Valois dukes of Burgundy: Inaugural Lecture*, University of Hull Publications, 1965. Indispensable for sections referring to the court and for their copious bibliography are the same author's *Philip the Bold*, 1962; *John the Fearless*, 1966; *Philip the Good*, 1970; *Charles the Bold*, 1973; all London.

For the court alone see Otto Cartellieri, *Am Hofe der Herzöge von Burgund*, Basle, 1926, translated as *The Court of Burgundy*, 1929, which summarizes a number of his previous articles, e.g. the court theatre (not treated above), 'Theaterspiele am Hofe Karls des Kühnen' in *Germanisch-romanische Monatschrift*, IX, 1921. Cartellieri was one of the few professional historians with an interest for and understanding of jousts and tourneys, the ceremonial aspect of which has been studied by S. Anglo, 'Anglo-Burgundian Feats of Arms at Smithfield, June 1467' in *Guildhall Miscellany*, II, no. 7, 1965, and *The Great Tournament Roll of Westminster*, Oxford, 1968. For the archaeology of the court nothing can equal Florens Deuchler, *Die Burgunderbeute, Inventar der Beutestücke aus den Schlachten von Grandson, Murten und Nancy 1476/1477*, Bern, 1963. This work is worth consulting even if the reader is ignorant of German for its splendid illustrations of the widest range of objects from precious to trivial, e.g. the reconstructed mask of the court fool, p. 350. For other princely courts in fifteenth-century France, see F. Piponnier, *Costume et vie sociale, la cour d'Anjou XIVe–XVe siècle*, Paris, 1970, informative, too, on subjects other than costume. For dress see M. Beaulieu and J. Baylé, *Le costume en Bourgogne de Philippe le Hardi à la mort de Charles le Téméraire (1364–1477)*, Paris, 1956; P. Wescher, 'Fashion and Elegance at the court of Burgundy' in *CIBA Review*, LI, July 1946. On the study of individual portraits and the pictorial taste of many courtiers E. Panofsky, *Early Netherlandish Painting. Its origin and character*, Harvard, 1958, supersedes most previous publications, although there still remains much to be done, as indicated by K. B. McFarlane's critique of the portrait of Sir John Donne of Kidwelly in his posthumous book *Hans Memling*, Oxford, 1971. Within the vast literature relating to illuminated MSS. produced at or for the court, special interest attaches to O. Pächt, *The Master of Mary of Burgundy*, London, 1947, together with *La miniature flamande, le mécénat de Philippe le Bon*, ed. H. Liebaers and L. M. J. Delaissé, Brussels, 1959, and *Miniatures médiévales de la librairie de Bourgogne au cabinet des manuscrits de la bibliothèque royale de Belgique*, ed. L. M. J. Delaissé, H. Liebaers, and F. Masai, Geneva, 1959. Intensive research on particular themes has produced valuable information; e.g. A. H. van Buren, 'Books for a Burgundian courtier; evidence for two Flemish illuminators' shops' in *The Princeton University Library Chronicle*, XXXIV, 2, 1973. For the influence of literature on society, commoners as well as knights, see G. Doutrepont, *La Littérature française à la cour des ducs de Bourgogne*, Paris, 1909, and his *Les mises en prose des épopées chevaleresques du XIVe au XVe siècle*, Brussels, 1939, and Geneva, 1966. For the literary and ethical interests encouraged by the Duchess Isabelle see C. C. Willard, 'Isabel of Portugal and the French translation of the Triunfo de las Donas' in *Revue belge de philologie et d'histoire*, XLIII, 2, 1965; 'The concept of true nobility at the Burgundian court' in *Studies in the Renaissance*, XIV, 1967; 'Isabel of Portugal, patroness of humanism' in *Miscellanea di studi e ricerche sul quattrocento francese*, Turin, 1967, with valuable footnotes.

For music sacred and secular see E. A. Bowles, 'Instruments at the court of Burgundy' in *Galpin Society Journal*, VI, 1953; J. Marix, *Les musiciens de la cour de Bourgogne au XVe siècle*, Paris, 1937, and her *Histoire de la musique et des musiciens sous le règne de Philippe le Bon*, Collection d'études musicologiques, vol. XXVIII, Strasbourg, 1939. And on Burgundian music in a wider context see A. Pirro, *Histoire de la musique de la fin du XIVe à la fin du XVIe siècle*, Paris, 1940.

Four Lorenzo de' Medici

The best bibliography on the Medici is in S. Camerani, *Bibliografia Medicea*, Florence, 1964.

The earliest contemporary life of Lorenzo was written by Niccolo Valori, surviving in manuscripts presented to Lorenzo's children. It was published by L. Mehus, *Laurentii Medicei Vita*, Florence, 1749, and is discussed by M. Martelli in *La Bibliofilia*, 66, 1964. There are valuable nearly contemporary comments on Lorenzo in 'Storie Fiorentine' of Francesco Guicciardini, edited in Guicciardini's *Opere* by V. de Caprariis, Milan and Naples, 1953. The best collection of correspondence in English translation is in J. Ross, *Lives of the Early Medici as told in their Correspondence*, London, 1910.

The most solid of the older biographies is A. von Reumont, *Lorenzo de Medici, the Magnificent*, English trans., 2 vols., London, 1876. E. Armstrong, *Lorenzo de Medici and Florence in the Fifteenth Century*, 2nd edn., London, 1923, is a wise book and there is a shorter biography by C. M. Ady, *Lorenzo dé Medici and Renaissance Italy*, London, 1955. N. Rubinstein, *The Government of Florence under the Medici, 1434–1494*, Oxford, 1966, supersedes all previous works, as does R. de Roover, *The Rise and Decline of the Medici Bank*, Cambridge, Mass., 1963.

The best introduction to Lorenzo's artistic patronage is in E. H. Gombrich, 'The Early Medici as Patrons of Art' in *Italian Renaissance Studies*, ed. E. F. Jacob, London, 1960. There is no up-to-date account in English of Lorenzo's writings. The most penetrating, though controversial, recent researches are contained in M. Martelli, *Studi Laurenziani*, Florence, 1965.

Five Francis I

PRIMARY SOURCES

No household ordinance for the reign of Francis I has survived; but there are a number of manuscript household accounts in Paris at the Archives Nationales (in the KK series) and at the Bibliothèque Nationale. These may be usefully compared with accounts of the same kind for earlier reigns published in L. Douët-D'Arcq, *Comptes de l'hôtel des rois de France aux XIVe et XVe siècles*, Paris, 1855. Francis I's building expenses will be found in L. de Laborde, *Les Comptes des bâtiments du roi (1528–71)*, 2 vols., Paris, 1877. Appointments to court offices may be traced in the *Catalogue des actes de François Ier*, 10 vols., Paris, 1887–1908; the eighth volume of this work contains the King's itinerary. Important glimpses of the court are contained in contemporary diplomatic dispatches, as for example in *Relations des ambassadeurs vénitiens sur les affaires de France au XVIe siècle*, ed. N. Tommaseo, 2 vols., Paris, 1838; *Letters and Papers, Foreign and Domestic, of the reign of Henry VIII, 1509–47*, ed. Brewer, Gairdner, and Brodie, 21 vols., London, 1862–1910; and *State Papers of Henry VIII*, 11 vols., London, 1830–52. Among contemporary narrative sources, the following are relevant: *Mémoires du Maréchal de Florange*, ed. R. Goubaux and P. A. Lemoisne, 2 vols., Paris, 1913; *Le Journal d'un bourgeois de Paris sous le règne de François Ier*, ed. V.-L. Bourrilly, Paris, 1910; and *Cronique du roy Françoys premier de ce nom*, ed. G. Guiffrey, Paris, 1860; Brantôme, *Oeuvres complètes*, ed. L. Lalanne, 11 vols., Paris 1864–82; and *Mémoires de Martin et Guillaume Du Bellay*, ed. V.-L. Bourrilly and F. Vindry, 4 vols., Paris, 1908. Catherine de Médicis' letter of advice to her son, Charles IX, will be found in *Lettres de Catherine de Médicis*, ed. H. de La Ferrière-Percy, Paris, 1885, vol. 2, pp. 91–92. For Francis I's art patronage see *The Life of Benvenuto Cellini*, ed. J. Pope-Hennessy, London, 1949, and G. Vasari, *The Lives of the Painters, Sculptors and Architects*, ed. W. Gaunt, 4 vols., London, 1963. An indication of the original contents of the King's collection at Fontainebleau is provided by P. Dan, *Le Trésor des merveilles de la maison royale de Fontainebleau*, Paris, 1642. For his library see H. Omont, *Anciens inventaires et catalogues de la Bibliothèque Nationale*, vol. 1, Paris, 1908.

SECONDARY SOURCES

The best general work on the reign of Francis I is still that of H. Lemonnier in E. Lavisse, *Histoire de France*, vol. 5, Paris, 1903. For a brief account of the constitutional aspects see R. J. Knecht, *Francis I and Absolute Monarchy*, London, 1969. The structure of the court is described by R. Doucet, *Les institutions de la France au XVIe siècle*, Paris, 1948, and by G. Zeller, *Les institutions de la France au XVIe siècle*, Paris, 1948. For royal entries see B. Guénée and F. Lehoux, *Les Entrées royales françaises de 1328 à 1515*, Paris, 1968; J. Chartrou, *Les Entrées solennelles et triomphales à la renaissance, 1484–1551*, Paris, 1928; A. Huon, 'Le Thème du Prince dans les entrées parisiennes au XVIe siècle' in *Les Fêtes de la renaissance*, ed. J. Jacquot, Paris, 1956; and more generally R. Strong, *Splendour at Court*, London, 1973. Other aspects of court ceremonial are examined by S. Anglo, 'Le Camp du Drap d'Or et les entrevues d'Henri VIII et de Charles Quint' in *Les Fêtes de la renaissance*, ed. J. Jacquot, vol. 2, Paris, 1959; J. G. Russell, *The Field of Cloth of Gold*, London, 1969; M. Bloch, *Les Rois thaumaturges*, Paris, 1961; and R. E. Giesey, *The Royal Funeral Ceremony in Renaissance France*, Geneva, 1960. Court manners are discussed in W. L. Wiley, *The Gentleman of Renaissance France*, Cambridge, Mass., 1954, and A. Lefranc, *La vie quotidienne au temps de la renaissance*, Paris, 1938. For literary attacks on the court see P. M. Smith, *The Anti-Courtier Trend in Sixteenth Century French Literature*, Geneva, 1966. The best general survey of Francis I's artistic patronage is A. Blunt, *Art and Architecture in France 1500–1700*, Harmondsworth, Middlesex, 1957. See also two valuable exhibition catalogues: the first on *L'Ecole de Fontainebleau*, Paris, 1972; the second, on *La Collection de François Ier*, Paris, 1972. Among many works on the palaces of Francis I the following are particularly useful: F. Gébelin, *Les Châteaux de la renaissance*, Paris, 1927, and F. Herbet, *Le Château de Fontainebleau*, Paris, 1937. The role of the architect is examined by P. Lesueur, *Dominique de Cortone dit Le Boccador*, Paris, 1924; L. H. Heydenreich, 'Leonardo da Vinci, Architect of Francis I' in *Burlington Magazine*, XCIV, 1952; and C. Pedretti, *Leonardo da Vinci: The Royal Palace at Romorantin*, Cambridge, Mass., 1972. For individual painters see P. Mellen, *Jean Clouet*, London, 1971; J. Shearman, *Andrea del Sarto*, Oxford, 1965; K. Kusenberg, *Le Rosso*, Paris, 1931; L. Dimier, *Le Primatice*, Paris, 1928. For the King's artistic patronage and the agents he employed see J. Adhémar, 'The Collection of Francis the first' in *Gazette des Beaux Arts*, 6th series, XXX, 1946; and his 'Aretino: artistic adviser to Francis I' in *Journal of Warburg and Courtauld Institutes* XVII, 1954; also M. G. de la Coste-Messelière, 'Battista della Palla, conspirateur, marchand ou homme de cour?' in *L'Oeil*, vol. 29, 1965. For one interpretation among several see D. and E. Panofsky, 'The Iconography of the Galerie François Ier at Fontainebleau' in *Gazette des Beaux Arts*, 6th series, LII, 1958. An important study of the Fontainebleau bronzes is S. Pressouyre, 'Les Fontes de Primatice' in *Bulletin Monumental*, 1969. A useful background to Francis I's patronage of scholarship is provided by *French Humanism 1470–1600*, ed. W. L. Gundersheimer, London, 1969. For special aspects see A. Lefranc, *Histoire du Collège de France*, Paris, 1893; L. Delaruelle, *Guillaume Budé*, Paris, 1907; E. Armstrong, *Robert Estienne, Royal Printer*, Cambridge, 1954. On the court and religion see P. Imbart de la Tour, *Les Origines de la réforme*, 4 vols., Paris, 1905–14; L. Febvre, *Au Coeur religieux du 16e siècle*, Paris 1957; P. Jourda, *Marguerite d'Angoulême*, 2 vols, Paris, 1930; *Aspects de la propagande religieuse* by G. Berthoud and others, Geneva, 1957; and G. Berthoud, *Antoine Marcourt*, Geneva, 1973.

Six The Austrian Habsburgs

A comprehensive history of the Imperial Habsburg court remains unwritten, as indeed does any survey of the whole interplay of society, culture, and politics in this period. But the subject has so many ramifications that specialized literature is enormous, though very little of it can be found in English. For a first orientation in the history of the Habsburgs see A. Wandruszka, *The House of Habsburg*, trans. C. and H. Epstein, London, 1964. Standard German-language histories of the Habsburg realm – the most recent is by E. Zöllner, *Geschichte Österreichs*, Munich, 1962 – tend to be thin on life at court and on the underlying features of government. Many of the stories are reproduced in E. Vehse, *Memoirs of the Court, Aristocracy and Diplomacy of Austria*, trans. F. Demmler, 2 vols., London, 1856. For anything like a continuous narrative the English reader must go back to the prolific Archdeacon Coxe: W. Coxe, *History of the House of Austria*, 2 vols., London, 1807. Biographies ought to be a good *entrée*, but only one of the seven emperors discussed in the text has a satisfactory modern treatment: V. Bibl, *Maximilian II, der rätselhafte Kaiser*, Hellerau bei Dresden, 1929. Older writers were obsessed by politics or impossibly prolix for today's tastes; good examples are F. B. von Bucholtz, *Geschichte der Regierung Ferdinand des ersten*, 9 vols., Vienna, 1831–38, and F. Hurter, *Geschichte Kaiser Ferdinands II . . . bis zu dessen Krönung*, 11 vols., Schaffhausen, 1850–67. Nor are the politicians much better served; nothing at all adequate exists on Eggenberg or Trautmannsdorf. Two serviceable old works are J. von Hammer-Purgstall, *Khlesls, des Cardinals . . . Leben*, 4 vols., Vienna, 1847–51, and A. Wolf, *Fürst Wenzel Lobkowitz*, Vienna, 1869; compare the recent general article on favourites by J. Bérenger, 'Le ministériat au XVIIe siècle' in *Annales Economies, Sociétés, Civilisations*, XXIX, Paris, 1974. There is a series of modern histories of the aulic administration: T. Fellner, *Die österreichische Zentralverwaltung*, ed. H. Kretschmayr, Abteilung I, 2 vols., Vienna, 1907; L. Gross, *Die Geschichte der deutschen Reichshofkanzlei*, Vienna, 1933; O. von Gschliesser, *Der Reichshofrat*, Vienna, 1942; H. F. Schwarz, *The Imperial Privy Council in the seventeenth century*, Cambridge, Mass., 1943. Administration embraces maladministration, and the remarkable story of Rudolf II's chamberlain Philipp Lang: F. Hurter, *Philipp Lang . . . eine Criminal-Geschichte aus dem Anfang des siebzehnten Jahrhunderts*, Schaffhausen, 1851.

The best evidence comes, of course, from chroniclers who knew the situation at court, though they often assume too much about their surroundings to be really illuminating. F. C. Khevenhüller, *Annales Ferdinandei*, 12 vols. in 7, Leipzig, 1721–26, is a mine of uneven information. G. Gualdo Priorato, *Historia di Ferdinando III Imperatore*, Vienna, 1672, and *Historia di Leopoldo Cesare*, 2 vols., Vienna, 1670, is a typically pedestrian paid historiographer, but the anonymous *Life of Leopold late Emperor of Germany*, London, 1706, offers livelier fare, as does its expanded German counterpart: E. G. Rinck, *Leopolds des Grossen . . . wunderwürdiges Leben und Thaten*, Leipzig, 1709. Obscurer works may throw shafts of light: the story of Rudolf's musicians, for example, comes from J. J. Beckovský, *Poselkyně starých příběhův českých*, ed. A. Rezek, 3 vols., Prague, 1879–80. Some travellers from western Europe are very readable, especially Esprinchard: L. Chatenay, *Vie de J. Esprinchard*, Paris, 1957; E. Browne, *An Account of Several Travels through a great part of Germany*, London, 1677; C. Patin, *Travels through Germany, Bohemia . . . and other parts of Europe*, Eng. trans., London, 1696; and C. Freschot, *Mémoires de la cour de Vienne*, Cologne, 1705. Other observers confided information to their masters which has since been printed as source material, above all the Venetian ambassadors: *Relazioni degli ambasciatori veneti . . .*, ed. E. Albèri, 1st series, no. 6, Florence, 1839–63; *Die Relationen der Botschafter Venedigs . . . im 17. Jahrhundert*, ed. J. Fiedler, 2 vols., Vienna, 1866–67; and the papal nuncios (too extensive to be cited here, but listed in L.-E. Halkin, 'Les archives des nonciatures' in *Bulletin de l'Institut Historique Belge de Rome*, XXXIII, 1961). A similar, but isolated, account is O. Redlich, 'Das Tagebuch E. Pufendorfs' in *Mitteilungen des Instituts für Österreichische Geschichtsforschung*, XXXVII, 1916. An invaluable contemporary description of the court and its composition is *The Particular State of the Government of the Emperour, Ferdinand the Second*, London, 1637, originally published in Latin (*Status particularis . . .*); the Latin edition includes an account of the situation in Prague in 1609 by one Daniel Eremita.

On the cultural role O. Brunner, *Adeliges Landleben und europäischer Geist*, Salzburg, 1949, though only tangential, has already become a classic. I have tried to interpret the strange court of Rudolf in *Rudolf II and his World*, Oxford, 1973, with further bibliography. A good insight into the largely unexplored private world of Leopold is given by T. von Karajan, 'Kaiser Leopold I und Peter Lambeck' in *Almanach der kais. Akademie der Wissenschaften*, XVIII, 1868. There is much on the Imperial collections in A. Lhotsky, *Die Geschichte der Sammlungen*, 2 vols., Vienna, 1941–45. Works about individual artists are numerous – four on Arcimboldo alone in recent years. Best introduction to the many facets of Habsburg patronage are the articles and documents printed over nearly a century in a journal originally entitled *Jahrbuch der Kunsthistorischen Sammlungen des allerhöchsten Kaiserhauses*, nowadays known as *Jahrbuch der Kunsthistorischen Sammlungen in Wien*. On Imperial piety see A. Coreth, *Pietas Austriaca*, Vienna, 1959; for the opposed phenomenon of the *Hofjude* see S. Stern, *The Court Jew*, Philadelphia, 1950. One curious aspect of court privilege is examined by A. von Wretschko, *Die Verleihung gelehrter Grade durch den Kaiser*, Weimar, 1910. On music in general consult L. von Köchel (of Mozart fame!), *Die kaiserliche Hof-Musikkapelle in Wien*, Vienna, 1869; and R. Haas, *Musik des Barocks*, Potsdam, 1928; more specifically: *Musikalische Werke der Kaiser Ferdinand III, Leopold I und Josef I*, ed. G. Adler, 2 vols, Vienna, 1892–93. The latest history of the court library is *Geschichte der Österreichischen Nationalbibliothek*, ed. J. Stummvoll, Vienna, 1968.

Seven The Tudors

Place of publication is London unless otherwise stated.

BIBLIOGRAPHIES:
A great many books and articles touching on the Tudor court are appraised in Mortimer Levine, *Bibliographical Handbooks: Tudor England, 1485–1603*, Cambridge 1968, which should be supplemented by Conyers Read, *Bibliography of British History: Tudor Period*, 2nd edn., Oxford, 1959.

RECORD SOURCES
The most relevant records are the accounts of different officials of the royal household preserved in the Public Record Office among the Exchequer, King's Remembrancer, Various Accounts, Wardrobe and Household. For Henry VIII's reign much of this material has been abstracted for *The Calendar of Letters and Papers, Foreign and Domestic, Henry VIII*, 37 vols., 1864–1932. For the years after 1547, however, there is no comparable publication. Among many published documents the most useful are *A Collection of Ordinances and Regulations for the Government of the Royal Household*, Society of Antiquaries of London, 1790; F. Madden, *Privy Purse Expenses of the Princess Mary*, 1831; and John Nichols, *The Progresses and Public Processions of Queen Elizabeth*, 3 vols., 1823.

CHRONICLES
Many sidelights on the court are contained in Edward Hall, *The Union of the Two Noble and Illustre Famelies York and Lancaster*, ed. H. Ellis, 1809; there is also an edition by C. Whibley, 1934; Polydore Vergil, *Anglica Historia*, ed. Denys Hay, Camden Soc. 3rd series, vol. 74, 1950; Charles Wriothesley, *A Chronicle of England, 1485–1559*, ed. W. D. Hamilton, Camden Soc. N.S., vols. 11 and 20, 1875–77; Raphael Holinshed, *Chronicles*, ed. H. Ellis, 6 vols., 1807–8; and John Stow, *Chronicles*, 1605 edn.

THE SOVEREIGNS
S. B. Chrimes, *Henry VII*, 1972, J. J. Scarisbrick, *Henry VIII*, 1968, and W. K. Jordan, *Edward VI: the Young King*, 1968, have superseded earlier lives. For Mary I there is no satisfactory alternative to H. F. M. Prescott, *Spanish Tudor: the life of Bloody Mary*, 1940. J. E. Neale, *Queen Elizabeth*, 1934, is a classic, though unlike the above volumes gives no references. There have been several lives of the Queen in the past ten years, of which the latest, and the longest, is Paul Johnson, *Elizabeth I: a study in power and intellect*, 1974. Of the studies of Henry VIII's queens the most outstanding are Garrett Mattingly, *Catherine of Aragon*, 1942, and Lacey Baldwin Smith, *A Tudor Tragedy: the life and times of Catherine Howard*, 1961. P. Friedmann, *Anne Boleyn: a chapter in English history, 1527–36*, 2 vols., 1884, is authoritative if dull. An understanding of the religious background is fundamental and the best guide is A. G. Dickens, *The English Reformation*, 1964.

THE ROYAL HOUSEHOLD
Specialist studies on the organization and finance of the royal household include A. P. Newton, 'Tudor Reforms in the Royal Household' in *Tudor Studies presented to A. F. Pollard*, ed. R. W. Seton-Watson, 1924; W. C. Richardson, *Tudor Chamber Administration, 1485–1547*, Baton Rouge, La., 1952; Neville Williams, 'Sessions of the Clerk of the Market of the Household' in *Trans. of the London and Middlesex Arch. Soc.*, vol. 19, 1957; and Allegra Woodworth, 'Purveyance for the royal household in the reign of Queen Elizabeth' in *Trans. of the American Philosophical Soc.*, N.S., vol. 35, 1945. G. R. Elton, *The Tudor Revolution in Government*, Cambridge, 1953, has important sections dealing with the changes in household administration under Thomas Cromwell.

THE COURT
Sydney Anglo, *Spectacle, Pageantry and Early Tudor Policy*, Oxford, 1969, contains fresh ideas and is well documented for the period to 1558. Joycelyn G. Russell, *The Field of Cloth of Gold*, 1969, though concerned with a single event sheds light on the personalities of the early court of Henry VIII. Neville Williams, *Henry VIII and his Court*, 1971, surveys developments during a seminal reign and his *All the Queen's Men*, 1972, discusses the position of courtiers under Elizabeth I. David Mathew, *The Courtiers of Henry VIII*, 1970, is a series of short studies.

SCHOLARSHIP
There has been renewed interest in the humanities at court and their effect on politics. Notable studies are Arthur B. Ferguson, *The Articulate Citizen and the English Renaissance*, Durham, N.C., 1965; J. E. Paul, *Catherine of Aragon and her friends*, 1966; and W. Gordon Zeeveld, *Foundations of Tudor Policy*, Cambridge, Mass., 1948. An important reassessment is G. R. Elton, *Reform and Renewal: Thomas Cromwell and the Common Weal*, Cambridge, 1973.

THE ARTS AND MUSIC
From a growing literature in a formerly neglected field should be noted Erna Auerbach, *Tudor Artists*, 1954; E. K. Chambers, *The Elizabethan Stage*, 4 vols., Oxford, 1923 – especially vol. 1; John Dent, *The Quest for Nonsuch*, 1962; A. Hughes and F. Abraham, *Ars Nova and the Renaissance*, 1960; J. Stevens, *Music and Poetry in the Early Tudor Court*, 1941; and Roy Strong, *Holbein and Henry VIII*, 1967. The best survey for the second half of the century is A. L. Rowse, *The Elizabethan Renaissance: the Cultural Achievement*, 1972.

Eight Philip IV of Spain

The court of Philip IV has more often been treated as a source of picturesque anecdote than as a subject for serious investigation. The standard work on the subject in English is still Martin Hume, *The Court of Philip IV*, London, 1907, and for Hume Spain was 'cursed with the gayest and wickedest court since that of Heliogabulus'. But if he was always liable to succumb to the more picturesque aspects of his theme, he was widely read in Spanish manuscript sources, and his book remains a lively, if not always reliable, account of the reign. In Spanish, José Deleito y Piñuela has collected a vast mass of detailed information about life in the court and the capital in a series of volumes, especially *El Rey Se Divierte*, Madrid, 1935, and *Sólo Madrid es Corte*, Madrid, 1953. These are largely based on contemporary literature, newsletters, and the reports of foreign travellers. Of these, the 'Voyage d'Antoine Brunel en Espagne (1655)' in *Revue Hispanique*, 30, 1914, and François Bertaut, 'Journal du Voyage d'Espagne (1659)' in *Revue Hispanique*, 47, 1919, are the fullest and most interesting. The more famous memoirs of Mme D'Aulnoy, reprinted in the *Revue Hispanique*, 67, 1926, are not to be trusted.

Historians of art and the theatre have shown more interest in the court of Philip IV than political and social historians. But Antonio Domínguez Ortiz has made a useful brief survey of court finances, 'Los gastos de la Corte en la España del Siglo XVII' in his *Crisis y Decadencia de la España de los Austrias*, Barcelona, 1969; and there is useful information on court offices and ceremonial in Antonio Rodríguez Villa, *Etiquetas de la Casa de Austria*, Madrid, 1913. The character of Olivares and of his relationship with the royal family and leading court figures is vividly analysed by Dr Gregorio Marañón in *El Conde-Duque de Olivares*, Madrid, 1936. I hope to continue the reassessment of Olivares begun by Marañón with a study of his political career which I am now preparing.

Carl Justi, *Diego Velázquez and his Times*, trans., London, 1889, remains easily the best general account of the cultural and artistic life of the court, but Justi has by no means said the last word. Much more, for instance, is known now than in Justi's time about the court theatre and theatrical design, as a result in particular of the pioneering work of N. D. Shergold, *A History of the Spanish Stage*, Oxford, 1967, and of Professor J. E. Varey, who produced with Professor Shergold an important illustrated edition of one of the court plays, Juan Vélez de Guevara's *Los Celos Hacen Estrellas*, London, 1970.

There is still surprisingly little good work on the Court architecture of the reign; and although Gómez de Mora's plans of the Alcázar were discovered in the Vatican Library some twenty-five years ago, they have so far received little attention from seventeenth-century historians, and have rarely been reproduced. The history of the Buen Retiro has still to be properly studied, but there is a valuable pioneering article on the Hall of the Realms by Elías Tormo y Monzó, reprinted in his *Pintura, Escultura y Arquitectura en España*, Madrid, 1949. Nor has Philip IV's patronage of the arts received the attention it deserves, although Svetlana Alpers shows in *The Decoration of the Torre de la Parada*, London, 1971, the kind of opportunities that exist. A good starting point is provided by the 1686 inventory of 1457 paintings in the Alcázar published with a commentary by Yves Bottineau in the *Bulletin Hispanique*, 58 and 60, 1956 and 1958.

Nine Charles I of England

Place of publication is London unless otherwise stated.

The *Calendars of State Papers Domestic* and, even more, the *Calendars of State Papers Venetian* for the period are an indispensable source of information of many sorts. Invaluable too are the contemporary letters in Thomas Birch, *The Court and Times of Charles the First*, ed. R. F. Williams, 2 vols., 1848, which also contains the *Memoirs of the Mission in England of the Capucin Friars 1630–1669*. I drew also on *The Letters, Speeches and Proclamations of King Charles I*, ed. Sir C. Petrie, 1935; *The Letters of Queen Henrietta Maria*, ed. M. A. E. Green, 1857; the Marshal de Bassompierre's *Memoirs*, trans. J. W. Croker, 1819; Bulstrode Whitelocke, *Memorials*, 1682; Nehemiah Wallington, *Historical Notices*, ed. R. Webb, 2 vols., 1869; Sir Henry Herbert, *The Dramatic Records*, ed. J. Q. Adams, Ithaca, N.Y., 1917; Dorothea Townshend, *The Life and Letters of Mr Endymion Porter*, 1897; and L. P. Smith, *The Life and Letters of Sir Henry Wotton*, 2 vols., Oxford, 1966.

Contemporary pamphlets used, in addition to those named in the text, include *A True Discourse of all the Royal Passages . . . at the . . . Marriage of Charles . . . and . . . Henrietta Maria*, 1625; *The entertainment of . . . Charles into his ancient city of Edinburgh*, 1633; Sir Charles Cornwallis, *A Discourse of Prince Henry*, 1641; *The Life and Death of King Richard the Second*, 1642; *A briefe Declaration . . . of . . . a College of Divines . . . at Chelsey*, 1645; John Milton, *Eikonoklastes*, 1649; Sir B. Gerbier, *A Manifestation*, 1651.

Secondary sources include I. D'Israeli, *Commentaries on the Life and Reign of Charles the First*, ed. B. Disraeli, 2 vols., 1851, and *Curiosities of Literature*, 3 vols., 1866; G. R. Elton, *Studies in Tudor and Stuart Politics and Government*, Cambridge, 1974; F. Guizot, *History of Charles the First*, trans. W. Hazlitt, 1856; C. Hibbert, *Charles I*, 1968; J. P. Kenyon, *The Stuarts*, 1958; and H. R. Trevor-Roper, in *Religion, the Reformation and Social Change*, 1967. I made particular use of Nicholas Tyacke's important essay 'Puritanism, Arminianism and Counter-Revolution' in *The Origins of the English Civil War*, ed. C. S. R. Russell, 1973.

For the literature of the period, in addition to the works of authors mentioned in the text, I was helped by G. E. Bentley, *The Jacobean and Caroline Stage*, 7 vols., Oxford, 1941–68; Stephen Orgel, *The Jonsonian Masque*, Cambridge, Mass., 1965; Roy Strong and Stephen Orgel, *Inigo Jones; the theatre of the Stuart Court*, 2 vols., 1973; J. Summers, *The Heirs of Donne and Jonson*, 1970; and C. V. Wedgwood, *Poetry and Politics under the Stuarts*, Cambridge, 1962, and essays in *Truth and Opinion*, 1960. The unpublished poems and plays of Sir Thomas Salusbury are extant in the National Library of Wales MS. Peniarth 5 390D.

For the other arts I am deeply indebted to John Charlton, *The Banqueting House, Whitehall*, 1964; John Harris, 'Inigo and the Courtier Style' in *Architectural Review*, CLIV, July 1973; John Harris, Stephen Orgel, and Roy Strong, *The King's Arcadia: Inigo Jones and the Stuart Court*, 1973; Sir Oliver Millar, *Rubens: The Whitehall Ceiling*, Oxford, 1958, *The Triumphs of Caesar*, 1960, reprinted 1963, *The Pictures in the Collection of H.M. the Queen. Pt. I, The Tudor, Stuart and Early Georgian Pictures*, 1963, and above all his splendid catalogue *The Age of Charles I*, 1972; David Piper, *Van Dyck*, 1968; Graham Reynolds, *The Raphael Cartoons*, 1972; H. R. Trevor-Roper, *The plunder of the arts in the seventeenth century*, 1971; Roy Strong, *Van Dyck's Charles I on Horseback*, 1972, and *Splendour at Court*, 1973; Sir John Summerson, *Architecture in Britain 1530–1830*, Harmondsworth, 1953, reprinted 1970; Ellis Waterhouse, *Painting in Britain 1530–1790*, Harmondsworth, 1953; M. Whinney and O. Millar, *English Art 1625–1714*, Oxford, 1957; and John White, *The Raphael Cartoons*, Oxford, 1972.

Ten Urban VIII

The only work in English which is solely devoted to Urban VIII is W. N. Weech, *Urban VIII*, London, 1905, but it is a slight work, principally devoted to politics, and is now out of date. A. Leman, *Urban VIII et la Rivalité de la France et de la maison d'Autriche de 1631 à 1635*, Paris and Lille, 1920, is similarly largely concerned with one aspect of politics in this pontificate but does throw interesting light on the character of the Pope and on the process of decision-making at Rome. Although they deal with an earlier period, G. Carocci, *Lo Stato della Chiesa nella seconda metà del secolo XVI*, Milan, 1961, and J. Delumeau, *Vie économique et sociale de Rome dans la seconde moitié du XVIe siècle*, Paris, 1959, provide useful insights and much invaluable background material. The best modern accounts of the court of Urban VIII will be found in F. Haskell, *Patrons and Painters: A Study in the Relations between Italian Art and Society in the Age of the Baroque*, London, 1963, and, despite its uncritical attitude, in L. von Pastor, *The History of the Popes from the Close of the Middle Ages*, ed. R. F. Keir, vols. XXVIII, XXIX, London, 1899–1910. P. Pecchiai, *I Barberini*, Rome, 1959, is, on the whole, hostile to all the Barberini, with the exception of Cardinal Francesco, but is comprehensive and often very entertaining. Details of the Barberini Palace and the other great palaces of Rome are to be found in V. Golzio, *Palazzi Romani dal Rinascità al Neoclassico*, Rome, 1971, and in A. Blunt, 'The Palazzo Barberini: The Contributions of Maderno, Bernini and Pietro da Cortona' in the *Journal of the Warburg and Courtauld Institutes*, vol. XXI, 1958. On the artists of Rome see R. Wittkower, *Art and Architecture in Italy, 1600–1750*, London, 1965, and ed. M. von Platen, *Queen Christina of Sweden: documents and studies*, Stockholm, 1966; on Cortona, G. Briganti, *Pietro da Cortona*, Florence, 1962, which contains a wealth of interesting material about Rome at the time of Urban VIII and about the *virtuosi* of the papal court. On nepotism and its cost see M. Rosi, 'La Congiura di Giacinto Centini contro Urbano VIII' in *Archivio della R. Società romana di Storia Patria*, vol. XXII, and J. Grisar, S. J., 'Päpstliche Finanzen, Nepotismus und Kirchenrecht unter Urban VIII' in *Miscellanea Hist. Pontificiae*, 1943, vol. VII. On the Roman commune, E. Rodoconachi, *Les Institutions Communales de Rome*, Paris, 1901, is still useful.

The vast bulk of source material relating to Urban VIII has never been printed. I have used O. Pollak, *Die Kunsttätigkeit unter Urban VIII*, 2 vols., Vienna, 1928, 1931, which contains much material on the arts, on patronage, and on public religious ceremonies. Obviously useful in this context is G. Baglione, *Le Vite de' Pittori, scultori, architetti, ed intagliatori*, Naples, 1733. Everyone who has written on the court of Urban VIII has followed Pastor in pillaging eds. N. Barozzi and G. Berchet, *Relazioni degli Stati Europei Lette al Senato dagli Ambasciatori Veneti nel secolo decimosettimo*, 3rd series (Italia), vol. I (Roma), Venice, 1877, since it is a source of such vivid quotations. It needs always to be borne in mind, however, that this is essentially a *Venetian* source and so inclined to be hostile. Another common source is F. Baldinucci's *Life of Bernini*. For English readers there exists an excellent translation by C. Engass, London, 1966, and, in quoting from Baldinucci, I have used this particular edition. Some quotations in the text are taken from the MSS. 'Avvisi di Roma', which give a good idea of the display, show, and magnificence of the papacy as experienced by the contemporary observer. Particularly rich are those for 1629–30, which will be found in the Vatican Library in MS. Urb. Lat. 1100.

Eleven Louis XIV

This essay is based on published memoirs, on independent archival research, and on monographs derived from archival research on specific aspects of the reign and the court. Of the greatest importance are the memoirs, so-called, of Louis XIV himself, consisting of his intructions to the Dauphin and sundry related pieces, the most complete collection of which are those edited by P. A. Grouvelle, *Oeuvres de Louis XIV*, 6 vols., Paris, 1806, and by J. Longnon, *Mémoires pour les années 1661 et 1666*, Paris, 1923, and *Mémoires de Louis XIV*, Paris, 1928. They should, however, be read in conjunction with Paul Sonnino's article, 'The Dating and authorship of Louis XIV's *Mémoires*' in *French Historical Studies*, III, 1964, the introduction to the same author's translation of Louis' *Mémoires for the Instruction of the Dauphin*, New York and London, 1970, and his article on 'Louis XIV's *Mémoires pour l'histoire de la guerre de Hollande*' in *French Historical Studies*, VIII, 1973. A selection of Louis' letters to Philip V are published in Grouvelle, *Oeuvres*, vols. V and VI, and many more in H. M. A. Baudrillart, *Philippe V et la cour de France*, 5 vols., Paris, 1890–1900, but the whole series is not yet in print.

In the use of the memoirs of the reign care must be taken. Some are authentic, such as those of Madame de la Motte for the Queen Regent's court; others, such as those purported to be by Madame de Maintenon, are worthless. Those of Saint-Simon are built, in part, on the journal of the Marquis de Dangeau mentioned in the text, and Voltaire, in his *Siècle de Louis XIV*, while stressing the prejudices of Saint-Simon, has pointed to isolated instances where Dangeau's journal is demonstrably erroneous, he having at times permitted domestics to write up the events of the day. On the whole, however, the Dangeau journal (published in 19 vols. in 1854) is a remarkable achievement, invaluable for court life at Versailles after 1684. Voltaire himself used Dangeau and the then unpublished Torcy memoirs as well as a variety of documents and oral evidence; his *Siècle de Louis XIV* is an important contribution to the role the King played in the encouragement of arts and sciences.

For the fabric of Versailles the many works of Pierre Nolhac are indispensable; for the symbolism see L. Hautecoeur, *Les Jardins des dieux et des hommes*, Paris, 1959; and, more generally for the various palaces and the life at court, J. G. P. M. Levron, *Parcs et châteaux royaux de l'Ile de France*, Paris, 1965, and *Les Courtisans*, Paris, 1960. See also P. Verlet, *Versailles*, Paris, 1961; B. Teyssèdre, *L'Art au siècle de Louis XIV*, Paris, 1967; R.-A. Weigert, *L'époque Louis XIV*, Paris, 1962; E. Guillou, *Versailles, le palais du soleil*, Paris, 1963; and W. D. Howarth, *The Seventeenth Century*, in the series *Life and Letters in France*, Edinburgh, 1965. The essays in Jacques Saint-Germain, *Louis XIV secret*, Paris, 1970, are more significant than the title might imply, particularly for the security precautions taken when Louis went hunting. On the social hierarchy see F. Bluche and P. Durye, *L'Anoblissement par charges avant 1789*, Paris, 1962, and Roland Mousnier, *Les Institutions de la France sous la monarchie absolue (1598–1789)*, vol. I, *Société et état*, Paris, 1974, is particularly useful. For the King's role in Church and government the works of F. Olivier-Martin, *Histoire du droit français des origines à la Révolution*, Paris, 1948, M. Bloch, *Les Rois thaumaturges*, 2nd edn., Paris, 1961 and G. Durand, *États et institutions: XVIe–XVIIIe siècles*, Paris, 1969, are essential, as are the many articles which have appeared in the periodical *XVIIe Siècle* since its inception in 1949.

Sections of the nobility have been studied by two younger scholars: R. C. Mettam has published some of his findings on the role of the high nobility in *France: A Companion to French Studies*, ed. D. G. Charlton, London, 1972; and Robert Oresko's interest in the role of the 'foreign princes' will be documented in his forthcoming work on the relationships between France and the princes of Monaco.

For Louis' *métier* as a ruler see the contributions in *Louis XIV and the Craft of Kingship*, ed. John C. Rule, Columbus, Ohio, 1969; *William III and Louis XIV*, ed. Ragnhild Hatton and J. S. Bromley, Liverpool and Toronto, 1968; *Studies in Diplomatic History*, ed. Ragnhild Hatton and M. S. Anderson, London, 1970; and R. Mousnier, *Le Conseil du roi*, Paris, 1970.

An unusual, stimulating survey is by F. Dornic, R. and S. Pillorget, and P. Cogny, *La France de Louis XIV 1650–1715*, Paris, 1970; and a most finely written and illustrated volume is by A. Adam, R. Mandrou, J. Meuvret, and G. Mongrédien, *La France au temps de Louis XIV*, Paris, 1966. For Louis' relationship to Paris see, apart from O. Ranum in *Louis XIV and the Craft of Kingship* (cited above), L. L. Bernard, *The Emerging City. Paris in the Age of Louis XIV*, Durham, N.C., 1970.

For bibliographical information see articles by John B. Wolf and Ragnhild Hatton in *Journal of Modern History*, XXXVI, 1964, and XLV, 1973, respectively; also Ragnhild Hatton, *Louis XIV and his World*, London and New York, 1972.

Twelve Peter the Great

The most detailed general work on Peter in English, though a patchy and now outdated one, is E. Schuyler, *Peter the Great, Emperor of Russia*, 2 vols., London, 1884; while B. H. Sumner, *Peter the Great and the Emergence of Russia*, London, 1950, is a balanced, accurate, and perceptive short account. V. Klyuchevsky, *Peter the Great*, London, 1958, is an English translation of part of the author's great *Kurs russkoi istorii*: it is concerned in the main with social and administrative change. The most complete and up-to-date general assessment in any language is R. Wittram, *Peter I, Czar und Kaiser*, 2 vols., Göttingen, 1964, a balanced account of a largely narrative type based upon a vast knowledge of the subject. The changes in Russia's intellectual life and in her relations with Western Europe which were already under way before Peter's accession are briefly but excellently discussed in S. F. Platonov, *Moskva i Zapad*, Berlin, 1926. The Tsar's character and personality are dissected in the same writer's *Pyotr Velikii, lichnost' i deyatelnost'*, Leningrad, 1926, and in Klyuchevsky's article 'Pyotr Velikii sredi svoikh sotrudnikov', reprinted in his *Ocherki i rechi*, Moscow, n.d. The comments of foreign observers are often very illuminating in this and other connections: the most useful are to be found in J.-G. Korb, *Diary of an Austrian Secretary of Legation at the Court of Czar Peter the Great*, London, 1863, reprinted 1968; J. Perry, *The State of Russia under the present Czar*, London, 1716, reprinted 1967; and F. C. Weber, *The Present State of Russia*, London, 1722–23, reprinted 1968. Peter's religious policies and attitudes, one of the most difficult aspects of his reign to understand, are treated in detail and with great competence in J. Cracraft, *The Church Reform of Peter the Great*, London, 1971; and the building of the new capital is discussed briefly, from a purely architectural and artistic standpoint, in C. Marsden, *Palmyra of the North: the first days of St. Petersburg*, London, 1952. The best general account in English of the intellectual history of the period is probably that in the relevant chapters of P. Milyukov, *Outlines of Russian Culture*, 3 vols., Philadelphia, 1942; while Peter's efforts to use architecture, painting, and the arts in general for the glorification of his regime are interestingly discussed in N. A. Baklanova, 'Otrazhenie idei absolyutizma v izobrazitel'nom iskusstve pervoi chetverti XVIII v.' in the collection *Absolyutizm v Rossii*, Moscow, 1964. The spectacular rise in the European prestige of Russia and still more of her ruler during the later years of the reign can be followed in the excellent accounts by A. Lortholary, *Le Mirage russe en France au XVIIIe siècle*, Paris, n.d., and H. Doerries, *Russlands Eindringen in Europa in der Epoche Peters des Grossen*, Berlin, 1939.

Thirteen Maria Theresa

The main source for Maria Theresa's reign in general is still A. von Arneth, *Geschichte Maria Theresias*, 10 vols., Vienna, 1862–79. E. Guglia, *Maria Theresia. Ihr Leben und Ihre Regierung*, Munich, 1917, contains useful additional material and references on cultural matters. These biographies can be supplemented by the published volumes of Maria Theresa's correspondence, nearly all edited by Arneth, and by her 'Political Testament', re-edited by J. Kallbrunner, Vienna, 1952, the more important part of which is available in an English translation in C. A. Macartney, *The Habsburg and Hohenzollern Dynasties in the Seventeenth and Eighteenth Centuries*, London, 1970. The diaries of the court chamberlain, J. J. Khevenhüller-Metsch, *Aus der Zeit Maria Theresias*, 8 vols., Vienna, 1904 ff., are a source of major importance for most aspects of the reign. Up-to-date interpretative accounts in English include C. A. Macartney, *Maria Theresa and the House of Austria*, London, 1969, and E. Wangermann, *The Austrian Achievement, 1700–1800*, London, 1973.

The sources for the architectural achievement of the reign are scattered. Fundamental for the palace and garden of Schönbrunn are K. Bielohlawek, 'Schönbrunn. Ein Beitrag zur Geschichte seines Baues u. seiner formalen Erscheinung' in *Jahrbuch des Kunsthistorischen Instituts des öst. Bundesdenkmalamtes*, XIV, 1920, Beiblatt; E. Susini, 'Schönbrunn' in *Etudes germaniques*, April–June 1965; J. Dernjač, *Zur Geschichte von Schönbrunn. Studien*, Vienna, 1885; E. Hainisch, *Der Architekt Johann Ferdinand Hetzendorf v. Hohenberg*, Vienna, 1949; M. Poch-Kalous, 'Wiener Plastik im 19. Jahrhundert' in *Geschichte der Stadt Wien*, Neue Reihe, VII/I, Vienna, 1970.

The main source for Maria Theresa's court theatre is O. Teuber, 'Das k.k. Hofburgtheater seit seiner Begründung' in *Die Theater Wiens*, II/1, Vienna, 1896. For the *Nationaltheater* see also C. Glossy, *Das Burgtheater unter seinem Gründer Joseph II*, Vienna, 1926, and H. Kindermann, *Theatergeschichte der Goethezeit*, Vienna, 1948. Illuminating primary sources which should not be neglected are J. H. F. Müller's autobiography *Abschied von der k.k. Hofschaubühne*, Vienna, 1802, and R. Payer v. Thurn, *Joseph II. als Theaterdirektor*, Vienna, 1920. For Gluck and the Reform opera, the best sources in English are A. Einstein, *Gluck*, London, 1964, and P. Howard, *Gluck and the Birth of Modern Opera*, London, 1963. Calzabigi's letter in *Mercure de France*, no. 34, 21 August 1784, is very important. The prefaces to the editions of Gluck's operas in the Kassel edition of his *Sämtliche Werke* are all extremely informative. For the introduction of French comedy, C. S. Favart, *Mémoires et correspondances littéraires, dramatiques et anecdotiques*, II, Paris, 1808, contains much important material.

Nearly all the relevant material available to date on Gottsched's relations with Vienna was published by T. W. Danzel, *Gottsched und seine Zeit. Auszüge aus seinem Briefwechsel*, Leipzig, 1848. For Klopstock's Vienna project, see R. Hamel's Introduction to 'Herrmann's-Schlacht' in J. Kürschner's 'Klopstocks Werke' in *Deutsche Nationalliteratur*, 46, IV, Berlin, 1888, and Klopstock's 'Gelehrtenrepublik' in *Klopstocks Sämtliche Werke*, VIII, Leipzig, 1855. The possibility of an appointment in Vienna for Lessing is best studied on the basis of his correspondence from 1771 to 1776 in *G. E. Lessings Sämtliche Schriften*, 3rd edn., rev. F. Muncker, XVII–XXI, Leipzig, 1904–7.

For the scientists employed at Maria Theresa's court, see *Gerard van Swieten und seine Zeit*, ed. E. Lesky and A. Wandruszka, Vienna, 1973; J. Wiesner, 'Jan Ingen-Housz in Wien' in *Osterreichische Rundschau*, III, May–July 1905; and E. M. Kronfeld, 'Jacquin' in *ibid*.

Most of the important sources for the patronage of the fine arts have been used by W. Wagner in *Die Geschichte der Akademie der Bildenden Künste in Wien*, Vienna, 1967, and by A. Novotny in *Staatskanzler Kaunitz als geistige Persönlichkeit*, Vienna, 1947. But there is still more to be discovered by studying the archival sources in *Allgemeines Verwaltungsarchiv* (Vienna), *Studienhofkommission*, F.61, Konv. Akademie der Bildenden Künste, especially Anton Maron's undated proposals (*c.* 1772) on teaching methods to be employed in the academy. For the rearrangement of the Habsburg collection of paintings see A. Lhotsky, 'Die Geschichte der Sammlungen' in *Festschrift des Kunsthistorischen Museums*, II, Vienna, 1941–45.

Fourteen Louis XV

Court history offers many a trap for the unwary reader for its sources are frequently less scholarly than anecdotal, inconsequential, or hagiographical, providing rather more colour than accuracy. As an age of advancing *sensibilité*, encouraging the frank expression of emotions, Louis XV's reign sets a particularly seductive snare. However, Alfred Cobban's *History of Modern France*, vol. 1, Harmondsworth, 1957, remains a most accomplished example of how to write good history, and is the best short introduction to eighteenth-century France available in English, while Pierre Gaxotte's *Le Siècle de Louis XV*, new edn., Paris, 1958, provides the best biography of the whole reign. There is no equivalent, however, for the period of Louis' majority of Dom. H. Leclerq's monumental though slightly indigestible *Histoire de la régence pendant la minorité de Louis XV*, 3 vols., Paris, 1921.

Among contemporary commentators pride of place must go to the incomparable Duc de Saint-Simon, whose *Mémoires*, ed. A. de Boislisle, 41 vols., Paris, 1879–1928, though highly prejudiced, vividly illuminate the regency of his friend, Philippe of Orléans. Recently Lucy Norton has pleasantly edited and translated a selection of these memoirs, London, 1967–72. Among others who lived in, and wrote of, this period from widely differing viewpoints are the Marquis d'Argenson, who was foreign minister in the 1740s, *Journal et mémoires*, ed. E. J. B. Rathéry, 9 vols., Paris, 1859–67; the barristers E. J. F. Barbier, *Chronique de la régence et du règne de Louis XV 1718–63*, 8 vols., Paris, 1885, and M. Marais, *Journal et mémoires de Mathieu Marais sur la régence et le règne de Louis XV, 1715–1737*, ed. M. de Lescure, 4 vols., Paris, 1863–68; and two aristocratic witnesses, the Duc de Cröy, *Journal inédit du duc de Cröy, 1718–1784*, ed. the Vicomte de Grouchy and P. Cottin, 4 vols., Paris, 1906, and the Duc de Luynes, *Mémoires du duc de Luynes sur la cour de Louis XV*, ed. E. Soulié and M. L. Dussieux, 17 vols., Paris, 1865.

Recent scholarly monographs dealing with aspects of the King's role in government include M. Antoine, *Le Conseil du roi sous le règne de Louis XV*, Paris, 1970, and J. Egret, *Louis XV et l'opposition parlementaire, 1715–1774*, Paris, 1970, while the secrets of Louis' personal diplomacy are revealed in the *Correspondance secrète du comte de Broglie avec Louis XV, 1756–1774*, ed. D. Ozanam and M. Antoine, 2 vols., Paris, 1956–61.

Of the personalities of the period we still lack a definitive biography of the King. Philippe of Orléans, too, deserves a more detailed and academic treatment than that given him by P. Erlanger, *Le Régent*, Paris, 1938, or C. E. Engel, *Le Régent*, Paris, 1969. Nancy Mitford's *Madame de Pompadour*, revised edn., London, 1968, offers a reliable portrait, beautifully illustrated, of the court's leading figure after the King himself. Pompadour is also the subject of volumes by J. Levron, *Pompadour*, trans. C. E. Engel, London, 1963, and P. Nolhac, *Louis XV et Madame de Pompadour*, Paris, 1928. The latter has also contributed a book on *Louis XV et Marie Leczinska*, Paris, 1904. Other biographies which are relevant and informative, though none are outstanding include M. Cheke, *The Cardinal de Bernis*, London, 1958; H. Cole, *The First Gentleman of the Bedchamber*, London, 1965, a biography of the Duc de Richelieu; S. Loomis, *Du Barry*, London, 1960; I. MacInnes, *Painter, King and Pompadour*, London, 1965, the painter in question being François Boucher; and S. Zweig, *Marie-Antoinette*, trans. from German to French, Paris, 1965, which throws some light on Louis XV's court in the last years of the reign.

The elaborate routine of life at Versailles is unravelled in two volumes: C. Kunstler, *La Vie quotidienne sous Louis XV*, Paris, 1953, and J. Levron, *Daily Life at Versailles in the Seventeenth and Eighteenth Centuries*, English trans., London, 1968.

The age of the Rococo may be studied in a volume of that title by T. Pignatti, English trans., London, 1969; in G. Savage, *French Decorative Art, 1638–1793*, London, 1969; and P. Verlet, *Les Meubles français du XVIIIe siècle*, Paris, 1966. Some indication of the elegance and splendour of the age may be glimpsed from the small paperback volume by A. G. Palacios, *The Age of Louis XV*, trans. from the Italian, London, 1969.

Finally, the changing intellectual climate is the subject of two volumes written almost a century apart. F. Rocquain, *L'Esprit révolutionnaire avant la Révolution, 1715–1789*, was first published in Paris in 1878 and has recently and deservedly been reprinted, Geneva, 1971, while J. H. Brumfitt, *The French Enlightenment*, London, 1972, provides an up-to-date treatment.

INDEX